ARMIN LANGE, Dr. theol. (1995), University of Münster, is Professor for Second Temple Judaism at the University of Vienna and a member of the international team editing the Dead Sea Scrolls. He has recently published the first volume of his *Handbuch der Textfunde vom Toten Meer* (Mohr Siebeck 2009).

EMANUEL TOV, Ph.D. (1974) in Biblical Studies, Hebrew University, is J.L. Magnes Professor of Bible at the Hebrew University and the former Editor-in-Chief of the Dead Sea Scrolls Publication Project. He has published several books on textual criticism and on the Scrolls.

MATTHIAS WEIGOLD is a member of the research project 'The Meaning of Ancient Jewish Quotations and Allusions for the Textual History of the Hebrew Bible' at the University of Vienna.

The Dead Sea Scrolls in Context

Integrating the Dead Sea Scrolls
in the Study of Ancient Texts, Languages,
and Cultures

Volume Two

Edited by

Armin Lange, Emanuel Tov, and Matthias Weigold

In association with Bennie H. Reynolds III

BRILL

LEIDEN • BOSTON
2011

This book is printed on acid-free paper.

Library of Congress Cataloging-in-Publication Data

The Dead Sea scrolls in context : integrating the Dead Sea scrolls in the study of ancient texts, languages, and cultures / edited by Armin Lange, Emanuel Tov, and Matthias Weigold in association with Bennie H. Reynolds III.
     p. cm. – (Supplements to Vetus Testamentum, ISSN 0083-5889 ; v. 140)
Proceedings of a conference jointly organized by the Hebrew University of Jerusalem and the University of Vienna in Vienna on February 11-14, 2008.
   Includes bibliographical references.
   ISBN 978-90-04-18903-4 (hardback : alk. paper)
1. Dead Sea scrolls–Congresses. 2. Qumran community–Congresses. 3. Judaism–History–Post-exilic period, 586 B.C.-210 A.D.–Congresses. I. Lange, Armin, 1961- II. Tov, Emanuel. III. Weigold, Matthias. IV. Universitah ha-'Ivrit bi-Yerushalayim. V. Universität Wien. VI. Title. VII. Series.

BM487.D44538 2011
296.1'55–dc22

                                                                    2010037469

ISSN 0083-5889
ISBN 978 90 04 20293 1 (vol. 1)
ISBN 978 90 04 20292 4 (vol. 2)
ISBN 978 90 04 18903 4 (set)

PRINTED BY DRUKKERIJ WILCO B.V. – AMERSFOORT, THE NETHERLANDS

CONTENTS

THE DEAD SEA SCROLLS AND
JEWISH LITERATURE AND CULTURE OF THE
RABBINIC AND MEDIEVAL PERIODS

THE DEAD SEA SCROLLS AND EARLY CHRISTIANITY

THE DEAD SEA SCROLLS AND
THE ANCIENT MEDITERRANEAN AND
ANCIENT NEAR EASTERN WORLDS

INTRODUCTION

It is a pleasure for the editors of the "Dead Sea Scrolls in Context" proceedings to introduce our readers to their second volume. We expressed our gratitude to all those colleagues, institutions, and individuals who made both the conference and its proceedings possible already in the introduction to the first volume. In addition, we would like to thank Dr. Nóra Dávid who supported us with the editorial work on the second volume. As with the first volume, if not indicated otherwise, abbreviations follow *The SBL Handbook of Style: For Ancient Near Eastern, Biblical, and Early Christian Studies* (ed. P.H. Alexander et al.; Peabody: Hendrickson, 1999).

The first volume of the conference proceedings focused on new methodologies applied to the Dead Sea Scrolls, the relevance of the Dead Sea Scrolls for the textual history of the Hebrew Bible, for ancient Semitic languages, for interpreting the individual books of the Hebrew Bible, and for Second Temple Jewish literature written in Hebrew or Greek. The second volume of the Vienna conference proceedings explores the contexts of Jewish history, culture, and archeology, Jewish thought and religion, Jewish literature and culture of the rabbinic and medieval periods, early Christianity, and the ancient Mediterranean and ancient Near Eastern worlds. While the first volume focused mainly on methodological, linguistic, and literary topics, the second volume is concerned with questions of material culture, political, cultural, and religious history, as well as the non-Jewish cultural and religious environments of the Dead Sea Scrolls.

The volume begins with the archeological and historical contexts of the Dead Sea Scrolls ("Jewish History, Culture, and Archeology and the Dead Sea Scrolls"). *Hanan Eshel* ז״ל ("Qumran Archeology in Light of Two Rural Sites in Judea") contextualizes the Qumran settlement archeologically by comparing it with the Second Temple ruins of Horvat Mazad (a way station on the road between Jerusalem and Jaffa) and the remnants of the country villa at Khirbet el-Muraq. Eshel shows that the Qumran settlement is very different from both sites and hence could have neither been a way station nor a Roman villa. That the Qumran settlement was not a Roman manor house is further supported by a comparison to a group of sites that contain courtyard installations and that were defended by a tower surrounded by a glacis. The architectonic similarities of these sites are not indicative of their functions. Structures of this sort were used for a variety of purposes in the Second Temple period. Another archeological context is discussed in an unconventional paper by *Minna and Kenneth Lönnqvist* ("Parallels to Be Seen: Manuscripts in Jars from Qumran and Egypt"). Based on research by J.T. Milik, these scholars compare the Qumran scroll jars from Cave 1 with cylindrical jars from Deir el-Medina and suggest that it was a common practice in antiquity to store ancient manuscript in jars. In their comparison with the Deir el-Medina jars, Lönnqvist and Lönnqvist find confirmation that the Qumran community was founded in the middle of the second century B.C.E. and consider the possibility that the scroll jars from Qumran may have served as portable archives or genizoth over a longer period of time. *Nóra Dávid* ("Burial in the Book of Tobit and in Qumran") discusses archeological evidence from Qumran in the context of Second Temple Jewish literature. She compares the archeological evidence from the Qumran graveyards with the information about burials in the book of Tobit. Dávid argues that as part of their asceticism the Qumran community practiced the average way of burying the dead as the poor of the country did. Although the random burials depicted in the book of Tobit may be similar in execution to Qumran graves, the motivation for this particular form of burial in the book of Tobit was not ascetic in nature but was simply the easiest and quickest way of burying the dead.

With historiography, *Edward Dąbrowa* ("The Hasmoneans in the Light of the Qumran Scrolls") points to yet another field of study for which the Dead Sea Scrolls might be helpful. By comparing the allusions to historical events and persons from the Hasmonean period with what we know about these events from other sources, Dąbrowa searches for the attitudes that the authors of the Qumran Dead Sea Scrolls had to past and present events and persons. He shows that the Qumran authors were not particularly interested in history. "Past events and historical figures, even if known to them, were only used as illustrative material to promulgate their own theological beliefs" (509).

By addressing "Jewish Thought and Religion in Light of the Dead Sea Scrolls," the next part of the conference proceedings studies the Dead Sea Scrolls in the context of Second Temple Judaism as well. Three papers by Esther G. Chazon, Daniel Stökl Ben Ezra, and Russell C.D. Arnold address questions of prayer, liturgy, and ritual while two papers by Sandra Jacobs and Alex P. Jassen are dedicated to the idea of the end of prophecy and the covenant of the rainbow as well as circumcision. *Esther G. Chazon* ("Shifting Perspectives on Liturgy at Qumran and in Second Temple Judaism") discusses prayers and liturgical texts from Qumran in the context of Second Temple and rabbinic prayers and liturgical texts. She shows that the non-sectarian Qumran scrolls in particular document a sizeable, continuous liturgical tradition stretching from the second century B.C.E. to the third century C.E. In some instances these scrolls document perhaps even a precursor or direct antecedent of a later rabbinic benediction or liturgical practice. The Dead Sea Scrolls unambiguously attest regular, public prayer in the two centuries prior to the Temple's destruction. The establishment of the new institution of obligatory Jewish prayer by the rabbis after the Second Temple's destruction was not *ex nihilo* but happened against a rich background of considerable, well-steeped, liturgical precedent and tradition. In comparison with rabbinic and Second Temple Jewish literature, *Daniel Stökl Ben Ezra* ("When the Bell Rings: The Qumran Rituals of Affliction in Context") develops a typology for rituals of affliction in Second Temple Judaism. He distinguishes between rituals and rites of affliction. Rituals of affliction include a) incantations, b) independent purifications, c) punishments, d) Yom Kippur, e) burials and mourning rites, and f) covenant renewal ceremony. Rites of affliction include a) apotropaic prayers, b) minor purifications, c) confessions, and d) curses. Although being part of an overall ritual continuity in Second Temple Judaism, some rituals of affliction that are prominent in Second Temple, rabbinic, and/or early Christian texts are rare in the Qumran scrolls. Absent or rarely mentioned in the Qumran Dead Sea Scrolls are regular fast days (with the exception of Yom Kippur), rites to handle collective emergencies, and individual healings. The latter absence is all the more interesting as a study of the bacterial remains in Qumran toilets points to the ubiquitous presence of sickness among the people of Qumran. *Russell C.D. Arnold* ("The Dead Sea Scrolls, Qumran, and Ritual Studies") applies concepts of ritual studies of contemporary communities to the Qumran *yaḥad*. He points to the pervasiveness of ritual in the *yaḥad*. Based on the examples of calendrical rites, rites of passage, and feasts and fasts, Arnold argues that rituals structured the *yaḥad*'s existence. Calendrical rites provided opportunities for the priestly *yaḥad* to be obedient to divine law and to ensure their coordination with the workings of the cosmos, until the end comes. Rites of passage served the purpose of identity construction, instruction and indoctrination as well as social control. Communal meals reinforced the members' shared experience and united them around common goals and a common identity thus strengthened the *yaḥad*'s group identity. They furthermore ritually enacted the hierarchical ranking that served to keep members in line.

Beyond the theme of ritual studies, *Sandra Jacobs* ("Expendable Signs: The Covenant of the Rainbow and Circumcision at Qumran") asks why the covenant of the rainbow and circumcision play minimal roles in the sectarian texts from Qumran although both are priestly signs. She suggests that the sign of the rainbow, with its inherent symbolism of sexuality and fertility, was of no value to men in the *yaḥad* community, who otherwise enforced increased levels of ritual purity and sexual restraint. Identifying themselves as "the elect, remnant of Israel," the members of the *yaḥad* had little interest in the covenant of the rainbow and the sign of circumcision as both included people beyond the *yaḥad* as well. Neither circumcision nor the covenant of the rainbow supported their self-defined elitism. In comparing the Dead Sea Scrolls with other Second Temple Jewish literature, *Alex P. Jassen* ("Prophecy after 'the Prophets': The Dead Sea Scrolls and the History of Prophecy in Judaism") revisits the question of whether or not prophecy ceased in the Second Temple period. His comparison shows that for some individuals or communities few features distinguished their own activity from that of the ancient prophets while for others their models of divine-human communication were radically different from ancient prophecy. In the Qumran community, no explicit prophetic terminology is applied to the activity of communal leaders. Nevertheless a rich world of human-divine communication exists at Qumran which expresses itself in new models that are either absent or underrepresented in biblical prophecy. These modes of human-divine communication were regarded by the community not merely in continuity with the ancient prophets, but as equivalent to prophetic activity.

The next part of the conference proceedings ("The Dead Sea Scrolls and Jewish Literature and Culture of the Rabbinic and Medieval Periods") addresses the difficult question of the extent to which the Dead Sea Scrolls are of importance for the understanding of Jewish culture and religion after the destruction of the Second Temple and thus shifts the reader's attention to later periods in the history of Judaism. *Lawrence H. Schiffman* ("Second Temple Literature and Rabbinic Judaism") probes the continuities and discontinuities between Second Temple and rabbinic Judaism. Of that which was composed or transmitted in the Second Temple period, the rabbis did not read anything beyond the Hebrew Bible. Nevertheless, Schiffman observes rich parallels between Second

Temple and rabbinic texts for which a rigorous debate between the Pharisees, as the spiritual ancestors of the Tannaim, and other Jewish groups is responsible. Although it was quieted when the Pharisaic-rabbinic movement emerged as the consensus group, various aspects of the common Judaism of Second Temple times were preserved in the rabbinic movement and its literature due to this debate. The Dead Sea Scrolls play a crucial role in documenting this debate between the Pharisees and other parts of Second Temple Judaism. *Günter Stemberger* ("Mishnah and Dead Sea Scrolls: Are there Meaningful Parallels and Continuities?") narrows the question of continuities and discontinuities between Second Temple and rabbinic Judaism to the relation of the Mishnah to the Dead Sea Scrolls. Admitting a gap between Second Temple and rabbinic Judaism, Stemberger finds substantial evidence for a continuity of halakhic traditions from the time before 70 c.e. to the rabbis. Most of these traditions are not specifically Pharisaic, but more representative of a "common" Judaism. Furthermore, Qumran texts which polemically oppose laws identical with or very close to what we find in the Mishnah, sometimes confirm the information we have from Mishnaic or other rabbinic texts on halakhic controversies between the Pharisees and the Sadducees. Stemberger emphasizes though that not everything opposed by the people of Qumran and accepted by the Pharisees is *eo ipso* a specifically Pharisaic law. It may represent a wider consensus opposed only by some priestly groups. *Paul Heger* ("Rabbinic Midrashei Halakhah, Midrashei Aggadah in Qumran Literature?") emphasizes the differences between rabbinic midrash and interpretations of legal and narrative biblical texts at Qumran in a debate with Steven D. Fraade. He argues that Fraade's use of the term midrash is not appropriate for describing the mode of interpreting both legal and narrative topics in the Qumran collection. Heger finds a fundamental distinction between the rabbinic and Qumranic methods of interpretation. He argues that Qumran scholars adhered to the simple interpretation of the biblical rules without any consideration of the practical difficulties posed by the law. In contrast, rabbinic interpretations were based on the rabbis' understanding of the texts and of the general principle of the Torah as well as an awareness of the necessity of adapting the traditional rules and customs to actual circumstances. While in Qumranic interpretation of legal and narrative texts their simple meaning was implemented in disregard of practical issues, rabbinic halakhot were based on the rabbis' reflections. Scriptural interpretation was used as a means of justification. *Moshe J. Bernstein* ("The *Genesis Apocryphon* and the Aramaic *Targumim* Revisited: A View from

Both Perspectives") moves the discussion about rabbinic contexts of the Dead Sea Scrolls to the relationship of 1QapGen ar with the Targumim of rabbinic times. Bernstein does not classify 1QapGen ar as a Targum. The composer(s) of the *Genesis Apocryphon* employed citations or paraphrases of biblical texts not deriving from its primary base text. Some of these citations or paraphrases are stylistic in nature while drawing attention to the analogous circumstances of the various biblical stories. In this approach, the *Genesis Apocryphon* (and other Second Temple works of the same genre) might have served as a model for certain features of the Palestinian Aramaic Targumim.

The contribution of *Stefan C. Reif* ("The Genizah and the Dead Sea Scroll: How Important and Direct is the Connection?") discusses yet another Jewish context of the Dead Sea Scrolls by comparing the Qumran collection with the finds from the Genizah of the Karaite Ezra Synagogue in Cairo. Both collections are uniquely extensive and cover lengthy periods. Both collections represent, at the least, an important part of the Jewish and related literatures of their day. Both collections testify to a considerable degree of literacy, usually in at least two languages, and a tendency to create Jewish linguistic dialects. In contradistinction to these commonalities, the Qumran collection does not include many documents that are interested in the many mundane areas that are well represented in the Cairo Genizah. The Cairo Genizah does, furthermore, not testify to a rejection of establishment figures, notions and practices as the Qumran Dead Sea Scrolls do. The four texts discovered both in the Qumran collection and the Cairo Genizah were transmitted in a live manuscript tradition and illustrate that ideas recorded in and around Qumran had the opportunity of finding surroundings in which to hibernate, or perhaps simply to exist in low key, before being adopted by the Karaite movement between the ninth and twelfth centuries. *Meir Bar-Ilan* ("Non-Canonical Psalms from the Genizah") studies a collection of poetic texts from the Cairo Genizah which was regarded by David Flusser and Shmuel Safrai as a Qumranic text. Bar-Ilan shows that this collection of psalms has parallels in the Qumran corpus but does not originate in the Qumran community. More likely it was composed in the first century after the destruction of the Second Temple in non-rabbinic circles.

Having addressed rabbinic and post-rabbinic Jewish contexts of the Dead Sea Scrolls, the next part of the conference proceedings ("The Dead Sea Scrolls and Early Christianity") is dedicated to early Christianity as a religious group which grew out of Judaism but moved away from it after the Qumran settlement and the Second Temple were destroyed by Roman armies. *Karl P. Donfried* ("Paul the Jew and the Dead Sea Scrolls") understands Paul primarily as a Jew and shows that the thoughts expressed in the Dead Sea Scrolls shaped him significantly. Being educated as a Pharisee, Paul nevertheless encountered the *yaḥad*. According to Donfried, the *yaḥad* facilitated Paul's break from the rationalist Pharisaic stream of Judaism and provided him with a context in which he was able to interpret and articulate his Damascus experience. The encounter with the *yaḥad* would have thus allowed Paul to become the apostle for the Gentiles. While Donfried is concerned with an overall reading of Paul, *Cecilia Wassen* ("'Because of the Angels': Reading 1 Cor 11:2–16 in Light of Angelology in the Dead Sea Scrolls") focuses on 1 Cor 11:10 and interprets it in light of the angelology of the Dead Sea Scrolls in particular and Second Temple Judaism in general. The Dead Sea Scrolls show that the phrase "because of the angels" in 1 Cor 11:10 points to a belief in the presence of angels among the Corinthian Christians. In Qumran and Corinth, such an angelic presence demanded a proper dress code—in Corinth men with unveiled heads and women with veiled heads. For both the Dead Sea Scrolls and Paul divine-human unity is expressed through imitation of the divine. It is likely that Paul encourages imitation of the angels in the context of this communion. The lost glorious nature of Adam—which can be likened to an angelic state of being—was partly attainable for the Qumran sectarians and Paul already in the present. In 1 Cor 11:2–16, Paul applies these ideas to the creation of Adam and his original angelic looks. With regard to appearance, men are naturally closer to the divine beings whom they resemble than women. In imitation of the male angels, women have to hide their long hair in order to attain the same authority as men have to prophesy and praise together with the angels.

Renate J. Pillinger ("Dead Sea Scrolls and Early Christian Art") carries the argument beyond the New Testament to the Christianity of the first centuries C.E. She directs the attention of her readers to an unexplored field of research, i.e. the importance of the Dead Sea Scrolls for the understanding of early Christian art. By way of the select examples of the Giants, Melchizedek, messianic thought and motifs, John the Baptist and baptism, communal meals, and resurrection, Pillinger points to convergences and divergences between ideas and motifs expressed in the Dead Sea Scrolls and early Christian artwork. *Agnethe Siquans* ("Hermeneutics and Methods of Interpretation in the Isaiah Pesharim and in the *Commentary on Isaiah* by Theodoret of Cyrus") illustrates the importance of the Dead Sea Scrolls for the understanding of the Christianity of late antiquity by comparing the interpretation of the book of Isaiah in the *Isaiah Commentary* of Theodoret of Cyrus and in the Isaiah pesharim. Siquans finds parallels between the pesharim and Theodoret in their subject matter and their hermeneutical strategy: Both identify figures mentioned in the biblical text with persons (or groups) of their own time; both understand Isaianic rhetoric metaphorically and apply the Isaiah text to their own situations; both quote other biblical texts to support their arguments. Next to these parallels, Siquans observes fundamental differences between the pesharim and Theodoret as well. These differences are due to different eschatological expectations of the pesharists and Theodoret which motivate their respective interpretations. Focusing on the recent past, the present, and especially the near future, the Qumran pesharim find their exegetical objective in the (eschatological) salvation history of the Qumran community. Theodoret reads Isaiah with regard to the time of the prophet himself, with regard to the time of Jesus and the apostles, and with regard to his own time. As a Christian exegete, Theodoret presupposes the fulfillment of Isaiah's prophecies in Jesus Christ. Theodoret finds his exegetical objective hence on a spiritual level.

While most of the contexts discussed already in the conference proceedings have enjoyed extensive scholarly interest, the question of the extent to which the Dead Sea Scrolls are of importance for the understanding of their non-Jewish cultural environments and vice versa was far removed from the center of the discussion about the finds from the Judean desert. In the last part of the proceedings ("The Dead Sea Scrolls and the Ancient Mediterranean and Ancient Near Eastern Worlds") we try to rectify this situation at least to some extent. *Gebhard J. Selz* ("Of Heroes and Sages: Considerations on the Early Mesopotamian Background of Some Enochic Traditions") reads the Enochic traditions of Second Temple Judaism in light of Sumerian and Akkadian evidence from Mesopotamia. Selz argues that the official transmission of texts in Mesopotamia was supplemented by a wealth of oral traditions. The Jewish Enoch traditions are rewritings of these ancient Mesopotamian concepts. More extensive study of such backgrounds will uncover more interpretative possibilities than traditional exegesis has. Another Mesopotamian influence on a text from the Qumran collection is traced by *Ursula Schattner-Rieser* ("Levi in the Third Sky: On the 'Ascent to Heaven' Legends within their Near Eastern Context and J.T. Milik's Unpublished Version of the *Aramaic Levi Document*"). She surveys an unfinished manuscript of Józef Tadeusz Milik about the *Aramaic Levi Document* (*ALD*) and provides in an appendix Milik's text and French translation of the first 48 verses of this text according to his reconstruction. Schattner-Rieser shows that the heavenly journeys of the *ALD* attest to two celestial concepts, one involving three heavens and the other one involving seven. The motifs of three and seven heavens are of Mesopotamian origin. The *ALD* demonstrates that Jewish ascent to heaven legends share vocabulary, cosmology (the architectural representation of the heavenly realm), and eschatological ideas (the belief in a final judgment of the righteous) with Persian legends and Babylonian cosmography. Jewish ascent to heaven legends thus depend on ancient oriental sources. *Ida Fröhlich* ("Qumran Biblical Interpretation in the Light of Ancient Near Eastern Historiography") asks how forms and methods of historical memory that are attested in the Dead Sea Scrolls correlate with those known from other ancient Near Eastern cultures. She compares, furthermore, the attitudes towards history that are displayed in the Dead Sea Scrolls with the ones known from ancient Near Eastern literature. Both in the Qumran and ancient Near Eastern literatures, the basis on which historical facts and events are evaluated is an ethical viewpoint. In both literatures, historical overviews represent a semiotization of the history in the name of ethics.

Moving from the ancient Near East to Coele-Syria and the Greco-Roman worlds, the contributions of Jan Dušek, Bernhard Palme, Armin Lange and Zlatko Pleše, as well as George Branch-Trevathan examine the legal, hermeneutical, and utopian contexts of the Dead Sea Scrolls. *Jan Dušek* ("Protection of Ownership in the Deeds of Sale: Deeds of Sale from the Judean Desert in Context") compares clauses warranting the protection of ownership in deeds of sale from the various sites around the Dead Sea with those in Aramaic, Hebrew, Nabataean, Greek, and Syriac legal documents from the fifth century B.C.E. until the third century C.E. from Palestine, Egypt, and Syria. He identifies three legal groups. 1) A comparison of deeds of sale from Wadi Daliyeh (satrapy of Transeuphrates) and from Elephantine (satrapy of Egypt) shows that within the Persian Empire the law protecting purchased property was not identical in all satrapies. 2) Aramaic, Nabatean, Greek, and Syriac deeds of sale from Wadi Daliyeh, Naḥal Ḥever, and Dura Europos spreading from the fourth century B.C.E. to the third century C.E. reflect the same—or similar—legal tradition of the protection of the buyer's rights. This legal tradition is attested in Palestine and Syria, especially in Aramaic or its later dialects, but also in Greek texts, under Persian, Nabataean and Roman administration. It stands to reason, therefore, that the Roman administration in Palestine and Syria did not interfere excessively with local legal traditions. 3) Aramaic and Hebrew deeds of sale from Naḥal Ḥever

and Wadi Murabbaʿat, which were written during the second Jewish war
(131–135 C.E.), reflect the same legal tradition as the documents from the
second group but also display the influence of Greek (Ptolemaic?) legal
traditions. In Palestine, this Greek legal influence seems to have coexisted with the earlier Aramaic legal tradition in at least the first and second centuries C.E. *Bernhard Palme* ("Public Memory and Public Dispute:
Council Minutes between Roman Egypt and the Dead Sea") explores the
Greco-Roman legal context of the Dead Sea Scrolls. He shows how the
Babatha archive, especially the extract of council minutes from P. Babatha
12 (5/6Ḥev12) written 124 C.E. in Petra, helps to better understand the
political and judicial institutions in the Roman Near East in general
and in Roman Egypt in particular. *Armin Lange und Zlatko Pleše* ("The
Qumran Pesharim and the Derveni papyrus: Transpositional Hermeneutics in Ancient Jewish and Ancient Greek Commentaries") compare the
hermeneutics of the Derveni papyrus—a lemmatic commentary to an
orphic poem dating to late the fifth or early fourth century B.C.E.—with
the ones of the pesharim. Lange and Pleše detect a common hermeneutical pattern underlying the exegetical techniques of both metatexts. The
Derveni papyrus isolates individual elements from an Orphic theogony
and recontextualizes them into the discourse of philosophical cosmology.
The Qumran pesharim isolate individual elements from the prophetic
scriptures of Judaism and recontextualize them into the (eschatological)
history of the Essene movement. Being distinct in their aims, both metatexts nevertheless overcome estrangement from their authoritative religious traditions by transposing one narrative into the context of another
one. Lange and Pleše describe this shared hermeneutical approach as
transpositional hermeneutics. Transpositional hermeneutics is a dialectical process in which both the primary and secondary narratives undergo
structural adjustments and acquire new meanings. As a cross-cultural
phenomenon, transpositional hermeneutics developed independently in
Greek and Jewish cultures. *George Branch-Trevathan* ("Why Does 4Q394
Begin with a Calendar?") asks, in comparison with the use of solar symbolism in the Greco-Roman cultures of the late Hellenistic and early
imperial periods, why *MMT* includes a solar calendar. He argues that
sections B and C of *MMT* portray the *yaḥad* as an utopian or eschatological community. In connecting the solar calendar to this idealistic depiction of the community, it participates in a widespread use of solar symbolism in utopian and eschatological discourse in Greco-Roman culture.
MMT's use of a solar calendar is comparable to the use of solar symbolism
in Iambulus' travel narrative *Commonwealth of the Sun*, in Aristonicus'

Heliopolitae, and in the propaganda of the Roman emperor Augustus. In the discursive context of the Hellenistic and early Roman periods, a solar calendar powerfully symbolized the utopian and eschatological claims made in the rest of *MMT*.

In our perception, both the Vienna conference on "The Dead Sea Scrolls in Context" and its proceedings show that the Dead Sea Scrolls can be best understood in light of Second Temple and rabbinic Judaism as well as early Christianity and the eastern Mediterranean and ancient Near Eastern cultures surrounding them. The Dead Sea Scrolls shed new light not only on the Hebrew Bible and its textual, canonical, and reception histories, but also on Second Temple and rabbinic Judaism, early Christianity, and the eastern Mediterranean and ancient Near Eastern cultures.

Armin Lange, Bennie H. Reynolds III,
Emanuel Tov, and Matthias Weigold
Jackson, Jerusalem, and Vienna, January 2011

JEWISH HISTORY, CULTURE, AND ARCHEOLOGY
AND THE DEAD SEA SCROLLS

QUMRAN ARCHEOLOGY
IN LIGHT OF TWO RURAL SITES IN JUDEA

Hanan Eshel ז״ל
Bar-Ilan University

In recent years, archeologists seeking alternatives to the "consensus" identification of Khirbet Qumran as a settlement of a religious community, have proposed that the site was a way station inn or a Roman villa.[1] In this short note, I compare Qumran to two sites: (1) Horvat Mazad, which served as a way station on the road between Jerusalem and Jaffa in the Second Temple period and (2) Khirbet el-Muraq, which is the only country villa from the end of the Second Temple period to have been found in Judea to date. This comparison demonstrates how different Khirbet Qumran is from both of these sites.[2] Following this comparison, I examine courtyard installations that have been uncovered in Judea in which a tower surrounded by a glacis has been built into one of the external walls.

Horvat Mazad is located on the road between Jerusalem to Jaffa (fig. 1). The site was surveyed by Moshe Fisher, Benjamin Isaac and Israel Roll as part of a project investigating Roman roads from Jerusalem to Jaffa.[3] Moshe Fisher supervised three seasons of excavations at Horvat Mazad in 1972, 1978, and 1980. Two levels of Second Temple period occupation were uncovered in Horvat Mazad: a Hasmonean layer and a Herodian one (fig. 2). In the Hasmonean period, a tower was built at the site. In the Herodian period, a surrounding wall was added. A number of rooms were constructed along the length of the southern wall. One *miqwah* was built in this period as well.[4] The site was built to function as a station

---

[1] M. Broshi and H. Eshel, "Qumran and the Dead Sea Scrolls: The Contention of Twelve Theories," in *Religion and Society in Roman Palestine: Old Questions, New Approaches* (ed. D.R. Edwards; New York: Routledge, 2004), 162–169.

[2] On the archeology of Khirbet Qumran, see R. de Vaux, *Archaeology and the Dead Sea Scrolls* (London: Oxford University Press, 1973); J.-B. Humbert and A. Chambon, eds., *Fouilles de Khirbet Qumrân et de Aïn Feshkha*, vol. I (Fribourg: Academic Press, 1994).

[3] M. Fisher, B. Isaac, and I. Roll, *Roman Roads in Judea*, vol. 2: *The Jaffa-Jerusalem Roads* (British Archeological Reports International Series 628; Oxford: Tempus Reparatum, 1996), 212–216.

[4] M. Fisher, "The Road Jerusalem-Emmaus in light of the Excavation in Horvat

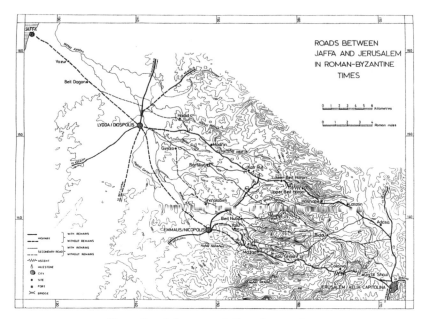

Fig. 1. Roads between Jaffa and Jerusalem
(according to Fisher, Isaac, and Roll).

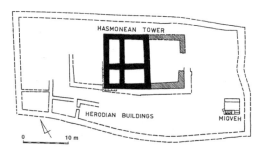

Fig. 2. Plan of Horvat Mazad (according to Fisher).

along the road that connected Jaffa to Jerusalem. Wayfarers would have stopped at this location to eat and to replenish their provisions before continuing on their way to Jerusalem. It may be supposed that some travelers would have occasionally spent the night at Horvat Mazad, when they had miscalculated the pace of their journey and realized that they

---

Mazad," in *Greece and Rome in Eretz-Israel* (ed. A. Kasher, G. Fuks, and U. Rappaport; Jerusalem: Ben-Zvi, 1989), 185–206 (Hebrew).

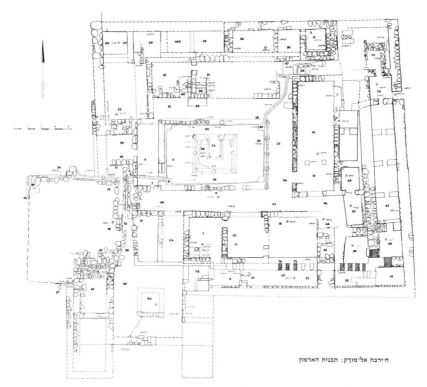

חירבת אל-מורק; תכנית הארמון

Fig. 3. Plan of Khirbet el-Muraq (according to Damati).

would not be able to reach Jerusalem before sunset. There is no similarity at all between Khirbet Qumran and Horvat Mazad, other than the fact that a tower was constructed at both sites.

We now turn to Khirbet el-Muraq, which is also called "The Palace of Hilkiya," because of an inscription found on a cornerstone at this site, which reads: ΕΛΚΙΑΣ ΣΙΜΩΝΟΣ ΕΓΡΑ(ΨΕ)—"Hilkiya son of Simon [wrote] the inscription." The site is located west of Hebron at the western part of the Judean mountains, overlooking the Shephela and the coastal plains. Khirbet el-Muraq was excavated by Emanuel Damati, who supervised five seasons of excavations at the site, between 1969 to 1983.[5] The installation at Khirbet el-Muraq was built around a central courtyard with a peristyle (a row of columns surrounding the courtyard; fig. 3). In the middle of the courtyard stood an elevated *triclinium*, surrounded by

5 E. Damati, "Khirbet el-Mûraq," *IEJ* 22 (1972): 173; idem, "The Palace of Ḥilkiya," *Qadmoniot* 15 (1982): 117–120 (Hebrew).

Fig. 4. Picture of Khirbet el-Muraq (according to Damati).

additional columns. An open *triclinium* of this sort has not been found in any other site in the land of Israel. The site was built in the time of Herod and appears to have been in use until the Bar Kokhba revolt. North of the *triclinium* there were a number of rooms that served as a bath house, including a hot room with a hypocaust dug into the rock; a warm room decorated by a mosaic floor featuring a colorful rosette at its center; and a cold room in which was dug a pool with stairs, which looks like a *mikvah* (room 30 in the plan).

A tower surrounded by a glacis was built into the western wall. An ornate gatehouse was built near the tower, in the southern wall of the site (locus 90). The peristyled courtyard had a mosaic floor. The *triclinium* was surrounded by an aqueduct, which Damati believes was intended to cool the diners. Pieces of red, green, and yellow stucco were found in the palace, and Nabatean capitals were found at the site (fig. 4).

Most of the features found at the palace of Hilkiya are absent at Qumran. Other than the fact that both sites have a courtyard structure incorporating a tower surrounded by a glacis, they are entirely dissimilar. No *triclinium* was built at Khirbet Qumran; no pillars were found at the site, nor was a bath house built there (fig. 5). There are no mosaic floors or Nabatean capitals, and there was no stucco ornamentation at Khirbet Qumran.

Fig. 5. Plan of Khirbet Qumran (according to Hirschfeld).

We now turn to a discussion of Second Temple era courtyard installations in Judea that feature a tower surrounded by a glacis. In 1991, Shimon Riklin excavated a site named Ofarim in western Samaria, east of
Jaffa. He uncovered a tower surrounded by a glacis, with a small courtyard to its east (fig. 6). The artifacts found in this installation include pottery from the first century B.C.E. and four coins from the time of Alexander Jannaeus (103–76 B.C.E.).[6] Riklin pointed out the architectural similarity between the site at Ofarim and the eastern building at Qumran. In

---

  [6] S. Riklin, "A Hasmonean Site at Opharim," in *Judea and Samaria Research Studies*
3 (ed. Z.H. Erlich and Y. Eshel; Ariel: The College of Judea and Samaria, 1994), 127–136
(Hebrew); idem, "When did the Essenes Arrive at Qumran? An Architectural Answer,"
in *Studies in the Land of Judaea* [פרקים בנחלת יהודה: קובץ מחקרים בגיאוגרפיה היסטורית] (ed.
Z.H. Erlich; Ofra: Moriah Press, 1995), 263–266 (Hebrew); idem, "The Courtyard Towers
in the Light of Finds from ʿOfarim," *Atiqot* 32 (1997): 95–98 (Hebrew).

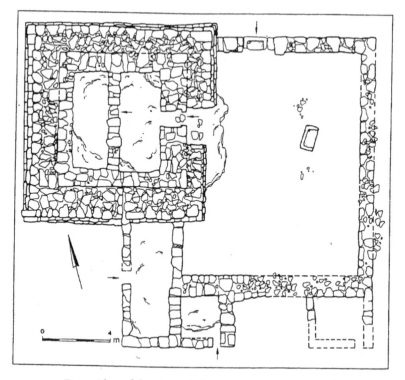

Fig. 6. Plan of the site in Ofarim (according to Riklin).

1994 and 1995 he published popular articles in which he suggested that the evidence he had found at Ofarim ought to be used for learning about the archeology of Khirbet Qumran.

Following Riklin's excavation, Yizhar Hirschfeld published an article in which he collected data about structures that had been found in Judea that included a central courtyard in which a tower surrounded by a glacis had been incorporated into one of its sides.[7] Hirschfeld identified ten structures of this type (fig. 7). In his view, these comprise a well-defined group, and are all to be identified as private villas. On the basis of the perceived similarity between Qumran and these other installations, Hirschfeld proposed that Khirbet Qumran was a "large Manor house" that had belonged to one of the friends of Herod.

---

[7] Y. Hirschfeld, "Early Roman Manor Houses in Judaea and the Site of Khirbet Qumran," *JNES* 57 (1998): 161–189.

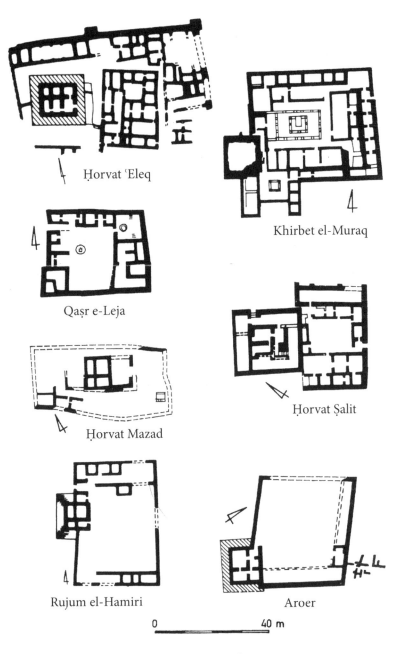

Fig. 7. Sites with courtyards, towers,
and glacis (according to Hirschfeld).

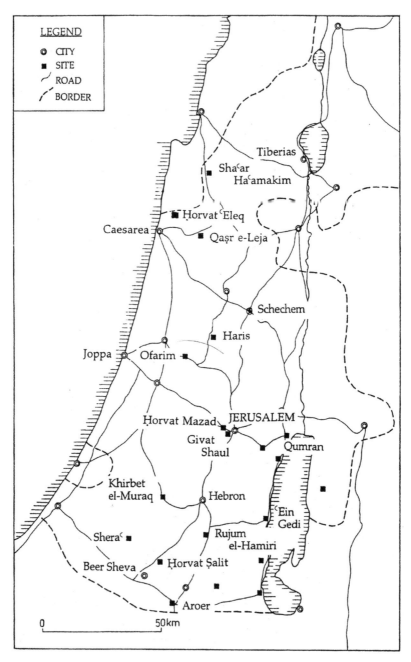

Fig. 8. Map of sites with courtyards, towers,
and glacis (according to Hirschfeld).

The ten Judean sites designated by Hirschfeld are:[8] (1) Ofarim; (2) Khirbet el-Muraq; (3) Rujum el-Hamiri;[9] (4) Aroer;[10] (5) Qumran; (6) Qasr e-Leja; (7) Horvat ʿEleq; (8) Horvat Salit; (9) Horvat Mazad; (10) Qasr et-Turabeh (fig. 8). The first five locations on this list are indeed Second Temple period sites with courtyard installations featuring a tower surrounded by a glacis. In my opinion, however, the remaining five sites ought not be placed in this group. Qasr e-Leja has been surveyed, but not yet excavated. It lies north of the other sites that have a courtyard and a tower surrounded by a glacis. It seems that this site is later than the Second Temple period and is to be dated to the second or third century C.E. Moreover, there was no glacis constructed around the tower found in the corner of Qasr e-Leja. There is no basis for including this structure in the group of sites of this type.[11]

Horvat ʿEleq is a multi-layered site. Hirschfeld's depiction of this site includes structures from a number of periods.[12] The tower surrounded by a glacis that was built at Horvat ʿEleq was not built into one of the sides of the courtyard structure, and so it should not be included in the list of sites similar to Qumran.[13]

The site of Horvat Salit was in use during the Bar Kokhba revolt, and it too differs from the sites of the type under discussion. The fortified structure here is attached to the courtyard installation, but the tower is much larger than those in the first five sites listed by Hirschfeld, and it is not surrounded by a glacis.[14]

---

[8] Ibid. See also Y. Hirschfeld, "Qumran in the Second Temple Period: A Reassessment," in *Qumran, the Site of the Dead Sea Scrolls: Archaeological Interpretations and Debates* (ed. K. Galor, J.-B. Humbert, and J. Zangenberg; STDJ 57; Leiden: Brill, 2006), 223–239, 233 n. 30; idem, *Qumran in Context: Reassessing the Archeological Evidence* (Peabody: Hendrickson, 2004), 222–225.

[9] On Rujum el-Hamiri, see Y. Barouch, "The Roman Castles in the Hills of Hebron," in *Judea and Samaria Research Studies* 4 (ed. Z.H. Erlich and Y. Eshel; Ariel: The College of Judea and Samaria, 1995), 137–143 (Hebrew).

[10] On Aroer in the period of the Second Temple, see M. Hershkovitz, "Aroer at the End of the Second Temple Period," *ErIsr* 23 (1992): 309–319 (Hebrew).

[11] Hirschfeld himself determined that the site at Qasr e-Leja was from the second or third century C.E. See Y. Hirschfeld, *The Palestinian Dwelling in the Roman-Byzantine Period* (Jerusalem: Franciscan Printing, 1995), 52–53.

[12] I am grateful to Dr. Orit Peleg, the current supervisor of the excavations at Horvat ʿEleq, for this information.

[13] Y. Hirschfeld, *Ramat Hanadiv Excavations: Final Report of the 1984–1998 Seasons*, (Jerusalem: Israel Exploration Society, 2000), 235–293.

[14] On Horvat Salit, see G. Bijovsky, "The Coins from Ḥorbat Ẓalit," *Atiqot* 39 (2000): 155–169.

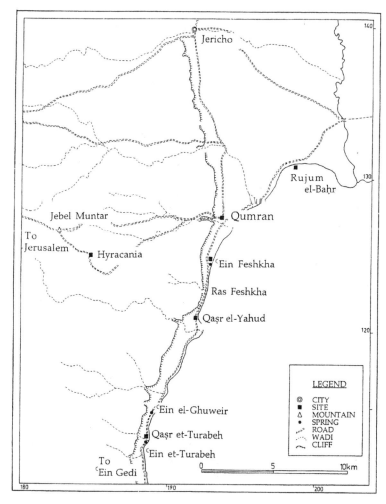

Fig. 9. Road map of the Qumran region (according to Hirschfeld).

As I have already shown in the beginning of this article, Horvat Mazad does not belong to this group either. The tower at this site is in the center of the installation, and it is not surrounded by a glacis.

The final site listed by Hirschfeld is Qasr et-Turabeh. It is located on the shore of the Dead Sea, about 12 km south of Khirbet Qumran (fig. 9). This site was excavated in its entirety by Pesah Bar-Adon in 1971. The square installation at this site includes a tower surrounded by a glacis attached to its southern wall (fig. 10). Alongside the western and northern walls of the structure there are rows of monoliths, i.e., stone

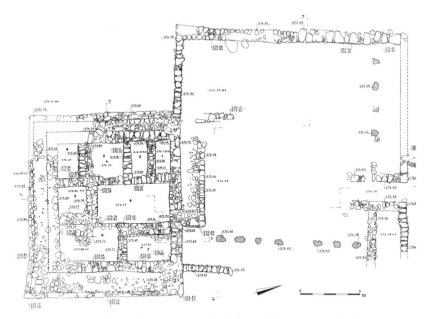

Fig. 10. Plan of Qasar et-Turabeh (according to Bar-Adon).

pillars, which are typical architectonic features of the Iron Age. Bar-Adon found 37 indicative ceramic artifacts at the site. Thirty-two of these are from the Iron Age II, including a complete juglet. The items appear to date from the seventh century B.C.E. Bar-Adon found only five potsherds from the Hasmonean era in his excavation.[15] The architectonic components as well as the pottery found at Qasr et-Turabeh indicate that the structure was originally built in the Iron Age II, and continued to function as a way station into the Second Temple period.

A comparison between Khirbet Qumran and the sites enumerated by Hirschfeld yields many more dissimilarities than similarities: None of the other sites that have a courtyard installation with a tower surrounded by a glacis feature ten miqwaot, as Qumran does.[16] The other sites do not have manufacturing installations like those found at Qumran (such as the potters' workshop). We have not found anything elsewhere similar to the

---

[15] P. Bar-Adon, "Excavations in the Judean Desert," *Atiqot* 9 (1989): 41–49 (Hebrew).

[16] Following R. Reich's identification of ten *miqwaot* at Qumran, see R. Reich, "*Miqwa'ot* (Ritual Baths) at Qumran," *Qadmoniot* 30 (1997): 125–128; see also J. Magness, *The Archaeology of Qumran and the Dead Sea Scrolls* (Studies in the Dead Sea Scrolls and Related Literature; Grand Rapids: Eerdmans, 2002), 134–162.

dining hall and the dishes found in the southern part of Khirbet Qumran. We have not found another site that is in the proximity of a cemetery with over 1100 burials. Not one of the other sites has an aqueduct of the type found at Qumran. Thus, despite the architectonic similarity between Khirbet Qumran and the other four Judean sites with a courtyard tower and glacis, it is clear that Qumran is very different from these other sites.

To date, we have uncovered five Judean sites featuring a courtyard installation in which a courtyard surrounded by a glacis has been incorporated into one of its walls. These five sites may be placed into four categories: The installations at Rujum el-Hamiri and Aroer were constructed for defensive purposes. These sites were constructed at strategic locations, and it is likely that they were inhabited by professional soldiers who served in the Hasmonean and Herodian armies. In contrast, the installation at Ofarim was built for the defense of a private individual and his family, who resided near their orchards in the fruit harvesting season. Evidence for this can be found in the tiny dimensions of the structure at Ofarim, which is much smaller than any of the other installations. Khirbet el-Muraq was a country villa or a palace. As noted above, it is the only country villa to have been found in Judea from the Second Temple period. At Qumran, the courtyard installation with the tower and glacis served a religious community that used the site at the end of the Second Temple period. It appears that the idea of building courtyard structures protected by a tower and surrounded by a glacis began already in the First Temple period, at the end of Iron Age II, as indicated by the excavations of Qasr et-Turabeh.

I would like to conclude this study with a general statement about archeological method. From a scientific standpoint, it is not legitimate to ask "what would we have thought about the site of Khirbet Qumran if the scrolls had not been discovered?" No responsible archeologist would assert that it is preferable to determine the date of a particular structure by deliberately disregarding the artifacts found in it, such as pottery or coins. In the same way, it would not be valid to suggest that the walls of a building be ignored in evaluating the purpose of the structure. Archeological method demands that a proposed explanation address all of the finds uncovered at a particular site. Thus, attempting to explain the purpose of the buildings at Khirbet Qumran, while ignoring the scrolls found near the site, is a game that is not relevant to serious inquiry.[17]

---

[17] H. Eshel, "Qumran Archaeology" (review of Y. Hirschfeld, *Qumran in Context*), *JAOS* 125 (2005): 389–394.

In summary, in this note I first compared Khirbet Qumran to a way station from the Second Temple era that was found west of Jerusalem. We saw that this site, Horvat Mazad, bears no architectonic similarity to Qumran. I then compared Qumran to Khirbet el-Muraq, which is the only known country villa from the Second Temple period. And, again, we saw that these sites were very different from one another. Finally, we compared Khirbet Qumran to a group of sites that contain courtyard installations that were defended by a tower surrounded by a glacis. We saw that the architectonic similarities of these sites was not indicative of the functions of the sites, but that structures of this sort were used for a variety of purposes in the Second Temple period.

PARALLELS TO BE SEEN:
MANUSCRIPTS IN JARS FROM QUMRAN AND EGYPT[*]

Minna Lönnqvist and Kenneth Lönnqvist
Universities of Helsinki and Oulu, Finland

Cylindrical Jars with and without Manuscripts from Qumran

The famous story of the Bedouin shepherd of the Ta'amireh tribe discovering ancient manuscripts in the caves at Qumran in 1947 does not provide us with secure archaeological documentation of the find. However, the Bedouin account is the only evidence at our disposal that manuscripts were actually found in jars in 1947 in the area (fig. 1).[1] Nevertheless, there are several other accounts of hiding and discovering manuscripts in jars around Eastern Mediterranean, Mesopotamia and Kurdistan, including the Bible and rabbinic literature. It is, for instance, known that manuscripts were found in jars near Jericho already in antiquity, and in the Dead Sea region in the Middle Ages, but there is no exact information as to whether these discoveries were associated with Qumran in specific.[2]

That the Bedouin's story of the Qumran discovery is largely credible is supported by the archaeological accounts from Egypt. Already in 1949 R. de Vaux,[3] followed by J.T. Milik in 1950[4] and B. Couroyer in

---

[*] We wish to express our deep gratitude to the Soprintendenza per i Beni Archeologici del Piemonte e Museo Antichità Egizie, Turin, Italy, to Chief Curator Dr. E. D'Amicone, Dr. Marcella Trapani, the museum assistants and the library staff, who gave us access to the Deir el-Medina archaeological material, the excavation documents and helped us to find relevant literature in October 2005.

[1] In his account the Bedouin, however, dates the discovery to 1945. See, e.g., W.H. Brownlee, "Muhammad ed-Deeb's Own Story of his Scroll Discovery," *JNES* 16 (1957): 236–239.

[2] Eusebius, *Hist. eccl.* 6.16.3, and O. Eissfeldt, "Der Anlass zur Entdeckung der Höhle und ihr ähnliche Vorgänge aus älterer Zeit," *TLZ* 74 (1949): 597–600 (597–598).

[3] R. de Vaux, "La grotte des manuscrits hébreux," *RB* 56 (1949): 586–609 (592).

[4] J.T. Milik, "Le Giarre dei Manoscritti della Grotta del Mar Morto e dell'Egitto Tolemaico," *Bib* 31 (1950): 504–508.

Fig. 1. Qumran Cave 1, the Site of the Bedouin
Discovery. Photograph: K. Lönnqvist.

1955,[5] pointed to the fact that apart from Qumran the tradition of hiding manuscripts in jars is especially well testified in Egypt, and that the only excavated finds of scrolls in jars were from Egypt. The date of the excavated manuscript finds varied from the Ramesside to the Ptolemaic and early Christian era. These finds contained papyri and parchment documents written in Hieratic, Demotic, Aramaic, Greek and Coptic. Most of the finds are scrolls, while the later texts were often in codex-form, like the early Christian and Gnostic literature (see table 1).

---

[5] B. Couroyer, "A propos des dépots de manuscrits dans des jarres," *RB* 62 (195): 76–81.

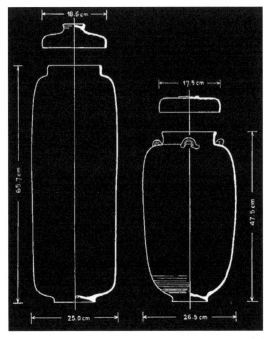

Fig. 2. The Qumran Cave 1 Jars Containing Manuscripts. (The Hebrew University Collection of Qumran Jars. After Sukenik 1955, 21.)

Table 1. A Short Summary of Jars Containing Scrolls or Codices Found in Egypt

Ramesses III (Hieratic)	1 occurrence
Sixth century B.C.E. (Saqqara and Hermopolis, both Aramaic)	2 occurrences
Ptolemaic/Hellenistic (1 Elephantine in Greek and Demotic, 1 Deir el-Medina in Greek and Demotic + 1 Deir el-Medina in Greek and Demotic)	3 occurrences
Early Christian/Gnostic texts (2 Nag Hammadi, 1 Fayum, 1 Kôm-Išgây)	4 occurrences

The two jars associated (fig. 2) with the original discovery of Cave 1 at Qumran were purchased by E. Sukenik with some manuscripts from a Bethlehem dealer for the Hebrew University of Jerusalem.[6] During the subsequent cave excavations at Qumran, L.G. Harding and R. de Vaux

---

[6] E.L. Sukenik, ed., *The Dead Sea Scrolls of the Hebrew University* (Jerusalem: Magnes, 1955).

found in Cave 1 dozens of broken pottery pieces of the same type as these intact jars, further reinstating the Bedouin discovery. In addition, the linen wrappings that were still attached to some pieces of pottery support the authenticity of the Bedouin discovery.[7] The excavations by R. de Vaux[8] in the 1950s and by Y. Magen and Y. Peleg[9] in 1993–2004 at the settlement of Qumran have produced cylindrical jars of the type found in the nearby caves. The common cylindrical jar types, then, have been used as an argument to connect the scroll caves with the main settlement at Qumran.

In Qumran studies, the cylindrical jars were for long generally thought to be unique to the Qumran region in Palestine. But in the last few years R. Bar-Nathan has pointed to similarities between the Qumran storage jars and the ceramic repertoire of the Hasmonaean and Herodian winter palaces at Jericho and Masada.[10] In addition, according to J. Magness, there are cylindrical jars from Qalandiya north of Jerusalem and Quailba (Abila) in Jordan.[11] The Masada jar finds are, however, more comparable in shape to the cylindrical jars from Cave 1 than the Jericho jars. For example, the "bag-shaped" jar type from Jericho, despite sharing some common features, is not comparable to the two cylindrical jars in the Hebrew University Collection that came to be called the "scroll jars."[12] Late Roman so-called bag-shaped amphora types of Peacock's Class 48 (Zemer 53) produced in Palestine, Gaza and Egypt do also bear some resemblance to the Qumran jars in their elongated shape, but they are later than the Qumran and the Jericho finds.[13] Therefore, beside the Qumran region the only hitherto known comparable and contempo-

---

[7] G.L. Harding in *DJD* I (1955): 7.

[8] See, e.g., J.-B. Humbert and A. Chambon, eds., *Fouilles de Khirbet Qumrân et de Aïn Feshka*, vol. I: *Album de photographies, répertoire du fonds photographique, synthèse des notes de chantier du Père Roland de Vaux OP* (NTOA.SA 1; Fribourg: Éditions Universitaires, 1994).

[9] Y. Magen and Y. Peleg, "Back to Qumran: Ten Years of Excavation and Research, 1993–2004," in *Qumran, the Site of the Dead Sea Scrolls: Archaeological Interpretations and Debates: Proceedings of a Conference Held at Brown University, November 17–19, 2002* (ed. K. Galor, J.-B. Humbert, and J. Zangenberg; STDJ 57; Leiden: Brill, 2006), 55–113.

[10] R. Bar-Nathan, "Qumran and the Hasmonaean and Herodian Winter Palaces of Jericho: The Implication of the Pottery Finds on the Interpretation of the Settlement at Qumran," in *Qumran, the Site of the Dead Sea Scrolls*, 263–277.

[11] J. Magness, "Qumran: The Site of the Dead Sea Scrolls: A Review Article," *RevQ* 22 (2005–2006): 641–664 (662–663).

[12] Cf. also ibid., 662.

[13] D.P.S. Peacock and D.F. Williams, *Amphorae and the Roman Economy: An Introductory Guide* (London: Thames & Hudson, 1991).

raneous cylindrical jars from the Dead Sea area are those from Masada called Masada group 2. These jars belong to the so-called last occupation (68–73/74 C.E.)[14] of Masada by the Zealots, or the *sicarii* according to Flavius Josephus (*J.W.* 4.398–400; 7.275–279, 303–406). Although the shape of the Qumran and Masada jars is the same, *the Masada jars did not contain manuscripts*. Based on the evidence from Masada, Bar-Nathan explains that the cylindrical jars from Qumran are from the first century C.E. This generalizing conclusion is, on the one hand, problematic, as we shall see in due course when studying the analyses of the clay that the Qumran pottery was made of, the existing parallels of cylindrical jars, as well as the dating of the texts that were discovered inside the jars. It is true that Bar-Nathan is right concerning the dating of some later examples of cylindrical jars found at the settlement, but this conclusion does not necessarily apply to the date of all the cylindrical jars that came from the Qumran caves, or the origin of burying scrolls in jars at the site. Therefore, there is a further problem that needs to be considered, i.e., how did, in fact, the jar type end up in Masada: Was it actually acquired from Qumran by the last fighters? Or did some Qumran occupiers join the last fighters? Moreover, how should one then interpret the fate of the cities in the vicinity such as Ein Gedi (Engaddi), which the *sicarii* destroyed?[15] Interestingly, Y. Yadin found on Masada a version of the *Songs of the Sabbath Sacrifice* (Mas1k) comparable to that from the Qumran Cave 4 (4Q400–405) and Cave 11 (11Q17). Yadin indeed believed that the occupiers of Qumran were Essenes and that the find from Masada was a proof that some Essenes participated in the Jewish revolt against Romans and joined the last fighters of the Zealots/*sicarii* on Masada.[16] J. Magness agrees with Yadin's deduction.[17] On the other hand, in the light of the present evidence we would only conclude that the common jar type and the manuscript find indicate that there were some contacts with the last occupants of Masada and Qumran.

J. Gunneweg and M. Balla analysed the origin of (the clay of) 61 jars from Qumran Caves 1, 2, 3, 4, 6, 7, 9, 10, 28, 31, 38 and 39 by using the Neutron Activation Analysis (NAA).[18] Of the 61 jars studied, 34 jars

---

[14] Bar-Nathan, "Qumran and the Hasmonaean and Herodian Winter Palaces."

[15] Josephus, *J.W.* 4.402.

[16] Y. Yadin, *Masada: Herod's Fortress and Zealots' Last Stand* (New York: Random House, 1966), 172–174.

[17] Magness, "Qumran: The Site of the Dead Sea Scrolls: A Review Article," 663.

[18] J. Gunneweg and M. Balla, "Neutron Activation Analysis: Scroll Jars and Common Ware," in *Khirbet Qumrân et 'Aïn Feshkha*, vol. II: *Études d'anthropologie, de physique et*

were of the elongated cylindrical shape—often called "scroll jars." The height of the jars varied from 35 cm to 78 cm. Some jars had handles and/or lids, whereas others lacked them. Similar jars were also analyzed from the Qumran settlement, but the function of these cylindrical jars discovered in the settlement—according to the authors—may have been different as the jars are of different size and thus may have been used for storage of other materials. Also in J. Magness' opinion the cylindrical jars from Qumran were used for storing other materials such as food and drink beside manuscripts.[19] The NAA samples of the clays point to the fact that generally the jars and ceramics from the settlement and caves were locally produced: probably in the Jericho-Dead Sea region or near Hebron from the Mozza clay, not representing the *terra rossa* type of clay. However, there is an intriguing but unidentified clay substance in a small group of Qumran jars which may have come from elsewhere. It should furthermore be noted that there are clear examples of clay "finger-prints" typical of the Nabataean pottery among the other types of jars from Qumran.[20]

Manuscript Jars from Egypt: The Deir el-Medina Finds

It is apparent that J.T. Milik's pioneering article on the similarities be-tween the Qumran jars and the jars from Deir el-Medina published in 1950 has fallen on "deaf ears" because it was written in Italian.[21] Milik emphasized, as we did in 2002,[22] that by then—before the publications

---

de chimie (ed. J.-B. Humbert and J. Gunneweg; NTOA.SA 3; Fribourg: Academic Press, 2003), 3–57.

[19] Magness, "Qumran: The Site of the Dead Sea Scrolls: A Review Article," 663.

[20] Gunneweg and Balla, "Neutron Activation Analysis."

[21] See n. 4 above.

[22] Milik, "Giarre dei Manoscritti," 507–508 says that: "*Vasi di tipo analogo ci sono però nell'Egitto contemporaneo,*" or that jars that are typologically similar and contemporary are from Egypt; and "*la similitudine morfologica delle giarre di Dêr et-Medîna e del Mar Morto è evidente,*" or that the morphological similarities between the Deir el-Medina jars and the Dead Sea jars are obvious; that "*L'esame più esteso della ceramica ellenistica dell'Egitto rileverà senza dubbio raffronti più numerosi e più esatti e confermerà con ogni probabilità l'ipotesi della provenienza dall'Egitto di questo tipo di vasellame della ceramica palestinese*" or in English "that a more fuller examination of the Hellenistic pottery of Egypt finds without any doubt so numerous and exact comparisons and confirms in all probability the hypothesis of an Egyptian origin for this type of Palestinian pottery vessel." See also M. Lönnqvist and K. Lönnqvist, *Archaeology of the Hidden Qumran: The New Paradigm* (Helsinki: Helsinki University Press, 2002), 73–78.

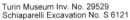

Turin Museum Inv. No. 29529　　　Turin Museum Inv. No. 29530
Schiaparelli Excavation No. S 6121　　Schiaparelli Excavation No. S 6122

Fig. 3. The Deir el-Medina Jars from Schiaparelli's
Expedition to Egypt in 1905. Published with
permission of The Egyptian Museum at Turin, Italy.

of other parallels from Israel—the closest typological and functional
parallels to the smaller Qumran jar type from Cave 1 were found in
Egypt. Milik's list of Egyptian parallels contained two cylindrical vessels
that are now housed in the Egyptian Museum in Turin in Italy (fig. 3).

In 1905, E. Schiaparelli's excavation team found these two clay jars still
closed and sealed with ropes in a house at the village of Deir el-Medina
in Western Thebes in Egypt. The house was associated with a large tomb
that may have been a part of the Temple of Hathor. An archive of Greek
and Demotic papyri was recovered from the two jars.[23] The authors of this
paper had an opportunity to closely study these Deir el-Medina jars in the
Egyptian Museum of Turin in Italy in 2005.[24] Both jars have three small

---

[23] G. Botti, *L'Archivio demotico da Deir el-Medineh* (2 vols.; Catalogo del Museo Egizio
di Torino, Serie Prima: Monumenti e Testi 1; Florence: Le Monnier, 1967). B. Bruyère,
Rapport sur les fouilles de Deir el Médineh (1935–1940) (Fouilles de l'Institut Français
d'Archéologie Orientale du Caire 20; Cairo: Institut Français d'Archéologie Orientale,
1948), 27, n. 1.

[24] Schiaparelli's two jars meet the following description: Jar A (Inv. No. 29,529), height
39 cm, diameter 23 cm, thickness 0.8–0.6 cm. The lid is of "anelliform" being 13 cm in
diameter. Jar B (Inv. No. 29,530) is 39 cm in height, with a diameter of 24.5–24.3 cm and
thickness of 0.5 cm. The diameter of the lid is 17.5 cm. The smaller Hebrew University jar
that is thought to originate in Qumran Cave 1 is 47.5 cm in height, 26.5 cm in diameter

Fig. 4. The Deir el-Medina Jar No. 29,529 from Schiaparelli's
Expedition to Egypt in 1905. Published with permission of The
Egyptian Museum at Turin, Italy. Photograph: K. Lönnqvist.

loop-handles close to the neck of the vessel. At the time of the original
discovery, the handles of the jars were used to close the lid with a rope.
The clay of both jars is fine *rossa* with some white inclusions, typical of
the Mediterranean *terra rossa* pottery. The function of the Deir el-Medina
jars was to preserve a family archive, and as such probably intended to be
a *portable archive*. These jars contained altogether 33 papyrus scrolls, 95
folios of which nine documents are in Greek and 45 in Demotic. The
papyri dated between 188 and 101 B.C.E. include liturgical texts, deeds
of sale, marital and divorce contracts, property agreements of funerary
organisations, cancellation of debts, etc. The manuscripts found in the
jars are thus from the Ptolemaic/Hellenistic era, and secure a date for
both the use of the private archive and its subsequent deposit.[25]

---

and its lid is 17.5 cm in width (fig. 1 above). The jar is therefore 8.5 cm taller than the Deir
el-Medina jars and ca. 2 cm wider in diameter.

   [25] Botti, *L'Archivio demotico*.

With the kind assistance of Dr. Marcella Trapani from the Egyptian Museum at Turin, we also discovered in 2005 that, in addition to Schiaparelli's 1905 find, another family archive had been discovered in jars in 1922 by E.B. Coxe Jr. under C. Fisher's archaeological expedition at Deir el-Medina in a house dating to the Ptolemaic period. This find was unknown to R. de Vaux and J. Milik. The expedition found altogether 32 Demotic papyri in two jars (of "beet form") in a house built against the pylon of the nineteenth dynasty tomb at Draʿ-Abu-el-Naga. The documents dated from the years 317–217 B.C.E. also being Ptolemaic/Hellenistic. With regard to the contents, the find resembles Schiaparelli's discovery: leases of houses, marriage contracts and divorce settlements, statements of accounts, mortgages, gifts and services for mummies. The jars and some of the manuscripts are now in the University of Pennsylvania Museum at Philadelphia, some in the Cairo Museum, but unfortunately, we have no information about the pottery vessels.[26]

MANUSCRIPT JARS FROM EGYPT: THE ELEPHANTINE FINDS

The Deir el-Meidna jars are not isolated examples in the material culture of ancient Egypt. In addition, it is elucidating to bring forth the archaeological fact that some Greek and Demotic papyri were also found in jars in 1906 during the German excavations at Elephantine in Upper Egypt. There were five papyri dating from 311/310–284/283 B.C.E. and nineteen from the years 225/224–223/222 B.C.E.[27]—the dates falling more or less into the same period as the latter finds by E.B. Coxe Jr. and C. Fisher from Deir el-Medina. Because these Greek and Demotic papyri from

---

[26] C.S. Fisher, "A Group of Theban Tombs," *University of Pennsylvania: The Museum Journal* 15 (1924): 28–49; N. Reich, "Marriage and Divorce in Ancient Egypt: Papyrus Documents Discovered at Thebes by the Eckley B. Coxe Jr. Expedition to Egypt," *University of Pennsylvania: The Museum Journal* 15 (1924): 50–57; repr. (with corrections) in *Mizraim* 1 (1933): 135–139; M. El-Amir, *A Family Archive from Thebes: Demotic Papyri in the Philadelphia and Cairo Museums from the Ptolemaic Period*, vol. 1: *Transliteration and Translation* (Cairo: General Organisation for Government Printing Offices, 1959). See also J.R. Abercrombie, "A History of the Acquisition of Papyri and Related Written Material in the University (of Pennsylvania) Museum" (ca. 1980; published only electronically: http://www.sas.upenn.edu/religious_studies/rak/ppen/paphist.htm).

[27] O. Rubensohn, *Elephantine-Papyri* (Ägyptische Urkunden aus den königlichen Museen in Berlin: Griechische Urkunden: Sonderheft; Berlin: Weidmann, 1907), 4–5, 34. The jars were oval and elongated, 32 cm in height.

Elephantine were found in jars, E.G. Kraeling, who published some of the Jewish Aramaic papyri from Elephantine, suspected that they were probably originally stored and found in jars owing to their exceptionally good state of preservation.[28] They had been purchased by C.E. Wilbour from locals in 1893[29] in the same manner as Dr. Sukenik had done with the Qumran manuscripts, and therefore the exact circumstances of the discovery are unknown. It should be noted that these Aramaic papyri from Elephantine in the Brooklyn Museum collection date from the fifth century B.C.E. and belonged to the Jewish military colonists living at Elephantine. Other fifth century documents of the Jewish colony were also published by A.E. Cowley.[30] Although these Jewish manuscripts are earlier than the manuscript jar finds made at Elephantine, Deir el-Medina and Qumran, Kraeling's suggestion that the manuscripts at the Brooklyn Museum collection had been originally stored in jars, does not have to be very far-fetched if we look at the finds in table 1. There are two known occurrences of Aramaic texts in jars dating from the sixth century B.C.E. found at Saqqara and Hermopolis.

The Persian domination of Egypt obviously influenced the contents of the writings of the Jewish colonies, and the languages used. As exemplified in the Elephantine documents, Aramaic and Greek were commonly used in the area in official texts in the Persian and Graeco-Roman period. The same situation obtains at Qumran even though the majority of the Qumran texts were composed in Hebrew. The Aramaic used in the Elephantine papyri belongs to the so-called Imperial Aramaic used during the Persian era until the conquest of Alexander the Great, after which Greek largely replaced Aramaic in official texts in the Near East.[31] The Qumran Aramaic dialect contains, in contrast to Imperial Aramaic, fixed Hebrew loanwords, but no Greek ones.[32] As far as the writing materials are concerned, the Elephantine texts were written on papyrus, which is,

---

[28] E.G. Kraeling, ed., *The Brooklyn Museum Aramaic Papyri: New Documents of the Fifth Century B.C. from the Jewish Colony at Elephantine* (New Haven: Yale University Press, 1953), 51.

[29] Ibid., 9.

[30] A.E. Cowley, ed., *Aramaic Papyri of the Fifth Century B.C.* (Oxford: Clarendon, 1923).

[31] See, e.g. K. Beyer, *The Aramaic Language: Its Distribution and Subdivision* (trans. J.F. Healey; Göttingen: Vandenhoeck & Ruprecht, 1986), 14–19.

[32] C. Müller-Kessler and F. Schiller *apud* K. Lönnqvist, "Winds of Change: Impressions from an International Conference called: *The Dead Sea Scrolls in Context, Integrating the Dead Sea Scrolls in the Study of Ancient Texts, Languages, and Cultures*," QC 16 (2008): 1–13 (13).

in fact, frequently encountered at Qumran, too (also at Cave 1), although the majority of the Dead Sea Scrolls were written on parchment. Furthermore, it is important to recall here that the Dead Sea area, like the rest of Palestine, was under Ptolemaic rule for an entire century in the Hellenistic period. The foreign domination continued in the Roman era, when Mark Antony bequeathed Jericho and her balsam groves with other areas to Queen Cleopatra, the Ptolemaic ruler of Egypt.[33]

As contacts and movement of people between Jewish communities and under different political dominations were common in antiquity, influences were naturally transmitted. Papyrus Padua 1, for instance, indicates that there were contacts between the Jews of Elephantine and those of another garrison city at Migdol in the Delta region.[34] After the Jewish temple of Elephantine was destroyed,[35] Jews from Elephantine may have relocated to areas such as the Delta region whereas others may even have returned to Palestine. The Jewish philosopher Philo the Alexandrian describes the life of the community of Jewish Therapeutae at Marea, another military colony in the Delta area.[36] These Jewish Therapeutae had doctrinal teachings and customs similar to the ones we encounter in the Qumran texts, and which the contemporary Essenes in Palestine had.[37]

Manuscript Jars from Egypt: The Nag Hammadi Finds

The provenance studies of the Qumran "scroll jars" conducted by J. Gunneweg and M. Balla do not take into account Milik's previously mentioned references to the typologically and morphologically comparable jars with manuscripts found in Egypt. The authors only mention a later jar find including Gnostic and Coptic manuscripts from Chenoboskion

---

[33] Josephus, *J.W.* 1.361–362.

[34] See also E. Bresciani, "Papiri aramaici egiziani di epoca persiana presso il Museo Civico di Padova," *RSO* 35 (1960): 11–24.

[35] A letter dating from 407 B.C.E. is a petition for authorization by Elephantine Jews to build a new temple to replace the old one, and includes a detailed description of the destruction of the first one. See, J.B. Pritchard, ed., *The Ancient Near East*, vol. 1: *An Anthology of Texts and Pictures* (Princeton: Princeton University Press, 1973), 279–281. See also Cowley, *Aramaic Papyri*, 31.

[36] Philo, *On the Contemplative Life.*

[37] See G. Vermes and M.D. Goodman, eds., *The Essenes According to the Classical Sources* (Oxford Centre Textbooks 1; Sheffield: JSOT Press, 1989), passim.

in Egypt.[38] This find from Egypt, also listed by Milik, is obviously the same as the Nag Hammadi (or Naj ʿḤammādī) discovery, as the site was called Chenoboskion in antiquity. The discovery of the famous Nag Hammadi Christian apocryphal and Gnostic codices in Upper Egypt in 1945 is a surprisingly similar story to the contemporary Qumran finds.[39]

The Bedouins at Nag Hammadi found a jar containing ancient manuscripts while digging for fertilizers, but it was destroyed and what remains is a description and drawing.[40] The colour of the bowl is deep reddish brown, connecting it to the *terra rossa* of the Deir el-Medina jars in Turin. The height is comparable with the taller jar from Qumran Cave 1,[41] but it is apparent that the Nag Hammadi jar was not as narrow as the Cave 1 jar. The Bedouin drawing points clearly to the existence of a wide amphora-type vessel which allegedly accommodated the original manuscripts. As far as the Nag Hammadi finds are concerned, they also contained much later religious texts, though not Jewish, but Gnostic Christian. The esoteric nature of both the Qumran texts and the Nag Hammadi texts has been noticed by several scholars.

The Storage of the Manuscripts for Their Preservation

In the cases of Qumran and Egypt the dry desert climate has been a major factor contributing to the preservation of the ancient manuscripts, though it is by no means the only factor. Both the Qumran jars and the Deir el-Medina jars, which are cylindrical in shape, have pottery saucers or bowls as a lid. In Qumran the bowls were turned upside down to protect the contents. As mentioned, the Nag Hammadi jar had a comparable lid—now in the Schøyen collection in Norway—to the

---

[38] Gunneweg and Balla, "Neutron Activation Analysis." See also J. Michniewicz and M. Krzyśko, "The Provenance of Scroll Jars in the Light of Archaeometric Investigations," in *Khirbet Qumrân et ʿAïn Feshkha*, vol. II, 59–99.

[39] J.M. Robinson, "The Discovery of the Nag Hammadi Library and its Archaeological Context," *BA* 42 (1979): 206–224.

[40] Ibid. The Bedouins describe its size as having been 60 cm in height, 30 cm in diameter at the bottom and the mouth having been 15–20 cm. Only the lid is preserved and is of a parallel bowl-type, such as the Qumran jar lids. The lid of the Nag Hammadi find belongs to the Schøyen Collection (MS 1804/7) in Oslo, Norway. It is 23.3 cm in diameter, the ring foot being 7.7 cm in diameter at the base. The description of the jar and the bowl-like lid is on pp. 212–213.

[41] Sukenik, *Dead Sea Scrolls of the Hebrew University*, fig. 6.

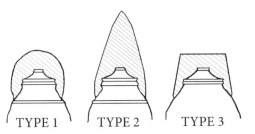

Fig. 5. Types of Clay Jar-Sealings and Lids in
Archaic Egypt. Following Emery, *Archaic Egypt*, 210
fig. 123. Redrawn and digitized by K. Lönnqvist.

Qumran bowls. Outside Qumran a single bowl of the type used in the
jars allegedly found in Cave 1 has also been discovered in Beit Zur on the
way to Bethlehem.[42]

It should be noted that already in the beginning of the First Dynasty in
Egypt, it was common to seal large wine jars by placing a round bowl-like
pottery cap in an inverted position over the mouth (see fig. 5). It could
have been further sealed with a lump of clay to protect the contents.[43] In
addition, the Deir el-Medina jars have loop handles near the neck of the
vessel comparable to the smaller jar purchased by Sukenik to the Hebrew
University (fig. 2). In the case of the Deir el-Medina jars the loop handles
functioned to tighten the closing mechanism of the lid with a rope or a
thong. It is likely that this was also the case in the smaller jar from Cave 1
at the Hebrew University collection. This closing mechanism prevented,
e.g., animals from entering the jars.

Manuscripts Dating Jars

A distribution map of the jars discovered containing manuscripts from
the Graeco-Roman era (see fig. 6.) demonstrates that the archaeological
finds from the period concentrate in Egypt. The Egyptian finds with
dated manuscripts discovered *in situ* provide a secure dating for the use
of the jars. The closing date of the deposit of the Deir el-Medina jars
and archive found by Schiaparelli's team is ca. 101 B.C.E. (*terminus post*

---

[42] R.W. Funk, "The 1957 Campaign at Beth-Zur," *BASOR* 150 (1958): 8–20.
[43] W.B. Emery, *Archaic Egypt: Culture and Civilization in Egypt Five Thousand Years
Ago* (London: Penguin Books, 1991), 207–210.

Fig. 6. Archaeological Find Locations for Jars Containing
Scrolls from the Graeco-Roman Period. White Coloured
Circles: Qumran, Deir el-Medina and Elephantine.

quem), but this does not rule out the possibility that this private portable archive with the cylindrical jar types was already in use in 188 B.C.E. and remained so until the archive was closed. The dating of the manuscripts found in the Deir el-Medina jars demonstrates that the jar type is most likely dating from the second century B.C.E. of the Ptolemaic era.

It is believed that the famous Isaiah scroll from Qumran Cave 1 (1QIsa[a]) was originally deposited in the jars which Sukenik bought. Other documents associated with the Qumran Cave 1 discovery are the *War Scroll* (1QM) and fragments of the *Thanksgiving Scroll* (*Hodayot*) (1QH[a]).[44] In addition, the finds from Cave 1 also include the *Community*

---

[44] Sukenik, *Dead Sea Scrolls of the Hebrew University.*

Rule (1QS) and *Pesher Habakkuk* (1QpHab). As the manuscript discoveries from Deir el-Medina consisted of family archives, the contents are not directly comparable with the Qumran texts that belonged to a religious community. Instead, it is possible to compare the composition of the Deir el-Medina archives with the fifth century B.C.E. Jewish Aramaic papyri from Elephantine in Upper Egypt.[45] However, apart from civil and judicial transactions, the Deir el-Medina papyri did also contain some liturgical and religious documents which—as religious documents—are comparable with the *Thanksgiving Scroll* from Qumran Cave 1 (1QH^a).

The radiocarbon date of the Isaiah Scroll (1QIsa^a) is 356–103 BC, with calibrated age ranges 250–103 Cal BC (with 76% probability). Palaeographic studies have dated it to 150–125 B.C.E., which is closer to the lower calibrated radiocarbon age. The *Community Rule* (1QS) dates to 2041±68 BP and *Pesher Habakkuk* (1QpHab) written on papyrus dates to 2054±22 BP. The former is calibrated to 206 Cal BC–Cal AD 111 (with 98% probability), and the latter to 120–5 Cal BC (with 97% probability). The former age, and part of the latter, is within the range of the lower calibrated radiocarbon date of the Isaiah Scroll (1QIsa^a) and is in accordance with its palaeographic dating. The lower calibrated radiocarbon ages of the *Community Rule* (1QS) and *Pesher Habakkuk* (1QpHab) around the turn of the millennium and the Common Era, however, could even indicate a date towards the end of the Qumran settlement and the First Jewish Revolt (66–73 C.E.).[46] It is interesting to observe that the Isaiah Scroll (1QIsa^a), which was probably stored in jars, is apparently of the same age as the second century B.C.E. jars from Deir el-Medina. However, the dating of the manuscripts found in jars by E.B. Coxe Jr. under C. Fisher's archaeological expedition concurs with the higher calibrated radiocarbon age of the Isaiah Scroll (1QIsa^a), but not with the lower one or the latest palaeographic dates, which agree with the Schiaparelli find.

Comparison of the radiocarbon dates of the Qumran texts from Cave 1 with the dating of the Deir el-Medina cylindrical jars comprising manuscripts allows us to tentatively date the Cave 1 jars in the Hebrew University collection to the second century B.C.E., i.e., to the Hellenistic

---

45 See nn. 28–30 above.

46 A.J.T. Jull et al., "Radiocarbon Dating of Scrolls and Linen Fragments from the Judean Desert," *Radiocarbon* 37 (1995): 11–19, esp. table 2. See also J. van der Plicht, "Radiocarbon Dating and the Dead Sea Scrolls: A Comment on 'Redating,'" *DSD* 14 (2007): 77–89, esp. 83.

era. This is also the dating which Milik originally supported, although he did not have the latest radiocarbon datings from the Cave 1 manuscripts available.

CONCLUSIONS

The Hellenistic date of the use of the Deir El-Medina archives discovered by Schiapparelli's team, and the calibrated radiocarbon dates as well as the palaeographic dates for the texts from Qumran Cave 1 are in agreement. In our view this implies that the jars—at least the smaller comparable one—allegedly found in Cave 1 at Qumran and now in the Hebrew University collection date from the second century B.C.E., like Milik originally suggested. In the light of this evidence we may suggest that the dating of 1QIsa³ to ca. 180–125 B.C.E. is more plausible than a third century B.C.E. date, and this could also be the case with *Pesher Habakkuk*. This has interesting repercussions as far as the establishment of the Qumran community and settlement is concerned, according to de Vaux's original view. The authors of this paper agree with a mid-second century B.C.E. date for the founding of the Qumran community, also suggested by the recently published numismatic evidence from Qumran, possibly even a date as early as the first half of the second century B.C.E.[47]

The question remains whether the scrolls of Cave 1 were written in or outside the Qumran community/region. That the Qumran Cave 1 jars— at least the smaller one—seem to date from the second century B.C.E. poses considerable complications, for instance, to the theory that second century B.C.E. or older scrolls would have been hidden during the First Jewish War in 68–73/74 C.E. in centuries old ceramic vessels. We have no evidence either in favour of the view that the people, who inhabited Qumran in the main occupation period, in the first century C.E. (Period II) would have used "old" ceramic types from the second century B.C.E. This discrepancy of storage of manuscripts in jars during the First Revolt was also noted in J. Gunneweg's and M. Balla's studies. If jars and documents would have been hidden in the caves at such a very late date would, nevertheless, not change the plausibility that the custom to store manuscripts in jars had been introduced at an earlier date and

---

[47] K. Lönnqvist and M. Lönnqvist, "The Numismatic Chronology of Qumran: Fact and Fiction," *NumC* 166 (2006): 121–165.

that jars may have served as *portable archives* or as *genizoth* over a longer period of time.

The cylindrical jar type used for the storage of the Qumran Cave 1 manuscripts is typical of the Dead Sea area in Palestine, and there is no reason to reject the notion that the Masada jar of the same type could originally have come from Qumran. As far as the archaeological evidence is concerned, Egypt also provides cylindrical jars containing manuscripts from the same period, and the archaeological evidence of the storage of the manuscripts in jars with particular closing mechanisms goes way back in Egypt.

BURIAL IN THE BOOK OF TOBIT AND IN QUMRAN

Nóra Dávid

University of Vienna

> "Precious in the sight of the Lord is the
> death of His pious ones."
>
> (Ps 116:15)

The type of burials found at Qumran differ from the common way of burying the dead in the Second Temple period.[1] Instead of the well-built mostly rock-cut family tombs, the community used very simple shaft tombs. We can search for the reasons why the community used this type of burial, but as only a small number (ca. 4.5 percent) of the tombs have been excavated up to now, it is difficult to draw significant conclusions on the basis of the unearthed material.[2] If we accept the common view that the Essenes lived at the site of Khirbet Qumran, we must probably speak about an ascetic community, living according to the rules set down in the *Rule of the Community* and the *Temple Scroll*, etc.

The Cemetery of Khirbet Qumran[3]

The cemetery of Khirbet Qumran reflects some kind of deliberateness in the burials,[4] which differs from the average Second Temple method. Behind this we should expect some imprint in the written texts from

---

[1] For the most detailed and complex introduction to the burial customs of the Second Temple period see R. Hachlili, *Jewish Funerary Customs, Practices and Rites in the Second Temple Period* (JSJSup 94; Leiden: Brill, 2005).

[2] For the detailed history of research of the cemetery of Khirbet Qumran see: B. Schultz, "The Qumran Cemetery: 150 Years of Research," *DSD* 13 (2006): 194–228.

[3] The main cemetery is located 30–40 meters east of the settlement (fits the Mishnaic law: *m. B. Bat.* 2:9), and divided into several parts: three extensions (so-called "fingers"), to the north, east and south; and the so-called north hill. The cemetery contains about 1100–1200 graves, well arranged in ordered rows, most of them oriented north-south. On the surface, the graves are marked by heaps of stones, and a large headstone. The tombs are simple shaft tombs, dug into the marl-terrace, to an average depth of 0.8–2.5 meters.

Qumran. But there we can only find a few allusions to the belief in afterlife and the proper way of caring for the corpse. One finds hardly anything about the proper way of burying it or about the cemetery. The lack of textual evidence could theoretically be solved by appeal to the archaeological evidence, but in the case of the Qumran cemetery the data are limited.

In order to find out any information about the possible intentional arrangement of the burials in the Qumran cemetery we have to look for parallels. The search for archaeological parallels—i.e., similar burials and cemeteries—has already been done.[5] The parallels discovered share three general similarities: the arrangement of the tombs, the lack of remarkable custom of placing grave-goods with the corpse, and the typical simple execution of the mostly individual tombs. But besides these similarities it is difficult to discover any shared intentions or other matching-points. To explain this method of burying the dead in this simple way, scholars mainly mention two possibilities: these tombs were common prior in time to the elaborated rock-cut tombs,[6] or they were used by the poor of the settlements.[7] In the case of Qumran I can support the second,

---

At the bottom of the graves, a *loculus* (burial niche) was dug out on one side, where the one body was placed. This *loculus* was sealed by stone slabs, or mud bricks, then filled up with soil. For a more detailed description of the tombs see: J. Magness, *The Archaeology of Qumran and the Dead Sea Scrolls* (Grand Rapids: Eerdmans, 2002), 168–175; Hachlili, *Jewish Funerary Customs*, 13–20; H. Eshel et al., "New Data on the Cemetery East of Khirbet Qumran," *DSD* 9 (2002): 135–165.

[4] The similarity of the elaboration and the strictly ordered rows of the graves reflect that these burials were not accidental, but well planned and organized.

[5] P. Bar-Adon, "Another Settlement of the Judean Desert Sect at ʿEn el-Ghuweir on the Shores of the Dead Sea," *BASOR* 227 (1977): 1–25; H. Eshel and Z. Greenhut, "Ḥiam el Sagha, A Cemetery of the Qumran Type, Judaean Desert," *RB* 100 (1993): 252–259; K.D. Politis, "Rescue Excavations in the Nabatean Cemetery at Khirbat Qazone 1996–1997," *ADAJ* 62 (1998): 611–614; idem, "The Nabatean Cemetery at Khirbet Qazone," *NEA* 62 (1999): 1–28; idem, "The Discovery and Excavation of the Khirbet Qazone Cemetery and its Significance Relative to Qumran," in *Qumran, the Site of the Dead Sea Scrolls: Archaeological Interpretations and Debates: Proceedings of a Conference Held at Brown University, November 17–19, 2002* (ed. K. Galor, J.-B. Humbert, and J. Zangenberg; STDJ 57; Leiden, Brill, 2006), 213–219; É. Puech, "The Necropolises of Khirbet Qumran and ʿAin el-Ghuweir and the Essene Belief in Afterlife," *BASOR* 312 (1998): 21–36; B. Zissu, "'Qumran Type' Graves in Jerusalem: Archaeological Evidence of an Essene Community?" *DSD* 5 (1998): 158–171; idem, "Odd Tomb Out: Has Jerusalem's Essene Community Been Found?" *BAR* 25/2 (1999): 50–55.

[6] A possible suggestion of it is to be read in Puech, "Necropolises," 28.

[7] J.E. Taylor, "The Cemeteries of Khirbet Qumran and the Women's Presence at the Site," *DSD* 6 (1999): 285–323 (312–313); Zissu, "'Qumran Type' Graves in Jerusalem," 166.

because—if we accept the common view, that the community lived at the site of Khirbet Qumran from 200 B.C.E. until 70 C.E.[8]—in terms of time, the community already should have become familiar with the practice of burying the dead into caves, from which they had enough in the vicinity.

The second reason—as we will see below—is easier to explain; also the individuality of the tombs supports it. As Rachel Hachlili notes: "Qumran is a desert site suitable for people seeking isolation."[9] The community of the Essenes living at the site could be something like a sect or monastic order, living an ascetic life of poverty. If this was the common way of burying the dead of the people who could not afford themselves a costly burial into rock-cut tombs in the Second Temple Period, it is reasonable to accept the explanation. Even if the skeletal research on the bones from the cemetery of Qumran shows that people buried there came from an upper layer of the society,[10] they most probably did not bury their dead because they could not have afforded themselves the costly burial into rock-cut tombs, but because they did not want to do so. Nevertheless, Brian Schultz has challenged this interpretation saying: "One striking difference [between the similar burials and the Qumran cemetery], however, is the high degree of uniformity in the orientation of the burials at Qumran, higher than at any other of the cemeteries, even of Khirbet Qazone where all the burials are said to be north-south."[11]

At this point, in order to better understand the burial practices of the Qumran community, we must also look for parallels in written sources. As we do not know any texts belonging to the group living at Qumran besides the scrolls from the site, we can only try to examine the sources possibly written in the same period. As some of the texts found in Qumran were most probably written before the establishment of the community at the Khirbeh, the criteria for being contemporary can be a date of composition somewhere between the end of the third century B.C.E. to the first century C.E., i.e., the end of the Second Temple period.[12]

---

[8] The basic periodization of the chronology of Qumran was made by Roland de Vaux. According to this the first period of habitation (Period Ia) began in ca. 130 B.C.E., and the last (Period III) ended in 73 or 74 B.C.E. Later Jodi Magness dated the beginning of habitation to ca. 100–50 B.C.E. Magness, *The Archaeology of Qumran*, 68.

[9] Hachlili, *Jewish Funerary Customs*, 476.

[10] O. Röhrer-Ertl, F. Rohrhirsch, and D. Hahn, "Über die Gräberfelder von Khirbet Qumran, inbesondere die Funde der Campagne 1956," *RevQ* 19 (1999): 3–46 (13).

[11] Schultz, "The Qumran Cemetery," 198.

[12] About the problem and method of dating the texts from Qumran see e.g.: J.C. VanderKam, *The Dead Sea Scrolls Today* (2nd ed.; Grand Rapids: Eerdmans, 2010), 15–20; G. Vermes, *The Dead Sea Scrolls in English* (London: Penguin Books, 1995), XXIII–XXV.

In this paper my aim is to search for possible parallels in the book of Tobit.[13] In the history of research of the book of Tobit Qumran has its own importance. Before the discoveries at Qumran, Tobit was known only in Greek versions. The Aramaic and Hebrew fragments of the book from Cave 4 changed that. It is especially significant that the Aramaic fragments cover 42 percent of the verses of the longer Greek text from codex Sinaiticus and the Hebrew covers 13 percent of them.[14] There are no significant differences between the text of the Septuagint and the fragments from the caves, but the fact that the community read the book has its own significance. Origen wrote in his *Epistula ad Africanum* (240 C.E.), that "Concerning it [the book of Tobit], we must recognise that Jews do not use Tobit."[15] But, as we can see after the discovery of the Tobit fragments from Qumran, at least some Jews did.

DEATH AND BURIAL IN THE BOOK OF TOBIT

Death plays an important role in the book of Tobit. It is not merely one motif among others in the story, but a thread running through the entire book. It comes out not only in Tobit's pious acts of burying dead fellow-Jews killed in the Assyrian court, but also as a central motif of the proper burial of the corpse of the ancestors, or the importance of the only son for the parents to carry out their desire of the proper final rest. The desire for a proper final resting place is well represented in the prayer of Tobit:

> So now deal with me as you will; command my spirit to be taken from me, so that I may be released from the face of the earth and become dust. For it is better for me to die than to live, because I have had to listen to undeserved insults, and great is the sorrow within me. Command, O Lord,

---

Especially about the dating of the *Temple Scroll* see: Y. Yadin, *The Temple Scroll*, vol. 1: *Introduction* (Jerusalem: The Israel Exploration Society, 1983), 386–390.

[13] The general agreement about the dating of the book is the third or early second century B.C.E. For a detailed analysis of the problem of dating the book of Tobit see: e.g. F. Zimmermann, *The Book of Tobit* (New York: Harper, 1958), 21–27; J.A. Fitzmyer, *Tobit* (CEJL; Berlin: de Gruyter, 2003), 51–52; B. Ego, *Buch Tobit* (JSHRZ II/6; Gütersloh: Gütersloher Verlagshaus, 1999), 899–900; eadem, "Tobit (Buch)," *TRE* 33:573–574. For the whole text and the fragments see: J. Fitzmyer in *DJD* XIX (1995): 1–76.

[14] J.A. Fitzmyer, "Fragments of Tobit from Qumran Cave 4," *CBQ* 57 (1995): 655–675 (659).

[15] Origen, *Ep. Afr.* 19 (SC 302:562).

that I be released from this distress; release me to go to the eternal home, and do not, O Lord, turn your face away from me. For it is better for me to die than to see so much distress in my life and to listen to insults.

(Tob 3:6 NRSV)

In the book of Tobit the reader meets two main aspects, or levels of burials. The first is the burial as a pious act, honouring the dead.[16] This act of Tobit is listed among others already at the beginning of the book after the taking of the firstfruits and tithes to Jerusalem, the almsgiving, and the exemplary family life. These passages are the following: 1:17–18; 2:3–8; 4:3–4; 6:15; 14:2, 10–13. It occurs for the first time in 1:17: "if I saw the dead body of anyone of my nation tossed beyond the wall of Nineveh, I would bury it." It reflects "the Jewish horror of corpses left unburied,[17] especially those of fellow Jews."[18] Later also the proper way of burial is emphasized.[19] This verse is the first, of which we have an Aramaic fragment from Cave 4: "the wall of Nineveh" (4Q196 1), which surely must be a part of the verse quoted. Verse 18 tells the same, but the accent is on the new Assyrian king Sennacherib, who forbade burying the corpses and pursued Tobit, that increased the risk of Tobit's deeds. In chapter 2 the son is also involved: he is the one who notices the body. Here we can read a whole burial-story with all its preparation and after-effects, to which I will return later. In chapters 4, 6 and 14 the burial is mentioned and discussed in another way: the proper burial of the father and the mother by the son. Tobit asks his son several times to bury him and his wife after their death properly. It was an obligation

---

[16] As for the burial as ethical task in the book of Tobit see: J. Bolyki, "Burial as an Ethical Task in the Book of Tobit, in the Bible and in the Greek Tragedies," in *The Book of Tobit: Text, Tradition, Theology* (ed. G. Xeravits and J. Zsengellér; JSJSup 98; Leiden: Brill, 2005), 89–103. He classifies the burial motif in the book as an ethical norm in three directions: "obedience towards God, piety towards outsiders and setting an example and assuming solidarity, strengthening the internal cohesion of the community towards the members of their people" (100).

[17] In the *Temple Scroll* (11QT[a] [11Q19] LXIV) the case of the guilty of a capital crime is discussed: he must be hung on the tree, but the corpse can not hang on the tree by night, but must be buried on the day of the death, because: "those hanged on the tree are accursed by God and men; you shall not defile the land which I give you for an inheritance" (11QT[a] LXIV:11–12).

[18] Fitzmyer, *Tobit*, 118. See also at Josephus Flavius, *Contra Apionem*: "not leaving (a corpse) unburied" (*C. Ap.* 2.211).

[19] Already in the Old Testament there was, above all, the traditional concern for the proper burial of all the dead; the height of disgrace was not to be buried (Deut 28:26; 1 Kgs 14:11; Qoh 6:3; Isa 14:20; Jer 7:33; 22:18–19; Ezek 29:5; 39:15). Fitzmyer, *Tobit*, 118. See also in the later rabbinic tradition about *mēt miṣwâh* in b. *Meg.* 3b.

of the son to bury the parents in honour. Tobit asks Tobiyah to bury Sarah into the same tomb as him,[20] following the ancient custom of burying the wife and husband—or even more members of the family—together.[21]

The second aspect is the hiding of the body of Tobiah by Raguel in 8:9–12 and 8:18 for the case if the bridegroom dying on the night of the wedding. The father of Sarah was afraid that the eighth groom of his daughter would die too and they would "become laughing-stock and object of ridicule" (8:10). He really wanted to hide the corpse from the other people, so on the night of the wedding (after the couple went to bed) he asked his servants to help him digging a grave, so that before sunset they would have been able to bury the corpse of Tobiah. Later in the night he asked a maidservant to check whether he was still alive or not. When he made sure that the couple was alive, he asked the servants to fill up again the hole in the ground "before dawn would come" (8:18).[22]

As we can see, the aim of the burial is completely different from the first "type." The one thing in common is the way; let's say the "duration in time" of the burial. In both cases it takes a very short time, only maybe a few hours to prepare a grave, which, in this case, could only be a simple shaft grave dug out of the ground for one individual. Tobit went out alone to dig the grave, and also Raguel sent only few servants, but according to the Greek short recension, Raguel himself went out alone and "dug a grave" (Καὶ ὥρυξεν τάφον, 8:9).[23]

As I have mentioned, a whole burial-scene is told in chapter 2. The intention to act piously gives birth to another pious act: the son being sent out to look for the poor of their "kinsfolk" to invite them to join the Pentecost-dinner finds a murdered fellow-Jew. Tobit ran out to find a place for him "in one of the outhouses until the sun would set" (2:4); after returning he bathed, and ate his dinner in grief. After sunset he

---

[20] Θάψον αὐτὴν παρ' ἐμοὶ ἐν ἑνὶ θάφῳ (Tob 4:4).

[21] A detailed description of family tombs and about the burial of women can be found in: Hachlili, *Jewish Funerary Customs*, 235–337.

[22] The Greek expression for "rebury the grave" in Tob 8:18 is χῶσαι τὸν τάφον. At other loci the burial as act is expressed by verbs formed from θάπτω, which basically means to bury, and the making of the grave is from ὀρύσσω. In the Latin text the verb *sepeliō* is used, which has the original meaning: to put into a grave, to bury. Some of these terms are with the original meaning of "to dig," they most probably refer to the making and usage of simple shaft tombs.

[23] For the different textual versions of the book of Tobit see: S. Weeks, S. Gathercole, and L.T. Stuckenbruck, eds., *The Book of Tobit: Texts from the Principal Ancient and Medieval Traditions* (Berlin: de Gruyter, 2004).

went out and "dug a grave and buried him." After everything, according to the longer Greek version: he went home, bathed again and went to the courtyard to sleep (2:9). We can see the importance of purifying after getting in contact with a corpse. Tobit not only bathes, but sleeps in the courtyard in order not to defile the house as a closed unit with the possible uncleanness. The point is not stressed in the longer Greek version, but is in the shorter: "because I was defiled, I lay down to sleep beside the courtyard wall" (2:9). The Vetus Latina reads: "and I washed again in that hour after I had buried; I entered my house and laid down to sleep near the wall." The notion—following the Jewish law—of the defiling nature of the corpse is unambiguous, but the way of purifying is not. In the different texts we find three different ways: 1) to bathe after the burial and to lay in the courtyard (longer Greek version); 2) not to bathe, but sleep in the courtyard (shorter Greek version); 3) to bathe, but sleep in the house (Vetus Latina).[24]

Purity Rules Regarding Corpse-Contamination in Qumran

From the very few sources we have from Qumran relating death and burial, the most important ones are the purity rules concerning the corpse. In the Qumran scrolls the corpse is represented as the highest source of impurity. As also in later Jewish tradition, it is referred to as "the father of uncleanness," or as Rashi states "father of the fathers of uncleanness."[25] This view is represented in the *Temple Scroll* (11QT^a), where the majority of these purity rules can be found (mostly in cols. XLVIII–L). We find in col. XLV a ban on anybody who had contacted the impurity of the dead (*tamē la-nefeš*), in order not to enter the city of the sanctuary. In 11QT^a XLVIII types of non-Jewish mourning rituals show up as counter-examples. The "holy men of JHWH" can not behave as gentile people, so they cannot bury their dead within their city limits, but they have to separate a place for them, just like for people contaminated with other uncleanness. Here we can see the authors' aim of expressing the holiness of the community, and the high pollution rate of the dead, even for the land. After the land, a closer unit follows. The house is the

---

[24] Tob 2:9. For the texts see: Weeks, Gathercole, and Stuckenbruck, *The Book of Tobit*, 98–99.
[25] See Rashi on *b. Pesaḥ.* 14b and 17a.

closest space for a person (only later do the persons themselves count, the pregnant woman, with a *fetus* inside). After someone dies, besides the house itself where it occurs, even all the people, food and vessels in it become unclean, and must to be purified. The main features of this purification are the bathing in water, the sprinkling of the waters of purification (made of the ashes of the red heifer) and the washing of clothes. The *termini* are the first, the third and the seventh days. The vessels should be washed on the third and seventh days only, while the men even on the first day should wash themselves and their clothes. By the evening of the seventh day everybody and everything becomes clean. The same rules should also be applied for people getting in contact in opened field with a corpse, with bones, or even if they touched a grave!

The other important text from the caves of Qumran regarding the impurity of the corpse-contaminated person is 4QRitPur A (4Q414) 2. As Esther Eshel has stressed, this fragment—which mentions the importance of cleansing on the first day—was "composed according to the law found in the Temple Scroll."[26] So we have a contemporary legal text with similar regulations regarding the need of cleaning on the first day. As for the significance of the purification on the first day, Jacob Milgrom understood it as "the first day ablution is to allow the impurity bearer to remain in the city."[27] This is why the corpse-contaminated are not listed in the *Temple Scroll* (11QT^a XLVI:16–18) among those quarantined or expelled from the city because of impurities such as the leper, the gonorrheic, etc.[28] But in 11QT^a XLV:17 there is the clear ban of entering the city for everyone unclean through contact with the dead.[29]

---

[26] E. Eshel, "4Q414 Fragment 2: Purification of a Corpse Contaminated Person," in *Legal Texts and Legal Issues: Proceedings of the Second Meeting of the International Organization for Qumran Studies, Cambridge 1995* (ed. M. Bernstein, F. García Martínez, and J. Kampen; STDJ 23; Leiden: Brill, 1997), 3–10.

[27] J. Milgrom, "Studies in the Temple Scroll," *JBL* 97 (1978): 501–523 (515).

[28] On the contrary, Josephus mentions the corpse contaminated among the defiled who needs isolation: *Ant.* 3.261–262. Also the Torah proscribes that he had to be expelled from the Temple city (Num 5:2–3). What could be the reason, for the author of the *Temple Scroll* to differ from it? According to Milgrom, it could be the *pshat* reading of the biblical text, therefore, the phrase "and then he may return to the camp" occurs in all other cases, but not at the mentioning of the corpse contamination. Milgrom, "Studies in the Temple Scroll," 515.

[29] This law is opposed to the laws of the Sages. For further details see Yadin, *The Temple Scroll*, 1:293.

PURITY RULES REGARDING
CORPSE-CONTAMINATION BESIDES QUMRAN

As we see in the book of Tobit, purification after being in contact with a corpse is important. He washes himself after hiding the body on the Pentecost-evening, and also after the burial of that night. Furthermore, he sleeps in the court and not in the house. The *Temple Scroll* addresses the issue of corpse-contamination as follows: "anyone who entered the house shall bathe in water and wash his clothes on the first day" (11QT[a] XLIX:17). So purification on the first day is needed, and as we further read also on the third and seventh days. The above mentioned fragment of 4QRitPur A (4Q414) also confirms this rule. If we look to Jewish tradition and law, we encounter contradictory examples.[30] For example, the rules of the purifying water in Numbers read as follows:

> Whoever in the open field touches one who has been killed by a sword, or who has died naturally, or a human bone, or a grave, shall be unclean seven days. For the unclean they shall take some ashes of the burnt purification offering, and running water shall be added in a vessel; then a clean person shall take hyssop, dip it in the water, and sprinkle it on the tent, on all the furnishings, on the persons who were there, and on whoever touched the bone, the slain, the corpse, or the grave. The clean person shall sprinkle the unclean ones on the third day and on the seventh day, thus purifying them on the seventh day. Then they shall wash their clothes and bathe themselves in water, and at evening they shall be clean.   (Num 19:16–19 NRSV)

So the Torah does not prescribe the purification for the first day. Also the later rabbinic tradition does not stress the importance of cleansing on the first day.[31] As we can see the regulations are the same in Qumran and in the mind of the author of the book of Tobit, and unambiguously differ from mainstream Judaism.

---

[30] L.H. Schiffman, "The Impurity of the Dead in the Temple Scroll," in *Archaeology and History in the Dead Sea Scrolls: The New York University Conference in Memory of Yigael Yadin* (ed. idem; JSPSup 8; JSOT/ASOR Monograph Series 2; Sheffield: JSOT Press, 1990), 135–156 (146–148).

[31] The seven-day period of impurity after the contamination from a corpse in the rabbinic times is based on the laws of the Torah. The detailed description of this system can be found in H.K. Harrington, *The Impurity Systems of Qumran and the Rabbis: Biblical Foundations* (SBLDS 143; Atlanta: Scholars Press, 1993), 141–179.

To sum up:

- The widely known sources of the "mainstream Judaism"—i.e. the Bible and rabbinic literature—reflect a system of purifying ritual, which prescribes cleaning on the third and seventh days.
- On the contrary, the Dead Sea Scrolls (11QTª, 4QRitPur A [4Q414], and the Tobit manuscripts 4Q196–200) reflect the importance of the cleansing also on the first day after the contamination from a corpse.
- Besides the Dead Sea Scrolls our only source for the purification on the first day is the book of Tobit.
- Besides this parallel of the purity rules, there is a practical parallel too. However, this is hypothetical, we do not know what these tombs looked like, we can only deduce from the way of their execution from the description of the text. On the basis of that, those tombs could only be simple shaft tombs dug into the ground.

Certainly my aim is not to prove that the author of the book of Tobit was familiar with the so-called "Qumran-type" tombs, but to demonstrate that this simply elaborated form of burial was known and practiced in the Second Temple period also outside of Khirbet Qumran. Archaeological proofs besides the cemetery of Khirbet Qumran come from the above referred sites, but it does not mean at all, that it was used nowhere else as the burial method of the poor. Moreover, most probably the community of Qumran expressed its desire to be simple and poor also in their death, as in their life: living as an ascetic group in the desert.

OPEN QUESTIONS

First of all, one could easily ask while reading the book of Tobit: where did Tobit bury the corpses? His faithfulness to Jewish law is strongly represented and stressed in the book, but here, the author makes no mention of the place of the burials. The reader can expect at the least, a reminder that he kept the rules of purity and buried the dead outside of the city. Burial into heathen cemeteries was also not proper. This question can give birth to another: if a proper burial was so important for Tobit, why did not he prepare a tomb for himself and for his wife still in his life, though as we read at the beginning of the story he was a wealthy man. In Tob 4:3–4 Tobit orders his son to bury him after his death, and, when his mother dies, bury her at his side. Burying couples close together was a widespread custom already since Abraham and Sarah, but it was most probably not practiced into simple shaft tombs, but rather into the well known burial niches of the Second Temple period. Caves suitable for similar family burials were often bought already in the lifetime of the head of the family, in order to insure the most proper place for the eternal rest. The sentence in 4:17 ("Be generous with bread and wine on the graves of virtous men, but not for the sinner.") also reflects to a more developed and subtle cult of the dead, which is difficult to link with the practice of the simple shaft graves.

On the basis of the above, we can sum up that in the book of Tobit the reader meets a really conscious and deliberate way of placing to the final rest. The author mentions burials neither into the widespread burial caves, nor into the simple shaft tombs, but often refers to a highly developed system of thanatology.

As for the eschatology what we can read out of the book,[32] the vocabulary used for the descriptions is really similar to the usage of the expression of death and afterlife in the Dead Sea Scrolls: death is conceived of as a release from "the face of the earth" and a becoming "dust" (3:6). Going to the "everlasting home" (3:6),[33] also the Hades (3:10), and the "darkness" (4:10) is mentioned.[34]

Epilogue

In order to conclude and place this study into a more general context, I would like to mention a contemporary phenomenon. In several cemeteries where sisters who used to live in one convent are buried, one can observe that their tombs are markedly different from the others. All the graves are simple—marked only with heap of soil and a wooden cross.[35] Although the nuns lived in poverty, they could have afforded

---

[32] Fitzmyer, *Tobit*, 48–49; G.W.E. Nickelsburg, "Tobit and Enoch: Distant Cousins with a Recognizable Resemblance," *SBLSP* (1988): 54–68.

[33] S. Beyerle, " 'Release Me to Go to My Everlasting Home ...' (Tob 3:6): A Belief in Afterlife in Late Wisdom Literature?" in *The Book of Tobit* (ed. Xeravits and Zsengellér), 71–89 (76–82).

[34] [33] For a detailed analysis of the terminology of death and afterlife in the Qumran corpus see: N. Dávid, "The Terminology of Death at Qumran," in *With Wisdom as a Robe: Qumran and Other Jewish Studies in Honour of Ida Fröhlich* (ed. K.D. Dobos and M. Kőszeghy; Hebrew Bible Monographs 21; Sheffield: Sheffield Phoenix Press, 2009), 339–348.

[35] The average graves are marked with decorated stone or marble structures.

more expensive and elaborate monuments. In my opinion, they chose simplicity. Even in death they wanted to lie in simple poverty. In this way, they could also express the aim of differing from the mainstream or stress the unimportance of property, wealth or exterior. The community of Qumran may have had similar ideas about burying their dead. Their lack of description for or stress on the proper way of burial also supports this idea: they practiced the average way of burying the dead, as the poor of the country did. The random burials depicted in the book of Tobit may be similar in execution to these, but not in rationale. The reason behind the burials in Tobit was not the separation from the local practice, but simply, that it was the easiest and quickest way of burying the dead. Despite this contradiction, similarities between burial practices at Qumran and in the book of Tobit call attention to possible trends in Jewish thought and practice.

THE HASMONEANS IN THE LIGHT
OF THE QUMRAN SCROLLS[*]

EDWARD DĄBROWA
Jagiellonian University in Kraków

Ever since the Qumran scrolls were discovered, researchers have been trying to date them. Despite repeated attempts, no definite answer has been found. Likewise, controversy surrounds their place of origin and the nature of the whole collection.[1] Both questions are not without consequence for our subject of interest. But space constraints forbid a detailed presentation of the various scholarly positions in this essay. All researchers agree in principle that most of the texts were written in the second to first centuries B.C.E. At that time Judea was ruled by the Hasmoneans. Given their role first in organizing and then leading an armed uprising against the Hellenistic religious reform during the reign of Antiochus IV, and also in creating and strengthening an independent Jewish state, it is only natural to inquire about how their actions were perceived by their contemporaries.

Searching for a picture of the Hasmonean period in the Qumran documents may hardly seem an original proposition, since similar attempts have been made many times and their more or less satisfactory results are common knowledge.[2] But our purpose is neither to offer more examples for historical allusions hidden in the Qumran scrolls nor to suggest a new

---

[*] I would like to acknowledge assistance of Professor Mark Geller with linguistic correction of this paper. Any errors of fact or interpretation are my sole responsibility.

[1] See A.I. Baumgarten, "Crisis in the Scrollery: A Dying Consensus," *Judaism* 44 (1995): 399–413; A. Lange, "The Qumran Dead Sea Scrolls-Library or Manuscript Corpus?" in *From 4QMMT to Resurrection: Mélanges qumraniens en hommage à Émile Puech* (ed. F. García Martínez, A. Steudel, and E. Tigchelaar; STDJ 61; Leiden: Brill, 2006), 177–193 (186–193); cf. also E. Tov, "The Corpus of the Qumran Papyri," in *Semitic Papyrology in Context: A Climate of Creativity: Papers from a New York University Conference marking the Retirement of Baruch A. Levine* (ed. L.H. Schiffman; Culture and History of the Ancient Near East 14; Leiden: Brill, 2003), 85–103 (98–99).

[2] Cf. J.H. Charlesworth, *The Pesharim and Qumran History: Chaos or Consensus?* (Grand Rapids: Eerdmans, 2002); H. Eshel, *The Dead Sea Scrolls and the Hasmonean State* (Studies in the Dead Sea Scrolls and Related Literature; Grand Rapids: Eerdmans, 2008).

interpretation, but to present some observations on the attitudes of the Qumran texts' authors towards the events and persons of the Hasmonean period, as well as to the past.

With the slow publication of Qumran manuscripts over more than half a century, it was impossible to form a full picture of the historical events to which they referred. Although each of the successively published texts that contained historical references or allusions immediately became the subject of many commentaries and interpretations, they were all geared primarily to establishing the chronology of the community that created them. It was only the publication of the pesharim, which contained an especially large number of historical allusions that cast more light on the community's attitudes toward developments in the world surrounding it.[3] Now that the publication of the manuscripts is almost complete (there are a few privately owned scrolls which still await publication), we can engage in a full, systematic analysis of the historical information contained in all of them and, moreover, reliably assess their value and nature. Numbering about 900 manuscripts, the Qumran corpus has enabled experts to identify at least several dozen references to historical figures and events relating to the Judea of the Hasmoneans. In addition, the documents contain many allusions to members of the ruling dynasty, although their real sense is difficult to establish, not least for the obscure language the authors used.[4]

---

[3] Cf. W.H. Brownlee, "The Historical Allusions of the Dead Sea Habakkuk Midrash," *BASOR* 126 (1952): 10–20 (12–16); J.M. Allegro, "Further Light on the History of the Qumran Sect," *JBL* 75 (1956): 89–95; idem, "*Thrakidan*, the 'Lion of Wrath' and Alexander Jannaeus," *PEQ* 91 (1959): 47–51; J.D. Amusin, "The Reflection of Historical Events of the First Century B.C. in Qumran Commentaries (4Q161; 4Q169; 4Q166)," *HUCA* 48 (1977): 123–152; I.R. Tantlevskij, "The Historical Background of the Qumran Commentary on Nahum (4QpNah)," in *Hellenismus: Beiträge zur Erforschung von Akkulturation und politischer Ordnung in den Staaten des hellenistischen Zeitalters: Akten des Internationalen Hellenismus-Kolloqiums, 9.–14. März 1994 in Berlin* (ed. B. Funck; Tübingen: Mohr Siebeck, 1996), 329–338.

[4] The best-known example of such a text is the excerpt from the *Pesher Habakkuk* referring to the Wicked Priest (1QpHab VIII:8–13). At first, most scholars narrowed the title down to a single person. It took A.S. van der Woude ("Wicked Priest or Wicked Priests? Reflections on the Identification of the Wicked Priest in the Habakkuk Commentary," *RevQ* 17 [1982]: 349–359) to argue that the text can just as well apply to a number of figures since the designation of Wicked Priest was used for several members of the Hasmonean family; cf. Brownlee, "Historical Allusions," 10–16; idem, "The Wicked Priest, the Man of Lies, and the Righteous Teacher—the Problem of Identitiy," *JQR* 73 (1982): 1–37 (1–15). See also F. García Martínez, "Was Judas Maccabaeus a Wicked Priest? Marginal Notes on 1QpHab VIII 8–13," in idem, *Qumranica Minora*, vol.1: *Qumran Origins and Apocalypticism* (ed. E.J.C. Tigchelaar; STDJ 63; Leiden: Brill, 2007),

The history of the Qumran community featured two watershed events: its creation and the conflict between the Teacher of Righteousness (or the Righteous Teacher)[5] and the Wicked Priest. According to the *Damascus Document* (CD 1:5–10), the community was founded 390 years after the Jews went into Babylonian captivity, with the Teacher of Righteousness appearing twenty years later. The chronology of events known to us suggests that the earlier occurrence may be dated at 197 B.C.E.; the latter at 177–175 B.C.E.[6] Both dates suggest a close link between the Qumran community and the Hellenistic religious reform during the reign of Antiochus IV Epiphanes.[7] Unfortunately, no other Qumran document fully

---

53–66. This proposition became a major part of the so-called Groningen Hypothesis about the beginnings of the Qumran community (cf. F. García Martínez, "Qumran Origins and Early History: A Groningen Hypothesis," *FO* 25 [1988]: 113–136; repr. in *Qumranica Minora*, 1:3–29; idem and A.S. van der Woude, "A 'Groningen' Hypothesis of Qumran Origins and Early History," *RevQ* 14 [1989–1990]: 521–541 [521–524]). Although van der Woude's premises for his hypothesis have since been questioned (T. Lim, "The Wicked Priests of the Groningen Hypothesis," *JBL* 112 [1993]: 415–425), the idea that the title of the Wicked Priest might have been applied to different individuals has not been rejected, see Lim, "Wicked Priests," 424; I. Fröhlich, *"Time and Times and Half a Time": Historical Consciousness in the Jewish Literature of the Persian and Hellenistic Eras* (JSPSup 19; Sheffield: Sheffield Academic Press, 1996), 164–165; A.S. van der Woude, "Once Again: The Wicked Priests in the Habakkuk Pesher from Cave 1 of Qumran," *RevQ* 17 (1996): 375–384; J.J. Collins, "The Time of the Teacher: An Old Debate Renewed," in *Studies in the Hebrew Bible, Qumran, and the Septuagint Presented to Eugene Ulrich* (ed. P.W. Flint, E. Tov, and J.C. VanderKam; VTSup 101; Leiden: Brill, 2006), 212–229.

[5] Cf. Charlesworth, *Pesharim and Qumran History*, 28–30.

[6] According to Charlesworth the dates in the *Damascus Document* cannot be used as a serious historical argument (ibid., 87: "... the 390 years, mentioned in CD 1:5–6, is not a mathematical computation but an adaptation from Ezekiel 4:5 which may be, nevertheless, not far off the mark.").

[7] H. Ulfgard, "The Teacher of Righteousness, the History of the Qumran Community, and Our Understanding of the Jesus Movement: Texts, Theories and Trajectories," in *Qumran between the Old and New Testaments* (ed. F.H. Cryer and T.L. Thompson; JSOTSup 290; Copenhagen International Seminar 6; Sheffield: Sheffield Academic Press, 1998), 310–346 (314–318); M. Geller, "Qumran's Teacher of Righteousness—a Suggested Identification," *Scripta Judaica Cracoviensia* 1 (2002): 9–19 (10–13); Charlesworth, *Pesharim and Qumran History*, 25–67; M.O. Wise, "Dating the Teacher of Righteousness and the *floruit* of his Movement," *JBL* 122 (2003): 53–87 (63–65). Based on chronological data in the *Damascus Document*, N. Kokkinos ("Second Thoughts in the Date and Identity of the Teacher of Righteousness," *Scripta Judaica Cracoviensia* 2 [2004]: 7–15) believes that the Teacher of Righteousness flourished and the Qumran community was created in the latter half of the third century B.C.E. On the other side Charlesworth (*Pesharim and Qumran History*, 27 n. 35) expresses an opinion that "CD represents the life and concepts of Jews similar to those at Qumran, but living elsewhere in ancient Palestine."

supports this dating. This is the reason for the considerably diverging scholarly opinions on the dating and identities of the Teacher of Righteousness[8] and of the Wicked Priest. Each of these figures is of key importance in establishing the chronology of the Qumran community. Since no text mentions the Teacher of Righteousness by name, scholars concentrate instead on identifying the Wicked Priest, who the account of the conflict suggests must have been one of the ruling Hasmoneans.[9] Naming the Wicked Priest would make approximate timing of the conflict possible.[10] In support of their proposed identifications of the Wicked Priest, proponents look for arguments not only in the Qumran documents, but especially in 1 Maccabees or in the works of Josephus Flavius. Each of those accounts was written at a different time and for a different purpose. This being the case, it is debatable whether we can indeed fully rely on them to solve a dating question that is of fundamental importance for the history of the Qumran community and for its relations with the Hasmoneans.

To solve this issue, we need first to focus on all historical references in the Qumran texts that relate to the Hasmoneans. One can hardly imagine that the documents would have neglected to mention the Hasmoneans in some capacity if much of the community's history including its paramount event coincided with their reign. Of much help in such an investigation is the list of historical allusions and references in Qumran scrolls compiled by M.O. Wise.[11] Each item in this list carries a body of additional information concerning:

---

[8] See ibid., 30–40, 87–93; Eshel, *Dead Sea Scrolls and the Hasmonean State*, 29–61.

[9] A presentation of all hypotheses on the identity of the Wicked Priest falls outside our scope here, so we stop at indicating the publications where they are comprehensively discussed or where relevant bibliography is given. See Collins, "Time of the Teacher," 212 nn. 1–4, 218–227; D.N. Freedman and J.C. Geoghegan, "Another Stab at the Wicked Priest," in *The Bible and the Dead Sea Scrolls: The Second Princeton Symposium on Judaism and Christian Origins*, vol. 2: *The Dead Sea Scrolls and the Qumran Community* (ed. J.H. Charlesworth; Waco: Baylor University Press, 2006), 17–24 (17 n. 1). Some more new publications appeared also in recent years; cf. ibid., 19–22.

[10] The key juncture in establishing the identity of the Wicked Priest is a description of the circumstances of his death: 1QpHab IX:1–2, 9–12. Cf. Collins, "Time of the Teacher," 218–229.

[11] Wise, "Dating the Teacher of Righteousness"; cf. also G.L. Doudna, *4Q Pesher Nahum: A Critical Edition* (JSPSup 35; Sheffield: Sheffield Academic Press, 2001), 701–705; Eshel, *Dead Sea Scrolls and the Hasmonean State*, 3–4.

(a) the person, process, or event, (b) the date or temporal span for that reference, whether exact or approximate, (c) the manuscript containing the reference or allusion, (d) the actual wording of such, in the original language and in translation, (e) the suggested origin of the work, whether sectarian or nonsectarian, (f) any miscellaneous comments.[12]

Apart from the first two entries (a–b), of all these items, the information about the origin of the respective texts (e) is most important for our search because the form and content of a reference or allusion largely depend on whether its author was part of the community or an outsider.

An analysis of the data collated by Wise reveals that the scrolls mention the names of only some of the Hasmoneans: Alexander Jannaeus, Alexandra Salome, Hyrcanus II, and Aristobulus II. The names appear mainly in texts classified as "non-sectarian." In documents numbered among those created at Qumran ("sectarian"), references and allusions to the Hasmoneans are devoid of any clear dating clues. Out of a total of more than a dozen relevant allusions, most come from a mere handful of texts, mainly from the pesharim. The historical references of the commentaries serve usually as examples of actions and practices deserving condemnation and just punishment by God.[13] In the other types of preserved Qumran documents, only very few historical allusions can be found.[14] Those that do appear are of limited use to the historians.

---

[12] Wise, "Dating the Teacher of Righteousness," 66–67. Cf. also Charlesworth, *Pesharim and Qumran History*, 19–25.

[13] On historical allusions in the pesharim: Charlesworth, *Pesharim and Qumran History*, 80–83.

[14] Such documents include the fragmentarily preserved texts 4Q245, 4Q448, and 4Q523 which mention King Jonathan or Jonathan. The hottest dispute arose from a fragment in 4Q448 that mentions King Jonathan. The publishers of the fragment identified him as Alexander Jannaeus because on his coins he used the name Jonathan: E. Eshel, H. Eshel, and A. Yardeni, "A Qumran Composition Containing Part of Ps. 154 and a Prayer for the Welfare of King Jonathan and his Kingdom," *IEJ* 42 (1992): 199–229 (216–219); H. Eshel and E. Eshel, "4Q448, Psalm 154 (Syriac), Sirach 48:20, and 4QpISAᵃ," *JBL* 119 (2000): 645–659 (652–657). This identification was contradicted by G. Vermes, ("The So-Called King Jonathan Fragment [4Q448]," *JJS* 44 [1993]: 294–300 [298–300]), who tried to offer arguments for Jonathan, the brother of Judah Maccabaeus. Yet his position failed to win approval and now most scholars accept identification of King Jonathan with Alexander Jannaeus: A. Lemaire, "Le roi Jonathan à Qoumrân (4Q448, B–C)," in *Qoumrân et les Manuscrits de la Mer Morte: Un cinquantenaire* (ed. E.-M. Laperrousaz; Paris: Cerf, 1997), 57–70 (70); E. Main, "For King Jonathan or Against? The Use of the Bible in 4Q448," in *Biblical Perspectives: Early Use and Interpretations of the Bible in Light of the Dead Sea Scrolls: Proceedings of the First International Symposium of the Orion*

In some cases, they may even be an editor's suggested reconstructions of damaged portions of the text.[15]

Such limited usefulness of historical allusions in the scrolls also applies to the pesharim, as attempts to read their precise message must be considered less than successful. One reason for this difficulty is that their authors recalled historical events completely at random, summoning examples from the past when they needed to express more clearly a theological thought. Besides, even when referring to a specific person, social group, or event, they conceal his or its identity under cryptic names or sobriquets, only some of which have been plausibly deciphered.[16] But even then, such suggested interpretations and identifications remain largely hypothetical since they are based on arguments drawn from sources outside Qumran, such as 1 Maccabees or from Josephus' historical writings. Any determinations reached in this way may be seriously in error because information from non-Qumran sources allows scholars to match virtually any proposed identification of the Wicked Priest with Maccabeans and Hasmoneans ranging from Judah the Maccabee[17] to Aristobulus II and Hyrcanus II. Studied separately, Qumranite and non-Qumranite texts present two quite different historical pictures with far fewer common elements than generally believed. Each author

---

Center for the Study of the Dead Sea Scrolls and Associated Literature, 12–14 May, 1996 (ed. M.E. Stone and E.G. Chazon; STDJ 28; Leiden: Brill, 1998), 113–135; J.C. VanderKam, "Identity and History of the Community," in *The Dead Sea Scrolls after Fifty Years: A Comprehensive Assessment* (ed. P.W. Flint and J.C. VanderKam; 2 vols.; Leiden: Brill, 1998–1999), 2:487–533 (531); Charlesworth, *Pesharim and Qumran History*, 104–105; Wise, "Dating the Teacher of Righteousness," 69–70; J.C. VanderKam, *From Joshua to Caiaphas: High Priests after the Exile* (Minneapolis: Fortress, 2004), 335; Collins, "Time of the Teacher," 227–228; G. Vermes, "Historiographical Elements in the Qumran Writings: A Synopsis of the Textual Evidence," *JJS* 58 (2007): 121–139 (136); G.G. Xeravits, "From the Forefathers to the 'Angry Lion': Qumran and the Hasmoneans," in *The Books of the Maccabees: History, Theology, Ideology: Papers of the Second International Conference on the Deuterocanonical Books, Pápa, Hungary, 9–11 June, 2005* (ed. idem and J. Zsengellér; JSJSup 118; Leiden: Brill, 2007), 211–221 (214–217).

[15] The historical references contained therein mainly come down to mentions of the names of some Hasmoneans in lists of priests or to identifying with Judean kings the figures mentioned in texts, cf. Wise, "Dating the Teacher of Righteousness," 67–69 nn. 1–6.

[16] Cf. Amusin, "Reflection of Historical Events," 139, 151–152; Brownlee, "Wicked Priest," 1–3; Fröhlich, "*Time and Times,*" 160–163; Doudna, *4Q Pesher Nahum,* 615–618; Charlesworth, *Pesharim and Qumran History,* 40–41, 94–109. See also the recent study on this subject by M.A. Collins, *The Use of Sobriquets in the Qumran Dead Sea Scrolls* (Library of Second Temple Studies 67; London: T&T Clark, 2009).

[17] Cf. García Martínez, "Judas Maccabaeus," 53–56.

looked at events through his particular lens and used his own idiom to narrate them. Different, too, were the purposes the various writings were meant to serve.[18]

For the most part, the Qumran manuscripts reflected the views and religious concepts of the community that produced them. Its members had consciously elected to isolate themselves from the outside world and its affairs. Dramatic though some of them might have been, such affairs could not divert their attention from theological discourse: indeed, they reinforced the community's determination in following their chosen path. Another notable trait in their attitude was a near complete lack of interest in the past other than that of their community.[19] It may seem that even their own history was known only superficially and did not inspire deeper interest. Only a handful of past episodes were deemed important enough to be recalled on various occasions. The Qumran texts clearly indicate that such events included the conflict between the Teacher of Righteousness and the Wicked Priest, leading to the martyrdom of the earlier. Occurrences like these were regarded by Qumran authors as the root cause of all misfortunes that happened to Judea ever since. Through the lens of these events, the Qumran authors interpreted both the past and their surrounding realities in a highly emotional way.

Most historical allusions in Qumran documents, particularly in the pesharim, concern broadly understood religion. For the Hasmonean period, most such allusions—chiefly in the pesharim—refer to religious struggles between the king who is described as the Lion of Wrath or Angry Lion[20] and a group called the Seekers-After-Smooth-Things[21] (these designations most probably stood for Alexander Jannaeus[22] and the Pharisees,[23] respectively). The allusions offer not a word, however,

---

[18] Cf. Collins, "Time of the Teacher," 217–218.

[19] Charlesworth, *Pesharim and Qumran History*, 67: "It should now be clear that no Qumran scroll is identified as a book dedicated to history or a text defined by an interest in history." Cf. ibid., 70–77, 115–116.

[20] 4QpNah (4Q169) 3–4 i 5–8; 4QpHos^b (4Q167) 2 2.

[21] Cf. 4QpNah (4Q169) 3–4 i 2, 7; ii 2, 4; iii 3, 6–7; 4Qpap pIsa^c (4Q163) 23 ii 10.

[22] Allegro, "Further Light," 92–93; idem, "*Thrakidan*," 47–51; Amusin, "Reflection of Historical Events," 140–146, 151; Tantlevskij, "Historical Background," 329–336; Charlesworth, *Pesharim and Qumran History*, 99–106; Xeravits, "From the Forefathers to the 'Angry Lion,'" 212; *contra* Doudna, *4Q Pesher Nahum*, 604–607.

[23] L.H. Schiffman, "Pharisees and Sadducees in *Pesher Naḥum*," in *Minḥah le-Naḥum: Biblical and Other Studies Presented to Nahum M. Sarna in Honour of His 70th Birthday* (ed. M. Brettler and M. Fishbane; JSOTSup 154; Sheffield: JSOT Press), 272–290

about the cause of the struggles. The Seekers-After-Smooth-Things re-
currently appear in Qumran manuscripts (also under different designations).[24] The Qumran authors display unconcealed hostility to them, as
they also do to their adversaries, the Sadducees.[25] Another frequently
mentioned group is the Kittim, now identified with the Romans.[26] The
names of the Hasmoneans usually dispense with any additional information, which is due to the fragmentary state of preservation of most
of the texts where they appear. Only in a few instances does such information clearly point to individuals. Most of these instances deal with
Alexander Jannaeus.[27] Only rarely are the events connected with the
feud between Hyrcanus II and Aristobulus II mentioned. How often
the Hasmoneans are mentioned does not, however, signal any special
attention given to them by the Qumran authors. The names merely

---

(274–277); M.P. Horgan, "Pesharim," in *The Dead Sea Scrolls: Hebrew, Aramaic, and Greek
Texts with English Translations*, vol. 6B: *Pesharim, Other Commentaries, and Related Doc-
uments* (ed. J.H. Charlesworth; The Princeton Theological Seminary Dead Sea Scrolls
Project; Tübingen: Mohr Siebeck, 2002), 1–193 (144, 149 n. 13); J.C. VanderKam, "Those
Who Look for Smooth Things, Pharisees, and Oral Law," in *Emanuel: Studies in Hebrew
Bible, Septuagint, and Dead Sea Scrolls in Honor of Emanuel Tov* (ed. S.M. Paul et al.;
VTSup 94; Leiden: Brill, 2003), 465–477; Charlesworth, *Pesharim and Qumran History*,
20 n. 11, 97–99; Xeravits, "From the Forefathers to the 'Angry Lion,'" 212, *contra* Doudna,
4Q Pesher Nahum, 654–656.

[24] Cf. Horgan, "Pesharim," 119, 144, 149 n. 13.

[25] Cf. Schiffman, "Pharisees and Sadducees," 284–286.

[26] Allegro, "Further Light," 93; Amusin, "Reflection of Historical Events," 139–140;
Doudna, *4Q Pesher Nahum*, 608–612; H. Eshel, "The Kittim in the *War Scroll* and in the
Pesharim," in *Historical Perspectives: From the Hasmoneans to Bar Kokhba in Light of the
Dead Sea Scrolls: Proceedings of the Fourth International Symposium of the Orion Center
for the Study of the Dead Sea Scrolls and Associated Literature, 27–31 January, 1999* (ed.
D. Goodblatt, A. Pinnick, and D.R. Schwartz; STDJ 37; Leiden: Brill, 2001), 29–44 (41–
43); Charlesworth, *Pesharim and Qumran History*, 73 n. 229, 103, 109–112.

[27] Cf. 4QpNah (4Q169) 3–4 i 5–8; 4QpHos[b] (4Q167) 2 1–7; 4Q448; 4Q523 (cf.
Wise, "Dating the Teacher of Righteousness," 70 n. 8). Especially contentious is 4Q448.
According to some scholars (Eshel, Eshel, and Yardeni, "Qumran Composition," 214–
216; Eshel and Eshel, "4Q448," 652–657; É. Puech, "Jonathan le prêtre impie et les débuts
de la comunauté de Qumrân: 4QJonathan (4Q523) et 4QpsAp (4Q448)," *RevQ* 17 (1996):
241–270 (253, 257), it is a prayer on behalf of Alexander Jannaeus. Yet critics point out
that such interpretation is unfounded and go on to present arguments to show that it
should be seen as a prayer for the well-being of the Qumran community, and in fact
meant against Alexander Jannaeus (Lemaire, "Le roi Jonathan," 62, 66–70; Main, "King
Jonathan," 113–135; Xeravits, "From the Forefathers to the 'Angry Lion,'" 213–217).
According to Charlesworth this text is favorable to Alexander Jannaeus, but it is not a
Qumran composition. The text was probably brought to Qumran by somebody who fled
Jerusalem ca. 88 B.C.E. during Jannaeus' repressions against the Pharisees (Charlesworth,
Pesharim and Qumran History, 103–105).

serve as chronological reference points. In the few cases where the Hasmoneans attract the authors' attention, it is only to condemn them as those Judean rulers whose actions contributed to a decline of religious life.[28] Indeed, this dimension is the main focus for Qumran authors, who chose to ignore all other aspects of social and political life. The large number of references to developments in the first half of the first century B.C.E. leads scholars to date most documents containing such mentions to that period.[29] This hypothesis is of considerable importance to our discussion as it suggests that most historical allusions in Qumran documents indeed concern contemporary events known to the authors from first-hand experience. By contrast, references to events and figures from the preceding period are few and in most cases not quite certain.[30]

The foregoing remarks suggest that the Qumran authors did not exhibit a particular interest in history. Past events and historical figures, even if known to them, were only used as illustrative material to promulgate their own theological beliefs. This peculiar attitude toward the past is further confirmed by an absence of any historical texts among Qumran scrolls. It is therefore unjustified to suppose that by merely using allusions and references to selected past events the Qumran authors aimed to show causal relationships between them or to offer an objective, true-to-life description of people. Random references to historical events, sprinkled with highly subjective opinions, can in no respect provide a solid foundation on which to build credible historical interpretations.[31] It must therefore be concluded that students of Judean history under the

---

[28] J. Sievers, *The Hasmoneans and their Supporters: From Mattathias to the Death of John Hyrcanus I* (South Florida Studies in the History of Judaism 6; Atlanta: Scholars Press, 1990), 88–92; Xeravits, "From the Forefathers to the 'Angry Lion,'" 211–221. Considered the best-known example of critics of the Hasmoneans is the *Pesher Habakkuk* (1QpHab); cf. van der Woude, "Wicked Priest," 349–359.

[29] Wise, "Dating the Teacher of Righteousness," 82–87. Based on this dating, a hypothesis has been proposed about the presumable date of death of the Teacher of Righteousness. See Doudna, *4Q Pesher Nahum*, 753–754; Collins, "Time of the Teacher," 212–218, 228–229. Cf. Charlesworth, *Pesharim and Qumran History*, 38, 90–91.

[30] Of 31 historical allusions identified in the manuscripts, only six refer to the second century B.C.E. figures and events. All are found in texts classed "non-sectarian": Charlesworth, *Pesharim and Qumran History*, 109–118; Wise, "Dating the Teacher of Righteousness," 67–69 nn. 1–6. Still, it should be remembered that more than a half of those allusions are hypothetical: see ibid., 67 n. 1 (= 4Q245 1 i 9), 68 nn. 3–4 (= 4Q245 1 i 10) and n. 5 (= 4Q331 1 i 7).

[31] Cf. Charlesworth, *Pesharim and Qumran History*, 116–118; Eshel, *Dead Sea Scrolls and the Hasmonean State*, 181–187.

Hasmoneans cannot find in Qumran scrolls any important information not already known from other sources. Consequently, the texts cannot be treated as sources to verify or question the credibility of known historical accounts dealing with that period.

JEWISH THOUGHT AND RELIGION
IN LIGHT OF THE DEAD SEA SCROLLS

SHIFTING PERSPECTIVES ON LITURGY
AT QUMRAN AND IN SECOND TEMPLE JUDAISM[*]

ESTHER G. CHAZON
The Hebrew University of Jerusalem

Two revolutions—one in Qumran studies, the other in the field of Jewish liturgy—began in the same year nearly two decades ago. In the spring of 1990, Ezra Fleischer published his monumental article, "On the Beginnings of Obligatory Jewish Prayer."[1] This article overturned the previous consensus built upon Joseph Heinemann's model of a gradual, evolutionary development of Jewish liturgy from Second Temple times to late antiquity.[2] Fleischer established a different paradigm that views the statutory liturgy as a completely new form of worship created *ex nihilo* by the rabbis at Yavneh at the end of the first century C.E., *after* the temple's destruction. Fleischer's paradigm raises questions about the relevance of Second Temple texts, including the Dead Sea Scrolls, for the history of Jewish prayer and poses a special challenge to scholars of Second Temple Judaism.

Just a few months after Fleischer's article appeared, Emanuel Tov was appointed editor-in-chief of the Dead Sea Scrolls, ending the forty-year reign of the original editors and ushering in a decade of rapid publication by a greatly expanded international team. In November, 2001 Tov announced the completion of the publication of the Dead Sea Scrolls. In fact, a few more volumes of *Discoveries in the Judaean Desert* appeared after 2001. The final volume of previously unpublished scrolls (*DJD* XXXVII), an edition of Aramaic texts by Émile Puech, was released

---

[*] I wish to thank Emanuel Tov for providing the most up-to-date Scrolls publication data, and Steven Fraade, Zeev Weiss, and Dena Ordan for their helpful comments on this paper.

[1] *Tarbiz* 59 (1990): 397–441 (Hebrew). See the review by R. Langer, "Revisiting Early Rabbinic Liturgy: The Recent Contributions of Ezra Fleischer," *Proof* 19 (1999): 179–194 and the responses by Fleischer, "On the Origins of the 'Amidah: Response to Ruth Langer," and Langer, "Considerations of Method: A Response to Ezra Fleischer," *Proof* 20 (2000): 380–387.

[2] J. Heinemann, *Prayer in the Period of the Tanna'im and the Amora'im: Its Nature and Patterns* (Jerusalem: Magnes, 1964) (Hebrew); idem, *Prayer in the Talmud: Forms and Patterns* (trans. R.S. Sarason; Berlin: de Gruyter, 1977).

in November 2008. With this last edition, sixty-one years after the initial discovery of the first Qumran cave, the age of Scrolls publication has drawn to a close. One of the great challenges in the post-publication era is to integrate the Scrolls into the study of all related disciplines and associated corpora with a goal of attaining a better picture of Jewish culture, religion, and society in the formative Second Temple period and beyond.

In the spirit of taking up the research challenges of the twenty-first century, this paper sets forth the key issues in the current study of Qumran prayer and early Jewish liturgy with an eye to pinpointing mutual concerns. The final part of the paper elucidates these issues in a concrete example at the intersection of the two fields.

QUMRAN STUDIES

I begin with the most recent stage of Qumran research. Now that nearly all the Dead Sea Scrolls have been published, we are in a position to take stock of the entire corpus of 1500 scrolls, 930 from Qumran alone, most of which are recent acquisitions in the last 30 *DJD* volumes. Three main issues are crucial at this major juncture in Qumran research.

The first is the provenance of the texts in the Qumran "library." Although this issue has been at the forefront of Qumran studies since the early 1990s, the provenance of many of the texts remains an open question. Recent calculations put the distinctively Qumranic compositions authored by members of the sect at only about 25 % of the Qumran corpus.[3] This surprisingly low figure completely changes our picture of the Qumran library and of the sect who collected it. The library is far less sectarian in origin than envisioned prior to the publications of the 1990s, which brought to light more biblical and previously known

---

[3] For figures on the distribution of the Qumran library (based on 800 manuscripts) see P.R. Davies, G.J. Brooke, and P.R. Callaway, *The Complete World of The Dead Sea Scrolls* (London: Thames & Hudson, 2002), 77 and D. Dimant, "The Qumran Manuscripts: Contents and Significance," in *Time to Prepare the Way in the Wilderness: Papers on the Qumran Scrolls by Fellows of the Institute for Advanced Studies of the Hebrew University, Jerusalem, 1989–1990* (ed. eadem and L.H. Schiffman; STDJ 16; Leiden: Brill, 1995), 23–58 (figures on pp. 31–32, 58). See also eadem "The Library of Qumran: Its Content and Character," in *The Dead Sea Scrolls Fifty Years After Their Discovery: Proceedings of the Jerusalem Congress, July 20–25, 1997* (ed. L.H. Schiffman et al.; Jerusalem: Israel Exploration Society, 2000), 170–176.

apocryphal works such as Tobit and the *Testament of Naphtali*. The same period also saw publication of methodological studies that identified many texts as non-sectarian on the basis of such criteria as language, use of the tetragrammaton, a different calendar or ideology.[4] Besides the biblical scrolls, which make up about 25 % of the library, the remaining non-sectarian texts—approximately 400 manuscripts—belong to a vast, largely unknown body of Jewish literature. The *Reworked Pentateuch*, *Paraphrase of Gen and Exod*, *Prayer of Enosh*, *Admonition on the Flood*, *Apocryphon of Jeremiah*, and *Time of Righteousness* are just a few of the hundreds of formerly lost Jewish works preserved by the Qumran community. To date, the provenance of a number of major texts in almost every genre is still under debate; these include the *Temple Scroll*, 4QInstruction, the *Songs of the Sabbath Sacrifice*, the *Barkhi Nafshi* psalms,[5] and even the prayers in the decidedly sectarian *War Scroll*.

Most recently, skepticism about the prospects of determining origin, together with post-modern perspectives, have shifted scholarly attention away from the discussion of origins.[6] But this historical pursuit is too

---

[4] A number of programmatic, methodological studies set down criteria for determining a work's provenance. See C.A. Newsom, "'Sectually Explicit' Literature in Qumran," in *The Hebrew Bible and Its Interpreters* (ed. W.H. Propp, B. Halpern, and D.N. Freedman; Winona Lake: Eisenbrauns, 1990), 167–187; E.G. Chazon, "Is *Divrei Ha-me'orot* a Sectarian Prayer?" in *The Dead Sea Scrolls: Forty Years of Research* (ed. D. Dimant and U. Rappaport; STDJ 10; Leiden: Brill, 1992), 3–17, and eadem, "Prayers from Qumran and Their Historical Implications," *DSD* 1 (1994): 265–284; Dimant, "The Qumran Manuscripts." See now C. Hempel, "Kriterien zur Bestimmung 'essenischer Verfasserschaft' von Qumrantexten," in *Qumran kontrovers: Beiträge zu den Textfunden vom Toten Meer* (ed. J. Frey and H. Stegemann; Einblicke 6; Paderborn: Bonifatius, 2003), 71–85, and in the same volume, A. Lange, "Kriterien essenischer Texte," 59–69.

[5] See F. García Martínez, "Temple Scroll," *Encyclopedia of the Dead Sea Scrolls* (ed. L.H. Schiffman and J.C. VanderKam; 2 vols.; Oxford: Oxford University Press, 2000), 2:927–933; D. Dimant, "Between Sectarian and Non-Sectarian: The Case of the 'Apocryphon of Joshua,'" in *Reworking the Bible: Apocryphal and Related Texts at Qumran: Proceedings of a Joint Symposium by the Orion Center for the Study of the Dead Sea Scrolls and Associated Literature and the Hebrew University Institute for Advanced Studies Research Group on Qumran, 15–17 January, 2002* (ed. E.G. Chazon, D. Dimant, and R.A. Clements; STDJ 58; Leiden: Brill, 2005), 105–134; M.J. Goff, *The Worldly and Heavenly Wisdom of 4QInstruction* (STDJ 50; Leiden: Brill, 2003), 6–23, 228–232; E.M. Schuller, "Prayers and Psalms from the Pre-Maccabean Period," *DSD* 13 (2006): 306–318.

[6] The shift away from origins and onto such questions as the scrolls' readership and reception was evident in the Qumran sessions at the 2007 Annual Meeting of the Society of Biblical Literature; for example, James Davila's paper on "Counterfactual History and Other New Methodologies" and Alison Schofield's on "From the Wilderness to a Door of Hope: Thematic (Re)Conceptualization of the Wilderness in Liturgical Texts." For a fine example of the contribution of the new approaches see M. Grossman, *Reading for History in the Damascus Document: A Methodological Study* (STDJ 45; Leiden: Brill, 2002).

important to abandon. A great deal is at stake in the case of each work under debate. There are serious implications for the ideological make-up of the Qumran community vis à vis other groups as well as for the history and transmission of biblical exegesis, Jewish law, and liturgy. It makes a huge difference, for instance, whether or not the *Songs of the Sabbath Sacrifice* are Qumranic in origin. If Qumranic, these songs may be understood as designed to serve as a spiritual substitute for sacrifice in the defiled Temple.[7] A sectarian, apocalyptic context may then be posited for the *merkabah* mystic and liturgical *Qedushah* traditions they attest.[8] If they are non-Qumranic in origin, then we must look to another author, social context, and liturgical function. A few scholars have suggested a priestly origin with links to the Jerusalem Temple cult but there are other possibilities.[9] I return to this significant case below. For now, we should bear in mind that the balance of manuscripts has shifted but not the essential fact that the library contains Qumranic as well as non-sectarian works.

---

[7] A.S. van der Woude, "Fragmente einer Rolle der Leiden für das Sabbatopfer aus Höhle xi von Qumran," in *Von Kanaan bis Kerala: FS J.P.M. van der Ploeg* (ed. W.C. Delsman et al.; AOAT 211; Neukirchen-Vluyn: Neukirchener Verlag, 1982), 311–337; J. Maier, "*Shîrê 'Ôlat hash-Shabbat*: Some Observations on their Calendric Implications and their Style," in *The Madrid Qumran Congress: Proceedings of the International Congress on the Dead Sea Scrolls, Madrid 18–21 March, 1991* (ed. J. Trebolle Barrera and L. Vegas Montaner; 2 vols.; STDJ 11.1–2; Leiden: Brill, 1992), 2:543–560. Maier, however, suggests (ibid., 559–560) that the Sabbath Songs also may have been used by priests outside of Qumran and that similar compositions may have been recited by priests not "actually engaged in service" at the Jerusalem Temple. Eyal Regev recently postulated that the Jerusalem Temple was "the cradle of fixed prayer in Israel" (see below p. 520) but that the Qumran prayers, including the Sabbath Songs, are sectarian (Qumranic or another sectarian group).

[8] I. Gruenwald, *From Apocalypticism to Gnosticism: Studies in Apocalypticism, Merkavah Mysticism and Gnosticism* (BEATAJ 14; Frankfurt: Lang, 1988), 145–170; R. Elior, "Mysticism, Magic, and Angelology-The Perception of Angels in Hekhalot Literature," *JSQ* 1 (1993): 3–53 and eadem, *The Three Temples: On the Emergence of Jewish Mysticism* (trans. D. Louvish; Portland: Littman Library of Jewish Civilization, 2004), esp. 11, 15–16 where she updates her view of the Songs' provenance and places this liturgy in the category of literature "preserved" but not authored at Qumran (see below) which, in her opinion, "represents the ancient centuries-old, priestly literature, the exclusive heritage of the Temple priesthood, preserved by the Zadokite priests and their allies." See now P. Alexander, *Mystical Texts* (Companion to the Qumran Scrolls 7; London: T&T Clark, 2006). For the new assessment of the Songs' non-Qumranic authorship by the text's editor, C.A. Newsom, see her article, "'Sectually Explicit,'" 179–185. The first edition, C.A. Newsom, *Songs of the Sabbath Sacrifice: A Critical Edition* (HSS 27; Atlanta: Scholars Press, 1985) is an indispensable tool.

[9] See my comments on Maier and Elior, respectively, in nn. 7 and 8 above as well as Alexander, *Mystical Texts*, 128–132, and pp. 520–522 below.

The second key issue in current Qumran research is the internal development within the Qumran community during the course of its 200 year history. Recent studies on the literary growth of the Community's own writings such as the *Community Rule*, the *War Scroll*, and the *Hodayot* point to an evolution in the sect's thought and practice.[10] There is also a growing appreciation of ostensibly contradictory materials in the vast and diverse Qumran library. Differences in such matters as calendar, the penal code, liturgies for the annual covenant ceremony, and deterministic theology signal an *internal* dynamic within the Qumran community not fully appreciated beforehand.[11] In addition, scholars now ponder the sect's continuous accretion and readership of non-Qumranic literature throughout its long history, its on-going intellectual and economic contacts with non-members, those officially in the lot of the "sons of darkness," and the impact of such persistent permeability on developments in sectarian practice, thought, and literature. These internal sectarian developments not only make a fascinating

---

[10] For example, P. Alexander and G. Vermes in *DJD* XXVI (1998): 1–4, 9–12 ("The Recensional History of Serekh ha-Yaḥad"); S. Metso, *The Textual Development of the Community Rule* (STDJ 21; Leiden, Brill, 1997) and eadem, "Methodological Problems in Reconstructing History from Rule Texts Found at Qumran," *DSD* 11 (2004): 315–335; E. Eshel and H. Eshel, "Recensions and Editions of the War Scroll," in *Dead Sea Scrolls Fifty Years After*, 351–364; J. Duhaime, *The War Texts: 1QM and Related Manuscripts* (Companion to the Qumran Scrolls 6; London: T&T Clark, 2004); R Yishay, "Prayers in Eschatological War Literature from Qumran: 4Q491–4Q496," *Meghillot* 5–6 (2008): 129–147 (Hebrew); E. Schuller, "Hodayot," in *DJD* XXIX (1999): 69–75; A.K. Harkins, "The Community Hymns Classification: A Proposal for Further Differentiation," *DSD* 15 (2008): 121–154 and eadem, "Sixty Years of Scholarship on the Community Hymns from 1QHª," in *Qumran Cave 1 Revisited: Texts from Cave 1 Sixty Years after Their Discovery: Proceedings of the Sixth Meeting of the IOQS in Ljubljana* (ed. D.K. Falk et al.; STDJ 91; Leiden, Brill, 2010), 101–134; E.G. Chazon, "Liturgical Function in the Cave 1 Hodayot Collection," in *Qumran Cave 1 Revisited*, 135–149.

[11] See, for example, Newsom, "'Sectually Explicit,'" 177–178; J.C. VanderKam, *Calendars in the Dead Sea Scrolls: Measuring Time* (London: Routledge, 1998), 79–90, 110–112; J. Ben-Dov, "Jubilean Chronology and the 364-Day Year," *Meghillot* 5–6 (2008): 49–59 (Hebrew); J.M. Baumgarten, "The Cave 4 Versions of the Qumran Penal Code," *JJS* 43 (1992): 268–276; Metso, "Methodological Problems"; B. Nitzan, "The Benedictions from Qumran for the Annual Covenantal Ceremony," in *Dead Sea Scrolls Fifty Years After*, 363–371. One wonders, for example, how the Qumran sect reconciled the different approaches to determinism versus moral choice present in its library particularly with respect to non-sectarian works used in Qumranic religious practice (e.g., the petitionary prayers in the *Words of the Luminaries*, 4Q504–506) or in the composition of sectarian writings (e.g., 4QInstruction in the *Community Rule's Treatise of the Two Spirits*). See, for example, Goff, *Worldly and Heavenly Wisdom*, 117–120 and the sources cited there.

subject of inquiry in their own right but are also a factor in sorting out Qumran's relationship to the outside world, which is the next point to be addressed.

The third major issue that arises now that the full scope of the Qumran corpus is available concerns the relationship between the Qumran community and the various authors, groups, and institutions whose works it preserved. Initially, this inquiry requires looking at the interface between Qumran thought and praxis according to the sect's own writings and the ideas and practices represented in the clearly non-sectarian works. What did the Qumran community borrow, from whom, in what way, and for what purpose?[12] Careful attention to different nuances in the shared material can provide clues about how the Qumran community read and adapted certain traditions, practices, and ideas; why it chose them and instituted various changes; and which groups, institutions, and social contexts influenced the sect during its formative years and entire history. Remarkably, the shared material extends across a broad spectrum of non-Qumranic works. It includes not only Bible, rewritten Bible, and apocalypses, but also sapiential, legal, poetical and liturgical texts. In the area of prayer alone, the scholarly literature is replete with comparisons between scrolls of diverse provenance and apocryphal, rabbinic, and early Christian texts regarding specific prayers, formulae, prayer-times, and other liturgical practices, some of which I discuss below.[13] After focusing inward on the Qumran corpus for many years due to the exigency of the publication project, the time is ripe to turn our gaze outward to the other corpora, which have served us well for deciphering

---

[12] Clear-cut, long-standing examples of borrowing are the citations of *1 Enoch*, the *Aramaic Levi Document*, and the book of *Jubilees* in the *Damascus Document* (CD 2:18–19; 4:15–19; 16:4, respectively); see J.C. Greenfield, "The Words of Levi Son of Jacob in Damascus Document IV, 15–19," *RevQ* 13 (1988): 319–322. For the influence of the previously unknown non-sectarian work, 4QInstruction, on the *Treatise of the Two Spirits* in the *Community Rule*, and on some of the *hodayot* in 1QH^a, see E. Tigchelaar, *To Increase Learning for the Understanding Ones: Reading and Reconstructing the Fragmentary Early Jewish Sapiential Text 4QInstruction* (STDJ 44; Leiden: Brill, 2001), 194–207 and M.J. Goff, "Reading Wisdom at Qumran: 4QInstruction and the Hodayot," *DSD* 11 (2004): 263–288. See Newsom, "'Sectually Explicit,'" 180–181, for the influence of the *Songs of the Sabbath Sacrifice*, which she considers non-sectarian, on 4QBerakhot, a sectarian covenant ceremony, and on the *Songs of the Sage*, an apotropaic liturgy apparently of sectarian origin.

[13] See pp. 522–527 below and the literature cited there. See further Chazon, "Liturgical Function," for the deployment of a traditional closing blessing formula by the sectarian editor of 1QH^a. For other sectarian adaptations of originally non-Qumranic material see n. 12 above.

individual scrolls, but need to be revisited in their own right and in light of all the new finds. Arguably, the most far-reaching goal in the next stage of research is redrawing the map of Second Temple Judaism with the benefit of the fully published corpus of Dead Sea Scrolls.

Jewish Liturgy

I turn now to the key questions in Jewish liturgical studies on which the Dead Sea Scrolls impact. Perforce, they are issues in the early history of the liturgy, that of the rabbinic period. The Scrolls' publications of the last fifteen years have already engendered a number of shifting perspectives on Jewish prayer as I demonstrate below.

The first and most fundamental question for the early history of Jewish liturgy is this: Did the Jewish population outside of Qumran engage in any regular, public prayer before the destruction of the Temple in 70 C.E.? Whereas just fifteen years ago we might have wondered how the Dead Sea Scrolls could teach us anything about prayer and religious practice outside of Qumran, scholars are currently asking how the Scrolls illuminate this issue. The change is predicated on a shift in scholars' understanding of the origins of many scrolls. More specifically, scholars now think that the overwhelming majority of texts from the Qumran library, including dozens of prayers, are non-sectarian in origin.

For the 2004 International SBL meeting, Eileen Schuller surveyed the Qumran corpus and composed a list of the pre-Maccabean prayers and psalms, which she published with some modifications in *DSD* 13 (2006).[14] Schuller is careful to put on her list only those texts that meet at least one of the hard criteria for non-Qumranic provenance such as a pre-Qumranic manuscript date, the use of the tetragrammaton, or a calendar that diverges from the sectarian solar calendar. The list has 24 items, 8 of which are collections, yielding a total of at least 100 non-biblical psalms; prayers embedded in narrative works such as the *Aramaic Levi Document*; and, most relevant for the present inquiry, annual and daily liturgies. The latter include the *Festival Prayers* (1Q34^{+bis}, 4Q507–509), the weekly liturgy of the *Words of the Luminaries*, the *Daily Prayers* in 4Q503, and the more vigorously debated *Songs of the Sabbath Sacrifice*.[15]

---

[14] "Prayers and Psalms," 314–316.

[15] Schuller puts in italics "texts whose provenance is the subject of considerable uncertainty or disagreement" ("Prayers and Psalms," 313–316). A strong case for non-sectarian

The non-Qumranic liturgical collections are direct evidence for religious practice outside of Qumran and open a window onto Second Temple Judaism. They place before us set texts of communal prayers for fixed prayer times—annual festivals, Sabbaths, and regular weekdays. They unambiguously attest regular, public prayer in the two centuries prior to the Temple's destruction. This essentially positive finding for some regular public prayer invites the next two questions, respectively, about the extent of this phenomenon during the Second Temple period and the connection to the statutory Jewish liturgy established by the rabbis after the Temple's destruction.

The second question is, then, in which institutions, locations, and groups other than the Qumran community—was regular, public prayer taking place during the Second Temple period? This question naturally entails, at least in its initial investigation, an effort to fit the data from the Scrolls into the framework of known groups and institutions.

Indeed, in this endeavor, much attention has been focused lately on the Jerusalem Temple. Eyal Regev's 2005 article, "Temple Prayer as the Origin of Fixed Prayer (On the Evolution of Prayer during the Period of the Second Temple)," is indicative of this approach.[16] Even after reconsidering all the evidence Regev amasses for prayer in the Temple—from Ben Sira's account of popular prayer at the end of the sacrificial service (Sir 50:17–19; cf. Luke 1:10; Josephus, *Ag. Ap.* 2.196) to the Mishnah's description of the priests' daily prayer in the Chamber of Hewn Stone and of Levitical song upon conclusion of the daily offering (*m. Tamid* 5:1; 7:3)—I still have serious doubts about whether this activity on the temporal and geographic perimeters of the cult is really "the origin of fixed prayer" in Israel.[17] Nonetheless, Regev's work—like that of Johann Maier and Daniel Falk before him—does open the door, I suppose, to

---

provenance can be made, however, for the italicized texts that use the tetragrammaton, such as the morning and evening prayers in 4QapocrMoses[c]? (4Q408), or whose calendar differs from the sectarian calendar, for example, 4QpapPrQuot (4Q503) and the *Festival Prayers* (for the latter see Newsom, " 'Sectually Explicit,' " 177–178 and Chazon, "Prayers from Qumran," 271–272, 282 n. 68).

[16] *Zion* 70 (2005): 5–29 (Hebrew). A literal translation of the Hebrew title would be, "The Temple as the Cradle of Fixed Prayer in Israel: Factors and Processes in the Development of Prayer in the Second Temple Period."

[17] For this locus of song and prayer *outside* the inner priestly "sanctuary of silence" see I. Knohl, "Between Voice and Silence: The Relationship between Prayer and Temple Cult," *JBL* 115 (1996): 17–30 and the revised Hebrew version in *Mehqerei Talmud: Talmudic Studies Dedicated to the Memory of Professor Ephraim E. Urbach* (ed. Y. Sussman and D. Rosenthal; Jerusalem: Magnes, 2005), 2:740–753.

considering this, albeit peripheral, Temple prayer activity as *one* possible source of inspiration for the post-destruction institutionalization of Jewish liturgy.[18] It also ties in with a growing awareness that not all fixed, public prayer came into being as a substitute for sacrifice. This new perspective on regular public prayer "alongside of Temple worship," to quote Eileen Schuller, is actually a necessary implication of the non-sectarian liturgies discovered at Qumran.[19] To see these two forms of worship—public prayer and sacrifice—as co-existent, symbiotic, or even complementary does not, however, require locating them together at the Temple.

Nor does regular public prayer appear to have been conducted in Second Temple period synagogues, at least not in Judaea and much of the Diaspora. The choice of the term *synagoge*, "(place of) assembly," for Judaean and some Diaspora synagogues as well as the simple, participant-oriented architectural design of the buildings indicate a general, multi-purpose communal use, rather than a specifically religious function. Admittedly, a number of Diaspora synagogues are called *proseuche*, "(place of) prayer"; however, even for those, as for all other ancient synagogues, the epigraphic and literary sources amply document a variety of communal activities including public Torah reading and study but not regular prayer services.[20]

---

[18] Johann Maier's article, "Zu Kult und Liturgie der Qumrangemeinde," *RevQ* 14 (1990): 543–586, was seminal in systematically differentiating between priestly, Levitical, and lay liturgies. See D.K. Falk, *Daily, Sabbath, and Festival Prayers in the Dead Sea Scrolls* (STDJ 27; Leiden: Brill, 1998), 53–54, 90–92, 123–124, 215, 253–255 and idem, "Qumran Prayer Texts and the Temple," in *Sapiential, Liturgical and Poetical Texts From Qumran: Proceedings of the Third Meeting of the International Organization for Qumran Studies* (ed. idem, F. García Martínez, and E.M. Schuller; STDJ 34; Leiden: Brill, 2000), 106–126. See also D. Levine, "A Temple Prayer for Fast Days," in *Liturgical Perspectives: Prayer and Poetry in Light of the Dead Sea Scrolls: Proceedings of the Fifth International Symposium of the Orion Center for the Study of the Dead Sea Scrolls and Associated Literature, 19–23 January, 2000* (ed. E.G. Chazon; Leiden: Brill, 2003), 95–112, and the thesis of D.D. Binder, *Into the Temple Courts: The Place of the Synagogues in the Second Temple Period* (Atlanta: Scholars Press, 1999), 31–38, 404–415, 477–493.

[19] Schuller, "Prayers and Psalms," 317. See also Falk, "Qumran Prayer Texts," 106–108, 124–126 and his discussion there of the classic model of prayer as a substitute for sacrifice.

[20] See L.I. Levine, *The Ancient Synagogue: The First Thousand Years* (2nd ed.; New Haven: Yale University Press, 2005), 1–173. Levine reports that "Of the fifty-nine references to Diaspora synagogues, thirty-one, i.e., some 53%, refer to a *proseuche*," and that this term "is used almost exclusively in Hellenistic Egypt, the Bosphorus, and Delos" (138). For the use of *synagoge* for this institution in Rome, Greece, Asia Minor, and Cyrene see pp. 102–103, 106, 115–120, 138–139. I agree with Levine (165 nn. 156–157) that Josephus' mention of prayer in Tiberius' *proseuche* on a fast day during the war likely refers

Clearly, other institutions, groups, and locations need to be considered. Proposals put forth in recent studies suggest a range of possibilities: from the town plazas and open public spaces throughout Palestine seen by Lee Levine as the venue for the communal activities that later found a home in the first-century synagogue[21] to the proto-Qumranic, priestly circles associated with works like the book of *Jubilees* and *1 Enoch* that Israel Knohl put forth as candidates.[22] Still other options exist—in the field, taking account of archaeology, historical geography, and demography; and in the literature, for example, in sapiential works associated with wisdom schools. The Wisdom of Ben Sira, apocryphal Psalm 154, and the Wisdom of Solomon all contain numerous references to regular prayer practices in addition to offering religious poetry. In short, a complex picture of the social map of public prayer is emerging, and there is need for much future work in this area.

The third question about the impact of current Scrolls research on our understanding of early Jewish prayer is this: What evidence is available now for the structure, form, and content of the later institution of Jewish

---

to ad hoc prayer (*Life* 290–295; this is the only occurrence of *proseuche* for Judaea) and that Agatharchides' reference to Sabbath prayer "in the temples" of Jerusalem (Josephus, *Ag. Ap.* 1.209) is probably to the Jerusalem Temple (I understand the *Damascus Document*'s reference to a "house of prostration" in a similar vein, see CD 11:21–12:1). I do not agree with Levine's assessment (ibid.), however, that prayer *per se* (as distinct from Torah reading) necessarily was "an integral part of Diaspora worship." For an inventory of synagogues until the first century C.E. see P. Richardson, "An Architectural Case for Synagogues as Associations," in *The Ancient Synagogue From Its Origins Until 200 C.E.: Papers Presented at an International Conference at Lund University, October 14–17, 2001* (ed. B. Olsson and M. Zetterholm; Stockholm: Almquist & Wiksell, 2003), 90–117; consult the articles in that volume for the current state of the research.

[21] Levine, *Ancient Synagogue*, 28–44. It is telling that the Mishnah still describes the lay counterpart (*ma'amadot*) to the priestly courses serving at the Temple as gathering "in their towns," without mentioning synagogues (*m. Ta'an.* 4:2, note also that *m. Bik.* 3:2 describes those bringing first-fruits to Jerusalem as gathering in the town square of the *ma'amad's* city). The fact that the *ma'amadot* ceremony consisted of public Torah reading, not prayer, is both significant and in keeping with the data for Palestinian (and Diaspora) non-sacrificial religious activity during the Second Temple period. At Qumran, the one Second Temple site in Palestine where we know daily communal prayer took place, there is no synagogue building and we are left to imagine where prayer services were held: the open space on the plateau beside the main complex is as good a candidate as the communal dining room (locus 77), small benched room (4) or adjacent, nondescript hall (30) that were suggested by Levine, "Ancient Synagogue," 65 and Richardson, "Architectural Case," 111–112.

[22] Knohl, "Between Voice and Silence," 29–30 (751–753 in Hebrew version). I thank Israel Knohl for sharing his further update on *1 Enoch* in his response to this paper at the Vienna conference.

liturgy, if not in its entirety then at least in substantial parts? From the pioneering work of David Flusser, Shemaryahu Talmon, and Moshe Weinfeld to more recent studies by Johann Maier, Bilhah Nitzan, Daniel Falk, and others, dozens of suggestions have been made for identifying specific, traditional Jewish prayers in the Dead Sea Scrolls and associated literature, most notably in Ben Sira and 1–2 Maccabees.[23] While I do not find all of those identifications convincing, I do see a significant number of close correspondences for certain prayers, formulae, and practices. Three sterling examples will suffice to illustrate my point.

1. The liturgical collections from Qumran, both those of sectarian and non-sectarian origin, attest the systematic use of blessing formulae to open and close liturgical prayers during the Second Temple period. For example, a blessing formula such as "Blessed is the God of Israel" opens each of the evening and morning prayers in 4Q503 and closes many of them, occasionally adding "You" or "Your name" to the formula. Similarly, each weekday prayer in the *Words of the Luminaries* and each of the *Festival Prayers* conclude with a "Blessed is the Lord" formula. This formal function closely accords with the rabbinic liturgical benediction, which imposes an opening and closing blessing framework on the

---

[23] S. Talmon, "The 'Manual of Benedictions' of the Sect of the Judaean Desert," *RevQ* 2 (1960): 475–500; idem, "The Emergence of Institutionalized Prayer in Israel in the Light of the Qumran Literature," in idem, *The World of Qumran From Within: Collected Studies* (Jerusalem: Magnes, 1989), 200–243. D. Flusser, "Sanktus und Gloria," in *Abraham unser Vater: Juden und Christen im Gespräch über die Bibel: FS O. Michel* (ed. O. Betz, M. Hengel, and P. Schmidt; AGSU 5; Leiden: Brill, 1963), 128–152; idem, "Qumran and Jewish 'Apotropaic' Prayers," *IEJ* 16 (1966): 194–205; idem, "'He Has Planted It [i.e., the Law] as Eternal Life in Our Midst,'" *Tarbiz* 58 (1989): 147–153 (Hebrew). M. Weinfeld, "Traces of Kedushat Yotzer and Pesukey De-Zimra in the Qumran Literature and in Ben Sira," *Tarbiz* 45 (1976): 15–26 (Hebrew); idem, "The Prayers for Knowledge, Repentance and Forgiveness in the 'Eighteen Benedictions'—Qumran Parallels, Biblical Antecedents, and Basic Characteristics," *Tarbiz* 45 (1979): 15–26 (Hebrew); idem, "The Morning Prayers (*Birkhoth Hashachar*) in Qumran and in the Conventional Jewish Liturgy," *RevQ* 13 (1988): 481–494; "Prayer and Liturgical Practice in the Qumran Sect," in *Dead Sea Scrolls: Forty Years*, 241–258; idem, "The Angelic Song Over the Luminaries in the Qumran Texts," in *Time to Prepare the Way in the Wilderness*, 131–157; see also L.H. Schiffman, "The Dead Sea Scrolls and the Early History of Jewish Liturgy," in *The Synagogue in Late Antiquity* (ed. L.I. Levine; Philadelphia: ASOR, 1987), 33–48. Maier, "Zu Kult und Liturgie"; B. Nitzan, *Qumran Prayer and Religious Poetry* (trans. J. Chipman; STDJ 12; Leiden: Brill, 1994), and eadem, "The Dead Sea Scrolls and the Jewish Liturgy," in *The Dead Sea Scrolls as Background to Postbiblical Judaism and Christianity* (ed. J.R. Davila; STDJ 46; Leiden: Brill, 2003), 195–219; Falk, *Daily, Sabbath, and Festival Prayers*, and idem, "Qumran and the Synagogue Liturgy," in *The Ancient Synagogue*, 404–433. See also Chazon, "Prayers from Qumran," and the specific examples given below.

obligatory prayers (principally, the *Shema* Benedictions and the *Amidah*).[24] Furthermore, the liturgies from Qumran show that the formal, liturgical use of closing blessings and the second person address to God as "You" in the benedictory formulae are innovations vis à vis the classic biblical blessing, which opens a spontaneous expression of praise *about* God.[25] These are two Second Temple period developments that serve as forerunners of the rabbinic liturgical benediction.

---

[24] Heinemann, *Prayer in the Talmud*, 77–103. Heinemann differentiates between the rabbinic opening formula, "Blessed are You, Lord, King of the Universe, who has done …" and the concluding participial eulogy pattern, "Blessed are You Lord who makes …," which was also used as an alternate opening formula, for example, at the beginning of the *Shema* Benedictions, "Blessed are You, Lord, King of the Universe, who forms light and creates darkness, makes peace and creates all." The Scrolls now show (contrast Heinemann, ibid., 93) that in this earlier period both the relative clause and the active participle were used alternately in closing as well as opening blessings, and that both forms could be couched either in the second or third person (on the second person address to God see also below). For the Qumran data see E.M. Schuller, "Some Observations on Blessings of God in Texts From Qumran," in *Of Scribes and Scrolls: Studies on the Hebrew Bible, Intertestamental Judaism and Christian Origins Presented to J. Strugnell on the Occasion of His Sixtieth Birthday* (ed. H.W. Attridge, J.J. Collins, and T.H. Tobin; Lanham: University Press of America, 1990), 133–143; E.G. Chazon, "A Liturgical Document from Qumran and Its Implications: 'Words of the Luminaries' (4QDibHam)" (Ph.D. diss., The Hebrew University of Jerusalem, 1992), 100–101 (Hebrew); Nitzan, *Qumran Prayer*, 72–80; Falk, *Daily, Sabbath, and Festival Prayers*, 37–42, 79–84, 182–185. In addition to the three non-sectarian liturgies from Qumran cited above, it is important to observe that at least two sectarian liturgical collections employ concluding blessings (*Songs of the Sage*, 4Q511 63 iv 1–3, and 1QH[a], for which see Chazon, "Liturgical Function") and several regularly employ opening blessing formulae (e.g, the Purification Rituals in 4Q512 and 4Q284; 4QpapRitMar [4Q502]; and many of the hymns in the *Hodayot*, see H. Stegemann, "The Number of Psalms in *1QHodayot*[a] and Some of Their Sections," in *Liturgical Perspectives*, 191–234). These sectarian examples demonstrate that the Qumran Community followed accepted liturgical conventions in writing its own prayers. Some features of the various formulae are discussed further below.

[25] For the biblical pattern and its use as the prototype for the rabbinic opening blessing see Heinemann, *Prayer in the Talmud*, 82–89. In the Bible, closing blessings are only used to mark the end of each book of Psalms (41:14; 72:19; 89:53; 106:48) and a few individual psalms (68:36; 72:18; 135:21). The Second Temple apocryphal works known before the discovery of the Dead Sea Scrolls provided just a few instances of closing blessings (Tob 13:19; *Pss. Sol.* 2:37; 5:19; 6:6; 3 Macc 7:23) and of blessings with a second person address to God (Tob 3:8, 15–17; LXX Dan 3:3, 29). For the latter as a late biblical expression occurring in Ps 119:12 and 1 Chr 29:10 see A. Hurvitz, *The Transition Period in Biblical Hebrew* (Jerusalem: Bialik Institute, 1972), 144–145. The second person address to God is employed in some closing blessings of the *Daily Prayers* and in the *Songs of the Sage*; it is regularly part of the opening blessing formulae in the Purification Ritual and the *hodayot* (see n. 24 above). Tellingly, a supralinear correction changes the typical *hodayot* formula, "I thank you, Lord" to "Blessed are You" in one hymn (1QH[a] XIII:22) and the

2. The New Year liturgy in the *Festival Prayers* from Qumran and the Friday prayer in the *Words of the Luminaries* now attest the liturgical recitation of a petition for the in-gathering of the Diaspora at those fixed prayer times. Not only does the liturgical practice correspond to that in later Jewish daily and festival prayer but, there is a common tradition of formulating this petition with Isa 11:12. The latter tradition underlies the *Festival Prayers* from Qumran and other exemplars of this petition from the Second Temple period. Notable examples inlcude Sir 36:13, 2 Macc 1:27, and *Pss. Sol.* 8:28, as well as the rabbinic daily *Amidah*, which uses Isa 11:12 in the tenth benediction's petition for in-gathering (*b. Ber.* 29a) and Isa 56:8 in its eulogy (*y. Ber.* 2:4, 5a; cf. Sir 51:12).[26] To illustrate their close correspondence and common tradition, I quote the text from Qumran followed by the talmudic sources for the tenth *Amidah* benediction:

> You shall assemble [our banished ones] for an appointed time of [...],
> and our dispersed ones for the season of [... may you] ga[ther].[27]
>   (4Q509 3 3–4)

> Our dispersed ones You shall gather from four (corners) ...
>   (abbreviated Eighteen Benedictions, *b. Ber.* 29a, cf. *y. Ber.* 4:3, 8a)
> (Blessed are You, God) who gathers the banished ones of Israel.[28]
>   (eulogy, *y. Ber.* 2:4, 5a)

---

second person pronoun (אתה) is added supralinearly to the opening blessing formula in the morning and evening liturgy of 4Q408 (frg. 3 + 3a), which is a liturgy similar to 4QpapPrQuot (4Q503). The data from Qumran thus provide early evidence for a growing tendency toward the second person address to God in opening and closing blessings.

[26] The hymn of praise in Sir 51:12 is probably a later addition because it is absent from the Greek and ancient Hebrew manuscripts. Sir 36:13 and 2 Macc 1:27 combine Isa 11:12; 49:5–6. The *Festival Prayers* from Qumran provide a closer linguistic parallel than the petition in the weekday *Words of the Luminaries*, which is formulated with Deut 30:1–4. For a fuller discussion and tables of the parallel texts see E.G. Chazon, "'Gather the Dispersed of Judah:' Seeking a Return to the Land as a Factor in Jewish Identity of Late Antiquity," in *Heavenly Tablets: Interpretation, Identity and Tradition in Ancient Judaism* (ed. L. LiDonnici and A. Lieber; JSJSup 119; Leiden: Brill, 2007), 159–175.

[27] The extant verb, ואספתה, could be taken as a perfect with consecutive *waw* denoting the past (E. Qimron, "Prayers for the Festivals from Qumran: Reconstruction and Philological Observations," in *Hamlet on a Hill: Semitic and Greek Studies Presented to Professor T. Muraoka on the Occasion of his Sixty-Fifth Birthday* [ed. M.F.J. Baasten and W.T. van Peursen; OLA 118; Leuven: Peeters, 2003], 383–393) or as a perfect with conversive *waw* denoting the future, as in Maurice Baillet's translation, which accords with his reading of [ץ]ק[ב]ת[in line 4 and the allusion to Isa 11:12 in lines 3–4 (*DJD* VII [1982]:185–187).

[28] The full version in the Palestinian prayer rite preserved in the Cairo Genizah reads:

3. The *Daily Prayers* from Qumran bear a striking similarity in form, content, language, and function to the rabbinic Benediction on the Luminaries (*b. Ber.* 11b–12a).[29] Both sets of benedictions offer praise twice a day at sunrise and sunset for the creation and daily renewal of the heavenly lights, using the verbs להאיר, "to shine" (e.g., 4Q503 10 3) and לחדש, "to renew" (4Q503 29–32 9). Both follow the practice of mentioning darkness as well as light in the morning and evening blessings. Both add traditional Sabbath themes (rest, delight, holiness, and election) in the special form of the benedictions for the Sabbath days.[30] Both contain a description of the praise offered by and in unison with the angels, which is known in the statutory liturgy as the *Qedushah* of the *Yotser*, the blessing to God "who forms (*Yotser*) light and creates darkness." Clearly, these texts represented the same religious phenomenon, reflect a shared liturgical tradition, and are similar enough to enable the Qumran scroll to shed light on Jewish liturgy, for example, on the antiquity of the *Yotser Qedushah* and the Babylonian custom of its *daily* recitation.[31] As impressive as the parallels

---

Sound the great ram's horn (Isa 27:13) for our freedom,
Hold up a signal (Isa 11:12a) to gather our exiled ones,
(Gather us together from the four corners of the earth [Isa 11:12b] to our land)
Blessed are You, God, who gathers the banished ones of His people Israel (Isa
    56:8).

Y. Luger, *The Weekday Amidah in the Cairo Genizah* (Jerusalem: Orhot, 2001), 114–118; see also S. Schechter, "Geniza Specimens," *JQR* (Old Series) 10 (1898): 654–659; for the similar version in the Babylonian rite see the early (ninth century C.E.) prayer book, *Seder Rab Amram Ga'on* (ed. D.S. Goldschmidt; Jerusalem: Mossad Harav Kook, 1971), 25 (Hebrew). The petition for in-gathering recited on festivals is worded differently in both the Palestinian and Babylonian prayer rites. For the latter see e.g., *Amram* (ibid., 126): "Bring near our scattered among the nations (Joel 4:2) and assemble (Ps 147:2) our dispersed (Isa 11:12) from the ends of the earth (Jer 31:8)." This formulation of the petition might already be attested by the version of the abbreviated Eighteen Benedictions recorded in the Palestinian Talmud (*y. Ber.* 4:3, 8a), "our scattered ones You will gather."

[29] For the full text in early prayer books see Schechter, "Geniza," 654; J. Mann, "Genizah Fragments of the Palestinian Order of Service," *HUCA* 2 (1925): 269–323; Goldschmidt, *Amram*, 13–14, 52, 71.

[30] 4Q503 24–25 5; 37–38 13–15; 40–41 4–6; see E.G. Chazon, "On the Special Character of Sabbath Prayer: New Data from Qumran," *Journal of Jewish Music and Liturgy* 15 (1992–1993): 1–21. The dates of the month assigned to the Sabbath prayers in 4Q503 render this liturgy inapplicable, in its present form, to every month of the year; however, the character of these evening and morning blessings suggests that blessings like them were recited daily by the worshippers who used this liturgy (see E.G. Chazon, "The Function of the Qumran Prayer Texts: An Analysis of the Daily Prayers [4Q503]," in *Dead Sea Scrolls Fifty Years After*, 217–225).

[31] E.G. Chazon, "The Qedushah Liturgy and its History in Light of the Dead Sea Scrolls," in *From Qumran to Cairo: Studies in the History of Prayer: Proceeding of the*

are both quantitatively and qualitatively, some differences in detail such as the astronomical terminology in the *Daily Prayers* from Qumran,[32] on the one hand, and the absence of the thrice-holy/*qedushah* verse in that scroll, on the other, lead me to question whether we actually have here an ancient version of this Jewish prayer. "Precursor" would be a more apt term.

The three examples given above are part of what now amounts to a critical mass of liturgical formulae, prayers and practices with striking parallels to their counterparts in the statutory Jewish liturgy. This picture is not unlike what Joseph Heinemann described as "common liturgical property,"[33] but on a far grander scale and with the highly significant contribution of early, non-sectarian liturgical collections. Thus, the Scrolls have uncovered a sizeable, continuous liturgical tradition stretching from the second century B.C.E. to the third century C.E., and in some instances perhaps even a precursor or direct antecedent of a later rabbinic benediction or liturgical practice. These results would appear to have implications for the early history of Jewish liturgy and for refining Ezra Fleischer's historical model of the liturgy's creation *ex nihilo* at Yavneh. They suggest that the establishment of the new institution of obligatory Jewish prayer by the rabbis after the Second Temple's destruction was not *ex nihilo* but rather came against a rich background of considerable, well-steeped, liturgical precedent and tradition.

PENITENTIAL PRAYER

The final section of this study focuses on one particular genre, that of penitential prayer, also known as communal confession or supplication.[34] This genre cuts across Second Temple literature up until, and including, early rabbinic prayer. It provides an opportunity to address together,

Research Group Convened Under the Auspices of the Institute for Advanced Studies of the Hebrew University of Jerusalem, 1997 (ed. J. Tabory; Jerusalem: Orhot, 1999), 7–17.

[32] The terminology is explained by J.M. Baumgarten, "4Q503 (Daily Prayers) and the Lunar Calendar," *RevQ* 12 (1986): 399–406.

[33] Heinemann, *Prayer in the Talmud*, 56; see his second chapter on "The Development of Prayers and the Problem of the 'Original Text,'" 37–76.

[34] See "Appendix A: Designations for Penitential Prayer," which also lists the prayers of this genre, in M.J. Boda, *Praying the Tradition: The Origin and Use of Tradition in Nehemiah 9* (BZAW 277; Berlin: de Gruyter, 1999), 198–202.

in a holistic fashion, the corresponding issues on the agendas of both Qumran research and Jewish liturgical studies as outlined above. These issues are the non-sectarian provenance of liturgical texts discovered at Qumran; the interface between sectarian, early non-sectarian, and later rabbinic prayer; and the social map of regular, public prayer during the Second Temple period.

Penitential prayer has been the subject of a number of major studies in the last few years as well as of a three-year consultation at the Society of Biblical Literature. These have produced a general consensus about the genre's origin at the very beginning of the Second Temple period, a basic list of prayers of this type, and an accepted working definition. The definition has been formulated by Rodney Werline as follows:

> Penitential prayer is a direct address to God in which an individual, group, or an individual on behalf of a group confesses sins and petitions for forgiveness as an act of repentance.[35]

The chief exemplars of this genre are considered to be: Ezra 9:6–15; Neh 1:5–37; 9:5–37; Dan 9:4–19; Bar 1:5–3:18; the Prayer of Azariah in LXX Dan 3:2[25]–21[45]; 3 Macc 2:1–20; Esther's prayer in the Septuagint (LXX Esth 14); and the Greek Prayer of Manasseh.

In the Qumran corpus, scholars generally class the following *non-sectarian* texts as penitential prayers: the Hebrew Prayer of Manasseh in the *Non-Canonical Psalms* (4Q381 33 + 35); the *Festival Prayers*, especially the one for the Day of Atonement (4Q508 3); the weekday prayers in the *Words of the Luminaries*; and 4QCommunal Confession (4Q393) which was first published in 1994.[36] Significantly three of these are in liturgical collections, of which two are collections for fixed prayer times. The time of recitation is not specified in the fourth text (4Q393), but its content and language better suit a regular rather than an ad hoc occa-

---

[35] "Defining Penitential Prayer," in *Seeking the Favor of God*, vol. 1: *The Origins of Penitential Prayer in Second Temple Judaism* (ed. M.J. Boda, D.K. Falk, and R.A. Werline; SBLEJL 21; Atlanta: SBL, 2006), xv. A petition for removal of the problem plaguing the petitioner(s) usually ensues. See R.A. Werline, *Penitential Prayer in Second Temple Judaism: The Development of a Religious Institution* (SBLEJL 13: Atlanta: Scholars Press, 1998), 2–3 and Boda, *Praying the Tradition*, 28–29.

[36] See especially E. Schuller, "Penitential Prayer in Second Temple Judaism: A Research Survey," in *Seeking the Favor of God*, vol. 2: *The Development of Penitential Prayer in Second Temple Judaism* (ed. M.J. Boda, D.K. Falk, and R.A. Werline; SBLEJL 22; Atlanta: SBL, 2007), 1–15. For 4Q393 see D.K. Falk, "4Q393: A Communal Confession," *JJS* (1994): 184–207.

sion. What is most striking about this list of scrolls is that it informs us unequivocally about the application of penitential prayer to fixed prayer times already in the second to first centuries B.C.E. and indicates that this liturgical regularization was taking place outside of the Qumran community.

Yet, the vast majority of penitential prayers in Second Temple literature are still for times of acute distress and particularly for recitation during special, ad hoc public assemblies called to deal with the crisis, which was understood as divine punishment for sin.[37] This original, emergency use persisted throughout the rabbinic period as seen in the fast-day ritual in tractate *Ta'anit* (Mishnah, Tosefta and both Talmuds), continuing even when the rabbis fixed penitential prayers in their Day of Atonement and daily liturgies (see below). Thanks to the Scrolls, we now know that the regular, liturgical use of penitential prayer also goes back to the middle of the Second Temple period. Furthermore, the Scrolls, especially the *Words of the Luminaries*, demonstrate how penitential prayer was adapted from ad hoc occasions to a new religious practice of daily communal prayer that was a harbinger of future developments in rabbinic liturgy. For instance, by shifting the emphasis away from sin and onto petitions for on-going spiritual and physical needs, the *Words of the Luminaries* tempered the penitential mode of prayer and accommodated it to a routine daily liturgy in a manner comparable to the incorporation of petitions for knowledge, repentance, forgiveness, and redemption in the daily *Amidah* prayer.[38]

Of the issues laid out above, the most difficult to solve is that of mapping the groups and settings in which penitential prayer was taking place on an ad hoc or regular basis during the Second Temple period. When surveying all the extant penitential prayers, it is striking how many of these there are for times of acute distress and how broad this

---

[37] Although some scholars prefer to see the genre's *Sitz im Leben* in covenant ceremonies like those in Ezra-Nehemiah, (and later, in 1QS I:16–II:23), the crisis is very much in view in all the exemplars in late biblical and apocryphal literature. See Werline, *Penitential Prayer*, 3–6, 194–195, and the recent assessments of research by S.E. Balentine, "'I Was Ready to Be Sought Out by Those Who Did Not Ask,'" and M.J. Boda, "Form Criticism in Transition: Penitential Prayer and Lament, Sitz im Leben and Form," both in *Seeking the Favor*, 1:1–20 and 1:181–192, respectively.

[38] E.G. Chazon, "The *Words of the Luminaries* and Penitential Prayer in Second Temple Times," in *Seeking the Favor*, 2:177–186. See also the discerning comments by Heinemann, *Prayer in the Talmud*, 197–199 on the confessional in the rabbinic daily, Day of Atonement, and emergency fast-day liturgies, as well as Weinfeld, "Prayers for Knowledge, Repentance and Forgiveness."

practice was both geographically and chronologically. Although each of those occasions was ad hoc, the practice itself was regularly implemented in frequently occurring crisis situations and may, therefore, be seen as habitual. Some evidence of penitential prayer on annual holidays now comes from separate quarters thanks to the non-sectarian *Festival Prayers* from Qumran that broaden the context in which to view the holiday penitential prayer in Baruch (Bar 1:14). The establishment of penitential prayers for certain yearly festivals and as the regular program for public emergencies may have laid the groundwork for the appropriation of penitential prayer in the weekday liturgy of the *Words of the Luminaries*, a practice not attested again until the rabbinic period.

The limited number of annual and daily penitential prayers from the Second Temple period makes it extremely difficult to determine how narrow or broad these practices were or which groups engaged in them. Some clues may be forthcoming from tracking all the examples of penitential prayer and from recent work on the groups behind the genre and its provenance. For instance, Dalit Rom-Shiloni finds the origins of this genre in what she calls "orthodox" circles of the mid-late sixth century B.C.E., by which she means the deuteronomistic historiographers, priests mainly of the Holiness school, and prophets like Jeremiah and Ezekiel.[39] Her finding fits the picture of the authors and settings of the penitential prayers throughout the Second Temple period both in Palestine and the Diaspora as exemplified by Ezra, Nehemiah, Baruch, and 3 Maccabees.[40] The Scrolls afford an opportunity to see how an anti-establishment group adopted but radically reinterpreted the genre in its own practice, as in its annual covenant ceremony,[41] while absorbing traditional exemplars of the genre like those in the *Festival Prayers* and the *Words of the Luminaries*, which apparently hailed from non-separatist circles that plausibly had closer ties than the Qumran community to the power base and Temple cult in Jerusalem.

---

[39] "Social-Ideological *Setting* or *Settings* for Penitential Prayer," in *Seeking the Favor*, 1:51–68.

[40] Both prayers in 3 Macc are recited by priests; the decidedly penitential prayer in 2:1–20 is said by the high priest in the Jerusalem Temple.

[41] For the Qumran covenant ceremony see n. 37 above and Falk, *Daily, Sabbath, and Festival Prayers*, 219–222.

Conclusion

The case of penitential prayer can provide a model for future research. It is an example of intensive research and consultation on a specific type of prayer and religious practice in every quarter of Second Temple Judaism over the course of the entire period, also taking account of earlier biblical tradents and later rabbinic trajectories. The map of Second Temple Judaism is richer and more detailed as a result. We have gained insights into the various groups employing this type of prayer, different nuances in separate quarters, and the application of ad hoc penitential practice to routine festival and daily communal prayer in non-sectarian circles. These matters lie at the heart of the key issues and mutual concerns of both Qumran research and Jewish liturgy. In conclusion, I propose adding another dimension to Qumran studies in the twenty-first century: not only the perspective of the entire corpus, its integration with all associated corpora, and a look at the interface between Qumran and the outside world, but also a new stage of collaborative, interdisciplinary research that will bring together scholars in the related disciplines and push the envelope on the outstanding, critical issues in the fields of Qumran and Jewish liturgy.

WHEN THE BELL RINGS:
THE QUMRAN RITUALS OF AFFLICTION IN CONTEXT

Daniel Stökl Ben Ezra
CNRS Aix-en-Provence

In the last twenty years, the disciplines of religious studies and e.g., political science, have seen the emergence of the thriving new perspective of "ritual studies." There is now a *Journal of Ritual Studies* and a *Ritual Studies Monograph Series*. Many institutions of higher education offer introductory classes to ritual studies.[1] There are many interesting focuses and perspectives through which ritual studies can throw light on religious behavior. Here, I shall limit myself to one of the endeavors of this new discipline: the attempt to develop a typology of ritual activity. In recent years, much progress has been made in the study of Qumran religion by studies cataloguing and systematizing Qumran liturgical texts.[2] Rituals, however, are larger than words. Ritual studies are particularly interesting for their attention to the non-verbal aspects of ritual and even for wholly non-verbal rituals. I do not want to say that these aspects have been completely neglected in previous studies,[3] yet, as is usual for a discipline dominated by philology, the study of words has clearly been preferred to that of ritual action.[4]

---

[1] See also the huge long-term *Sonderforschungsbereich* "Ritual Dynamics" in Heidelberg with more than 50 collaborators (see http://www.ritualdynamik.uni-hd.de/en/index.htm).

[2] Let me only mention B. Nitzan, *Qumran Prayer and Religious Poetry* (trans. J. Chapman; STDJ 12; Leiden: Brill, 1994) and D.K. Falk, *Daily, Sabbath, and Festival Prayers in the Dead Sea Scrolls* (STDJ 27; Leiden: Brill, 1998). Many of the important works written by E. Chazon, D. Flusser, J. Maier, E. Schuller and M. Weinfeld deal with the history of tradition, the antecedents to, the heirs of, as well as the parallel developments to the prayer texts discovered at Qumran.

[3] Much of the work of D.K. Falk, e.g., focuses on the relation of ritual and chronological as well as socio-historical aspects.

[4] This is also exemplified by the revolution in Qumran Studies caused by the work of L.H. Schiffman that brought halakhah back to the place of primordial importance such an issue should have in the study of a Jewish religious community.

Among the pioneers and driving forces for the success of ritual studies are scholars such as Ronald Grimes and the late Catherine Bell.[5] In her *Ritual: Perspectives and Dimensions*—arguably the best introduction to ritual studies—Bell proposed a typology of rituals and her work has been rather influential..[6] To my knowledge, the first application of Bell's typology to Qumran texts was an article by Rob Kugler.[7] Two brief articles by James Davila survey the texts of the Old Testament Apocrypha and Pseudepigrapha.[8] The most extensive work so far is the recent dissertation *The Social Role of Liturgy in the Religion of the Qumran Community* by Russell Arnold that admirably elaborates on Kugler's study.[9]

I shall proceed in three steps. The first part addresses problematic aspects in Bell's typology, focusing one of her types: "rites of affliction." In the second part, I briefly investigate Arnold's (and Kugler's) applications of Bell's typology and propose my own. In the third and final part, I shall make some observations resulting from comparisons of Qumran's rites of affliction with those of other forms of early Judaism and Christianity. Special consideration will be given to the paradox of the existence of

---

[5] C. Bell, *Ritual: Perspectives and Dimensions* (New York: Oxford University Press, 1997); eadem, *Ritual Theory Ritual Practice* (New York: Oxford University Press, 1992); R. Grimes, *The Beginnings of Ritual Studies* (Columbia: University of South Carolina Press, 1994). See also R.A. Rappaport, *Ritual and Religion in the Making of Humanity* (Cambridge: Cambridge University Press, 1999); J.Z. Smith, *To Take Place: Toward Theory in Ritual* (Chicago Series in the History of Judaism; Chicago: University of Chicago Press, 1987).

[6] Bell, *Ritual: Perspectives and Dimensions*, 91–137.

[7] R. Kugler, "Making All Experience Religious: The Hegemony of Ritual at Qumran," *JSJ* 33 (2002): 131–152.

[8] J.R. Davila, "Ritual in the Jewish Pseudepigrapha," in *Anthropology and Biblical Studies: Avenues of Approach* (ed. L.J. Lawrence and M.I. Aguilar; Leiden: Brill, 2004), 158–183 (*non vidi*) (conference paper available online at http://www.st-andrews.ac.uk/academic/divinity/ritual_pseud.html). Davila articulates his larger project in his paper "Ritual in the Old Testament Apocrypha" (draft for discussion at the Symposium on Anthropology and the Old Testament, Glasgow, 27 August 2004), 1–7 (here 1), online: http://www.st-andrews.ac.uk/academic/divinity/RitApoc.htm.

[9] R.C.D. Arnold, *The Social Role of Liturgy in the Religion of the Qumran Community* (STDJ 60; Leiden: Brill, 2006), cf. his contribution "The Dead Sea Scrolls, Qumran, and Ritual Studies" in this volume. See also E. Larson, "Worship in Jubilees and Enoch" in *Enoch and the Mosaic Torah: The Evidence of Jubilees* (ed. G. Boccaccini and G. Ibba; Grand Rapids: Eerdmans, 2009), 369–383 and the communication of "Ritual in Jubilees" by M.A. Daise in the same venture. See also: M.A. Daise, "Ritual Density in Qumran Practice: Ablutions in the *Serekh Ha-Yaḥad*," in *New Perspectives on Old Texts: Proceedings of the Tenth Annual International Symposium of the Orion Center for the Study of the Dead Sea Scrolls and Associated Literature, 9–11 January, 2005* (ed. E.G. Chazon and B. Halpern-Amaru; STDJ 88; Leiden: Brill, 2010), 51–66.

rituals of affliction in the ritual behavior of a group that believes in predetermination. After all, the main aim of these rituals is normally an effort to change the current miserable situation, a seemingly futile endeavor for people with a deterministic worldview.

Bell suggests distinguishing the following six groups of rituals:[10]

1. Rites of passage / life-cycle rites are rites (such as birth or marriage) that deal with the sociocultural and/or biological events of human life.[11]

2. Calendrical and commemorative rites (such as Passover) "give socially meaningful definitions to the passage of time."[12]

3. Rites of exchange and communion (e.g. community meals) secure "the well-being of the community and the larger cosmos" and "redefine the culture's system of cosmological boundaries ... while simultaneously allowing the crossing or transgression of those very same boundaries."[13]

4. Rites of affliction (e.g. response to meteorological disaster) "attempt to rectify a state of affairs that has been disturbed or disordered: they heal, exorcise, protect, and purify."[14]

5. Rites of feasting, fasting, and festivals (such as Lent, Ramadan or Carnival) emphasize the public display of religiocultural sentiments.[15]

6. Political rituals (enthronization, military parades) "specifically construct, display and promote the power of political institutions ... or the political interests of distinct constituencies and subgroups."[16]

We should not forget, however, that Bell states herself that this list is *not* exhaustive.[17] We should therefore add a seventh category:

7. X (other).

---

[10] Bell, *Ritual: Perspectives and Dimensions*, 91–137.

[11] Ibid., 94.

[12] Both, *rites de passage* and calendrical rites "impose cultural schemes on the order of nature," while commemorative rites "recall the important historical events" (ibid., 102, 103, 104). These recurring rites often "express the most basic beliefs of the community" (ibid., 105). Calendars and festival calendars also define boundaries.

[13] Ibid., 114.

[14] Ibid., 115.

[15] Ibid., 120.

[16] Ibid., 128.

[17] Ibid., 92 and 135. This has not been exploited in the applications of Bell to early Judaism by Arnold, Davila or Kugler.

Bell's typology is appealing because of its brevity and its clarity. This clarity, however, might only be apparent. My main methodological critique of Bell is that she seems to employ two different sets of criteria, functionalist and phenomenological, to establish her typology. For example, category Five, "Rites of feasting, fasting and festivals" is defined in largely phenomenological terms (rituals with mass feasting or fasting), while category six "political rites" is rather functionalist and category two "calendrical rites and commemorative rites" is a mixture of both. Many of the calendrical rites are feasts, fasts or festivals. She is well aware that many rituals may be categorized in multiple rubrics, yet, it seems to me, that not only the polyvalent functions of one ritual foster the problem of classifying rituals in one or another category but also that her six categories are not so to speak six brands of apples but a mix of apples *and* *oranges*. The Shiite Ashura could be classified among the calendrical and commemorative rites (2) as well as rite of affliction (5) or among the rites of feasting, fasting, and festivals (4). It can easily assume political aspects (6) when Hizbollah publicly displays its power in demonstrations on this day.

An emergency rite such as a public fast prescribed in *Mishnah Ta'anit* could fit category four "rites of affliction," as well as category five "rites of feasting, fasting, and festivals." Yom Kippur fits both categories as well as "calendrical and commemorative rites," i.e., categories two, four and five. In the fifth and fourth century B.C.E., it was to some extent even a political rite as it was *the* rite performed by the High Priest, the acting ruler of Yehud that also established his claim to the high-priesthood, shown by his special garments, the legendary feast at the end of the day and in much later times by the struggle about who would control the garments. He is the only one to perform this ritual, so the one who performs it is recognizably the High Priest.

Let us now have a closer look at Bell's category "Rituals of Affliction." "Of" in this expression has to be understood as adversative "against," so very different from the other terms she uses in her typology (e.g. rites of feasting and fasting).[18] Bell defines rituals of affliction as rites that "attempt to rectify a state of affairs that has been disturbed or disordered: they heal, exorcise, protect, and purify."[19] They "redress the devel-

---

[18] Davila seems to have misunderstood this when he includes also "vision-quests" in the category of rituals of affliction. Vision quests are preparatory rituals for visional experiences that often involve self-affliction.

[19] Bell, *Ritual: Perspectives and Dimensions*, 115.

opment of anomalies or imbalances."[20] According to Bell, we speak primarily of emergency rites and the majority of rituals (but not the totality) concerns the individual.[21] It is therefore frequently regarded as the most "magical" sort of rites. Among the main problems for which these rites are "needed," she lists meteorological disorders, physical or psychological health problems and impurities but also e.g., sins. Her wide range of examples for these three subtypes include the exposition of divine statues to the burning sun in times of drought in China for meteorological disorders, Shamanistic healing rites from Korea, Western psychoanalysis, and the Red Indian Ghost Dance for physical or psychological health problems. The third subcategory, purifications, includes those performed after contact with untouchables or foreigners among Indian Brahmans, and others after menstruation in Hinduism, Shintoism, medieval Christianity and Judaism. Bell also includes recurring calendric events such as the annual fire-walking of statues in China, purification before Shabbat, as well as the *Kumbha Mela* of India, the largest religious gathering in the world celebrated every twelve years with tens of millions of participants.

In my opinion, the inclusion of regular purification before Shabbat shows a problem. The *main* focus is Shabbat, not the purification or an affliction. When an Orthodox bishop washes his hands before proceeding to the liturgy, or Muslims perform the *wuduʿ* and wash the face, hands and feet before beginning the statutory prayer, the purifications are minor matters preparing and introducing the essential ritual. As Bell states herself, her typology largely disregards context and what I would call the intertextuality of ritual. I would add that her typology also seems to disregard hierarchy. Accordingly, I shall distinguish between independent rituals and minor rites that are part of a ritual in my analysis.

Naturally, any attempt to approach religion by categorizing all rituals of *all* religions is a daunting enterprise. For some religions this typology, which was developed out of the experience with a selection of religions, might be a sort of a Procrustean bed. For example, Bell's typology does not really have a category for daily prayer, demonstrating her background outside of Jewish orthodox or Christian monastic traditions. Yet, one should approach models from the social sciences pragmatically with

---

[20] Ibid.

[21] "[I]n some cases it may also involve the intercession of powerful beings to rectify intrusions and imbalances that go beyond the body of a single person" (ibid.).

questions such as: Are they useful? What is the surplus knowledge gained by their application? Let us therefore regard the actual application of Bell in the work of Russell Arnold.

In his recent book on Qumran rituals, Russell Arnold (who accepts Bell's typology without much discussion) comes up with three subtypes for "rituals of affliction": a) curses, b) apotropaic prayers and incantations and c) purifications. Each of these three types is further distinguished into two subtypes: There are curses against humans and those against supra-humans. Apotropaic prayers address evil as such while incantations are directed against specific demon(s). And finally, purifications can treat specific causes (such as genital or corpse impurity) or be calendrically cyclical.[22]

Arnold's classification differs at some points from Kugler's earlier attempt—without always stating why. Arnold is certainly right in the first point to add apotropaic prayers and incantations, rites of affliction *par excellence*.[23] With regard to our distinction between rituals and rites, incantations are normally independent emergency rituals for specific occasions,[24] while most apotropaic prayers are rites subordinate to and part of complex and recurring rituals.[25] Only for the former do we have texts arguably composed by the *yaḥad*.[26]

---

[22] Arnold, *The Social Role of Liturgy*, 159–186.

[23] Ibid., 165–168. On apotropaic prayers, see D. Flusser, "Qumrân and Jewish 'Apotropaic' Prayers," *IEJ* 16 (1966): 194–205; E. Eshel, "Apotropaic Prayers in the Second Temple Period," in *Liturgical Perspectives: Prayer and Poetry in the Light of the Dead Sea Scrolls: Proceedings of the Fifth International Symposium of the Orion Center for the Study of the Dead Sea Scrolls and Associated Literature, 19–23 January, 2000* (ed. E.G. Chazon; STDJ 48; Leiden: Brill, 2003), 69–88.

[24] E. Eshel refers to 4Q560, 8Q5, 11Q11, all non-sectarian compositions. 4Q560 is an Aramaic magic formula for a person plagued by illness and sins: J. Naveh, "Fragments of an Aramaic Magic Book from Qumran," *IEJ* 48 (1998): 252–261. 8Q5 is a very fragmentary text beginning בשמכה] [ג]בור אני מירא ומע׳. 11Q11 speaks to an individual and mentions demon(s) (I:10; II:3–4), an aggressive angel (מלאך תקיף, IV:5), healing (רפואה, II:7), and exorcism language (משביע, III:4; IV:1; cf. I:7), God's name (II:8), Salomon (II:2), and Raphael (V:3).

[25] In addition to the sectarian texts mentioned below, Eshel refers to Num 6:24–26, the prayer of Levi in the *Aramaic Levi Document* (4Q213a), 11Q5 XIX:13–16 (*Plea for Deliverance*) and XXIV (Ps 155), and *Jub.* 6:1–7 and 12:19–20 as non-Sectarian apotropaic prayers. In Judaism, Mezuzot and Tefillin are frequently thought to contain apotropaic aspects, but this is not clear in Qumran, see P.S Alexander "Magic and Magical Texts," *Encyclopedia of the Dead Sea Scrolls* (ed. L.H Schiffman and J.C. VanderKam; 2 vols.; Oxford: Oxford University Press, 2000), 1:502–504 (here 502).

[26] Eshel, "Apotropaic Prayers," 84. She refers to 4Q510–511, 4Q444, 6Q18 and 1QHᵃ 4 as examples for apotropaic prayers from sectarian or para-sectarian texts found at Qumran.

Second, Kugler's rituals of affliction encompass also the Day of Atonement and "additional rites of affliction" such as e.g., communal confession.[27] As stated above, the polyvalence of Yom Kippur makes this day a problematic case for Bell's typology. Despite the fact that Yom Kippur is a recurring event and has much in common with "calendrical rituals" or "feasting, fasting and festivals," Yom Kippur is also the central rite to handle two of the main afflictions mentioned by Bell: impurity and sin.[28] Both impurity and sin are particularly closely connected in Qumran. I would, therefore, side with Kugler in putting Yom Kippur among the "rituals of affliction."[29]

Third, I would follow Kugler in classifying communal confessions and other rites dealing with the expiation or atonement of sin equally as "rites of affliction."[30] Since they rarely stand on their own and are usually parts of more complex liturgies such as daily prayer, they are rites rather than rituals.

Fourth, despite the fact that Kugler and Arnold agree that curses are rites of affliction, I regard them as a borderline case. These rites do not *rectify* a disorder but, as Arnold correctly states, they "*establish* ... boundaries between members and outsiders."[31] With exception to the excommunication rite in the *Damascus Document*,[32] they are not full-fledged rituals in themselves, but rites that form rather extensive parts of the initiation and covenant ceremony. They define "we" versus "them" in a dualistic, black and white perspective. In comparison to later Jewish and Christian liturgies such as the "*Birkat*" *Haminim*,[33] curses are prominent in Qumran.[34] Functionally, curses might be classified under

---

[27] Kugler, "Making All Experience Religious," 146.

[28] Ibid., 147.

[29] Arnold treats Yom Kippur under "feasts and fasts" (*The Social Role of Liturgy*, 101–105). We could also deduce from analogy with one of the examples mentioned by Bell, the annual fire-walking of statues in China that seems to be a similar yearly purgation ritual, Bell, *Ritual: Perspectives and Dimensions*, 118.

[30] E.g. 4Q393, CD 9:13, 15:4, 1QS I:24–26.

[31] Arnold, *The Social Role of Liturgy*, 160. See also the contribution of J.S. Anderson "Curses and Blessings: Social Control and Self Definition in the Dead Sea Scrolls" in the first volume of these proceedings.

[32] See below. *Serekh ha-Yaḥad* speaks of exclusion of members for grave sins for a limited time or for good, without giving the details of a ritual for excommunication.

[33] Cf. also Gal 1:8–9, 1 Cor 16:22 and *Did.* 10:6. R. Deichgräber and S. Hall, "Formeln, Liturgische II. Neues Testament und Alte Kirche," *TRE* 11:262, 265 refer to Tertullian, *Scorp.* 1 and *Praescr.* 6.

[34] See M. Bar Ilan "Segen und Fluch IV. Judentum," *TRE* 31:84–88 who refers to *m. Soṭah* 7:8, the synagogue inscription from Ein Gedi, *b. Meg.* 31b, the "*Birkat*" *Haminim*,

Bell's calendaric and commemoration rites that do serve the function of establishing cosmic order, especially when they are part of the yearly covenant renewal ceremony and turn also against angelic forces. Arnold subsumed the initiation and covenant ceremony under life cycle rites and Qumran daily prayer among the calendrical rites. These are reasonable choices that demonstrate again the problems inherent in Bell's typology. If curses are rites of affliction, we could classify the yearly covenant renewal ceremony that employs them amply as a ritual of affliction. I would, however, hesitate to do so, as the covenant renewal ceremony can be categorized as almost every single one of Bell's six types and as the affliction treated here (possible apostasy, threats from the outside) is minor with regard to the other functions of the ritual.

Finally, let us ask whether there are some other candidates for the category of rituals of affliction not mentioned by either Kugler or Arnold: I would think in particular of a) punishments, and b) funerals, mourning and purification rites after death. Let me briefly expound each of them:

Punishments are clearly emergency rituals attempting to rectify a disorder. Afflictions are imposed upon an individual that has afflicted the community by transgressing its codes. The most current punishment in the very developed penal system of Qumran is deprivation of participation in the pure food, which comes close to some sort of fasting.[35] This practice is not unlike the exclusion of penitents from the Eucharistic service in Late Antique Christianity. Kugler puts the punishments in Bell's "festivals, feasting and fasting" as their "main social function was to socialize community members 'in physical practices that reproduce central doctrinal traditions and identities.'"[36] But Bell's examples for

---

piyyutim of Yannai and medieval Ashkenazi curses against non-Jews on Yom Kippur. On the latter, see I. Yuval, "Vengeance and Damnation, Blood and Defamation: From Jewish Martyrdom to Blood Libel Accusations," *Zion* 58 (1993): 33–90 (Hebrew).

[35] For analyses of the texts chiefly from *Serekh ha-Yaḥad* and the *Damascus Document*, see e.g. J.M. Baumgarten, "The Cave 4 Versions of the Qumran Penal Code," *JJS* 43 (1992): 268–276; idem, "Judicial Procedures," *Encyclopedia of the Dead Sea Scrolls* 1:457–460; C. Hempel, "The Penal Codes Reconsidered," in *Legal Texts and Legal Issues: Proceedings of the Second Meeting of the International Organization for Qumran Studies, Cambridge 1995* (ed. M. Bernstein, F. García Martínez, and J. Kampen; STDJ 23; Leiden: Brill, 1997), 337–348; L.H. Schiffman, *Sectarian Law and the Dead Sea Scrolls: Courts, Testimony and the Penal Code* (Chico: Scholars Press, 1983); M. Weinfeld, *The Organizational Pattern and the Penal Code of the Qumran Sect: A Comparison with Guilds and Religious Associations of the Hellenistic-Roman Period* (NTOA 2; Fribourg: Éditions Universitaires, 1986).

[36] Kugler, "Making All Experience Religious," 139.

feasting and fasting rituals demonstrate that she had mainly those rituals in mind where everybody is acting in the *same* way, either feasting
a potlatch or fasting in Ramadan. Here, however, the *yaḥad* has been
afflicted by the sin of one of its members and reacts very pointedly by
temporarily afflicting this specific member. More severe forms of punishment than food deprivation are excommunication[37] and the death
penalty.[38] In my view, all these punishments attempt to "rectify a state
of affairs that has been disturbed" and they function as rites of affliction.[39]

A second type of rituals that might belong here are rituals dealing
with death. Death may be regarded as the worst of sicknesses, one of
the major afflictions that—as other maladies—does not only affect the
victim itself but also his or her family and close ones with deep distress.
Most cultures have developed rituals addressing this problem. As most
anthropologists, Bell classifies rites dealing with death as life-cycle rites.
Rites dealing with pollution resulting from death, however, she regards
as a prominent rite of affliction.[40] This division of two often closely
connected rite complexes shows again that we speak of a borderline case.
In any case, in Qumran texts, life-cycle rites including rites dealing with
death seem to be underrepresented. This phenomenon dovetails with
the absence of other life-cycle rites.[41] Circumcision, e.g., is extremely
rarely noted.[42] The so called *Ritual of Marriage* (4Q502) has nothing to
do with a marriage.[43] If we focus on Qumran literature one might be

---

[37] For the ritual of excommunication, see 4QDᵃ (4Q266) 11 5–16 (וכול המואס במשפטים)
(par. 4QDᵉ [4Q270] 7 ii).

[38] CD 9:1; 9:23–10:3 par. 4QDᵃ (4Q266) 8 ii 8–9 par. 4QDᵉ (4Q270) 6 iii 16. Cf. also
the non-community texts: 4QBibPar (4Q158) 9 1; 4QOrdinᵃ (4Q159) 2–4 + 8 5–6 and
8–9; 4QJubᶠ (4Q221) 4 4 (*Jub.* 33:13); 4QHalakha A (4Q251) 8 3–6; 4QRPᵇ (4Q364)
13 3 (Exod 21:15); 11QTᵃ (11Q19) XXXV:4–8; LI:16–18; LXIV:2–13; LXVI:2–8; 4QTᵇ
(4Q524) 1 and 14 2–3.

[39] See the two emic explanations for the punishment of the "stubborn son," decontam-
ination of the collective and admonition to all in 11QTᵃ (11Q19) XIV:5–6: ורגמוהו כול אנשי
עירו באבנים וימות ובערתה הרע מקרבכה וכול בני ישראל ישמעו ויראו.

[40] Bell, *Ritual: Perspectives and Dimensions*, 115.

[41] I have dealt with this issue in my paper "When the Bell Rings: The Qumran Life-
Cycle Rituals // Rites de Passage" (presented at the SBL Annual Meeting in Boston, 20–
25 November 2008) that I plan to publish elsewhere.

[42] Lev 12:3 is quoted in 4Q4QDᵃ (4Q266) 6 ii 6 and 4QRPᵉ (4Q367) 1a–b 4. Cf. the
circumcision of Abraham in CD 16:6 par. 4QDᵉ (4Q270) 6 ii 18–19 par. 4QDᶠ (4Q271) 4
ii 7.

[43] J.M. Baumgarten, "4Q502, Marriage or Golden Age Ritual?" *JJS* 34 (1983): 125–135;
M. Satlow, "4Q502, a New Year Festival?" *DSD* 5 (1998): 57–68. In this light, Arnold's
focus on the Qumran initiation ritual for this category seems a wise decision.

tempted to say that in Turnerian terms Qumran was a liminal community largely neglecting essential events of individual life such as birth or death. This idealized impression from the texts stands in blatant contrast to the archaeological remains. The adjacent cemetery with more than 1000 tombs suggests that a substantial number of people who lived at the site also died there. Burials must have been quite frequent a ritual, every two or three months or so, and at least some people as well as the site itself must have been afflicted by corpse impurity quite regularly.[44] The *Temple Scroll*, a text appreciated by the Qumranites, details rules of purification after death, yet we know nothing from the scrolls about their burial and mourning rites.[45]

To sum up part two: In addition to Arnold's incantations and independent purification rituals, I would regard Yom Kippur[46] and the punishments prescribed in the penal code as *rituals* of affliction and apotropaic prayers, small scale purifications and confessions as *rites* of affliction. In addition, burial and mourning rites, curses and the covenant renewal ceremony are borderline cases. This new model would look as follows:

1. Rituals of Affliction
    a. incantations
    b. independent purifications
    c. punishments
    d. Yom Kippur (borderline with calendrical rituals)
    e. (burials and mourning rites [borderline with *rites de passage*])
    f. (covenant renewal ceremony [borderline with nearly all types of ritual])[47]
2. Rites of Affliction
    a. apotropaic prayers
    b. minor purifications
    c. confessions
    d. (curses [borderline with political rituals])

---

[44] If Qumran was occupied during roughly 150 years, around six people would have died each year giving a population estimation of 200 in average and one burial every two months—a frequent ritual.

[45] R. Hachlili, "Cemetery," *Encyclopedia of the Dead Sea Scrolls* 1:125–129.

[46] Despite its overlapping with calendrical rites as part of the festival calendar.

[47] For the initiates that are introduced to the *yaḥad* in this ritual, it is a *rite de passage* (see Arnold). As it is a yearly recurrent event, it is also a calendrical ritual. It gives sense to time passing. It establishes a political and cosmic hierarchy and its boundaries of insiders and outsiders as well as leaders, members and novices.

In the final part, I would like to make some more general observations on the basis of a macrocomparison of the map of Qumran rites of affliction with that of early Judaism. As Davila has shown, all of the rites and rituals of affliction attested for Qumran are part and parcel of many streams of Second Temple and rabbinic Judaism. On the micro-level there might be differences, but rarely do they distinguish Qumran from all other forms of Second Temple Judaism. Curses are certainly of higher importance at Qumran. Inner participation as condition for purification in 4Q512 and 4Q414 is attested also in John the Baptist. Baumgarten is wrong in juxtaposing a sad Sectarian Yom Kippur to a joyous Pharisaic one. Both include aspects of joy and sorrow.[48]

If we turn tables, however, we can observe that a substantial number of rituals of affliction attested in Second Temple, rabbinic (and early Christian) texts are absent from the Qumran scrolls. And it is here where our macrocomparison, with the help of Bell's typology, might prove heuristically fruitful. To use the expression of the title of this paper: it is now, when the Bell rings.

a. As others have remarked, the absence of evidence for regular fast days except Yom Kippur is truly exceptional. Zechariah 8 mentions four yearly fasts and rabbinic and patristic sources give evidence that some late Antique Jewish and Christian groups celebrated fasts accordingly.[49] The *Didache* knows of two weekly Jewish and Christian fasts.[50] In the third and fourth century the various forms of Lent emerge, in the fourth century Roman Christianity introduces the Ember Days, in the fifth or sixth Eastern Syriac Christians inaugurate the fast of the Ninevites. In the Qumran texts, arguably all occurrences of fasting and self-affliction refer to Yom Kippur.[51] Perhaps the ruling deterministic ideology may have

---

[48] See D. Stökl Ben Ezra, *The Impact of Yom Kippur on Early Christianity: The Day of Atonement from Second Temple Judaism to the Fifth Century* (WUNT 163; Tübingen: Mohr Siebeck, 2003), 35.

[49] M. Ta'an 4; y. Ta'an 4:5, 20b; b. Roš Haš. 18b; Jerome, *Comm. Zach.* 8:18–19 (CCSL 76A:820), referring to the 17 Tammuz, 9 Av, 3 Tishri and 10 Tevet; Philaster of Brescia, *Diversarum Hereseon Liber* 149 (written between 385 and 391 C.E.): "*absolute praedicauit, ut mysteria Christianitatis in ipsis quattuor ieiuniis nuntiata cognosceremus. Nam per annum quattuor ieiunia in ecclesia celebrantur, in natale primum deinde in pascha, tertio in ascensione, quarto in pentecosten*" (CSEL 38:120:24–121:4 [F. Marx 1888]).

[50] Cf. also Matt 9:14–15.

[51] N. Hacham, "Communal Fasts in the Judean Desert Scrolls and Associated Literature," in *Historical Perspectives: From the Hasmoneans to Bar Kokhba in Light of the Dead*

fathered the opinion that fasts cannot alter divine predestination anyhow. Yom Kippur was only retained since it was the only fast ordained in the Torah. That Yom Kippur was highly significant for the group's identity is also visible in the memories attributing a persecution of the group to this day as foundational event as well as in the future expectations of a divine redemption on Yom Kippur may have played a role.[52]

b. In addition to the *absence of* regular fast days, I do not know of any evidence for other rites to handle collective emergencies. Descriptions and prescriptions of emergency public fasts abound in early Jewish and Christian literature.[53] How did the Qumranites react ritually when the Jewish War broke out and news of the developments in Jerusalem and the Galilee arrived there? Had texts like the *War Scroll* a liturgical *Sitz im Leben* in such a situation? Many crises in antiquity, as today, are meteorological disasters. Rituals in times of meteorological catastrophes are among Bell's first examples for affliction rituals. They are widely attested in early Judaism and Christianity. Jesus calms the storm.[54] Hanina ben Dosa prays for rain.[55] The Mishna and Talmudim include a whole tractate describing such a ritual (*Ta'anit*). And Gregory of Nazianzus reports of ritual responses during an episode of a severe drought.[56] Handling weather and meteorological mishaps do not however seem to play a role in Qumran ritual life.[57] Could this observation be used as an argument

---

Sea Scrolls: Proceedings of the Fourth International Symposium of the Orion Center for the Study of Dead Sea Scrolls and Associated Literature, 27–31 January, 1999 (ed. D.M. Goodblatt, A. Pinnick, and D.R. Schwartz; STDJ 37; Leiden: Brill, 2001), 127–145. Can we infer from the name "*the* festival of *the* fasting/affliction" (מועד התענית) for the Day of Atonement that this was the only day Qumranites fasted? The plural forms in 4QShir[a] (4Q510) 1 4–8 par. 4QShir[b] (4Q511) 10 1–6 and 4QShir[b] 8 5 and 121 2 and 11QapocrPs (11Q11) IV:12 may, perhaps, refer to affliction/humiliation in general, but this is not certain. The late H. Eshel, however, has argued that 4QpPs[a] (4Q171) 2 9–11 refers to a communal fast in a dreadful drought in 65 B.C.E., a fast, that was kept not only by the Qumranites but in general, see *The Dead Sea Scrolls and the Hasmonaean State* (Jerusalem: Yad Ben-Zvi, 2004), 135 (Hebrew) and p. 149 in the English translation (Studies in the Dead Sea Scrolls and Related Literature; Grand Rapids: Eerdmans, 2008).

[52] See 1QpHab XI:7–8, 11QMelch (11Q13) II:7–8 and Stökl Ben Ezra, *The Impact of Yom Kippur*, 97–100.

[53] E.g. in Jonah 3–4; 1 Macc 3:46–55; *m. Ta'anit*.

[54] Mark 4:35–40 par.

[55] *B. Ta'an*. 24b.

[56] Gregory of Nazianzus, *Or. Bas.* 16.

[57] Almost all references to rain appear in narratives of Enoch and retellings of the story of the flood. But see 1Q34 3 and 1QH[a] XVI:16–17: "But You, O my God, have placed Your words in my mouth, as showers of early rain, for all [who thirst] and as a spring of living

that the people behind the scrolls lived in the desert of Qumran, where they could lead a life largely independent of the follies of the weather gods?

c. If Joe Zias' analyses of the bacterial remains in Qumran toilets prove true, sickness must have had a ubiquitous presence among the inhabitants of Qumran—having caused a considerable number of fatalities according to the cemetery data.[58] In the Qumran texts, however, individual healing seems to be a minor affair.[59] Most references to healing are halakhic developments on how to decide whether somebody has to be regarded as healed and therefore pure or not.[60] Almost all other passages address God as healer in very general and/or eschatological terms or speak of the object of healing in a very general plural: "they" or "them." The majority of extra-biblical references about individual healing are in texts that have been written in Aramaic who were owned but not produced by the community: e.g. Pharaoh's afflictions due to Sara and Nabonidus' illness.[61] The incantation 4Q560, the only text that one might compare to a medical treatise, is part of this alien Aramaic wisdom, too. Were it not for 11QapocrPs (11Q11), the one exception mentioned above, one might think that healing prayers were completely futile in the eyes of people believing in predetermination.[62]

---

waters. The heavens shall not fail to open, 17 nor shall they run dry, but shall become a stream pouring out up[on] water and then to seas without en[d.]" 11QSefer ha-Milḥamah (11Q14) 1 ii 7–11 par. 4QSefer ha-Milḥamah (4Q285) 8 4–7: "God Most High will bless you and shine his face upon you, and he will open for you 8 his rich storehouse in the heavens, to send down upon your land 9 showers of blessing, dew and rain, the early rain and the latter rain in its season, and to give you frui[t], 10 produce, grain, wine and oil in abundance; and the land will produce for you [d]elightful fruit 11 so that you will eat and grow fat." Both translations are taken from E. Tov, ed., *The Dead Sea Scrolls Electronic Library* (Leiden: Brill, 2006). Cf. also 4QBer[a] (4Q286) 3 a–d 4.

[58] J. Zias, "Toilets at Qumran, the Essenes, and the Scrolls: New Anthropological Data and Old Theories," RevQ 22 (2005–2006): 631–640.

[59] For healing in Second Temple Judaism, cf. L.P. Hogan, *Healing in the Second Temple Period* (NTOA 21; Göttingen: Vandenhoeck & Ruprecht, 1992). M.O. Wise, "Healing" *Encyclopedia of the Dead Sea Scrolls* 1:336–338.

[60] E.g. 4QRP[c] (4Q365) 18–20 and 4QD[a] (4Q266) 6 i–iii; 4QD[g] (4Q272) 1 i–ii; 4QpapD[h] (4Q273) 4 ii (cf. CD 13:4–7); on the 4QD texts see C. Hempel, *The Laws of the Damascus Document: Sources, Tradition and Redaction* (STDJ 29; Leiden: Brill, 1998), 43–50.

[61] 1QapGen ar (1Q20) XX:12–32 and 4QPrNab ar (4Q242).

[62] The earliest extent inventory of a Christian or Jewish library is that of the monastery of Elias in Egypt, which includes a medical treatise as the one and only non-purely religious book.

d. The reality of the people in Qumran is only very partially described in its texts. On the one hand, the society described by the texts found in Qumran was clearly a highly ritualized one. We have evidence for a great number of very diverse rituals. Blessings and curses, praises and hymns fill pages and pages. Yet, the Qumran texts talk very little about the actual performance of the rituals and give very few hints about the details with regard to where, how, who—actions, actors, places, etc. Speaking in Roman Catholic terms, there are very few rubrics. The amount of "black ink" widely outdoes that of "red ink." The two major exceptions are only apparent exceptions: Temple rituals (including the red cow)[63] and the Qumran initiation ritual. Temple rituals, however, are theory—not practice—for anyone who is not in control of the Temple and they do not belong to the life of the community in the strict sense. And a closer look at the initiation or the covenant renewal ritual reveals that despite a considerable amount of words, the details of where, who, when remain unknown. Did they sing the curses, whisper or scream a sentence like ארור אתה לאין רחמים? Similarly, the great mass of texts on purification rituals deceives in the sense that we have very little information about how exactly these rituals were performed. The greater part of ritual lore and expertise was not transmitted through written form, and probably not even orally, but by non-verbal action and mimesis. With regard to Qumran ritual, the extant texts constitute only the tip of the iceberg. Nevertheless, we should try to get an idea of this iceberg. Arnold and Kugler have the merit to have opened the door to a promising discussion to which this paper hopes to be another small contribution.

---

[63] J. Bowman, "Did the Qumran Sect Burn the Red Heifer?" *RevQ* 1 (1958): 73–84; J.M. Baumgarten, "The Red Cow Purification Rites in Qumran Texts," *JJS* 46 (1995): 112–119.

THE DEAD SEA SCROLLS, QUMRAN, AND RITUAL STUDIES

RUSSELL C.D. ARNOLD
DePauw University

The present study has two primary objectives. First, I present what I consider to be some of the benefits of bringing a ritual studies approach to the study of the Dead Sea Scrolls and the *yaḥad* community associated with Khirbet Qumran.[1] Second, I discuss some lessons we learn from employing a ritual studies approach with respect to Qumran that can enhance our investigations of the lives of other communities from Ancient Israel to Early Judaism and Christianity.

DEFINITIONS OF RITUAL AND LITURGY

Before I get too deeply into this discussion, I should pause to present my working definitions of the key terms, ritual and liturgy. A good place to begin for a definition of ritual comes from Roy Rappaport: "the performance of more or less invariant sequences of formal acts and utterances not encoded by the performers."[2] I would modify this definition slightly to include the symbolic element of ritual for the performer. I define ritual as an action or series of actions, governed by culturally determined guidelines or rules, which is understood by the participants as significant beyond the mundane or regular practice of such an act. The difference, for example, between a bath for the sake of washing and a ritual bath or ritual washing may or may not be evident from the action itself. The behavior may be more formal and more consistent from one

---

[1] Many of the conclusions described in this first part of the paper are based on the results of my Ph.D. dissertation research, which surveyed the entire range of ritual and liturgical material associated with the Dead Sea Scrolls community. Cf. R.C.D. Arnold, *The Social Role of Liturgy in the Religion of the Qumran Community* (STDJ 60; Leiden: Brill, 2006).

[2] R.A. Rappaport, "The Obvious Aspects of Ritual," in *Ecology, Meaning, and Religion* (Richmond: North Atlantic Books, 1979), 175.

person to the next, but what truly makes it a ritual washing, is that it is infused, by the participant and/or by the culture, with meaning that goes beyond cleaning off the dirt. This does not mean that such a ritual washing does not actually clean off the dirt, but only that it does more than that. For a ritual to be successful, therefore, the participants in the ritual ought at least to know that what they are doing carries more significance than the act in itself. At the same time, the participants are not necessarily aware of the full significance of the ritual, such that certain rituals may, from an outsider's perspective, be seen to function to establish boundaries or unify or solidify the identity of the members or any number of other things that could not be precisely articulated by the participants in the ritual. Obviously, since we have no access to individual Qumran practitioners, we must rely on the textual evidence from the Dead Sea Scrolls that indicates the symbolic significance of these actions.

I use the term liturgy to describe an element used in rituals. Liturgy is the spoken component of any particular ritual. Many of our texts give only this liturgical component with a short introduction indicating a ritual context, usually a time referent.[3] In other cases we have texts that both provide the wording/liturgy and more detail about the ritual context and ritual action.[4] In other cases we have clearly liturgical texts without any indication of their ritual context.[5] The fact that most of our knowledge of Qumran ritual derives from liturgy is primarily a result of the evidence that we have, that is, texts. Secondarily, it is an outgrowth of the Qumran community's strong emphasis on the importance of proper speech.[6]

---

[3] E.g. "[On the] 17th day of the mon[th in the] evening, they bless ..." (4Qpap-PrQuot [4Q503] 29–32 i 12). See also the *Words of the Luminaries* and the *Songs of the Sabbath Sacrifice*. Translations throughout the paper are mine unless otherwise indicated.

[4] See for example the initiation and covenant renewal ceremony in 1QS I–III; V–VI. For a recent challenge to connecting these two sections of 1QS see M.A. Daise, "The Temporal Relationship between the Covenant Renewal Rite and the Initiation Process in 1QS," in *Qumran Studies: New Approaches, New Questions* (ed. M.T. Davis and B.A. Strawn; Grand Rapids: Eerdmans, 2007), 150–160. Other examples may be found in the ritual purification texts (4Q512, 4Q414, and 4Q284).

[5] Psalms and the *Hodayot* are the best examples of such liturgical material.

[6] I discuss this idea in more detail in R.C.D. Arnold, "Qumran Prayer as an Act of Righteousness," *JQR* 95 (2005): 509–529.

THE NATURE OF THE *YAḤAD*
AND ITS CONNECTIONS TO QUMRAN

Much recent scholarship has taken up, once again, the complicated questions about the nature of the community or communities associated with the Dead Sea Scrolls, as well as their connections with the Qumran site.[7] At the heart of much of this discussion is the relationship between the varied but connected legal traditions of the *Community Rule* (1QS, 4QS) and the *Damascus Document* (CD, 4QD) as well as the variants found within these traditions.[8] I am, by no means, intending to solve this complicated issue here in these few pages. For my purposes here I take as starting points for my study the following conclusions that seem to me to be well supported by the evidence and by most scholars: 1) Despite some differences between the S and D traditions, the many similarities indicate that they represent different perspectives within a larger ideological community, 2) A connection exists between the Scrolls, especially those from caves 1 and 4, and the Qumran site, although the *yaḥad* was not exclusive to Qumran, 3) While it is not certain that Qumran was the headquarters of the *yaḥad*, it held, at least for some of its history, a community of members who likely sought to live according to the *yaḥad*'s prescriptions.[9] Recognizing the complexity associated with mapping out the different communities within the larger Dead Sea Scrolls movement, I use the term Qumran Community to refer to those who participated in the Qumran complex and saw themselves as part of the *yaḥad* associated with the S tradition. By focusing on the part of the *yaḥad* at Qumran, we can tentatively include data from the archaeological remains and the physical context, where relevant, to better understand the community's ritual life together.[10]

---

[7] See especially the recent issue *DSD* 16/3 (2009) devoted entirely to these questions. A summary of the articles and their positions can be found in M.A. Knibb, "The Community of the Dead Sea Scrolls: Introduction," *DSD* 16 (2009): 297–308.

[8] These include also other rule texts such as 4Q265, 5Q13, etc. For a recent discussion of radial-dialogic approach to the legal corpus see A. Schofield, "Between Center and Periphery: The *Yaḥad* in Context," *DSD* 16 (2009): 330–350.

[9] J.J. Collins, "Beyond the Qumran Community: Social Organization in the Dead Sea Scrolls," *DSD* 16 (2009): 351–369.

[10] Obviously, there are difficulties in connecting an array of texts that develop over time and in different locations with the practices at Qumran with great certainty. My purpose here is to highlight how bringing the textual and archaeological evidence into conversation with a ritual studies approach can help us achieve a thicker description of the life of the community. As such, I concede that different conclusions about the dating

Ritual Density

One of the first things that we notice about Qumran is the pervasiveness of ritual in the life of the community. As many as one-fourth of the non-biblical texts discovered in the Qumran caves can be classified as ritual or liturgical. Although there are a number of ways ritual types can be categorized, Catherine Bell's system helps us to see the breadth and depth of Qumran's ritual practice.[11] Although there are certainly overlaps between some of these categories, they remain useful for addressing both the characteristics and the functions of the whole range of ritual practice.[12] Bell's categories are as follows: Calendrical Rites,[13] Rites of Passage,[14] Feasts and Fasts,[15] Rites of Affliction,[16] Political Rites,[17] and Rites of Exchange and Communion.[18] After mentioning some of the Qumran examples from these categories, Rob Kugler describes the density of Qumran ritual as follows:

---

or context of one of the texts or some of the material remains would yield different results. I contend, however, that applying ritual studies approaches would be productive in any case.

[11] C. Bell, *Ritual: Perspectives and Dimensions* (Oxford: Oxford University Press, 1997).

[12] See the article by D. Stoekl Ben Ezra in this volume for an assessment of the category of Rites of Affliction.

[13] This is the largest category found in the Dead Sea Scrolls. There are rites associated with daily cycles (*Daily Prayers* and *Words of the Luminaries*), weekly cycles (*Songs of the Sabbath Sacrifice*), and yearly cycles (*Festival Prayers* and the covenant renewal ceremony in 1QS).

[14] The initiation of new members is presented as a rite of passage in 1QS. There is no mention of rituals associated with birth, circumcision, or death and the possible reference to marriage in 4Q502 is highly questionable. See M. Baillet in *DJD* VII (1982): 81–105; J.M. Baumgarten, "4Q502, Marriage or Golden Age Ritual?" *JJS* 34 (1983): 125–135; M.L. Satlow, "4Q502 A New Year Festival?" *DSD* 5 (1998): 57–68.

[15] Communal meals are represented especially in 1QS VI:1–8 and 1QSa II:17–22. Somewhat surprisingly there is no mention of fasts other than the biblically prescribed fast on the Day of Atonement.

[16] Such rites either protect against elements of disorder whether they be spiritual forces or physical ailments or impurities. Qumran's purification rituals (4Q414, 4Q512, 4Q284) and curses (1QS II:4–18, 4Q586 7, 4Q280 2) fall in this category.

[17] Political rites establish hierarchies, social structures, and the authority of leaders. At Qumran, these elements are strongest in the ranking of members associated with the covenant renewal ceremony and the regular communal meals. Authority of the priests is reinforced in practices described in 1QM and 1QSb.

[18] These rites establish or express connections between humans and those in the divine realm, angelic realm, and/or human realm. At Qumran, Psalms and the *Hodayot* hymns provide a kind of social cohesion and connection with the divine. Other texts, such as *Songs of the Sabbath Sacrifice*, also establish communion with the angels.

From the way they measured their time to the way they consumed their meals, from their rising in the morning to their laying down at night, from the way they prayed to the way they saw to the purity of their bodies, from their entry into the community to their departure from it, the people of Qumran patterned their actions in "more or less invariant sequences of formal acts and utterances" aimed at bringing them closer to God.[19]

The pervasiveness and importance of ritual at Qumran makes it an important test case for the application of ritual studies approaches to historical communities in antiquity. We are also fortunate to have a relatively large amount of material, much of it written by its own members, about the religious life of a narrow, relatively localized community that thrived for only a couple centuries.

Once we recognize the pervasiveness of ritual and liturgical texts at Qumran we are left with the question of what to do with these texts. My interest is to follow the methodological challenge set forth by Lawrence Hoffman: to move beyond text-focused, philological, historical, and form-critical approaches and treat ritual and liturgical texts themselves and other texts about the practice of ritual as evidence of a living community of practitioners.[20] Hoffman draws on insights from the work of the anthropologist, Clifford Geertz, who claims that the task of interpreting culture is to understand what is meant, or what is being said, by a particular ritual or practice.[21] Hoffman presents the holistic study of liturgy as a similar process of using all textual and material evidence to sort out what is signified by the liturgy, what is being said, not just *in* the liturgy, but also *by* the liturgy.[22] Looking at Qumran ritual practice we see how ritual and liturgy can communicate through the doing, not just the meaning of the words to be recited. This is at the heart of what we can learn from ritual studies. No action is univalent, especially ritual action.

---

[19] R. Kugler, "Making All Experience Religious: The Hegemony of Ritual at Qumran," *JSJ* 33 (2002): 131–152. Notice that Kugler uses Rappaport's definition of ritual as cited above in n. 2.

[20] L. Hoffman, *Beyond the Text: A Holistic Approach to Liturgy* (Notre Dame: University of Notre Dame Press, 1987). Hoffman argues that liturgical texts are a remarkable expression of a community's worldview and indicate the nature of the community's relationships with the divine/holy, and with those outside the community.

[21] C. Geertz, *The Interpretation of Cultures* (New York: Basic Books, 1973).

[22] Hoffman's interpretations of rabbinic liturgical practice were hindered by the lack of sufficient concrete information describing the social structures governing the rabbinic communities. By comparison, such social information regarding the *yaḥad* is quite abundant, although by no means as complete as we might like.

We turn now to some examples that highlight how ritual studies improve our understanding of the complex and multivalent meanings of ritual and liturgical practice at Qumran. In the interest of time and space we will not discuss rituals from all six categories. Instead we will focus our attention on examples from the first three: calendrical rites, rites of passage, and feasts and fasts.

Calendrical Rites As Systems

Calendrical rites are among the most varied and pervasive rituals found at Qumran. The scrolls contain liturgies designed to mark every one of the key calendrical units: Evening and morning (*Daily Prayers* [4Q503], 1QS X, 4Q408); Days of the week (*Words of the Luminaries* [4Q504, 506]); Sabbaths (weeks) of the quarter (*Songs of the Sabbath Sacrifice* [4Q400–407, 11Q17]); Festivals of the Year (*Festival Prayers* [1Q34, 4Q507–509 + 505]). Each of these texts establishes a fixed periodic sequence of rituals, liturgies to be recited in a regular order. The prayer for the fifth day will always be read after the prayer for the fourth day. Ritual studies tell us that, as a ritual system, each individual ritual should be interpreted in terms of the whole system. Arnold van Gennep argues that the individual elements of a ritual have no inherent symbolic meaning, but can only be understood as part of a sequence, related to what came before and what came after.[23] In order to understand how the different elements affect the interpretation of the system, Pierre Smith highlights what he calls the focalizing element of a ritual system, i.e. that action or idea that frames the symbolic message of the ritual.[24] Consequently, two

---

[23] A. van Gennep, "On the Method to Be Followed in the Study of Rites and Myths," in *Classical Approaches to the Study of Religion: Aims, Methods and Theories of Research* (ed. J. Waardenburg; 2 vols.; Religion and Reason 3; The Hague: Mouton, 1973–1974), 1:287–300.

[24] P. Smith, "Aspects of the Organization of Rites," in *Between Belief and Transgression: Structuralist Essays in Religion, History and Myth* (ed. M. Izard and P. Smith; Chicago: University of Chicago Press, 1982), 103–128. Since Smith puts such emphasis on finding the focalizing elements of the ritual, he believes that it is important first to consider the rituals in their most stripped down form. By understanding the central thrust of the ritual, then one can understand the meaning or purpose of the accumulating glosses and the various accessories associated with the ritual in its full-blown form. While I agree with Smith about the importance of locating an overarching purpose in order to understand the various elements of the ritual, it must be noted that the basic elements of the ritual may not always be clear and are subject to the scholar's interpretation. It may also be true that some elements attached to rituals may be either unrelated or perhaps counterproductive.

identical elements that appear in the rites of different communities may, in fact, have different meanings based on their importance within each system, in relation to each focalizing element. Smith states, "[I]n a general way, a single type of ritual act, such as sacrifice, initiation, prayer, or the display of ritual masks, can be integrated, either centrally or accessorily, to various systems, differently interconnected among themselves, and in this way receive different colorings or orientations, pertinent for its analysis."[25] Elsewhere I have argued for an alternative understanding of confession at Qumran on this basis.[26]

The discovery of a large number of calendars, and the fact that the particulars of the community's calendar seems to have been a prominent boundary marker, invests these calendrical rites with important reinforcements to community identity.[27] This is true even with those texts that are likely to have originated outside the *yaḥad* because their use at Qumran would make them part of the larger sectarian calendrical ritual system.[28]

The importance of the calendrical system, as a system, is evident because the Qumran calendar is based on divine commands concerning the appointed times. God had created these cycles and ordained that the precise times be appointed for such liturgies. Maintaining the proper times is described as central to walking in the ways commanded by God in the *Community Rule*:

> They (i.e. potential members) shall not depart from any one of the words of God *concerning their times; they shall neither rush nor delay the times of any of their appointed times*, they shall not turn aside from any of the true precepts to go either to the right or to the left.[29]

---

[25] Ibid., 110.

[26] R.C.D. Arnold, "Repentance and the Qumran Covenant Ceremony," in *Seeking the Favor of God*, vol. 2: *The Development of Penitential Prayer in Second Temple Judaism* (ed. M.J. Boda, D.K. Falk, and R.A. Werline; SBLEJL 22; Atlanta: SBL, 2007), 159–175.

[27] See for example, the dispute over the Day of Atonement between the Wicked Priest and the Teacher of Righteousness in 1QpHab XI:6–8. S. Talmon, "Yom Hakkippurim in the Habakkuk Scroll," *Bib* 32 (1951): 549–563. See also idem, "Calendar Controversy in Ancient Judaism: The Case of the 'Community of the Renewed Covenant,'" in *The Provo International Conference on the Dead Sea Scrolls: Technological Innovations, New Texts, and Reformulated Issues* (ed. D.W. Parry and E. Ulrich; STDJ 30; Leiden: Brill, 1999), 279–395, 388 n. 35.

[28] In other words, texts such as *Words of the Luminaries* and *Festival Prayers*, once incorporated into the practice of the *yaḥad*, would have come to be understood as part of the calendrical system.

[29] 1QS I:13–15, emphasis added. See also 1QS III:9–11 "Let him order his steps to walk perfectly in all the ways commanded by God *concerning the times appointed*

The hymn in col. X indicates that specific acts of speech were required at these appointed times. Blessings and prayers were to be offered at the appointed times. It also indicates that such words were to be offered "according to the precept engraved forever":

> at their appointed times I will bless him with the offering of the lips
> according to the precept engraved for ever ...
> All my life the engraved precept shall be on my tongue as the fruit of
> praise and the portion of my lips.[30]

The *yaḥad* developed its liturgical practice both by adopting liturgies used in the temple service, and by creating new liturgies for their own use. This practice, they believed, was done according to God's eternal precept both in terms of precise time for such ritual, and perhaps also in terms of the content of the liturgy. The *Songs of the Sabbath Sacrifice* reveal the *yaḥad*'s concern to indicate the legitimacy of its own priest-hood and to ensure the continued functioning of their service in con-junction with the heavenly service, even at a time when the service in the temple was disrupted by impurity.[31] With all this in mind, we recog-nize that the *yaḥad*'s calendrical rites are best understood, not primar-ily as independent acts of prayer establishing communication with God on these special occasions, but rather as opportunities for the priestly *yaḥad* to be obedient to divine law and to ensure their coordination with the workings of the cosmos, until the end comes. Such an understanding only emerges by focusing on the ritual system, rather than on each prayer individually.

---

for them, and stray neither to the right nor to the left and transgressing none of his words."

[30] 1QS X:5–6, 8. This translation follows G. Vermes, *The Complete Dead Sea Scrolls in English* (New York: Penguin, 1997), 112. The first person references in this hymn are ascribed to the *maśkîl*, a member of the community who played a leadership role in liturgical matters.

[31] One way that this is accomplished in the *Songs of the Sabbath Sacrifice* is through a series of rhetorical questions in Song 1, "How shall we be reckoned among them? How shall our priesthood (be considered) in their dwellings? [And our] ho[liness] with their holiness? How does the offering of our tongue of dust compare with the knowledge of the divine [beings]?" (4Q400 2 6–7). While these questions might seem to indicate distance between the human members and the angelic priests, in the context of the system established by the collection of weekly songs these questions marvel at the reality of the close connection between the two. "By identifying themselves with the cult of the heavenly temple they could exalt their own rank above the priesthood of the mere earthly temple in Jerusalem." J.R. Davila, *Liturgical Works* (Eerdmans Commentaries on the Dead Sea Scrolls 6; Grand Rapids: Eerdmans, 2000), 90.

RITES OF PASSAGE AND COMMUNITY FORMATION

The only rite of passage about which we have evidence is the initiation ceremony described in some detail in the *Community Rule*. To understand this central ritual of the community, we shall draw on a variety of approaches that focus on the real effects on the lives of the participants involved as they are integrated into the life of the community.[32] The ritual has six parts, although we will only discuss how the first three (Preparation, Entrance of New Initiates, Blessings and Curses) contribute to identity construction, instruction and indoctrination, and social control.[33]

Identity Construction

The first section of the *Community Rule* (1QS I:1–15) establishes the framework that governs the transformation of new initiates from sons of darkness into sons of light. In order to approach the community for membership, these initiates were expected to have rejected the ways of wickedness and now to freely offer themselves to perfect obedience to the laws of God[34] with a total commitment of their strength, knowledge, and wealth for the benefit of the community (1QS I:11–12).[35] Beginning the initiation process for entrance into the *yaḥad* required repentance. Repentance was undertaken on two fronts. First, a person who offered himself to join the *yaḥad* was expected to "turn from all evil ... and to separate from the congregation of the men of wickedness" (1QS V:1–2). Second, he was to return to the covenant (1QS V:22), to the law of

---

[32] Speech act theory, initiated by J.L. Austin and developed by John Searle, highlights the different ways speech can do things. The real effects of speech acts on the participants are called perlocutionary effects. J.L. Austin, *How to Do Things with Words* (New York: Oxford University Press, 1965); J.R. Searle, *Speech Acts* (Cambridge: Cambridge University Press, 1969).

[33] The final three stages are: Entrance into the *Serekh*, Purification and Instruction, and Rebuke and Dismissal. For a more detailed discussion see Arnold, *Social Role of Liturgy*, 52–81.

[34] 1QS V:2, 9 explicitly indicate that initiates are to follow the law as interpreted by the sons of Zadok, the priests, and the men of the *yaḥad*. Two of the manuscripts of the *Rule of the Community* from Cave 4 lack explicit reference to the sons of Zadok, but retain reference to the interpretive authority of the men of the *yaḥad*. For more information about the differences between the Cave 1 and Cave 4 manuscripts see S. Metso, *The Textual Development of the Qumran Community Rule* (STDJ 21; Leiden: Brill, 1997).

[35] This exhortation is reminiscent of the three-fold commitment in the Shema (Deut 6:5). Notice also the reference in 1QS I:2 to heart and soul, and the contrast between love and hate.

Moses (1QS V:8), and to the truth (1QS VI:15). This language indicates that repentance was a boundary issue;[36] no one who had not completed their repentance could be considered for membership and participate in the rest of the ceremony.[37] The ritual itself reenacted the passage from darkness to light that marked the transformation of one's social identity made possible by one's repentance. Once an initiate crossed over into the covenant, he became identified with the children of light who receive blessings rather than the sons of darkness who receive curses (1QS II:1–9).

Instruction and Indoctrination

The introduction to the initiation ritual in 1QS I:1–15 also indicates the instructional effects of this ritual. The first half of the introduction uses general terms of obedience and seeking God: loving what God loves and hating what God has rejected (I:3–4). The second half uses some of the same verbs, but it applies them in distinctly sectarian ways. Here, they are to love the children of light and hate the children of darkness, to be united in the council of God, and to walk in perfection (I:9–11). Newsom claims, "What the introduction models in its structure is that as persons are brought into the community, so is their language."[38] This indicates that, in this preparation phase, potential members were taught the meaning of obedience in the particular world of the *yaḥad*. Specifically, they were taught how to interpret the commitments from Deuteronomy employed in the first half of the introduction. They were also taught how to talk, the modes of discourse modeled by the members.[39] The transformation of their use of language goes hand in hand with the indoctrination into the sectarian worldview of the *yaḥad*.

---

[36] The *Damascus Document* (CD 4:2; 6:5; 8:16; 9:29) identifies the members of the *yaḥad* as "the ones who have repented" (שבי ישראל).

[37] The fact that the *yaḥad* settled in the wilderness, in fulfillment of Isa 40:3 (1QS VIII: 14; IX:20), may indicate that they viewed themselves as living in a liminal state outside of the normal structure of society in order to complete the transition to a renewed covenant. As such, the entire community would experience the strength of the community bond and the separation from society described by Victor Turner as *communitas*. V. Turner, *The Ritual Process: Structure and Anti-Structure* (Chicago: Aldine, 1969).

[38] C.A. Newsom, *The Self as Symbolic Space: Constructing Identity and Community at Qumran* (STDJ 52; Leiden: Brill, 2004), 113.

[39] This follows Thomas Csordas' work on the instruction about community discourse, T.J. Csordas, "Genre, Motive, and Metaphor: Conditions for Creativity in Ritual Language," *Cultural Anthropology* 2 (1987): 445–469.

Social Control

The initiation ritual also established the strict discipline that served as the mechanism for social control within the life of the strictly hierarchical community. Upon crossing over to enter the covenant, initiates were warned against "turning aside because of any fear, terror, or testing" (1QS I:17). The authority of the priests and Levites was established by the next stages of the liturgy. The priests recited all God's mighty and righteous deeds, followed by the Levites rehearsing Israel's failures and a formulaic confession recited by the initiates (1QS I:21–II:1). This historical liturgy reminds the initiates of what was expected of them by contrasting the perfection of God's righteousness with the transgressions of Israel over the years. The not so subtle message is to heed the warning, avoid the pitfalls of Israel's past, and achieve perfect righteousness. The set of blessings and curses that followed (1QS II:1–10) reinforced the strict boundary between insiders and outsiders by granting blessings to those destined for the lot of God and curses for the lot of Belial.

The pronouncement of the second set of curses against those who enter insincerely (1QS II:11–18) addressed the dangerous possibility that some who claimed to be of the lot of God, might actually be shown otherwise. This was a warning to any initiates who held on to any thoughts about maintaining their independence within the *yaḥad*. Membership in the *yaḥad* required complete submission to its authority and discipline in all things. If someone were to keep apart by telling himself privately that he would be okay even if he "walked in the stubbornness of his heart,"[40] this would confirm that he did not belong to the children of light in the first place. His deeds would show him to be of the lot of Belial and deserving of the curses directed toward that lot. In this way, this second curse reframed the first. The first set of curses, which seemed to be directed only against the evil outsiders, might have actually applied to some of those crossing over. Every one of them was required to be on their guard against falling away from the path of righteousness. They were also expected to be alert to the failures of others among them, reproving and rebuking them when necessary in order to maintain the high standards of perfection required of members of the community.[41]

---

[40] Deut 29:18–19 is quoted here.

[41] 1QS V:24–VI:1 presents rules governing reproof based on Lev 19:17, which reads, "you shall not hate your brother in your heart; you shall surely rebuke your neighbor, and you shall bear no sin because of him."

Meals and Community Structures

The last example to discuss is the community meal. Much has been written about the character of the communal meal as either a sacred meal, an eschatological banquet, or a Hellenistic symposium.[42] For our purposes we have time only to highlight the complexity of the ritual surrounding the meal and the many political and communal effects of it.

The clearest description of the Qumran meal is found in 1QS VI:1–8.[43] Notice the juxtaposition of emphasis on the unity and togetherness of all members and reminders of the strict hierarchy headed by the priest.

> In these things they shall walk at all their dwellings/sojourns all who are located each with his neighbor. And they shall hear/obey from the smallest to the greatest regarding work and money. And *together* they shall eat and *together* they shall bless and *together* they shall take counsel. In every place which there are there ten men from the council of the *yaḥad*, there shall not cease from with them a man who is a priest and each according to his rank shall sit before him and thus (i.e. according to rank) they shall ask for their counsel for everything or on any matter. And when they shall set the table to eat or the new wine to drink, the priests shall send his hand first, to cause to bless the firstfruits of the bread and the new wine. And there shall not cease, in any place which there are ten men, a man who interprets the Torah day and night always alternating one with his neighbor. And the Many shall watch over *together* a third of every night of the year to read in the book and to interpret judgment(s) and to bless *together*.[44]

---

[42] P. Bilde, "The Common Meal in the Qumran Essene Communities," in *Meals in a Social Context: Aspects of the Communal Meal in the Hellenistic and Roman World* (ed. I. Nielsen and H.S. Nielsen; Aarhus: Aarhus University Press, 1998), 145–166; K.G. Kuhn, "The Lord's Supper and the Communal Meal at Qumran," in *The Scrolls and the New Testament* (ed. K. Stendahl; Westport: Greenwood, 1975), 65–93; J. Magness, "Communal Meals and Sacred Space at Qumran," in *Shaping Community: The Art and Archaeology of Monasticism* (ed. S. McNally; BAR International Series 941; Oxford: Archaeopress, 2001), 15–28; J. Pryke, "The Sacraments of Holy Baptism and Holy Communion in the Light of the Ritual Washings and Sacred Meals at Qumran," *RevQ* 5 (1966): 543–552; J. van der Ploeg, "The Meals of the Essenes," *JSS* 2 (1957): 163–175. The main challengers of such designations are L.H. Schiffman, "Communal Meals at Qumran," *RevQ* 10 (1979): 45–56, and A.R.C. Leaney, *The Rule of Qumran and Its Meaning: Introduction, Translation and Commentary* (NTL; Philadelphia: Westminster, 1966). Sorting out the various positions presented in the above articles requires deciphering how each author defines these terms. Given the theologically charged nature of such terms, and the lack of their clear use at Qumran to describe the meals, we will leave this discussion for another occasion.

[43] The other key text informing our understanding of the meal is 1QSa II:17–22.

[44] Italics added to highlight the repetition of the term יחד (*yaḥad*) both to refer to the community and the ideal of togetherness within the community.

The first thing we notice here is the complicated interplay between eating and blessing, taking counsel, and interpreting the Torah. Although it is indeed difficult to determine precisely how these elements would have fit together within the ritual event, we must recognize that the community perceived a strong connection between eating, blessing, and instruction.

Our evidence shows that Qumran's communal meals were restricted only to members in good standing.[45] Initiates, those being punished, and of course non-members were all excluded from participation. Those who could participate were constantly reminded of the importance of acting together as a community. The passage above employs the term יחד (yaḥad) six times, highlighting the communal nature of this activity. The members ate together, blessed together, and took counsel together. The combination of these activities reinforced the members' shared experience and united them around common goals and a common identity.[46]

At the same time that the communal meals strengthened the yaḥad's group identity, they ritually enacted the hierarchical ranking that served to keep members in line. The priest's ultimate authority was not to be questioned or usurped, even by the messiah of Israel who was to come.[47] Each member's place within the community was daily reinforced by where he sat, when he was questioned by the priest, when he gave a blessing for the food, and when he could eat.[48] These constant reminders of the ranking ensured that members would take seriously the annual examinations that were part of the covenant ceremony. This brief examination of Qumran's meals recognizes the many layers on which they work. The meals contain elements of instruction and counsel, blessing, and purity of the food and those eating it. In addition, they serve as both rites of communion (emphasizing common identity) and political rites (establishing order).

---

[45] Arnold, *Social Role of Liturgy*, 90–92.

[46] "The common meal appears to have been a strong expression of the Qumran-Essene communities common history, experiences, identity and solidarity. It manifested the congregation as the only legitimate expression as the 'true,' 'pure,' 'holy' chosen people" (Bilde, "Common Meal," 162).

[47] This is evident in the description of the eschatological banquet in 1QSa II:14–22.

[48] It is interesting for our purposes to note that the nature and purpose of the blessing before eating seems to have been completely overshadowed by the importance of maintaining the proper order according to the ranking.

Implications for Ritual Study of Other Communities

What lessons do we learn from applying ritual studies approaches to the *yaḥad* that would be useful for understanding the religious life of other groups in antiquity?

First of all, I believe our study provides additional evidence that approaches developed to describe practices in the modern world can be successfully adapted to suit historical groups. Doing this effectively requires an approach to the study of texts that is sensitive to the relationship between text and practice. The text is not itself the ritual. We are not witnesses to the ritual itself, and we cannot ask follow-up questions of the text and receive further explanation. Ritual texts, therefore, must be assessed regarding whether they are meant to be prescriptive or descriptive. If they are prescriptive, it remains possible that the texts represent idealized rituals, rather than those actually practiced. At Qumran, given the evidence throughout for significant social conformity in the service of righteousness, we can be fairly certain the rituals prescribed were generally practiced as prescribed. In studying other communities, however, the absence of such strong internal forces would introduce more uncertainty about the correlation between text and practice. In other words, aspects of a community's social dynamics (conformity, authority, permeability of boundaries, etc.) are extremely important in making judgments about the degree of connection between the text before us and the ritual lives of the people behind the texts.[49]

Another issue raised by this work, especially important for ritual studies and the Pentateuch, involves the relationship between ritual and religious law or halakhah. Gruenwald describes halakhah as "an applied philosophy of life. It organizes into a ritual manner every aspect of life in systemic categories that create ritual clusters."[50] Since both ritual and law are concerned with appropriate behavior at appropriate times according to divine command, we propose that ritual theories might be applied to all aspects of biblical law, not only what we separate out as ritual.

---

[49] One useful typology of communities with respect to social dynamics is described by M. Douglas, *Natural Symbols: Explorations in Cosmology* (London: Barrie & Rockliff: Cresset, 1970). Charts that illustrate her typology can be found in S.R. Isenberg and D.E. Owen, "Bodies, Natural and Contrived: The Work of Mary Douglas," *RelSRev* 3 (1977): 1–16; B.J. Malina, *Christian Origins and Cultural Anthropology: Practical Models for Biblical Interpretation* (Atlanta: Knox, 1986).

[50] I. Gruenwald, *Rituals and Ritual Theory in Ancient Israel* (The Brill Reference Library of Ancient Judaism 10; Leiden: Brill, 2003), 33.

One thing we find at Qumran is that righteousness (an all encompassing obedience to the law of God and the community) is the goal. What we call ritual is just a part of that, but is not distinguished from other behavior. So, for example, it is not only ritual acts like prayer that fill in the gap left by the temple, but also things like purity, study, and sectarian life in general.[51] With this in mind we should broaden our focus when applying ritual studies to biblical books like Deuteronomy or Leviticus. Obviously, ritual studies will be useful in understanding the laws surrounding sacrifice, but we should consider carefully how it might help understand laws related to sexual behavior, agriculture, or damages.

With respect to the interpretation of specific rituals, one of the most important principles we learn from Qumran is to treat all ritual practices as part of a system (or in some cases multiple systems). This systemic approach requires that we do not treat individual practices or individual symbols apart from their context(s). A fine example of careful consideration of context in discussion of baptism in the early church has been carried out by Richard E. DeMaris.[52] DeMaris challenges the simple assertion that baptism was *the* entry rite for early Christians, instead treating it more broadly as a type of boundary crossing ritual that played a part in the process of reformulating social relationships and establishing new kinship ties within the church.[53] In this way, DeMaris places baptism within the larger system of rites that facilitate this transition. DeMaris' next chapter contextualizes baptism in a different way by placing the practice of baptism in the Corinthian church within the system of Corinth's dynamic traditions of using water for religious purposes.[54] Understanding the rite in this context opens our eyes to the possible political or polemical functions of water baptism particularly in Corinth.

With respect to the study of ritual practices from Ancient Israel, our study of the *yaḥad* challenges us to think beyond the simple focus on ritual sacrifice in connection with the temple cult. To be sure, the temple and its ritual practices pervaded Ancient Israelite conceptions of religion. However, none of the biblical texts unambiguously presents the tradition of the temple priests. Again, a systems approach helps us understand each ritual practice as it relates to the temple practice in

---

[51] L.H. Schiffman, "The Dead Sea Scrolls and the Early History of Jewish Liturgy," in *The Synagogue in Late Antiquity* (ed. L.I. Levine; Philadelphia: ASOR, 1989), 34.

[52] R.E. DeMaris, *The New Testament in Its Ritual World* (London: Routledge, 2008).

[53] Ibid., 14–22.

[54] Ibid., 37–56.

a radial-dialogic way.[55] At the same time, we must go beyond simple explanations that focus only on sacrifice as a means for atonement and prayer as a replacement for sacrifice.[56] We can begin to ask about how the priests understood their purpose vis-à-vis the lives of the people. We can investigate the social effects of the various systems of sacrifice and the impact centralization had on those systems. We also think more carefully about how differences between the worldviews and settings of the Priestly Code (P), the Holiness Code (H), and the Deuteronomic Code (D) affect the meaning of the same ritual practices set within these different systems.

Finally, as we are all aware, it is important to recognize the cultural distance between us and the ancient communities we study. Reading ritual studies of modern societies helps us to recognize the otherness of our subjects, and to better understand societies that had much higher ritual density. In this regard, Qumran may not be representative of mainstream Second Temple Judaism, but it is certainly closer to it than we are. Our study of Qumran gives us a more historically near parallel from which to draw. The relative wealth of information about Qumran gives us more questions to ask, and a greater desire to dig deeper. For example, investigations of meal rituals in various Pauline communities could be usefully compared to the *yaḥad* with respect to any indications we have of social hierarchy and communal identity. The comparison could help us better understand the theological, political, and social implications of the contested ritual practice of the Lord's Supper in 1 Cor 11. Recognizing the depth of ritualization and the multivalence of its meanings and functions within the *yaḥad* forces us to not be satisfied with simplistic theological or social interpretations of ritual practice in other contexts. We must strive for the thickest descriptions possible of the complex ritual lives of the communities that are the subject of our study.

---

[55] This concept is developed concerning the *yaḥad* in Schofield, "Between Center and Periphery."

[56] For an example of a more sophisticated study of biblical sacrifice see J. Klawans, *Purity, Sacrifice, and the Temple: Symbolism and Supersessionism in the Study of Ancient Judaism* (Oxford: Oxford University Press, 2006).

EXPENDABLE SIGNS:
THE COVENANT OF THE RAINBOW
AND CIRCUMCISION AT QUMRAN[*]

SANDRA JACOBS
University College, London

The covenant of the rainbow and circumcision are two Priestly signs that have minimal roles in the sectarian texts from Qumran. The purpose of this paper is to explore the general significance of these images in order to understand their relative absence in the Dead Sea Scrolls. This analysis suggests that the sign of the rainbow, with its inherent symbolism of sexuality and fertility, was of no value to men in the יחד (*yaḥad*) community, who were otherwise intent on enforcing increased levels of ritual purity and encouraging greater sexual restraint.[1] By identifying themselves as "the elect, remnant of Israel," neither the covenant of the rainbow, nor the sign of circumcision,[2] served to enhance their self-defined elitism.[3] While circumcision was attested on a widespread basis in Judea and Egypt in the Persian period, it attracted harsh condemnation in Graeco-Roman society. Accordingly, its practical application was of no significant doctrinal value to the writers of the scrolls.

The Hebrew קֶשֶׁת *qešet*, or bow, denotes either the concrete image of an instrument for hunting or a rainbow and was used also "figura-

---

[*] This material was presented in the first year of my PhD at the University of Manchester under the supervision of Bernard Jackson. Further thanks also to Russell Arnold, Shani Berrin-Tzoref, Adrian Curtis, Esther Eshel, Diana Lipton, Shula Medalie, Lawrence Schiffman and Daniel Stoekl Ben Ezra for their insights which have been incorporated into this printed version of the paper. Biblical Hebrew translations are from the NJPS.

[1] See H.K. Harrington, *The Purity Texts* (Companion to the Qumran Scrolls 3; London: T&T Clark, 2004) and E. Regev, "Moral Impurity and the Temple in Early Christianity in Light of Ancient Greek Practise and Qumranic Ideology," *HTR* 97 (2004): 383–411.

[2] As practised also by the descendants of Ishmael and Esau, among others.

[3] Particularly since the sectarian texts were not concerned with the welfare of humanity in general, unlike the account of the covenant of the rainbow, where the promise never to destroy the earth by means of a flood was would apply to Noah's "offspring to come" (Gen 9:9), "to every living creature among all flesh" (Gen 9:15) and "to all flesh that is on earth" (Gen 9:17).

tively as a symbol of power, sovereignty, war."[4] Its representation as an effective symbol of male sexuality and virility, however, was rooted in Neo-Assyrian political imagery,[5] where "the fully taut bow, the *qaštum malītum*, is a bow whose reed has been pulled back while it gathers the necessary energy for the shot."[6] In both the biblical corpus and eighth-seventh century Assyrian Royal inscriptions, the concrete and symbolic meanings were, on occasions, used interchangeably.[7] The biblical image of the קשת בענן "the bow in the clouds" in Gen 9:13 appears immediately after the flood, when God states: "I have set my bow in the clouds and it shall serve as a sign of the Covenant between me and the earth."[8] This "sign of the Covenant between me and the earth" is extended to "every living creature among all flesh" in Gen 9:15.[9] At Qumran, this sign appears only in 4QAdmonFlood (4Q370) I:7:

ויאש אל [אות ברית וא]ת קשתו נתן [בענן ל]מען יזכור ברית [ ]

his bow he set [in the clouds so] that he would remember the covenant[10]

It is also mentioned in 1QapGen ar XII:1: והואת לי לאת בעננה "and it was for me a sign in the cloud." Thus Lawrence Schiffman concludes that these references to the rainbow were not part of the core sectarian traditions found at Qumran, but rather recalled earlier tradents:

> These materials, we should note, are not part of the mainstream Qumranic sectarian compositions but indicate that the Qumran sectarians were heir to a pre-sectarian tradition regarding this venerable ancestor of Israel. The

---

[4] T. Kronholm and H.-J. Fabry, "קשת, *qešet*," *TDOT* 12:202.

[5] S.M. Paul, "The Shared Legacy of Sexual Metaphors and Euphemisms in Mesopotamian and Biblical Literature," in *Sex and Gender in the Ancient Near East: Proceedings of the 47th Rencontre Assyriologique Internationale, Helsinki, July 2–6, 2001* (ed. S. Parpola and R.M. Whiting; 2 vols.; Helsinki: The Neo-Assyrian Text Corpus Project, 2002), 2:489–499.

[6] היא קשת שיתרא משוך לאחור תוך שהוא צובר את נרגיא הדרושא לירייה *qaštum malītum* ש/קשת מלאה (I. Eph'al, "Lexical Notes on Some Ancient Military Terms," *ErIsr* 20 [1989]: 115–119 [117]).

[7] This is apparent in Neo-Assyrian treaty convention and also (for example) in Gen 49:22–24, which are discussed below.

[8] את קשתי נתתי בענן והיתה לאות ברית ביני ובין הארץ.

[9] Gen 9:15 states: "I will remember My covenant between me and you and every living creature among all flesh, so that the waters shall never again become a flood to destroy all flesh." This is recalled in *Jub.* 6:15–16: "And He gave to Noah and his sons a sign that there should not again be a flood on the earth. He set His bow in the cloud for a sign of the eternal covenant that there should not again be a flood on the earth to destroy it all the days of the earth."

[10] C. Newsom in *DJD* XIX (1995): 85–97, where the explicit parallels between 4Q370 and Gen 6:5; 7:11, 14, 22, 23; 9:11, 13, 15 are identified further (87–88).

brief allusion to this covenant in the *Zadokite Fragments* (CD III, 1–4) reflects this pre-sectarian tradition.[11]

What, then, did a bow in the clouds represent in the context of pre-sectarian Judean tradition? Harry Hoffner explains that masculinity was determined by two criteria: Firstly, a man's physical strength in battle and secondly, his ability to reproduce children, or biblically speaking, ללדת בנים to "beget" sons.[12] Both achievements were represented by the image of a bow and its arrows in ancient Hurrian, Hittite, Ugaritic and Mesopotamian traditions. In Neo-Assyrian convention the figurative use of the bow and arrow was evoked in written expressions and in engraved reliefs from the eighth-seventh century kings, as recently documented by Cynthia Chapman.[13] As such the expression to "break the bow," which conveyed the desire to cut off the reproductive powers of one's enemy and thereby extinguish his future dynastic succession, was frequently evoked in treaty curse formulations. Aššur-nerari V of Assyria's treaty with Mati'ilu of Arpad, for example, states:

> May Mati'ilu's (sex) life be that of a mule, his wife extremely old; may Ištar, the goddess of men, the lady of women, take away their bow, bring them shame and make them bitterly weep: "Woe, we have sinned against the treaty of Aššur-nerari, King of Assyria."[14]

The interaction between the Assyrians and Judeans, particularly after Sennacherib's conquest of Lachish, is historically relevant to the cultural proliferation of this symbolism.[15] A relief from a panel located in the South West Palace of Sennacherib, excavated at Nebi Yunis (Nineveh), Northern Iraq, depicts soldiers active in the Assyrian Royal Guard.

---

[11] L.H. Schiffman, "The Concept of Covenant in the Qumran Scrolls and Rabbinic Literature," in *The Idea of Biblical Interpretation: Essays in Honor of James L. Kugel* (ed. H. Najman and J.H. Newman; JSJSup 83; Leiden: Brill, 2004), 257–278 (258).

[12] H. Hoffner, "Symbols of Masculinity and Femininity: Their Use in Ancient Near Eastern Sympathetic Magic Rituals," *JBL* 85 (1966): 326–334.

[13] C. Chapman, *The Gendered Language of Warfare in the Israelite-Assyrian Encounter* (HSM 62; Winona Lake: Eisenbrauns, 2004). My thanks here particularly to Diana Lipton, who initially brought the symbolism of these sources to my attention.

[14] S. Parpola and K. Watanabe, eds., *Neo-Assyrian Treaties and Loyalty Oaths* (SAAS 2; Helsinki: Helsinki University Press, 1988), 12.

[15] Irrespective of the fact that Sennacherib's claim, in the annuls of his third campaign, of having taken 200,150 Judeans captive is considered to be an improbably high exaggeration: "200150 *nišī ṣeher rabi zikar ù/u sinniš*" (R. Borger, *Babylonisch-Assyrische Lesestücke* [3rd ed.; AnOr 54; Rome: Pontifical Biblical Institute, 2006], 74). Cf. A. Faust "The Extent of Sennacherib's Campaign to Judah in 701 B.C.E.: A New Examination" (paper presented at the Anglo-Israel Archaeological Society Lecture in the British Museum on 21 February 2008).

Fig. 1. Soldiers or Bodyguards During the Reign of Sennacherib[16]

In addition, the emasculation of men and their evocation as women was a recognised political and ideological "spin" in the language of ancient Near Eastern warfare. Chapman concludes that "the parallel usage of femininity as a simile for weakness in both biblical and Neo-Assyrian curses demonstrates the essential rather than the accidental nature of

---

[16] Relief Number ME 124901 is reproduced with courtesy of the trustees of the British Museum. This panel was one of a group found between the palace of Sennacherib (reigned 704–681 B.C.E.) and the Temple of Ishtar, the principal goddess of Nineveh. The full scene

gendered language in military cursing."[17] It is this "essential" nature of this symbolism that influenced the Priestly redaction of Gen 9:12–18, if not also the pre-sectarian interpretation of God's covenant with Noah. As Joseph Blenkinsopp has observed "it is therefore not, as Wellhausen, Gunkel and many others have suggested, the equivalent of burying the hatchet, a signifying of the end of hostilities with God hanging his war bow in the clouds."[18]

Nor is the association of the bow with reproductive sexuality found exclusively in ancient Near Eastern and Priestly representations. Ezekiel's description of his vision of God also conveys this understanding of the symbolism:

> From what appeared his loins up, I saw a gleam, as of amber—what looked like fire encased in a frame; and from what appeared his loins down, I saw what looked like fire. There was radiance all about him, like the appearance of the bow (כמראה הקשת) which shines in the cloud on a day of rain, such was the appearance of the surrounding radiance. (Ezek 1:26–28)

This bow was clearly no "instrument of hunting" nor a weapon of war and like the subsequent Second Temple literary traditions,[19] it recalled the reproductive continuity promised by the sign of that earlier bow in the clouds of Gen 9:16. Jacob's death-bed blessing to Joseph in Gen 49:22–25 provides a good example of the interchangeable use of the concrete and figurative sense of this bow:

---

shows the king and his entourage in formal court dress, where these two figures formed part of the royal bodyguard. The Museum's accompanying description states further: "The archer on the left is one of the lightly-armed soldiers who were probably drawn from the Aramaic-speaking communities that had been conquered in and around the Assyrian heartland. The spear-man on the right wears a turban fastened by a headband with long ear-flaps, and a short kilt curving upwards above his knees. His clothing tells us that he comes from around the environs of either Judah or Israel. An almost identical uniform is worn by the men of Lachish, in the kingdom of Judah, as represented in panels showing Sennacherib's siege of the city in 701 BC from another part of the palace."

[17] Chapman, *Gendered Language*, 86.

[18] J. Blenkinsopp, *The Pentateuch: An Introduction to the First Five Books of the Bible* (London: SCM Press, 1992), 86.

[19] Compare also Sir 26:10–12: "Keep strict watch over a headstrong daughter, or else, when she finds liberty, she will make use of it. Be on guard against her impudent eye and do not be surprised if she sins against you. As a thirsty traveller opens his mouth and drinks from any water near him, so she will sit in front of every tent peg and open her quiver to the arrow." Also as in *b. Ḥag.* 15a: והאמר שמואל: כל שכבת זרע שאינו יורה כחץ אינו מזרעת, "Samuel said: A spermatic emission that does not shoot forth like an arrow cannot germinate."

Joseph is a wild ass, a wild ass by a spring;[20] wild colts on a hillside.
Archers bitterly assailed him, they shot at him and harried him, yet his
  bow stayed taut[21]
and his arms were made firm by the hands of the mighty ones of Jacob—
There, the Shepherd, The Rock of Israel—The God of your father who
  helps you
and Shaddai who blesses you, with blessings of heaven above, blessings of
  the deep that couch below, blessings of the breast and of the womb.

Nowhere in the biblical corpus is Joseph associated with either military activity or success on the battle-front. Suggestively, the attraction of Potiphar's wife provides the more appropriate interpretative key for this blessing, so that ותשב באיתן קשתו "his bow stayed taut" indicates rather that Joseph's sexual capacity remained potent.[22] Naturally "the blessings of the breast and of the womb" are also more relevant to this figurative interpretation of Joseph's bow as his reproductive powers, rather than as a weapon of war. It is justified therefore to conclude that this symbolism of the bow as a symbol of male virility and sexuality was familiar to pre-sectarian Judean scribes even if its explicit association was absent in the scrolls preserved at Qumran.[23]

Such symbolism would have been essentially avoided by men whose focus on sexual restraint and reified notions of purity was crucial to their idealized (if not, normative) ritual agenda. Any emphasis upon the universal nature of the sign of the rainbow would have been detrimental to the recognition of their community as "the elect, remnant of Israel,"

---

[20] This recalls the imagery evoked in the considerably earlier genre of Sumerian potency incantations: "Incantation: Wild ass who has had an erection for mating, who has dampened your ardour? Violent stallion whose sexual excitement is a devastating flood, [W]ho has bound your limbs? Who has slacked your muscles?" R.D. Biggs, ŠÀ. ZI. GA: Ancient Mesopotamian Potency Incantations (TCS 2; Locust Valley: Augustin, 1967), 17, incantation no. 1, lines 12–14.

[21] Compare also 4QCommGen C (4Q254) 7: ¹ [...] ² [... (Gen 49:24–25) And his] bow [remain]ed steady (ותשב באיתן קשתו[]) [...] ³ [... the Shepher]d, the stone of Israel. [...] ⁴ [... blessings of the heaven] from ab[ov]e, [...] ⁵ [...].

[22] Certainly this is the interpretation in b. Soṭah 36b, commenting on Gen 49:24, where Rabbi Yoḥanan states in the name of R. Meir, that "his bow (i.e. penis) subsided," while in y. Hor. 2.46d Rabbi Shmuel states, "his bow (קשתו) stretched forth and retracted."

[23] However Herodotus' (Hist. 11.141) account of the Assyrian retreat in Egypt, which he explained was due to swarms of field-mice devouring the bow-strings of their soldiers, is unlikely to have been known to Judean scribes and is also considered to be "a muddled and fanciful tradition." See K.A. Kitchen, "Egypt, the Levant and Assyria in 701 BC," in Fontes atque Pontes: FS H. Brunner (Ägypten und Altes Testament 5; Wiesbaden: Harrassowitz, 1983), 243–253 (245). I am indebted to Russ Arnold for kindly reminding me of this, after I had delivered the paper.

who were "caused to sprout from Israel and from Aaron, a shoot of the planting."[24] The importance of this self-designation is particularly highlighted by the various plant metaphors that denote exclusively the צמח צדיק, the "righteous branch" of the Davidic dynasty.

This "narrowing down of the metaphor to refer only to the community of the elect, the true remnant of Israel," is highly characteristic of Qumran literature,[25] yet has its origins in earlier biblical tradition. This convention was summarized recently by Nicholas Wyatt who succinctly outlined this typology, or "reiterated threefold pattern," in which the elements of blessing and covenant, sin and renewal are recalled:[26]

The Universal Covenant of Noah

Gen 1:1–2:24   The "primordial covenant" with Adam.
Gen 6–8   The account of the flood and the destruction of mankind.
Gen 9:1–17   The covenant with Noah, symbolized by the rainbow.

The Covenants of Abram/Abraham

Gen 15:1–21   The initial covenant with Abram.
Gen 16   Hagar's expulsion and the birth of Ishmael.
Gen 17:1–21   The Covenant of Circumcision with Abraham.

The Covenants of Israel at Sinai

Exod 19–24   The initial Mosaic Covenant Code to the Israelites.
Exod 32   The apostasy of the golden calf.
Exod 34:1–33   The second set of tablets issued to Moses.

In this sequence the universal covenant symbolized by the rainbow was first issued to כל־נפש חיה בכל בשר "every living creature among all flesh"

---

[24] השאיר שארית לישראל ... פקדם ויצמח מישראל ומאהרן שורש מטעת (CD 1:5–7 par. 4QD^a [4Q 266] 2 i 9–12).

[25] H. Ulfgard, "The Branch in the Last Days: Observations on the New Covenant Before and After the Messiah," in *The Dead Sea Scrolls in Their Historical Context* (ed. T.H. Lim; Edinburgh: T&T Clark, 2000), 233–247 (235). The differentials between the איש טהר (the pure man) and the טהר יתר (the more scrupulous, pure man), are further discussed in Harrington, *Purity Texts*, 75–76.

[26] N. Wyatt, "Circumcision and Circumstance: Male Genital 'Mutilation' in Ancient Ugarit" (paper presented in the series "Mary Douglas Seminars on Anthropology and the Bible" organized by the Institute of Jewish Studies at University College, London, 6 February 2008). This outline was provided by Professor Wyatt on the accompanying hand-out to this lecture, and is reproduced here with his permission. It has since been published as: "Circumcision and Circumstance: Male Genital Mutilation in Ancient Israel and Ugarit," *JSOT* 33 (2009): 405–431.

(Gen 9:15), i.e., all mankind. It was then limited to Abraham and his entire household. In the Priestly narrative, this later specified Abraham's descendants from Isaac and then Jacob with the exclusion of Ishmael, the sons of Keturah and Esau. By Exodus the covenant is addressed only to the Israelites. This developing pattern of covenant, sin and renewal is endemic also in the writings of the scrolls, as Craig Evans notes, "Israel's ancient covenant, and here it is primarily the Sinai covenant that is in view, and its renewal constitute the Qumran community's very *raison d'être*."[27] Evans concludes that,

> simply put, the distinctive feature of the understanding of Covenant at Qumran is the reduction of the number of the elect. There is now a chosen people drawn out from the people of Israel: a chosen from the chosen, as it were. Those who adhere to the law according to the terms spelled out in the sectarian writings are the elect who stand in the Covenant.[28]

Given that in the primeval and patriarchal biblical traditions, both fertility and circumcision were crucial elements in the narrative, how can we understand their relative absence as defining signs of the covenant in the Dead Sea Scrolls? Lawrence Schiffman explains:

> the Abrahamic covenant has one further ingredient, the practise of circumcision. This fact, which we encounter so extensively in rabbinic literature, is attested rarely in the scrolls. However, CD XII uses the phrase "covenant of Abraham" as a direct reference to circumcision,[29] so closely associated with Abraham in Genesis 17:10–15, 23–27.[30]

Indeed physical circumcision is explicit only in the *Damascus Document* (CD 16:4–6) as follows:

---

[27] C.A. Evans, "Covenant in the Qumran Literature," in *The Concept of Covenant in the Second Temple Period* (ed. S.E. Porter and J.C.R. de Roo; JSJSup 71; Leiden: Brill, 2003), 55–80 (55).

[28] Ibid., 80.

[29] As, for example in *m. 'Abot* 3:15, where בריתו של אברהם "the covenant of Abraham," likewise, denotes circumcision: "R. Eliezer of Modin has said: He who profanes the sacred, despises the festivals, shames his neighbour in public, removes the covenant of our father Abraham and reveals interpretations of Torah which are not in keeping with the *halakhah*, even if he possesses knowledge of Torah and good deeds, he has no portion in the world to come." See R. Hall's discussion of this Mishnah and its similarity to the statements in Philo (*Migr.* 89–93) and in *b. Yoma* 85b, in "Epispasm and the Dating of Ancient Jewish Writings," *JSP* 2 (1988): 71–86 (81–82).

[30] Schiffman "Concept of Covenant," 260, where he adds: "This covenant may be mentioned in 4Q378 (4QapocrJosh) 22 I 4, (restoring *habber]it*), or this may only be a general allusion to the covenant with Abraham."

4 ... וביום אשר יקים האיש על נפשו לשוב
5 אל תורת משה יסוד מלאך המסטמה מאחריו אם יקים את דבריו
6 על כן נימול [ב]אברהם ביום דעתו *vacat*

4 ... And on the day on which one has imposed upon himself to return
5 to the law of Moses, the angel Mastema will turn aside from following him, should he keep his word.
6 This is why Abraham circumcised himself on the day of his knowledge
   vacat

Otherwise, circumcision appears only as a metaphor in the scrolls. This includes 1QS, the סרך היחד, or *Rule of the Community*, which states as follows:

> Justice and uprightness, compassionate love and seemly behaviour in all paths. No one should walk in the stubbornness of his heart in order to go astray following his heart and his eyes and the musings of his inclination instead he should circumcise in the Community the foreskin of his tendency (למול ביחד עורלת יצר) and of his stiff-neck in order to lay a foundation of truth for Israel, for the Community of the eternal covenant.
> (1QS V:4–6)[31]

It is in this context that Martin Abegg concludes that

> this matter does not attain to the stature of later rabbinic—where the word covenant itself (ברית) is understood as circumcision—or New Testament discussions is demonstrated by the metaphorical use of the word for "foreskin" in all of its occurrences in Qumran literature in reference to the spiritual condition of the heart.[32]

This preoccupation with "the spiritual condition of the heart," not forgetting הצנע לכת בכול דרכיהם "seemly behaviour in all paths," further highlights the lack of interest of the covenant of circumcision in the rewritten biblical traditions found at Qumran.

What were the reasons for this distinct shift? Circumcision is commonly explained in the following terms:

> the very first covenantal promise had also been accompanied by a visible proof, the rainbow, described as *ot haberit* (Gen. 9.12). Similarly, [circumcision was] a visible sign ... to distinguish those descendants of Abraham

---

[31] Also compare גזורו עורלת בשרכון "circumcise your fleshy foreskin" in the *Aramaic Levi Document* (1:3), which is discussed in relation to Gen 34:15, Ezek 44:6–9, and 1QpHab XI:12–13 by J.C. Greenfield, M.E. Stone, and E. Eshel, *The Aramaic Levi Document: Edition, Translation, Commentary* (SVTP 19; Leiden: Brill, 2004), 113–116.

[32] These are 1QS V:5, 26; 1QpHab XI:13; 4Q177 II:16; 4Q266 6 ii 6; 4Q434 1 i 4; 4Q504 4 11, cited by M.G. Abegg, "The Covenant of the Qumran Sectarians," in *The Concept of Covenant in the Second Temple Period*, 81–97 (82).

who are the hereditary beneficiaries of the promise from those who are not.[33]

As such Josephus states, with reference to the birth of Isaac to Abraham: "Furthermore, to the intent that his posterity should be kept from mixing with others, God charged him to have then circumcised and to perform the rite on the eight day after birth" (*Ant.* 1.191–192 [Thackeray, LCL]).[34] Yet, in practical terms, this cannot have been the case. Hence Michael Fox argues that at its earliest implementation, differentiating between the descendants of Isaac and Ishmael (if not also Abraham's other sons) could not have provided either the impetus, or rationale, for this rite:

> It is not an identity sign designated belonging to the covenanted people, for first of all, no one would see it. (There is no point referring the custom to a time when people went naked, for that custom was certainly not relevant for P and even in the earliest times Israelites did not go naked). Anyway it would not be of much use in distinguishing the Israelites from their neighbours, because many of them were also circumcised. And Ishmael, who as P takes pains to emphasize is not part of the covenant, is also circumcised. For practical purposes circumcision could at most distinguish the Israelites from the Philistines, who are not an issue for P.[35]

---

[33] B.S. Jackson, *Studies in the Semiotics of Biblical Law* (JSOTSup 314; Sheffield: Sheffield Academic Press, 2000), 239. This view is expressed earliest by Tacitus, *Hist.* 5.5.2: "They [i.e. the Jews] adopted circumcision to distinguish themselves from other peoples by this difference." Translated in L. Feldman and M. Reinhold, *Jewish Life and Thought among the Greeks and Romans: Primary Readings* (Edinburgh: T&T Clark, 1996), 380.

[34] Here Louis Feldman observes: "Josephus was evidently well aware that this might lead to a charge of misanthropy, however, so he immediately adds that elsewhere he will explain the reason—that is, presumably, the rational or symbolic meaning of this practice. The announced work has not come down to us, but in it Josephus might well have pointed to the separation of the reputedly wise Egyptians, who, he says, themselves practise circumcision (*Ag. Ap.* 1.164–170 and 2.141–142). In any case, it is significant that whereas Josephus elsewhere draws upon the *Book of Jubilees*, he omits the strong statement in *Jubilees* (15:26), presumably directed against the Hellenizers of the period" (L.H. Feldman, *Josephus's Interpretation of the Bible* [Hellenistic Culture and Society 27; Berkeley: University of California Press, 1998], 245–246). Here *Jub.* 15:26–27 states: "Anyone who is born, the flesh of whose private parts has not been circumcised by the eighth day does not belong to the people of the pact which the Lord made with Abraham but to the people (meant for) destruction. Moreover, there is no sign on him that he belongs to the Lord, but (he is meant) for destruction, for being destroyed from the earth, and for being uprooted from the earth because he has violated the covenant of the Lord our God." Translation of J.C. VanderKam, *The Book of Jubilees* (2 vols.; CSCO 510–511; Scriptores Aethiopici 87–88; Leuven: Peeters, 1989), 2:92.

[35] M.V. Fox, "The Sign of the Covenant: Circumcision in the Light of the Priestly 'ôt Etiologies," *RB* 81 (1974): 557–596 (595). Likewise, William Propp concludes that "because circumcision set Jews apart in the later Greco-Roman and Christian worlds, most people assume that the original intent, the 'covenant sign' of Genesis 17 was to

Fox's argument is supported by the evidence that male circumcision is attested in both in Egypt and in the Levant as either an initiation or pre-puberty rite, although references to circumcision in Egypt are exceptional in the earlier dynastic periods. By the fifth century, however, Herodotus writes that:

> but my better proof was that the Colchians and Egyptians and Ethiopians are the only nations that have from the first practised circumcision.[36] The Phoenicians and the Syrians of Palestine acknowledge of themselves that they learned the custom from the Egyptians; and the Syrians of the valleys of Thermodon and Parthenius, as well as their neighbours the Macrones, say they learned it lately from the Colchians.[37]   (Herodotus, *Hist.* 2.104)

Among the circumcised Philo includes Jews, Egyptians, the Arabians, the Ethiopians and "nearly all the nations that dwell in the southern parts of the world" (*QG* 3.47–48). Of particular significance is the tradition recorded in Jeremiah, which further confirms the widespread origins of the rite.

> Lo, the days are coming—declares the Lord—when I will take note of everyone circumcised in the foreskin: of Egypt, Judah, Edom, the Ammonites, Moab and all the desert dwellers who have the hair of their temples clipped. For all these nations are uncircumcised, but all the house of Israel are uncircumcised of heart.[38]   (Jer 9:24–25)

Such admonitions characterize, if not typify, the metaphorical allusions to circumcision as a means to achieving both physical and mental restraint in pre-Qumranic thought.

Yet it was only after the Greek conquest of the Persian province of Judea that circumcision then did "effect a heightening of tribal consciousness and can be used, as in Hellenistic and Roman times, to identify a member of the people."[39] This came about when "physical demarcation was especially acute in a society in which public nudity during work and at play was prevalent and in which the perfection of the unaltered male

---

distinguish Jew from Gentile, or Israelite from foreigner. But this is wrong" (W.H. Propp, "Circumcision: The Private Sign of The Covenant," *BRev* 20/4, [2006]: 22–29 [23]).

[36] Colchis was east of the Black Sea and south of the Caucasus Mountains: "Though this area is far from Egypt, it seems that Egypt received immigrants from this district at the close of the Old Kingdom" (Feldman and Reinhold, *Jewish Life and Thought*, 378 n. 73).

[37] Translation ibid., 378. This view is reported also by Josephus (*Ag. Ap.* 1.168–172).

[38] Where the emphasis upon: כי כל־הגוים ערלים וכל־בית ישראל ערלי לב "For all these nations are uncircumcised, but all the house of Israel are uncircumcised of heart" is significant.

[39] Fox, "Sign of the Covenant," 595.

physique was prized,"[40] and would have been noticeable particularly in the Roman bath house and gymnasium.[41] The response of a number of Jewish men to these social pressures is evident from the accounts of epispasm: surgery undertaken to reverse the appearance of their circumcision[42] in order to disguise what was otherwise considered as a physical deformity.[43] In addition to the repugnance for circumcision and the intense social stigma that this rite conveyed, Robert Hall explains that the two drachma tax levied in the aftermath of the Jewish wars (68–72 C.E.) for any circumcised man, provided a further incentive to undergo epispasm.[44] Moreover, in Alexandria, citizenship additionally required the removal of circumcision, as was evident in 3 Macc 2:30–31; 3:21; 7:10–15.[45]

Thus, once "circumcision is likewise singled out in Hellenistic Jewish, pagan and Christian literature as the premier mark of the Jew, and specifically of the convert to Judaism,"[46] does it constitute what Shaye Cohen has termed a "tribal mark or ethnic habit."[47] This negative perception of circumcision (reinforced also by Paul and in the transmission of the gospels)[48] would have done little to enhance its appeal in Judean society.

---

[40] R. Abusch, "Circumcision and Castration under Roman Law in the Early Empire," in *The Covenant of Circumcision: New Perspectives on an Ancient Jewish Rite* (ed. E. Wyner Mark; Brandeis Series on Jewish Women; Hanover: Brandeis University Press, 2003), 75–86 (75). See also Feldman and Reinhold, *Jewish Life and Thought*, 377–380.

[41] See R. Hall, "Epispasm: Circumcision in Reverse," *BRev* 8/4 (1992): 52–57 (52).

[42] As in 1 Macc 1:11–15; 2 Macc 4:12; *T. Mos.* 8:3; Josephus, *Ant.* 12.241; 1 Cor 7:18; *t. Šabb.* 15:9; *b. Yebam.* 72a.

[43] As understood, for example, by Petronius, *Satyricon* 68:8: "He [a slave] has only two faults, and if he were rid of them he would be simply perfect. He is circumcised and he snores." Translated in Feldman and Reinhold, *Jewish Life and Thought*, 379.

[44] Hall, "Epispasm and the Dating of Ancient Jewish Writings," 76–78. This is also evident from the tradition recounted by Suetonius, *Dom.* 12:2: "Besides other taxes, that on the Jews were levied with utmost rigour, and those were prosecuted who without publically acknowledging that faith yet lived as Jews, as well as those that concealed their origin and did not pay the tribute levied on their people. I recall being present in my youth when the person of a man ninety years old was examined before the procurator and a very crowded court, to see whether he was circumcised." Translated in A.M. Rabello, "The Ban on Circumcision as a Cause of Bar Kokhba's Rebellion," *Israel Law Review* 29 (1995): 176–214 (181).

[45] Hall, "Epispasm and the Dating of Ancient Jewish Writings," 77.

[46] P. Friedriksen, "The Circumcision of Gentiles and Apocalyptic Hope: Another Look at Galatians 1 and 2," *JTS* 42 (1991): 532–564 (536).

[47] S.J.D. Cohen, *Why Aren't Jewish Women Circumcised? Gender and Covenant in Judaism* (Berkeley: University of California Press, 2005), 15.

[48] Both Gal 6:14–15 and Acts 15:19–29 indicate that circumcision was, firstly, recog-

Given the self-identification of the community represented at Qumran as "the elect remnant of Israel," it is understandable that a rite that was as prevalent in the surrounding, pagan society such as circumcision (and one which was not originally the unique the mark of the Jew) was of little use in the promotion of their sectarian ideals. Moreover, the fact that circumcision was perceived as a physical deformity additionally explains the need to develop its role primarily (if not exclusively) in metaphorical terms thus avoiding explicit mention of its actual application.

In pragmatic terms it therefore seems unlikely that the requirement for circumcision was absent in the סרך היחד, the *Community Rule*, because it was simply taken for granted, as a normative Judean rite assumed by the sectarian scribes.[49] This is, even though, as Russell Arnold and Daniel Stoekl Ben Ezra pointed out when this paper was delivered in Vienna, the more general life-cycle rituals (birth, initiation, marriage, death, etc.) are largely absent in the scrolls, with exception to the initiation rite and covenant renewal ceremony in 1QS VI:13–15 and I:18–II:18 respectively. These factors do not preclude the reality that male circumcision was never exclusively an Israelite tradition but was common in Second Temple Judean society and its surrounds and that, furthermore, by the Graeco-Roman period was publically vilified and considered a disfiguring social stigma. This historical context explains why the covenant of circumcision assumed significance only as a metaphor and was not valued in and of itself as a requirement for the future redemption of Israel in the Dead Sea Scrolls. Like the covenant of the rainbow, addressed initially to all mankind, both signs were clearly irrelevant, if not detrimental to, the particular elitism advanced by the men of Qumran.

---

nised as a Jewish characteristic, and secondly that it was not required for converts to the Christian faith.

[49] In accordance with Mosaic law suggested in Gen 17:10–14; Exod 4:24–26; etc.

PROPHECY AFTER "THE PROPHETS": THE DEAD SEA SCROLLS AND THE HISTORY OF PROPHECY IN JUDAISM

ALEX P. JASSEN
University of Minnesota

INTRODUCTION

Recent scholarship on ancient Judaism has witnessed a renewed interest in the question of ongoing prophetic activity in Second Temple and rabbinic Judaism. Perhaps the most representative examples of this trend are the two articles by Frederick Greenspahn and Benjamin Sommer that appeared in the *Journal of Biblical Literature* in 1989 and 1996, respectively.[1] Greenspahn's contribution sought to build upon earlier treatments by Ephraim Urbach, Thomas Overhalt, and David Aune in reconsidering what had long been deemed a closed discussion: did prophecy indeed cease in the early post-exilic period as everyone from the rabbis to Wellhausen and beyond had imagined?[2]

Greenspahn's examination covers two sets of data: (1) explicit evidence attesting to ongoing prophetic activity or the belief in its continued existence well beyond the exile and (2) reexamination of several passages from Second Temple and rabbinic literature that seem to claim the opposite. Considering the second group, Greenspahn correctly observes that what one group thinks should be the case is not evidence for the actual social reality in other segments of society.[3] Several years later, Sommer

---

[1] F.E. Greenspahn, "Why Prophecy Ceased," *JBL* 108 (1989): 37–49; B.D. Sommer, "Did Prophecy Cease? Reevaluating a Reevaluation," *JBL* 115 (1995): 31–47.

[2] E.E. Urbach, "מתי פסקה הנבואה?" *Tarbiz* 17 (1945–1946): 1–11; D.E. Aune, *Prophecy in Early Christianity and the Ancient Mediterranean World* (Grand Rapids: Eerdmans, 1983), 103–106; T. Overholt, "The End of Prophecy: No Players without a Program," in *The Place Is too Small for Us: The Israelite Prophets in Recent Scholarship* (ed. R.P. Gordon; SBTS 5; Winona Lake: Eisenbrauns, 1995), 527–538. For full bibliography, see A.P. Jassen, *Mediating the Divine: Prophecy and Revelation in the Dead Sea Scrolls and Second Temple Judaism* (STDJ 68; Leiden: Brill, 2007), 11–19; idem, "Prophets and Prophecy in the Qumran Community," *AJSR* 32 (2008): 299–334.

[3] Greenspahn, "Prophecy," 40 (so also Aune, *Prophecy*, 103).

argued that Greenspahn and his predecessors got it all wrong. While offering a corrective to Greenspahn's over-reading of some texts, Sommer asserts that the evidence from ancient Judaism does not present a portrait of uninterrupted prophetic activity. Rather, he argues, "new ways to ascertain or proclaim YHWH's will arose, but these methods display an even more acute sense of distance from full-fledged prophecy."[4]

Both Greenspahn and Sommer draw upon a wide range of biblical, Second Temple, and rabbinic sources in their inquiries. What is conspicuously absent from both articles, however, is a serious consideration of the evidence from the Dead Sea Scrolls.[5] To be sure, Greenspahn's article appeared before the full availability of the scrolls, and Sommer's was likely written before the full impact of the availability of the scrolls was felt outside of Qumran studies. Yet, there is virtually no engagement even with the scrolls that were widely available, a situation found elsewhere in the scholarly literature on this subject.[6] The Dead Sea Scrolls have rightly been understood to have revolutionized so many fields of inquiry in the study of the Bible, and ancient Judaism and Christianity. Yet, they have failed to enter fully into the discussion of prophecy in ancient Judaism. What do the Dead Sea Scrolls teach us about prophecy and how can this help us understand the larger context of Second Temple Judaism?

INTEGRATING THE DEAD SEA SCROLLS

Discussions of prophecy in the scrolls generally focus on the reception of ancient prophecy in the community—as in pesher literature, for example—or to a lesser extent in prophecy at the end of days.[7] The

---

[4] Sommer, "Prophecy," 43.

[5] Greenspahn cites 1QS VIII:16 as evidence for the equation of prophecy and the holy spirit ("Prophecy," 37 n. 4) and notes the existence of "lying prophets" in the Hodayot (ibid., 41). Sommer briefly notes the importance of inspired exegesis at Qumran as a new (non-prophetic) way to access the divine will ("Prophecy," 43–44).

[6] See, e.g., G. Stemberger, "Propheten und Prophetie in der Tradition des nachbiblischen Judentums," in *Prophetie und Charisma* (ed. W.H. Schmidt and E. Dassmann; Jahrbuch für Biblische Theologie 14; Neukirchen-Vluyn: Neukirchener, 1999), 145–174. In discussing Qumran (145–149), he focuses almost entirely on the issue of the eschatological prophet and false prophecy, thereby limiting the potential contribution of the Qumran evidence to his larger study.

[7] For full discussion and bibliography on the study of prophecy in the Dead Sea Scrolls, see Jassen, *Mediating*, 3–4. To this earlier discussion should be added M. Nissinen, "Transmitting Divine Mysteries: The Prophetic Role of Wisdom Teachers in the Dead Sea Scrolls," in *Scripture in Transition: Essays on the Septuagint, Hebrew Bible, and Dead Sea*

dearth of scholarship on ongoing prophetic activity has in large part been driven by the nature of the evidence provided by the scrolls. References to contemporary prophecy employing explicit prophetic terminology (e.g., נביא, חזה) are rare. Such terminology is primarily employed to refer to biblical prophecy.[8] Thus, there is seemingly no (or little) evidence to consider.

Any attempt to discuss prophecy in the Dead Sea Scrolls and its larger contribution to the study of Second Temple Judaism must begin by overcoming this terminological pitfall. Just because the Qumran community restricts its use of explicit prophetic terminology to ancient prophets does not mean that it does not regard prophecy as a live institution.[9] Moving beyond the terminological constraints, we must inquire as to how the community envisions continued modes of human-divine communication. At the same time, however, this discussion should include only those forms of human-divine communication that the community deems to be commensurate with the activity of the ancient prophets. The abundance of material in the Qumran corpus that reconceptualizes ancient prophets and prophetic activity provides a critical starting point for charting the community's own conceptualization of prophecy.[10]

My suggestion, therefore, is to move away from the terminological constraints and emphasize (1) prophetic-revelatory phenomena and (2) new modes of transformed prophetic activity. The evidence provided by the scrolls, some of which I will examine here, indicates that the Qumran community recognizes a distinction between ancient prophecy and the

---

Scrolls in Honour of Raija Sollamo (ed. A. Voitila and J. Jokiranta; JSJSup 126; Leiden: Brill, 2008), 513–533; K. de Troyer, A. Lange, and L.L. Schulte, eds. *Prophecy after the Prophets? The Contribution of the Dead Sea Scrolls to the Understanding of Biblical and Extra-Biblical Prophecy* (CBET 52; Leuven: Peeters, 2009).

[8] See Jassen, *Mediating*, 25–131, for treatment of the uses of explicit biblical terminology in the scrolls (נביא, חזה, משיח, איש האלהים, and עבד).

[9] See, e.g., H. Barstad, "Prophecy at Qumran?" in *In the Last Days: On Jewish and Christian Apocalyptic and its Period* (ed. K. Jeppsen, K. Nielsen, and B. Rosendal; Aarhus: Aarhus University Press, 1996), 104–120, who restricts his study to explicit biblical terminology. Barstad's conclusion that prophecy was not a live phenomenon at Qumran is therefore based on a limited set of evidence and ignores the much wider and variegated world of prophecy at Qumran.

[10] For fuller exposition of this methodology, see Jassen, *Mediating*, 4–11, idem, "Prophets and Prophecy." See the similar approach in G.J. Brooke, "Prophecy and Prophets in the Dead Sea Scrolls: Looking Backwards and Forwards," in *Prophets, Prophecy, and Prophetic Texts in Second Temple Judaism* (ed. M.H. Floyd and R.D. Haak; Library of Hebrew Bible/Old Testament Studies 427; New York: T&T Clark, 2006), 151–165. On the issue of terminology, see also Nissinen, "Transmitting," esp. 515–517.

contemporary related phenomenon. At the same time, the community views itself and its activity as commensurate with ancient prophetic practice. In this sense, I agree with Sommer's assertion that Jews in the Second Temple period developed alternative ways to mediate the divine word and will. Unlike Sommer, however, I am proposing that the Qumran corpus indicates that these alternative models were in fact regarded as prophecy.

In this article, I examine several texts from among the Dead Sea Scrolls that provide insight into the Qumran community's view regarding ongoing prophetic activity and the nature of its application. I then offer some suggestions regarding how these insights can be employed to understand better related phenomena in wider segments of Second Temple Judaism.[11]

READING FOR PROPHECY WITHOUT PROPHETIC TERMINOLOGY: THE CASE OF THE *HODAYOT* (*THANKSGIVING HYMNS*) AND JOSEPHUS

Let me now discuss one particular text that I think illustrates well many of the suggestions that I am making. 1QH^a XII:5–29 (Sukenik: col. IV) describes a bitter conflict between a leader of the Qumran community (possibly the Teacher of Righteousness) and the community's enemies.[12] The main thrust of the hymn is to condemn the opponents for their illegitimate attempt to change the law and, as we so often find in sectarian polemics, for just being all-around bad people. This invective, however, is couched in a much larger assessment of the competing claims to divine access by the hymnist (and by extension the sect) and the opponents. As we would expect, the hymnist claims to have direct access to the divine, while the opponents are condemned as illegitimate and misguided in their relationship with the divine.

---

[11] One important area not addressed here is scriptural interpretation as prophecy. On this, see Jassen, *Mediating*, passim; idem, "Prophecy and Prophets."

[12] Some parallel Cave 4 content is preserved, though no significant variants exist (4Q430 1–7 par. 1QH^a XII:13–19; 4Q432 8 1 par. 1QH^a XII:10). This hymnic unit is generally understood as half of a larger hymn that continues in XII:29–XIII:4 by describing the failings of humans (see J.A. Hughes, *Scriptural Allusions and Exegesis in the Hodayot* [STDJ 59; Leiden: Brill, 2006], 103–104). Fuller treatment of this hymn can be found in Jassen, *Mediating*, 280–290; idem, "Prophecy and Prophets." Translations follow M. Wise et al. in *Poetic and Liturgical Texts* (ed. D.W. Parry and E. Tov; The Dead Sea Scrolls Reader 5; Leiden: Brill, 2005).

What is interesting here, however, is that it is the enemies who are described with explicit prophetic terminology (lines 10, 20: חוזי רמיה, "seers of deceit" and חוזי תעות, "seers of error"; line 16: נביאי כזב, "lying prophets").[13] In contrast, the hymnist never identifies himself as a prophet. Rather, he continually maintains that only he has access to God and only he has been the recipient of true revelation. The hymnist's claims are asserted at the very beginning (lines 5–6):

> I give thanks to you, O Lord, for you have made my face to shine by your covenant, and [ ] I seek you, and as an enduring dawning, as [perfe]ct light (לאור | תו[ם]), you have revealed yourself (הופעתה) to me.

Two circuitous terms are employed here to describe the hymnist's intimate relationship with the divine. First, the peculiar locution לאור | תו[ם] is often understood as the singular form of the Urim and Thummim—oracular devices employed to access the divine will—and thus attests to the hymnist's claims of divine access.[14] Second, the experience of divine revelation is expressed with the seldom used verb יפע.[15] This twofold circumscribed language underscores the hymnist's claim of revelation at the same time as it identifies it as entirely unique.

The rest of the hymn serves to emphasize this point further while simultaneously rejecting the alternative claims of the opponents. Thus, lines 6–7 assert that the enemies are led by "mediators of deceit," while in line 8 the hymnist reaffirms his closeness to God by identifying himself as a conduit for divine strength—"You displayed your might through me." The following lines present the core element of the conflict and provide further contrast between the competing revelatory claims. The enemies are condemned again as "mediators of a lie" (מליצי כזב) and also "seers of deceit" (וחוזי רמיה), the latter term using the explicit prophetic epithet חזה. The long invective against the enemies' attempt to seek divine sanction for alteration of the law continues in line 16 with the claim that they incorrectly sought the intervention of "lying prophets" (נביאי כזב).[16]

---

[13] See also the use of מליץ, "mediator" (lines 7, 9), which may have a prophetic nuance (S. Holm-Nielsen, *Hodayot: Psalms from Qumran* [ATDan 2; Aarhus: Universitetsforlaget, 1960], 161 n. 29; Hughes, *Scriptural Allusions*, 107; Nissinen, "Transmitting," 531).

[14] First suggested by E.L. Sukenik, מגילות גנוזות: מתוך גניזה קדומה שנמצאה במדבר יהודה: סקירה שניה (Jerusalem: Bialik Institute, 1950), 43. On the restoration, see Jassen, *Mediating*, 370 n. 30.

[15] For its revelatory use, see Deut 33:2; Pss 50:2; 80:2; 94:1 (cf. 1QH[a] XVII:31; XXIII:5–7). See Holm-Nielsen, *Hodayot*, 80–81; Hughes, *Scriptural Allusions*, 106.

[16] Most scholars view the "lying prophets" as identical with the general opponents

In lines 22–23, the hymnist once again states that the enemies reject him notwithstanding his status as a recipient of divine revelation:

> For they esteem [me] not [thou]gh you display your might through me, and **reveal yourself** (ותופע) to me in your strength **as a perfect light** (לאורתום) ...

The entire expression parallels the earlier revelatory claims in lines 5–6 and 8 and therefore forms a "revelatory" *inclusio* for the intervening hymnic unit:

Table 1. The *Inclusio* Formed by 1QHª XII:5–6, 8 and 22–23

1QHª XII:5–6, 8	1QHª XII:22–23
אודכה אדוני כי^א האירותה פני לבריתכה ומ[ו]אדורשכה וכשחר נכון לאור[תו]ם הופעתה לי	כיא לא יחשבונ[י ע]ד הגבירכה בי ותופע לי בכוחכה לאורתום
(5) *vacat* I give thanks to you, O Lord, for you have made my face shine by your covenant, and [ ] (6) [ ] I seek you, and as an enduring dawning, **as [perfe]ct light, you have revealed yourself to me.**	For (23) they esteem [me] not [thou]gh you display your might through me, **and reveal yourself to me in your strength as a perfect light.**
ולא יחשבוני בהגבירכה בי	
(8) Neither did they esteem me; even when you displayed your might through me.	

The implication of this literary presentation is clear. The hymnist alone has received true revelation. The oppositional language employed through the intervening portions of the hymn frames the entire passage as the hymnist's explicit claim of revelation and a rejection of the competing claims of his would-be prophetic opponents.

The theme of illumination (אור) found at the beginning of the hymn (line 5) appears once more in the remainder of the hymn and generates another "revelatory" *inclusio* with material from the opening portion of the hymn:

---

throughout the hymn. It is clear, however, that the prophets are a separate group who are sought out by the opponents (see Jassen, *Mediating*, 286–287).

Table 2. The *Inclusio* Formed by 1QHᵃ XII:5 and 27

1QHᵃ XII:5	1QHᵃ XII:27
אודכה אדוני כיᵃ **האירותה** פני לבריתכה	ובי **האירותה** פני רבים
I give thanks to you, O Lord, for **you have made my face shine** by your covenant	But by me **you have illumined** the face of many (or the general membership)

This second *inclusio* transforms the hymnist from an individual recipient of revelation to a prophetic messenger. In line 5, the hymnist exclaims that God has made *his* face shine. As made clear by the ensuing content, the hymnist refers here to his receipt of revelation. In line 27, the same language and imagery is employed. Instead of the face of the hymnist being illumined, however, it is the face of the "many."[17] The preposition בי ("by me") identifies the hymnist as the agent of this divine illumination. The hymnist can only serve in this mediating capacity on account of his personal illumination as recounted in line 5. This entire revelatory *inclusio* (lines 5 and 27) encloses the earlier *inclusio* discussed above (lines 5–6 and 22–23). The latter identifies the individual revelation of the hymnist, while the former marks the transformation of this revelation from personal to public. In doing so, the hymnist is not merely one who has unmediated access to God; he is now entrusted with the responsibility to mediate the divine word and will to a larger audience.[18]

This hymn contains many elements that prove helpful in considering larger attitudes toward prophecy in the Qumran community and related segments of Second Temple Judaism. Foremost, this hymn demonstrates the importance of sensitivity to the use and non-use of prophetic terminology. The hymnist deliberately avoids referring to himself with a prophetic designation or more common revelatory language. Yet, there can be little doubt that he viewed his activity as recounted in this hymn as true revelation and as part of a larger institution of prophecy. This

---

[17] The term רבים here may merely designate a larger audience. Alternatively, it may be understood in its narrowly sectarian sense as the "members of the community" (1QS VI:7–21). See the similar expression ולהאיר פני רבים, "to illuminate the face of the many" in 1QSb IV:27.

[18] On the importance of the element of transmission in identifying prophetic activity, see Nissinen, "Transmitting," esp. 515–517; and idem, "Preface," in *Prophecy in Its Ancient Near Eastern Context: Mesopotamian, Biblical and Arabian Perspectives* (ed. idem; SBLSymS 13; Atlanta: SBL, 2000), vii.

terminological peculiarity can be explained in two ways. By "quietly" asserting his close relationship to God at the same time as he employs prophetic titles for his clearly unprophetic opponents, he simultaneously affirms his own status as a true prophet while warning others to be wary of individuals who claim such status. The interest in false prophecy here corresponds with related concerns in other Qumran and Second Temple literature.[19] The second explanation for the avoidance of prophetic titles is the community's recognition that prophecy, while very much a live phenomenon, differs from its ancient Israelite heritage.

The features described here are especially helpful in considering the importance of prophecy in another central body of Second Temple period writings—Josephus.[20] As in the Dead Sea Scrolls, if one were to restrict the discussion of prophecy in Josephus to classical prophetic terminology, only the biblical prophets would be in view. It is well known that Josephus employs a different set of titles for biblical prophets (προ-φήτης) and contemporary ones (μάντις).[21] At the same time, he is consistent in using the latter terminology for phenomena that he (and presumably others) regards as commensurate with the ancient prophetic institution. For example, when Josephus recounts Judah the Essene's prediction of the murder of Antigonus (J.W. 1.78–80), he identifies Judah with the latter terminology. Moreover, Judah's predictions are identified as προρ-ρηθέντων ("predictions") and μάντευμα ("oracles"), but never with the terminological designation "prophecies." At the same time, the activity of Judah the Essene comports with Josephus' more general understanding of the predictive role of prophets and prophecy.[22] While Judah's actions are prophetic, Josephus carefully refrains from identifying him as a prophet.

---

[19] Three texts from Qumran display concern with false and illegitimate prophecy: 4QList of False Prophets ar (4Q339), 4QapocrMoses^a (4Q375), 11QT^a (11Q19) LIV:8–18 (see Jassen, *Mediating*, 299–306). On more general trends in Second Temple Judaism, see Aune, *Prophecy*, 127–128, 137–138; Stemberger, "Propheten," 147–149.

[20] Scholars have devoted considerable attention to prophecy in Josephus: J. Blenkinsopp, "Prophecy and Priesthood in Josephus," *JJS* 25 (1974): 239–262; L.H. Feldman, "Prophets and Prophecy in Josephus," in *Prophets* (ed. Floyd and Haak), 210–239; R. Gray, *Prophetic Figures in Late Second Temple Jewish Palestine* (Oxford: Oxford University Press, 1993); Stemberger, "Propheten," 149–152.

[21] See J. Reiling, "The Use of ΨΕΥΔΟΠΡΟΦΗΤΗΣ in the Septuagint, Philo and Josephus," *NovT* 13 (1971): 146–156, 156; Blenkinsopp, "Prophecy," 240, 262; Gray, *Prophetic Figures*, 23–26. Exceptions are treated in D.E. Aune, "The Use of ΠΡΟΦΗΤΗΣ in Josephus," *JBL* 101 (1982): 419–421; Sommer, "Prophecy," 40 n. 36.

[22] On the predictive character of prophecy in Josephus, see Blenkinsopp, "Prophecy," 242–246; Feldman, "Prophets," 227–230; Gray, *Prophetic Figures*, 30–34.

Josephus provides us with an explanation for his use of distinct terminology. In *Ag. Ap.* 1.41, we find the well-known statement that the
"exact succession of prophets" ended in the time of Artaxerxes. Contrary
to some scholars who read this as a claim that prophecy ended, it merely
serves to mark a distinction in prophetic status.[23] While prophecy does
not cease, it is transformed to such an extent that later prophetic writings
are unfit for inclusion into the sacred history.[24] Prophecy as it was performed and perceived in the pre-exilic period had come to an end at some
point in the early post-exilic period. At the same time, new prophetic
models emerged that performed similar mediating functions. The critical
point is to be able to identify these modified forms of prophecy without
the convenient terminological designators.

Relocating Prophecy in Second Temple Judaism I: Prophecy and Law in the *Rule of the Community* and 1 Maccabees

The hymn discussed above provides additional information regarding
transformed modes of prophetic activity at Qumran. In this hymn, the
opponents are condemned for soliciting the aid of prophets in their
attempt to gain divine approval for modification of the law (1QH[a] XII:10–
11, 15–16). Throughout the sectarian polemic, the enemies are never censured for turning to prophets and contemporary revelation in judicial
matters. Indeed, the Qumran community based its entire legal system
on the progressive revelation of law. For the community, God revealed
the law originally to Moses on Sinai and continued to reveal the interpretation and amplification of the Torah to special individuals throughout each generation—the community representing the most recent stage
of this progressive revelation.[25] In the case of the enemies' similar claim,

---

[23] On the former understanding of this passage, see, for example, H.S.J. Thackeray,
Josephus: The Man and the Historian (New York: Ktav, 1968), 79; R. Beckwith, *The Old
Testament Canon of the New Testament Church and its Background in Early Judaism*
(London: SPCK, 1985), 371–372.

[24] See S.Z. Leiman, "Josephus and the Canon of the Bible," in *Josephus, the Bible, and
History* (ed. L.H. Feldman and G. Hata; Detroit: Wayne State University Press, 1989), 56.
A similar argument is advanced in Blenkinsopp, "Prophecy," 241; Gray, *Prophetic Figures*,
23–26.

[25] See N. Wieder, *The Judean Scrolls and Karaism* (London: East and West Library,
1962), 67–70; L.H. Schiffman, *The Halakhah at Qumran* (SJLA 16; Leiden: Brill, 1975),
23–32.

the very action of appealing to God for guidance on the application of the Torah is conceptualized as a prophetic experience (lines 15–16: ויבאו לדורשכה מפי נביאי כזב מפותי תעות, "they come to seek you through the words of lying prophets corrupted by error"). The larger question, however, is did the community also conceive of its own revelatory legislative activity as prophecy and its inspired legislators as prophets?[26]

As a way to think about this question, I would like to compare the primary statement regarding the community's attitude toward the role of the classical prophets in the progressive revelation of law as articulated in column VIII of the *Rule of the Community* and the community's own self-identity as recipients of progressive revelation as articulated in columns V and IX.[27] 1QS VIII.15–16[28] identifies two means by which the law as originally transmitted by Moses continues to be applied and amplified post-Sinai. This passage begins with the citation of Isa 40:3 that the community viewed as programmatic for its own retreat to the desert and study of the Torah. The Torah is then further explained as something that was commanded "to do" (לעשות)—that is, to observe.[29] The Torah of Moses, according to the *Rule of the Community*, is not self-sustaining in the sense that it can be observed in full without recourse to any external explication and amplification. The employment of "to do" introduces a two-fold model for how the Torah transmitted by Moses can be "applied" in full by the sectarian community, a model presumably demanded for the rest of Israel as well.[30]

First, the community is exhorted to observe the law "according to everything which has been revealed (הנגלה) (from) time to time" (line 15). This expression articulates the sectarian belief that the proper understanding of the Torah is apprehended through a system of periodic leg-

---

[26] For a much fuller exploration of this question, see A.P. Jassen, "The Presentation of the Ancient Prophets as Lawgivers at Qumran," *JBL* 127 (2008): 307–337.

[27] Translations of 1QS follow E. Qimron and J.H. Charlesworth, "Rule of the Community (1QS; cf. 4QS MSS A–J, 5Q11)," in *The Dead Sea Scrolls: Hebrew, Aramaic, and Greek Texts with English Translations*, vol. 1: *Rule of the Community and Related Documents* (ed. J.H. Charlesworth et al.; The Princeton Theological Seminary Dead Sea Scrolls Project; Tübingen: Mohr Siebeck, 1994), 1–107.

[28] Note that 4QSᵉ (4Q259) 1 iii 5–6 lacks text corresponding to 1QS VIII:15b–IX:12. Space does not allow a full exploration of the implications of this different recension (see Jassen, "Presentation," 320 n. 40, 332–333)

[29] On the understanding of the Torah as the antecedent of "to do" (rather than "study of the Torah"), see P. Wernberg-Møller, *The Manual of Discipline* (STDJ 1; Leiden: Brill, 1957), 129 and further discussion in Jassen, "Presentation," 320–321.

[30] Wieder, *Judean Scrolls*, 78. Compare 1QS I:1–3, which employs the identical language of "observing" (לעשות) the law of Moses.

islative revelations. This passage, however, seems to speak only in generalities, merely introducing the sectarian belief in progressive revelation as
a mechanism for comprehending the Torah and its post-biblical application.[31] Indeed, wedged between Moses and the prophets, these periodic
revelations seem to lack a recognized time-frame and easily identifiable
audience.

This general statement regarding the centrality of progressive revelation is followed by a description of the first post-Sinai stage—the
prophets: "and according to that which the prophets have revealed by his
holy spirit" (line 16). The prophets are here conceptualized as possessing the proper understanding of the Torah of Moses and empowered to
share this knowledge with Israel. This juridical knowledge is intimately
connected with their prophetic status. Following a general statement on
the sect's theory of progressive revelation, the prophets are described
as the initial historical link in the succession of these periodic revelations.

When we compare this passage to two separate statements regarding
the community's role in the progressive revelation, an interesting feature
emerges. The textual correspondences are outlined in table three:

Table 3. 1QS VIII:15–16 Compared to 1QS V:8–9 and IX:13

1QS VIII:15–16	1QS V:8–9	1QS IX:13
התורה ... ביד מושה	תורת מושה	לעשות את[23] רצון אל
The Torah ... through Moses	The Torah of Moses	To do God's will
א[ש]ר צוה	ככול אשר צוה	
Wh[ic]h he commanded	According to all that he commanded	
לעשות ככול הנגלה עת בעת	לשוב אל ... בכול לב ובכול נפש לכול הנגלה ממנה	ככול הנגלה לעת בעת
To do according to everything that has been revealed (from) time to time	To return ... with all heart and with all soul, according to everything that has been revealed from it	According to everything which has been revealed from time to time

---

[31] Wieder, *Judean Scrolls*, 78; Schiffman, *Halakhah*, 26.
[32] 4QS[e] (4Q259) lacks this word.

1QS VIII:15–16	1QS V:8–9	1QS IX:13
וכאשר גלו הנביאים ברוח קודשו	(לכול הנגלה ממנה) לבני צדוק	ולמוד את כול השכל הנמצא ...
And (to do) as the prophets revealed through his holy spirit.	(according to everything that has been revealed from it) to the Sons of Zadok (4QS^b, d: to [the multitude of] the council of the men of the Community)	He [the *maśkîl*] shall learn all the understanding which has been found ...

In both 1QS V and IX, a similar situation is described regarding the Torah and its need for interpretation as is found in 1QS VIII. Once again, the community's general principle of progressive revelation is first introduced as a way to facilitate full observance (1QS VIII:15, IX:13: לעשות; 1QS V:8: לשוב) of the Torah. In 1QS V and IX, however, the next stage is not identified as the prophets. Rather, the community takes the place of the prophets following the general description of the idea of progressive revelation. In 1QS V, the full application of the law is revealed to the Sons of Zadok, or, according to 4QS^b, d (4Q256, 258), "[the multitude of] the council of the men of the Community."[33] In 1QS IX:13 (par. 4QS^e [4Q259] 1 iii 8–10), the ability to do God's will is based on the *maśkîl*'s ability to "learn all the understanding which has been found ...," a reference to sectarian exegetical activity.[34] This fits well with the sect's own understanding of inspired exegesis as the way that the sectarian leaders gain access to the progressive revelation of law. Their revelatory activity, like the prophets before them, represents the realization of the progressive revelation of law through periodic revelations.

The identification of lawgiving as a prophetic task is not commonly found in ancient Judaism. Other contemporaneous and later traditions—such as the authors of the *Temple Scroll* and *Jubilees*, and the rabbis—conceive of a one-time revelation at Sinai in which the entirety of the law and its future amplification are made known.[35] The recognition that the

---

[33] See 4QS^b (4Q256) 4 7–8; 4QS^d (4Q258) 1 6–7. The restoration (לרוב) follows Qimron and Charlesworth (cf. P.S. Alexander and G. Vermes in *DJD* XXVI [1998]: 94, 97, who restore על פי, "in accordance with").

[34] On the understanding of this expression as a reference to the sectarian exegetical process, see Schiffman, *Halakhah*, 33–36.

[35] L.H. Schiffman, "The Temple Scroll and the Systems of Jewish Law in the Second

Qumran community regarded its own legislative-revelatory encounter as somehow prophetic compels us to inquire as to further echoes of this attitude in Second Temple Judaism.

Let me briefly discuss one relevant example. In 1 Macc 4:42–46, we are told about the legal dilemma presented to Judah and the Hasmonean army upon regaining control of the temple and encountering the defiled altar. According to Deut 12:2–3, all altars in Israel that had been used for idolatry must be destroyed. They presumably understood Deut 12:4 (לֹא תַעֲשׂוּן כֵּן לַיהוָה אֱלֹהֵיכֶם, "do not do as such to the Lord your God")—as the rabbis later would—as a prohibition against destroying the altar of the Lord, whereby תַעֲשׂוּן כֵּן ("do as such") refers back to the act of destruction in vv. 2–3.[36] They therefore attempt to apply legal-exegetical reasoning: because the altar has been used for idolatry it must be razed in accordance with Deut 12:2–3. Deuteronomy 12:4, however, says that the altar of the Lord cannot be treated in the same way. Thus, instead of razing the altar, they merely remove its stones and store them away.[37]

At the same time, they recognize that their solution is incomplete and the final status of the stone—and therefore the correct application of Deut 12:2–4—will ultimately need to be resolved. The final legal resolution is placed in the hands of a future prophet, most likely one who will emerge in eschatological times. Rather than apply further exegesis, juridical reasoning, or appeal to tradition—as found in a late rabbinic discussion of this event (see b. 'Abod. Zar. 52b)—Judah identifies the prophet as the final arbiter of the precise harmonization and application of Deut 12:2–4 is this particular context. The assignment of juridical functions to a prophet—particularly in the determination of the precise meaning of two biblical passages—should be situated in the same world as the Qumran community's own prophetic-legislative activity.[38]

Temple Period," in *Temple Scroll Studies: Papers Presented at the International Symposium on the Temple Scroll, Manchester, December 1987* (ed. G.J. Brooke; JSPSup 7; Sheffield: JSOT Press, 1989), 239–255.

[36] The straightforward reading of v. 4 condemns the de-centralized worship in vv. 2–3 (thus NJPS: "Do not worship the Lord your God in like manner"). For the rabbinic interpretation, see *Sipre Deut* 61; *t. Mak* 5(4):8.

[37] See J.A. Goldstein, *I Maccabees* (AB 41; Garden City: Doubleday, 1976), 285.

[38] Later rabbinic tradition would associate such a role specifically with the eschatological Elijah (e.g., *m. Šeqal.* 2:5; *m. B. Meṣi'a* 1:8; 2:8; 3:4–5; *b. Menaḥ* 63a).

RELOCATING PROPHECY IN SECOND TEMPLE JUDAISM II:
PROPHECY AND WISDOM IN THE PSALMS SCROLL AND BEN SIRA

The same hymn discussed above provides insight into an additional modified mode of revelation. As I have repeatedly emphasized, this hymn is about the contrasting prophetic-revelatory claims of the hymnist and his opponents. In addition to the broad strokes in which this debate is framed, we are provided with some more specific details regarding the sapiential framework of the prophetic-revelatory communication. Following the wider polemical tone of the hymn, this too is expressed in oppositional language. Thus, the enemies "hold back the drink of knowledge" in line 11 and reject the "vision of knowledge" in line 18. In contrast, toward the end of the hymn, the hymnist provides details regarding the medium of his revelation: "For you have given me understanding of the mysteries of your wonder, and in your wondrous council you have confirmed me" (lines 27–28). His revelation is experienced neither through visions or dreams; rather, for the hymnist the cultivation of divinely revealed wisdom characterizes his revelatory encounter.[39]

The receipt of divinely revealed wisdom as a prophetic-revelatory encounter is found in two additional sapiential contexts that testify to the worldview of the Qumran community and related segments of Second Temple Judaism—the description of David's literary production in the Psalms Scroll (11QPs[a] XXVII:2–11) and Ben Sira. Both of these texts explicitly identify the receipt of divinely revealed wisdom as a prophetic experience.

Column XXVII of the Psalms Scroll identifies David's literary output and highlights its divine origins.[40] The beginning of the passage underscores David's intellectual achievements and identifies God as the source of his wisdom (lines 2–3). David is thus able to compose 4,050 psalms (lines 4–10). The conclusion of the passage contains a second explanation for David's literary oeuvre—he was granted prophecy from God (line 11). This entire passage reinforces the belief in David's prophetic status and that all the Psalms were written under divine inspiration.[41]

---

[39] On sapiential revelation and the *Hodayot*, see further Jassen, *Mediating*, 366–371.
[40] J.A. Sanders in *DJD* IV (1965): 91–93.
[41] On the view of David as a prophet, see Josephus, *Ant.* 6.166; Acts 1:16; 2:25–31; Heb 11:32. See discussion in J.A. Fitzmyer, "David, 'Being Therefore a Prophet …'" (Acts 2:30)," *CBQ* 34 (1972): 332–339; P.W. Flint, "The Prophet David at Qumran," in *Biblical Interpretation at Qumran* (ed. M. Henze; Studies in the Dead Sea Scrolls and Related Literature; Grand Rapids: Eerdmans, 2005), 158–167; Nissinen, "Transmitting," 514–515.

This passage curiously blends sapiential and prophetic language, though seemingly with little explanation. A closer examination of the passage's literary frame (lines 2–4 and 11), however, reveals the significance of this feature. In the first half of the literary frame, David is described as wise (חכם), "a light like the light of the sun" (ואור כאור השמש), "literate/scribe" (סופר), "discerning" (נבון) (lines 2–3). Moreover, he has received an "enlightened and discerning spirit" (רוח נבונה ואורה) from God (lines 3–4).[42] Were we to stop here, we would think that David's literary output was the direct result of his sapiential acumen.

The concluding portion of the passage, however, provides further details about the prophetic character of David's sagacity. David wrote the psalms under prophetic inspiration bestowed upon him by God (כול אלה דבר בנבואה אשר נתן לו מלפני העליון—"all these he spoke through prophecy which was given to him from before the Most High," line 11). The literary frame merges the sapiential and the prophetic with a "revelatory" *inclusio*. The *inclusio* is reinforced by two paronomastic elements: The discernment (נבונה) that God gave (ויתן) David in the first half is mirrored in the second half by the prophecy (נבואה) given (נתן) to David by God. David's prophetic capabilities as identified in line 11 are the direct result of the sapiential revelation granted to him in line 3.

Let me now discuss briefly another example of the merging of the sage and prophet in our most well-known sage in Second Temple Judaism— Ben Sira.[43] In Sir 39:1–11, Ben Sira outlines the path traveled by a prospective sage, which unfolds in three successive stages.[44] The first stage involves education in both scriptural and sapiential content together with prayer and prudent obedience to God (vv. 1–5). Notwithstanding the sapiential nature of the curriculum, the point of enlightenment in this process is not a purely intellectual one. Rather, in v. 6, we are told that the fully realized sage is "filled with the spirit of understanding (πνεύματι συνέσεως)" from God. As commentators have noted, Ben Sira draws upon language and imagery similar to the receipt of the divine spirit that marks the onset of prophetic inspiration.[45] The ensuing lines provide a three-fold model for how the sage becomes a conduit through which this knowledge is transmitted to the larger community

---

[42] Note the prominence of the theme of illumination (אור), a feature likewise found in 1QH[a] XII.

[43] For fuller treatment, see Jassen, *Mediating*, 310–314.

[44] See B.L. Mack, *Wisdom and the Hebrew Epic: Ben Sira's Hymn in Praise of the Fathers* (CSJH; Chicago: University of Chicago Press, 1985), 93–101.

[45] Ibid., 98–99.

(39:7–11).[46] As the ancient prophets, the sage receives the divine word after a preparatory process and then proceeds to transmit the revealed world to others. Unlike the ancient prophet, however, revelation for the sage is a thoroughly sapiential experience.

The revelatory character of wisdom is further reinforced in Ben Sira's autobiographical note in 24:31–33. As one who has successfully followed the path of the ideal sage, Ben Sira comments on the final stage of this process—sapiential instruction. For Ben Sira, he is not merely a purveyor of wisdom. Rather, his transmittal of divinely revealed knowledge is conceptualized as pouring out knowledge "like prophecy" (ὡς προφητείαν) (24:33).[47] Ben Sira indicates the close proximity of his sapiential activity and ancient prophecy. In doing so, Ben Sira conceives of himself here as analogous to the ancient prophets and therefore in continuity with the prophetic tradition. At the same time, neither Ben Sira nor David in the Psalms Scroll is explicitly identified as a prophet. Rather, their activity is regarded as prophetic. This phenomenon corresponds with the same set of terminological distinctions found earlier in the Dead Sea Scrolls and Josephus.

Conclusion

I began this inquiry by revisiting the question of whether or not prophecy ceased in the Second Temple period. It is equally true that prophecy continues and that prophecy ceases. For some individuals or communities, little distinguishes their own activity from that of the ancient prophets. For others, their models of divine-human communication are radically different than ancient prophecy and are clearly understood as such. The Qumran community provides another way to think about prophecy that can open up additional areas of inquiry elsewhere in Second Temple Judaism. As we have seen, no explicit prophetic terminology is applied to the activity of communal leaders. If we move beyond these terminological limitations, however, and examine prophetic phenomena as conceptualized by the community, a rich world of human-divine communica-

---

[46] See P.W. Skehan and A.A. Di Lella, *The Wisdom of Ben Sira* (AB 39; Garden City: Doubleday, 1987), 452.

[47] The Syriac has "in prophecy" (the Hebrew is not extant). For full discussion of the implications of this variant reading and the range of meanings for the Greek formulation, see Jassen, *Mediating*, 312–313.

tion exists at Qumran. In particular, new models emerge that are either absent or underrepresented in biblical prophecy. Most importantly, these modes of human-divine communication are regarded by the community not merely in continuity with the ancient prophets, but as equivalent to prophetic activity. My brief discussion of prophecy in non-sectarian texts suggests that this approach can inform and be informed by wider currents in Second Temple Judaism and thereby construct a more integrated and nuanced portrait of prophecy in ancient Judaism.

THE DEAD SEA SCROLLS AND
JEWISH LITERATURE AND CULTURE OF THE
RABBINIC AND MEDIEVAL PERIODS

SECOND TEMPLE LITERATURE AND RABBINIC JUDAISM

LAWRENCE H. SCHIFFMAN
New York University

One of the central issues of the history of Judaism is the periodization of its early history. Behind this issue lurks a much more central question: to what extent may we trace continuity between the various bodies of Jewish literature and religious ideas that they embody? When we study the development of Judaism from the late books of the Hebrew Bible, through the texts of the Second Temple period, into rabbinic literature, to what extent do we observe continuity and to what extent do we see change? This question is made more complex by the variegated nature of Second Temple Judaism, so much so that some would prefer to use the designation "Judaisms."[1] So we deal not only with the vertical axis of historical change, but also with the horizontal axis of competing approaches to Judaism at various times—a phenomenon best documented and understood for the Hasmonean period but no doubt also present at other times as well. Within this complex framework, we seek to ask how the Judaism of the various Second Temple period sects, Apocrypha, pseudepigrapha, Josephus and Dead Sea Scrolls, relates to the Judaism of the Mishnah, Talmud and midrash—the rabbinic or Talmudic tradition. What has been continued, and what has been changed; what is old and what is new?[2]

To a great extent this question is complicated by a related issue. In the transition from the period of the Hebrew Scriptures into Second Temple times, the earlier period bequeathed a massive literary legacy to the subsequent history of Judaism—the Hebrew Bible. This religious, literary and historical legacy remains a permanent, indeed formative ingredient in all subsequent Jewish development. Yet although Second

---

[1] J. Neusner popularized this term. See his "Preface," in *Judaisms and their Messiahs at the Turn of the Christian Era* (ed. J. Neusner, W.S. Green, and E. Frerichs; New York: Cambridge University Press, 1987), i–x. This term has been discussed and critiqued by M. Satlow, "Defining Judaisms: Accounting for 'Religions' in the Study of Religion," *JAAR* 74 (2006): 837–860.

[2] Cf. L.H. Schiffman, *From Text to Tradition: A History of Second Temple and Rabbinic Judaism* (Hoboken: Ktav, 1991), 1–15.

Temple Judaism passed the Bible on to the rabbinic tradition, it did not pass on its own literary productions. We can speak of only one text from the Second Temple period as being in the hands of the Talmudic rabbis in its entirety, Ben Sira.[3] Beyond that, they did not have, or perhaps did not want to read, the Dead Sea Scrolls, Apocrypha and pseudepigrapha, nor the works of Philo and Josephus. This hiatus in culture, indeed an abyss from a literary point of view, remains unexplained. It appears on the surface to be a radically different development from the passing on of the corpus of Scripture to Second Temple times. However, the difference is not total. In fact, some twenty-two or so books are mentioned in the Hebrew Bible that did not survive into later periods.[4] The reason may be that these books were not accepted into the canon, which would have insured their preservation. Nevertheless, virtually nothing passed from Second Temple times to the Talmudic era, in stark contrast with the large body of biblical literature that was transmitted into Second Temple Judaism.

If there was no direct literary influence, as seems to be the case, we will have to content ourselves with seeking common ideas and approaches that were passed down as part of a general religious ambience. This is also the case because the halakhic and theological forebears of the rabbis were the Pharisees,[5] and so we have to expect that rabbinic literature and rabbinic Judaism are dependent primarily on the Pharisaic teachings. However, evidence points to no existing written texts, except for written notebooks of halakhic and aggadic literature.[6]

This situation is most probably the result of the penchant for oral tradition associated in the Dead Sea Scrolls,[7] Josephus[8] and later rabbinic literature with the approach of the Pharisees, even if the ideological notion

---

[3] M.Z. Segal, *Sefer Ben Sira ha-Shalem* (2nd ed.; Jerusalem: Bialik Institute, 1971–1972), 12–13, 37–42.

[4] Cf. C.F. Craft, "Books Referred to," *IDB* 1:453–454; J.S. Rogers, "Books Referred to in the Bible," *NIDB* 1:489–491.

[5] Schiffman, *Text to Tradition*, 177–179.

[6] S. Lieberman, *Hellenism in Jewish Palestine* (New York: Jewish Theological Seminary, 1962) 87, 204–205; H.L. Strack and G. Stemberger, *Introduction to the Talmud and Midrash* (trans. M. Bockmuehl; Edinburgh: T&T Clark, 1991), 41–42, 48–49.

[7] L.H. Schiffman, *Reclaiming the Dead Sea Scrolls: The History of Judaism, the Background of Christianity, the Lost Library of Qumran* (Philadelphia: JPS, 1994), 245–255; idem, "Pharisees and Sadducees in *Pesher Nahum*," in *Minhah le-Nahum: Biblical and Other Studies Presented to Nahum M. Sarna in Honour of his 70th Birthday* (ed. M. Brettler and M. Fishbane; JSOTSup 154; Sheffield: JSOT Press, 1993), 272–290.

[8] J.M. Baumgarten, *Studies in Qumran Law* (SJLA 24; Leiden: Brill, 1977), 13–35.

of oral revelation and transmission is actually stated only in the Tannaitic period.[9] At the same time, we can never rule out the possibility of the loss of putative Pharisaic texts whose popularity waned as oral tradition dominated Pharisaic Judaism.[10] Further, such texts would not have been preserved in the Qumran sectarian collection, especially as the sect was so anti-Pharisaic. But in any case, the Pharisees bequeathed no literary materials, only apparently extensive oral traditions, to the Talmudic enterprise. It is possible that as Pharisaic Judaism emerged as the only real survivor of the Second Temple period, books from that period were ignored or suppressed, under the category of ספרים חיצוניים, "outside (apocryphal) books."[11]

More should be said about explicit references to apocryphal works in rabbinic literature. In fact, rabbinic texts only mention two such works, one being Ben Sira, that the rabbis apparently knew and that is quoted.[12] Another is a certain book called "Sefer ben Laʿana,"[13] the contents of which we have absolutely no idea. The rabbis explicitly prohibit the reading of such books.[14] There is something of an exegetical controversy regarding the meaning of this prohibition. On the one hand, it might be a blanket prohibition forbidding the reading of these texts under any circumstances. The assumption would be that it is forbidden to write down any books other than those of Scripture and, therefore, to read them. The other interpretation holds that what was prohibited was the public reading of these books as part of the lectionary. In this case, it would be permitted to read such books privately. Such an approach would explain the quotation of Ben Sira by the rabbis.[15]

An interesting parallel that will serve as an example of this phenomenon is the fundamental agreement of the theme of *Jubilees*, namely that the patriarchs observed all the laws later to be given at Sinai, with some rabbinic statements[16] and a variety of aggadot. Apparently, this also was part of the common heritage of Second Temple Judaism and was echoed by some rabbis.

---

[9] Strack and Stemberger, *Introduction*, 36–40.

[10] M.S. Jaffee, "Writing and Rabbinic Oral Tradition: On Mishnaic Narrative, Lists and Mnemonics," *Journal of Jewish Thought and Philosophy* 4 (1994):123–146.

[11] *M. Sanh.* 10:1; *y. Sanh.* 10:1 (28b); *b. Sanh.* 100b.

[12] Above, n. 3.

[13] *Y. Sanh.* 10 (28a); cf. *Qoh. Rab.* to 12:12 that substitutes "Sifre ben Tigla."

[14] *M. Sanh.* 10:1. Cf. *b. Sanh.* 100b (*baraita*).

[15] Cf. I. Lipschutz, *Tifʾeret Yisraʾel* to *m. Sanh.* 10:1 (in Mishnah, ed. Vilna) who permits occasional reading of heretical books or those of other religions.

[16] An addition to the end of the tractate in *m. Qidd.* 4:14; *b. Yoma* 28b.

Numerous sectarian groups are in fact mentioned in rabbinic literature.[17] These groups, however, while apparently practicing modes of piety similar to those that we might expect based on what we now know from the Dead Sea Scrolls, seem in no way to be identifiable with the specific literary works that we have from the Second Temple period. Rather, it appears that the later rabbis were aware of the general nature of Judaism in the pre-70 C.E. period. Indeed, they blamed the phenomenon of sectarianism for the disunity that led to the destruction.[18] However, none of the reports that they preserve can be directly associated with the textual materials from Second Temple times. We can only assume, again, that they did not or would not read these materials.

It is necessary to stress that the sect of the Essenes is not mentioned by name in rabbinic literature unless one of the minor sects mentioned is identical to them, but this is not likely.[19] Attempts to claim that the Boethusians, *baytosim*, are in fact none other than the Essenes[20] have failed to garner significant support because of the philological difficulties involved.[21] While it is possible that some practices of the Essene sect might be described somewhere in rabbinic literature, we see as more fruitful an understanding that the Essenes, as described by Philo,[22] Josephus,[23] and Pliny the Elder,[24] most likely shared the Saducean-type halakhic tradition that is indeed polemicized against in rabbinic texts.[25]

One area in which rabbinic literature provides fruitful parallels to sectarian organization is that of the system of entry into the sect and the close link between purity law and sectarian membership. Further,

---

[17] K. Kohler, "Essenes," *JE* 5:224–227; M. Mansoor, "Sects," *EncJud* (1972) 14:1097–1089; C. Rabin, *Qumran Studies* (Scripta Judaica 2; Oxford: Oxford University Press, 1957), 38–52.

[18] *Y. Sanh.* 10:6 (29c).

[19] Kohler, "Essenes," 224–227.

[20] J.M. Grintz, "'Anshe 'ha-Yaḥad'—'Issiyim—Bet (Es)sene," *Sinai* 32 (1952/1953): 11–43 (Hebrew).

[21] Cf. R. Harari "Boethusians," *Encyclopedia of the Dead Sea Scrolls* (ed. L.H. Schiffman and J.C. VanderKam; 2 vols.; Oxford: Oxford University Press, 2000), 1:100–102.

[22] *Good Person* 75–87.

[23] *Ant.* 18.18–22; *J.W.* 2.119–161.

[24] *Nat.* 5.15.

[25] M.R. Lehmann, "The *Temple Scroll* as a Source of Sectarian Halakhah," *RevQ* 9 (1978): 579–588; Y. Sussmann, "The History of Halakha and the Dead Sea Scrolls: Preliminary Observations on *Miqṣat Ma'ase ha-Torah* (4QMMT)," *Tarbiz* 59 (1989/1990): 11–76 (Hebrew); idem, "The History of the Halakha and the Dead Sea Scrolls: Preliminary Talmudic Observations on *Miqṣat Ma'aśe ha-Torah* (4QMMT)," in *DJD* X (1994): 179–200.

a similar system was in effect for the *ḥavurah*, a term designating a small group of those who practiced strict purity laws, extending temple regulations into private life even for non-priests. Scholarly literature has tended to associate this group with the Pharisees,[26] most probably correctly, but the textual evidence seems to separate these terms. In any case, the detailed regulations pertaining to entering the *ḥavurah* are more closely parallel to the initiation rites of the Qumran sect than they are to the descriptions of the Essenes in Josephus with which they also share fundamental principles.[27]

Some practices of the Qumran sect are indeed mentioned in rabbinic polemics against heterodoxy, termed *derekh aḥeret* (literally, "another way").[28] But these practices are too few to indicate any kind of real knowledge of the Qumran sect or its practices or of other sectarian groups as a whole.

One interesting area is that of calendar disputes. For us, it is a commonplace that alongside the calendar of lunar months and solar years used by the Pharisaic-rabbinic tradition, others, including the Dead Sea sectarians and the authors of *1 Enoch* and *Jubilees*, called for use of a calendar of solar months and solar years.[29] While we are aware of the fact that numerous problems still beset attainment of a full understanding of the calendrical situation of Second Temple Judaism,[30] some part of it was clearly known to the rabbis. Rabbinic sources report that certain sectarians, Sadducees and Boethusians, practiced such a calendar, insisting that the holiday of *Shavuot* fall on a Sunday and, hence, that the start of the bringing of the *omer* barley offering commence on a Saturday night.[31] If indeed these rabbinic references are due to the calendar controversy of which we are aware from the scrolls and pseudepigraphal literature, then

---

[26] A. Oppenheimer, *The ʿAm ha-Aretz: A Study in the Social History of the Jewish People in the Hellenistic-Roman Period* (trans. I.H. Levine; ALGHJ 8; Leiden: Brill, 1977), 118–156.

[27] Rabin, *Qumran Studies*, 1–21.

[28] S. Lieberman, "Light on the Cave Scrolls from Rabbinic Sources," *PAAJR* 20 (1951): 395–404; repr. in *Texts and Studies* (New York: Ktav, 1974), 190–199.

[29] J.C. VanderKam, *Calendars in the Dead Sea Scrolls: Measuring Time* (The Literature of the Dead Sea Scrolls; London: Routledge, 1998), 43–90.

[30] See the full-length studies of J. Ben Dov, *Head of All Years: Astronomy and Calendars at Qumran in their Ancient Context* (STDJ 78; Leiden: Brill, 2008) and S. Stern, *Calendar and Community: A History of the Jewish Calendar: Second Century BCE–Tenth Century CE* (Oxford: Oxford University Press, 2001).

[31] *M. Menaḥ.* 10:3; *b. Menaḥ.* 65a–b; *Megillat Taʿanit* to 8 Nisan (ed. V. Noam, *Megillat Taʿanit: Versions, Interpretation, History: With a Critical Edition* [Between Bible and Mishnah; Jerusalem: Yad Ben-Zvi, 2003], 174–179 [Hebrew]).

it seems that the rabbis' knowledge was quite fragmentary or that they chose to pass on only a small part of the picture. From rabbinic sources one would never have gathered that this sectarian calendar was based on solar months and that it represented an entirely alternative system. All we would have known is that there was a disagreement regarding the date of *Shavuot*.

The bottom line of this discussion is that Second Temple literature was not transmitted to the rabbis in any direct way, with the possible exception of Ben Sira, and no Pharisaic teachings in a literary form survive for us from the Pharisees before 70 C.E. except in traditions embedded in later rabbinic texts.

From what we have said so far, one would assume that there simply is no relationship between Second Temple literature and the rabbinic corpus. After all, virtually nothing of Second Temple literature and certainly nothing of the Dead Sea Scrolls sectarian texts appear to have been known to the rabbis. But here is a great irony: when we examine the Judaism of the Dead Sea Scrolls sect as well as much of the literature that they gathered, we find both similarity and interaction with views discussed in rabbinic texts. Further, fundamental ideas expressed in the Apocrypha and pseudepigrapha find their way into the rabbinic tradition. Still to be appropriately explained is the fact that rabbinic literature includes a variety of reflections of historical data preserved for us by Josephus, either in his words or those of his sources, which are somehow reflected in the rather occasional historiographic comments of the sages. In what follows, we will concentrate on examples illustrated by materials preserved in the Qumran corpus, including some that stem from books otherwise included in the Apocrypha and pseudepigrapha.

JEWISH LAW

Sectarian law was characterized by a distinction between what was termed the "revealed law," that is, the written Torah, and the "hidden law," derived by sectarian exegesis and known only by the sectarians.[32] This concept is clearly different from the rabbinic concept of a dual Torah,

---

[32] L.H. Schiffman, *The Halakhah at Qumran* (SJLA 16; Leiden: Brill, 1975), 22–32; S. Tzoref (Berrin), "The 'Hidden' and the 'Revealed': Progressive Revelation of Law and Esoterica," *Meghillot* 7 (2009): 157–190 (Hebrew).

comprising a written law and an oral law. Further, the sectarian view makes no attempt to trace its second Torah to divine revelation at Sinai, seeing it, rather, as something that emerged from the life of the sect and its leadership. At the same time, it is hard to avoid the fact that the sectarian system and the Pharisaic-rabbinic dual Torah approach both provide for a supplement to the fundamental written Torah, solving in slightly different ways the difficult problem of applying the written Torah to the life of the community. Further, both groups share the notion that the second Torah was divinely inspired. It is true that the *Temple Scroll* seems to be based on a very different approach, assuming instead that only one Torah was revealed at Sinai, containing the author's interpretations and enshrining them in his law.[33] While this one-Torah system is at serious variance with that of the rabbis, what we might call the usual revealed/hidden approach of Qumran texts seems to share some of their fundamental concepts.[34]

It is well-known that Tannaitic literature provides two kinds of texts: those that are collections of apodictic laws arranged by subject matter, a form we term *mishnah*, and those that are biblically based, in which the work is organized according to Scripture, termed *midrash*. We have argued at length that the form of Qumran legal materials displays both of these options in what we might term proto-rabbinic mode. Laws, such as the Sabbath laws or laws of courts and testimony, or laws of forbidden sexual unions often appear as a series of apodictic laws organized by subject and titled accordingly. These parallel in form the Mishnaic tractates and even have similar titles. Further, texts like the *Temple Scroll* and some of the legal fragments that survive indicate that some authors chose to express their legal views in the order of Scripture.[35] There is one essential difference. Whereas in rabbinic literature, midrash exegesis must maintain a strict distinction between the words of the Bible and the words of the rabbinic explanations, the *Temple Scroll* felt free to rewrite the text in accord with sectarian assumptions about the Bible and its text.[36] Such an

---

[33] L.H. Schiffman, *The Courtyards of the House of the Lord: Studies on the Temple Scroll* (ed. F. García Martínez; STDJ 75; Leiden: Brill, 2008) 24–25.

[34] Cf. B.Z. Wacholder, *The Dawn of Qumran: The Sectarian Torah and the Teacher of Righteousness* (HUCM 8; Cincinnati: Hebrew Union College Press, 1983), 30–32.

[35] L.H. Schiffman, "Legal Texts and Codification in the Dead Sea Scrolls," in *Discussing Cultural Influences: Text, Context, and Non-Text in Rabbinic Judaism* (ed. R. Ulmer; Studies in Judaism; Lanham: University Press of America, 2007), 21–31.

[36] Y. Yadin, *The Temple Scroll* (3 vols.; Jerusalem: Israel Exploration Society, 1983), 1:71–88; L.H. Schiffman, "The Deuteronomic Paraphrase of the *Temple Scroll*," RevQ 15 (1991–1992): 543–568.

approach would, of course, have been an anathema to the rabbis. A further difference involves the very apodictic statements preserved in Qumran texts. Whereas in rabbinic literature such statements are composed in Mishnaic Hebrew, and therefore are linguistically distanced from the biblical texts upon which they might depend, many Qumran apodictic laws make use of the language of the Bible and even allow us to determine from their phraseology their biblical midrashic basis.

When we come to the actual subject matter of the laws, the situation is also complex. Some laws seem to be virtually the same, as, for example, the statement that the Sabbath begins on Friday at sunset and its derivation from Scripture.[37] While some of the laws are very similar, such as the requirements to wear clean clothes on the Sabbath,[38] some however, differ more extensively, such as the establishment of two separate Sabbath limits[39] or the setting up of courts of ten for judging issues of Jewish civil law.[40] In looking at such examples of legal difference, it is usually the case that they almost always derive from differing interpretation of Scripture from that which is found in the rabbinic corpus. This is certainly the case with the *Temple Scroll*, where large numbers of differences can be seen from rabbinic law and interpretation.

However, most interestingly, these differences often constitute a link between the Second Temple texts and the rabbinic corpus. In many cases only the opportunity to see the alternative interpretations in the Dead Sea Scrolls allows us to understand the religious/intellectual world within which the Talmudic views were being put forth. Much research remains to be done in this area. I will mention just one topic that I hope to study in detail at some point. It is clear that rabbinic laws pertaining to ritual purity and prayer are closely linked to Temple purity laws preserved in the *Temple Scroll* and other Qumran documents. There is simply no other way to understand these laws, even as presented in the Babylonian Talmud.

---

[37] CD 10:14–17 par. 4QD^e (4Q270) 6 v 1–3 (J.M. Baumgarten in *DJD* XVIII [1996]: 160; Schiffman, *Halakhah at Qumran*, 84–87).

[38] CD 11:3–4 par. 4QD^f (4Q271) 5 i 1 (Baumgarten in *DJD* XVIII [1996]: 180); Schiffman, *Halakhah at Qumran*, 106–109.

[39] CD 10:21; 11:5–7; 4QD^b (4Q267) 9 ii; Schiffman, *Halakhah at Qumran*, 91–98, 111–113.

[40] CD 11:4–6; 4Q266 8 iii 4–5; 4Q270 6 iv 15–16; L.H. Schiffman, *Sectarian Law in the Dead Sea Scrolls: Courts, Testimony and the Penal Code* (BJS 33; Chico: Scholars Press, 1983), 24–26.

It seems now to be fairly well accepted that ancient Judaism knew two separate approaches to Jewish law, that of the Sadducees/Zadokites and that of the Pharisaic-rabbinic tradition. The former priestly approach, as has been repeatedly shown, typified the codes of the Qumran sect and such works as *Jubilees* and, to some extent, the *Aramaic Levi Document*.[41] These trends were opposed by the Pharisaic-rabbinic tradition that is preserved for us in Talmudic literature. Due to the strictures of the Pharisees against writing down their traditions or other vicissitudes of preservation we do not have earlier exemplars of Pharisaic-rabbinic material except as represented in the later corpus of the Talmudic rabbis. Nonetheless, careful research methodology allows us to reconstruct the early layers of that material and in so doing often to reconstruct the Pharisaic views that were opposed, explicitly or implicitly, by the scrolls authors. Essentially, therefore, scrolls research has allowed us to uncover an earlier layer of history in which the approach later ensconced in rabbinic works competed with the priestly approach for dominance of the halakhic market. The importance of this perspective in understanding rabbinic literature cannot be underestimated.

This is especially the case when rabbinic literature itself preserves the evidence for the content of the priestly, Sadducean tradition. After the removal of those references to Sadducees (*Ṣeduqim*) that actually constitute intentional alterations by self-censoring Jewish scribes or by Christian censors in the age of printing, we can collect a series of passages that seem to describe this alternative halakhic tradition and which seem to be in general agreement with the information available to us from the scrolls and other Second Temple texts about this approach.[42] In this manner, some sense of the general authenticity of rabbinic materials

---

[41] L.H. Schiffman, "Sacrificial Halakhah in the Fragments of the *Aramaic Levi Document* from Qumran, the Cairo Genizah, and Mt. Athos Monastery" in *Reworking the Bible: Apocryphal and Related Texts at Qumran: Proceedings of a Joint Symposium by the Orion Center for the Study of the Dead Sea Scrolls and Associated Literature and the Hebrew University Institute for Advanced Studies Research Group on Qumran, 15–17 January, 2002* (ed. E.G. Chazon, D. Dimant, and R.A. Clements; STDJ 58; Leiden: Brill, 2005), 177–202; M. Himmelfarb, "Earthly Sacrifice and Heavenly Incense: The Law of the Priesthood in *Aramaic Levi* and *Jubilees*," in *Heavenly Realms and Earthly Realities in Late Antique Religions* (ed. R.S. Boustan and A.Y. Reed; Cambridge: Cambridge University Press, 2004), 103–122.

[42] E. Regev, *The Sadducees and their Halakhah: Religion and Society in the Second Temple Period* (Jerusalem: Yad Ben-Zvi, 2005), 59–202 (Hebrew), but he reaches a different conclusion than we do regarding the affinity of the Qumran texts and Sadducean law (212).

that report on the Second Temple period has been gained and scholars have begun to discard more skeptical approaches of the last generation. This is exemplified, perhaps exceptionally, by the collection of
Pharisee-Sadducee disputes in *Mishnah Yadayim*[43] and the parallel collection in *MMT*.[44] What is astounding here is the presence of a group
of traditions in both places, of course stated from the opposite perspective. In general terms, what becomes clear here is that rabbinic literature and Second Temple texts may often represent opposite sides of the
same coin, that is, two separate approaches to the same set of problems.
Without the use of Second Temple materials we would never have known
this.

PHYLACTERIES, *MEZUZOT* AND BIBLES

A distinct area of halakhah is that of scribal practice. Here it seems clear
that much of the scribal art transcended sectarian religious affiliation.
This would explain why scribal law in rabbinic texts and indeed in later
Jewish tradition is so close to that found when we investigate the actual
artifacts—the Dead Sea Scrolls and other biblical texts from the Judean
desert.[45] Without going into details here, rabbinic Judaism received a
scribal tradition from the earlier Jewish community and, for the most
part, simply passed it down, following virtually the same mechanics for
the production of hides, their preparation, writing, and the storage of
scrolls. Further, if we investigate the *mezuzot*[46] and phylacteries,[47] we can
see the intersection of the common scribal arts with the varying interpretations regarding the contents. Apparently, the sectarians were willing to
include passages from before and after those required by the Pharisaic-
rabbinic tradition, which did not allow any additional material.[48] But the

---

[43] *M. Yad.* 4:6–8.

[44] Cf. E. Qimron in *DJD* X (1994): 147–175.

[45] E. Tov, *Scribal Practices and Approaches Reflected in the Texts Found in the Judean Desert* (STDJ 54; Leiden: Brill, 2004), 258.

[46] J.T. Milik in *DJD* VI (1977): 80–89.

[47] Y. Yadin, *Tefillin from Qumran (X Q Phyl 1–4)* (Jerusalem: Israel Exploration Society, 1969); Milik in *DJD* VI (1977): 34–79; Tov, *Scribal Practices*, 256–258. See the full list ibid., 256 n. 314.

[48] D. Nakman, "The Contents and Order of the Biblical Sections in the *Tefillin* from Qumran and Rabbinic *Halakhah*: Similarity, Difference, and Some Historical

commonality in the preparation and construction of phylacteries, for example, and in the practice of *mezuzah*, shows clearly that these were elements inherited from the common Judaism of Second Temple times. This is the case despite the fact that rabbinic traditions connect these religious objects closely to oral law,[49] an approach eschewed by the Qumran sectarians and other Sadducees/Zadokites.

The variegated textual character of Second Temple biblical materials contrasts greatly with rabbinic statements on the subject and with what seems to be the evidence of Pharisaic influence at Masada and in the Bar Kokhba caves. Rabbinic texts assume a much greater standardization of the biblical text than what is in evidence in the Qumran materials and in the secondary use of biblical material in the scrolls. Further, the Septuagint and the use of biblical materials in the Apocrypha and pseudepigrapha often support the looser construction of biblical texts known to us from Qumran, where a variety of texts and text types coexisted.[50] While clearly this is in contrast to what we have observed in rabbinic texts, despite some textual variants in biblical materials preserved there, we cannot be totally certain that Pharisaic Jews in Second Temple times would have had Bibles as standard as those assumed by the Mishnah and Talmud. Josephus does write as though this is the case,[51] in the last part of the first century C.E., but it is not possible for us to be certain about the Pharisees of the early period.

Conclusions," *Cathedra* 112 (2004): 19–44 (Hebrew); idem, "*Tefillin* and *Mezuzot* at Qumran," in *The Qumran Scrolls and their World* (ed. M. Kister; 2 vols.; Between Bible and Mishnah; Jerusalem: Yad Ben-Zvi, 2009), 1:143–155 (Hebrew).

[49] Many of the details of their construction are termed *halakhah le-Mosheh mi-Sinai,* "a law (communicated) to Moses from Sinai."

[50] E. Tov, "Groups of Biblical Texts Found at Qumran," in *Time to Prepare the Way in the Wilderness: Papers on the Qumran Scrolls by Fellows of the Institute for Advanced Studies of the Hebrew University, Jerusalem, 1989–1990* (ed. D. Dimant and L.H. Schiffman; STDJ 16; Leiden: Brill, 1995), 85–102; idem, "Hebrew Biblical Manuscripts from the Judaean Desert: Their Contribution to Textual Criticism," *JJS* 39 (1988): 5–37; E. Ulrich, "Pluriformity in the Biblical Text, Text Groups, and Questions of Canon," in *The Madrid Qumran Congress: Proceedings of the International Congress on the Dead Sea Scrolls, Madrid 18–21 March, 1991* (ed. J. Trebolle Barrera and L. Vegas Montaner; 2 vols.; STDJ 11; Leiden: Brill, 1992), 1:23–41.

[51] *Ag. Ap.* 1.28–29; 42–43. A. Kasher, *Josephus Flavius, Against Apion: A New Hebrew Translation with Introduction and Commentary* (2 vols.; Jerusalem: Merkaz Zalman Shazar, 1996), 1:60–62, 72 (Hebrew).

HERITAGE OF BIBLICAL EXEGESIS

Certainly prominent and basic to the continuity between Second Temple and rabbinic Judaism is the area of biblical exegesis. After all, biblical interpretation stands as the basis for Judaism throughout its history and all its manifestations. But even here, as we will see, the issues are complex.

One area of almost complete continuity is that of translation of the Bible. Here we deal with two versions, the Greek translation (LXX) and the Aramaic Targumim.

Regarding the Greek, one might gather from the Tannaitic parallel[52] to the account of the seventy-two elders in the *Letter of Aristeas* that the rabbis, on the one hand, saw the translation as a tragic step in the Hellenization of the Jews, but at the same time approved of the actual translation, at least of the modifications supposedly made by the elders for polemical reasons. On the other hand, scholarly investigation of these variants shows that the account reflects no actual familiarity with the Septuagint[53] which, like the other Greek Jewish literature, was apparently lost to the rabbinic Jewish community by this time. This is despite the fact that after the Septuagint, additional Jewish translations were created or adapted to bring the Greek closer to the Masoretic Text that was now the standard for Jews.[54] Clearly, the Greek Bible simply became identified with Christianity, despite the use of the Septuagint by Josephus and/or his assistants.

Regarding Aramaic the situation is more complex. Although the small fragment of *Targum Leviticus* found at Qumran[55] has exegetical parallels with the later Leviticus Targumim and rabbinic exegesis,[56] the actual Targum text from Qumran was not taken up by the rabbis. This is more apparent from examination of the *Job Targum*, the other Targum text preserved (very substantially) at Qumran.[57] Here we see that, like the *Targum Job* preserved by the rabbinic community, this is a very literal trans-

---

[52] *B. Meg.* 9a–b.

[53] E. Tov, "The Rabbinic Traditions concerning the 'Changes' Inserted in the Septuagint Translation of the Pentateuch and the Question of the Original Text of that Translation," in *I.L. Seeligmann Volume: Essays on the Bible and the Ancient World* (ed. A. Rofé and Y. Zakovitch; 3 vols.; Jerusalem: Rubinstein, 1983), 2:371–393 (Hebrew).

[54] E. Tov in *DJD* VIII (1995): 102–158.

[55] J.T. Milik in *DJD* VI (1977): 86–89.

[56] M. Kasher in *DJD* VI (1977): 92–93.

[57] J.P.M. van der Ploeg and A.S. van der Woude with the collaboration of B. Jongeling, eds. and trans., *Le Targum de Job de la Grotte XI de Qumrân* (Leiden: Brill, 1971).

lation.[58] Tannaitic tradition mentions that both Rabban Gamliel I and II buried Job Targums[59] because of the belief that translation was part of the oral law that was forbidden to be written. No mention of sectarian provenance appears, and in any case there is nothing at all sectarian about the Qumran *Job Targum*. Yet there is no literary relationship between these two Job Targums. The Second Temple version apparently fell into disuse and was replaced by a later one. All in all, then, rabbinic tradition continued the pattern of translation, but initially rejected it in the form of a written text. All pre-70 C.E. Targumim were lost and later texts, composed or at least recorded after the rabbis loosened up their prohibition of writing the oral law, replaced the old, lost ones.[60]

Another area to look at is in the vast library of Second Temple books containing non-literal exegesis of the Bible of the type usually termed rewritten Bible or expansions on the biblical text. In some of the exegetical presumptions of these texts, they seem similar to rabbinic aggadah. Here we need to distinguish form from content. Whereas the Second Temple texts of the pseudepigrapha and numerous Dead Sea Scrolls allow the authors to invade the actual biblical texts, as is done in the *Genesis Apocryphon*, *Jubilees* and for halakhah in the *Temple Scroll*, it seems that the barrier between written and oral texts for the rabbis meant that such books were totally forbidden.

The rabbis seem to maintain this distinction strictly, even with the gradual abeyance of the prohibition of writing the oral law, so that not a single literary contact can be traced between these texts and rabbinic literature.[61] However, where we also see parallels is in the examination of the specific units of interpretation and sometimes in the actual content. In general terms, we can see specific passages that use exegetical

---

[58] M. Sokoloff, *The Targum to Job from Qumran Cave XI* (Bar-Ilan Studies in Near Eastern Languages and Culture; Ramat-Gan: Bar-Ilan University, 1974), 6–8.

[59] *T. Šabb.* 13:2 (S. Lieberman, ed., *Tosefta Seder Moʿed* [New York: Jewish Theological Seminary of America, 1962], 57); S. Lieberman, *Tosefta Ki-Fshuṭah* (New York: Jewish Theological Seminary of America, 1955), 3:203–204.

[60] L.H. Schiffman, "Translation as Commentary: Targum, Midrash and Talmud," in *La Bibbia nelle Culture dei Popoli: Ermeneutica e Comunicazione: Atti del Convegno Internazionale, Pontificia Università Urbana, 10–11 maggio 2007* (ed. A. Gieniusz and A. Spreafico; Vatican City, Rome: Urbaniana University Press, 2008), 32–45.

[61] Apparently some textual materials reached the medieval Jewish community. See L.H. Schiffman, "Second Temple Literature and the Cairo Genizah," *PAAJR* 63 (1997–2001): 139–161; M. Himmelfarb, "Some Echoes of *Jubilees* in Medieval Hebrew Literature," in *Tracing the Threads: Studies in the Vitality of Jewish Pseudepigrapha* (ed. J.C. Reeves; SBLEJL 6; Atlanta: Scholars Press, 1994), 115–141.

techniques similar to those of the rabbis later on. What is striking, however, is that often in these examples the interpretations of the rabbis are different. At times, there are common interpretations and these were no doubt part of the traditions inherited by the rabbis from Second Temple times. Often, however, rabbinic tradition directly contradicts such interpretations found in earlier books.

One type of scrolls exegesis with no real resonance in rabbinic literature is the pesher. This form of contemporizing exegesis argues for a two-step process of prophecy and assumes that the earlier prophets did not really speak to their own times but to Second Temple historical circumstances.[62] Despite some homiletical flourishes here or there, this form of exegesis and most of its content has little relevance in rabbinic literature

Sectarian versus Rabbinic Theology

Both Second Temple texts and rabbinic literature were heir to the complex and often contradictory theological views of the various biblical books. However, it goes without saying that such basic theological ideas of Judaism as God as the creator, revelation of the Torah, or hope in a coming redemption are shared by both corpora. The more important question is whether ideas that are unique to Second Temple period texts and that represent substantive development from or differences with common biblical notions are continued in rabbinic Judaism. Does Tannaitic Judaism in its theology inherit Second Temple literature or does it trace its continuity with the last days of the Hebrew Bible through some other pathway?

An interesting example of this issue is that of the extreme predestination and dualism taught in the sectarian Dead Sea Scrolls.[63] This set of beliefs assumes that God has preplanned the entire course of the cosmos and certainly of humans who are divided into two lots, as are the heavenly beings, who struggle eternally against one another. A person's actions, for good or evil, seem in this system to be beyond his own power, and yet he is punished for transgressing God's law, even including prescriptions that are not known beyond the sect. There is no basis for such ideas in the Hebrew Scriptures, and it is widely assumed that these concepts are

---

[62] Schiffman, *Reclaiming*, 223–241.

[63] J. Duhaime, "Determinism," *Encyclopedia of the Dead Sea Scrolls* 1:194–198; idem, "Dualism," *Encyclopedia of the Dead Sea Scrolls* 1:215–220.

somehow influenced by Persian dualism. When we arrive at the rabbinic corpus we find that predestination is not accepted, although human free will can be countermanded by God.[64] There is no cosmic dualism, but rather we find an inner spiritual dualism of the good and evil inclination (יצר) in each person.[65]

Later, this concept would merge with Hellenistic notions and the two inclinations would be closely identified with the spiritual and physical aspects of humanity.[66] But free will is the basis of God's judgment of people and all are fully informed of their obligations.

Another example of a notion found in the scrolls, also in Second Temple texts, is the notion that prophetic or revelatory phenomena did not end with the story line of Scripture circa 400 B.C.E. but rather continued beyond, into Greco-Roman times.[67] This point of view seems to underlie a lot of material from the period. Yet it is virtually absent from rabbinic literature. The only remnant, the בת קול, some kind of echo of a divine voice, is explicitly declared to be null and void.[68] Clearly the system of oral Torah and its internal development obviated notions of direct divine inspiration, even if weak. Perhaps most importantly, the rise of Christianity seems to have emphasized for the rabbis their notion that the end of the biblical period meant the end of prophecy and the end of writing of scriptural books.

A few words, however, need to be said about eschatology and messianism. Both of these themes are very important in rabbinic literature, with extensive materials devoted to them.[69] This is not to speak of the apocalyptic-type messianic materials that appear in post-Talmudic writings and that in large part resemble such texts as the Qumran *War Scroll*.[70]

---

[64] E.E. Urbach, *The Sages: Their Concepts and Beliefs* (trans. I. Abrahams; 2 vols.; Jerusalem: Magnes, 1987), 1:255–285.

[65] Ibid., 1:471–483.

[66] Cf. ibid., 1:214–254.

[67] A.P. Jassen, *Mediating the Divine: Prophecy and Revelation in the Dead Sea Scrolls and Second Temple Judaism* (STDJ 68; Leiden: Brill, 2007), 279–288.

[68] For sources and bibliography see A. Rothkoff (Rakefet), "Bat Kol," *EncJud* (1972) 4:324–325.

[69] Urbach, *Sages*, 1:49–90; J. Neusner, *Messiah in Context: Israel's History and Destiny in Formative Judaism* (Philadelphia: Fortress, 1984); L.H. Schiffman, "Messianism and Apocalypticism in Rabbinic Texts," in *The Cambridge History of Judaism*, vol. 4: *The Late Roman-Rabbinic Period* (ed. S.T. Katz; Cambridge: Cambridge University Press, 2006), 1053–1072.

[70] L.H. Schiffman, "War in Jewish Apocalyptic Thought," in *War and Peace in the Jewish Tradition* (ed. idem and J.B Wolowelsky; Orthodox Forum Series; New York: Yeshiva University Press, 2007), 477–495.

Here we must distinguish two separate issues, the question of the nature of the messianic figure or figures, on the one hand, and that of the nature of the messianic expectations, on the other. Put simply, we need to ask first how many and what kinds of messiahs are expected and, second, what kind of events are supposed to lead up to the messianic era, and, third, what its nature will be.

Second Temple texts contain three different views of the messianic figure.[71] Some texts present what I would term non-messianic messianism, in which the eschatological future is assumed to come into being but no leader is specifically mentioned. We cannot be certain that in these instances no such leader is expected; it is simply that no messianic figure occurs in the texts. A second variety, perhaps the most common, is that in which it is assumed that there will be one messiah of Davidic extraction. The third approach, known to us from certain of the Qumran sectarian texts as well as from the *Testaments of the Twelve Patriarchs*, is the notion of two messiahs, one of Aaron and one of Israel. I emphasize the words "of Israel" because many books simply assume that the Israel messiah is Davidic, a notion with which I have disagreed based, I hope, on a thorough study of the evidence. In any case, Talmudic Judaism assumes that there must be a messianic figure, even though some rabbis argued that the messiah had already come.[72] The dominant point of view is that of one messiah, a scion of David, expected to bring about the messianic era. No serious parallel at all can be quoted for the notion of a priestly messiah from rabbinic literature. Talmudic tradition does, however, speak of a second messiah, a messiah son of Joseph.[73] No amount of searching will reveal the prehistory of this Josephite messiah (referred to in some later apocalyptic texts as a son of Ephraim) in any Second Temple text.[74] The upshot of this is that the dominant notion in Second Temple times, carried over into rabbinic tradition, was the expectation of one Davidic messiah who would bring about the redemption and rule over Israel as the messianic king. While this approach has extensive rabbinic parallels, other competing approaches seem to

---

[71] L.H. Schiffman, "Messianic Figures and Ideas in the Qumran Scrolls," in *The Messiah: Developments in Earliest Judaism and Christianity* (ed. J.H. Charlesworth; Minneapolis: Fortress, 1992), 116–129; idem, "The Concept of the Messiah in Second Temple and Rabbinic Literature," *RevExp* 84 (1987): 235–246.

[72] *B. Sanh.* 98b.

[73] *B. Sukkah* 52a.

[74] Contra I. Knohl, "'By Three Days, Live': Messiahs, Resurrection, and Ascent to Heaven in *Hazon Gabriel*," *JR* 88 (2008): 147–158.

have become extinct and not to have crossed the literary abyss that we spoke of before, between Second Temple texts and the rabbinic tradition.

On the other hand, a significant difference of opinion among Second Temple texts regarding the onset of the messianic era itself is carried over into rabbinic texts. Two trends have always been observable in Jewish messianism:[75] the first trend, the restorative or naturalistic trend, assumed that the messianic era would usher in a return to the great glories of the ancient Jewish past. A second trend, the catastrophic or utopian, assumed that the messianic era would usher in an era of total perfection, one that never had existed before, in which all evil and suffering would be eradicated. While the naturalistic messianic approach assumed that the messianic era could be created by the gradual improvement of the world, the catastrophic or utopian assumed that a great war, often termed the Day of the Lord, would lead to the total destruction of the wicked and the onset of the eschaton. Both of these views existed in Second Temple texts, but Dead Sea Scrolls materials particularly emphasized the catastrophic and apocalyptic—the assumption that the great war of the Sons of Light against the Sons of Darkness, in which all but the sectarians would be destroyed, would bring on the messianic era.

This very dispute is reflected in rabbinic texts where we find Talmudic sources supporting the onset of the messianic era under either peaceful or violent means. Further, some texts speak of a naturally improving world, where others speak of perfection attained through miracles that bring on the messianic era. Both trends visible in Second Temple literature appear in the rabbinic corpus. In this case, it is simple to account for this situation. This dispute regarding the messianic era was part of the common Judaism of the Greco-Roman period and accordingly passed, with no literary framework necessary, into the thought of the rabbis. We may observe here that rabbinic thought in the aftermath of the Great Revolt and the Bar Kokhba Revolt tended to the more quietistic approaches to messianism. With time, however, the apocalyptic militant notions resurfaced in Amoraic times.

There was also a debate during Second Temple times about the significance of the messianic era and its nature. Clearly, to those who advocated

---

[75] G.G. Scholem, *The Messianic Idea in Judaism and Other Essays on Jewish Spirituality* (New York: Schocken, 1971). Cf. S. Talmon, "Types of Messianic Expectation at the Turn of the Era," in *King, Cult and Calendar in Ancient Israel* (Jerusalem: Magnes, 1986), 202–224.

the Davidic messiah, he was to accomplish the restoration of Jewish military power and national independence, and to rebuild the Temple, which was the goal of the messianic era. On the other hand, it was expected by others, who emphasized the two-messiah concept in which the messiah of Aaron was most prominent, that the true purpose and perfection of the eschaton would be the restoration of the Temple to the standards of holiness and sanctity which it deserved. (We must remember that the Second Temple texts were composed while the Temple still stood.) In the aftermath of two Jewish apocalyptic revolts and the destruction of the land twice at the hands of the Romans, the rabbis sought a restoration of the Davidic glories of old, of a political entity secure and independent. Apparently, in their view this would insure the proper rebuilding of the Temple. Yet they did not see the Temple as the central act in the messianic drama, rather as a part of the process. For this reason, the Aaronide messiah has no parallel in rabbinic literature. This is the case despite the fact that Eleazar the Priest appeared with Bar Kokhba on coins,[76] conjuring up the messianic pair of the *nasi* and *kohen*.

History of Liturgy and Poetry

From First Temple times it is apparent that prayer was a significant part of the individual piety of a fair number of Israelites. Individual prayer was accompanied apparently by poems written for the collective people of Israel.[77] Such prayers seem definitely to have attained a place in the psalmody of the Temple by the Second Temple period. In various Second Temple texts there are individual and collective prayers, and toward the end of the Second Temple period, prayer was becoming institutionalized increasingly, at least as appears from the Tannaitic evidence. From the set liturgical texts preserved at Qumran,[78] it seems that daily statutory ritual

---

[76] Y. Yadin, *Bar-Kokhba: The Rediscovery of the Legendary Hero of the Second Jewish Revolt against Rome* (New York: Random House, 1971), 24–25.

[77] M. Greenberg, *Biblical Prose Prayer as a Window to the Popular Religion of Ancient Israel* (Berkeley: University of California Press, 1983).

[78] D.K. Falk, *Daily, Sabbath, and Festival Prayers in the Dead Sea Scrolls* (STDJ 27; Leiden: Brill, 1998); B. Nitzan, *Qumran Prayer and Religious Poetry* (trans. J. Chapman; STDJ 12; Leiden: Brill, 1994); E.G. Chazon, "Hymns and Prayers in the Dead Sea Scrolls," in *The Dead Sea Scrolls after Fifty Years: A Comprehensive Assessment* (ed. P.W. Flint and J.C. VanderKam; 2 vols.; Leiden: Brill, 1998), 1:244–270; eadem, "Prayers from Qumran and their Historical Implications," *DSD* 1 (1994): 265–284.

had become part of the life of the sectarians who had separated from the sanctuary that they regarded as impure and improperly conducted. These texts appear not to be of sectarian content and may typify wider trends in the Jewish community. Further, the scrolls give evidence of the twice daily recital of the Shema[79] and the use of *mezuzot* and phylacteries, some of which were prepared very much in the same way as the Pharisaic-rabbinic tradition requires.

Additional parallel details indicate the possibility that some Tannaitic practices derived from those in evidence in Qumran liturgical texts. Both corpora require that a benediction of lights be part of the service each morning and afternoon-evening. This seems to be the only required benediction in the preserved Qumran daily prayer texts. However, it seems to be equivalent to one of the two blessings before Shema required by the rabbis.[80]

Qumran liturgical texts include also supplication texts similar to later rabbinic propitiatory prayers, and festival prayers seem to share similar motifs. But we must emphasize that not a single prayer preserved in the scrolls is part of the rabbinic liturgy, and no text of rabbinic prayer was found in the sectarian collection. Again, the parallels in practice seem to derive from the common Judaism of Second Temple times, not from any literary or otherwise direct connection.

The literature of the Second Temple period seems to have played a major role in the development of *piyyut*, Hebrew liturgical poetry from the Byzantine period. Previous to the Dead Sea Scrolls, the evidence for Hebrew poetry in the post-biblical period was given scant attention. Hence, the significance of the poems in 1 Maccabees, for example, and even in the New Testament, not to mention early Jewish liturgy preserved in rabbinic texts or reconstructed from the later prayer texts, was ignored. It was assumed that biblical psalmody was a dead-end tradition to be succeeded later by a de novo form of Hebrew liturgical poetry that developed virtually ex nihilo. When the first scrolls were discussed, the *Hodayot* were taken to be a bad version of Psalms poetry,[81] following the age-old anti-Jewish trope of the decline of Hebrew literature after the "Old

---

[79] In the poem at the end of the *Rule of the Community* (1QS X:10). Cf. Schiffman, *Reclaiming*, 293.

[80] L.H. Schiffman, "The Dead Sea Scrolls and the Early History of Jewish Liturgy," in *The Synagogue in Late Antiquity* (ed. L.I. Levine; New York: Jewish Theological Seminary, 1987), 33–48.

[81] See B.P. Kittel, *The Hymns of Qumran: Translation and Commentary* (SBLDS 50; Chico: Scholars Press, 1981), 6, 14–20.

Testament." No one seemed to realize that we were dealing with the next stage in the dynamic history of Hebrew poetry. Indeed, elements of what are now known as Qumran religious poetry point in various directions toward the style—not content—of the later *piyyut*. This is clear now especially as regards the reuse of biblical material to form post-Hebrew Bible poems and the tendency to create grammatical forms not previously known. But *piyyut*, as a corpus related closely to rabbinic literature, takes the rabbinic liturgical character and its content as a starting point and is suffused with rabbinic midrashim and legal rulings, even if some of them are at variance with those taken as normative in the rabbinic legal texts.

Conclusions

How can we explain the contradictory observations that we are making in this presentation? On the one hand, we have emphasized the lack of a literary pipeline from Second Temple times into rabbinic texts, beyond that of the Hebrew Scriptures themselves. On the other hand, we have pointed to rich parallels and apparent intellectual interaction between those who left us Second Temple texts and those who were apparently the spiritual ancestors of the Tannaim, namely the Pharisees. It would seem that here it is the existence of a "common Judaism"[82] that provides the answer.

First, however, we must return to the vertical and horizontal axes of which we spoke earlier. From the point of view of the historical, or vertical axis, the Second Temple materials are of course earlier texts, and, as we have indicated, they were not read by the rabbis. Hence, we cannot expect them to have had great direct influence. From the point of view of the horizontal axis, we deal with the various approaches to Judaism, and, as we noted over and over, Pharisaic-rabbinic Judaism was at odds with the sectarian and apocalyptic trends, both in Second Temple times and after the destruction. Therefore, what we really seek is not dependence, but dialogue and disputation, and sometimes polemic. We lack adequate documentation of the Pharisaic side to do more than to retroject from

---

[82] The term is taken from E.P. Sanders, *Judaism: Practice and Belief, 63 BCE–66 CE* (London: SCM Press, 1992), 45–47. Cf. S.S. Miller, *Sages and Commoners in Late Antique 'Erez Israel: A Philological Inquiry into Local Traditions in Talmud Yerushalmi* (TSAJ 111; Tübingen: Mohr Siebeck, 2006), 12 n. 41 and 21–28.

rabbinic literature. However, the license to perform such a reconstruction is inherent in the anti-Pharisaic polemics of the Second Temple texts, especially the Dead Sea Scrolls. We therefore suggest a rigorous debate replete with polemics back-and-forth, of which our texts constitute a small sample. This polemic must have been quieted greatly in the aftermath of the destruction when the Pharisaic-rabbinic approach emerged as the consensus. From this point on, in an atmosphere of rabbinic debate, various aspects of the common Judaism of Second Temple times were preserved in the rabbinic movement and its literature. In this way all kinds of ideas crossed the literary abyss we discussed, even without the rabbis' having read Second Temple texts. It is these ideas that constitute the heritage of Second Temple literature and the Dead Sea Scrolls. For the rabbis, however, these texts were vastly outnumbered and overpowered by the Pharisaic heritage, transmitted as an unwritten tradition, that served as the real basis of rabbinic Judaism.

MISHNAH AND DEAD SEA SCROLLS: ARE THERE MEANINGFUL PARALLELS AND CONTINUITIES?

Günter Stemberger
University of Vienna

A central problem in our understanding of Palestinian Judaism in antiquity is the amount of continuity between the time before the destruction of the Temple and the rabbinic period. The assumption or negation of such continuity influences our interpretation of the Mishnah and other early rabbinic texts. Before the discovery of the Dead Sea Scrolls and, above all, the legal texts among them very little was known about the halakhah in the Second Temple period. Texts like the book of *Jubilees*, Josephus or the Gospels were among the few sources dating from the period; their reliability, especially with regard to the actual practice, was much discussed. Mishnah and Tosefta were considered by many as the main sources even for the time when the Temple still stood, based on the widely accepted hypothesis that the anonymous halakhah in the early rabbinic texts has very ancient roots and continues the halakhic tradition of the Pharisees. There was little possibility of controlling this hypothesis. The situation has radically changed with the discovery of the Scrolls. They offer much material that can be interpreted in favour of such continuity; thus, they have been used in order to attribute high antiquity to certain Mishnaic halakhot and, by generalisation, to claim Second Temple, more specifically Pharisaic, origins for much of the Mishnaic system.

Ever since the discovery of the *Damascus Document* in the Cairo Genizah, the halakhic parallels in the Mishnah have been discussed. In 1922, Louis Ginzberg drew on rabbinic materials to identify the author of the *Damascus Document* as a Pharisee.[1] This position has long since

---

[1] L. Ginzberg, *Eine unbekannte jüdische Sekte* (1922; repr. Hildesheim: Olms, 1972); posthumously published in a revised and updated English version: *An Unknown Jewish Sect* (New York: Jewish Theological Seminary, 1970); C. Rabin, *Qumran Studies* (Scripta Judaica 2; London: Oxford University Press, 1957), considered the authors of the text as Proto-Pharisees.

been abandoned, but it remains an "eloquent testimony to the common elements between Qumran and Pharisaic law."[2] After the discovery of the Dead Sea Scrolls, their halakhic aspects have long been rather neglected in comparison with the doctrinal and organizational elements of the people behind them. Early pioneers of research into the halakhah in the Qumran texts were Joseph Baumgarten and Lawrence Schiffman, whose work concentrated on the Qumran Sabbath Code.[3] Both authors have continued their research into Qumran halakhah over the decades and everyone interested in the field stands in their debt. Among talmudic scholars not specialized in Qumran, we must of course mention the pioneering work of Yaakov Sussmann on the halakhic context of *Miqṣat Maʿaśeh ha-Torah*, first published in Hebrew and then in an abridged English version in the official edition of 4QMMT.[4] Israeli scholars have ever since contributed substantial studies in practically all halakhic aspects of the Scrolls.

Some might consider it problematic to speak of halakhah at Qumran, since the term never occurs in the Scrolls. That the designation "seekers of smooth things" (דורשי חלקות) is a pun on the halakhot of their opponents, commonly considered as Pharisees or Proto-Pharisees, has some probability, but cannot be proven. But the term remains most convenient for speaking of the halakhic rules in Qumran texts and its use is justified as long as it does not presuppose a closed halakhic system as that of the rabbis and allows for different halakhic approaches within the texts.

1. A Common Halakhic Basis

As is to be expected, the groups behind the Scrolls shared many, if not most of their halakhot with other Jewish groups of their time. As Schiffman noted long ago:

---

[2] J.M. Baumgarten in *DJD* XVIII (1996): 18.

[3] J.M. Baumgarten, *Studies in Qumran Law* (SJLA 24; Leiden: Brill: 1977; a collection of earlier papers); L.H. Schiffman, *The Halakhah at Qumran* (SJLA 16; Leiden: Brill, 1975); idem, *Sectarian Law in the Dead Sea Scrolls: Courts, Testimony and the Penal Code* (BJS 33; Chico: Scholars Press, 1983).

[4] J. Sussmann, "The History of the Halakha and the Dead Sea Scrolls: Preliminary Talmudic Observations on *Miqṣat Maʿaśeh ha-Torah* (4QMMT)," in *DJD* X (1994): 179–200 (Hebrew version with extensive annotation: *Tarbiz* 59 [1989–1990]: 11–76, with an English abstract on pp. I–II).

Because the tannaim also used exegesis as a method for the derivation of law, the sectarian and Rabbinic traditions often share the same *midrash halakhah*. Also parallels to the sectarian *halakhah* can be found in minority views or old *halakhot* mentioned by the tannaim.[5]

Many of the Sabbath laws studied by Schiffman are very close to what is known from the Mishnah.[6] The same holds true for most other fields of halakhah. The importance of the Scrolls in this regard lies in the confirmation of the antiquity of these laws which cannot be regarded as post-70 rabbinic developments.

It would be uncritical to suppose such halakhic continuity wherever not clearly contradicted by the texts. Many halakhot look similar, but may have quite different intentions. To give just one example: In *y. Šabb.* 1:4, 3d, we read in the name of R. Jeremiah: "Yose ben Yoezer of Seridah and Yose ben Yohanan of Jerusalem decreed that the territory of the gentiles should be unclean, and likewise that that is the case for glass utensils."[7] We find the same tradition quoted in *b. Šabb.* 15a and with the following commentary on it:

> Lo, it was the rabbis of the eighty years before who made that decree ... Eighty years prior to the destruction of the Temple the decree was made that the lands of the gentiles and utensils made out of glass were subject to uncleanness.

This has been paralleled with the passage from the *Damascus Document* 4QD[a] (4Q266) 5 ii 4–6, 8–9:

> 4 [...] his brethren, the priests, in the service, but he shall n[ot ... Anyone]
> 5 of the Sons of Aaron who was in captivity among the gentiles [...]
> 6 to profane him with their uncleanliness. He may not approach the [holy] service [...]
> 8 Anyone of the Sons of Aaron who migrates to se[rve the gentiles, ...]
> 9 ⟨to teach⟩ his people the foundation of the nation, and also to betray (?) [...

Joseph Baumgarten understands this passage of "priests who were in captivity among gentiles or who emigrated into foreign lands where they were subject to gentile powers"; they "are disqualified for the Temple service and as guides 'for the foundation of the nation.'" But since their

---

[5] Schiffman, *Halakhah at Qumran*, 135.

[6] Cf. L. Doering, *Schabbat: Sabbathalacha und -praxis im antiken Judentum und Urchristentum* (TSAJ 78; Tübingen: Mohr Siebeck, 1999).

[7] Translations of rabbinic texts follow those of J. Neusner; they are slightly adapted wherever the context necessitates a more literal translation.

interpretation of the Law actually originated in Damascus, Baumgarten concluded

> that two distinctions might have limited the application of the law. One is the special status of Syria which … was regarded like the land of Israel in some religious matters. The second is the likelihood that the law was intended for priests living among gentiles, not those living in Jewish communities in gentile lands.[8]

Baumgarten does not refer to the talmudic passage, but Eyal Regev does so and sees a halakhic parallel between these two texts.[9] He concludes that the halakhic tradition attributed to Yose ben Yoezer is historically reliable (as are three halakhic traditions connected with him in *m. 'Ed.* 8:4) and go back to the second century B.C.E.; "the halakhic divergence between the Pharisees and the Qumran sectarians had begun in the days of Yose ben Yoezer."[10] He even considers identifying Yose ben Yoezer with the "Man of Lies" mentioned in the *Damascus Document* and in the pesharim.[11] Such historical conclusions certainly go much too far; but I even doubt the comparability of the halakhah: The Qumran text does not speak of foreign lands as such, which disqualify for priestly service, but of priests in captivity among the Gentiles or even willingly migrating to serve them. Not the country of the Gentiles, but the close contact with Gentiles disqualifies the priests. This is far from the general statement attributed to Yose about the impurity of Gentile countries as such.

There are many other halakhot in Mishnah and Qumran which have much in common but still have to be differentiated. Thus, for example, Aharon Shemesh sees important parallels between some halakhot in the field of agriculture in Qumran and in rabbinic texts.[12] In this particular case I doubt that the Mishnah can be used to such an extent as Shemesh does to fill the lacunae of the Qumran texts.

---

[8] Baumgarten in *DJD* XVIII (1996): 9–10. I have quoted his translation (ibid., 50).

[9] E. Regev, "Yose ben Yoezer and the Qumran Sectarians on Purity Laws: Agreement and Controversy," in *The Damascus Document: A Centennial of Discovery: Proceedings of the Third International Symposium of the Orion Center for the Study of the Dead Sea Scrolls and Associated Literature, 4–8 February, 1998* (ed. J.M. Baumgarten, E.G. Chazon, and A. Pinnick; STDJ 34; Leiden: Brill, 2000), 95–107.

[10] Ibid., 104.

[11] Ibid., 105.

[12] A. Shemesh, "The History of the Creation of Measurements: Between Qumran and the Mishnah," in *Rabbinic Perspectives: Rabbinic Literature and the Dead Sea Scrolls: Proceedings of the Eighth International Symposium of the Orion Center for the Study of the Dead Sea Scrolls and Associated Literature, 7–9 January, 2003* (ed. S.D. Fraade, A. Shemesh, and R.A. Clements; STDJ 62; Leiden: Brill, 2006), 147–173.

2. Pharisees and Sadducees behind
the Laws Mentioned in the Scrolls

Before the discovery of the Scrolls, it was well-nigh impossible to control the reliability of rabbinic texts regarding disputes between the Perushim, or the sages, and the Sadducees, or Boethusians. The Dead Sea Scrolls have changed the situation considerably, most dramatically since the publication of 4QMMT, where several halakhic positions attributed to the Sadducees, or Boethusians, in rabbinic texts seem to be defended by the we-group of this text so crucial for the early history of Qumran. Yaakov Sussman, in his already mentioned highly influential article, "The History of the Halakha and the Dead Sea Scrolls," stated that

> comparison of the DS Scroll's halakhic rulings with the halakhic traditions preserved in rabbinic literature reveals that the halakha of 4QMMT is clearly *anti-Pharisaic* and most probably *Sadducean*. This Halakha, in contrast to Pharisaic Halakha, is stringent, uncompromising and harshly formalistic.

He suggests that

> the Essenes (who may well be *Bet Sin* [Boethusians] mentioned in rabbinic literature) followed a Sadducean halakhic tradition. This sect was thus engaged in a dual struggle: an ethical, social and theological conflict with the Sadducees ("Manasse" in their writings), and a halakhic and theological conflict with the Pharisees ("Ephraim").[13]

This equation of the Qumran halakhah with that of the Sadducees and the identification of their halakhic opponents with the Pharisees was accepted with some nuances by many scholars. The Scrolls thus seemed to offer incontrovertible evidence for the direct continuity between early Pharisaic and rabbinic halakhah in essential points. But soon doubts were voiced against a too-straight identification of the halakhic issues involved. I shall briefly summarize the main issues.

a. *Streams of Liquid*

The most hotly debated problem is the equation of the Qumranic *muṣa-qot* with the rabbinic *niṣṣoq*. In *m. Yad. 4:7* we read: "The Sadducees say, We cry out against you, O ye Pharisees, for ye declare clean an unbroken

---

[13] Sussmann, abstract of the article in *Tarbiz*, II.

stream of liquid (*ha-niṣṣoq*)." *M. Yad.* 4:7 seems to correspond to *MMT* B 55–58:

[ו]אף על המוצקות אנחנו אומר[ים] שהם שאין בהם [ט]הרה ואף המוצקות אינם
מבדילות בין הטמא [ל]טהור כי לחת המוצקות והמקבל מהמה כהם לחה אחת

> And concerning the streams [of a liquid poured from a clean vessel into an unclean vessel]: we say that in them there is no [p]urity. And (concerning) the streams: they do not separate between the impure and the pure. For the liquid of the streams and that which receives them (are) alike, a single liquid.

The equation of *niṣṣoq* and *muṣaqot* was most thoroughly discussed by Yaakov Elman.[14] As Elman states

> that single equation of *niṣṣoq* = *muṣaqot*, when viewed systemically, yields contradictory consequences in both the rabbinic/Pharisaic and Qumranic systems of purities ... When we look beyond the mesmerizing lexical equation of *muṣaqot* and *niṣṣoq*, there appears in its place a wealth of possibilities, of varying degrees of likelihood; some, I think, are more probable than the one currently accepted.[15]

John Strugnell and Elisha Qimron, the editors of 4QMMT, suggest:

> Since the word ואף is repeated in this passage, we must distinguish two separate rulings concerning streams. 1. Streams poured into an unclean vessel are unclean. 2. These streams are to be considered as connecting a pure liquid and an impure liquid (so that if the receptacle contains an impure liquid, then the liquid in the upper vessel is also rendered unclean).[16]

If we compare this text with *m. Yad.* 4:7, quoted above, 4QMMT contests the Pharisaic position that a *niṣṣoq* does *not* connect the impure vessel below with the pure vessel above. But even in the opinion of the rabbis (and perhaps already of the Pharisees), at least in some cases *niṣṣoq does* cause impurity, i.e. where a *niṣṣoq* is made up of a viscous liquid, such as honey: "Any unbroken streak (*niṣṣoq*) is clean, except for the thick honey and porridge. The House of Shammai say, Also: one of porridge made from grits or beans, because it shrinks backwards" (*m. Makš.* 5:9).

---

[14] Y. Elman, "Some Remarks on 4QMMT and the Rabbinic Tradition, Or, When Is a Parallel Not a Parallel?" in *Reading 4QMMT: New Perspectives on Qumran Law and History* (ed. J. Kampen and M.J. Bernstein; SBLSymS 2; Atlanta: Scholars Press, 1996), 99–128.

[15] Elman, "Some Remarks," 105.

[16] J. Strugnell and E. Qimron in *DJD* X (1994): 162.

In such cases at least some of the honey or other viscous liquid which was already outside the upper vessel, returns into it once it is put again into an upright position; thus, the liquid confers impurity to the contents of the upper vessel. Elman rightly sees here a problem and doubts the equation of rabbinic *niṣṣoq* with Qumranic *muṣaqot*.

The second part of *m. Yad.* 4:7 "The Pharisees say, We cry out against you, O ye Sadducees, for ye declare clean a channel of water (*'ammat ha-mayim*) that flows from a burial ground" is frequently read in the light of *m. Ṭehar.* 8:9: "A jet of liquid (*ha-niṣṣoq*), [water on] an incline, and dripping moisture, do not serve as a connective (*ḥibbur*) for uncleanness and for cleanness; but a pool of water serves as a connective for uncleanness and for cleanness."

The connection of these two texts with the second part of the statement of 4QMMT that a *niṣṣoq* does not serve as a connective for uncleanness and for cleanness is even more problematic. It is irrelevant for the continuation in *m. Ṭehar.* 8:9: "but a pool of water serves as a connective for uncleanness and for cleanness." The question of two connected pools or ritual baths where the drawn water of the lower one is rendered ritually valid by the pure water of the other is hardly on the mind of the author of 4QMMT in this passage, unless *muṣaqot* includes not only free-falling streams of liquid, but encompasses all streams of liquid including water in pipes and channels, something the rabbis would never consider as *niṣṣoq*. Elman therefore proposes to abandon the tempting *niṣṣoq-muṣaq* equation and offers a range of interpretive options without reaching a final conclusion. But his whole discussion makes it abundantly clear how problematic a neat connection of Qumranic concepts with those of the rabbis can be.[17]

b. *Animal Bones*

M. Yad. 4:6 quotes in the same context of the controversies between Pharisees and Sadducees Rabban Johanan ben Zakkai speaking to the Sadducees:

> Have we naught against the Pharisees save this!—for lo, they say, The bones of an ass are clean, and the bones of Johanan the High Priest are unclean. They said to him, As is our love for them so is their uncleanness—that no man make spoons of the bones of his father or mother.

---

[17] Elman, "Some Remarks," 107–127.

This may be paralleled with *MMT* B 21–23: "And concerning the hide[s] and bones of the impure animal: one must not make [from their bones] and from the h[i]de[s] handles of a v[essel]" (cf. 11QT^a L:4–6); the bones of unclean animals impart impurity. It is not quite clear who the speakers in the Mishnah passage ("they say") are; thus the use of this passage in the comparison between Qumran and the Mishnah is not as clear as might be wished.

c. Ṭevul Yom / *Red Heifer*

Another well known controversy between the Ṣadduqim and the sages (Pharisees?) concerns the degree of purity required of the priest who was to burn the Red Heifer. According to rabbinic teaching the person became pure for rituals outside the temple (but not for eating *terumah*) immediately after the ritual bath, without waiting for sunset—what the rabbis call *ṭevul yom*. M. *Parah* 3:7 presents this as a controversial decision which had to be enforced against the convictions of the Sadducees:

> The elders of Israel used to go forth before them (the priests and their assistants) on foot to the Mount of Olives. There was a place of immersion there (*bet ṭevilah*), and they had [first] rendered unclean the priest that should burn the Heifer, because of the Sadducees: that they should not be able to say, It must be performed only by them on whom the sun has set (*bim'orave shemesh*).

Priestly tradition required of a person who had taken a ritual bath to wait until sundown before being considered pure (Lev 11:29–38; Num 19:9). This also seems to be the teaching of *MMT* B 13–17 on the Red Heifer:

> 13 And concerning the purity of the bull of the purification offering:
> 14 he who slaughters it and he who burns it and he who gathers its ashes and he who sprinkles the [water of]
> 15 the purification offering; all these at the set[tin]g of the sun (*le-ha'arivut ha-shemesh*) become pure.
> 16 so that he who is pure might sprinkle upon the (one who is) impure.

Lester Grabbe accepts that

> the concept of the *ṭĕvûl yôm*, if it existed, would indeed have been rejected by both the Ṣadduqim and the authors of MMT and the Temple Scroll. Nevertheless, neither of the two passages in MMT mentions the *ṭĕvûl yôm* concept explicitly.[18]

---

[18] L.L. Grabbe, "4QMMT and Second Temple Jewish Society," in *Legal Texts and Legal Issues: Proceedings of the Second Meeting of the International Organization for Qumran*

Both the Mishnah and *MMT* refer to the purity of the one who slays the Red Heifer, a point not in the biblical text. More essential is the understanding of להעריו]בו[ת השמש:

> this reading requires a partial textual reconstruction. Although the reconstruction is not unreasonable, it is less than certain. It seems premature to leap to the conclusion that the author must be attacking the rabbinic idea of the *ṭĕvûl yôm*.[19]

It is certainly still highly probable to read *m. Parah* 3 in the context of 4QMMT, but this is far from certain.[20]

d. Calendar—Shavuot

In *m. Menaḥ.* 10 it is discussed whether the details of reaping and offering of the Omer, the first sheaf of barley from which the fifty days until Shavuot are counted, differ depending on the day when it occurs, a Sabbath or a weekday. R. Ishmael is for differentiation, but the sages say that there was no difference whether it was a Sabbath or a weekday. When reaping the sheaf on an evening which is the beginning of the Sabbath, the person who is going to reap the sheaf explicitly asks the bystanders:

> "On this Sabbath?" They say, "Yes." "On this Sabbath?" They say, "Yes." "Shall I reap?" They say, "Reap!" "Shall I reap?" They say, "Reap!"—three times for each and every matter. And they say to him, "Yes, yes, yes." All of this for what purpose? Because of the Boethuseans, for they maintain: "The reaping of the [barley for] the offering of the first sheaf of barley is not [done] at the conclusion of the festival."   (*m. Menaḥ.* 10:3)

Studies, Cambridge, 1995 (ed. M. Bernstein, F. García Martínez, and J. Kampen; STDJ 23; Leiden: Brill 1997), 89–108, 91.

[19] Ibid., 92.

[20] J. Neusner has even argued that the concept of the *ṭevul yom* (or at least most halakhic rules connected with this concept) was developed in the period of Usha, ca. 140–170 C.E.: *A History of the Mishnaic Law of Purities*, part 22: *The Mishnaic System of Uncleanness* (SJLA 6.22; Leiden: Brill, 1977), 148–149, 176–177, 212–213. Against Neusner's position see J.M. Baumgarten, "The Pharisaic-Sadducean Controversies about Purity and the Qumran Texts," *JJS* 31 (1980): 157–170, 169–170. See also H. Birenboim, "*Tevul Yom* and the Red Heifer: Pharisaic and Sadducean Halakah," *DSD* 16 (2009): 254–273, who argues that the Pharisees wanted to enable the common people in the preparation of the ashes by not considering the red heifer as a sacrifice; they therefore required a minor degree of purity of the priest officiating in the rite than the Sadducees or the Qumran sectarians would have done.

As is well known, the explicit reason for the difference is the interpretation of Sabbath in Lev 23:15 (*mi-moḥarat ha-shabbat*). Does one
offer the first sheaf after the weekly Sabbath or after the first holy day of
Nisan? Does one count "Sabbaths" or "weeks"? Lester Grabbe has rightly
observed:

> no suggestion is made in this or any other context that the differences
> between the groups arose from using a different calendar. If this were the
> case, not only would *Šavuʿot* be on a different day, but so would all the other
> festivals (cf. 1QpHab 11:4–7). Indeed, if they were supposed to be using
> a different calendar, one would expect many other calendrical disputes
> to have arisen and to be mentioned. Yet only Pentecost seems to be in
> question.[21]

Not the calendar is the point of dispute between the Boethusians and
those people who defend the common procedure, but the question
whether the correct understanding of Lev 23:15 warrants doing work
("reaping") on the Sabbath or not. The Qumran calendar is a radical solution of the problem—it is simply impossible that the day when the Omer
is to be reaped, ever falls on a Sabbath. The Boethusians, as depicted in
the Mishnah, seem to advocate a less radical procedure, namely, to post-
pone the reaping of the barley in this case to the next day. The Dead Sea
Scrolls in this case point to the same problem, but offer a different solution.

3. Some Conclusions

Let us return to the question in the title of my article. The Dead Sea Scrolls
have certainly provided us with a wealth of material for the study of the
prehistory of Mishnaic law. Qumran texts which polemically oppose laws
identical with or very close to what we find in the Mishnah, sometimes
confirm the information we have from Mishnaic or other rabbinic texts
on halakhic controversies between the Pharisees and the Sadducees. It
is common to use such cases in order to confirm the direct continuity
between Pharisaic and rabbinic halakhah. But we should beware: Not
everything opposed by the people of Qumran and accepted by the Pharisees is *eo ipso* a specifically Pharisaic law. It may represent a wider consensus opposed only by some priestly groups.

---

[21] Grabbe, "4QMMT," 97–98.

More important are the many undisputed halakhot attested to in Qumran texts that turn up again in rabbinic tradition. Here we do have substantial evidence for a continuity of halakhic traditions from the time before 70 to the rabbis, most of them not specifically Pharisaic, but more representative of a "common" Judaism (although not necessarily observed by everybody). At the same time we have to be careful in the evaluation of this parallel material to put it into the right context of halakhic systems; we certainly cannot indiscriminately fill in gaps in one corpus of texts with information from the other: Further research will have to evaluate as much the differences within seemingly parallel halakhot as their common aspects. There are meaningful parallels and continuities between the Dead Sea Scrolls and the Mishnah; but they certainly cannot be used as an excuse to return to an a-historical conception of the halakhah. We have to look for continuity *and* change; the gap between the Second Temple and the time afterwards has become much smaller, but it remains.[22]

---

[22] For a more general discussion of the problems dealt with in this paper see A. Shemesh, *Halakhah in the Making: The Development of Jewish Law from Qumran to the Rabbis* (The Taubman Lectures in Jewish Studies 6; Berkeley: University of California Press, 2009); idem, "Halakhah Between the Dead Sea Scrolls and Rabbinic Literature," in *The Oxford Handbook of the Dead Sea Scrolls* (ed. T.H. Lim and J.J. Collins; Oxford: Oxford University Press, 2010), 595–616 (the article is based on the aforementioned book).

RABBINIC MIDRASHEI HALAKHAH, MIDRASHEI AGGADAH IN QUMRAN LITERATURE?

Paul Heger
University of Toronto

Introduction

In response to Steven Fraade's articles about exegesis in rabbinic and Qumran literature, this paper will attempt to demonstrate that Fraade's use of the term "midrash" is not appropriate for describing Qumran's mode of interpreting both legal and narrative topics.[1]

The Etymological Meaning of the Terms דרש and מדרש in Scripture, Rabbinic, and Qumran Corpora

The term דרש has many meanings in Scripture and is thus difficult to define. In rabbinic literature, too, the term can have multiple meanings, although it is most often used to refer to the complex rabbinic exegesis, in many instances really *eisegesis*, of Scripture, for both halakhic and narrative issues. Similarly, in Qumran literature the term דרש has a variety of meanings, and is generally defined according to the particular context.[2]

---

[1] Steven D. Fraade, "Looking for Legal Midrash at Qumran," in *Biblical Perspectives: Early Use and Interpretation of the Bible in Light of the Dead Sea Scrolls: Proceedings of the First International Symposium of the Orion Center for the Study of the Dead Sea Scrolls and Associated Literature, 12–14 May, 1996* (ed. M.E. Stone and E.G. Chazon; STDJ 28; Leiden: Brill, 1998), 59–79 and idem, "Looking for Narrative Midrash at Qumran," in *Rabbinic Perspectives: Rabbinic Literature and the Dead Sea Scrolls: Proceedings of the Eighth International Symposium of the Orion Center for the Study of the Dead Sea Scrolls and Associated Literature, 7–9 January, 2003* (ed. idem, A. Shemesh, and R.A. Clements; Leiden: Brill, 2006), 43–68.

[2] For example, in 1QS VI:24 the phrase ושפטו במדרש יחד is translated by F. García Martínez and E.J.C. Tigchelaar, eds., *The Dead Sea Scroll Study Edition* (2 vols.; Leiden: Brill, 1997–1998), 1:85 as: "they shall judge in an examination of the Community" and by G. Vermes, *The Complete Dead Sea Scrolls in English* (New York: Allen Lane/Penguin,

The term מדרש appears only once in Scripture, in 2 Chr 24:27, bordering the period of our inquiry. The term may have been coined to refer to something added to the original text, and would correspond to the rabbinic concept of מדרש, which refers to an interpretive method that, according to Brewer, attempts "to find a hidden meaning, which may completely ignore the plain meaning of the text."[3] Thus, מדרש is the antithesis of the simple meaning of the text,[4] as we observe from its use in rabbinic literature,[5] and in Rashi's writings.[6]

1997), 107: "the Court of Inquiry." This is not merely translation but an interpretation that corresponds to the translator's particular understanding of the text.

[3] D. Instone Brewer, *Techniques and Assumptions in Jewish Exegesis before 70 CE* (TSAJ 30; Tübingen: Mohr Siebeck, 1992), 16.

[4] Rabbi Ishmael's and his school's rejection of the Akiban complex exegesis does not imply that he uses only simple sense interpretation. Rather, he, too, uses midrashic modes of interpretation, albeit of a different sort. Rabbi Ishmael and Rabbi Akiba, along with their respective schools, differ in their midrashic methods only in some instances. In principle, both employ hermeneutic systems that are not evident from the text, and that are, at times, blatantly opposed to it. We do not encounter any suggestion that Rabbi Ishmael does not accept the Sabbath rules, and it would be absurd to assume this about Rabbi Ishmael, although *m. Ḥag.* 1:8 declares that "The halakhot of the Sabbath, the offerings of the holidays and the unlawful use of sacred property are like mountains suspended by a hair, since there are many halakhot supported by a limited scriptural texts." The thirteen middot (methods) of interpretation, which form the basis of the rabbinic exegetical system, are attributed to Rabbi Ishmael, and some of them are definitely used in ways incompatible with a simple sense interpretation. See a deliberation about the method of *gzerah shavah* (one of the thirteen middot) on p. 642 n. 39 below. See also n. 48 a complex midrashic interpretation attributed to Rabbi Ishmael. Unless indicated otherwise, translations of the Hebrew Bible are from the NIV and translations of the Dead Sea Scrolls are from E. Tov, ed., *The Dead Sea Scrolls Electronic Library* (Leiden: Brill, 2006). Translations of rabbinic literature are mine.

[5] For example, it is written in *m. Šeqal.* 6:6: עולות הבשר לשם והעורות לכהנים זה מדרש דרש יהוידע כהן גדול "[the halakhah that] the meat of the holocaust offerings is dedicated to God [burnt on the altar] and their skins belong to the priests originates from a Midrash by the High Priest Jehoiada." It is then explained that in Lev 5:19 the term אשם is written three times אשם הוא אשם אשם לה', once with the extension לה' meaning "to God," an apparent contradiction, since the denomination אשם implies an offering consumed by the priests, and the term with the suffix "to God," implies that it should be burnt for God upon the altar. Jehoiada, the High Priest resolved this contradiction, as is written in 2 Kgs 12:17: כסף אשם וכסף חטאות לא יובא בית ה' לכהנים יהיו "the money from the guilt offerings and the sin offerings was not brought into the Temple of the Lord; it belongs to the priests." Through an additional convoluted conjecture, these rituals were applied to the skins of the holocaust offerings, despite the fact that all the cited verses refer to guilt and sin offerings.

[6] Rashi employs two literary styles to distinguish between the two systems of interpretation. For example, in his comments on Gen 15:5: Rashi states: ויוצא אתו החוצה לפי פשוטו הוציאו מאהלו לחוץ לראות הכוכבים ולפי מדרשו אמר לו צא מאצטגנינות שלך שראית באצטלות שאינך עתיד להעמיד בן "[It is written]: 'He took him outside' according to its simple-sense meaning [it says]: he took him outside his tent to see the stars, and according to its Midrash [it

The usual rabbinic interpretative literary style proceeds, according to Brooke, in a manner "in which the extract of scripture is explicitly cited and then given interpretation."[7] The thirteen techniques of exegesis, the middot, are introduced with the term דרש, demonstrating that מדרש is an interpretation founded on these techniques, and is distinct from מקרא, the simple, literal interpretation of the Torah. The meaning of מדרש in Qumran literature is entirely distinct from the terms מדרשי הלכה and מדרשי אגדה used in rabbinic literature. It is important to keep in mind that contemporary uses of the term midrash is shaped by the rabbinic perspective. For this reason, it is not appropriate to apply this term to discussions of the style, structure, aim and outcome of Qumran's exegesis. It is important to maintain an awareness of such distinctions when comparing the two systems of interpretation.

PHILOSOPHICAL/THEOLOGICAL DISTINCTIONS IN THE APPROACH TO SCRIPTURAL INTERPRETATION OF LEGAL ISSUES

Biblical texts include many lacunae, inconsistencies and indeterminate ordinances. The challenge of interpreting these texts fell to Qumran, as it did to the Rabbis, and later to the Karaites. The core of my thesis is that there is a fundamental distinction between the rabbinic and Qumranic applied methods of interpretation, notwithstanding several similarities in the exegesis of the two corpora, which have been pointed to by Fraade and others. The Tannaim, and plausibly the Pharisees too, considered pragmatic issues in their halakhic decisions. Only at a later stage did they attempt to find exegetical justifications for their decisions. Often, these were far-fetched and removed from the simple meaning of the text. At times, the justifications even contradicted the plain

---

says]: He [God] said to him [Abraham] get out from (ignore) your astrological divination that you will not have a son." This explanation provides first a simple interpretation followed by a midrashic interpretation. But in his comments on the verse fragment: כי באפם הרגו איש "they have killed a man [in singular mode] in their anger" (Gen 49:6), Rashi begins with the midrashic interpretation, as follows: אלו חמור ואנשי שכם ואינם חשובין כולם אלא כאיש אחד ... זהו מדרשו ופשוטו אנשים הרבה קורא איש כל אחד לעצמו באפם הרגו כל איש שכעסו עליו "These are Hamor and the people of Shechem, [and Scripture uses the single mode, because] they are all worth like one person; this is its midrashic interpretation, but its simple meaning is: he calls many people in singular, each on his own, [intending to say] they killed each person of whom they were furious."

   [7] G.J. Brooke, "4Q252 as Early Jewish Commentary," *RevQ* 17 (1996): 385–401 at 389.

meaning of the text. The *lex talionis* serves as a good example of this practice, and demonstrates the meaning of the rabbinic concept of "midrash,"
which can be completely at odds with Scripture.[8] In contrast, Qumran scholars adhered, as much as possible, to the simple interpretation
of the biblical rules, without any consideration of the practical difficulty posed by the law.[9] Qumran could not envisage that God would
allow an interpretation of the Torah that overturns its plain meaning.
Thus, for example, Qumran did not accept that one is permitted to
desecrate the Sabbath in order to save a life or to defend oneself at
war.[10]

Each school of thought saw its own approach as true to the divine
intentions. The Qumranites believed that by interpreting the biblical
commands literally (or in a manner that seemed to them literal, at any
rate),[11] they were adhering most closely to the divine commandments,
and that their opponents had falsified the divine intentions through
contorted interpretations. The instances in which Qumranic halakhot
do not seem to be closely aligned with a simple reading of the
text (as in the case, for example, of the additional first fruits holidays

---

[8] Scripture (Lev 24:19) decrees that the punishment for causing bodily harm to
another is an "eye for an eye," and goes on to explain: כאשר יתן מום באדם כן ינתן בו "as
he has injured the other, so he has to be injured" (Lev 24:20). Nevertheless, the rabbis
(*m. B. Qam.* 8:1 and *b. B. Qam.* 83b) declare: החובל בחברו חייב עליו משום חמשה דברים
בנזק בצער ברפוי בשבת ובבשת "If one injures his neighbour he is liable to pay five types of
compensation: damage, pain, healing, loss of working capability and shame." See P. Heger,
*Cult as the Catalyst for Division: Cult Disputes as the Motive for Schism in the Pre-70
Pluralistic Environment* (STDJ 65; Leiden: Brill, 2007) 69 n. 96, for the method of the
rabbinic interpretation of this rule.

[9] L. Doering, "Parallels without Parallelomania: Methodological Reflections on Comparative Analysis of Halakhah in the Dead Sea Scrolls," in *Rabbinic Perspectives*, 13–42 at
16, quotes K. Müller, "Anmerkungen zum Verhältniss von Tora und Halacha im Frühju-
dentum," in *Die Tora als Kanon für Juden und Christen* (ed. E. Zenger; Herders biblische Studien 10; Freiburg: Herder, 1996), 257–291, who deliberates about the impact of
the exigencies of life on halakhah. I fully agree that this concept was a primary, if not a
dominant factor in many rabbinic halakhic decisions, whereas its influence on Qumran
halakhah was marginal; such considerations were a factor in the creation of the particular
rules for the Yahad community.

[10] In *b. Yoma* 85a it is asked: מניין לפקוח נפש שדוחה את השבת "How do we know that
saving a life overrides the Sabbath [rules]?" The seven weak answers offered by the rabbis
demonstrate a clear lack of biblical support for this ruling. See Heger, *Cult*, 240 nn. 197–
198 and 253 n. 46 for details about this deliberation.

[11] M.J. Bernstein, "4Q252: From Re-Written Bible to Biblical Commentary," *JJS* 45
(1994): 1–27 at 19–20, writes in a similar circumstance: "The author of 4Q252 is of the
opinion that the *sensus literalis* of a prophetic blessing like that of Jacob is by definition
eschatological."

or the form and content of the phylacteries),[12] may denote earlier customs that were practiced by the entire community and were thus outside the realm of debate.[13]

Rabbinic Philosophy

The rabbinic interpretations were based on the rabbis' understanding of the texts and of the general principle of the Torah, the *Grundnorm*,[14] as well as an awareness of the necessity of adapting the traditional rules and customs to actual circumstances. The rabbis believed that God had granted them authority to interpret the Torah according to their understanding. In the renowned Akhnai narrative,[15] God endorses the rabbis' authority to interpret Scripture even when it conflicts with the actual divine intention.[16] To support their halakhic rulings, the sages alleged that their exegesis of the biblical commands was in accordance with the

---

[12] See Heger, *Cult*, 384 n. 139 for an extended deliberation about this issue.

[13] See ibid., 136–137 n. 371 about the probability that a host of Sabbath rules, lacking any scriptural support, were ingrained in ancient traditions. For example, there is no biblical support for the prohibition against carrying anything outside one's house, nor against carrying inside (CD 9:7–8). See the relevant text of *m. Ḥag.* 1:8 in n. 4.

[14] In modern language we would say that the "Law" consists of universally accepted principles, which are applied by the judge in each case. The sages perceived themselves as having the same liberty of decision with respect to the norms of the universal divine "Law." J. Roth, *The Halakhic Process: A Systemic Analysis* (New York: Jewish Theological Seminary of America, 1986), 9, calls this divine law the *Grundnorm* (a term used by the positivist Hans Kelsen), stating that the sages considered themselves to be its sole legitimate interpreters.

[15] The story in *b. B. Meṣiʿa* 59b recounts a miraculous divine intervention that sided with Rabbi Eliezer's opinion, which conflicted with that of the majority of sages. Rabbi Joshua, in the name of the sages, stood up [in defiance] and declared: "[The Torah] is no longer in heaven [cf. Deut 30:12] … it was already given [to the people of Israel] on Mount Sinai; we are not [obligated to listen to the voice from heaven, since you wrote already in the Torah [given at] Sinai: 'accept [the decision of] the majority' (the rabbis interpreted this most ambiguous biblical verse to serve their objective in this occurrence; they interpreted it differently in other instances), [which decided against Rabbi Eliezer's opinion, and we have now the authority to decide the correct halakhah]." The story reaches its climax when Elijah tells a Rabbi that God smiled at that juncture and declared: "My children were victorious over me," acknowledging the rabbi's exclusive authority to interpret Scripture.

[16] D. Weiss Halivni, *Peshat and Derash: Plain and Applied Meaning in Rabbinic Exegesis* (Oxford: Oxford University Press, 1991), 50, in comparing Talmud with another mode of study, writes that the interpretations of Talmud exegesis "frequently alter the substantive meaning of the text."

middot, the statutory rules of interpretation. Thus, they were able to present their halakhot as preserving the Scriptural commands and not transgressing the law in Deut 13:1 that states: "do not add to it [the Torah] or take away from it."

The rabbinic halakhot were founded mainly on the rabbis' reflections, and the hermeneutics were used as a means of justification.[17] Indeed, the rabbis saw the midrash functioning not as a "creative interpretation מדרש יוצר," but as an "integrative interpretation מדרש מקיים" that supports the *a priori* ideological decision.[18] The rabbinic maxim (*b. Ber.* 4b) "And both [sages, who dispute a halakhah] attained their [contended opinion] by interpreting [differently] the identical biblical verse," suggests that the rabbis were not relying on the literal meaning of the texts,[19] and instead allowed for the legitimacy of more than one possible interpretation, hence the axiom: "Both [conflicting halakhic utterances] are the words of the living God" (*b. Giṭ.* 6b); the forsaken opinion was appreciated and preserved, despite the adversities generated by the prohibition to record them in writing.

---

[17] D. Weiss Halivni, *Midrash, Mishnah and Gemara: The Jewish Predilection for Justified Law* (Cambridge: Harvard University Press, 1986), 68, perceives the Mishnah as "apodictic, unjustified law" and the Gemara, which attempted to reveal biblical support, as "justificatory law."

[18] This is the translation appearing in M. Elon, *Jewish Law: History, Sources, Principles* (trans. B. Auerbach and M.J. Sykes; 4 vols.; Philadelphia: JPS, 1994), 1:283. A. Yadin, "Resistance to Midrash? Midrash and *Halakhah* in the Halakhic Midrashim," in *Current Trends in the Study of Midrash* (ed. C. Bakhos; JSJSup 106; Leiden: Brill, 2006), 35–58, uses alternative terminology to address this issue, stating that the midrash has priority over halakhot or vice-versa.

[19] The source of the quoted citation is a *baraita* in *b. Šabb.* 117b: כמה סעודות חייב אדם לאכול בשבת שלש רבי חידקא אומר ארבע אמר רבי יוחנן ושניהם מקרא אחד דרשו ויאמר משה אכלהו היום כי שבת היום לה' היום לא תמצאוהו בשדה רבי חידקא סבר הני תלתא היום לבר מאורתא ורבנן סברי בהדי דאורתא "How many meals must a person eat on Sabbath? [A.] Three. Rabbi Hidka says: four. Said Rabbi Johanan: and both deduced it by the interpretation of the identical [biblical] verse; [it is written in Exod 16:25] 'Eat it today, Moses said, because today is a Sabbath to the Lord. You will not find any on the ground today.' Rabbi Hidka thinks that since it is written three times 'today' it intends to say that one must eat three meals during the day and one during the evening, and the Rabbis think that the three meals include the one at the evening." The Amora Rabbi Johanan speculates on the motives of the Tannaim, which are not divulged; we may assume that their opinions were not founded on the exegesis of the biblical verse, but rather on actual fact, that is, on how many meals were seen to represent an appropriate celebration of the Sabbath. *Mek. de Rabbi Shimʿon b. Yoḥai* 20 interprets Deut 5:11 (v. 12 in KJV): "Observe the Sabbath day by keeping it holy," that one fulfills this command by eating on Sabbath festive food of better quality and distinct from the food consumed on weekdays, among other similar symbolic acts, like wearing clean clothes, etc. See a similar rule in CD 11:3 regarding clean clothes.

Qumran Philosophy

Qumran scholars were antagonistic to this "midrashic" method,[20] calling those who practiced it דורשי חלקות "seeking flattery" and/or accus-
ing them of רמיה "deceit." They were aware of the system, and found
it to be misleading and wrong. Instead, they adhered, as much as possible, to the simple and straightforward meaning of the biblical rules,
without any consideration of practical consequences. When the vague-
ness or lacuna of the scriptural text required some compounded form
of exegesis, they relied on simple, logical considerations, very different
from the rabbinic complex exegetical method. For example, regarding
the prohibition against marrying one's niece, the author demonstrates
first that Scripture equates man and woman with respect to incest prohibitions,[21] and then presents the consequence: "[Though] the law of
prohibited marriages is written for males, it applies equally to females"
(CD A 5:9–10). The prohibition against polygamy is explained in a
similar manner,[22] as is the qumranic prohibition against intermarriage
between priests and lay Israelites.[23] In contrast to the rabbi's multi-layered
system of interpretation, founded on Scripture's multi-vocal character,

---

[20] Cf. G.J. Brooke, *Exegesis at Qumran: 4Q Florilegium in its Jewish Context* (JSOTSup
29; Sheffield: JSOT Press, 1985), 2.

[21] We read in CD A 5:8: ומשה אמר אל אחות אמך לא תקרב שאר אמך היא "But Moses said:
Do not approach your mother's sister, she is a blood relation to your mother." It refers to
the interconnected verses Lev 18:12 and 13: ערות אחות אביך לא תגלה שאר אביך הוא and ערות
אחות אמך לא תגלה כי שאר אמך הוא "Do not have sexual relations with your father's sister;
she is your father's close relative" and "Do not have sexual relations with your mother's
sister, because she is your mother's close relative." This simple and logical extension of a
rule is comparable to the rabbinic maxim דבר הכתוב בהוה "The Torah cited what is the
most common," a rational, legitimate rule, not included in the midrashic middot system.
See *Mek. Mishpatim* 20 regarding the extension of the biblical prohibition against cooking
a kid in its mother's milk, to apply to all animals.

[22] CD A 4:21–5:1 refers first to the cosmological reality, as recorded in Scripture: יסוד
הבריאה זכר ונקבה "the principle of creation is one man and one woman," and confirmed
again by the divine instruction to save one male and one female of each species in
Gen 7:9: שנים שנים באו אל התבה זכר ונקבה "two by two went into the ark male and
female."

[23] Qumran scholars claimed first by logical comparison that the biblical prohibitions
of כלאים and שעטנז, against mixing wool and flax in garments, mating different species
of animals, and sowing different plant species together: כשכתוב קודש [ישראל] [ועל בהמה
טהו]רה כתוב של[וא] להרביע]ה כלאים ועל לבושים שלוא יהיה] שעטנז ושל[וא לזרוע] [שדו וכרמו
כלא[י]ם (4QMMTᵈ [4Q397] 6–13 12–14) relates equally to all types of mixed unions,
including those between humans of distinct genealogies: ב[ג]לל שה[מה קדושים ובני אהרן
קדושי קדושים "But they [i.e. the Israelites] are holy, and the sons of Aaron are the holiest
of the holy."

Qumran believed in a single correct interpretation, and saw all others as illegitimate and false. Indeed, we do not encounter internal halakhic disputes in Qumran literature.

Rabbinic and Qumran Styles of Justifying Halakhot

In rabbinic literature, the explanation/justification is always associated with the citation of the biblical text. Qumran literature does not typically quote a biblical support for its halakhot, even when it uses the words כתוב or אמר, to refer to the text.

Fraade finds this odd, but I see this as a logical consequence of Qumran's interpretive method. Since Qumran adhered to the simple meaning of familiar texts, which seemed evident to the authors and the intended readership[24] (and which they probably assumed was similarly clear to their contenders),[25] citation was seen as superfluous, even in their polemic 4QMMT writing.[26] On the other hand, when the halakhah is not evident from the biblical text, the phrases אנו חושבים/אומרים "we think/say" are used to indicate that the halakhah is, in their opinion, what Scripture intends. What some scholars assume to be an incorrect biblical citation in Qumran is actually just an element of their halakhic writing style, which

---

[24] Fraade, "Looking for Narrative Midrash," 64 suggests that the different forms of Qumran and rabbinic writings may be due to the differences between the intended audiences. R.A. Kugler, "Hearing 4Q225: A Case Study in Reconstructing the Religious Imagination of the Qumran Community," *DSD* 10 (2003): 81–103 at 82 and 84, writes that we can determine the community's response to the "Parabiblical scrolls," "because they were built from literature the group knew better than any other . . ., the Jewish Scriptures." This affirmation is equally valid for the subject of our assertion, as he states: "even when echoes of Scripture are barely whispered, the full scope of a story's testimony is evoked as well in the recipient's imagination." As said above, I challenge the pertinence of the label "Parabiblical Scrolls."

[25] M. Bernstein, "The Employment and Interpretation of Scripture in 4QMMT: Preliminary Observations," in *Reading 4QMMT: New Perspectives on Qumran Law and History* (ed. J. Kampen and M. Bernstein; SBLSymS 2; Atlanta: Scholars Press, 1996), 29–51 at 43, writes: "The author of MMT believes that the correct interpretation of the biblical text" corresponds to their halakhah regarding the rules of the leper in *MMT*, in which the expression כתוב appears.

[26] M. Bernstein, "Pentateuchal Interpretation at Qumran," in *The Dead Sea Scrolls after Fifty Years: A Comprehensive Assessment* (ed. P.W. Flint and J.C. VanderKam; 2 vols.; Leiden: Brill, 1998–1999), 1:128–159 at 143, writes regarding some rules in *MMT*: "it is clear that these laws are based on Lev 19:23 and 27:32 respectively." Bernstein perceives, as do I, that Qumran does not see it as necessary to offer a citation when the source of a law is obvious. However, unlike me, Bernstein does not see this approach as generally true of Qumran.

incorporated "biblicized" vocabulary and phrasing that became part of the spoken language of the community.[27]

The Gemara never asks how we know that one must not work on Sabbath or that one is obligated to dwell in a booth on Sukkoth. The relevant biblical verses for these principles are well known and do not require citation. However, the specific types of work prohibited on the Sabbath and the detailed rules regarding the building of the booths, warrant the disclosure of a biblical source and an appropriate interpretation. Both the Tannaim and the Qumranites had complete confidence in their understanding of the Torah's ultimate intention, and therefore did not consider it essential to divulge justifications for their decisions.[28] The absence of these verses from Qumran literature suggests that they were assumed to be well-known. That is, the connection between the biblical verse and its interpretation seemed evident to them. Only in those instances in which their halakhah does not seem perfectly clear from the biblical text, do they add an explanation, or an explicit exegesis, as G. Brooke points out.[29] On the other hand, the rabbinic midrashic system, with its complex rules and methods of interpretation, must be explicitly associated with the biblical verses, since without this one would be unable to connect the halakhah with the relevant verses.

---

[27] T.H. Lim, "The Chronology of the Flood Story in a Qumran Text (4Q252)," *JJS* 43 (1992): 288–298 at 289 writes: "There is no straightforward way of distinguishing between a quotation and a rewriting of the biblical verse." M. Bernstein, "4Q252 i 2 לא ידור רוחי באדם לעולם: Biblical Text or Biblical Interpretation?" *RevQ* 16 (1993–1995): 421–427 at 421, defines the question differently: "when is the reflection of a biblical text which does not conform to MT, and which appears in a 'non-textual' source, to be viewed as a variant text, and when may treat it as a paraphrastic interpretation of an underlying text which may have resembled MT?" See also n. 24 above.

[28] J. Neusner, *A History of the Mishnaic Law of Purities*, part 21: *The Redaction and Formulation of the Order of Purities in Mishnah and Tosefta* (SJLA 6.21; Leiden: Brill, 1977), 312, writes: "Our order [i.e. of the Mishna] is remarkably uninterested in Scriptural proofs for its propositions." He asserts that the mishnaic writings were used for "the transmission of teachings on behalf of which is claimed divine revelation" (ibid., 313). I perceive them rather as reflecting the sages' understanding of the Torah's ultimate intention, and not as the transmission of a particular revelation.

[29] Brooke, "4Q252 as Early Jewish Commentary," 389, perceives implicit and explicit exegesis in Qumran literature. He explains these differences in application by saying that the implicit exegesis "is likely to have been intended or to reflect what may have been more widely acceptable or accepted than the more particularist explicit exegesis" (398). In fact, this is quite similar to my own hypothesis in this respect, since he, too, distinguishes between what was more acceptable and what was less so. I disagree with Brooke, however, regarding his notion of a shift from implicit to explicit exegesis. I perceive both methods as co-existent, with each applied according to functional suitability.

THE PARTICULAR *PESHER* STYLE

Only the *pesher* writings, the esoteric *nistar*, transmitted through revelation and impossible to deduce from the simple understanding of the text, consistently cites the relevant biblical text.[30] *Pesher* is not concerned with the literary, etymological or halakhic interpretation of the text.[31] Instead, it is concerned with the particulars of the period, event, circumstances or personality referred to by the text. Thus, it is an entirely distinct genre as suggested by many scholars.[32]

Pesher Habakkuk, the model *pesher*, actualizes the entire book of Habakkuk,[33] thus rendering it pertinent to their period.[34] *Pesher* is an

---

[30] Lim, "Chronology," 297: "Inferential exegesis of the kind that is described above [regarding the chronology of the Flood in 4Q252] is not paralleled in either the continuous or thematic pesher," and he indicates the difference: "prophecies are revelatory whereas the flood story is conducive to chronological enumeration."

[31] Bernstein, "4Q252: From Re-Written Bible," 3, writes about the *pesharim*: "their exegesis does not strive at all to achieve a contextual and literal understanding of the biblical text, but rather its historical or eschatological actualization."

[32] S.D. Fraade, "Rewritten Bible and Rabbinic Midrash as Commentary," in *Current Trends in the Study of Midrash*, 59–78 at 60, states that the midrash and the Dead Sea Scrolls have in common the practice of a boundary line between received scripture and its interpretive retelling by a dialogical shuttle between them. According to my understanding, he refers in this instance to the *pesher* writings in his expression "Dead Sea Scrolls," since in his study "Looking for Narrative Midrash," 61–62 he perceives a minor engagement with Scripture in Qumran writings. For example, referring to a parallel interpretation of a midrash and Qumran writing, he observes the midrash's engagement with the words of the Torah, distinguishing this approach from Qumran's rule, according to which "the dialogical engagement with the scriptural text of Exodus 19 does not appear to have occupied the same performative place as it did among the early rabbinic sages." He also writes specifically at 52 that such Qumran texts as the *Community Rule*, *MMT*, the *Temple Scroll* and the *War Scroll* "never directly and exegetically engage the texts of Scripture." There seems to be an inconsistency between his two statements, unless we assume that in his assertions regarding the common character of the Dead Sea Scrolls and rabbinic midrash, with respect to the engagement with Scripture, he indeed refers to the *pesher* genre. He does not consider, however, that this class of writing is *sui generis*, and is not a conventional interpretation. Thus, one cannot draw conclusions about other types of writings from this text, which Fraade attempts to do.

[33] The question of whether the author of the *Pesher Habakkuk* believed that the prophecy refers exclusively to his period, as L.H. Schiffman states in "Contemporizing Halakhic Exegesis in the Dead Sea Scrolls," in *Reading the Present in the Qumran Library: The Perception of the Contemporary by Means of Scriptural Interpretations* (ed. K. De Troyer and A. Lange; SBLSymS 30; Atlanta: SBL, 2005), 35–41 at 35 or, as J. Jokiranta writes in "Pesharim: A Mirror of Self Understanding," in ibid., 23–34, that the prophet Habakkuk was referring to his period, but that his universal prophecy remained relevant is open to debate. Jokiranta's perception of the "actualization" of the *pesharim* seems to me more reasonable, since it does not limit the applicability of Scripture to a particular period, and preserves the idea of Scripture's eternal significance.

ex-cathedra direct utterance that has a particular meaning, and while it does not require any justification, the citation of the source is essential for its association with Scripture. The *nigleh* halakhic texts, whose biblical source is well known, do not require thorough citations but only an occasional justification. This explains the genre's distinct style and structure. Qumran's halakhot were also seen as presenting an absolute truth, which left little room for debate.

Both *pesher*'s and Qumran's halakhot require little or no justification, since these were believed to be derived from revelation, or are considered self-evident. In contrast, rabbinic midrash is usually structured as a direct or indirect answer to a particular question, and includes supporting evidence, allowing for a wide range of possible interpretations (as substantiated above on p. 636). This openness to multiple ways of understanding a text is why halakhic disputes are so common, and why in rabbinic literature justifications are required.

Intermediate Summary

As I demonstrated, the two methods of interpretation—Qumran and rabbinic—are extremely different from one another. This becomes manifest, ultimately, in the differences between the rulings offered by each. For example, Qumran requires a distance of three days' walk from Jerusalem to permit profane slaughter of animals suitable for offering,[35] while the Rabbis limit this prohibition to the Temple precinct.[36] Instead of

---

[34] For example, the רשע in 1QpHab V:9 is identified as the renowned הכוהן הרשע in 1QpHab IX:9 and the צדיק as the מורה הצדק in 1QpHab V:10.

[35] We read in 11QTᵃ (11Q19) LII:13–16: לא תזבח שור ושה ועז טהורים בכול שעריכה קרוב למקדשי דרך שלושת ימים כי אם בתוך מקדשי תזבחנו לעשות אותו עולה או זבח שלמים ואכלתה ושמחתה לפני במקום אשר אבחר לשום שמי עליו "You shall not slaughter an ox, or sheep or he-goat which are pure in any of your gates which are nearer than three day's walk from my Temple, but instead you shall slaughter it inside my Temple, making it into a burnt-offering or peace offering; and you shall eat and rejoice before me in the place where I shall choose to put my name upon it."

[36] We read in *Sipra*, *Dibura de Nedaba* 13: ושחטו ושחט אותו ושחט אותו מה תלמוד לומר לפי שנאמר וכי ירחק ממך המקום וזבחת ברחוק מקום אתה זובח ואי אתה זובח בקרוב מקום פרט לחולין שלא ישחטו בעזרה "[The term] slaughter [is written] three times [at the commands of the fellowship offering (Lev 3:2, 8 and 13)], what does it teach? Since it is written 'if the place [the Lord chooses] is too far away from you … you may slaughter (Deut 12:21)' [it teaches us] you may slaughter [profanely] at a distant place, and you must not slaughter [profanely] at a close place, [and that means] that except of the Temple's precinct [you may slaughter] unconsecrated [animals/birds suitable for offerings]."

deliberating about the precise measure of distance that is considered far
from Jerusalem, as implied in Scripture,[37] the rabbis, driven by a pragmatic consideration, sought to define the range in terms of that which is
not close, which they determine refers to anything outside the Temple's
precinct. The same pragmatic approach underlies the rabbinic interpretation of the biblical dictum of an eye for an eye, which imposes pecuniary
compensation for the injuries despite Scripture's explicit instruction.[38]

A rule often used by the rabbis is *gzerah shavah*, one of the thirteen
middot, which derives the meaning of a word or term based on the use
of the same or a similar word or term in a different, unrelated text.[39]
Qumranic interpretations, such as the prohibition against marrying one's
niece are logical and self evident, founded on the same reasoning as the
rabbinic maxim (not included in the *middot*) which states that "The
Torah cited what is the most common."[40] In some instances, Qumran
may have utilized more elaborate exegesis, but we have no indication
of their character. Thus, our assumptions must be based on Qumran's
general adherence to the simple meaning of the text, which represents
the antithesis of the rabbinic midrashic system. The name "midrash" is,
therefore, inappropriate for describing Qumran's halakhic interpretation.

Discussion of Fraade's Examples

Fraade cites the rule of reproof as evidence for his theory of legal midrash
in Qumran literature.[41] The example cited by Fraade correlates, in my
opinion, to the Qumranic mode of interpretation. The two relevant biblical verses are difficult to interpret,[42] and the traditional commentators

---

[37] A three days walk is a typical distance unit as we encounter in Exod 5:3; 15:22, Num 10:33; 33:8, Josh 9:16; Jonah 3:3.

[38] See the relevant biblical text above in n. 8.

[39] In a complex deliberation in *b. Ber.* 35a about the meaning of the undefined term תבואה in Lev 19:25 regarding the use of the fruits of a tree on the fifth year, a *gzerah shavah* is used: נאמר כאן להוסיף לכם תבואתו ונאמר להלן ותבואת הכרם מה להלן כרם אף כאן כרם "It is written here, at the fruit of the fifth year (Lev 19:25) "your harvest will be increased" and it is written there, at the prohibition to plant two kinds of seed (Deut 22:9) "the fruit of the vineyard," like there it refers to a vineyard, so it is here too." Though the two verses relate to two distinct, unrelated topics, a *gzerah shavah* is applied.

[40] See the explanation of this concept above in n. 21.

[41] Fraade, "Legal Midrash," 69.

[42] We read in Lev 19:17–18: לא תשנא את אחיך בלבבך הוכח תוכיח את עמיתך ולא תשא עליו חטא "Do not hate your brother in your heart; Rebuke your neighbour frankly so

and the Talmud offer a great variety of interpretations.[43] The *Damascus Document* elegantly integrated the two verses into one law, to be interpreted as follows: "do not hate your brother in your heart [when you see him sinning, as you should hate a sinner], but rebuke him so that you should not incur in the sin" (Lev 19:17) [of having failed to rebuke him] "and of seeking revenge or bearing a grudge" (Lev 19:18, paraphrased).[44]

The second example cited by Fraade refers to the time addition to the Sabbath. CD 10:14–17 quotes the rule,[45] and justifies it with the scriptural dictum: כי הוא אשר אמר שמור את יום השבת לקדשו "because this is what is meant by the passage, 'Observe the Sabbath day to keep it holy'" (Deut 5:12). However, the *Damascus Document* does not discuss the hermeneutics of how this conclusion was derived from the text. This example offers a simple, logical interpretation of the biblical verse:

---

you will not share in his guilt"; and לא תקם ולא תטר את בני עמך ואהבת לרעך כמוך "Do not seek revenge or bear a grudge against one of your people, but love your neighbor as yourself." The command "do not hate your brother in your heart," seems to have no logical connection to the succeeding decree "Rebuke your neighbour frankly so you will not share in his guilt," which, it would seem, should have followed v. 18: "Love your neighbour as yourself." The association of rebuking with avoiding sin is equally perplexing. The sin's essence is not defined, nor is the identity of the sinner. Both the rabbis and Qumran may have been uncomfortable with the contradiction posed by the juxtaposition of this verse with the obligation to hate the sinners, as is stated in Ps 139:21: "Do I not hate those who hate you, O Lord, and abhor those who rise against you?"

[43] For example, Ibn Ezra understands the text in a similar way to the *Damascus Document*: You should rebuke your neighbour, and thus give him the possibility of denying his sin, because to make a wrongful accusation is also a sin. For Ramban the sin consists of not preventing the future sinning of your neighbour; he might have improved his ways, if you had rebuked him, and therefore you are partly responsible for his sin. Ramban offers an additional explanation: if you do not reprove your friend, thereby giving him a chance to remedy his offense against you and reconcile with him, you will continue to hate him, and thus transgress the law that forbids one to "hate your brother in your heart" (Lev 19:17). Modern scholars have also recognized the nebulous nature of this phrase.

[44] We read in CD 9:6–8: אם החריש לו מיום ליום ובחרון אפו בו דבר בו דבר מות ענה בו יען "If he kept silent אשר לא הקים את מצות אל אשר אמר לו הוכח תוכיח את רעיך ולא תשא עליו חטא day by day and then in anger against his fellow spoke against him in a capital case, this testifies against him that he did not fulfill the commandment of God which says to him, '*You shall reprove your fellow and not bear the sin yourself.*'"

[45] על הש[ב]ת לשמרה כמשפטה אל יעש איש ביום {מל} השישי מלאכה מן העת אשר יהיה גלגל השמש רחוק מן השער מלואו כי הוא אשר אמר שמור את יום השבת לקדשו "About the Sa[bb]ath, how to keep it properly. *vac* A man may not work on the { } sixth day from the time that the solar orb is above the horizon by its diameter, because this is what is meant by the passage …"

the term שמור implies to "guard" something precious, and one must be similarly careful in guarding against the desecration of the Sabbath. Qumran's role model,[46] the returnees from Babylon, introduced a spirit of awe to the fulfillment of the divine commands.[47] Qumran incorporated a similar attitude of awe and fear in its approach to ritual observance, and the time added to the Sabbath derived from this attitude, meant as an extra caution against potential transgressions. This approach is similar to the one adapted by the rabbis in their method of creating "a hedge for the Torah" (*m. 'Abot* 1:1).

In contrast to Qumran's simple understanding of the scriptural term שמור, the corresponding rabbinic midrashic method cited by Fraade is construed on an extremely complex system.[48] The rule can be deduced from different biblical verses, and different rules can be derived from the same verse. The midrashic interpretation is not inherent to the biblical command; it is an *eisegesis* rather than an *exegesis*; one can understand Qumran's opposition to halakhot reached by such methods.

---

[46] See S. Talmon, *The World of Qumran from Within: Collected Studies* (Jerusalem: Magnes, 1989), 40–43. He writes, for example: "this compilation (i.e. CD IV:2–6) was in fact a Qumran parallel of the biblical reports to the returned exiles" (40). He denotes the Covenanters' "conceptual proclivity to identify with and present themselves as biblical Israel" (41). And states that the term יחד "serves as a socioreligious term that defines solely the community of the erstwhile exiles" (43).

[47] We read in Ezra 10:3: והחרדים במצות אלהינו וכתורה יעשה "those who fear the commands of our God. Let it be done according to the Law." See an extensive deliberation about the meaning of the concept חרד in the context in Heger, *Cult*, 82 and n. 140.

[48] We read in *Mek.*, Jethro 7: "[It is written in Exod 20:8]: זכור "Remember [the Sabbath" and in Deut 5:12]: שמור "Guard [the Sabbath"]; remember it before it comes and guard it after it is gone; from that we deduce that one adds from the profane to the holy," without any logical explanation for this deduction. Other midrashim add to this one, but have no clear connection to the extension of the Sabbath's duration. *B. Roš. Haš.* 9a quotes another convoluted midrash that attempts justifying the same rule. We read there: "Wherefrom does Rabbi Ishmael deduce the rule to add from the profane to the holy? [A.] he deduces it from Lev 23:32: 'you shall afflict your souls in the ninth day of the month.' Could it be that it applies to the ninth [day of the month [since it is written in v. 27 that the holiday is on the tenth day?] No, it is written in the evening. If on the evening, could it intend after dark? No. It is written on the ninth day [and after dark, it is already the tenth]. How do you reconcile it? He starts to deny himself [from food/fast] on the early evening, when it still day, and from this we learn that one adds from the profane to the holy. From that we know that one has to add at its start, but how do we know that you have to add also at its end? We deduce it from the phrase 'from evening to evening.' From that we know that the rule refers to the Day of Atonement (the subject of Lev 23:32), but how do we know that it is valid equally for the Sabbaths? Because it is written 'abstain from work'. How do we know that it is valid equally for the holidays? Because it is written your Sabbath. What does it mean? Whenever there is an abstention from work, one must add from the profane to the holy."

Fraade's third example, Qumran's prohibition, according to his interpretation, to offer on Sabbath other than the particular Sabbath offerings,[49] includes the specific holiday offerings. I have written an extended
study in which I discuss this complex issue. I argue there that Qumran's
rule is based on a simple logical interpretation of Num 28:9–10, whereas
the rabbinic concept of מוסף, the key for the rabbinic interpretation of
this biblical verse, conflicting with Qumran's rule, does not exist in Scripture.[50]

STYLE AND STRUCTURE OF NARRATIVES
IN QUMRAN AND RABBINIC LITERATURES

The structural and stylistic distinctions between rabbinic and Qumran
narrative writings are reflective of the differences in the legal/halakhic
lemmas of the two. A comparison of Qumran narratives with the rabbinic midrashic parallels substantiates this hypothesis.[51] In 4QpsJub[a]
(4Q225),[52] there is no connection to a biblical verse, and no specific information regarding what Mastema said to God. *Jubilees* offers a more elaborate narrative,[53] again without a connection to a biblical verse or a biblical
support. The identical tale appears in *b. Sanh.* 89b,[54] this time as part of a

---

[49] We read in CD A 11:17–18: אל יעל איש למזבח בשבת כי אם עולת השבת כי כן כתוב מלבד
שבתותיכם "No one should offer any sacrifice on the Sabbath except the Sabbath whole-
burnt-offering, for so it is written, '*besides your Sabbaths*' (Lev 23:28)." In fact, Scripture
reads: מלבד שבתת ה', probably to avoid writing the divine name.

[50] "Sabbath Offerings According to the Damascus Document-Scholarly Opinions and
a New Hypothesis," *ZAW* 118 (2006): 62–81.

[51] It seems to me that the reservations regarding comparisons, advanced by L. Doering,
"Parallels," 28–29 on the congruence of rabbinic and Qumran writings and by Y. Elman,
"Some Remarks on 4QMMT and Rabbinic Tradition: Or, When is a Parallel not a
Parallel?" in *Reading 4QMMT*, 99–128, do not affect our particular narrative.

[52] We read in 4Q225 2 i 9–10: ויבוא שר המשטמה אל אלוהים וישטים את אברהם בישחק "and
the Prince of Mastema (Animosity) came to God and accused Abraham with regard to
Isaac."

[53] We read in *Jub.* 17:16: "And the prince Mastema came and said before God, 'Behold,
Abraham loves Isaac his son, and he delights in him above all things else; bid him offer
him as a burnt-offering on the altar, and Thou wilt see if he will do this command, and
Thou wilt know if he is faithful in everything wherein Thou dost try him.'"

[54] We read in *b. Sanh.* 89b: "[It is written in Gen 22:1] And it came to pass after these
things (In Hebrew the term דבר means both word and thing). [Q] After which things?
Said Rabbi Joḥanan in the name of Rabbi Jose ben Zimra: After the words of Satan, as it
is written (Gen 21:8) and the child grew and was weaned etc., Satan charged before the

full-fledged narrative in its final phase (this gradual development is typical of rabbinic folktales and narratives, which is similar to the general accretion process of folktales).[55] In contrast to the narratives in 4Q225 and in *Jubilees*, the rabbinic Midrash, a creative interpretation, opens and concludes with supporting biblical verses.[56]

The parallel narrative in rabbinic and Qumran literature about Canaan's curse demonstrates the same distinction. The smooth integration of biblical and non-biblical[57] language in 4QCommGen A (4Q252)[58] denotes that the biblical sections became elements of a discourse, rather than a new rewrite of the Bible. Indeed, 4Q252 demonstrates the characteristics of an oral tradition,[59] with its narration and elucidation of a biblical story. Unlike the succinct style of Qumran, the rabbinic midrash reveals a particular structure[60] that includes a) the citation of the biblical verse and then its exegesis, and b) the justification of the exegesis by way of citing another biblical verse. We observe the explicit association

---

Holy, be He blessed: Master of the world, you graced with favour this old man, granting him a fruit of the womb at the age of hundred years, [but] from the feast he celebrated, he did not deem it proper to offer you one dove or one chick. God answered him: though he has done everything for his son, if I tell him to slaughter his son before me, he would do it immediately, [and that what is written] and God tempted Abraham and said: 'Take your son (Gen 22:2).'"

[55] The renowned story of the Akhnai hearth that started with a vague indication of a dispute between the sages, grew by accretion in the Tosefta, Jerusalem Talmud, and became an extraordinary ideologically significant, fully developed literary narrative, in its latest stage, in *b. B. Meṣiʿa* 59b. See the story in Heger, *Cult*, 123 and the process of accretion in P. Heger, *The Pluralistic Halakhah: Legal Innovations in the Late Second Commonwealth and Rabbinic Periods* (SJ 22; Berlin: de Gruyter, 2003), 12, 14, and 15.

[56] Gen 22:1 at the beginning, which has no connection or hint to the proposed interpretation, and 22:2 at its conclusion.

[57] See above n. 24 on this issue.

[58] We read in 4Q252 II:5–7:ויקץ נוח מיינו וידע את אשר עשה לו בנו הקטן ויומר ארור כנען עבד עבדים יהיה לאחיו ולוא קלל את חם כי אם בנו כי ברך אל את בני נוח "And Noah awoke from the wine and he knew what his youngest son had done. And he said: 'cursed be Canaan; he will be for his brothers, a slave of slaves.' But he did not curse Ham, but only his son, for God has blessed the sons of Noah."

[59] See Kugler, "Hearing 4Q225," 83.

[60] We read in *Gen. Rab.* 36:7:ויקץ נח מיינו נתפרק יינו מעליו וידע את אשר עשה לו בנו הקטן בנו הפסול הדא הוא דכתיב כי מזבח הנחושת קטן מהכיל "[It is written in Gen 9:24] 'And Noah awoke from the wine,' [the somewhat awkward biblical sentence is explained as meaning]: he freed himself from the wine's impact 'and he knew what his youngest son had done'; [the phrase his youngest son means] his unfit/blemished son, [and this meaning of the term קטן corresponds] to what is written: 'because the bronze altar was too small to hold' [the many offerings (1 Kgs 8:64), understood as: it was unfit for its function]."

of the midrash with the biblical verses and the clear distinction between the biblical text and the exegesis, all of which is in contrast to the uninterrupted flow of Qumran's narrative structure.

Qumran does not attempt to reveal illusory biblical support for the supplementary details, because such support cannot be deduced through simple interpretation[61] or logical considerations.[62] Qumran vehemently opposed this method with regard to halakhic issues, seeing this mode of interpretation as a falsification of the divine command. However, Qumran does accept this approach, albeit unenthusiastically, with regards to the innocuous haggadot. The scarce number of such narratives and the almost exclusive use of Aramaic language[63] (the vernacular of the masses)

---

[61] Bernstein, "4Q252: From Re-Written Bible," 13, writes regarding Qumran's simple exegesis that "the author of 4Q252 is willing to explain the [biblical] text straightforwardly on the principle that events in the Torah are not always narrated chronologically."

[62] I do not agree with Bernstein, "Pentateuchal Interpretation," 135, who perceives *Jubilees* and the *Genesis Apocryphon* as "works which interpret substantial segments of the Pentateuch." These writings do not interpret or explain the text; they add details that are outside of the text. On the other hand, for example, the addition of the days of the week in 4Q252, can be deduced through logical considerations regarding their calendar, and may be perceived as interpretation or commentary. See Lim's similar assertion in n. 31 ("Chronology," 297). In "4Q252: From Re-Written Bible," 2, Bernstein seems to be more cautious in this regard; he writes that "works as Jubilees or the Genesis Apocryphon often present inferential simple sense interpretation to their reader." I agree with Bernstein that this statement concurs with the character of these writings in some instances, but in others they present details that must be considered as *eisegesis* that have no integral association with the relevant biblical texts.

[63] Most scholars agree that *1 Enoch* was originally written in Aramaic, in contrast to Qumran's philosophic/theological writings, which were written exclusively in Hebrew. D. Dimant, "4Q127: An Unknown Jewish Apocryphal Work?" in *Pomegranates and Golden Bells: Studies in Biblical, Jewish, and Near Eastern Ritual, Law, and Literature in Honor of Jacob Milgrom* (ed. D.P. Wright, D.N. Freedman, and A. Hurvitz; Winona Lake: Eisenbrauns, 1995), 805–813 at 805–806, writes that the Qumran writings in Aramaic "contain mostly narratives and pseudepigraphic visions, lacking the specific features attributable to the literature of the community," and concludes: "these facts strongly emphasize the importance of Hebrew as a vehicle of religious expression at Qumran." In a more recent article, "The Qumran Aramaic Texts and the Qumran Community," in *Flores Florentino: Dead Sea Scrolls and Other Early Jewish Studies in Honour of Florentino García Martínez* (ed. A. Hilhorst, É. Puech, and E. Tigchelaar; JSJSup 122; Leiden: Brill, 2007), 197–205, she writes: "the Aramaic texts contain nothing of the specifically sectarian terminology or ideology" (199), that no Aramaic texts deals with issues after the flood and the patriarchs (203) and that one should "consider these (Aramaic) texts [found at Qumran] as a specific group" (205). P.E. Lapide, *Hebrew in the Church: The Foundations of Jewish-Christian Dialogue* (trans. E.F. Rhodes; Grand Rapids: Eerdmans, 1984), 1, writes: "In the days of Jesus the common language of most Palestinian Jews was Aramaic ... But Hebrew remained the language of worship, of the Bible, and of religious discourse; in a word, it remained the sacred language well into the period of the early church."

for this type of literature, in contrast with the exclusive use of Hebrew for Qumran's literature, may explain the atypically neutral attitude toward the haggadic writings.

DISCUSSION OF FRAADE'S EXAMPLES OF NARRATIVE MIDRASH

Example 1: Blessings and Curses Renewed

I am doubtful of whether the Qumranic custom of blessings and curses in 1QS I:16–II:19 is at all related to or derived from the scriptural lemma in Deut 28,[64] regarding blessings and curses. The Qumran custom was devised for a specific, limited period, as explicitly stated in the concluding verse II:19, "They shall do as follows annually, all the days of Belial's dominion: the priests shall pass in review." The substance of the curses is distinct from that of those listed in Deuteronomy (the blessings are not mentioned at all in Deuteronomy). The assumption that the ordinance regarding the recitation of the blessings by priests, and that of curses the Levites, is derived from a biblical command is possible, but the source is not necessarily Deuteronomy. Indeed, many duties listed in Qumran literature are meant to be carried out by the priests and Levites, who are given priority status over the Israelites, in conformity with the biblical rules. Even according to Fraade's assumption that there is an association with the Deuteronomic command, the addition of the priests for the blessings, absent in Scripture, can easily be explained according to a simple logical consideration: "if the Levites recite the curses, the priests must recite the blessings," as Fraade himself suggests, again, in compliance with the biblical order of things. Qumran followed the model of Chronicles, which added details missing in Kings.

---

[64] Fraade mentions both chapters. However, the public ceremony on the Gerizim and Ebal mountains does not cite the list of the blessings, nor does it mention who recites these (although verse 12 does indicate which tribes stand on Mount Gerizim for the blessings.) The blessings and curses in chap. 28 do not relate to a ceremonial event and certainly have no connection the annual Qumran ceremony.

Example 2: Revelation Retold:
Three Days Abstention from Sexual Intercourse

Qumran's argumentations: אנו חושבים/אומרים, כתוב, אמר present a direct exegetical engagement with biblical passages, contrary to Fraade's assertion. However, this is done in a manner different to that of the rabbis. Expressions cited above, and שתבין בספר מושה, ואף כתוב בספר מושה and the accusation כיא לוא בקשו ולוא דרשהו בחוקוהי affirm that interpretation, not revelation, was the foundation of their halakhot.[65] The required period of three days abstention from sexual intercourse before entering the Temple demonstrates the straightforward logical approach of Qumran versus the rabbinic midrashic complex method. Leviticus 15:16–18 does not indicate the degree of purity one attains the day after intercourse. Deuteronomy 23:11–12 allows entering the undefined camp (מחנה) the next day.[66] Because the Temple is considered the most holy camp,[67] however, it is logical to assume that more than one day's abstention is required prior to entering this holy space. Rabbinic literature reveals inconsistencies in scriptural texts and offers complex solutions.[68] Of course, these speculations regarding Qumran's exegesis are not absolute, and one cannot rule out the fact that Qumran may have understood these biblical commands differently.

---

[65] See P. Heger, "The Development of Qumran Law—*Nistarot*, *Niglot* and the Issue of 'Contemporization,'" *RevQ* 23 (2007–2008): 167–206 at 178–186.

[66] We read in Lev 15:16: ואיש כי תצא ממנו שכבת זרע ורחץ במים את כל בשרו וטמא עד הערב "When a man has an emission of semen, he must bathe his whole body with water, and he will be unclean till evening." And in Deut 23:12: והיה לפנות ערב ירחץ במים וכבא השמש יבא אל תוך המחנה "But as evening approaches he is to wash himself, and at sunset he may return to the camp."

[67] We read in 4QMMTᵃ (4Q394) 3–7 ii 16–17: שהמקדש משכן אוהל מועד הוא וירושלים הוא מחנה והחוצה למחנה הוא חוצה לירושלים "The Temple is the place of the Tent of Meeting, and Jerusalem is the camp; and outside the camp is outside Jerusalem."

[68] In fact, we read in Exod 19:10–11: "And the Lord said to Moses, Go to the people and consecrate them today and tomorrow. Have them wash their clothes and be ready by the third day, because on that day the Lord will come down on Mount Sinai in the sight of all the people." In v. 15, however, we read: "Then he [i.e. Moses] said to the people, "Prepare yourselves for the third day. Abstain from sexual relations." *Mek.*, Jethro 3 poses the question: "We have not heard that God said to abstain from sexual relations," a question, which the *Mek.* resolves through the use of a *gzerah shavah*: the phrase היו נכונים "be ready" appears in Exod 20:11, at the divine utterance to Moses and in v. 15 at Moses' command to the Israelites. Since there it refers to abstention from intercourse, one may assume a similar meaning here. The weakness of this argument is clear; the abstention appears at Moses' command and is not part of the divine command. There are additional, unconvincing attempts at resolving this issue as well.

CONCLUSION

Fraade's classification of Qumran writings is based on his familiarity with the rabbinic midrashic interpretive system which he perceives as normative. Thus, he sees the Qumranic style as divergent, and requiring explanation/justification. In analyzing Qumran literature and ideology, however, it is important to remove oneself from any predisposition, and to judge Qumran writings on their own merit.

I eliminated the problematic designation "Rewritten or Paraphrased Bible" through my proposition that we perceive these writings as composed in a "biblicized" language or as mnemonic drafts, prepared by individuals, where the biblical verses became elements of the composition.[69]

Pesher writings, originating from the same period, are composed in a style similar to that of the rabbis. But these do not constitute midrash. Instead, these writings are *sui generis* and exclude the speculation of progression, as proposed by Fraade.[70]

As opposed to Fraade's conjecture that the relationship between author and audience is a possible crucial motive for the differences between rabbinic and Qumranic literary style,[71] my proposition perceives the relationship between the interpretation and the original biblical text as the essence of the distinction.

---

[69] See Heger, *Cult*, 104–121.
[70] Fraade, "Looking for Narrative Midrash," 63.
[71] Ibid., 64.

THE *GENESIS APOCRYPHON* AND THE ARAMAIC *TARGUMIM* REVISITED: A VIEW FROM BOTH PERSPECTIVES[1]

MOSHE J. BERNSTEIN
Yeshiva University

I. INTRODUCTION

Some of the questions that arise from any attempt to juxtapose the *Genesis Apocryphon* and the Aramaic versions of the Pentateuch are fairly obvious, and many of those have been discussed since the first publication of the *Apocryphon* in 1956. Others, however, could only be asked after the *Apocryphon* and works related or similar to it from the Second Temple era had been studied, as they have been now, for many years. I shall take the opportunity offered by this presentation to address both types of questions.

When the *Apocryphon* was first presented to the scholarly world by Avigad and Yadin, it appeared to be a very peculiar text: an Aramaic pre- and non-rabbinic document which retold stories from Genesis in a fashion at times similar to the way in which later rabbinic literature would in the genres usually labeled as targum and midrash. Those initial editors of the *Apocryphon*, however, in their introduction to the text and its translation did not focus on its relationship with the later rabbinic targumim. They appropriately, if not always accurately, saw fit to contextualize it within the Second Temple literature to which we are now certain that it belongs, describing it "as a sort of apocryphal version of stories from *Genesis*, faithful, for the most part, to the order of the chapters in Scripture. ... The work is evidently a literary unit in style and structure, though ... it may be perhaps be divisible into books—a Book of Lamech, a Book

[1] I am grateful to participants in the Vienna conference who responded to the original presentation of this paper and impelled me to rethink and reformulate certain of its details and to Professor Edward M. Cook, Dr. Aaron Koller, and Dr. Shani Tzoref who were kind enough to read and comment on the penultimate draft.

of Enoch, a Book of Noah, a Book of Abraham."[2] The fact, however, that it was a Bible-oriented work written in Aramaic drew other scholars to search for points of contact with the later targumim, and several articles, beginning at the earliest stages of *Apocryphon* scholarship, have addressed the possible relationship between it and the targumim.[3] To begin this discussion I should like to review some of those early forays into the comparative analysis of the targumim and *Apocryphon* and to show how some of the paths which were followed were not only ultimately unproductive, but also misleading to our proper understanding of this Second Temple era work.

II. THE EARLY YEARS

The observations that were made of the *Apocryphon* vis-à-vis the later targumim were usually superficial, ranging from the unsurprising fact that certain portions of the *Apocryphon* were closer to the Hebrew text than others, and therefore were more similar in those places to the Aramaic versions, to similarities or differences in the ways that each of them translated the underlying biblical Hebrew text. Thus in what was probably the first article to approach this issue in the very first year

---

[2] N. Avigad and Y. Yadin, *A Genesis Apocryphon: A Scroll from the Wilderness of Judaea: Description and Contents of the Scroll, Facsimiles, Transcription and Translation of Columns II, XIX–XXII* (Jerusalem: Magnes, 1956), 38.

[3] M.R. Lehmann, "1Q Genesis Apocryphon in the Light of the Targumim and Midrashim," *RevQ* 1 (1958–1959): 249–263; G.J. Kuiper, "A Study of the Relationship between 'A Genesis Apocryphon' and the Pentateuchal Targumim in Genesis 14₁₋₁₂," in *In Memoriam Paul Kahle* (ed. M. Black and G. Fohrer; BZAW 103; Berlin: Töpelmann, 1968), 149–161; P. Grelot, "De l''Apocryphe de la Genèse' aux 'Targoums': sur Genèse 14,18–20," in *Intertestamental Essays in Honour of Józef Tadeusz Milik* (ed. Z.J. Kapera; Qumranica Mogilanensia 6; Cracow: Enigma Press, 1992), 77–90. I have discussed some of the treatments of the assignment of the *Apocryphon* to the targumic genre in "The Genre(s) of the Genesis Apocryphon," at the International Conference on the Aramaic Texts from Qumran, Maison Méditerranéenne des Sciences de l'Homme, Aix-en-Provence, France, June 30–July 2, 2008. That essay, together with responses to it, has been published in the proceedings of the conference, *Aramaica Qumranica: Proceedings of the Conference on the Aramaic Texts from Qumran in Aix-en-Provence 30 June–2 July 2008* (ed. K. Berthelot and D. Stökl Ben Ezra; STDJ 94; Leiden: Brill, 2010), 317–343. Some of my formulations in the early portion of this paper will resemble my remarks in that one. At the same conference, I was the respondent to Thierry Legrand's paper "Exégèses targumiques et techniques de réécriture dans l'*Apocryphe de la Genèse* (1QapGen ar)," and his paper and my response to it have also appeared in that volume (225–252). In my view, much of Legrand's discussion can be said to belong to the area of midrash as much as of targum, and this is the focal point of the divergence in our analyses.

of *Revue de Qumran*, Manfred Lehmann observed that even outside of cols. XXI:23–XXII:26, which "are easily recognized for keeping fairly close to the Massoretic text [*sic*] … we find shorter or longer passages of literal translations of the Biblical text interwoven in the midrashic portions."[4] This is doubtless true, and Lehmann's observation that at times the Aramaic phraseology differs from the Hebrew only by virtue of its having been shifted from the third person biblical narrative to the first person version in the *Apocryphon* was certainly correct. Note, on the other hand, the instinctive dichotomizing of the *Apocryphon* into "targumic" and "midrashic" segments; the generic sophistication and hyper-sophistication which we have developed in discussing the Qumran scrolls and other Second Temple literature over the last half century is of course lacking, so the convenient reference points of those two rabbinic genres, targum and midrash, are taken as the touchstones.[5]

Lehmann, like others after him, moves from this assertion about literal translations in the *Apocryphon* to a claim that the *Genesis Apocryphon* was somehow an ancestor of the later targumim, particularly the Palestinian ones, which are not as strictly limited to rendering the biblical text as is *Onqelos* and which intersperse their translations of the text with midrashic material. A half century ago, in the very childhood of Qumran scholarship, some analogies were too strong to resist and some of the flaws in this analysis may not have been as obvious as they appear to be to us today.

Shortly after Lehmann's article appeared, Matthew Black explicitly questioned Avigad and Yadin's characterization, wondering "whether, in fact, this is an adequate or even correct description of the character of this old Aramaic text," and suggesting that "too much stress on the apocryphal

---

⁴ Lehmann, "1Q Genesis Apocryphon," 252.

⁵ This view was not limited to the literature in scholarly journals. André Dupont-Sommer, in one of the standard early translations of the Scrolls, in the edition that appeared after the *Apocryphon* had been published (and after Lehmann's article), remarks on the material in the *Apocryphon* parallel to Gen 14 (*The Essene Writings from Qumran* [trans. G. Vermes; Oxford: Blackwell, 1961], 291 n. 2):

> [T]he story in the *Genesis Apocryphon* is even told in the third person as in the Bible, and no longer in the first person singular as in the preceding sections. *In fact the additions and modifications are so relatively insignificant that it may almost be regarded as a simple paraphrase of the biblical text in the targumic manner* [my emphasis, M.J.B.]. Chapter xiv of Genesis is generally thought to be an interpolation of fairly recent date and already midrashic in style; the author of the *Genesis Apocryphon* saw no need to add new midrashic development to this ancient midrash.

character of the scroll may have the effect of obscuring or even misrepresenting its essential nature."[6] Black suggests that this Aramaic document might be "an early specimen of a written Aramaic Pentateuch Targum from Palestine, perhaps a prototype and forerunner of the old Palestinian Targum ... and of the so-called Fragment Targum."[7] But within a few pages, the tentative hypothesis becomes an assertion that "like any other Targum text, the Aramaic translation is simply following the sections of Scripture in their canonical order."[8] Black's surprising (to us) conclusion is "The new scroll is almost certainly our oldest written Palestinian Pentateuch Targum."[9]

The next decade did not bring major progress in this area, as not only were the views expressed by Lehmann not corrected, but they were taken even further and sometimes with a greater sense of certitude. Gerald Kuiper, in his "A study of the relationship between 'A Genesis Apocryphon' and the Pentateuchal Targumim in Genesis 14$_{1-12}$," sets out to test Black's conclusion.[10] After comparing the targumim of the first portion of Gen 14 with each other, and establishing some "working hypotheses" regarding their interrelationships (hypotheses, incidentally, which would probably not be acceptable in current targumic scholarship either), he turns to the *Apocryphon* and writes,

> In G[enesis] A[pocryphon], as in the tgg, the Aram. paraphrase follows the Hebr. verse by verse, though this is most marked in columns XXI and XXII, and contains verses-proper and free midrashic additions. ... In the verses-proper there is agreement in GA with all the Pal. tgg as well as with the Hebrew text. The agreement with one tg is particularly marked with N[eofiti], but is also found with P[seudo-]J[onathan].[11]

These so-called "agreements" are, on the whole, extremely superficial and are of the sort that might be expected among any group of translations or

---

[6] M. Black, *The Scrolls and Christian Origins: Studies in the Jewish Background of the New Testament* (New York: Scribner, 1961), 193.

[7] Ibid., attributing this idea to Paul Kahle.

[8] Ibid., 195. We should note that the evidence for the targumic nature of the scroll derives almost entirely from the Abram material, especially col. XXII, which is much closer to the biblical text than the material in col. II, the only other one published at that time.

[9] Ibid., 198. Some years later, Black changed his mind about the generic identification, writing of the *Apocryphon*, "The new Aramaic document is a kind of *midrash* on Gen. xii and xiv" (*An Aramaic Approach to the Gospels and Acts* [3rd ed.; Oxford: Clarendon, 1966], 40).

[10] Kuiper, 149. On p. 155, he quotes Black as calling attention to the agreement of the *Apocryphon* "with the pre-Onkelos Palestinian Pentateuchal Targum."

[11] Ibid., 155.

paraphrases of the same Hebrew material into Aramaic. Kuiper's remark, "As is the case in all tgg, GA occasionally follows literally the Hebrew text. Thus there is every indication of accord between GA and the Pal. tgg in the verses-proper,"[12] demonstrates quite overtly his presumption that the *Genesis Apocryphon is* a targum. The same observation, however, regarding such accord between the *Apocryphon* and the later Aramaic versions may enable us to understand how the *Apocryphon* is operating if we make the opposite assumption, namely that it is *not* a targum. The unique readings in the *Apocryphon* that do not coincide with any of the known Aramaic versions of Genesis are explained by Kuiper as being "characteristic of independently and freely developing tgg."[13] In other words, the identical passages indicate the *Apocryphon*'s dependence on earlier versions, or at least traditions, while the divergent ones are also a feature of targumic composition. Somehow this just does not seem right.

Kuiper describes the *Genesis Apocryphon* further, once again in terms that highlight its asserted identification as a targum in non-specific generalities:

> In GA, as in the Pal. tgg, we find midrashic additions. Among the shorter additions some agree with the tgg, and others have affinities to Palestinian traditions as has been noted in the discussion of the unique renderings. GA also includes unique, longer additions, another characteristic of the Pal. tgg. In the presentation of midrashic additions, some of which coincide with those in the Pal. tgg, while others are unique and often reflect likeness to Palestinian traditions, the nature of GA is revealed as the same as that of the Pal. Pent. Tg tradition.[14]

In this characterization, the attempt to encompass all of the *Genesis Apocryphon* under the rubric of "targum" requires that the very lengthy, non-biblical narratives that it contains be forcibly squeezed into the same category as the occasionally substantial, but never very lengthy, midrashic pluses which are found in the Palestinian targumim. They are simply not of the same order of magnitude.

It is perhaps unfair to reach back forty and fifty years to set up a straw man just to knock it down. I am doing it, however, not to denigrate the scholarship of that era, but rather to establish a framework for my ensuing analysis. And I therefore conclude this opening portion of my paper with Kuiper's conclusion, one which is far from proven in my view:

---

[12] Ibid., 155–156.
[13] Ibid., 156–157.
[14] Ibid., 158.

> It is clear that GA is a targumic text. Following the Hebr. text, the Aram. translation inserts midrashic material. It parallels the free translation of the Pal. tgg and is unlike the literal translation of O[nqelos]. ... Our conclusion is the tentative thesis that GA is a unique recension of the Pal. Pent. Tg tradition, to be placed next to those of PJ, N, C[airo] G[eniza], Pa[ris], and Vat[ican]-L[e]ips[ig]-Nor[emberg]-Bom[berg]; that this recension is related to N; and that it, as well as the other Pal. Pent. tgg, lies behind the authoritative translation of O.[15]

We are now told that the *Apocryphon* is actually a recension, a witness to the targumic translation and interpretive traditions which should be juxtaposed to those of the later surviving targumim, and, even beyond that, that it is related to *Targum Neofiti*, whose manuscript, we should recall, dates to the early sixteenth century! We observe that the flaws in the methodologies of both Lehmann and Kuiper have to do not just with their inaccurate preconceptions of the *Genesis Apocryphon*, but probably their misevaluations of the Aramaic versions as well. In the 1950s and 1960s there were many prevalent theories regarding the history and interrelationships of the targumim that we have had to unlearn since then as well.

III. The Current State of the Question

Suffice it to say that these early exaggerated conclusions regarding the *Genesis Apocryphon* and its potential connection to the Aramaic versions have, on the whole, fallen by the wayside. But the ways in which we think about that theoretical link have not. If we examine, for example, the currently regnant edition of the *Apocryphon*, the third edition of the outstanding commentary by Joseph A. Fitzmyer, there are two features which attempt to present the data relevant to studying that connection. First, Fitzmyer presents a far more sober discussion of "The Genesis Apocryphon and the Classical Targums" in the introduction to the edition,[16] and second, in his translation he italicizes all text which he deems to be Aramaic translation of the biblical Hebrew text of Genesis. Although these techniques are both fundamentally mechanical in nature, and the second is occasionally debatable, they present the student of the *Apocryphon* with raw data for analysis.

---

[15] Ibid., 160–161.

[16] J.A. Fitzmyer, *The Genesis Apocryphon of Qumran Cave 1 (1Q20): A Commentary* (3rd ed.; BibOr 18/B; Rome: Pontifical Biblical Institute, 2004), 38–45.

Fitzmyer presents a detailed list of passages "where one finds what may be regarded as an Aramaic translation of the Hebrew text of Genesis, or at least parts of it,"[17] being careful to distinguish between translation and what he calls "allusion." In any retelling of the biblical story, language is likely to be used that can be seen as "alluding to" or reflecting the biblical version. He then follows with an even more elaborate comparative chart of the language of all the Aramaic versions and the *Apocryphon* in those passages.[18] Fitzmyer moves directly from this chart to his conclusion:

> When one surveys the above data, it is evident that the *Genesis Apocryphon*, though a literal translation of the Hebrew text in places or in isolated phrases, is more frequently a paraphrase of the biblical text. The phrases that are literally translated are incorporated into its own expanded account. Therefore it cannot be regarded simply as a targum. In its use of Genesis, it is farthest removed from the literal character of *Tg. Onqelos*, and its paraphrase resembles some of the midrashic insertions in *Tg.Ps.-Jonathan*. ... [S]ome of the translations and interpretations of the Genesis text found in it are at the root of interpretations given in the later targums. Nevertheless, there is no way to prove this, since no direct literal dependence of the targums on the *Genesis Apocryphon* can be shown.[19]

Although in his care and unwillingness to go beyond where the data take him, Fitzmyer is light-years beyond the somewhat careless methodology of Lehmann and Kuiper, we may ask whether on a certain level his technique and the questions that he is asking of the text in this area have progressed very far beyond those of the earlier generation.[20] We are still lining up Aramaic words against Aramaic words and trying to discern whether there are any patterns of replication or imitation which could lead us to the conclusions that were asserted, although unproven, by scholars such as Lehmann and Kuiper. We are asking the questions and giving the answers from the perspective of the Aramaic targumim, and not from the perspective of the *Apocryphon*. For example, "its paraphrase resembles some of the midrashic insertions in *Tg.Ps.-Jonathan*." Why not

---

[17] Ibid., 39.

[18] Ibid., 40–43.

[19] Ibid., 43.

[20] To be sure, Fitzmyer (ibid., 43–45) follows his above-cited remarks with brief observations meant to show that the *Apocryphon* belongs to an earlier stage of translation style than do the rabbinic targumim, noting such features in the *Apocryphon* as greater literality in certain instances; the absence of ית to render Hebrew את; the use of construct chains rather than -ד; and the absence of "buffer" terms like מימרא when referring to God. But all of these are comparatively unsurprising and do not advance our understanding of the fundamental ways in which the *Apocryphon* and the targumim are, or are not, alike.

"some of the midrashic insertions in *Targum Pseudo-Jonathan* resemble those in the *Apocryphon*"?

And it should be noted that, despite the work of Fitzmyer and others in clarifying the nature of the *Apocryphon*'s genre as non-targumic, Grelot could still write in 1992, admittedly far more cautiously than Lehmann and Kuiper, "On pourrait donc soutenir qu'à partir de cet endroit, l'auteur final a collecté de véritables passages targoumiques, du moins pendant un certain temps (on a le début de Gen 15)."[21] His notion of a "final author" for the *Apocryphon* is one with which, as will be seen, I am in agreement. But I am less certain about the collection of targumic passages. He concludes, having focused in his discussion on a few verses from Genesis whose version is found in col. XXII of the *Apocryphon*:

> Dans les versets examinés ici, l'*Apocryphe de la Genèse* se présente comme un véritable *Targoum*: il ne transpose pas les récits en faisant d'eux des documents autobiographiques. Mais on remarque au passage que les variants introduites dans le texte primitif et les minimes additions qu'on y relève ne dépassent pas [88] la manière d'agir du T[argoum] J[onathan], dans toutes ses variantes. On peut en induire que la pratique du *Targoum*, en marge de la lecture synagogale de l'Écriture, existait déjà au temps où le texte araméen de Gen 14–15 a été collationné pour prendre place dans l'ensemble du livre.[22]

Although arguing more subtly than his predecessors, Grelot fundamentally asserts on the basis of the presence of the translation of the Hebrew verses into the Aramaic of the *Apocryphon* that there were already targumim in existence when the *Apocryphon* was put into its final form.[23] Why need the presence of Hebrew verses rendered into Aramaic demonstrate the existence of whole targumim?[24] Why should we not rather allow for

---

[21] Grelot, "De l'Apocryphe de la Genèse' aux 'Targoums,'" 77.

[22] Ibid., 87–88.

[23] J.E. Miller, "The Redaction of Tobit and the Genesis Apocryphon," *JSP* 8 (1991): 53–61 (56), makes a similar claim, asserting, "The only non-pseudepigraphic section on [*sic*] the scroll is the later part of the Abram section, which may be thought of as targum, *and probably derived from a targum available to the redactor*" [emphasis mine, M.J.B.]. He observes further, ibid. n. 6, that only Dupont-Sommer (above n. 5) "recognizes the third person narrative as targumic."

[24] I am not asserting that there were no complete or partial targumim of the Pentateuch in circulation prior to the period when the *Apocryphon* was written, only that the contents of the *Apocryphon* cannot prove their existence or non-existence one way or the other. The overall evidence of the Qumran corpus for the existence of such targumim is also negligible in my view, despite the substantial remains of 11QtgJob. Furthermore, while it is quite reasonable to presume that oral traditions of interpretation and translation

the possibility that the author of the *Apocryphon* translated Hebrew into Aramaic wherever he chose to employ the language of the biblical text in his Aramaic narrative?

IV. Reformulating the Issue
in Light of Recent Scholarship

I think that if we accept Fitzmyer's broad conclusions, as I believe we should, any meaningful discussion of the *Genesis Apocryphon* and the Aramaic targumim must begin with a different set of questions and operate from a very different vantage point from the one taken in the past if we are going to be able to learn anything new. In the remainder of this paper, I shall lay out some methodological reflections, preliminary observations, and suggestions for further investigation. The first one is that we should begin with the *Apocryphon*; I believe that one of the initial flaws in Lehmann's original study is manifest in the title—"The Genesis Apocryphon in the Light of the Targumim and Midrashim"— rather than targumim and midrashim in light of the *Genesis Apocryphon*. The historical sequence must be a significant factor in our analysis.

It is also clear that when we examine the *Apocryphon* for passages that translate, rather than paraphrase or summarize, the text of the Hebrew Bible, we find far more in the second, Abram segment (Part II), cols. XIX–XXII, than we do in the Lamech-Noah segment, cols. 0–XVII (what I shall refer to as Part I).[25] Even if we include passages where the biblical narrative has been changed from third person to first in keeping with the narrative style of most of the *Apocryphon*, there are far fewer examples of *translated biblical text* in Part I of the *Apocryphon* than in Part II. This is one of several ways in which Part I and Part II differ, and which demonstrate, in my view, that they derive from different sources, a position that I have addressed in a recent article.[26] They are probably also

---

in Aramaic existed in this era, to think of them as "targumim" would probably be an historically misleading methodological error.

[25] The rather unusual designation col. 0 is employed for the fragments of the first extant column of the *Apocryphon* based on the arrangement of the pieces of 1Q20 which extend to the right of what had been referred to as col. I since the initial publication. The term, which has been adopted by all current students of the *Apocryphon*, was suggested by Michael Wise and Bruce Zuckerman when they presented this data at the 1991 SBL Annual Meeting in Kansas City.

[26] "Divine Titles and Epithets and the Sources of the *Genesis Apocryphon*," *JBL* 128

of somewhat different genres, a fact that raises further generic questions about the *Apocryphon* as a whole which I dealt with at the conference on Aramaic texts from Qumran at Aix-en-Provence in July 2008.[27]

Furthermore, Part I of the *Apocryphon* can be characterized, on the whole, as very loosely attached to the biblical text, beyond the presence or absence of literally translated stories. If we align the biblical narrative with that of the *Apocryphon*, there is very little in the surviving, very fragmentary material of cols. 0–XVII that can be matched closely with the biblical text: virtually none of cols. 0–V, for example, where the story, as far as we can tell, involves the Watchers, the birth of Noah, and predictions of the future destruction of the earth that are made to Enoch and, through him, to Methuselah and Lamech, can be said to match the biblical text.[28] It is thus not very "targumic." There are a few passing points of contact with the biblical text in Noah's self-introduction in col. VI, but nothing really recognizable as translation other than perhaps VI:23 [ואש]כחת אנה נוח חן רבו וקושט, which is obviously modeled on Gen 6:8 ונח מצא חן בעיני ה' transformed into first person speech.[29] Only after the story of the flood are there a few close parallels to what we might call targumic versions of the Hebrew.[30] The absence of the systematic employment of translated biblical material makes it less likely that what seems at first glance to be biblical text should be treated as such.

Part II of the *Apocryphon* is, as a narrative, more tightly bound to the biblical text than Part I, and this is true even for Abram's first person narrative, cols. XIX–XXI:23, before the story begins to be told in the third person. It is very clear that Part II is not of the same nature as Part I in this regard and that it is the fact that Part II is closer to the

---

(2009): 291–310. I endeavor to show there that the two parts of the *Apocryphon* refer to God by two almost completely discrete sets of epithets, a feature that I believe points in the same direction as the observations about closeness to the biblical text and translations of biblical passages.

[27] "The Genre(s) of the Genesis Apocryphon," (above, n. 3).

[28] My own preferred terminology is to refer to this type of material as "parabiblical," and not to use the overworked term "rewritten Bible" for it. Some of the remarks that I made in "'Rewritten Bible': A Generic Category Which Has Outlived Its Usefulness?" *Text* 22 (2005): 169–196 regarding "rewritten Bible," as well as on the *Genesis Apocryphon* as belonging to that category, will have to be reworked in light of my recent work on the *Apocryphon*, including the paper on its genre(s) referred to in n. 3.

[29] Fitzmyer, *Genesis Apocryphon*, 149, calls this a "reflection," while the echoes of Gen 6:9 in VI:6 he refers to as an "allusion."

[30] Language in that segment of Part I of the *Apocryphon* that clearly reflects the underlying biblical text is virtually limited to the following: X:12 (Gen 8:4), XI:17 (Gen 9:2–4), XII:1 (Gen 9:13), XII:10–12 (Gen 10:22, 6, 2).

biblical text than Part I that gives the impression that there is something "targumic" about it. Since I am in agreement with Fitzmyer that there is no evidence for formal Aramaic translations prior to the *Apocryphon*, I should like to offer an hypothesis to explain the targum-like features of Part II without resorting to the presumptions that the author or composer of that material had targumim in front of him, in oral or written form, from which he drew the "translations" in the text.

I believe that the answer to the questions posed by this "pseudo-targumic" material lies indirectly in the issue of the genre of the *Genesis Apocryphon*. Vermes included in his narrow definition of "rewritten Bible," one with which I happen to be in strong sympathy, works in which "the midrashist inserts haggadic development into the biblical narrative—an exegetical process which is probably as ancient as scriptural interpretation itself." His list includes "the Palestinian Targum and Jewish Antiquities, Ps.-Philo and Jubilees, and the … Genesis Apocryphon."[31] Putting aside the ones for which we do not have any Semitic original extant, we are left with the Palestinian targumim, *Jubilees* and the *Apocryphon*. Generically, it must be admitted that the Palestinian targumim differ radically from *Jubilees* and the *Apocryphon*, to the degree that I believe virtually all scholars in subsequent discussions of "rewritten Bible" omit those Aramaic versions from the list, because of the radical divergence between the formal shape of the targumim from that of all other works which are called "rewritten Bible."[32]

The targumim, like the other ancient versions, are translations of the Hebrew text, in almost all circumstances bound to the shape and language of the Hebrew text regardless of whatever other material they may add to it. That is why it is clear to me that the *Genesis Apocryphon* cannot be a targum. And if we did not have the Aramaic targumim as a later model with which to confuse the translation material found in the *Apocryphon*, we should have understood the role of those "translation passages" in it much more readily because we might then have compared it to the other "rewritten Bible" of which we have some Hebrew remains, *Jubilees*. And we might have succeeded in doing so even without the

---

[31] G. Vermes, *Scripture and Tradition in Judaism: Haggadic Studies* (2nd ed.; StPB 4; Leiden: Brill, 1973), 95.

[32] The one exception of which I am aware (although there may be others) is G.J. Brooke, who, in the last sentence of the entry "Rewritten Bible" in the *Encyclopedia of the Dead Sea Scrolls* (ed. L.H. Schiffman and J.C. VanderKam; 2 vols.; Oxford: Oxford University Press, 2000), 2:777–781 (780b), writes "Once both the form and the content of the biblical books were fixed in Hebrew, 'rewritten Bible' continued only in the Targums."

Hebrew fragments of *Jubilees*. I suggest that as an experiment you go through your text of *Jubilees*, in whatever language you prefer to read it, and mark off the passages that are more or less the equivalents of biblical verses.[33] I do not believe that it matters whether they are precise citations or close paraphrases. Their presence is indubitable. You will see that one of the techniques of the author of *Jubilees* is to use texts from the Hebrew Bible as part of his narrative and often to expand them or interrupt them with non-biblical material.

In a similar fashion, the introduction of biblical texts into a rewritten Bible like the *Apocryphon* probably has nothing to do with its being written in Aramaic or with the targumim, but is likely to be a consequence of the way the authors of rewritten Bible composed. If the *Genesis Apocryphon* had been composed in Hebrew, I suspect, we should not have been surprised by the presence in its retelling of Part II (which, incidentally, shares more of certain features with *Jubilees* than does Part I) of biblical texts which have been integrated into the narrative. When we read the *Apocryphon* in Aramaic and come across biblical verses, we need to concentrate on the fact that they are *biblical verses* and not be misled by the fact that they are *biblical verses in Aramaic* into thinking that we are reading an Aramaic translation of the Bible, a targum.[34]

V. The Employment of Biblical Texts
in the Composition of the *Apocryphon*

There is one further issue about the use of biblical texts in the *Apocryphon* that I should like to address, and that is the compositional use of biblical material that does not derive from the immediate context of the narrative,

---

[33] The same kind of experiment can also be done with the Latin text of Pseudo-Philo's *Liber antiquitatum biblicarum* in which biblical texts are occasionally employed as part of the narrative. To the best of my knowledge, no one has suggested that it ought to be characterized as a "targum." And in fact, H. Jacobson, the editor of the most recent comprehensive text and commentary of pseudo-Philo, *A Commentary on Pseudo-Philo's Liber Antiquitatum Biblicarum: With Latin Text and English Translation* (2 vols.; AGAJU 31; Leiden: Brill, 1996) approached the issue "biblical quotations" in the work in just such a fashion in "Biblical Quotation and Editorial Function in Pseudo-Philo's *Liber Antiquitatum Biblicarum*," *JSP* 5 (1989): 47–64.

[34] See "Appendix: Further Reflections Beyond Vienna," at the end of this essay for further ramifications of this point.

but material that we might describe as "targumic" nonetheless.[35] How has the style or idiom of the author been affected by his knowledge of the Hebrew Bible? I should like to make it clear that I am not the discoverer of this phenomenon, but I do not believe that there has been any previous significant discussion of it. Fitzmyer alludes to some of the passages that I shall mention in his commentary, but does not italicize them in his translation because they do not derive from the Genesis material that is the fundamental framework of the *Apocryphon*. I am not certain that broad conclusions can be drawn from them, but preliminary observations should be made.

In Noah's description of the offerings which he made before leaving the ark in 1QapGen X, the language of line 15 "I poured their blood on the base of the altar" reflects the language of Lev 4:7 and elsewhere (although it pertains in Leviticus to sin-offerings and Noah's sacrifices here are completely immolated). His words "I placed on it *fine wheat flour mixed with oil* together with incense *for a meal-offering*" are a close echo of Lev 14:21. Either the author is consciously resorting to the legal language of Leviticus to describe Noah's actions or, permeated with knowledge of the Bible, he is citing those texts unconsciously. Likewise, at XI:16–17 where God permits Noah to eat flesh as well as the produce of the earth, the *Apocryphon* "renders" Gen 9:3 כל רמש אשר הוא חי לכם יהיה **לאכלה** הא אנה [י]**הב לך** ולבניך **כולא למאכל בירקא**, with **כירק עשב נתתי לכם את כל ועשב די ארעא**.[36] But then instead of proceeding to translate Gen 9:4 **אך** בשר בנפשו דמו לא תאכלו ("You must not eat flesh with its life-blood in it"), it appears to introduce instead the Aramaic equivalent of Lev 3:17 **וכל דם לא תאכלו**, "You may not eat any blood," since the *Apocryphon*'s formulation has the word "all" but no reference to flesh or life. It is not clear what might have impelled him to draw material from a legislative passage in Leviticus rather than a virtually identical one immediately at hand.

In 1QapGen XI:11, Noah declares that he went out (presumably from the ark) and "walked upon the earth, by its length and by its breadth," perhaps in response to a divine command for him to do so that does not

---

[35] Jacobson, "Biblical Quotation and Editorial Function," discusses the same phenomenon in Pseudo-Philo.

[36] Because of the biblical language underlying the Aramaic, I should strongly prefer the reading כירקא, rather than בירקא that is usually read, but Daniel Machiela, who reviewed the photographs carefully in response to my query, has insisted that בירקא must be read. I still find the sentence difficult to translate with that reading.

survive in the remains of the manuscript. A few lines later, in XI:15, God
appears to Noah and says אל תדחל יא נוח עמך אנה ועם בניך די להון כואתך
לעלמים ("Do not fear, O Noah, I am with you and with your sons who
will be like you forever"). Both of these passages are virtual replications
of material referring to Abram later in Genesis, 13:17 "Arise and walk
through the land by its length and by its breadth"[37] and 15:1 "Do not fear,
O Abram; I am your shield." The latter passage, indeed, actually appears,
with an expansion that we might label as targumic, in the Aramaic of the
Apocryphon at XXII:30–31 אל תדחל אנה עמך, "Do not fear; I am with you
and I shall be for you support and strength, and I am a shield over you
and your buckler against anyone stronger than you." As I have suggested
elsewhere, in both of these cases, the employment of the language of the
Abram material in a Noah context is part of an effort to include Noah as
another "patriarch" in the chain of tradition.[38]

These first examples derive from Part I of the *Apocryphon* which is
less closely linked to the biblical text than is Part II. But in Part II
as well, for all its closeness to the Hebrew Bible of Gen 12–15, the
narrator employs biblical language borrowed from other passages in the
Pentateuch. Where the Hebrew of Gen 12:10 ויהי רעב בארץ has no definite
article on the word for "famine," and lacks the word "all," the *Apocryphon*
at XIX:10 והוה כפנא בארעא דא כולא has "the famine was in this whole
land," and is likely to be based on Gen 41:57 כי חזק הרעב בכל הארץ, "for the
famine was severe in the whole land," which has both of those features.
The fact that the continuation of that line in the *Apocryphon* employs the
idiom of the Joseph narrative, Gen 42:2 הנה שמעתי כי יש שבר במצרים, in
its rewriting, ושמעת דעבורא הוא במצרין, "I heard that there was grain in
Egypt," makes the first association a bit more plausible. These could very
well be the sorts of "unconscious harmonization" of which I have written

---

[37] In the Noah passage, ארעא probably means "earth," while in the Abram one it means "land."

[38] "From the Watchers to the Flood: Story and Exegesis in the Early Columns of the
Genesis Apocryphon," in *Reworking the Bible: Apocryphal and Related Texts at Qumran:
Proceedings of a Joint Symposium by the Orion Center for the Study of the Dead Sea
Scrolls and Associated Literature and the Hebrew University Institute for Advanced Studies
Research Group on Qumran, 15–17 January, 2002* (ed. E.G. Chazon, D. Dimant, and
R.A. Clements; STDJ 58; Leiden: Brill, 2005), 39–63 (60–61). For other allusions to
Noah in patriarchal contexts, cf. my "Noah and the Flood at Qumran," in *The Provo
International Conference on the Dead Sea Scrolls: Technological Innovations, New Texts,
and Reformulated Issues* (ed. D.W. Parry and E. Ulrich; STDJ 30: Leiden: Brill, 1999),
199–231 (220–221).

elsewhere rather than conscious efforts at analogizing the sections, but, whatever we call them, they occur because the author of the *Apocryphon* knew his Hebrew Bible very well.[39]

The scene between Sarai and Pharaoh contains several instances of language deriving from other pentateuchal passages. When the *Apocryphon*, XX:17, adds to Gen 12 the very significant remark ולא יכל למקרב בהא ("[Pharaoh] was unable to touch her"), it is using the language of Gen 20:4 ואבימלך לא קרב אליה, "Abimelech did not approach her,"[40] whereas the words ואף לא ידעהא ("and he knew her not") are just the sort of supplement that we should have called targumic if we were looking at the *Apocryphon* from the vantage point of the targumim. The purpose of its introduction is very likely to fill the gap in the biblical narrative which does not furnish the information, crucial to the later Jewish reader, that Sarai remained untouched by Pharaoh, and the language perhaps underscores a connection between the two stories of her abduction. The author of the *Apocryphon* likewise creates a further point of contact between those stories when Lot's command to Hirqanosh to tell the king to send Sarai back to her husband, "and he will pray for him and he will live" (XX:23) is modeled on the Abimelech narrative, Gen 20:7 "and let him pray for you and live."

Pharaoh's summons to his various wise men and magicians to cure him (XX:18–19) has "he *sent and called all the Egyptian wise men* and *all the magicians* with all the doctors of Egypt" and is thus probably not modeled only on Exod 7:11 "Pharaoh *called the wise men and magicians*," but on Gen 41:8 as well, "*He sent and called all the magicians of Egypt and all its wise men*." And the inability of those practitioners to help is formulated in language that is very close to that of Exod 9:11 ולא יכלו החרטמים לעמוד לפני משה מפני השחין כי היה השחין בחרטמים ובכל מצרים ("The magicians were unable to stand before Moses because of the boils, for the boils were upon the magicians and all Egypt"). The *Apocryphon* writes, XX:20 "The doctors and *magicians* and all the wise men *were unable to stand* to cure him because the spirit was plaguing all of them and they fled." Here I suspect a more conscious modeling or

---

[39] "Re-Arrangement, Anticipation and Harmonization as Exegetical Features in the Genesis Apocryphon," *DSD* 3 (1996): 37–57.

[40] Professor Cook pointed out correctly that קרב ב- in Aramaic must be translated "touch," rather than "approach." It is thus very interesting that the *Apocryphon* has successfully "conflated" in its rewriting both Gen 20:4 ואבימלך לא קרב אליה and Gen 20:6 לא נתתיך לנגע אליה, the former in root, and the latter in meaning.

employment of the later verses, with the language drawn from the stories of the two later Pharaohs, in the time of Joseph and the time of the Exodus, being employed consciously by the composer of the *Apocryphon*. It is a linguistically subtle way to make the theologically sophisticated observation that the behavior and fates of the three Egyptian kings are linked in some fashion.

Finally, Abram's prayer of thanks in XXI:2–4 והללת לשם אלהא וברכת אלהא ואודית תמן קודם אלהא על כול נכסיא וטבתא די יהב לי ודי עבד עמי טב ודי אתיבני לארעא דא בשלם recalls Jacob's vow in Gen 28 and its fulfillment. Fitzmyer notes correctly that ארעא דא, "this land," derives from God's promise to Jacob in Gen 28:15 והשבתיך אל האדמה הזאת, but fails to observe that the addition of בשלם, "in peace," is borrowed from Jacob's words Gen 28:21 ושבתי בשלום אל בית אבי, "I shall return in peace to my father's home."[41] It is interesting that *Jub.* 13:15–16 "he blessed the Lord his God who had brought him back in peace," also seems to have been influenced in part by Gen 28:21, although not by Gen 28:15, and the same modeling, or borrowing, technique is taking place in both examples of rewritten Bible.

VI. A Further Hypothesis

While I am confident that these suggestions regarding the apparent presence of biblical verses in Aramaic in the *Genesis Apocryphon* are plausible and worthy of consideration as an hypothesis, I should like to propose a more speculative theory regarding the possible relationship of the Aramaic targumim to the *Apocryphon*. Whereas the early discussions about their possible connection were often very specific and binary, e.g., was the *Genesis Apocryphon* a "targum" or was it a "midrash," I think that asking the question about their relationship in a more nuanced fashion might generate different sorts of answers. Although I believe that they belong to different genres, and I do not suggest including the targumim under the rubric of rewritten Bible (as Vermes and Brooke do), we can still ask whether there is a link between the two genres, rewritten Bible and Palestinian targum, and whether one contributed to the development of the other in some fashion. And this question, too, can perhaps be answered in more than one way.

---

[41] Fitzmyer, *Genesis Apocryphon*, 218.

Let me begin with a description of *Pseudo-Jonathan* by one of its fore-most students, Avigdor Shinan. In the conclusion of his 1992 book on that targum, he suggests that "its base is undoubtedly a targumic text, but in its present form it is already a different composition."[42] Denying that *Pseudo-Jonathan* should be classified as a midrash, he sees *Pseudo-Jonathan* as resembling, in its literary form, *Pirqe deRabbi Eliezer*, and would assign both of them to the initial stages of the revival of the genre "rewritten Bible" after the decline of classical haggadah.[43] He classifies *Pseudo-Jonathan* as "a former targum that is striving to become an Ara-maic composition of 'rewritten Bible'"; whose author made "a pioneering and incomplete attempt at writing" such a composition "based on a text of a targum."[44] The movement, according to Shinan, is therefore from a targumic text to something more akin to "rewritten Bible." In this histor-ical scenario, we should not realistically think of a connection between the *Genesis Apocryphon* and the Palestinian targumim since the move-ment of the latter toward the rewritten Bible genre takes place long after the *Apocryphon* and similar works from the Second Temple era are gone and forgotten.

My own suggestion, offered somewhat hesitantly, is that we should think about the possible relationship between a targum like *Pseudo-Jonathan* and the rewritten Bible form of the Second Temple period in an almost inverted fashion. Might the appearance of rewritten Bible in targumic form be explained, in part, by a connection between some Second Temple rewritten Bible texts and the Aramaic versions at an early stage of the Palestinian targumim? Might not the authors of some of the Palestinian targumim in the formative stages of their development, have modified the approach of the rewritten Bibles and adapted and shaped them to the targumic form, bound more tightly to the biblical verse than any of the earlier representatives of the rewritten Bible genre were? Rather than including the Palestinian targumim, especially the late *Pseudo-Jonathan*, among the other examples of rewritten Bible as Vermes did,[45]

---

[42] A. Shinan, *The Embroidered Targum: The Aggadah in Targum Pseudo-Jonathan of the Pentateuch* (Jerusalem: Magnes, 1992), 199 (Hebrew).

[43] Ibid., 200–201. Shinan thinks that both of these works are struggling to become full-fledged "rewritten Bible," with *Pirqe R. El.* still maintaining midrashic style somewhat, while *Tg. Ps.-J.* obviously has the constraints of the targumic form.

[44] Ibid., 202.

[45] For the dating of *Tg. Ps.-J.*, cf. any of the standard accounts, e.g., P.S. Alexander, "Targum, Targumim," *ABD* 6:320–331 (322–323); idem, "Jewish Aramaic Translations of Scripture," in *Mikra: Text, Translation, Reading and Interpretation of the Hebrew Bible in*

or suggesting that *Pseudo-Jonathan* marks an effort to return to the "rewritten Bible" form, as Shinan did, can we consider them, rather, as descendants of those Second Temple texts, albeit modified by the constraints of the targumic form, the shape of the biblical verse? This hypothetical construct would demand that the *Pseudo-Jonathan* or one of its ancestors had some now lost antecedent that was itself linked somehow to the Second Temple era. In suggesting such an approach, I have thus, ironically, returned to a position asserted by Lehmann regarding a genetic relationship between the *Apocryphon* and the targumim, but one that resembles his only in a formal sense. As indicated above, I offer this suggestion to scholars of both Second Temple literature and targum for further consideration with a good deal of hesitation.

VII. Conclusion

In conclusion, then, what have we shown in this discussion of the *Genesis Apocryphon* and the Aramaic targumim?

1. We have suggested that the way in which questions have been formulated regarding the potential relationship of the *Genesis Apocryphon* and the targumim has not been the most productive;
2. confirming Fitzmyer's verdict that the *Apocryphon* is certainly not a targum, we have suggested an alternative way of approaching the question of why there are biblical verses in Aramaic in the *Apocryphon*;
3. we have shown that the narrative technique of the composer(s) of the *Apocryphon* involved the employment of citations or paraphrases of biblical texts not deriving from his immediate context, and that sometimes the employment of those texts may be considered merely stylistic, while at other times they function to draw attention to the analogous circumstances of the various biblical stories;
4. we have suggested, very tentatively, that if we examine the material in historical perspective, the *Apocryphon* (or other Second Temple works of the same genre) might be said to have served as a model for certain features of the Palestinian Aramaic targumim.

Ancient Judaism and Early Christianity (ed. M.J. Mulder; CRINT 2.1; Assen: Van Gorcum, 1988), 217–253 (219–220, 243–245).

VIII. Appendix: Further Reflections Beyond Vienna

During the more than a year and a half since the presentation of the oral version of this paper, my ongoing research into the *Apocryphon* has taken me in a direction that I believe has ramifications, perhaps supplementary and perhaps contradictory, for some of the conclusions that I reached in this paper when I delivered it in Vienna. I have suggested that in addition to the ways that the *Genesis Apocryphon* has been approached in the past, it is also productive to analyze it as a literary entity (almost) independent of its relationship to the Hebrew Bible. Although my work along those lines is still in its incipient stages,[46] I should like to sketch some of the implications that such an approach to the *Apocryphon* might have for the questions discussed above regarding its possible relationship to Aramaic targumim.

Two things have become clear to me in the course of this analysis: first, our predisposition to the assignments of generic rubrics is intimately tied up with the goals of our study in any particular case; and second, and perhaps more paradoxical, we may be able to assign the same works productively to different genres without violating literary and academic canons. Thus my earlier work on the *Genesis Apocryphon*, including the body of this essay, always studied it from the perspective of its connection to the Hebrew Bible, engaging such issues as whether the more appropriate term to employ in discussing its genre is "rewritten Bible" or "parabiblical," and discovering that the attempt to assign a definitive generic designation to it could be stymied, as I was in my Aix-en-Provence paper.[47] My studies of its interpretive techniques and the ways in which the *Apocryphon* responds to exegetical stimuli in the biblical text likewise grew from treating the *Apocryphon* as one of Vermes's paradigmatic examples of "rewritten Bible." There is little doubt in my mind that this approach to the *Apocryphon* is both valid and valuable, and to ignore it is to turn a blind eye to some of the most prominent aspects, and perhaps even goals, of the text. It should furthermore also be clear that those somewhat primitive early generic discussions of "is the *Apocryphon* targum or

---

[46] I made my initial foray in a paper entitled "Narrator and Narrative in the Genesis Apocryphon" at the Fifteenth World Congress of Jewish Studies in Jerusalem, Israel in August 2009, and continued with "Genre Just Gets in the Way Anyway: Reading the Genesis Apocryphon Multigenerically," at the SBL Annual Meeting, Atlanta, 20–23 November 2010, and "The Narrative of the *Genesis Apocryphon*: Between Exegesis and Story," at the Association for Jewish Studies Annual Conference, Boston, 19–21 December 2010.

[47] Above, n. 3.

midrash?," although they have been less productive than the search for the exegetical methodology of the *Apocryphon*, belong to the same basic way of thinking about the text as well, emphasizing the ways in which its relationship to the Hebrew Bible resembles one or the other of the two later rabbinic genres of biblical interpretation.

If, however, we adopt a generic analysis that views the *Apocryphon* as an independent work that happens to stand on a biblical foundation, but without focusing on how close its connection is to the Bible, then the question of the snippets of "biblical text" employed by the author cannot have the same impact on our discussion that they have had when we read the *Apocryphon* as "rewritten Bible," and our analysis must be more judicious as a result. From the standpoint of the storyteller, sometimes the employment of "biblical" language may be important to the way he tells the story, but at other times there may be much less significance in the fact that he borrows the language of the Bible in telling his tale. In the latter instances it is the writer's intimate knowledge of the biblical text that enables him to employ it in the presentation of the narrative without any particular goal in mind. In such instances, the scriptural language is thus not necessarily privileged in any way by the narrator; its scriptural nature is often a coincidental, rather than a meaning-laden, phenomenon. Such a perspective on the *Apocryphon* moves it even further away from being considered as something related to the Aramaic targumim. And we can now make this assertion not only for texts which derive from other locations in the Pentateuch, as I suggested earlier, but even for the biblical text that underlies the story that the *Apocryphon* tells.

From this perspective, focusing on the story rather than its biblical connection, we have to be careful in the way that we characterize the seeming intertextualities created by the language used by the author of the *Apocryphon*, because they derive their significance primarily from the relationship of the *Apocryphon* to the Hebrew Bible. I am not suggesting that if the *Apocryphon* is an "independent" literary work then it cannot contain any significant intertextualities, but that we have to be wary of claiming that all of the echoes of biblical language must be intentional and significant. If one of the primary goals of the final author was to present a narrative that edified, engaged, or entertained, then even some of the apparent exegesis reflected in the *Apocryphon* may be coincidental. On the other hand, since the *Apocryphon* is clearly composed of sources, it is possible, and even likely, that some of the intertextualities that we notice may be the responsibility of the authors of those sources and not of the final hand of the work. And finally, it also appears that the original composers of different parts of the work may have had different attitudes to their presentation in terms of modeling on the biblical text (and, hence, employing biblical language), complicating our analysis in yet another fashion. In the final result, then, the way in which we respond to the presence or absence of a relationship of some sort between the *Genesis Apocryphon* and the Aramaic versions of the Bible may depend on the generic presuppositions with which we begin our analysis.

THE GENIZAH AND THE DEAD SEA SCROLLS: HOW IMPORTANT AND DIRECT IS THE CONNECTION?

Stefan C. Reif
University of Cambridge

Introduction

In the course of the past thirty-five years I have given literally hundreds of lectures about the Genizah (henceforth: G) manuscripts, not only to fellow scholars around the world but also to many thousands of non-specialists with interests in the history of Jewish religion and culture.[1] Especially among the latter kind of audience, as well as when I have dealt with the media, the question has often been raised about the relative importance of the G vis-à-vis the Dead Sea Scrolls (henceforth: DSS). How do they compare and is there any connection between them? Which is the more impressive collection and why? Has each had a revolutionary impact on broad areas of Hebrew and Jewish studies? I have at times answered somewhat flippantly and pointed out that the G texts are far more important not only because I was devoting virtually my whole career to curating and studying them but also because they were less theologically obsessed and therefore less dull. I have also made the point that the DSS have attracted wider attention because they are so closely linked in location and chronology with the world of Jesus and the emergence of early Christianity. But while making such comments, I have often had the thought that I really ought to apply myself more seriously to the topic and try to compare the two collections in an academically sound and historically balanced manner. I therefore greatly welcome the opportunity of undertaking precisely such a task in the current context ands hope that the results may prove to be of some value for DSS as well as G scholars.

---

[1] As is well known, almost three-quarters of all Genizah material is today to be found at Cambridge University Library and such material is fully discussed in S.C. Reif, *A Jewish Archive from Old Cairo: The History of Cambridge University's Genizah Collection* (Richmond, Surrey: Curzon, 2000).

Is such a comparison of any real value or is it an entirely artificial exercise? In explaining why the prayer marking the end of the Sabbath and the beginning of the new week is inserted in the benediction for knowledge that follows the first three standard benedictions of the daily Amidah recited on Saturday evening, an early talmudic passage deriving from the land of Israel records the categorical but insightful statement אם אין דיעה הבדלה מנין "without the intelligence here being requested of God the human being has no capacity for making distinctions" (*y. Ber.* 5.2 [9b]). All comparisons sharpen our minds about the items being compared and provide us with a clearer idea of their content and meaning. It therefore seems to me that a close examination of both collections and their relationship might assist our scholarly efforts in one manner or another, if not in a variety of ways. I could of course begin by delineating their similarities and differences with regard to Hebrew Bible texts and their literal and more fanciful interpretations, halakhah and liturgy. The truth is, however, that I briefly, and others in the context of broader studies, have already dealt seriously with such topics.[2] What I consequently prefer to do is something a little more unusual. I intend to concentrate here on other topics more related to the special nature of the two collections *qua* collections in order to see what lessons, if any, and of which sort, may be derived from such an analysis. I intend to pay particular attention to some inter-testamental items that are common to both collections. My treatment will be subsumed under the headings of disposal; survival; palaeography and codicology; contents and dating; languages and function; discovery, accessibility and location; description and exploitation; special finds; conclusions.

Disposal

How did these two collections come to be collected and stored? The contents of the G in Cairo had been stored for many centuries within one or more of the synagogues, usually in a room beside the special cabinet containing the Torah scrolls. They were apparently deposited there

---

[2] S.C. Reif, "Cairo Genizah," and the bibliography attached to it, *Encyclopedia of the Dead Sea Scrolls* (ed. L.H. Schiffman and J.C. VanderKam; 2 vols.; Oxford: Oxford University Press, 2000) 1:105–108.

without much concern for order or survival. On the contrary, the whole purpose was for them to rot away with the possible intention that they might then be removed to a cemetery for more permanent interment. Such a historical reconstruction matches archaeological finds that testify to a small room beside the synagogue that may well have been used for such a purpose. Originally scrolls appear to have been kept outside the main room of the synagogue and fetched from storage when needed and that same storage room perhaps also functioned as a *bet genizah*.[3] The whole historical issue is complicated by a failure to move the material to a cemetery, by its removal (on more than one occasion) during rebuilding works, and the interchange of material between synagogues of different rites and ideologies.

With regard to the DSS, some caves contain evidence of storage facilities, thus indicating an organized system for housing the scrolls, while in other cases there would seem to have been an emergency that required swift consignment to a special and possibly temporary home.[4] The scrolls from the Judean Desert were actually located not only in the areas around Khirbet Qumran but also in Wadi Daliyeh (15 kilometres north of Jericho), Masada, Wadi Murabba'at, Naḥal Ḥever, Wadi Seiyal, with some other items found in Naḥal Mishmar and Khirbet Mird. Here the complicating factors include the question of where they came from beforehand, whether they are one sect's library or a corpus of texts from variant sources, or whether they did at any stage constitute a *genizah* of some sort.[5]

In neither case was there any obvious order, any clear evidence of prior context, or any indication of future plans. We should not therefore think in terms of a systematic archive but of a somewhat haphazard collection and disposal.

---

[3] M. Bar-Ilan, "The Ark of the Scrolls in Ancient Synagogues," in *Libraries and Book Collections* (ed. M. Sluhovsky and Y. Kaplan; Jerusalem: Shazar, 2006), 49–64 (Hebrew), and I. Hamitovsky "From Chest to Ark: The Evolving Character of the Ark of the Scrolls in the Periods of the Mishnah and the Talmud," in *Kenishta: Studies of the Synagogue World*, vol. 3 (ed. J. Tabory; Ramat-Gan: Bar-Ilan University Press, 2007), 99–128 (Hebrew).

[4] L.H. Schiffman, *Reclaiming the Dead Sea Scrolls: The History of Judaism, the Background of Christianity, the Lost Library of Qumran* (Philadelphia: JPS, 1994), xxi.

[5] F. García Martínez, *The Dead Sea Scrolls Translated: The Qumran Texts in English* (trans. W.G.E. Watson; Leiden: Brill, 1994), xxxii–xxxv.

Survival

Obviously there is a distinct element of serendipity about what survives from among any collection of writings in the ancient or medieval world. It is therefore a questionable exercise to assume that what have become available to scholars are the most important collections of what once existed, since what is lost may well have presented a different picture. We can, however, reconstruct history and literature on the basis of a comparative study of the various pieces of evidence that we have, including, on the one hand, those works that were consistently transmitted through the ages, and, on the other, those that were for some time lost but have through archaeological and epigraphical discoveries been restored to us. While doing so, we must always acknowledge that the picture may be more complicated than can be painted at present. Interestingly, with regard to both the G and the DSS the climatic factor has played a major role. Both in Cairo and in the Dead Sea area the lack of rain and the low humidity have conspired to preserve items that would undoubtedly have perished in damper conditions. What is more, in both cases it would appear that those who abandoned their literary treasures were deliberately doing so, or were forced to do so, without any immediate prospect of their retrieval in any form or context. At the same time, the poor condition in which they have survived presents a major challenge to conservators, as well as to scholars attempting to reconstruct original sets of manuscripts and discrete works.[6]

In both cases, then, what has survived has done so by historical accident and may not be wholly representative of the total situation in which it originated. On the other hand, the two collections are so extensive, compared to what was known before their discovery, that they may justifiably be used to paint a more nuanced picture of the two respective backgrounds.

Palaeography and Codicology

Now that we have had the G for 110 years and the DSS for six decades we tend to forget the degree to which they filled enormous lacunae that existed in the history of Hebrew and Jewish manuscripts before

---

[6] Schiffman, *Reclaiming*, xx–xxi; Reif, *Jewish Archive*, 11–14.

their respective discoveries and exploitation. With regard to the Jewish world of the post-exilic period and talmudic periods—a total of about a thousand years—there was virtually nothing other than inscriptions to attest to the writing used for texts.[7] The Nash Papyrus stood in almost splendid isolation, accompanied by only a very few other texts.[8] As A. Cowley put it in an article published in 1903 that dealt with what he regarded as a papyrus that lacked "any great interest": "Hebrew papyri are so few that perhaps no apology is needed for printing them."[9] The many texts found in the Dead Sea area revolutionized the historical study of Hebrew writing and, indeed, the Nash Papyrus came to be dated a century or two earlier than had been customary. Such texts were of course written mostly in scroll format on animal skin, with only some papyrus material, and the famous *Copper Scroll* as a singular rarity.[10]

As far as the Middle Ages are concerned, the pre-G situation was that the vast majority of the manuscripts that provided the primary sources on which Jewish history—particularly Jewish literary history— was being built were dated no earlier than the fourteenth and fifteenth centuries. The G material brought major innovations with regard to the earlier form of Hebrew texts, whether on animal skin, cloth or papyrus, but also in the matter of the emergence of the Hebrew codex and the adoption of the new medium of paper. It has even been suggested that such material testifies to a revolution in Jewish literacy in and around the Jewish communities of the Eastern Mediterranean in about the tenth century.[11] Is one perhaps entitled to say something similar about the situation in Judea in the first pre-Christian century?

Both collections demonstrate a considerable degree of literacy among the communities that produced them, provide data for periods that were previously very ill-served by primary sources, and make major contributions to the history of Hebrew script and the physical transmission of what was written.

---

[7] B. Richler, *Hebrew Manuscripts: A Treasured Legacy* (Cleveland: Ofeq Institute, 1990), 14–19; C. Sirat, *Hebrew Manuscripts of the Middle Ages* (trans. N. de Lange; Cambridge: Cambridge University Press, 2002), 26–34.

[8] S.C. Reif, *Hebrew Manuscripts at Cambridge University Library: A Description and Introduction* (Cambridge: Cambridge University Press, 1997), 65.

[9] A. Cowley, "Hebrew and Aramaic Papyri," *JQR* 16 (1903): 1–8, with the quotation on the first page.

[10] García Martínez, *Dead Sea Scrolls Translated*, xlvii–xlviii.

[11] R. Brody, "The Cairo Genizah," in Richler, *Hebrew Manuscripts*, 111–133; S.C. Reif, *Problems with Prayers: Studies in the Textual History of Early Rabbinic Liturgy* (SJ 37; Berlin: de Gruyter, 2006), 181–206.

CONTENT AND DATING

The contents of the DSS may be divided into the three topics of biblical texts, apocryphal literature, and what, for want of a more accurate
term, might be called "sectarian" books. The biblical books (all represented with the exception of Esther) match the later Masoretic texts, or
the Septuagint or Samaritan versions, or the local Hebrew dialect presumably used by the Qumran sect. The apocryphal and pseudepigraphical items are the earliest testimony to the works later preserved primarily
by the Church but with some occurrence in rabbinic literature. They do
however include many items not previously known. The so-called "sectarian" items refer to the special interests of the group or groups that
apparently preserved these manuscripts. They cover theology, communal
behaviour, halakhah, eschatology, notions of the temple (purity, sacrifice,
dimensions and defence), biblical interpretation, liturgy, poetry and calendar. If we move beyond the area near Khirbet Qumran, the finds in
other caves contain, in addition, legal documents, letters and personal
archival material. Dating of all DSS texts gives a wide range of about the
fourth century B.C.E. to the eighth century C.E. but that is to include those
fewer items at the furthest points of the chronological graph. Most of
the manuscripts date from the second century B.C.E. to the second century C.E.[12]

The contents of the G touch on almost every area of activity on which
writing might have impinged within the Jewish communities of the Eastern Mediterranean of the "high" Middle Ages. They cover, on the literary side, Hebrew Bible, masoretic and grammatical treatises, synagogal
lectionaries and biblical interpretation, as well as talmudic, midrashic,
halakhic, liturgical and poetic texts. Most importantly for our purposes
here, there are also "sectarian," apocryphal and pseudepigraphical works.
Karaism as well as Rabbanism is well represented. The more documentary material relates to historical events and to mundane matters and
daily activities. Dating of the G manuscripts gives a wide range of about
the sixth century C.E. to the nineteenth century C.E. but that is to include
those fewer items at the furthest points of the chronological graph. The
great majority of items are to be dated from the early tenth to the late
thirteenth centuries.[13]

---

[12] García Martínez, *Dead Sea Scrolls Translated*, xxxii–xxxv and xlix–li; Schiffman,
Reclaiming, 31–35.
[13] Reif, *Jewish Archive*, 98–207; Brody, "Cairo Genizah," 124–126.

Somewhat remarkably, the active period in both cases is about 400 years and the broader spectrum about eight or nine centuries in excess of that period. The common subject content is wholly as expected but the mundane matters of life are much more extensively covered in the G than in the DSS.

Languages and Function

Almost 80 % of the DSS texts are in Hebrew, whether that used in the Hebrew Bible or that which may be called the post-biblical style that straddles the period between the latest biblical books and the earliest rabbinic formulations. Most of the remaining items are in the Aramaic that again represents the transitional period between biblical and late forms of the language, with both western (Palestinian) and eastern elements represented. The DSS record unique dialectical characteristics of importance for better understanding of the historical evolution of both languages, as well as a few Greek and Latin items. Since the DSS were found in different locations and were obviously not all part of the literary detritus of the same group at an identical period, their functions are varied. There are the religious texts relating to the life, practice, study and thought of Jews, or groups of Jews, of the Second Temple period, as well as documents relating to more mundane matters.[14]

The primary languages of the G texts are Hebrew, Aramaic and Arabic. The first two are represented in their biblical and post-biblical forms, with Aramaic texts in both Eastern and Western forms, while the Arabic language does occur in its classical form and script but is much more commonly represented in what has come to be known as Judeo-Arabic. Although Hebrew accounts for a large majority of the G fragments, Judeo-Arabic may be represented (sometimes only briefly) in anything between 40 % and 50 % of them and is the primary language in at least 30 % of them. More fascinatingly, the G material contains substantial evidence of those other special Jewish vernaculars that used Hebrew vocabulary and script to Judaize their own versions of another language, such as Judeo-Spanish, Judeo-Greek, Judeo-Persian and Judeo-German, and even some French glosses written in Hebrew script. The G texts relate to the whole way of life of the Jewish communities of the medieval Islamic

---

[14] García Martínez, *Dead Sea Scrolls Translated*, xxxii–xxxv; Schiffman, *Reclaiming*, 32–33.

world and also contribute significantly to scholarly understanding of their relationships with the Muslims and Christians of the time.[15]

While Hebrew and Aramaic remain at the centre of Jewish literary activity, the Greek and Latin of the Classical empire have effectively given way to the Arabic of the Islamic world. Dialectal variation within Hebrew and Aramaic are represented in the DSS but this has been extended into Jewish vernaculars in the G communities.

Discovery, Accessibility and Location

The period of some sixty years since the first discoveries of what are now known as the DSS has seen the involvement of Bedu tribesmen, dealers in antiquities, clergymen, scholars, journalists, museums, learned societies and governments in a process that was originally motivated as much by greed, sensation and conceit as it was by academic research and the pursuit of knowledge. The searches for the material in the areas around the Dead Sea went on from 1946 or 1947 until the early 1960s and, because of the break-up of Jerusalem and the area from there down to the Dead Sea into two political entities, belonging to Israel and Jordan, the material came to be located in two separate and virtually watertight compartments. The political situation dictated that access to the manuscripts was limited, especially to Jewish and Israeli scholars. After the Six-Day War of 1967, most of the manuscripts were relocated to the Shrine of the Book attached to the Israel Museum in the west part of Jerusalem. In response to widespread frustration with the failure to publish and make accessible all the manuscripts, new arrangements had been made by the Israel Antiquities Authority to rectify this situation and were already under way in 1991. Two American institutions, the Biblical Archaeological Society and the Huntington Library, pre-empted such plans by publishing photographs of all the material and effectively ensured that all the discoveries, amounting to approximately 900 items and many thousands of folios (the number depending on the system of counting), were quickly made available to all with an interest.[16]

On the matter of the Cairo G, Adolf Neubauer reported in 1876 to the Vice-Chancellor of the University of Oxford on the (second) Firkovich

---

[15] Reif, *Jewish Archive*, 214–224, with full bibliography on pp. 230–231.

[16] García Martínez, *Dead Sea Scrolls Translated*, xxvi–xliv; Schiffman, *Reclaiming*, 3–31.

Collection in St Petersburg and argued its special value for geonic history, the evolution of Hebrew grammatical study, and the biblical exegesis of Karaites and Rabbanites. He concluded with a remarkably prescient piece of advice for manuscript explorers and researchers. "May I be allowed," he asked, "to draw the attention of the University to the treasures which Rabbanite synagogues might offer from their numerous 'Genizoth' in the East? While searching for such MSS. a competent person might also reap a rich harvest of Mohametan and Syriac manuscripts."[17] From that statement alone it would appear that moves were already then afoot to acquire individual items for interested parties and, in the course of the subsequent decades until the end of the nineteenth century, a host of synagogue officials, communal personalities, dealers in antiquities, travellers, archaeologists, rabbis and scholars all played their parts in ensuring that such moves were successfully completed. The result was that some 70% of the contents of the Cairo G made its way to Cambridge (including the Mosseri and Westminster College collections), major collections found homes at the Jewish Theological Seminary in New York, the Russian National Library in St Petersburg, the British Library in London, the John Rylands University Library at the University of Manchester, the Bodleian Library in Oxford, and the Alliance Israélite Universelle in Paris, and smaller collections were housed in Budapest, the University of Pennsylvania in Philadelphia, Jerusalem, Cincinnati, Vienna, Washington D.C., Geneva, Strasbourg, Birmingham (U.K.), Kiev, and Frankfurt/Main. Initial efforts were made early in the twentieth century to conserve (in the contemporary fashion) and make available such material but this process then slowed down considerably until after the Second World War and the establishment of the State of Israel. The work of the Institute of Microfilmed Hebrew Manuscripts, the researches of S.D. Goitein, the establishment of the Genizah Research Unit at Cambridge University Library, as well as the foundation of the Friedberg Genizah Project, then led to comprehensive projects, now reaching completion, to make available all the collections, which total over 200,000 items.[18]

---

[17] A. Neubauer, "Report on Hebrew-Arabic Manuscripts at St. Petersburg," *Oxford University Gazette* 7, no. 237 (1876): 7.

[18] B. Richler, *Guide to Hebrew Manuscript Collections* (Jerusalem: Israel Academy of Science and Humanities, 1994), 61–64; Reif, *Jewish Archive*, 234–260; idem, "A Fresh Set of Genizah Texts," *SBL Forum*, n.p. [cited 26 February 2008]. Online: http://www.sbl-site.org/Article.aspx?ArticleId=582; and the website of the Friedberg Genizah Project, to be found at http://www.genizah-project.org.

The building of manuscript collections is not exclusively motivated by purely scholarly considerations but may also be subject to political developments and theological concerns. Libraries and museums with many important such sources may have to be inspired by special circumstances or determined personalities in order to devote their attention, staff and funding to some rather than to others.

Description and Exploitation

Many of the more major and lengthier items were published within the first few years of their discovery as a result of scholarly efforts on both sides of the armistice lines. "By June 1961," in the words of Larry Schiffman, "511 manuscripts of Cave 4 had been identified, arranged on 620 museum plates; 25 plates of material remained unidentified."[19] The work on the Israeli side had been virtually completed by 1956 but the team appointed in Jordanian East Jerusalem was making only slow progress by the time that the Six-Day War of 1967 overtook events. Some of the exclusively Christian team that had been working on the scrolls had to a degree tended to see the corpus in the light of Christian theological history rather than Jewish literary development. This situation did, however, change with the appointment by the Israel Antiquities Authority of a whole new international team led by Emanuel Tov of the Hebrew University of Jerusalem. The pace of research heated up considerably and the changing nature of the findings led to important new conclusions about Jewish religious history at the end of the Second Temple period. Fresh knowledge about the newly available material was applied to a growing sphere of topics and was incorporated into overall descriptions of Jewish life, language and ideology as they had evolved from early post-Exilic times until after the Bar Kokhba Revolt. To date, some 900 manuscripts have been listed.[20]

The initial explosion of G research matched the availability of the early discoveries and the interest found in them and therefore covered the period from the 1890s until the First World War. Work on individual items then continued in a less intensive fashion until the research of Goitein and his students began to make its published appearance in the

---

[19] Schiffman, *Reclaiming*, 16.
[20] García Martínez, *Dead Sea Scrolls Translated*, xxvi–xliv; Schiffman, *Reclaiming*, 3–31.

1950s and 1960s.[21] Even then, the vast majority of the G fragments, wherever they were located, remained unpublished, and what was published rarely appeared as a fully transcribed, translated and annotated item. For the reasons already explained in connection with conservation and availability, there then occurred the massive increase in publication of G texts that marked the three decades until the present. The statistics that apply to Cambridge are perhaps best illustrative of the situation. The bibliography of published items in the Cambridge Genizah Collections relating to the years 1896 to 1980 contains 34,211 entries, an average of just over 400 per year. The next volume of bibliography, relating to the years 1980 to 1997, contains 25,117 entries, this time averaging almost 1,400 annually, an increase of a thousand items per year.[22] Topics that were literary and historical (such as commentaries and chronicles) had given way to those that were more documentary (for instance, letters) while conventional literature had to a considerable extent moved over in favour of the more eccentric areas of, say, medicine and magic.[23]

In planning and conducting their research, scholars may often be guilty of forgetting that, as Voltaire put it so well some 235 years ago, "le mieux est l' ennemi du bien."[24] In the history of these two collections, progress for the good of the majority, in the form of briefer but more numerous descriptions, was often hindered by the selfish concerns of the individual who concentrated on detailed and fewer treatments. They were also adversely affected by political and theological considerations.

---

[21] S.D. Goitein, *A Mediterranean Society: The Jewish Communities of the Arab World as Portrayed in the Documents of the Cairo Geniza* (5 vols.; Berkeley: University of California Press, 1967–1988); S. Shaked, *A Tentative Bibliography of Geniza Documents Prepared under the Direction of D.H. Baneth and S.D. Goitein* (Paris: Mouton, 1964); "Genizah, Cairo," *EncJud* 16:1333–1342.

[22] S.C. Reif, ed., *Published Material from the Cambridge Genizah Collections: A Bibliography, 1896–1980* (Cambridge: Cambridge University Press, 1988); R.J.W. Jefferson and E.C.D. Hunter, eds., *Published Material from the Cambridge Genizah Collections: A Bibliography, 1980–1997* (Cambridge: Cambridge University Press, 2004).

[23] On medicine, see especially H.D. Isaacs, *Medical and Para-Medical Manuscripts in the Cambridge Genizah Collections* (Cambridge: Cambridge University Press, 1994) and the ongoing work of E. Lev, as exemplified in his recent publication, with Z. Amar, *Practical Materia Medica of the Medieval Eastern Mediterranean According to the Cairo Genizah* (Sir Henry Wellcome Asian Series 7; Leiden: Brill, 2008). In the field of magic, the pioneering work of S. Shaked is now being completed by G. Bohak; see also L.H. Schiffman and M.D. Swartz, eds., *Hebrew and Aramaic Incantation Texts from the Cairo Genizah: Selected Texts from Taylor-Schechter Box K1* (Semitic Texts and Studies 1; Sheffield: Sheffield University Press, 1992).

[24] *La Bégueule: Conte moral* (1772).

Another important lesson is that what we today consider of marginal significance to current scholarship may come to be regarded by our successors as of indispensable centrality to their academic analysis.

SPECIAL FINDS

Having made these general comparisons concerning the DSS and the G, we now come to the what are often regarded as the most remarkable connections between the two collections. When, in 1897, Solomon Schechter discovered among the Cambridge G texts two manuscripts (of the tenth and twelfth centuries) emanating from a sect that was clearly not pharisaic or rabbinic, he thought at first that they were Samaritan, then made a link with the Karaites, and only about a decade later finally opted for a view that identified them as "Zadokites," with origins among the Sadducees. He subsequently published them, thirteen years later, as *Fragments of a Zadokite Work*.[25] The degree to which other scholars differed demonstrates how difficult it was, and indeed is, to identify with any precision the nature of Jewish sects and their ideologies from Second Temple period times until, and including, the development of Karaism. Ginzberg saw the writers of Schechter's fragments as proto-Pharisees; Kohler as non-pharisaic Jews whose ideas had been transmitted by Dositheans; Büchler as proto-Karaites in Damascus in the seventh or eighth century; and George Margoliouth as "Sadducean Christians."[26] For his part, D.S. Margoliouth regarded them, as indeed he viewed all the G material, as valueless, no more than "the contents of a huge waste-paper basket."[27] With the discovery, almost exactly a century later, of the same work among the DSS, represented in a number of manuscripts that complement and expand the G versions in numerous ways (doubling the size of the work now available to researchers), it has become clear that the

---

[25] S. Schechter, ed., *Documents of Jewish Sectaries*, vol. 1: *Fragments of a Zadokite Work Edited from Hebrew Manuscripts in the Cairo Genizah Collection now in the Possession of the University Library, Cambridge, and Provided with an English Translation, Introduction and Notes* (Cambridge: Cambridge University Press, 1910).

[26] S.C. Reif, "The Damascus Document from the Cairo Genizah: Its Discovery, Early Study and Historical Significance," in *The Damascus Document: A Centennial of Discovery: Proceedings of the Third International Symposium of the Orion Center for the Study of the Dead Sea Scrolls and Associated Literature, 4–8 February, 1998* (ed. J.M. Baumgarten, E.G. Chazon, and A. Pinnick; STDJ 34; Leiden: Brill, 2000), 109–131.

[27] D.S. Margoliouth, "The Zadokites," *The Expositor* 6 (1913): 157–164, esp. 157, 159 and 164.

Damascus Document, as it came later to be called, was a popular religious tract in Second Temple times with Samaritan, Sadducean, Zadokite and apocryphal connections, which in many respects matched the religious ideas and practices reflected in many of the other Qumran texts. An authentic version then re-appears in tenth-century Cairo.[28]

The second example of the remarkable connections to which reference was just made concerns the apocryphal book of Ben Sira in its Hebrew version and, once again, the name of D.S. Margoliouth figures in the personal and scholastic aspects of the tale. Schechter in Cambridge and Margoliouth in Oxford had for a number of years disputed the value to be assigned to the rabbinic quotations of passages from Ben Sira. Margoliouth regarded them as no more than part of the "whole Rabbinic farrago"[29] while Schechter thought them part of an authentic transmission but, to his great chagrin, without, as yet, the kind of early medieval evidence that might substantiate his hypothesis. Any scholar with even the vaguest interest in Ben Sira is now wholly familiar with the story of the find made by Mrs Margaret Gibson and Mrs Agnes Lewis, Schechter's excited identification of it as Ben Sira, and his discovery, and publication with Charles Taylor, Master of St John's College and eminent Christian hebraist, of a number of folios of three discrete manuscripts in the haul that he brought from Cairo in 1897.[30] Other fragments, also emanating from the Cairo G, were located in various collections around the world, including those in Oxford, London and Paris, and it proved possible, on the basis of these nine early medieval manuscripts from Cairo, to reconstruct most of the Hebrew of a work that had been written some 1,200 years earlier in Hellenistic Judea.[31] If Bacher's rejection of D.S. Margoliouth's persistently negative theories ("which rose, like a soap bubble,

---

[28] M. Broshi, ed., *The Damascus Document Reconsidered* (Jerusalem: Israel Exploration Society, 1992); H. Stegemann, "Towards Physical Reconstructions of the Qumran Damascus Document Scrolls," in *The Damascus Document* (ed. Baumgarten, Chazon, and Pinnick), 177–200.

[29] D.S. Margoliouth, *An Essay on the Place of Ecclesiasticus in Semitic Literature* (Oxford: Oxford University Press, 1890), esp. 21.

[30] S.C. Reif, "The Discovery of the Cambridge Genizah Fragments of Ben Sira: Scholars and Texts," in *The Book of Ben Sira in Modern Research: Proceedings of the First International Ben Sira Conference 28–31 July 1996, Soesterberg, Netherlands* (ed. P.C. Beentjes; BZAW 255; Berlin: de Gruyter, 1997), 1–22.

[31] M.H. Segal, *Sefer Ben Sira Ha-Shalem* (2nd ed.; Jerusalem: Bialik Institute, 1958), 47–69 and 375–378; P.C. Beentjes, *The Book of Ben Sira in Hebrew: A Text Edition of all Extant Hebrew Manuscripts and a Synopsis of all Parallel Hebrew Ben Sira Texts* (VTSup 68; Leiden: Brill, 1997).

from the Sirach enquiry, only to burst after a short brilliancy")[32] was not enough to establish the authenticity of the Cairo G fragments of Ben Sira, then Yadin's discovery during the excavation of Masada in 1963–1964 of a version that matched most closely MS B from Cairo put paid to any serious negation of the reasons for Schechter's great excitement.[33] With regard to the transmission between the Second Temple period and the Middle Ages, P.C. Beentjes has offered the important assessment that the "Hebrew text of Ben Sira was sometimes treated as reasonably authoritative, so that a reasonable text was preserved throughout the ages."[34]

The *Aramaic Levi* is a third work that is represented both in G and DSS. Again, there is a Cambridge-Oxford connection since G texts were located in both Cambridge University Library and the Bodleian Library and published in 1900 and 1907 respectively.[35] It was Hermann Leonard Pass who was employed by Schechter, soon after the G's arrival in Cambridge, to describe the biblical items, and who then went on to sort, identify and describe the apocryphal and pseudepigraphical items, including the *Aramaic Levi*.[36] Pass had been an Orthodox Jew who studied at Jews' College in London and then converted to Anglican Christianity. Perhaps his personal religious predilections gave him a special interest in the inter-testamental period and in books such as the *Aramaic Levi*. Dating from the third or second century B.C.E., the *Aramaic Levi* takes a different attitude to priesthood from that of Ben Sira by linking Noah to Levi via Abraham and provides an image of the perfect ruler and priest. It was later used later as a source by *Jubilees* and the Greek *Testament of Levi*. Seven copies were found among the DSS, and a number of these reveal a textual overlap with the G fragments. The first of these DSS versions was published by J.T. Milik in 1955.[37] It is particularly important for the purposes of this study that the content of *Aramaic Levi* is not typical of many of the other Qumranic works but appears to be earlier and

---

[32] W. Bacher, "An Hypothesis about the Hebrew Fragments of Sirach," *JQR* 12 (1900): 92–108, 106, publishing a communication sent from Budapest in June 1899.

[33] Y. Yadin, *The Ben Sira Scroll from Masada: With Introduction, Emendations and Commentary* (Jerusalem: Israel Exploration Society, 1965).

[34] Beentjes, *Ben Sira in Hebrew*, 6.

[35] H.L. Pass and J. Arendzen, "Fragment of an Aramaic Text of the Testament of Levi," *JQR* 12 (1900): 651–661 on T-S 16.94; R.H. Charles and A. Cowley, "An Early Source of the Testaments of the Patriarchs," *JQR* 19 (1907): 566–583.

[36] *Cambridge University Reporter* no. 1360 (12 June 1901): 1088 and 1107–1108; Reif, *Jewish Archive*, 66.

[37] J.T. Milik, "Le Testament de Lévi en araméen: Fragment de la grotte 4 de Qumrân," *RB* 62 (1955): 398–406, 398–399.

to have circulated more broadly, perhaps even to have been regarded as more authoritative. As Michael Stone succinctly puts it, "[Aramaic Levi] should be attributed to a third-century wing of Judaism from which the Qumran sectarians are but one group of descendants."[38] Interestingly, it has only been fairly recently that two thorough studies and complete text editions have been published, one of them by Israeli scholars, Jonas Greenfield, Michael Stone and Esther Eshel, and the other by Henryk Drawnel, who teaches at the Catholic University of Lublin.[39] The textual overlaps between the Qumran and G fragments appear to point to some form of continuous transmission.

When Pass was sorting the apocryphal and pseudepigraphical items in the Taylor-Schechter Genizah Collection, ultimately to be placed in box (now binder) T-S A45, he also identified three Hebrew fragments of the book of Tobit. Between 1900 and 1978, no further scholarly note was taken of these, other than in brief mentions made in articles by Alexander Scheiber.[40] In 1978, Simon Hopkins, then a research assistant in the Genizah Research Unit at Cambridge University Library, included brief descriptions and photographs in his published hand-list of T-S A45.[41] On the Qumranic side, Tobit was found in Cave 4, in four Aramaic texts and in a Hebrew version. About a fifth of the book is represented and the fragments have been dated between the first century B.C.E. and the first century C.E.[42] Unlike what has been described above with regard to the other three works stored in Cairo and at Qumran, the textual situation in the case of Tobit does not permit us to conclude that there was a direct recensional link between the two sets of fragments. There are three Cambridge G texts. The first of them (T-S A45.26) is written on vellum in

---

[38] M.E. Stone, "Levi, Aramaic," *Encyclopedia of the Dead Sea Scrolls* 1:486–488. See also Schiffman, *Reclaiming*, 167.

[39] J.C. Greenfield, M.E. Stone and E. Eshel, *The Aramaic Levi Document: Edition, Translation, Commentary* (SVTP 19; Leiden: Brill, 2004); H. Drawnel, *An Aramaic Wisdom Text from Qumran: A New Interpretation of the Levi Document* (JSJSup 86; Leiden: Brill, 2004).

[40] A. Scheiber, "Materialien zur Wirksamkeit des Joseph b. Jakob Habavli als Schriftsteller und Kopist aus der Kaufmann-Genisa," *AcOr* 23 (1970): 115–130, 117 and 120; repr. in his collected essays *Geniza Studies* (Collectanea 17; Hildesheim: Olms, 1981), 326–341, 328 and 331; idem, "Qeṭa mi-Nusaḥ ʿIvri shel Sefer Ṭuviyah mi-Ginzey Kaufmann," *Sinai* 87 (1980): 97–99, 97.

[41] S. Hopkins, *A Miscellany of Literary Pieces from the Cambridge Genizah Collections: A Catalogue and Selection of Texts in the Taylor-Schechter Collection, Old Series, Box A45* (Cambridge: Cambridge University Library, 1978), 96–101 and 106–107.

[42] J.A. Fitzmyer, "The Aramaic and Hebrew Fragments of Tobit from Qumran Cave 4," *CBQ* 57 (1995): 655–675; idem in *DJD* XIX (1995): 1–76.

a semi-cursive Sephardi hand no later than the fourteenth century and
has been identified by Hopkins as following the same recension as the
printed editions of Constantinople 1516, republished in Basle 1542 by
S. Münster. Most specialists trace these to an earlier manuscript tradition,
that may go back to a period between the fourth and seventh centuries
and have been translated into Aramaic from the Hebrew or the Greek.[43]
The second fragment (T-S A45.29) may confidently be dated about 1200
since the semi-cursive handwriting on paper is well known in the G texts
as that of Joseph ben Jacob Ha-Bavli. The third (T-S A45.25)—the latest—
is also on paper and written in a cursive Sephardi hand of the fifteenth
century and both these latter texts follow the same recension as that
published by P. Fagius in Isny, 1542, and based on that of Constantinople,
1519. That recension is characterized by F. Zimmermann as a medieval
recasting, in the biblical idiom, for popular story-telling and it has been
suggested by L. Stuckenbruck that it may have originated in the shorter
Greek version of Codex Vaticanus.[44] According to J.A. Fitzmyer, none of
these medieval versions have any direct links with the Qumranic forms[45]
but Stuckenbruck has wisely added the assessment that "none are simply
direct translations of the texts known to us in Latin and Greek."[46] We
may therefore conclude that they were copied from later versions or from
original forms that are no longer preserved. Either way, there appears to
have been an ongoing, or recurring, tradition to transmit and utilize the
book of Tobit in Jewish circles.

---

[43] F. Zimmermann, *The Book of Tobit: An English Translation with Introduction and
Commentary* (New York: Harper, 1958), 133–136; R.A. Spencer, "The Book of Tobit in
Recent Research," *CurBS* 7 (1999): 168–173; S. Weeks, S. Gathercole, and L. Stucken-
bruck, eds., *The Book of Tobit: Texts from the Principal Ancient and Medieval Traditions:
With Synopsis, Concordances, and Annotated Texts in Aramaic, Hebrew, Greek, Latin, and
Syriac* (Fontes et Subsidia ad Bibliam pertinentes 3; Berlin: de Gruyter, 2004), 32.

[44] Zimmermann, *Tobit*, 137–138; Weeks, Gathercole and Stuckenbruck, *Tobit*, 56; and
L.T. Stuckenbruck, "The 'Fagius' Hebrew Version of Tobit: An English Translation Based
on the Constantinople Text of 1519," in *The Book of Tobit: Text, Tradition, Theology: Papers
of the First International Conference on the Deuterocanonical Books, Pápa, Hungary, 20–
21 May, 2004* (ed. G.G. Xeravits and J. Zsengellér; JSJSup 98; Leiden: Brill, 2005), 189–
194. It will be noted that, having now closely examined the manuscript handwriting,
I prefer slightly later dates for T-S A45.26 and T-S A45.25 than those suggested by
Stuckenbruck.

[45] J.A Fitzmyer, "Tobit, Book of," *Encyclopedia of the Dead Sea Scrolls* 2:948–950, 949.

[46] L.T. Stuckenbruck and S. Weeks, "The Medieval Hebrew and Aramaic Texts of
Tobit," in *Intertextual Studies in Ben Sira and Tobit: Essays in Honor of Alexander di Lella*
(ed. J. Corley and V. Skemp; CBQMS 38; Washington: Catholic Biblical Association of
America, 2005), 71–86, esp. 86.

CONCLUSIONS

In assessing the evidence provided by these two collections, it must be borne in mind that they constitute what they do merely by the accident of history and they have been housed and researched in great centres of learning by virtue of the special interests of those have made decisions about what to preserve and what to study. It should be recalled that one Cambridge librarian expressed the view in 1927 that a substantial part of the G collection should long before have been committed to the flames, if it had not been for the inherent conservatism of the scholar in charge of the University Library.[47] All this raises the question of how representative the two collections may be. In response to such caution, one should recall that all the literary material that we have inherited through standard, more continuous channels has survived because it suited the motivations of particular religious traditions to preserve it. In addition, the uniquely extensive nature, and lengthy period of coverage, of both collections supports the supposition that they do represent at least an important part of the Jewish and related literature of their day. They also testify to a considerable degree of literacy, usually in at least two languages, and a tendency to create Jewish linguistic dialects. It is perhaps fair to say that there is a gap in the DSS with regard to the many mundane areas so well represented by the G. On the other hand, the G does not testify to such a powerful rejection of establishment figures, notions and practices as that which is recorded at Qumran. What is more, what is today considered fascinating may be dull fare to tomorrow's specialist. This should also alert us to the fact that we can interpret only as well as current sources and academic fashions permit and that there is no shame in admitting that the situation may change drastically within a decade or two.

On the basis of all these considerations, it is tempting to conclude that the four so-called "sectarian" items that are found in both collections indicate that such literature was familiar, maybe even well-known, to the Jews of both periods and performed some sort of literary and religious function for them. It may not have been valued by the Pharisees and proto-Rabbis of the earlier period or by the talmudic authorities of the later one—it may indeed have been suppressed by them—but it did nevertheless attract some if not many groups of Jews. The languages in which it was preserved may have been altered in accordance with changing

---

[47] Reif, *Jewish Archive*, 242 and 257.

environments and there is every likelihood that what has been found represents only the tip of the iceberg. What we have to ask is whether there was a continuous stream of such non-establishment literature and whether it ever existed within a broader Jewish framework or only within groups who stood outside it. Some have argued that it was only when Karaism discovered sectarian scrolls in caves of the Judean desert, as reported by Timotheus, the Nestorian Catholicos of Baghdad, in 815, that they took over such earlier writings and their ideas, and that the Karaite over-arching desire to trace an historical link with the Jewish sects of the past was what motivated them. They contend that such links have not been convincingly established and the reports in the Muslim sources are confused, inconsistent and unreliable.[48]

In response to such objections, it may be countered that the recognized Jewish obsession with tradition, among Karaites no less, perhaps even more, than among Rabbanites, makes it unlikely that any group could simply pick up some manuscripts and adopt their contents forthwith. Furthermore, it seems that there were so many Jewish, Christian and Muslim sects that were not approved by those religious traditions that did ultimately become dominant in each of the three monotheistic faiths, that there is every chance that ideas that had been recorded in and around Qumran had the opportunity of finding friendly surroundings in which to hibernate, or perhaps simply to exist in low key, before being incorporated into the powerful Karaite movement between the ninth and twelfth centuries. There are so many laws relating to Sabbath, calendar, diet and priesthood, so much content with parallels in apocryphal and pseudepigraphical literature, and such a welter of ideas and terminology that Karaism shares with earlier groups that the argument for some sort of continuity seems a powerful one. My late, revered teacher, Naphtali Wieder, was indeed a pioneer in demonstrating the massive debt that Karaism owed to the literature preserved at Qumran. In addition, in the pre-Karaite period and in the early days of Karaism there was not always a clear demarcation between rabbinic and non-rabbinic ideas and practice and Karaism itself did not emerge suddenly as the creation of one individual or a few rebels as its enemies liked to claim.[49]

---

[48] A useful summary may be found in H. Ben-Shammai, "Some Methodological Notes concerning the Relationship between the Karaites and Ancient Jewish Sects," *Cathedra* 42 (1987): 69–84 (Hebrew).

[49] An equally useful summary is provided by Y. Erder, "When did the Karaites first Encounter Apocryphic [*sic*] Literature akin to the Dead Sea Scrolls?" *Cathedra* 42 (1987): 54–68 and 85–86 (Hebrew). This is expanded in his monograph *The Karaite Mourners of*

F. Astren has described its emergence in a clear and convincing fashion:

> The new Karaite movement emerged at the end of the ninth and tenth centuries as a nonhybrid alternative to both Islam and rabbinic Judaism. As a revitalization movement within Judaism it offered meaning in a world fractured by the political dissolution of the caliphate, by the economic decline of Iraq and the East, and by the demographic decline of Jewry as a consequence of Islamicization. By locating itself in opposition to rabbinic institutionalization and halakhic particularity, Karaism was able to attract remnants from Jewish and other sectarian movements as well as Judeo-Muslim hybrids who were unwilling to make the final commitment to Islam.[50]

If that is a correct historical assessment, it follows that the overall picture is what is important for our purposes and not whether this or that source has got its facts slightly tangled or its theological connections partly awry. Many non-establishment groups existed and they may well have preserved such literature as the four items under discussion. Some medieval manuscripts of those items have recensional parallels in Qumran while others have no recensional link, suggesting that they derive from alternative, live manuscript traditions. Whether, once they had fulfilled their purpose and been absorbed into the Karaite religious conglomerate, such pieces of literature were to be found only in that context is another matter. Perhaps they were, or is there not also a likelihood that rabbinic Judaism had, from time to time, its more ecumenical periods, as well as its bursts of increased literacy, and was able on occasion to encourage, or at least not to discourage too strongly, the reading and writing of such items in its midst or on its edges? Is it not equally plausible that there were other times within the history of a rabbinic community when such literature was angrily assessed as heretical and, as such, rapidly consigned to a *bet genizah*?

Zion and the Qumran Scrolls: On the History of an Alternative to Rabbinic Judaism (Tel Aviv: Hakibbutz Hameuchad, 2004) (Hebrew). Wieder's outstanding study of the similarities between Qumran and Karaite sources—*The Judean Scrolls and Karaism* (London: East and West Library, 1962)—appeared much earlier and has recently been reprinted, with the author's additions and corrections (Jerusalem: Ben-Zvi Institute, 2005).

[50] F. Astren, *Karaite Judaism and Historical Understanding* (Columbia: University of South Carolina Press, 2004), 39–40.

NON-CANONICAL PSALMS FROM THE GENIZAH

MEIR BAR-ILAN
Bar-Ilan University

The aim of this paper is to discuss a text comprised of non-canonical psalms that was published as early as 1902. Some 80 years later the text was "rediscovered" and a connection to Qumran posited, but subsequent scholarly debate and the speculative nature of the discussions make it clear that the historical circumstances and contexts of the entire issue from its very beginnings require further clarification. The main objective of this paper is to describe the document in relation to the background history of the Jews in Antiquity, as well as to discuss its relationship to Qumran and various liturgical and theological elements of Judaism.

A. STATE OF THE ART

Archimandrite Antonin (1817–1894) was the head of the Russian mission in the Holy Land during 1865–1894 and he was a collector of real-estate as well as manuscripts.[1] After Antonin's death, his collection went to the Oriental Institute at the University of St Petersburg. The Antonin collection contains about 1200 Hebrew manuscripts. It has been established that this collection is derived from the Cairo Genizah, though it also contains documents that Antonin collected from other sources.[2] This paper focuses on the analysis of a small text found in the Antonin collection at the Library in St Petersburg, Russia, that is assumed to have come from the Genizah, tentatively dated between the tenth to twelfth centuries.[3]

---

[1] A. Carmel, "Russian Activity in Palestine in the Nineteenth Century," in *Vision and Conflict in the Holy Land* (ed. R.I. Cohen: Jerusalem: Yad Ben-Zvi, 1985), 45–77.

[2] A.I. Katsh, The Antonin Genizah in the Saltykov-Schedrin Public Library in Leningrad (New York: Institute of Hebrew Studies, 1963).

[3] In the Antonin collection the siglum is B 798. At the Institute of Hebrew Manuscripts in Jerusalem the old siglum is 32269 while the modern one is Antonin B 68735 (and Photostat 4598). My thanks are due to Mr. B. Richler who helped me to trace these sigla.

Before analyzing this "new" text it is important to be aware of the conclusions of former studies, albeit of necessity presented here only briefly. The document was first discovered by Abraham Eliyahu Harkavy (1835–1919), who published it in 1902.[4] His main contribution was to draw initial attention to the text, but his very short introduction, which includes only minimal commentary, reveals his inability to trace its historical and cultural contexts. Harkavy, who was an expert in his own field, gaonic literature written in Arabic, did not have the academic background or knowledge to research this text comprehensively, and so his paper reads more like a puzzle than a piece of scholarship. Few have subsequently read or studied *HaGoren*, in which it was published, and it is no wonder that the text soon was forgotten.

After several decades, in 1982 David Flusser and Shmuel Safrai "rediscovered" the document (having been informed of its existence by others), and wrote a substantial study of it.[5] Once again, the primary text itself was published with few corrections made with regard to the original publication; photocopies of the original were provided, but with no accompanying sigla. Though the breadth of knowledge and professional reputation of these scholars cannot be refuted, nor the value of their contributions to their fields, the academic rigor of this specific study may indeed be questioned.

As is evident from the title of their paper, Flusser and Safrai asserted premature conclusions that were deduced on the basis of assumptions concerning the authority and the provenance of the text. Instead of positing an objective investigative query, they presented their conjecture as fact at the outset of their paper. These researchers were ready to link theories together in a manner confusing to an experienced scholar, not sufficiently differentiating between fact and hypothesis. It appears that had they had written their paper prior to the discovery of Qumran, like Harkavy, they would not have been able to make any significant statements about the text.

---

[4] A.E. Harkavy, "A Prayer by an Anonymous Writer in the Style of the Psalms," *HaGoren* 3 (1902): 82–85 (Hebrew).

[5] D. Flusser and S. Safrai, "A Fragment of the Songs of David and Qumran," *Bible Studies: Y.M. Grintz in Memoriam* (ed. B. Uffenheimer; *Te'uda* 2; Tel Aviv: Hakibbutz Hameuchad, 1982), 83–105 (Hebrew; English abstract: p. XV); repr. in D. Flusser, *Judaism of the Second Temple Period: Qumran and Apocalypticism* (Jerusalem: Magnes, 2002), 220–239; English translation in idem, *Judaism of the Second Temple Period*, vol. 1: *Qumran and Apocalypticism* (trans. A. Yadin; Grand Rapids: Eerdmans, 2007), 258–282.

Though the text appeared many centuries after (disappearance of) Qumran and its provenance is unknown (except for the fact that it is Egyptian), these scholars discuss its affinities with Qumranic, rabbinic, and Christian sources in a parallel fashion. While they state that the text refers to David as a messiah, the reader is not explicitly informed that the word "messiah" does not, in fact, appear in the text.

Flusser and Safrai's paper regrettably relays no systematic study of the text itself, though it contains many insights and is replete with "intuitive" thinking. Not only does the paper reveal a lack of rigorous preparation, but a number of significant aspects of the text upon which it is based were ignored. One must therefore approach this research with caution.

None other than the late Ezra Fleischer censured this study, adding his own comments and assessments to the existing critique.[6] Though Fleischer applauds Flusser and Safrai openly for their discovery, he criticizes almost every aspect of their scholarship, and in a long footnote condemns them for making a priori assumptions. Fleischer provides evidence that his colleagues copied the text inaccurately, and consequently some of their hypotheses are built on an erroneous reading. As one of the most renowned scholars of his day, Fleischer's work and achievements compel us to read his arguments with respect; indeed, it is not easy to refute him. While acknowledging that Fleischer was more aware of the linguistic aspects of this text than were earlier scholars, however, it is difficult to determine whether or not Fleischer was predisposed to date the text from the Middle Ages primarily because he specialized in that period. In any event, Flusser wrote a partial response to Fleischer,[7] although one must admit that most of Fleischer's claims remain unrefuted. This scholarly debate can be summarized as follows: Flusser and Safrai were of the opinion that the text under discussion is to some extent Qumranite, while Fleischer alleges that the text "definitely" originated during a later period, after the Arab conquest of the Land of Israel—that is, from the seventh century onward.

An additional scholar, Menahem Haran, has written about this text,[8] but the contributions of his research are minor, and his confidence in the

---

[6] E. Fleischer, "Medieval Hebrew Poems in Biblical Style," *Te'uda* 7 (1991): 200–248 (esp. 207–224) (Hebrew).

[7] Flusser, Judaism of the Second Temple Period: Qumran and Apocalypticism, 240–243 (Hebrew).

[8] M. Haran, The Biblical Collection: Its Consolidation to the End of the Second Temple Times and Changes of Form to the End of the Middle Ages, vol. 1 (Jerusalem: Bialik Institute, 1996), 154–169 (Hebrew).

assumed "Karaite" origin of the text seems speculative in a manner analogous to the insufficiently substantiated claims of his predecessors. Surprisingly enough, Haran, whose specialty is closely related to the biblical *Quellen* theory, discussed a number of texts from different manuscripts in the same study without differentiating between the unique history of each of the documents; one of them is the text from the Genizah that is the subject of this paper.

Summing up the present state of scholarship concerning this text is not easy, but the bottom line is that there is no agreement either on the provenance or the date of this text from the Genizah. The affiliation of the document with Qumran is debatable, and it is encircled by a cloud of hypotheses. In order to clarify the significance of this text, the entire subject must be reconsidered from the very beginning by examining the concrete textual evidence and determining what assumptions and conclusions can be made after the primary text itself is critically analyzed. Hereafter, therefore, follows a concise systematic examination of the text that will draw attention to its implications on the study of Qumran and of Judaism in Antiquity.

B. Features of the Text

1. *Technical: General*

The manuscript in hand is a complete document in itself, but it is clear from its structure, which lacks a beginning and an end, that it is a remnant of a longer piece. It consists of two pages, with writing on both sides of each page, resulting in a total of four pages of text. On each page there are two columns, or stanzas, in a layout that may be seen as typical of biblical psalms as they are written in modern typography. This way of writing is not typical of ancient documents, however, and there are additional characteristics of the text that make it unique in several aspects.

a. *Length*

The text is divided into four chapters according the four first days of the month of Iyar, but as mentioned, the beginning and the end of the manuscript are missing. The entire text that we possess is 998 words in length.

b. *The Name of the Lord*

The scribe wrote the name of the Lord as if this were a biblical text, not in an abbreviation such as יי, but rather יהוה. This way of writing the name of the Lord is very unusual in the rabbinic tradition, though there are a few parallels.[9]

2. *Liturgy: Four Hymns or Psalms*

When the text's structure is examined, it is clearly identifiable that portions of the manuscript were cut at the beginning as well as at its end. The intermediate selections are complete; they contain two full liturgies, so it can be reasonably surmised that the original text was composed of four liturgies (at least). At first glance the text appears to be a biblical psalm, but after only one line it becomes palpable that the author had neither the intention nor the skill to compose a biblical psalm. The author, rather, wrote poetry in his own personal style, idiosyncratic and unusual, and not biblical in any aspect.

The text is a liturgical piece, hence it should be analyzed according to its adherence to the accepted structure of liturgy as well as in relation to its content.

a. *A Different Prayer for Every Day*

In the heading of three liturgies, the date when the text should be recited is mentioned, as it is in Ps 91. In these selections the dates are sequential, however, so it is clear that the psalm recorded before those dated the fourth, third, and second of Iyar must have had the missing heading denoting it as intended for the first day in the month of Iyar.

The literary style of the liturgy for the first day of the month is slightly more elaborate and elevated than the other liturgies, as is evident from the prayer's alphabetic structure. This is unlike the other psalms, which indicates that this literary piece received special treatment and intellectual investment. Considering the enhanced ritual status of the first of the month in comparison to the other days in the month, it is apparent why the former is accorded special treatment; this phenomenon is demonstrated in the prayer-book, where on *Rosh-ḥodesh* the liturgy is much

---

[9] Ibid., 161 n. 32.

more complex. This state of affairs makes the singularity of the liturgy of the first day of Iyar easy to explain. However, when we come to discuss the designation of a different prayer for each day, this is a different subject that requires further critical attention.

The assignment of a special prayer for each and every day is a non-rabbinic feature of liturgy. Though it is possible to claim that this practice is derived from the Mishnah (*Ber.* 4:4), it is known that this idea did not spread among the rabbis. In rabbinic liturgy, as is evidenced in the daily prayer service, each and every weekday has the same liturgy (excluding the readings from the Torah), while only the psalm, *Shir shel Yom*, is different for each day of the week. This liturgy, though derived from temple rituals like the *Ma'amadot*,[10] was actually established in a post-Talmudic era. Another instance of this tradition is the *Hosha'anot*, where one is instructed to recite a different *Hosha'ana* poem every day during Sukkot. As far as can be determined, this custom comes from the days of the Gaonim (seventh to tenth centuries). It seems, in turn, that the practice of reciting a different *Hosha'ana* each day has its origin in the different sacrifices that were offered in the Temple each day during Sukkot. In any event, this provides further evidence that the idea of having a different liturgy for each day is non-rabbinic.

On the other hand, the practice of having a different liturgy for each day of the month is typical of the Qumran tradition. The most important text demonstrating this phenomenon is 4QpapPrQuot (4Q503), where it is stated: "and on the sixth of the mo[nth in the evening they shall bless and answer and s]ay, Ble[ssed be the God of] Israel" (III:18) etc.[11] In this fragmentary text we have evidence for a special prayer for the fifth, sixth, seventh, twelfth, fifteenth, sixteenth, seventeenth, eighteenth, twentieth, twenty-first, twenty-second, twenty-third, twenty-fifth, and twenty-sixth days of the month; this is not the sole text attesting to such a custom (another is 4QDibHam^a [4Q504] 8 recto). It should be noted that this practice is augmented by the fact that for every Sabbath, or at least in a number of them, there was a special liturgy for that specific Sabbath,

---

[10] Y. Ta'an. 4:3, 68b; b. Ta'an. 27b; J. Tabory, "Ma'amadot: A Second-Temple Non-Temple Liturgy," in Liturgical Perspectives: Prayer and Poetry in the Light of the Dead Sea Scrolls: Proceedings of the Fifth International Symposium of the Orion Center for the Study of the Dead Sea Scrolls and Associated Literature, 19–23 January, 2000 (ed. E.G Chazon; STDJ 48; Leiden: Brill, 2003), 235–261.

[11] B. Nitzan, *Qumran Prayer and Poetry* (Biblical Encyclopaedia Library 14; Jerusalem: Bialik Institute, 1996), 35–44 (Hebrew); J.R. Davila, *Liturgical Works* (Eerdmans Commentaries on the Dead Sea Scrolls 6; Grand Rapids: Eerdmans, 2000), 208–224.

as is revealed in 11QShirShabb (11Q17), 4QShirShabb[a] (4Q400), and 4QShirShabb[d] (4Q403); additional documents confirm the existence of the same custom.[12]

Thus, it is clear that the concept behind these non-canonical "new" psalms, as well as behind the liturgy of Qumran, is that of having a different prayer for every day; this idea is not found in the rabbinic tradition until a comparatively late period.

b. *The Benedictions*

There are three benedictions, or doxologies, in the text. Each is at the end of a chapter. This feature is only absent from the fourth chapter, where the end of the manuscript is missing. Making a benediction the literary closure of a piece is already present in the book of Psalms, but only at a later period did it become standard in rabbinic liturgical pieces such as the *Shemoneh Esre*. This practice is also attested to in Hekhalot literature (ca. fourth to fifth centuries), though its presence is not systematic. The structure and content of each of the benedictions, however, is different from any formerly known benedictions.

The first psalm ends as follows: ברוך אתה יהוה אל לעבדו בכל עת קוראיו which is unusual, not only in its Hebrew format but because of the unique repetition of God's name using different appellations. The second psalm ends with a doxology; there is no clear benediction, but the word ברוך is repeated not less than seven times. The third psalm ends with this benediction: ברוך אתה יהוה אל נא זוכר ברחמיו את ברית עבדו לנצח; once again we note a previously unknown benediction that has no parallel and just as with the ending of the first psalm, the name of the Lord is repeated in different forms. In the Jewish liturgical heritage from Qumranic, rabbinic, and Karaite sources, there are altogether about 170 benedictions. However, the benedictions under discussion are an example of a unique style that is unparalleled elsewhere.[13]

3. *Content*

There are at least three themes that are expressed in different forms in these psalms. These themes reveal the essence of the text, and in doing so provide a unique "fingerprint" of the author, and of the text itself.

---

[12] Nitzan, Qumran Prayer and Poetry, 38, 207–237; Davila, Liturgical Works, 147.
[13] Cf. *b. Ber.* 59b.

a. *Universalistic versus Nationalistic Liturgy*

Biblical as well as rabbinic liturgy may be divided into two different categories: a personal or a national liturgy on the one hand and a universalistic liturgy on the other. These two types of prayers can be discerned
in many texts; it is beyond the scope of this paper to provide examples
of both groups from biblical or rabbinic liturgies, though they abound.
Suffice it to say that a text that discusses "Israel" falls into the category of
those that are nationalistic in nature, while a text that discusses "all the
nations" has a universalistic appeal.

At the very beginning of this manuscript the Lord is described as one
"who knows the ways of all living," the one who separated light from
darkness in the world. In the first psalm it is stated that the "shoot of
Jesse," that is King David, is said to be the "king of all nations" the one who
smote "all kings of Midian" and who was stronger than all "the heroes of
Qedar." In the second psalm it is stated that "all nations will recount Your
glory" and later "all the inhabitants of the world" will learn from me (the
psalmist). In the third psalm it is stated: "for all will know the Lord, from
their great to their smaller people, since the Lord judges the whole world."

However, the first psalm represents the nation of Israel as "Your people," while in the second psalm Israel is called "the sheep that was slaughtered." The third psalm mentions "daughters of Jerusalem" and "His
Torah." These variations indicate that the themes of these psalms are
interwoven in a very unusual way. When juxtaposed to the nationalism
in the Shemoneh Esre, it becomes clear that the combination of themes
in the text under discussion is unusual.

The fourth psalm (from which the end is missing), in contrast, bears
the character of a personal prayer, resembling many personal prayers
in the book of Psalms. For that reason even a non-Jew may recite the
words of the fourth psalm with no hesitation. In summary, in terms
of the standard categorization of psalms according to theme, from the
nationalistic versus the universalistic point of view three psalms out
of four do not fit the standard models; clearly this issue merits more
study.

b. *Praising the Lord: His Might and Theodicy*

One aspect of any prayer, no doubt, is praising God, and one can see this
feature in almost any prayer in the Jewish liturgy. This is true, of course,
of the text in hand, where in many cases the prayer speaks to his God

recounting His deeds. Of special importance is the epithet שופט צדק that appears twice, in the first and the fourth psalms. In the fourth psalm this concept is even more pronounced: כי אתה הוא שופט הצדק/ולא יצא מלפניך משפט שקר ("since you are judge of justice and no false judgment will come out from you"); this statement can only be interpreted as theodicy. The fact that the second psalm begins with the tragedy of the slaughtered sheep followed by more prayers, petitions, and eulogy shows that the poet was thinking of the Deity in light of theodicy. The idea, of course, is not new, but weaving this theology into liturgical verses is a unique feature of this text.[14]

c. *Praising David*

In Jewish liturgy King David plays a role, since he is mentioned several times a day in rabbinic prayer. In Jewish tradition King David has an important position, not as a hero to be praised, but rather because of the belief that his descendent will save the Jewish people. In the Bible, the role of King David is even more prominent and elevated; see Ps 89:21 (4QPs^x [4Q98g]) or 132:11, where he is acclaimed.

In the text at hand, King David is praised much more extensively than in the Bible, and after reading a few verses it becomes evident that the author considered King David to be his hero. For example, in the second half of the first psalm twelve lines are devoted to praising King David in an unprecedented manner.

Before concluding the present discussion of the content of the prayers in this document, one should keep in mind that the majority of the liturgy of Qumran does not convey sectarian beliefs. That is to say, assuming fragments one may find are from a liturgical text, they do not necessarily reveal the text's theological background. A modern example of this phenomenon can be seen in present-day Jewish liturgies: Orthodox, Conservative, and Reform Judaism alike do not present their uniqueness in each and every sentence of their literature of worship. This is especially true when one reads only one or two pages out of an entire book, and this principle applies to the matter under discussion in a similar manner.

---

[14] Cf. *b. Ber.* 58b.

4. *Idiosyncratic Hebrew*

Flusser, Safrai, Fleischer, and Haran did their best to point out that some of the phrases in the text are common to and characteristic of Qumran. Such phrases are: נתיבי צדקך, חפצי רצונך, בחירי צדק, and perhaps one or two additional expressions. The number of these parallel phrases is small, however, and one needs to be aware of the broader picture before attempting to determine the significance of one specific aspect of the language.

The present text is composed in a unique and idiosyncratic form of Hebrew that utilizes unusual syntax and vocabulary. No doubt, translating the text is not easy. Some of the phrases are not known elsewhere, such as תקומי הארץ, מבטחות, גדולות גדולות, and more. Others are extremely rare, such as רוזני תבל.[15]

Another uncommon linguistic practice in the Hebrew text is the affinity of the author for expressing a single concept in two words, a formula that leads to a plethora of double-phrases. One might imagine that this practice implies that he is using a genitive construction, though this is not the case. This type of language is known from Qumran as well as from "classic" *piyyutim* (ca. fifth to eighth centuries). It is not clear whether this language formation exists in rabbinic texts, but it has been claimed that this type of phrasing was already present in the Bible.[16]

All in all, the Hebrew employed in this manuscript is neither biblical nor rabbinic, neither Qumranite nor Karaite. The text was written in atypical Hebrew that is one of a kind. Had but a few words been missing from the text, less than one percent, modern scholars would have been highly skeptical about any connection between these psalms and Qumran. It is true that even in Qumran more than one type of Hebrew was used,[17] but the reader should nonetheless be cautious and keep the significance of parallel phraseology in proportion.

---

[15] The last expression is found in a song attributed to Joshua in the book of Yashar. See D. Goldschmidt, ed., *Sepher hajaschar: Das Heldenbuch: Sagen, Berichte und Erzählungen aus der israelitischen Urzeit* (Berlin: Harz, 1923), 290.

[16] N. Aloni, *Tiberian School of Hebrew Grammar* (Jerusalem: Mass, 1995), 74 (Hebrew); Haran, *Biblical Collection*, 1:159 n. 29.

[17] J.F. Elwolde, "Developments of Hebrew Vocabulary between Bible and Mishnah," in *The Hebrew of the Dead Sea Scrolls and Ben Sira: Proceedings of a Symposium held at Leiden University 11–14 December 1995* (ed. T. Muraoka and J.F. Elwolde; STDJ 26; Leiden: Brill, 1997), 17–55 (nn. 14, 38).

5. *Poor Poetry*

When the text is analyzed from a poetical perspective, as a manuscript that appears to be poetic in nature, one cannot but be surprised at the fact that the writer attempted to create poetry notwithstanding the deficiency of his skills in this art. If one thinks of a poet, certainly of a prophet, as a sage who is assumed to have a total command of his own language, then in this case one would be disappointed. It is true that Harkavy wrote as the title of his paper that the text is composed in the style of the book of Psalms. A closer look at the text, however, readily reveals that this characterization is an overstatement. The most that can be claimed is that the author of the document was familiar with the book of Psalms, which is not a particularly daring assumption. Moreover, when reading the psalms in the manuscript under discussion, one may wonder why an author with such limited ability would attempt the poetic genre in the first place.

6. *Prophecy*

The role of prophecy in these psalms deserves special treatment, both because of its unprecedented character and because close study may provide a clue as to its nature.

Although the first psalm lacks a heading, the other three psalms begin with a header, or a superscript, that reads as follows: "On that date in the month I saw in a (holy) vision and all prophecies, and I prayed before the Lord and said." In the first psalm, since the superscript is missing, one cannot be certain of the connection between the author and the prophecy, that is, to whom to attribute the ensuing prophecy. The author does mention prophecy as a spiritual experience of "Your servant," however, which leads the reader to assume that the speaker is the author himself. That is to say, the author implies that he himself is a prophet, which is a very unusual phenomenon.

The problem of prophecy in this text should be divided into two different issues: a) an author who is a prophet; and b) a prayer that was made in relation to a prophecy. The statement that implies the speaker himself was a prophet raises the immediate question: when did this prophet live, or until what historical era did the Jews believe they had prophets among them? The other question is striking as well, though more uncommon: do we know of any other liturgical composition—a prophetic prayer or a prayer by a prophet—that is said to have been composed under the influence of a vision? Though there are many liturgical pieces in the Bible, it seems that the most relevant, if not the only parallel,[18] is Ps 89:20–38, in which a vision is related to a hymn and David is praised, as occurs in the first psalm in our text.[19]

In any event, the text under discussion is unique in terms of the prophetic tradition, especially when taking into consideration the fact that according to the rabbis of the first centuries, prophecy had disappeared a considerable time previously. In this text, on the contrary, the author speaks of prophecy as a living phenomenon, implying that he was not part of rabbinic tradition.

7. The Author

Harkavy was in doubt concerning the identity and chronology of the author of this text. In contrast to Harkavy's caution, Flusser and Safrai were confident that the text was composed by someone who attributed the psalms it contained to King David, and thus convinced that the text itself is pseudepigraphic. A close look at Flusser and Safrai's study reveals how much emphasis they put on this aspect of the manuscript. When reading the primary document without the aid of former studies, however, it becomes clear that the author does not explicitly clarify his identity at any point, nor does he imply that King David rather than he is the author of the psalms. On the contrary, the poet speaks of David in the third person. It is thus not surprising that Fleischer began his refutation of Flusser and Safrai's research exactly at this point. In other words, King David's authorship was attributed to the text without textual evidence.

The intellectual profile of the author is not easy to reconstruct and hence the following is but conjecture. The text itself indicates that the author had some knowledge of the Bible, especially the book of Psalms, though the Bible did not leave a noticeable imprint on his way of thinking or expression. His writing evidences knowledge of some of Qumranic literature as well as some of rabbinic liturgy, but to what extent cannot be determined. There is almost no indication that the author knew any rabbinic tract. Most of the text is not sectarian, a feature already noted in relation to Qumran. Non-rabbinic features of the text are the practice

---

[18] Cf. Jer 32:14–17.

[19] See P.W. Flint, "The Prophet David at Qumran," in *Biblical Interpretation at Qumran* (ed. M. Henze; Studies in the Dead Sea Scrolls and Related Literature; Grand Rapids: Eerdmans, 2005), 158–167.

of the scribe writing the biblical form of the name of the Lord and of recording a different prayer each day, but these features may be seen in rabbinic circles as well. The most notable difference between this author and the rabbis is his claim of seeing visions (and his unprecedented benedictions). Since the author was a prophet, he was thus not part of rabbinic society. It seems the author played a role in his congregation as the prayer leader, or perhaps as a religious leader in some other capacity.

C. Dating the Text

Some people consider the dating of any given text as the most important aspect in understanding its meaning, and this idea is increasingly valid the older the text is considered to be. Finding a "new" text that is not known through tradition is similar to an archeological discovery, and it is no wonder that scholars debate such matters, especially when an element that is sectarian, or in some way unusual, is involved. It seems that the goal of determining the date of the text in hand influenced the thinking of the scholars involved in analyzing its content, as they assumed that unless they ascertained when it was written, the publication would suffer a real lacuna. There is of course no problem in declaring the date of a text even before analyzing it, though some appear to think that first and foremost a conclusion as to the chronological context is required, and only afterwards can the text be properly analyzed. Needless to say, this type of scholarship is not the most optimal means of building knowledge.

Harkavy was of the opinion that the text was composed by "either David Alroi, or Abraham Abulafia or some other false prophet," postulating that perhaps it was composed between the twelfth to thirteenth centuries. Flusser and Safrai declared that the text was composed before the destruction of the Second Temple, which put its composition sometime between the first century B.C.E. and the first century C.E. Fleischer stated that: "certainly (the author) worked after the Arab conquest of the Land of Israel," implying an approximate date of between the seventh to ninth centuries. Haran was of the opinion that this text (along with another that is not studied here) was composed by a Karaite, without giving a specific date, though it may be surmised that his opinion was that the text was composed probably around the eighth to ninth centuries C.E. All this leaves the reader with the tentative conclusion, according to the span of time between these opinions, that the date of the text's composition is anywhere within a timeframe of around 1300 years! Contemplating this wide span may remind the reader of the analogous problem of *Hermes Trismegistus*, or else may lead one to consider the poor status of our knowledge of Hebrew textual historiography.

Attempting to solve the problem of dating seems formidable, especially when taking into account the aforementioned scholarship but, nevertheless, finding the *Sitz im Leben* is part of understanding a text and this leads us to discern unsatisfactory arguments in former studies. It seems that Fleischer puts excessive stress on the word Qedar, claiming that since Qedar was a common epithet for Arabs in the Middle Ages, this word suggests a Medieval date for the text. As Fleischer knew the origin of each and every Hebrew word, it appears that he was confident that his readers share this knowledge, and so he did not provide them with additional information about the term Qedar. Biblical Qedar is the name of one of the sons of Ishmael (Gen 25:13) and Isaiah made a prophecy against "heroes, children of Qedar" (Isa 21:16–17). In Ezek 27:21 Qedar is cited together with Arabia (and Sheba), and therefore it cannot be claimed that the mention of "heroes of Qedar" as enemies of King David in the first psalm can be taken as proof of its connection to Arabs, and thus denote a later date of composition. Thus, the fact that the presence of a particular biblical word is taken by Fleischer to suggest a late date looks as if it is based upon a self-convinced scholar's assumption. Moreover, Fleischer is well aware of the cry against idolatry in the second psalm but he does not interpret this as an indication of pre-Arab times. He is undoubtedly cognizant of the similarity between this text and a liturgical piece named "*Alenu*," but for some reason he fails to declare that this piece of liturgy originated in the Hekhalot literature,[20] perhaps because he ignored it (along with more than thirty poems in this literature). Given this evidence, it must be admitted that Fleischer's arguments are flawed, and consequently it is more legitimate to accept Flusser and Safrai's claims for an earlier date of composition.

Going "backwards" in time does not necessarily lead us to agree with Flusser and Safrai that the text under consideration originated in Qumran, however. On the contrary, the affiliations with Qumran literature, valid as they are, are too few to convincingly validate the claim the text came from Qumran. That is to say, just as Fleischer overemphasized the word Qedar to denote lateness, Flusser and Safrai "sinned" in the other

---

[20] M. Bar-Ilan, "The Source of 'Aleinu le-Shabe'ah' Prayer," *Da'at* 43 (1999): 5–24 (Hebrew).

direction, claiming Qumran provenance on very meager grounds (as well as attributing pseudepigraphy and messianism to the text without sufficient basis).

It seems that a key point in determining the chronology of this text is the phrase "the sheep that was slaughtered," words derived from Ps 44:23. Taking the usage of this phrase as denoting real history leads one to surmise that it reflects the aftermath of either the first or the second rebellion against the Romans (70 or 135 C.E.). As previously noted, there is no reason to assume that the author had any rabbinic training or that the way he expressed his thoughts reflects a world-view different than any other of his time and place. The author's claim to prophecy leads one to speculate that he could not be one of the rabbis who believed that prophecy had left Israel centuries before the second destruction. On the other hand, we know for a fact that there were many Jews, not including rabbis, who in the first and second centuries believed in a living prophecy.[21] Jews in those times might have had connections or even access to the Qumran library, and hence using Qumranic phraseology does not necessarily or automatically lead to Qumran itself. The main "source" of the text is the Bible, the common heritage of all Jews in Antiquity. Using words assumed to be taken from Qumran, on the one hand, and using words assumed to be taken from rabbinic circles (as claimed by Fleischer), on the other, hint at the theory that what we have at hand is a non-rabbinic and non-Qumranic (and needless to say, not a Karaite) text. Rather, the text at hand reflects a form of Jewish thinking at the end of the first century or in the second century that later was considered to be sectarian, though those who prayed in this manner, with this piece of liturgy, would not have considered themselves as such during their own times.

R. Yohanan (d. 279 C.E.) stated that the Jews went into exile (when Jerusalem was destroyed) only after they were separated into twenty-four (that is, numerous) sects of heresies.[22] This well-known statement has been accepted by modern scholarship as a kind of proof for the division of the Jews into sects, though none have really asked how to validate testimony given some 200 years after the event. For that reason, it is assumed that the words of R. Yohanan, true as they are, also reflect his

---

[21] D.E. Aune, Prophecy in Early Christianity and the Ancient Mediterranean World (Grand Rapids: Eerdmans, 1983); R. Gray, Prophetic Figures in Late Second Temple Jewish Palestine: The Evidence from Josephus (Oxford: Oxford University Press, 1993).

[22] Y. Sanh. 10:5, 29c.

own times. In other words, though it seems that after the destruction of the Second Temple in Jerusalem only the rabbis were left to preserve the national spirit, so to speak, the truth was that a number of other types of Jews were living at the time, as some scholars have already argued.[23]

In all, the text in hand is a reflection of one of the many Jews who lived in Palestine a century or so after the destruction of the Second Temple. In Antiquity there were numerous groups of Jews, many more than attested to by our sources, and the text from the Genizah affords additional evidence of the diversity of Judaisms in Antiquity.[24]

D. Some Methodological Remarks

Analyzing a text according to a pre-conceived opinion derived from prior scholarly expertise is nothing but an example of academic dogma, which is not far from fixed theological doctrine. Modern criticism should be free of such academic bias even when opinions of this nature are expressed by a respected scholar of great repute.

Although scholars are anxious to know the exact date of any text that comes from Antiquity, there are numerous additional questions that must be posed, such as: what data can be considered "proof" of the assumed date of a previously unknown text? Once again, we refer to a well-known methodological understanding: the fewer hypotheses the better in order to form solid conclusions, which need be established and backed up by a systematic analysis.

Former scholars have looked at the text under study here as a dichotomy: either it is from Qumran or it is a non-rabbinic text, assumed to be Karaite. Historical evidence allows more than only these two possibilities, however, and having two options does not exclude the option of a third. In other words, if the text is not rabbinic, that allows but does not of

---

[23] M. Black, "The Patristic Accounts of Jewish Sectarianism," *BJRL* 41 (1958–1959): 285–303; A.F.J. Klijn and G.J. Reinink, *Patristic Evidence for Jewish-Christian Sects* (NovT-Sup 36; Leiden: Brill 1973); M.D. Goodman, *Judaism in the Roman World: Collected Essays* (Ancient Judaism and Early Christianity 67; Leiden: Brill 2007), 33–46.

[24] A.F. Segal, *The Other Judaisms of Late Antiquity* (BJS 127; Atlanta: Scholars Press, 1987); G. Boccaccini, "Middle Judaism and its Contemporary Interpreters (1986–1992): Methodological Foundations for the Study of Judaisms, 300 BCE to 200 CE," *Hen* 15 (1993): 207–233; J.J. Collins, "Varieties of Judaisms in the Hellenistic and Roman Periods," *JR* 77 (1997): 605–611.

necessity entail the conclusion that it is a Karaite text, for one scholar, or a Qumranite text, for another.

The issue of authoritatively dating a text cannot depend upon a single phrase, nor on any one particular custom, since in Antiquity, like today, there were many diverse categories of Jews; it is not possible to determine exactly who belonged to what group. In order to understand ancient documents, therefore, instead of focusing solely on particular words, one should look for other phenomena, such as special liturgy, prophecy, and more.

This discussion concludes by drawing attention to a case analogous to the one under study, the critical history of a text whose discovery is similar in many aspects to the one being analyzed in this paper: *Die Weisheitsschrift*.[25] In both instances, texts from the Genizah led to ensuing critical debate over dating spanning centuries, where several hundred years stand between the contending opinions.

CONCLUSION

Though the text from the Genizah that is the subject of this study has already been published and analyzed, many of its aspects still need further clarification, and would benefit from additional, more thorough studies free of predetermined hypotheses.

The text under discussion is no more than a small fragment, but it does constitute testimony to a non-rabbinic Judaism, and as such its importance is unequivocal.

In conclusion, rather than discussing Judaisms in Antiquity on the scant existing evidence, one should look forward to collecting and analyzing additional texts in a mode free from pre-conceived characterizations; their number is larger than one would expect.

---

[25] S.Z. Schechter, "Genizah Fragments," *JQR* 16 (1904): 425–452; K. Berger, *Die Weisheitsschrift aus der Kairoer Geniza: Erstedition, Kommentar und Übersetzung* (Texte und Arbeiten zum neutestamentlichen Zeitalter 1; Tübingen: Francke, 1989); E. Fleischer, *The Proverbs of Sa'id ben Babshad* (Jerusalem: Ben-Zvi Institute, 1990), 241–263; G.W. Nebe, "Die wiederentdeckte Weisheitsschrift aus der Kairoer Geniza und ihre 'Nähe' zum Schrifttum von Qumran und zu Essenern," in *New Qumran Texts and Studies: Proceedings of the First Meeting of the International Organization for Qumran Studies*, Paris 1992 (ed. G.J. Brooke and F. García Martínez; STDJ 15; Leiden: Brill, 1994), 241–254; J.J. Collins, "Review of K. Berger, *Die Weisheitsschrift aus der Kairoer Geniza*," *JBL* 110 (1991): 148–150.

Appendix 1
Photographs of MS Antonin

APPENDIX 2
TRANSCRIPTION OF THE HEBREW TEXT[26]

שירי דוד החיצוניים

א גלוי לפניך צדיק ורשע ולא תבקש עליהם עידי אדם:
דיין דורות ושופט בצדק ידוע בדרכי כל חי:
חפצת בצדק ומאסת בעוול ולא יתיצבו הוללים לנגד כבודך:
והבדלתה עולם בין חושך לאור ובין טמא לטהור ובין צדק לשקר:
5 זריתה מעמך כל בני זרים וטהרת צאנך מן חיה טמאה:
חוכמת עוזך נתתה לעבדך כי מבין בכולם כחפצי רצונך:
טעתה צדקות בארץ אמת ומשפט הרביתה בעולמים:
ילמדו שיר כל עובדי שמך אשר יאמינו בדברי עבדך:
כנגד כל הארץ ירבו צדקתם ופועלי טובתם אשר אהבו בלבבם:
10 כוננת דרכם אל מצותך וישרתה כוחם בכל מעשי פלאך:
לעולם לעולם יעבדו את שמך ולנצח נצחים ירוממו את שמך:
מי כמעשיך ומי כפועליך ומי ידמה לך על רב כל מעשיך:
מחלת וסלחת על כל חטאתינו וכפרת באהבה על כל פשיענו:
ניבאת ברוחך על פי עבדך כי קרבתי קץ ועוד לא תאחר:
15 נשבעת מראש לדויד עבדך ומשחת ברחמך את שורש ישי:
סמכת זרועו בקדושתך כי היכין שבחך עד אפסי ארץ:
עמוד עולם שמתה את שמו וגודר פרץ ובונה חורבות:
פינה ממואסה אשר מאסו הבונים ועלית לראש מעל כל האומים:
פאר ועטרת הינחלתו ברינה והוד כל הגוים קראת את שמו:
20 צדק ומשפט הרביתה בימיו ושלום וברכות עד בלי מספר:
צהלו לפניך כל בחירי צדק כי ישמחו בא[רץ ח]{מ}דה:
קדשת על פיו את שם הגדול ושירות עוזך יספר כל היום:
רוב כל מלאכים עשית גדולתו ומלך כל האומים נתתו לנצח:
שברת לפניו כל מלכי מדין וטבעת במצולות כל שונאי נפשו:
25 תמכת ימינו על חרבו וחזקת זרועו על כל גיבורי קידר:
לא ימוט רגלו כי בטח בשמך ולא יכשל כוחו כי עזרתו באהבה:
אשרי הגבר אשר יבטח בדברך כי לעולם לעולם לא נכלמו פניו:

ב בך בטחתה נפשי חוניני ועניני: ברוך אתה יהוה אל עונה לעבדו בכל עת קוראיו:
אלהי הרחמן רחים עלינו: ברוך שם כבוד מלכותו לעולם ועד:
ברוך שם כבודו לעולם ועד: ברוך יהוה אלהי ישראל מן העולם ועד העולם
ואמר כל העם אמן: בחודש אייר בשנים בחדש ראיתי במראה וכל נבואיו
5 והתפללתי לפני יהוה ואמרתי:
יהי רחמן יהוה אלהינו על צאן הריגה אשר הרגום רועים ולא חמלו עליהם
חבוש ברחמך עצמות דכות ורפא באהבה את שברי נחלתך:
כי לטוב העולם העמדתני לפניך ולאור הגוים נתתני בעוזך:
כל האומים יספרו כבודך כי יראו צדקתך על יד נאמנך:
10 יקבצו סגונים וכל מלכי ארץ רוזני תבל ומושלי אדם:
לראות את גבורות ימינך ולהבין את סוף דברי קדשך:
וידעו כולם את גבורתך כי ידך יהוה עשה כל אלה:

---

[26] The Hebrew text is based on former readings but compared to the Photostats (that do not show each and every word). In comparison with Flusser's text there are eight emendations but only in two cases (2:11; 3:13) are these changes significant. Few minor typographical changes were made to clarify the reading.

ישמח צדיק כי יראה זאת   ויגיל לפניך בשירות והודאות:
ילמדו ממני כל יושבי תבל   וישובו אל דרכך ויעבדוך באימונה:
15 ויקדמו פניך בתודה   בזמירות ובשירות והודאות:
יגדלו כבודך בתוך מחנותם   וידעו כי אתה יהוה בראתם:
יבושו כל עובדי סמל   כי יחכמו בפסיליהם:
לא יעבדו עוד את אלילים   ולא ישתחוו לעד למעשה ידיהם:
והאלילים כליל יחלופו   מחמדיהם יאבדו לנצח:
20 ותתגדל ותתקדש מפי כל מעשך   מעתה ועד עולם:
כי עבדך יספר בנפלאותיך   כאשר כוחך ורוח דבריו:
כי אין לי שמחת כל דבר   כי אם דבריך ומראה כבודך:
אל תסתיר ממני ברחמך הרבים   ואל תמיתני בעבור אהבתך:
כי אהבתי מעון ביתך   מכל היכלי מלכים:
25 טוב לי תורתיך   מאלף אלפים וככרי זהב:
טוב לי קדוש דברך   מכל כלי חמדה:
טוב לי מצוות רצונך מכל אבנים טובות   ומרגליות חפצי מלכים:
ג אשרי שימצא כבוד בחפצי רצונך   ובעבורך אני אשאל מפניך:
וזה חפצי על כל בקשותי   כי אהיה לפניך תמיד:
ואהליך בצדקתך בלא עוון   וארדוף באמיתך כל יום כאשר יושר בעיניך:
אל תמנע ממני את שאלתי   ועשה בקשתי כחפצי רצונך:
5 אעמוד בהם עד עולם   לדעת כל נתיבי צדקך:
ברוך אל עושה זאת   ברוך פועל את כל אלה:
ברוך אשר בחר בעבדו   וימלא אותי כל משאלות לבי:
ברוך שם כבוד מלכותו לעולם   ברוך שם כבודו לעולם ועד:
ברוך יהוה אלהי ישראל מן העולם ועד   העולם ואמר כל העם אמן:
10 בשלשה בחדש אייר ראיתי במראה וכל נבואי
והתפללתי לפני יהוה ואמרתי:
ברוך מוריש ומעשיר   ומבורך משפיל ומרים:
מהקים מעפר דל   ומאשפות הירים אביון:
ויגדל כסאו מעל כל השרים   ויגביר כוחו על כל מושלים:
15 ויתן לו כל חמדת מלכים   וחיל גוים ואוצרות מלכים:
בנות מלכים לכבודו   ובנות ירושלם לתפארת מלכותו:
אשריו יאמרו כל העולמים   ולפניו ישתחוו כל תקומי ארץ:
ויבטחו ביהוה כי הגדיל לעשות   ולא יטעו עוד בהבל ומשגה:
כי כולם ידעו את יהוה   מגדולי אדם ועד קטני אינוש:
20 כי יהוה שופט בכל העולם   אחד משפיל ואחד מירים:
לאשר ירצה יתן   ולאביוני אדם ירש נחלה:
כי בידו נפש כל חי   ורוח כל בשר אליו ישתחוו:
שירו לו זמרו לו   שיחו כל נפלאותיו:
שירו לשמו בכל עת   כי לו נאה תפארת ועוז:
25 אשר היציל מצרה את נפש אוהבו   ומיד כל מרעים רוח חסידו:
כי בטח בשמו ובכבוד מראה   ובדברי קודשו ובכל דרכי חיים:
לעד נעבוד את שמו   ולנצח נצחים נגיד גבורתו:
ד כי הוא רופא לנשברי לב   וחובש את עצם דכים:
והוא הפך דוויה לשמחה   וזיע ורתת למבטחות גדולות:
כי לו ארץ ומלואה   תבל וכל יושבי בה:
כי מלפניו צוה על עבדו   הוד והדר וכבוד מלכותו:
5 אשר חפץ בטוב עמו   ושלח הרופא ורפא בשרם:
והכביד תורתו על פי עבדו   ומצות דברו על ידי נאמנו:
הרבה בלבו חכמה ובינה   ורב קדושתו עד בלי מספר:
מי דומה לו ומי כמותו   אשר לא שכח צעקת איביון:
וזכר ברחמיו עני ודל וגם אנכי כי זכרתי   גבורות ועוז ממשלתו ותפארת עזו:

10 לילה ויום אעמוד לפניו   ואברך את זכרו על כל מעשיו:
תתברך ותתרומם אדון כל הדורות   תתקדש ותתפאר מושיל בכל מעשיו:
תתיחד מלכי מפי כל משרתך   שופט צדק ודיין אמת:
ברוך אתה יהוה אל נא זוכר ברחמיו   את ברית עבדו לנצח:
ברוך שם כבוד מלכותו לעולם ועד: ברוך שם כבודו לעולם ועד:

15 ברוך יהוה אלהי ישראל מן העולם ועד העולם ואמר כל העם אמן:
בארבעה בחודש אייר ברוח ראיתי במראה הקודש וכל נבואיו
והתפללתי לפני יהוה ואמרתי:
ברוך כי שבר רשעים   והעמיד קרן צדיקים:
ודעתו וחכמתו בכל לבי   כי אתה הוא שופט הצדק:

20 ולא יצא מלפניך משפט שקר   כי אם אמת ואמונה:
תתן לאדם כדרכיו   וכפרי מעלליו תשיב לו:
אין כחש בכל מעשיך   ואין כזב בכל דברך:
כל פועלך תמים יחד   ועול בל ימצא במעשך:
כנהר שוטף הירביתה משפט   וכזרע מבורך הצמחתה צדקתך:

25 אשרי יוכה בקדושתך   יספר כבודך בכל יום:
עזרתי מלפני כבודך   לאוכל לנצח לעמוד ברצונך:
כי ת[מול ו]היום   אשרי שומרי פקודיך:

APPENDIX 3
ENGLISH TRANSLATION[27]

I. Revealed before you are the righteous and the evil;
     you want not for human witnesses:
Judge of generations, your rulings are just,
     knowing in the ways of all living things:
You desire justice and despise injustice;
     the boastful will not stand before your glory:
You divided the world into darkness and light,
     into pure and impure, justice and lie:
5 You cast off from your nation all aliens,
     purifying your flock of impure beasts:
You bestow upon your servant your mighty wisdom;
     he understands all according to your desire:
You have planted righteousness in the land of truth,
     multiplying justice throughout eternity:
All who worship your name will teach a song,
     all those who believe the words of your servant:
Their righteousness is increased in the sight of all the land
     and of those who do justice, whom they love in their hearts:
10 You have set their path toward your commandments,
     extending their might through your wondrous deeds:

---

[27] The English translation was made by Azzan Yadin. © All rights reserved to William B. Eerdmans and Magnes publishing companies. The translation is highly acclaimed but a few corrections have been made.

For all eternity they worship your name,
   glorifying it forevermore:
Who is like you in deeds, who in exploits,
   who is like you in your many great feats:
You have forgiven and absolved us all our sins,
   loving exonerated all our transgressions:
Your spirit prophesies through your servant;
   for you draw the end near, it will tarry no more:
15 You vowed of old to your servant David,
   mercifully anointing the shoot of Jesse:
You sustained his authority in your sanctity
   for he spread your praise to the ends of earth:
You set his name as an eternal pillar;
   he repairs the breach and rebuilds the ruins.
A cornerstone despised by the builders
   you have raised to the headstone above all nations:
Joyfully you crown him with glory,
   calling him the splendor of all nations:
20 You multiplied justice and the righteousness in his day,
   peace and blessings forever beyond counting:
All the elect of justice rejoiced before you
   for they will glory in the beloved land:
You have sanctified through him the holy name,
   and he recounts daily the songs of your might:
You made him greater than all the angels,
   establishing him as king of all nations forever:
You broke before him all the kings of Midian,
   drowning in the abyss all those who hate him:
25 You sustained his right arm, bearing the sword,
   giving strength to his arm over all the warriors of Qedar:
His leg will not stumble for he trusts in your Name;
   his power will not wane for you lovingly aided him:
Blessed is the man whose faith is in your teaching
   for he shall not be shamed forevermore:

II. My soul trusted in you, answer me in your grace.
   Blessed are you, O Lord God, who answers his servant at the time
    that he calls unto him:
  Merciful God, have mercy upon us.
   Blessed is the name of the glory of his kingdom forever:
  Blessed are you, O Lord God of Israel, for all eternity.
  And the entire people said: Amen.
  5 On the second day of Iyar I beheld a vision and all his prophecies,
    and I prayed before the Lord, saying:
  May your mercy, O Lord our God, rest upon the flock doomed to
    slaughter;
    the shepherds have killed it without mercy:

Mercifully bind the crushed bones;
    heal lovingly the wounds of your lot:
For you have placed me before you for the sake of the world;
    you have placed me in your might as a light to the nations:
All the nations will tell your glory,
    for they will see your justice on your faithful.
10 Let the rulers gather, all the kings of earth,
    the lords of the world and the rulers of man:
That they may see the might of your right hand
    and understand your holy words till the end:
All will know your might,
    for your hand, O Lord, has done all these:
Let the righteous man be gladdened when he sees this,
    rejoicing before you with hymns and gratitude:
Let all the inhabitants of earth learn from me,
    and return to your way and worship you in faith:
15 They will greet your presence with thanksgiving,
    with hymns and songs and giving thanks:
Magnifying your glory within their encampment
    let them know that you, O Lord, created them:
All who worship idols shall be shamed
    for they will come to recognize their statues:
No longer will they worship idols
    nor bow down to artifacts:
The idols will utterly pass away,
    their delights lost forever:
20 All your creatures will glorify and sanctify you
    from now and for all eternity:
Your servant will speak of your wondrous deeds
    according to his strength and the spirit of his words:
For I take joy in nothing
    save your teachings and the appearance of your glory:
For the sake of your great mercies, do not hide yourself from me;
    do not cause me to die for their love:
For I have loved your residence
    more than all the palaces of kings:
25 The teachings of yours are better for me
    than a myriad of gold bullion:
Your sacred words are better for me
    than any fine garment:
The commandments of your will are better for me
    than the precious stones and pearls, the desire of kings:

III. Blessed is he who finds glory in the wishes of your will;
    for your sake I shall indeed request of you:
And this is my desire above all my wishes
    that I reside in your presence forever:

And to walk in your righteousness without sin
   and pursue your truth every day, as is right in your eyes:
Do not deny me my request;
   fulfill my wish as though it were the wish of your will:
5 I will set myself in them for all eternity,
   knowing the paths of your righteousness:
Blessed be God who does this,
   blessed the one who performs these feats:
Blessed be He who selected his servant
   and who fulfills all the wishes of my heart:
Blessed be the name of the glory of his kingdom forever and ever,
   blessed be the name of his glory forever:
Blessed is the Lord God of Israel for all eternity.
   And the people respond. Amen.
10 On the third day of Iyar I beheld a vision and all his prophecies,
   and I prayed before the Lord, saying:
Blessed be He who impoverishes and enriches,
   blessed be He who lays low and raises on high:
For He had raised the lowly from the dust,
   the poor man from the refuse heap:
He made his throne greater than all ministers,
   his power mightier than all rulers:
15 He gave all that kings desire,
   the might of nations and treasures of kings:
Kings' daughters for his glory,
   daughters of Jerusalem for the glory of his kingdom:
His blessed ones speak for all eternity;
   all the mighty of earth will bow before him:
They will put their trust in the Lord for He has done mighty deeds,
   no longer going astray after vanity and error:
For all will know the Lord
   from the mightiest man to the most humble:
20 For the Lord is judge over the entire world;
   He sets one on high while laying the other low:
He gives to whom He will,
   providing an inheritance for the poorest of men:
For the soul of every man is in his power,
   and the spirit of all flesh will bow down to him:
Sing to him, raise your voices in song,
   speak all his great deeds:
Sing to his name at all times
   for splendor and might are befitting him:
25 He saved the soul of his beloved from the straits
   and the spirit of his righteous ones from all harm:
For he trusts in his Name and in the glory of the vision
   and in His holy words, in all the paths of life:

Forever will we worship his Name,
    speaking his might for all eternity:

IV. For He heals the brokenhearted,
    bandages the bones of the downtrodden:
He turns sorrow to joy,
    fear and trembling to refuge:
For his is the earth and all that is in it,
    the universe and all its inhabitants:
He has commanded his servant before him,
    the splendor and brilliance and glory of his kingship:
5 He wills the good of his people,
    sending the healer to heal their flesh:
He made weighty his teaching upon his servant,
    his commands by the agency of his trusted messenger:
He magnified wisdom and understanding in his heart,
    great sanctity without measure:
Who is like him? Who compares to him?
    For he has not forgotten the cry of the poor.
He recalls in his abundant mercies the poor and the downtrodden;
    I too recalled the mighty deed and power of his kingship, the
        splendor of his power:
10 Night and day I stand before him,
    blessing his memory for all his creatures:
May you be blessed and glorified, master of the generations,
    Sanctified and glorified, the governor of all creatures:
May the mouths of all your servants speak your unity,
    righteous and true judge:
Blessed are you, O Lord God,
    who kindly recalls his servant's covenant forever:
Blessed is the name of the glory of his kinship forevermore,
    blessed is the name of his glory forever:
15 Blessed is the Lord God of Israel for all eternity.
    And the people said: Amen.
On the fourth day of Iyar I beheld a vision and all his prophecies,
    and I prayed before the Lord, saying:
Blessed is He for He has broken the wicked
    and raised up the horn of the righteous:
His knowledge and wisdom are in my heart,
    for you are the righteous judge:
20 No false judgment will you proclaim
    but only truth and faithfulness:
You give to all according their ways,
    according to the fruit of their doings:
There is no deceit in your actions,
    no falsity in your words:

Your action is wholly pure,
    no injustice in your deeds:
You have multiplied your judgment like a flowing river,
    growing your righteousness like a blessed seed:
25 Blessed is he who receives your holiness;
    he will speak of your glory every day:
My support lies in the presence of your glory
    for eternity to stand in your will:
For yesterday and today
    blessed are they that keep your commandments:

THE DEAD SEA SCROLLS AND EARLY CHRISTIANITY

PAUL THE JEW AND THE DEAD SEA SCROLLS

Karl P. Donfried
Smith College

The contemporary discussion of "Paul and Judaism" continues in ways that are for the most part vague, imprecise and misleading and the very use of the phrase "Paul and Judaism" implies that Paul is an outsider. The time has come for a renewed focus on Paul as a Jew and to determine what streams within the diversity of Second Temple Judaism helped to shape his patterns of thought. I will suggest that the Dead Sea Scrolls contribute significantly to this process.

1. The Internal Diversification of Second Temple Judaism

E.P. Sanders and the alleged "new perspective of Paul" have been a dominant force in the contemporary discussion of Paul and Judaism. Although Sanders understanding of Judaism is seriously flawed he has helped shift the discussion to matters Jewish.[1] In his 1977 publication, *Paul and Palestinian Judaism*,[2] Sanders had many of the Dead Sea Scrolls available but made inadequate use of them. Today we have over 900 Qumran manuscripts at our disposal and these, together with their emerging interpretations, have transformed the "new perspective" into the "old perspective."[3] Additionally, research and publications related to the Judaisms of the late Second Temple period as well as the interactions among themselves, including the Jesus movement, are increasingly available.[4]

---

[1] See the detailed criticism by J. Neusner, "Comparing Judaisms: Review of E.P. Sanders, *Paul and Palestinian Judaism: A Comparison of Patterns of Religion*," *HR* 18 (1978): 177–191.

[2] E.P. Sanders, *Paul and Palestinian Judaism* (Philadelphia: Fortress, 1997).

[3] See K.P. Donfried, "Justification and Last Judgment in Paul-Twenty-Five Years Later," in idem, *Paul, Thessalonica and Early Christianity* (Grand Rapids: Eerdmans, 2002), 279–292; S.J. Gathercole, *Where is Boasting? Early Jewish Soteriology and Paul's Response to Romans 1–5* (Grand Rapids: Eerdmans, 2002); also, S. Westerholm, *Perspectives Old and New on Paul* (Grand Rapids: Eerdmans, 2004).

[4] See S. Talmon, "The Community of the Renewed Covenant: Between Judaism and

Sander's reconstruction of Judaism is unsound precisely because he presents a homogenized view that respects neither the internal diversification of Judaism nor the often harsh polemical tensions between the various Torah schools. A perspective shared by many is that Sanders constructed an illusionary and artificial pattern of so-called Palestinian Judaism.[5] To focus predominantly on rabbinic and talmudic traditions of the post-second century and then to retroject this pattern back into the first century is precisely what scholars have rejected with regard to the applicability of, for example, second and third century Gnosticism as a tool for understanding the background of such New Testament documents as 1 Corinthians.

Among the conventional captivities that must be broken in the study of Paul is the continued domination of such distorting descriptors as "Judaism" and "Christianity." Paul never uses the terminology "Christian/Christianity" and the New Testament only uses the terms "Christian/Christians" three times.[6] For contemporary scholars to use such non-New Testament language in discussing Pauline thought inserts characterizations from a much later period that are bound to lead to serious distortions. Paul refers to believers in Christ as "saints,"[7] i.e., holy ones, and he himself is part of a larger, broader Jewish Jesus movement that is never referred to as "Christianity" nor characterized by him in any such way. Along these same lines Ed Sanders gets if fundamentally wrong when he argues that this "is what Paul finds wrong with Judaism: it is not Christianity."[8] Such an assertion already carries with it the presupposition of a split between "Judaism" and "Christianity" in the first half of the first century that must be categorically rejected. It is necessary to recognize that Paul is not involved in an *extra-mural* battle between Christians and Jews but in an *intramural* set of disagreements that take place within the Judaisms of the late Second Temple period.

It is Paul the Jew and his intramural conflict with some of the Judaisms of his day that require sustained focus and concentration and it is

---

Christianity," in *The Community of the Renewed Covenant: The Notre Dame Symposium on the Dead Sea Scrolls* (ed. E. Ulrich and J. VanderKam; Christianity and Judaism in Antiquity 10; Notre Dame: University of Notre Dame Press, 1994), 3–24.

[5] See Neusner, "Comparing Judaisms."

[6] Acts 11:26; 26:28; 1 Pet 4:16.

[7] See, for example, 1 Cor 1:2 and Rom 1:7.

[8] Sanders, *Paul and Palestinian Judaism*, 552.

precisely at this point that the study of the Dead Sea Scrolls afford a new perspective for rethinking Paul by providing the detailed context of another Jewish community that overlapped with the Pauline communities both chronologically and theologically, i.e. the *yaḥad* at Qumran that self-identifies itself as the community of the new covenant.[9]

In this context Shemaryahu Talmon makes the crucial point that the Qumran community, the *yaḥad*, is a movement "prophetically inspired and inclined to apocalypticism" and that it "dissents from the emerging brand of Pharisaic Judaism at the turn of the era" which represents a rationalist stream that first surfaces in Ezra and Nehemiah. Both movements, the prophetic and the rational, generate further diversification and, by the turn of the era, this process culminated in the distinct nonuniformity and heterogeneity of Judaism.[10] Daniel Schwartz, deepening such observations, has argued that there is a fundamental dissimilarity between the Qumran sectarians and rabbinic Judaism with regard to the very *nature* of the law. The Qumran attitudes on the validity of contemporary divine revelation and on predestination as opposed to free will are all corollaries of what he argues is a fundamental contradiction between priestly realism and rabbinic nominalism. Priests did not, in fact, depend upon the law for their authority whereas the sages and the rabbis had their authority only through the law.[11]

Furthermore, several texts from Qumran accuse the Pharisees of following "false laws, finding ways around the requirements of the law, and pronouncing false verdicts in legal cases—practices leading to the virtual annulment of Jewish law in the view of the sect. Indeed, the very existence of such laws constitutes an annulment of the Torah, because it replaces Torah laws with the laws of the Pharisees." For the Qumran community tradition could not be authoritative "since all Israel had gone astray. The true way had been rediscovered by the sect's teacher," the Teacher

---

[9] CD 6:19; 8:21; 19:33; 20:12.

[10] Talmon, "Community," 22.

[11] D.R. Schwartz, "Law and Truth: On Qumran-Sadducean and Rabbinic Views of the Law," in *The Dead Sea Scrolls: Forty Years of Research* (ed. D. Dimant and U. Rappaport; STDJ 10; Leiden: Brill, 1992), 229–240. This perspective has been criticized by J.L. Rubenstein, "Nominalism and Realism in Qumranic and Rabbinic Law: A Reassessment," *DSD* 6 (1999): 157–183. While suggesting modifications, Rubenstein concludes that "Schwartz's categories may still contribute a great deal to our understanding of ancient Jewish law" (183).

of Righteousness.[12] One might already at this point invite the question whether this is not strikingly evocative of assertions posited by the Apostle Paul?

It is only when such dissimilar assumptions of the *yaḥad* and the rationalist stream are sorted out that one can begin to understand the nature of the dialogue—often polemical—that takes place between these two groups within the larger family of Second Temple Judaism. Both Talmon and Schwartz suggest that at key points Paul has perspectives that cohere remarkably well with that of the *yaḥad* over against the Pharisaic stream. While comparisons are important, our ultimate goal must be to assess whether a deeper penetration of the contextual reality of the Qumran community can allow us more profound access into the structure and logic of Pauline thought. The central question is this: can Paul be comprehended more accurately and effectively by careful study of such primary Qumran texts as the *Commmunity Rule* (1QS), the *Damascus Document* (CD), the commentaries/pesharim and the *Thanksgiving Hymns/Hodayot* (1QH), all of which chronologically precede the Jesus movement and its Pauline actualization? Will meticulous readings of these and similar texts help identify and expose dimensions of Pauline thought that might otherwise have been inadequately recognized?

2. The Dead Sea Scrolls: Distinctive Perspectives

2.1. ברית

In addition to the distinctive perspectives already alluded to, there is a significant variance in the use of ברית between the conceptual frameworks of the community of Qumran and that of the Pharisees, with the *yaḥad's* understanding of ברית virtually absent from the latter. According to Talmon the Rabbis "did not develop the notion that in their days, and with their community, God had renewed his covenant of old with the people of Israel. In contrast to the pointed *communal* thrust of the Covenanter's concept of ברית and specifically ברית חדשה the noun ברית, *per se* and in diverse word combinations, connotes in the Rabbinic vocabulary exclusively the act of circumcision. On the strength of this rite, every male infant is *individually* accepted into ברית אברהם אבינו, God's

---

[12] L.H. Schiffman, *Reclaiming the Dead Sea Scrolls: The History of Judaism, the Background of Christianity, the Lost Library of Qumran* (Philadelphia: JPS, 1994), 254.

ancient covenant with all Israel." This "specific technical connotation of ברית," he continues, "is not documented in *yahad* literature. On the other hand, the *communal* dimension of ברית which attaches to the concept of 'covenant renewal' in the Covenanters' theology, as reflected in the Foundation Documents, appears to be altogether absent from the Rabbinic world of thought."[13]

Given this strikingly different usage between these two Torah schools, it is of considerable interest to note Paul's evident affinity for the *yahad's* use of ברית, particularly in the context of an ecclesial comparison of the καινῆς διαθήκη with that of the old covenant in 2 Cor 3:6 and 14. For Paul the communal character of the new covenant is primary. It is also remarkable that the only two communities that give evidence to and interpret Jeremiah's ברית חדשה are the *yahad* and the early Jesus movement, especially as articulated in Paul.

2.2. Biblical Hermeneutics

Since, in contrast to the Rabbis, Qumran granted "normative importance to contemporary (since Sinai!) divine revelation"[14] it used the *pesher* method of biblical interpretation, a contemporizing form of interpretation in which the prophetic texts are understood as referring to present events in the life of the *yahad*. More specifically, in its use of biblical texts it divided the law into distinct categories, i.e., the revealed (*nigleh*) and hidden (*nistar*).

A further result of the *yahad's* prophetic hermeneutic is sharp criticism of Pharisaic rationalist interpretation. They are referred to as *dôr-shê halāqôt*, meaning literally "seekers after smooth things," but more properly understood as "interpreters of false laws." In CD 4:19–20 they are called "builders of the wall ...," a phrase remarkably similar to *m. 'Abot* 1:1 where it is taught that one should "Build a fence around the Torah." Similarly, in 1QH[a] XII:10–11 it is stated that "they planned evil [lit., "Belial"] against me to replace your Torah which You taught in my heart with smooth things [i.e. false laws] (which they taught) to Your people."

Not only does Paul participate in implicitly analogous criticisms, he reveals an exegetical method remarkably similar to that of the *yahad*. Each cite biblical texts in ways not unrelated. Joseph Fitzmyer has made

---

[13] Talmon, "Community," 14–15.
[14] Schwartz, "Law and Truth," 238.

a careful comparison of the introductory formulas used by Paul to introduce the Old Testament with those used in the Dead Sea Scrolls.[15] He also makes references to the study by B.M. Metzger in which a comparison is made between the formulas used to cite "Old Testament" quotations in the Mishnah and the New Testament.[16] Fitzmyer concludes his meticulous evaluation with the conclusion that Paul's introductory formulas are far closer to the *yaḥad's* method than to the Pharisaic-rabbinic approach of the Mishnah. He then raises two perceptive queries with regard to the mode of Pauline citation: "Can the mode have so radically changed from the pre-70 Palestinian custom to that of the Mishnaic in the course of some 150 years? Or is a different custom being followed?"[17]

In this connection one other comment is in order. In Otto Michel's important volume, *Paulus und seine Bibel*,[18] he concluded that no collections similar to Paul's *testimonia* lists or *florilegia* (e.g. Rom 3:10–18; 9:25–29; 15:9–12) could be found in the Jewish tradition.[19] The publication of 4QTest (4Q175) in 1956 raises in yet another way the intriguingly proximate relationship between Paul and the *yaḥad* of Qumran.

2.3. *The Language of Temple Purity and Sanctification*

As is unmistakably evident in the Qumran literature, the *yaḥad* understood itself as a replacement temple, a virtual temple, in view of the utter corruption of the Jerusalem Temple from which they had separated (CD 20:23; 1QS VIII:5). As a result there is a stringent application of purity within the *yaḥad* as is testified by the presence of multiple *Mikva'ot* at the community center. Noteworthy also is the Qumran community's refusal to distinguish between cultic and moral impurity. Magness states the matter well: "To the sectarians, purity and impurity were manifestations of the moral state of the individual."[20]

[15] J.A. Fitzmyer, "Paul's Jewish Background and the Deeds of the Law," in *According to Paul: Studies in the Theology of the Apostle* (New York: Paulist, 1993), 18–35, here 29–31. See also J.A. Fitzmyer, "The Use of Explicit Old Testament Quotations in Qumran Literature and in the New Testament," *NTS* 7 (1960–1961): 297–333.

[16] B.M. Metzger, "The Formulas Introducing Quotations of Scripture in the NT and the Mishnah," *JBL* 70 (1951): 297–307.

[17] Fitzmyer, "Paul's Jewish Background," 31.

[18] O. Michel, *Paulus und seine Bibel* (Gütersloh: Bertelsmann, 1929).

[19] Ibid., 43.

[20] J. Magness, *The Archaeology of Qumran and the Dead Sea Scrolls* (Studies in the Dead Sea Scrolls and Related Literature; Grand Rapids: Eerdmans, 2002), 137.

There is sufficient language in the Pauline letters to suggest that Paul also viewed his communities as being replacements for the temple and that he himself is deeply concerned with issues of purity. Most striking is the reference that "we are the temple of the living God" in the broader context of 2 Cor 6:14–7:1. Almost identical is the use of "temple" language in 1 Cor 3:16–17 and 6:19, particularly with the references to "you" in the plural pointing to the community rather than the individual. The former is especially instructive: "Do you not know that you are God's temple and that God's Spirit dwells in you? If anyone destroys God's temple, God will destroy that person. For God's temple is holy, and you are that temple" (NRSV). Application of such a manner of thinking can also be found in 1 Cor 5:1–13. The replacement temple community cannot tolerate immorality since the impurity of even one member will defile the entire church. Since "our paschal lamb, Christ, has been sacrificed," the "festival," presumably the sacred meal of the community, must be celebrated not with the old yeast of malice and evil but "with the unleavened bread of sincerity and truth." To guard against such impurity Deut 17:7 is invoked: "Drive out the wicked person from among you." The presence of God in this sacred community demands purity. Paul's *serekh*, i.e. his "order" or "rule" in 1 Thess 4:1–9 contains similar themes, including a corresponding pattern of uncleanness/impurity being opposed by sanctification/holiness.[21]

This use of temple and purity language in the Pauline letters raises a not unrelated question: the correlation of Paul's divine apostolic call and his priestly ministry. In Schwartz's analysis of the difference between the realism of Qumran and the nominalism of the Rabbi's he notes that "my basic thesis is that there is a symmetry between the respective natures of priests and rabbis themselves, on the one hand, and the natures of their respective attitudes toward law, on the other. Priests (in Judaism) are created by God, or by nature, if you will, and seem typically to have ascribed great authority to God or nature in the legal process. Rabbis, in contrast, created themselves, and even prided themselves on the lack of importance of pedigree among them; it is noteworthy that their approach to law leaves God and nature on the sidelines, objects of debate but not participants in it."[22] Or put another way, priestly "authority did not,

---

[21] See further on this K.P. Donfried, "Paul and Qumran: The Possible Influence of סרך on 1 Thessalonians," in idem, *Paul, Thessalonica and Early Christianity*, 221–232.

[22] Schwartz, "Law and Truth," 240.

in fact, depend upon the law. ... Sages and rabbis, on the other hand, had authority only through the law."[23]

Paul emphasizes his priestly role in Rom 15:16:

> Nevertheless on some points I have written to you rather boldly by way of reminder, because of the grace given me by God to be a minister of Christ Jesus to the Gentiles in the priestly service (ἱερουργοῦντα) of the gospel of God, so that the offering (ἡ προσφορά) of the Gentiles may be acceptable, sanctified by the Holy Spirit. (NRSV)

What exactly does Paul have in mind when he writes to the Romans about his "priestly service"?

In Phil 2:17 the term λειτουργία is used in a distinctly liturgical setting: "But even if I am being poured out as a libation over the sacrifice and the offering of your faith, I am glad and rejoice with all of you" (NRSV). It would therefore appear that Paul is describing himself as being involved in a distinctly liturgical act in Rom 15, viz., preaching the gospel to the Gentiles, and this coheres well with his formulation at the opening of Romans: "For God, whom I worship (λατρεύω) with my spirit in the proclamation of the gospel of his Son ..." (1:9). Fitzmyer is to be followed when he concludes that in "his mission to the Gentiles Paul sees his function to be like that of a Jewish priest dedicated to the service of God in his Temple." It is indeed likely that for Paul in this context ἱερουργέω means "to function as a priest," and that the "service of the priests in the Jerusalem Temple provides the background of Paul's metaphorical language."[24] In this act of worship, however, the priestly offering does not include animals but repentant Gentiles.

In his letter to the Philippians the Apostle described himself "as to the law a Pharisee" (3:5). That Paul would still hold to such a self-description at the time he is writing Romans is unimaginable since such a Pharisaic allegiance would have disallowed using the sacrificial language of the temple cult in such a metaphorical way. Is not a closer proximity to concepts situated within the *yahad* a more likely source of influence than that of the Pharisaic/rationalist stream, particularly since the Apostle to the Gentiles views his communities in Christ as replacements for the temple much as did the covenanters at Qumran?

---

[23] Ibid., 237.
[24] J.A. Fitzmyer, *Romans: A New Translation with Introduction and Commentary* (AB 33; New York: Doubleday, 1993), 711.

2.4. *Righteousness of God/Justification in the Context of Election*

The *yaḥad*'s confidence in predestination within a context of dualism differentiates them from the other Judaisms of the day. Those predestined for righteousness have been given the knowledge of God as one reads in 1QHᵃ XX:11–13: "And I, through my understanding, have come to know You, my God, through the spirit which You placed within me. ... In Your holy spirit You have [o]pened to me knowledge of the mystery of Your understanding."[25] As a result of this knowledge and as a consequence of the gift of "the spirit of the counsel of the truth of God" (1QS III:6–9), the elect or chosen of God "can discern the correct path and follow the divine will."[26]

Paul explicitly refers to the Thessalonians as ἐκλογή in 1 Thess 1:4 and in 4:9 that they have been "God taught" (θεοδίδακτος). As with Qumran so for Paul the theme of election is foundational from his earliest letter, 1 Thessalonians, to Romans, his last. In Rom 8:30 one reads: "And those whom he predestined (προώρισεν) he also called (ἐκάλεσεν); and those whom he called he also justified (ἐδικαίωσεν); and those whom he justified he also glorified (ἐδόξασεν)" (NRSV). In this text it is election/predestination that precedes the reference to "justification" and it is the theme of election/predestination that provides the appropriate context for understanding the function of "justification" in Pauline thought.

In addition to this remarkable commonality of language it is likely that the community at Qumran also contributed a set of conceptual tools for Paul's understanding of justification and the righteousness of God in light of the Christ event. I refer here especially to 1QS XI:9–15 and 1QHᵃ XII:36–40. One observes there that the theme of human sinfulness and wickedness, the assertion that "judgment shall be by the righteousness of God" and the emphasis on the mercy of a gracious God in whom human righteousness is rooted are remarkably analogous to Paul's teaching about justification by grace. A closer examination of this terminology is revealing. The term δικαιοσύνη θεοῦ, "the righteousness of God," is used by Paul in Rom 1:17; 3:5, 21, 22; 10:3; and 2 Cor 5:21, often in close connection with his comments on justification. It is not insignificant that the exact phrase "the righteousness of God," not found in the Old Testament, is used here as well as in 1QM IV:6 (צדק אל) and in

---

[25] The Translation is taken from Schiffman, *Reclaiming*, 152.
[26] Ibid.

1QS X:25 and XI:12 (צדקת אל). This prior use of the concept by the *yaḥad* would support the observation that δικαιοσύνη θεοῦ is not a Pauline creation. Further, at the beginning of the passage cited above, 1QS XI:9, there is a striking parallel to Paul's use of σαρκὸς ἁμαρτίας ("sinful flesh"; Rom 8:3): בשר עול ("perverse flesh"). Also related to the use of σὰρξ ἁμαρτίας in Rom 8:5–8 is עוון בשר, "the sin of flesh" in 1QS XI:9 and 12.

By the weaving of these themes into a more coherent unity, Qumran places them in a context different from that found in the Tanak. It is indeed possible that the *yaḥad* provided Paul with these emphases that he subsequently reformulated as a result of his encounter with the Risen Christ (Gal 1:15–16). One should not, of course, fail to notice the obvious differences between Paul and the *yaḥad*, the most notable being the centrality of the death and resurrection of Jesus Christ. Because the messiah has come, the righteousness of God has now already been revealed. For the *yaḥad*, who are still waiting for messiah(s), their radicalized obedience to Torah suggests that such a manifestation of the righteousness of God still remains a future expectation and goal. Thus Fitzmyer correctly recognizes that, from a Pauline perspective, this community's emphasis on the mercy and the righteousness of God "is transitional, because it is not yet the full-blown idea of Pauline justification by *grace through faith*."[27] For this reason one should also follow his lead in translating משפט as "judgment" and not as "justification."[28] "Judgment" allows Qumran to influence Paul's thinking without suggesting the broader connotation that "justification" implies.

2.5. The Works of the Law

The examples just cited have suggested a proximity between selected terminology found in the Dead Sea Scrolls and selected Pauline theological formulations. There is yet another phrase that Paul uses, ἔργα νόμου, ("works of the law"), that has been uncovered in the Qumran scrolls. Given the enormous controversy surrounding the meaning of this phrase, I wish in the context of this article, to make only two preliminary points:

---

[27] J.A. Fitzmyer, "Paul and the Dead Sea Scrolls," in *The Dead Sea Scrolls after Fifty Years: A Comprehensive Assessment* (ed. P.W. Flint and J.C. VanderKam; 2 vols.; Leiden: Brill, 1998–1999), 2:599–621, here 604 (italics in the original).

[28] Against, for example, S. Schulz, "Zur Rechtfertigung aus Gnaden in Qumran und bei Paulus," *ZTK* 56 (1959): 155–185, and G. Vermes, *The Complete Dead Sea Scrolls in English* (New York: Penguin, 1997), 115–116.

2.5.1 ἔργα νόμου

The phrase, ἔργα νόμου, has no parallel in the Tanak. However, the precise parallel phrase to Paul's ἔργα νόμου is found in the Qumran texts. In 4QMMT C 27 one reads מקצת מעשי התורה ("some works of the law"), in 4QMMT C 30–31 the emphasis falls on the correct practice of these deeds ("in your deed [בעשותך] you may be reckoned as righteous"). Particularly important here is that the phrase מקצת מעשי התורה is explicitly related to the pursuit of righteousness: the one who does "works of the law" is reckoned as righteous.

2.5.2 Torah in the Pauline Letters

Although Paul sharply and, at times, polemically criticizes the misuse of the Torah in his letters, I am unable to reach the conclusion that Paul has categorically rejected the Torah in light of the Christ event. One needs to recognize that Paul's polemic against the "works of the law" is frequently found within the context of a broader apologetic, as is the case in Rom 3:31 ("Do we then overthrow the law by this faith? By no means! On the contrary, we uphold the law" [NRSV]) and in Rom 7:12 ("So the law is holy, and the commandment is holy and just and good" [NRSV]). In my judgment the critical text for understanding Paul's new understanding of the Torah is found in Rom 8:3–4:

> For God has done what the law, weakened by the flesh, could not do: by sending his own Son in the likeness of sinful flesh, and to deal with sin, he condemned sin in the flesh, so that the just requirement of the law might be fulfilled in us (ἵνα τὸ δικαίωμα τοῦ νόμου πληρωθῇ ἐν ἡμῖν), who walk not according to the flesh but according to the Spirit.   (NRSV)

Critical is the interpretation of "just requirement" and that "the law might be fulfilled." While the "works of the law" are not the basis of righteousness—only Christ is—that does not deny a positive function for the law, properly understood, for those who are "in Christ." In such an interpretative context the term τέλος in Rom 10:4 would mean that Christ is the goal or intention of the Torah, not unilaterally its termination or end.[29]

---

[29] For a full discussion of the options see Fitzmyer, *Romans*, 584–585.

2.6. *Repentance and Predestination*

Schwartz understands repentance as "a sinner's decision to be perfect, no longer to sin."[30] For Paul, as can be seen in Rom 7,

> successful repentance is at least something of a fiction. As much as one tries, one really never really succeeds; the next day, or the next Day of Atonement, there is always a need to repent again. ... Similarly, Qumran writers who continually demanded "perfection of way" were led to conclude that man cannot save himself; "Man's way is not his own, and man shall not prepare his own steps, for the judgment is God's and perfection of way is in His hands" (1QS 11:10–11), "I know that righteousness is not for man, and perfection of way is not for the son of man; unto the Most High are all works of righteousness, and the way of man cannot be established unless God creates for him a spirit to make perfect the way of the sons of man" (1QH 4:30–32).[31]

Schwartz continues that for the rabbis, in contrast,

> what is important is not so much what really happens as the human decision to repent (just as human decisions of courts are granted supreme importance); if it doesn't work out, in the end, then one should try again ... And regarding the latter, human sin, God was considered to have allowed man an efficacious method of settling his account and starting anew—repentance.[32]

Paul's lack of repentance language and his virtual omission of forgiveness rhetoric suggest commonalities with the *yaḥad*. A closer examination of these phenomena might indicate a coherent deep structure that underlies these connections. Relevant to a more detailed examination of such a possible coherent deep structure are both Paul's analysis of sin in Rom 3 as echoed in 1QS XI:9–15 and 1QHᵃ XII:36–40[33] and the fact that atonement at Qumran can only be viewed in light of the *yaḥad*'s doctrine of predestination. Here, again, with regard to atonement language, Paul is considerably closer to the views reflected in texts like 1 QS III:15–23 than to those of the Pharisaic tradition. Precisely the *yaḥad*'s confidence in predestination, within a context of dualism, differentiates them from the other Judaisms of the day.[34]

---

[30] Schwartz, "Law and Truth," 239.
[31] Ibid.
[32] Ibid.
[33] See previous citation of these texts in main body of paper.
[34] See further J. Licht, "The Doctrine of the Thanksgiving Scroll," *IEJ* 6 (1956): 1–13.

Paul is so confident that the Thessalonian Christians have been taught by God that he can assure them that despite the hindrances created by Satan they are his "crown of boasting" at the coming of Jesus; "yes, you are our glory and joy!" (1 Thess 2:18–20 NRSV). A comparison with 1QS IV:6–8 is instructive: "And as for the visitation of all who walk in this spirit, it shall be healing, great peace in a long life, and fruitfulness, together with every everlasting blessing and eternal joy in life without end, a crown of glory (כליל כבוד) and a garment of majesty in unending light."[35] For communities such as these repentance and forgiveness language becomes largely superfluous.

3. Summary

In Paul's final letter, Romans, he writes: "I ask, then, has God rejected his people? By no means! I myself am an Israelite, a descendant of Abraham, a member of the tribe of Benjamin. God has not rejected his people whom he foreknew" (Rom 11:1 NRSV). This religious biography is written in the present tense and not the past; he continues as a member of the people of Israel.

If Jerome is correct, Paul was born in Gischala in the Galilee and was subsequently exiled to Tarsus where he grew up in a Jewish household and educated in the Hellenistic traditions of that city.[36] Upon going to Jerusalem to study as a mature young man he undoubtedly came under the influence of the Pharisees during a period of religious intensity and it undoubtedly to this that he refers in his singular use of the term "Pharisee" in Phil 3:5: "as to the law, a Pharisee." But before long he encountered a movement described by Talmon as "prophetically inspired and inclined to apocalypticism" that dissented "from the emerging brand of Pharisaic Judaism at the turn of the era."[37] Not only did the *yaḥad* facilitate Paul's break from the rationalist stream, it provided a context in which he was able to interpret and articulate his call by God to proclaim his son among the Gentiles (Gal 1:15).

---

[35] Vermes, *Complete Dead Sea Scrolls*, 102.
[36] Jerome, *Comm. Phlm.* 23; *Vir. ill.* 5.
[37] Talmon, "Community," 22.

"BECAUSE OF THE ANGELS":
READING 1 COR 11:2–16 IN LIGHT OF
ANGELOLOGY IN THE DEAD SEA SCROLLS

CECILIA WASSEN
Uppsala University

Many documents from the Dead Sea Scrolls display a great fascination in angels. Not only do the writers speculate about the appearance and function of angels in God's heavenly temple, but also about their role as intermediaries between God and humans. In this paper I propose that the angelology in the Scrolls can throw some light on Paul's arguments in 1 Cor 11:2–16 where he advises women to wear something on their heads as "authority," ἐξουσία, "because of the angels," διὰ τοὺς ἀγγέλους.[1]

With its multilayered, metaphorical language and play on words, the discourse of 1 Cor 11:2–16 offers well-known challenges to the interpreter. Paul argues that men should be unveiled and women veiled when praying or prophesying (11:5). As part of his argumentation he explains that the man, not the woman, is "the image and reflection of God" (11:7), that woman was made from man (11:8), and that she was created for the sake of man. "For this reason," Paul writes, "a woman ought to have authority on her head, because of the angels" (11:10). His explanation, which must have been perfectly lucid to the original audience, poses a special problem. The exegesis can be divided into two main strands of understanding with various nuances: (1) women have to protect themselves against "bad angels" following the speculations around the "sons of God" in Gen 6:1–4 who took wives among the "daughters of men";[2] (2)

---

[1] Literally, "a woman ought to have authority on her head" (cf. NRSV "a woman ought to have a symbol of authority on her head").

[2] See e.g., *1 En.* 1–36, the *Book of the Watchers*. For the view that woman might evoke lust amongst the angels, see e.g., L.J. Lietart Peerbolte, "Man, Woman, and the Angels in 1 Cor 11:2–16," in *The Creation of Man and Woman: Interpretations of the Biblical Narratives in Jewish and Christian Traditions* (ed. G.P. Luttikhuizen; Themes in Biblical Narratives 3; Leiden: Brill, 2000), 76–92. This interpretation is highly unlikely. One reason is that the phrasing almost parallels that of three passages in the Dead Sea Scrolls that similarly refer to the presence of angels in an assembly (see below). In these cases, the meaning clearly is "out of reverence for the angels." J.A. Fitzmyer ("A Feature of Qumran Angelology and the Angels of 1 Cor 11:10," in *Paul and Qumran: Studies in New Testament*

since angels traditionally are guardians of the order of creation, women should cover their hair as this corresponds to the creative order in reverence to the angels. Alternative interpretations include the view that women should imitate the angels who covered their faces with their wings according to Isa 6:2 and the view that the angels here are evil angels. My proposal builds on two of these ideas: the association of angels with creation, and the idea of humans imitating angels—although not in the sense previously suggested. I hold that the interpretive key to the crux is to be found in the beliefs surrounding the impact of angels in worship, an important dimension in this text that has largely been overlooked. In this regard, the various beliefs concerning angels in the Dead Sea Scrolls are highly illuminating, particularly the concept of communion with angels and the theme of imitation of angels. In addition, this study draws on other Jewish sources from Second Temple Judaism and early rabbinic literature. We begin, however, by examining the belief in a union with angels in worship in literature from Qumran. Subsequently we consider Paul's expression, "because of the angels" (1 Cor 11:10), which is strongly reminiscent of three passages in the sectarian documents from Qumran, as well as his appeal to creation. Then, we investigate the link between angels and head coverings in Corinth by taking the greater socio-cultural context into consideration. In conclusion, I suggest that Paul is advising the female participants to cover their distinctive female attribute, their hair, in imitation of male angels.

COMMUNION WITH ANGELS IN THE DEAD SEA SCROLLS

Angels appear frequently in hymns and liturgical material within the context of worship. The *Sabbath Songs* are evidently a rich source for the belief in communion with angels. Although a sectarian origin of the collection is debated, with nine copies discovered at Qumran it is clear that the *Songs* held an important place in the Qumran community.[3] In

---

Exegesis [London: Chapman, 1968], 31–47, 44) correctly, I believe, argued "Though this evidence from Qumran has not solved the problem of *exousia*, it has, we believe, made the interpretation of *dia tous angelous* as 'fallen angels' far less plausible." For a list of the various interpretations, see H. Conzelmann, *1 Corinthians: A Commentary on the First Epistle to the Corinthians* (trans. J. Leitch; Hermeneia; Philadelphia: Fortress, 1975), 188–190; L.T. Stuckenbruck, "Why Should Women Cover Their Heads Because of the Angels? (1 Corinthians 11:10)," *Stone-Campbell Journal* 4 (2001): 205–234.

[3] The sectarian composition *Berakot* (4Q286–290) exhibits influence from the *Sab-*

sublime, rhythmic language, using strange syntax,[4] the songs meditate on the angelic praise and the heavenly sanctuaries where carved images also praise God. The hymns bring the worshipers on a virtual journey through the seven levels of temples and into the inner most sanctuary where they, as it were, get to gaze on the heavenly chariot throne, and the angelic priesthood offering the Sabbath sacrifice. The precise function of these songs is contested: Carol Newsom suggests the purpose of the songs was to facilitate "communal mysticism."[5] Similarly, Philip Alexander unequivocally states "the temple is not merely an object of intellectual speculation or literary curiosity: it constitutes a divine, transcendent realm that is seen as the goal of mystical aspiration."[6] Highlighting the rhythmic language, Rachel Elior argues that it is designed "to express the invisible in poetic and musical terms and thus transplant him [the worshiper] to the supernatural worlds, to inspire in him a mystical ascent to the angelic world."[7] The *Songs* were, then, a vehicle for the participants to transcend the human realm and join the angelic host in worship.

---

bath Songs, thereby testifying to the importance of the *Songs*; see C.A. Newsom, "'Sectually Explicit' Literature from Qumran," in *The Hebrew Bible and its Interpreters* (ed. W. Propp, B. Halpern, and D.N. Freedman; Biblical and Judaic Studies 1; Winona Lake: Eisenbrauns, 1990), 167–187, 183–184; eadem, "Angelic Liturgy: Songs of the Sabbath Sacrifice (4Q400–4Q407, 11Q17, Mas1k)," in *The Dead Sea Scrolls: Hebrew, Aramaic, and Greek Texts With English Translations*, vol. 4B: *Angelic Liturgy: Songs of the Sabbath Sacrifice* (ed. J.H. Charlesworth and C.A. Newsom; The Princeton Theological Seminary Dead Sea Scrolls Project; Tübingen: Mohr Siebeck, 1999), 1–135, 4–5. We find in 4QBer[a] (4Q286) a similar numinous language as the *Sabbath Songs* with a focus on the heavenly temple and the angelic worship, though it is also concerned with God's earthly creation that takes part in the praise (4Q286 5a–c).

[4] Unstructured syntax with long chains of nouns and frequent use of participles is characteristic also of later Hekhalot literature; see L. Schiffman, *Reclaiming the Dead Sea Scrolls: The History of Judaism, the Background of Christianity, the Lost Library of Qumran* (Philadelphia: JPS, 1994), 358. For a general comparison between the Dead Sea Scrolls and later Jewish mystical texts, see J.R. Davila, "The Dead Sea Scrolls and Merkavah Mysticism," in *The Dead Sea Scrolls in their Historical Context* (ed. T.H. Lim; Edinburgh: T&T Clark, 2000), 249–264.

[5] C.A. Newsom, *Songs of the Sabbath Sacrifice: A Critical Edition* (HSS 27; Atlanta: Scholars Press, 1985), 19.

[6] P. Alexander, *The Mystical Texts: Songs of the Sabbath Sacrifice and Related Manuscripts* (Library of Second Temple Studies 61; Companion to the Qumran Scrolls 7; London: T&T Clark, 2006), 10.

[7] The quote is from the context of Elior's analysis of the seventh Sabbath song in which a divine covenant is renewed with both angels and humans; *The Three Temples: On the Emergence of Jewish Mysticism* (trans. D. Louvish; Oxford: The Littman Library of Jewish Civilization, 2004), 169.

We find the same notion of an angelic and human union in a range of texts from Qumran; a few examples will suffice. The concluding hymn in 1QS asserts that the angelic and human communities are united for ever (1QS XI:7–9):

> God has given them [secret knowledge] to his chosen ones [= humans] as an everlasting possession, and has caused them to inherit the lot of the Holy Ones [= angels]. He has joined their assembly [= humans] to the Sons of Heaven to be a council of the community, a foundation of the building of holiness, and eternal plantation throughout all ages to come.[8]

We may note here the blurry boundaries between humans and angels; the congregation in some sense, spiritually, already in the present lives together with the angels.[9] Similarly, the speaker in 1QH[a] XI:21–23 expresses the belief in the ability of humans to enter the angelic realm and praise with the angelic host:

> The perverse spirit You have cleansed from great transgression, that he may stand with the host of the holy ones, and enter into community (*yahad*) with the congregation of the sons of heaven. And for man, You have allotted an eternal destiny with the spirits of knowledge, to praise Your name together with shouts of joy, and to recount Your wonders before all Your creatures.[10]

Yahad here denotes a togetherness that embraces both humans and angels; this unity is possible through God's grace in forgiving the transgressions, so the faithful, now cleansed, can join the angels.[11] A final

---

[8] Translation by G. Vermes, *The Complete Dead Sea Scrolls in English* (New York: Allen Lane/Penguin, 1997), 115.

[9] The close union between angels and humans is sometimes expressed in language that makes it hard to distinguish between angels and humans. In the sectarian literature such as the *War Scroll* similar terminology is used for the earthly and heavenly warriors; they are grouped together into opposing camps, under all encompassing headings such as "the hordes of Belial" (1QM XI:8), "the lot of darkness" (XIII:5), "the army of Belial" (I:13), and the corresponding "lot of God" (XIII:5; XVII:7–8), or "lot of light" (XIII:9), and "our congregation" (XII:8–9). Furthermore, the common nature of the human and angelic participants is underscored in attributes common for both parties: both humans and angels are "the elect" (X:9; XII:1, 5); both are called "holy ones," and 1QM I:8–9 presents humans with typical angelic attributes: "then [the Sons of Rig]hteousness shall shine to all ends of the world, continuing to shine forth until the end of the appointed seasons of darkness" (cf. that partly preserved line 16: "the holy ones shall shine," which may refer to either humans or angels).

[10] All translations are from D.W. Parry and E. Tov, eds., *The Dead Sea Scrolls Reader* (6 vols; Leiden: Brill, 2004–2005), unless otherwise stated.

[11] Other passages from the Dead Sea Scrolls that point to a close communion between angels and humans include, for example, 11QSefer ha-Milḥamah (11Q14) 1 ii 11–15; 4QShir[b] (4Q511) 35 2–4; 1QSb IV:25–26; and 4QM[a] (4Q491) 11 i 12–16.

example is taken from the *Rule of the Blessings* (1QSb), which cloaks the traditional priestly blessing in Num 6:24–26 in an eschatological garb.[12] The blessing of the high priest in 1QSb IV:24–26 compares him to an Angel of Presence:[13]

> May you be as an Angel of Presence in the Abode of Holiness to the glory of the God of [hosts]. May you attend upon the service in the Temple of the Kingdom and decree destiny in company with the Angels of the Presence, in common council [with the Holy Ones] for everlasting ages and time without end.

Whether or not these blessings should be understood as expressions of realized or future eschatology, they give further evidence of the close bond between humans and angels. It is worth noting that many of the passages that assert a communion between the community and angels appear in hymns and prayers. This circumstance indicates that it was particularly during worship that the Dead Sea sectarians, like the Corinthians, would experience the presence of angels.[14]

The close communion with angels put stringent obligations on the sectarians; they aspired to live a perfect life of purity, holiness, and obedience, like the angels. Devorah Dimant demonstrates how the sectarians "conceived their own existence as analogical to that of angels" on many levels. Dimant points out that many functions of the sectarians have a striking resemblance to that of angels.[15] The stringent purity rules of the sect and the practice of celibacy, for example, may well be explained from

---

[12] As J.H. Charlesworth argues, since the sect believed it was living at the end times the blessings may have been recited in anticipation of the eschaton; see "Rule of the Community (1QS; cf. 4QS MSS A–J, 5Q11)," in *The Dead Sea Scrolls: Hebrew, Aramaic, and Greek Texts With English Translations*, vol. 1: *Rule of the Community and Related Documents* (ed. idem; The Princeton Theological Seminary Dead Sea Scrolls Project; Tübingen: Mohr Siebeck, 1994), 1–51, 2 n. 9.

[13] Translation by Vermes, *Complete Dead Sea Scrolls*. The official editor, J.T. Milik, presumed that the blessing was part of that for the Zadokite priests in the previous column. J.H. Charlesworth accepts this interpretation ("Blessings [1QSb]," in *The Dead Sea Scrolls: Hebrew, Aramaic, and Greek Texts with English Translations*, vol. 1: *Rule of the Community and Related Documents*, 119–131, 120). For the view that the blessing concerns the high priest, see C. Fletcher-Louis, *All the Glory of Adam: Liturgical Anthropology in the Dead Sea Scrolls* (STDJ 42; Leiden: Brill, 2002), 151–158.

[14] B. Frennesson, *"In a Common Rejoicing": Liturgical Communion with Angels in Qumran* (Studia Semitica Upsaliensia 14; Uppsala: University of Uppsala Press, 1999), 37–41. Frennesson provides a thorough analysis of all the liturgical Qumran texts related to angels; see also M. Davidson, *Angels at Qumran: A Comparative Study of 1 Enoch 1–36, 78–108 and Sectarian Writings from Qumran* (JSPSup 11; Sheffield: JSOT Press, 1992), 278.

[15] D. Dimant, "Men as Angels: The Self-Image of the Qumran Community," in *Religion*

their aim of living like angels. Also, as Elior demonstrates, the liturgy, rituals, and calendar of the Qumran community were designed to correspond to that of the heavenly cult.[16] Nevertheless, the sectarians did not only strive to imitate the angels in their behaviour and liturgy, but also in their appearance as we will see below.

"Because of the Angels"

The *War Scroll* (1QM), the *Rule of the Congregation* (1QSa), and the *Damascus Document* (D) refer to the presence of angels as explanations for disqualifying the physically disabled and the impure, from participating in communal activities. While D and 1QSa prohibit various categories of disabled members from entering communal meetings, M bars them from participating in the final battle (CD 15:15–17 par. 4Q266 8 i 6–9 par. 4Q270 6 ii; 1QSa II:3–9; 1QM VII:4–6). In wording similar to Paul's, they all refer to the presence of holy angels as the reason for the exclusion, as 1QSa II:3–9 reads:

> And no-one who is afflicted in the flesh, crippled in the legs or the hands, lame or blind or deaf or dumb, or stricken with a visible blemish in the flesh visible to the eyes; or a (tottering) old man who cannot maintain himself within the congregation, may en[ter] to stand firm [wi]thin the Congregation of renown, for holy angels [(are) in] their [Counc]il.[17]

In addition, the *War Scroll* also bans women and youth from entering the war camp (1QM VII:3–4). Although the reason for the exclusion of women is primarily related to concerns about purity, the law may also express uneasiness about them being present when angels are near.

---

and Politics in the Ancient Near East (ed. A. Berlin; Studies and Texts in Jewish History and Culture; Bethesda: University Press of Maryland, 1996), 93–103.

[16] According to Elior (*Three Temples*, 173), there was a "collaboration of priests and angels" in the cult.

[17] Translation based on J.H. Charlesworth and L. Stuckenbruck, "Rule of the Congregation (1QSa)," in *The Dead Sea Scrolls: Hebrew, Aramaic, and Greek Texts With English Translations*, vol. 1: *Rule of the Community and Related Documents*, 108–117. The translation has been modified to make it gender-inclusive, which seems appropriate in a document that mentions women and children several times; see Eileen Schuller, "Women in the Dead Sea Scrolls," in *Methods of Investigation of the Dead Sea Scrolls and the Khirbet Qumran Site: Present Realities and Future Prospects* (ed. M.O. Wise et al.; Annals of the New York Academy of Sciences 722; New York: New York Academy of Sciences, 1994), 115–131, 123.

It is commonly accepted that the lists of physical defects are based on Lev 21:17–23, which lists blemishes that render priests ineligible to serve in the temple. It is noteworthy that these lists not only include disabilities that would be physically disabling and hinder service, but also include blemishes that are aesthetically unattractive. While being similar to Lev 21, the Qumran lists go beyond these categories by adding new types of blemishes.[18] Taken together, these rules testify to the reality of angelic presence; this is not metaphorical, symbolic language; instead imperfect people were physically barred so that angels would not come in contact with them. This is the perspective we should bring with us when examining Paul's message to the Corinthians about angels.

ECSTASY AND ANGELS AT CORINTH

Given the background of fellowship with angels as expressed in the Scrolls, we can begin to appreciate the significances of the perceived angelic presence at Corinth. Was the belief in the joint worship with angels grounded in mystical experiences[19] in which the worshipers transcended the human realm, as was likely the case at Qumran? The information we receive about the worship in Corinth certainly suggest that this indeed was the case. The Corinthian worship was clearly of ecstatic

---

[18] For a detailed comparison of these lists and a discussion on various underlying causes, see C. Wassen, "What do Angels Have against the Blind and the Deaf? Rules of Exclusion in the Dead Sea Scrolls," in *Common Judaism: Explorations in Second-Temple Judaism* (ed. W. McCready and A. Reinhartz; Minneapolis: Fortress, 2008), 109–123.

[19] I am using the term mystical experiences in a wide sense with reference to personal experiences of transcendence and of perceived encounter with the divine that often take the form of visions or other forms of revelations. In modern terminology it involves an experience of an "altered state of consciousness" that is interpreted by the practitioner in religious terms. I accept April DeConick's definition of mysticism: "a tradition within early Judaism and Christianity centered on the belief that a person directly, immediately, and before death can experience the divine, either as a rapture experience or as one solicited by a particular praxis." She points out that the term mysticism is modern and that the ancients referred to these kinds of experiences as "apocalypse," i.e., revelation; see A.D. DeConick, "What is Early Jewish and Christian Mysticism?" in *Paradise Now: Essays on Early Jewish and Christian Mysticism* (ed. eadem; SBLSymS 11; Atlanta: SBL, 2006), 1–24, 2. Whether or not all ecstatic phenomena listed by Paul should be defined as mystical by definition is impossible to know, since of course we do not have first-hand descriptions (except for Paul's own in 2 Cor 12:1–5, in which case they fit the criteria). Certainly *glossolalia* and prophesying appear to be mystical experiences according to my description above. At any rate, for this study I cannot go into depth into this intriguing issue.

or mystical nature.[20] Paul speaks of persons empowered by the spirit speaking in tongues ("ecstatic utterances"), prophesying, and performing "deeds of power" and healings—spiritual activities that are clearly of charismatic and ecstatic nature.[21] In this setting the angels played a role. For Paul, speaking in tongues was speaking a different language; γλῶσσα normally means a language in the NT (1 Cor 12:28).[22] In spite of his cautions about using *glossolalia* in worship (1 Cor 14:13–19), Paul has a positive overall view of the practice (2 Cor 14:5, 18), claiming to speak it more than his addressees (14:18). The basis of his appreciation of this "gift" lies in its nature as the language angels (1 Cor 13:1).[23] In fact, *glossolalia* expresses "mysteries in the Spirit" (14:2), that is, as James Dunn explains, "mysteries of which only the angels in heaven have knowledge."[24] At the same time, this angelic language was hailed as a means not only of revelation, but also of prayer (1 Cor 14:2, 14–17).[25] Hence, through *glossolalia* the ecstatic worshipers perceived themselves being in the company with the angels, taking part in the angelic praise. Paul refers to such combined human and angelic worship in Phil 2:9–11, which poetically articulates

---

[20] For an examination of the charismatic nature of the experiences at Corinth (and elsewhere in the early Christian movement), see J.D.G. Dunn, *Jesus and the Spirit* (London: SCM Press, 1975), 199–342.

[21] *Glossolalia* has been described as "the language of the unconscious" (G. Theissen, *Psychological Aspects of Pauline Theology* [trans. J.P. Calvin; Philadelphia: Fortress, 1987], 267) since the speaker does not normally understand what he or she is saying (1 Cor 12:10; 14:2, 10–11). But, according to Paul the speaker may have the ability to understand the utterances, which is desirable (1 Cor 14:4, 13, 27–28). This, however, does not appear to be common since someone else may be given the ability to interpret the language (1 Cor 12:10; 14:27–28). The accusation of drunkenness in Acts 2:4–13 in connection to speaking in tongues gives further support to the ecstatic nature of the phenomenon. For a general discussion on the phenomenon, see Theissen, *Psychological Aspects*, 267–341; Dunn, *Jesus and the Spirit*, 242–248; J. Behm, "γλῶσσα," TDNT 1:722–724.

[22] Dunn, *Jesus and the Spirit*, 243–244.

[23] Theissen, *Psychological Aspects*, 308.

[24] Dunn, *Jesus and the Spirit*, 244.

[25] It can be deduced from 1 Cor 14 that glossolalic utterances were interpreted as both messages and prayers. Theissen (*Psychological Aspects*, 322–323) argues that through gestures, posture, and other nonverbal means, it would be evident for others whether the *glossolalia* concerned prayer or messages. 1 Cor 12:2–3 (introduction to the section on spiritual gifts) shows that confession to Jesus was also part of the ecstatic utterances and that mispronunciations by ecstatic people or misapprehensions could be dangers in these cases; see arguments by Theissen, *Psychological Aspects*, 308. Dunn (*Jesus and the Spirit*, 245) suggests that also Rom 8:26 refers to *glossolalia* as a way of communicating with God. Although *glossolalia* was understood to mediate heavenly messages, Paul still distinguishes between prophesying and speaking in tongues (1 Cor 14:1–5) based on the means by which the message is revealed (see below).

the cosmic nature of the confession to Jesus by the earthly and heavenly (as well as under-worldly) powers.[26]

Whereas praise or prayer could be expressed through speaking in tongues, prophecy appears to have taken the form of regular, intelligible language (1 Cor 14:1–4). Still, we do get hints about the means by which the revelations are received: Paul groups all these phenomena together under the umbrella terms "spiritual gifts," πνευματικά (12:1; 14:1); "gifts," χαρίσματα (12:4); "activities," ἐνεργήματα (12:6); manifestation of the spirit (12:7), which suggests that prophecy was no less the result of ecstatic, or mystical practices, than speaking in tongues. Consequently, in his commentary on 1 Cor 12:10, C.K. Barrett argues that prophecy "was uttered in ordinary though probably excited, perhaps ecstatic, speech."[27]

Although the specific term "angels," ἄγγελοι, only appears in 1 Cor 11:10 in the letter, there are further hints that they were seen as actively involved in the worship. Paul refers to "spirits," πνεύματα, in the plural a few times (1 Cor 12:10; 14:12; cf. Rev 22:6; Heb 1:7). Since πνεύματα in Hebrew, רוחות, is one of the most common designations for angels in the Dead Sea Scrolls, the simplest interpretation of the plurality of spirits is that it refers to angelic powers.[28] Furthermore, according to Earle Ellis, the spiritual gifts, πνευματικά, which includes prophecy, should be understood as the powerful manifestations of the spirits, the πνεύματα / angels, behind them.[29] Prophecy is also particularly linked to communication with angels elsewhere in the Corinthian correspondence where Paul speaks of "the *spirits* of the prophets" (1 Cor 14:32; cf. Rev 22:6). There is therefore reason to understand the uttering of prophecies and prayers of women and men under discussion in 1 Cor 11:2–16 within the context of the ecstatic nature of the Corinthian worship in general, and as part of the activities that were linked to communion with angels.

Paul himself was a mystic, as Alan Segal, amongst others, has superbly demonstrated.[30] Paul's mystical experience on the road to Damascus

---

[26] Theissen, *Psychological Aspects*, 308.

[27] C.K. Barrett, *A Commentary on the First Epistle to the Corinthians* (London: Black, 1968), 286.

[28] There are references to a dualism of spirits (e.g., 1 Cor 2:12; 12:10; 2 Cor 11:4, 15) that include also the evil spirits (1 Thess 5:21), but the plurality of good spirits—1 Cor 14:12; 14:32—can only mean good angels; see E.E. Ellis, *Prophecy and Hermeneutic in Early Christiantiy: New Testament Essays* (WUNT 18; Tübingen: Mohr Siebeck, 1978), 29–36.

[29] See ibid., 30–36. Ellis highlights, for example, that Paul uses "spirits" and "spiritual gifts" interchangeably in 1 Cor 14:1, 12.

[30] A. Segal, *Paul the Convert: The Apostolate and Apostasy of Saul the Pharisee* (New

(according to Acts 9:3–8; 22:6–11; 26:12–18) was likely one of the many "visions and revelations" (2 Cor 12:1, 8; cf. Acts 22:17–18) Paul professes to have had. Paul has seen the Lord (1 Cor 9:1), received a revelation, *apokalypsis*, of Jesus (Gal 1:12), and spoken directly with him (2 Cor 12:9), which goes beyond mere prayers; clearly Paul speaks of mystical experiences.[31] In 2 Cor 12:1–9, Paul records one event that we may call an altered state of consciousness (ASC), or ecstasy. Though Paul takes a pseudonymous stance, writing in the third person, he is most likely writing about himself. He interprets his experience in light of the ascent traditions of Jewish apocalyptic, mystical traditions, claiming to ascend to "the third heaven," which he also calls paradise. In line with these apocalyptic traditions that saw revelations of heavenly realities as secret, Paul shows restraint in his descriptions, only stating that he "heard things that are not to be told, that no mortal is permitted to repeat" (2 Cor 12:4; cf. 1 Cor 15:8; Gal 1:15–16).[32] Given that Paul refers to this experience in the context of boasting, as he says, one may safely conclude that some of the Corinthian addressees, particularly the "Spirit-people," οἱ πνευματικοί (e.g., 1 Cor 3:1; 14:37), claimed spiritual supremacy also based on mystical experiences. Paul speaks frequently of being "in Christ," and sometimes of Christ dwelling in the believers, which is not simply a metaphorical language but articulates a sense of intimacy and of a mystical bond between the believers and the divine.[33] Therefore, the reference to angels

---

Haven: Yale University Press, 1990), 34–71; idem, *Life and Death: A History of the Afterlife in Western Religion* (New York: Doubleday, 2004), 399–440.

[31] Segal points out (*Paul the Convert*, 58–71) that ecstatic visions are often transformative experiences, which is evident also in the case of Paul's so-called "conversion" (Gal 1:10–17; 2 Cor 3:18–4:6).

[32] Paul's experience follows a long-standing tradition of prophets receiving visions and revelations through ASC experiences, according to hints in the Hebrew Bible; see R.R. Wilson, *Prophecy and Society in Ancient Israel* (Philadelphia: Fortress, 1980); idem, "Prophecy and Ecstasy: A Reexamination" in *Community, Identity and Ideology: Social Science Approaches to the Hebrew Bible* (ed. C.E. Carter and C.L. Meyers; Sources for Biblical and Theological Study 6; Winona Lake: Eisenbrauns, 1996), 404–422. Also many revelations recorded by apocalyptic writers are likely based on ASC experiences; see discussion by DeConick, "Early Jewish and Christian Mysticism," 5–8; C. Rowland, with P. Gibbons and V. Dobroruka, "Visionary Experience in Ancient Judaism and Christianity," in *Paradise Now*, 41–56. As Ellis (*Prophecy and Hermeneutic*, 42–43) points out, the imagery of "the third heaven" and "Paradise" would naturally involve the presence of angels and of God (cf. Dan 7; 1 *En.* 20). Most scholars assume that Paul is speaking about himself (Segal, *Paul the Convert*, 36). See also analysis by Segal, *Life and Death*, 413–414.

[33] Paul uses the phrase "in Christ" 58 times (Ephesians, Colossians and the Pastorals excluded) with various connotations. Sometimes, the expression conveys the meaning

in 1 Cor 11:10 may primarily be an allusion to a communion—plausibly a mystical one—between humans and angels. Given the mystical, ecstatic framework and close relationship between angels and humans at Corinth that we will also find at Qumran, this raises the possibility that Paul is advising his community to imitate the angels just like the sectarians did. To consider this option we need to further consider the views on head coverings in antiquity.

Head Covering

It is a common misconception that women in Roman society in Antiquity would ordinarily be veiled in public.[34] The custom of wearing a veil appears, rather, to have belonged to the eastern fringes of the empire. Instead, both men and women usually appeared in public with bare heads.[35] In her in-depth study on the customs of head coverings in the Mediterranean antiquity, Linda Belleville demonstrates that decorum

of believers being in Christ (or "in the Lord") as for example, in Rom 6:11; 8:1; 12:5 ("we all are one body in Christ"); 1 Cor 1:2, 30; 15:18. A related expression is "in the Spirit" (Rom 8:9); also, believers are part of Christ's body (1 Cor 12:12–13). Conversely, Christ (or "his son") is present in Paul (Gal 1:16; 2:19–20) and in the believers (2 Cor 13:5; Rom 8:10). Related to this are the concepts of dying "united with him (Christ)" through baptism (Rom 6:1–11; cf. Rom 7:4; 8:17; 2 Cor 1:3–7; 4:10) and the transformation of believers who are becoming like Christ in his death (Phil 3:10; cf. Rom 12:2) and are being transformed into God's image (2 Cor 3:18; see below). For a detailed discussion on the mystical dimension of Paul's Christological expressions, see J.D.G. Dunn, *The Theology of Paul the Apostle* (Edinburgh: T&T Clark, 1998), 390–412. See also, J.D. Tabor, *Things Unutterable: Paul's Ascent to Paradise in its Greco-Roman, Judaic, and Early Christian Contexts* (Studies in Judaism; Lanham: University Press of America, 1986), 42; Segal, *Paul the Convert*, 63–64.

[34] Stuckenbruck argues that the often quoted Plutarch's statement about women covering their hair in public (*Quaest. rom.* 14) is speculative; "Why Should Women Cover Their Heads," 211.

[35] See L.L. Belleville "ΚΕΦΑΛΗ and the Thorny Issue of Head Covering in 1 Corinthians 11:2–16," in *Paul and the Corinthians: Studies on a Community in Conflict: Essays in Honour of Margaret Thrall* (ed. T.J. Burke and J.K. Elliott; NovTSup 109; Leiden: Brill, 2003), 315–331; C.S. Keener, *1–2 Corinthians* (New Cambridge Bible Commentary; Cambridge: Cambridge University Press, 2005), 91. Consequently, the argument that women unveiled their heads in order to dress like men (W.A. Meeks, "The Image of the Androgyne: Some Uses of a Symbol in Earliest Christianity," *HR* 13 [1974]: 199–200), or to manifest a transcendence of sexual differentiation, as M.Y. MacDonald ("Women Holy in Body and Spirit: The Social Setting of 1 Corinthians 7," *NTS* 36 [1990]: 161–181, 166) argues, is not compelling. For the hair styles of Roman women, see R. Ling, "The Arts of Living," in *The Oxford History of the Classical World* (ed. J. Boardman, J. Griffin, and O. Murray; Oxford: Oxford University Press, 1986), 718–747, 743–744.

even allowed women to participate in public with loose hair in certain
religious rites as well as at weddings and funerals.

There is evidence of women taking part in religious rites with bare
heads. For example, most of the women participants in the Dionysiac
rites painted in the Villa of Mysteries by Pompeii have bare heads with
their hair tied up.[36] Literary evidence also suggests that the maenads of
the cults of Dionysos, Sibyl, Cybele, and the Delphian Pythia had dishevelled hair.[37] When functioning in liturgical roles, however, such as offering sacrifices, both men and women commonly covered their heads.[38]
There is plenty of both literary and statuary evidence for this practice, including images of both Emperor Augustus and Empress Livia.[39]
Both male and female clergy covered their heads by pulling up their
togas, such as in the case of a statue at Pompeii depicting Plyaena,
priestess of Victory.[40] Paul's instruction to women to cover their heads
relates particularly to when they pray or prophesy (1 Cor 11:5), i.e., when
they perform an official function in the worship, and is therefore in
line with liturgical customs of the day.[41] But his reasoning cannot be
explained on the basis of social conventions alone, since Paul's command for men to pray and prophecy with bare heads appears to be contrary to the norms. This position is what makes up the most remarkable
aspect of Paul's address—not that women should cover their heads—
as both Belleville and Wire note.[42] Paul's insistence of marking gender distinctions in worship also differ from the social norms in general.[43]

---

[36] A.C. Wire, *The Corinthian Women Prophets: A Reconstruction through Paul's Rhetoric* (Minneapolis: Fortress, 1990), 183.

[37] See Stuckenbruck, "Why Should Women Cover their Heads," 211. E. Schüssler
Fiorenza (*In Memory of Her: A Feminist Reconstruction of Christian Origins* [New York:
Crossroad, 1983], 227), states "such a sight of dishevelled hair would be quite common
in the ecstatic worship of oriental divinities." This may explain the reason why women at
Corinth chose to prophesy and pray with un-covered hair.

[38] Ibid., 227.

[39] Belleville, "Thorny Issue of Head Covering," 220–221.

[40] Ibid.

[41] Belleville (ibid., 224) points out that "it is when a woman prays to God that a head
covering is called for."

[42] Ibid., 222. A possible underlying reason for why men should have bare heads is the
importance of the Exodus tradition (Exod 34:27–35) about Moses' unveiled face when
he saw the glory of God (see 2 Cor 3:12–18).

[43] There are exceptions; in the Isis cult women veiled their heads while the men had
shaven heads (Apuleius, *Metam.* 11.10); see Stuckenbruck, "Why Should Women Cover
Their Heads," 210–212.

Since social customs alone do not easily explain the reasons behind Paul's instructions it may be because they are mainly theologically motivated. Certainly his arguments are theological rather than practical; only at the very end does he bring up social customs in a last effort to persuade his readers (11:16). We should, therefore, closely consider his theological reasoning, which relates the issue of head covering to creation and to angels.

ADAM AND CREATION

Paul's key argument is that man is the image and glory, εἰκὼν καί δόξα, of God (1 Cor 11:7), while woman is the glory of man. Of course, Gen 1:27, to which Paul alludes, refers to the creation of *ādām* (carth-creature) in God's image, specifying that it includes male and female. Paul, ignores the plain meaning of the text, however, and interprets *ādām* as only male. He then continues by referring to the second creation story, "neither was man created for woman, but the woman for the sake of man," thus conflating the two creation stories.

Importantly, Paul adds "glory," δόξα, of God compared to Gen 1:27 which only reads "image," צלם. This phrase reflects developed speculations about the nature of Adam, known from other Jewish sources, according to which Adam was created in a perfect glorious state, even semi-divine or angelic, which humanity lost in the fall.[44] According to 2 *En.* 30:8–11 (first century C.E.)[45] and *T. Ab.* 11 (recension A) Adam was an angel. Thus 2 *En.* 30:10 reads,

> From invisible and visible substances I created man. From both his natures come both death and life. And (as my) image he knows the word like (no)

---

[44] See e.g., *Apoc. Mos.* 20:1–2 in an expansion of Gen 3:7, "And at very moment my eyes were opened and I knew that I was naked of the righteousness with which I had been clothed. And I wept saying, 'Why have you done this to me, that I have been estranged from my glory with which I was clothed?'" (translation by M.D. Johnson, "Life of Adam and Eve (First Century A.D.): A New Translation and Introduction," in *OTP* 2:249–295).

[45] *2 Enoch* is written originally in Greek, but preserved in Slavonic; see J.T.A.G.M. van Ruiten, "The Creation of Man and Woman in Early Jewish Literature," in *The Creation of Man and Woman*, 34–62, 55. A first century date is also suggested by F.I. Andersen, who also emphasizes that the provenance is unknown; see "2 (Slavonic Apocalypse of) Enoch (Late First Century A.D.) A New Translation and Introduction," in *OTP* 1:91–213, 95–97).

other creature. But even at his greatest he is small, and again at his smallest he is great. And on earth I assigned him to be a second angel, honored and great and glorious.[46]

According to the *Life of Adam and Eve* (first century C.E.),[47] God commanded the angels to worship "the image of God," that is Adam, a tradition that is developed also in rabbinic literature.[48] Some rabbinic traditions speculate about Adam's spectacular height, immortality, and superiority to angels.[49] Also Job 15:7–8 alludes to traditions concerning a semidivine first human being, "the firstborn of the human race," who listened to the council of God.[50] Philo describes the first man of Gen 1 as a "heavenly man" who was "stamped in the image of God" (referring to the mind of the human) whereas the forming of the man in Gen 2 represents the earthly man. Clearly Philo, like Paul, is developing pre-existing speculations about the glorious guise of Adam, or the first man.[51]

The angelic likeness of Adam may also be linked to the tradition that angels were present at the creation; thus Philo explains that when God says "let us make man (*ādām*) in our likeness" in Gen 1:27 God is speaking to the angels; this view is echoed in later rabbinic literature.[52] Earlier Jewish documents including *Jubilees* and some Qumran documents assume that angels were present at the creation, which at least allows for the possibility that God was assumed to be speaking to them when he says "in our likeness."[53] Importantly, 4QInstruction (4Q417 1 i 16–17 and 4Q416 2 iii) presents God and angels as taking part in the creative process of humans, but humans are fashioned in the likeness of angels, not God. 4QInstruction[b] (4Q416) 2 iii 16–17 reads:

---

[46] Translation ibid., 1:152.

[47] Johnson, "Life of Adam and Eve," 2:252.

[48] *L.A.E. Vita* 13–14; *Apoc. Mos.* 10:3; see M.E. Stone, *A History of Literature of Adam and Eve* (SBLEJL 3; Atlanta: Scholars Press, 1992); W.D. Davies, *Paul and Rabbinic Judaism: Some Rabbinic Elements in Pauline Theology* (4th ed.; Philadelphia: Fortress, 1980), 42.

[49] *B. Sanh.* 38b; 59b; *b. B. Bat.* 58a; *Gen. Rab.* 8:1; 17:5; 21:3; 24:2; *Lev. Rab.* 14:1; 18:2; *Pirqe R. El.* 11; *Pesiq. Rab.* 1b; 115a; see Davies, *Paul and Rabbinic Judaism*, 44–46; DeConick, "Early Jewish and Christian Mysticism," 19–20.

[50] See Davies, *Paul and Rabbinic Judaism*, 45. Although any identification between this "first man" and Adam of Genesis in Job 15 is not certain, it is likely that later readers did not make such distinctions.

[51] E.g., *Leg.* 1.31.

[52] *Opif.* 75; *Fug.* 68; *Mut.* 29–31; *Tg. Ps.-J.* on Gen 1:26; see discussion by Stuckenbruck, "Why Should Women Cover their Heads," 221–222.

[53] E.g., 4QBer[a] (4Q286) 3a–d presents the angels as being in charge of creation; so also 1QH[a] IX:10–20; 1QM X:11–14.

For as God is to a man, so is his own father and as angels (אדנים) are to a person so is his mother, for they are the oven of your origin. And just as he set them in authority over you and fashioned you according to the spirits so serve them.[54]

Traditions about the glorious nature of Adam are also evident in the Dead Sea Scrolls. In wording similar to Paul, the liturgical text *Words of the Luminaries* reads "You fashioned [Adam] our [fa]ther in the image of Your glory" (4Q504 I:4). The expression "the image of the glory" recalls Ezekiel's visions of God's glory, the visible manifestation of God (e.g., Ezek 1:28; 3:12; 10:4) and emphasises the glorious state of Adam. The expression "glory of Adam," כבוד אדם, appears in several documents from Qumran as part of the eschatological reward for the faithful, e.g., 1QS IV:22–23 reads "for those God has chosen for an eternal covenant, and all the glory of Adam shall be theirs without deceit." Here and elsewhere (CD 3:20; 1QHᵃ IV:27) this eschatological gift is associated with immortality. In 1QS XI:9–22 the writer elaborates upon the human, sinful nature: "I (belong to) wicked Adam, to the assembly of deceitful flesh" (XI:9). While the sectarians as humans partake in this sinful nature of Adam, the author explains how God also has cleansed his elect from this state; the message is that the elect through divine mercy have received a taste of the original glorious state of Adam. Paul shares this perspective that comes somewhere in between realized and future eschatology, explaining that through Christ, followers already have part in this gift, which he develops further in 1 Cor 15; 15:49 is noteworthy in particular: "just as we have borne the image of the man of dust, we will also bear (or, "let us bear") the image of the man of heaven" (cf. Rom 5:12–21; 8:30).[55]

---

[54] Based on the translation by B.G. Wold, *Women, Men, and Angels: The Qumran Wisdom Document* Musar leMevin *and its Allusions to Genesis Creation Traditions* (WUNT 2/201; Tübingen: Mohr Siebeck, 2005), 149–150; see also his discussion on 4Q417 1 i 15–18; 4Q416 2 iii 16–17 on pp. 124–156.

[55] This Adam-typology presents Adam and Christ as contrasting representatives of humanity. Whereas Adam brought death, Christ, the second Adam, will bring resurrection (1 Cor 15:42–53). For similarities and differences with Philo's treaties on a heavenly and earthly man, see Davies, *Paul and Rabbinic Judaism*, 44–57. Paul presents the two Adams within an eschatological framework based on the belief that the eschaton corresponds to the beginning (cf. *1 En.* 85–90; *Apoc. Mos* 21:6; 41:1–3); see J. Murphy-O'Connor, "The First Letter to the Corinthians," in *The New Jerome Biblical Commentary* (ed. R.E. Brown, J.A. Fitzmyer, and R.E. Murphy; Upper Saddle River: Prentice Hall, 1990), 798–815, 799. Christ as the second Adam, untainted by sin, repossesses the original glory of Adam that believers now are able to benefit from in the present. Tabor (*Things Unutterable*, 17) explains, "so Jesus (as a last Adam) is the first of a transformed race or *genus* of heavenly beings, immortal and glorified. That Jesus is human (i.e., mortal,

As many commentators note Paul's argumentation in 1 Cor 11:2–16 is a bit forced; while arguing that man is the image and glory of God, and that man was not made from woman and so on—to enforce hierarchy—he almost immediately qualifies his statement by explaining their mutual dependency on each other. It is as if he is uncomfortable with his own argumentation; indeed, elsewhere all believers have part in this glorified state; they are transformed into the image of Christ or "His son" (Rom 8:29; 1 Cor 15:49; Phil 3:21; cf. Col. 3:9) and in 2 Cor 3:18 into the image of the Lord (= God):[56]

> and all of us, with unveiled faces, seeing *the glory of the Lord* as though reflected in a mirror, are being *transformed into the same image from one degree of glory to another*; for this comes from the Lord, the Spirit.

Paul emphasizes the transformation of all the believers, so through union with Christ, they are being changed into the divine likeness, the image of God's glory, which recalls the creation of the original Adam. Like Moses who saw the glory of God and was transformed in Exod 33, Paul argues here, so are the believers. The transformation concerns renewal of the "inner nature," as opposed to the "outer nature," the body, which he explains in 2 Cor 4:17.[57] The change is a new creation, as he says in 5:17, which again recalls the Adam motif.[58] Such transformation is the outcome of a (mystical) union with Christ.

The similarity between the reference to Adam as the image and glory of God in 1 Cor 11:7 and "the glory of the Lord" in 2 Cor 3:18 is striking; clearly he alludes to the same glory available to believers through Christ.[59] But in 1 Cor 11 Paul applies the imagery only to the man; why?

"Adam") is crucial since his transformation to an immortal, glorious state is representative for all those who follow." Cf. Segal, *Paul the Convert*, 65–66.

[56] T.H. Lim, *Holy Scripture in the Qumran Commentaries and Pauline Letters* (Oxford: Clarendon, 1997), 170–171. In Paul's thought the idea of the glorification of the believers is clearly linked to the transformation that was part of his own ecstatic "conversion" experience. Alan Segal (*Paul the Convert*, 39–52) explains Paul's notion of transformation on the basis of Jewish mysticism; he argues "Like Enoch Paul claims to have gazed on the Glory, whom Paul identifies as Christ; Paul understands that he has been transformed into a divine state, which will be fully realized after his death" (ibid., 47; e.g., Phil 3:21). See also Tabor, *Things Unutterable*, 9–14.

[57] See Segal, *Life after Death*, 416–421; cf. Phil 3:12–21; the complete transformation of also the body lies in the future (1 Cor 15:41–54; Phil 3:21; 2 Cor 4:13–18).

[58] Cf. Rom 8.

[59] As Alan Segal explains, Paul interprets Adam's divine likeness as being identical to the glory which Christ received; see "The Risen Christ and the Angelic Mediator Figures in Light of Qumran," in *Jesus and the Dead Sea Scrolls* (ed. J.H. Charlesworth; New York: Doubleday, 1992), 302–322, 318.

Because in this case the focus is on the outer appearance only; in their outer appearance men/Adam is made in the glory and image of the Lord, women are not.

As we have seen, Jewish speculations about the first man, Adam, envisioned him semi-divine or angelic. Paul is likely drawing on this rich tradition and claims that the male body resembles that of angels. Paul frequently uses language of imitation; Christ followers are to imitate both Christ and Paul (who is imitating Christ): 1 Cor 4:16; 1 Thess 1:6; Phil 3:17; imitate other churches 1 Thess 2:14. In 1 Cor 11:10 "because of the angels" may then be a call for imitating angels.

What do we know about the appearance of angels? They are not sexless; though as the myth of the fallen sons of God in Gen 6 emphasizes, they are not supposed to be sexual in nature; the names of all the arch angels, such as Michael, Gabriel, Melchizedek and so forth, are male.[60] In the Dead Sea Scrolls, the primary roles of angels are that of priests serving in the temple and of warriors, both which identify them as male. The book of *Jubilees* claims that angels were created circumcised (*Jub.* 15:27–28), again leaving no doubt about their sex. This is the general view of angels to which also Paul subscribes when he refers to the creation of Adam as being in the image and glory of God.

In their close communion with angels, the Corinthians like the Qumranites, had to be careful about their appearance; women's hair is the feature that particularly represents their femaleness—a woman's hair is her glory, as Paul explains in 1 Cor 11:15. Therefore it has to be covered. If she does not veil herself, he argues, she might as well cut off her hair or even shave it (11:6). The point here is not so much to bring on shame, as commentators usually hold, but to make herself look male. Like at Qumran, the closeness to angels inspired worshippers to imitate them in inner and outer perfection. It may seem strangely foreign to us today; would people believe that angels really cared about how they looked? Yes, they would. To retain sacredness of space, decorum was extremely important. In the Dead Sea Scrolls no one who was blemished in any way was admitted into the meetings—angels demanded perfection in appearance and in action;

---

[60] See C. Wassen, "Angels in the Dead Sea Scrolls," in *Angels: The Concept of Celestial Beings-Origins, Development and Reception* (ed. F.V. Reiterer, T. Nicklas, and K. Schöpflin; Deuterocanonical and Cognate Literature Yearbook 2007; Berlin: de Gruyter, 2007), 499–523, 502–503; K. Sullivan, "Sexuality and Gender of Angels," in *Paradise Now*, 211–228.

no blemished priests were allowed to serve in the Jerusalem Temple in the presence of the divine (Lev 21:17–23); similarly here, when Christ-believers got together for worship they created a sacred space where the appearance before the divine, represented through angels, was extremely important. According to Paul, women, not looking angel-like as the original Adam, had to make an effort to imitate the angels by covering up their most distinctive female feature, their long hair.

Thus when Paul demands that a woman covers her head—"for this reason a woman ought to have authority on her head because of the angels"—I propose that he intends to make her look less female and more male. In this chapter (whether we like it or not) Paul asserts a hierarchical distinction between men and women by stating that the man is the head of the woman like Christ is the head of every man, and God is the head of Christ (1 Cor 11:3). "Head" here denotes both authority and origin, according to its metaphorical usage in Greek and Jewish literature.[61] Although many commentators[62] more recently have dismissed any notion of subordination in the verse in favour of a chain of origin, such chain would also point to hierarchical relationships (cf. 1 Cor 8:6).[63] Paul is certainly smoothing out the initial hierarchical claims in the subsequent discourse by highlighting the mutual dependency of man and woman on each other, and them being a source of origin of each other (11:11–12). Nevertheless, as a woman's head, the man has a certain authority over women in 11:2–3. This verse provides the basis of his argument, an initial statement on which he builds his arguments.[64] By covering her hair, a woman thus symbolically covers her femaleness and gains the same authority as a man to prophesy and pray with the angels.

---

[61] Barrett (*Commentary on the First Epistle to the Corinthians*, 249) holds, "Thus a chain of originating and subordination relationships is set up: God, Christ, man, woman." Similarly, Keener (*1–2 Corinthians*, 92) claims "both 'authority' and 'most honored part' fit Paul's Christology," pointing out that Paul assumes the normal structure of the household of his day.

[62] See G.D. Fee, e.g., *The First Epistle to the Corinthians* (NICNT; Grand Rapids: Eerdmans, 1987), 502–503.

[63] See Conzelmann, *1 Corinthians*, 183.

[64] Conzelmann argues that 11:3 is part of "not the doctrinal tradition of Christian creed ... but a speculative school tradition founded on a Hellenistic-Jewish basis and aimed at providing a *fundamental* ground on which to argue the special problem" (ibid., 182).

WOMEN, HAIR, AND ANGELS

This interpretation of 1 Cor 11 that traces the underlying issue to the uneasiness over the female appearance of women in the presence of angels finds support in the Jewish novella *Joseph and Aseneth*. In this tale, we find the same concern about the uncovered hair of a woman in the presence of angels. Upon Aseneth's repentance and conversion to Judaism an angel ("a man") appears and asks her to change clothing, from those of mourning into a new linen robe, which marks her new status (*Jos. Asen.* 14). When she appears wearing also a linen veil, the angels says: ' "Remove the veil from your head ... For you are a chaste virgin today, and your head is like that of a young man." And Aseneth removed the veil from her head."[65] Both *Joseph and Aseneth* and 1 Cor 11 address the same problem: should women be veiled in the presence of angels? Although the practical solution here is different than Paul's position, both authors agree that women have to look like men when encountering angels. In Paul's case by covering up the distinctive female feature, the hair, in the case of *Joseph and Aseneth*, by spiritual transformation that make women— again, with a focus on the head—appear as male.[66]

CONCLUSION

This study has examined beliefs surrounding angels in the Dead Sea Scrolls primarily, and other Jewish documents secondarily, as a background to understanding Paul's message about angels in 1 Cor 11:10. These beliefs are helpful in three aspects: first, the Dead Sea Scrolls help us understand the reality behind Paul's phrase "because of the angels." Angels were believed to be present in a very real sense both in Corinth and among the Qumran sectarians. Three of the Qumran documents

---

[65] Translation by C. Burchard, "Joseph and Aseneth (First Century B.C.–Second Century A.D.): A New Translation and Introduction," in *OTP* 2:177–247, 225–226.

[66] This story reflects a society in which women were wearing veils. A common suggestion for provenance is Egypt and the date may be anywhere form first century B.C.E. to second century C.E.; see ibid., 187–188. It is worth noting that also *Gos. Thom.* 114 expresses a similar view, although perhaps only on a spiritual level: "Jesus said: See I shall lead her (Mary), so that I will make her male, that she too may become a living spirit, resembling you males. For every woman who makes herself male will enter the Kingdom of Heaven." Translation from A. Guillaumont et al., *The Gospel according to Thomas: Coptic Text Established and Translated* (Leiden: Brill, 1959).

bar blemished people from participating in gatherings of the community and in the final war because of the presence of angels. Their presence put obligations on the worshipers. In both communities the appearance of the worshipers was important; at Corinth men should worship with unveiled heads and women with veiled heads, according to Paul. Second, both Paul and the Scrolls writers express a deep unity with the divine, and in both cases to some extent this claim was based on mystical experiences. As well, both sets of writings reflect the idea that divine-human unity is expressed through imitation of the divine. At Qumran the imitation of angels concerned both behaviour and outer appearance. Paul ordinarily encourages his audience to imitate Christ and himself. Nevertheless, given the motif of imitating the angels in the sectarian literature from Qumran, it is likely that Paul expresses a similar view in the context of the communion with angels and is encouraging the Christ-followers to imitate the angels. Third, the Dead Sea Scrolls as well as other Jewish documents from the Second Temple period, testify to the rich traditions that developed concerning the original glorious nature of Adam. In 1 Cor 11:2–16 the focus is on the original glory that belonged to humans once, but was lost; for both the sectarians and Paul this glorious state was in part attainable in the present, and can be likened to an angelic state of being. This concept seems to lie beneath Paul's explanation. In Cor 11:2–16 he narrows this motif to apply to the creation of Adam, the man, focussing on the appearance, the outer nature, alone. In this regard, men are naturally closer to the divine beings whom they look alike. Therefore, in imitation of the male angels, women have to hide their female, long hair in order to attain the same authority as men have in order to prophesy and praise with the angels.

DEAD SEA SCROLLS AND EARLY CHRISTIAN ART

Renate J. Pillinger
University of Vienna

From the outset I must state that I am not a specialist in the Dead Sea Scrolls; rather I simply number among those interested in the Scrolls. The present article should not be understood as a comprehensive comparison between early Christian art and the Dead Sea Scrolls but as a first consideration of the importance of one for the other. Using select examples, I would like to demonstrate some convergences and divergences between the Scrolls and early Christian art. In this way, I hope to point to a new and mostly unexplored field of research.

Direct contact between the first Christians and the Qumran community cannot, as yet, be verified. The Greek fragments from Cave 7 do not permit any reliable conclusion and, in addition, could have been placed there at a later date.[1] Nonetheless, the number of provisional commonalities are noteworthy—perhaps because of the shared (Jewish) context or roots—as well as the significant differences in their seemingly similar practices. Precisely this predicament shall be demonstrated by means of select early Christian images.

We shall begin with the *giants*, who are mentioned only briefly in Gen 6:4. The Septuagint text reads, "The giants were on the earth in those days, and also afterward, when the sons of God came in to the daughters of men, and they bore children to them. These were the mighty men that were of old, the men of renown."[2] But giants are not only known from the Hebrew Bible and its Greek translation. Gods also battle against giants in Graeco-Roman mythology.[3] The best known examples are the images on the Altar of Zeus from Pergamon, now in the Berlin Pergamon Museum, such as the goddess Athena subduing the giant Enkelados.

---

[1] See further K. Berger, *Qumran: Funde-Texte—Geschichte* (Stuttgart: Reclam, 2005), 32–33.

[2] English translation of LXX by R.J.P.

[3] See further F. Vian, *Répertoire des gigantomachies figurées dans l'art grec et romain* (Paris: Klinsieck, 1951).

In different caves from Qumran, a series of Aramaic scrolls of various Enochic texts were found[4] and among these Enochic texts is also the *Book of the Giants*.[5] In 4QEnGiants[b] ar (4Q530) II:2 and 4QEnGiants[c] ar (4Q531) 17 12 one of the giants is called Gilgamesh—just like the hero of the Babylonian Epic[6]—which probably goes back to an older tradition.

4QEnGiants[b] ar (4Q530) II:7–12 (Ohyah's dream), in which a garden is destroyed by water and fire, is suggestive of a connection between the giants and the flood. 2QEnGiants ar (2Q26) likewise mentions rising waters. The most conclusive citation however, remains 6QpapGiants ar (6Q8) 26 with the reference to Mount Lubar in line 1. According to the book of *Jubilees* Lubar is a mountain among the mountains of Ararat (cf. *Jub.* 5.28 and 7.1), i.e. the mountain peak on which Noah's ark landed.

Turning now to early Christian iconography, two images in particular are thought-provoking. One, in the *Vienna Genesis* codex (Pictura 3; fig. 1), is an illustration of the flood. There are fairly large humans in the water around the three-story ark in the center. Humans of similar proportions can be found on Folio 9[r] of the Ashburnham Pentateuch (fig. 2); in both of these examples one could consider a Jewish tradition of giants.[7]

Another prominent figure in the Dead Sea Scrolls is *Melchizedek*.[8] He too is mentioned in the Hebrew Scriptures. Genesis 14:18–20 tells how Melchizedek, king of Salem and priest of the Most High God, brings bread and wine to Abraham. According to 11QMelch (11Q13), Melchizedek is considered the precursor of the Messiah.[9]

---

[4] For the Enochic manuscripts in Qumran, see especially J.T. Milik, *The Books of Enoch: Aramaic Fragments of Qumrân Cave 4* (Oxford: Clarendon, 1976).

[5] For the *Book of Giants* in the Qumran library, see L.T. Stuckenbruck, *The Book of Giants from Qumran: Texts, Translation, and Commentary* (TSAJ 63; Tübingen: Mohr Siebeck, 1997). In the following the manuscripts of the *Book of Giants* from Qumran are quoted according to this edition.

[6] Cf. A. Schott, *Das Gilgamesch-Epos: Übersetzt und mit Anmerkungen versehen* (ed. W. von Soden; Stuttgart: Reclam, 2005) and the contribution of G.J. Selz to this volume.

[7] See especially K. Weitzmann, *Spätantike und frühchristliche Buchmalerei* (München: Prestel, 1977), 121. Weitzmann notes that various midrashim speak of "Giants of such largeness and strength that water alone would not be able to overcome them" ("Riesen von solcher Größe und Stärke, dass die Wasser allein sie nicht hätten überwältigen können").

[8] More details on Melchizedek can be found in 1QapGen ar (1Q20) XXII:15–17 and 11QMelch (11Q13) II:5, 8, 13 and III:5.

[9] Compare here A.S. van der Woude, "Melchisedek als himmlische Erlösergestalt in den neugefundenen eschatologischen Midraschim aus Qumran Höhle XI," *OTS* 14 (1965): 354–373 and the contribution of P. Bertalotto to the present proceedings.

In the New Testament, specifically John 1:41, Jesus is shown as the Christ, i.e. the Anointed One, i.e. the Messiah. According to Heb 5:6, 10 and 6:20, Christ is the High Priest "according to the Order of Melchizedek."[10] An early Christian mosaic (fig. 3) dated to the first third of the fifth century, located in Santa Maria Maggiore in Rome, fits this description. To the left of a *kantharos* stands Melchizedek with a bread basket in his hands, which he passes to Abraham. Abraham rides towards his right with his soldiers, and a bust with a nimbus, namely Christ, points to him from the blue-red sky.

The portrayals of Melchizedek from the sixth century Ravenna churches San Vitale and Sant Apollinare in Classe are quite distinct from the previous example. In San Vitale (fig. 4), Melchizedek is shown only with Abel, in Sant Apollinare in Classe (fig. 5) he is pictured with Abel, Abraham, and Isaac at the altar—in both cases clearly a Eucharistic reference.

We additionally learn of the expectation of the *Messiah* from the Qumran scrolls, though in no way is the Messiah presented in a uniform manner. In 1QSa (1Q28a) II:12–14, for example, the Anointed One is subordinated to the Priest; in CD 12:23–13:1 one awaits the "manifestation of the Anointed of Abraham and Israel," thus perhaps two or even three messianic figures are present in this text, while 11QMelch (11Q13) II:18 cites the Anointed of the Spirit.[11]

Even the New Testament speaks of such an "anointed one," as previously shown in the example of Melchizedek. John 1:41 identifies this "anointed one" as Christ, and as we shall see, Christ's own resurrection plays a significant role in the resurrection of others.

The Messiah images in early Christian art are diverse. Thus, for example, the Messiah is depicted as a *shepherd* with his herd of sheep in a fifth century mosaic in the so-called Mausoleum of Galla Placidia in Ravenna. The shepherd, with a nimbus and wearing a golden tunic and purple pallium, holds a golden cross-staff (fig. 6).

We also see the Messiah-figure in a kenotic form, namely as a *small child*. His birth scene is almost always depicted with the ox and donkey,

---

[10] Unless otherwise indicated all quotations of biblical references are taken from the RSV.

[11] See J. Maier, *Die Qumran-Essener: Die Texte vom Toten Meer* (3 vols.; München: Reinhardt, 1995–1996), 3:239 s.v. "Gesalbter." Cf. also the contributions in R.S. Hess and M.D. Caroll, eds., *Israel's Messiah in the Bible and the Dead Sea Scrolls* (Grand Rapids: Baker, 2003).

as narrated in the apocryphal text *Ps.-Mt.* 14.[12] A roughly eight-pointed *star* is frequently depicted, as on a textile fragment in the Metropolitan Museum of New York (fig. 7).[13] The star also appears on ivory pieces: in the Nativity scene on the back of Maximian's kathedra in Ravenna (fig. 8), and a panel in London showing the Adoration of the Magi, below the manger with Salome (fig. 9).

Moreover, the star is found in the Adoration of the Magi; among other examples[14] are the early fifth century mosaics on the triumphal arch of Santa Maria Maggiore in Rome (fig. 10), and, from the sixth century, in Ravenna's Sant Apollinare Nuovo (fig. 11). Sometimes it is shown in a combination of these two scenes, as in the sarcophagi in the Museo Pio Cristiano (MPC) of the Vatican (fig. 12).[15]

The star even appears in the apocryphal narrations of the Annunciation. We see the star in the image of Mary spinning the purple wool next to the Visitation scene on an orbiculus in London's Victoria and Albert Museum (fig. 13). From the Abegg Foundation in Riggisberg near Bern is the so-called *Marienseide*, a silk textile with images from the Virgin's life, such as the Annunciation at the fountain by the angel of the Lord, as told in *Ps.-Mt.* 9 (fig. 14).[16] A fresco in Rome's Catacombs of Priscilla (fig. 15) deals with the typological depiction of the pronouncement, namely the announcement of the Messiah by a prophet (Balaam or Isaiah).[17] The prophet, indicating the star, is in front of the Mother of God with the child Jesus. In Cubiculum O of the New Catacombs in the Via Latina,[18] we see the painting of the prophet pointing to the star as an autonomous composition.

In all of these cases, the star designates Christ. The latter two examples raise the possibility of interpreting the star as a messianic symbol in several other images from the Hebrew Bible. Such might be the case for

---

[12] G. Schneider, *Evangelia infantiae apocrypha: Apokryphe Kindheitsevangelien* (Fontes Christiani 18; Freiburg: Herder, 1995), 226–229.

[13] A. Stauffer, *Textiles of Late Antiquity* (New York: Metropolitan Museum of Art, 1995), 45, nos. 26 and 38 with figure.

[14] Compare also Vatican, MPC 124 and the textile from New York cited in n. 14 above.

[15] See also F. Mancinelli, *Römische Katakomben und Urchristentum* (Florence: SCALA, 1981), 62, fig. 115.

[16] A. de Santos Otero, *Los evangelios apócrifos: Edición crítica y bilingüe* (3rd ed.; Biblioteca de autores cristianos 148; Madrid: EDICA, 1979), 201.

[17] According to Num 24:19 (cf. Isa 60:1–6). Cf. also E. Kirschbaum, "Der Prophet Balaam und die Anbetung der Weisen," *RQ* 49 (1954): 129–171.

[18] A. Ferrua, *Katakomben: Unbekannte Bilder des frühen Christentums unter der Via Latina* (Stuttgart: Urachhaus, 1991), 145, fig. 145.

the Sacrifice of Isaac on an amulet from the Tamerit private collection.[19] Also in Cubiculum O of Via Latina's New Catacombs is the image of a young man (fig. 16), whose physiognomy is that of the youthful Jesus, holding a *virga* or staff and passing through the Red Sea—under a star. Such might also be the case with the three Babylonian youths who had refused to pay homage to Nebuchadnezzar as carved on the Milan sarcophagus,[20] or the image of Daniel in the lion's den woven in a textile from Düsseldorf[21]—here Daniel is even between two stars. In all of these examples, we could only encounter a typology, with the star as an indicator of the coming Messiah in Jesus Christ, thus exclusively an *interpretatio christiana*.

On a sarcophagus in the Cathedral of Palermo,[22] the apostles are standing with crowned heads and their right arms stretched out in acclamation. Each apostle has a five-pointed star adjacent to his head.[23]

With respect to a star as a messianic symbol, in the Qumran scrolls, one must certainly include the reference to Num 24:17 ("... a star shall come out of Jacob, and a scepter shall rise out of Israel") in CD 7:18–20.[24] A link to Christian star symbolism can also be found in the Bar Kokhbah coins of the Second Revolt which also use the star as a messianic symbol.[25]

---

[19] See E. Lässig, "Ein Amulett mit Reiterdarstellung und Opferung des Isaac: Papyrussammlung der Österreichischen Nationalbibliothek, Privatsammlung Tamerit, M 63," in *Realia Coptica: Festgabe zum 60. Geburtstag von Hermann Harrauer* (ed. U. Horak; Wien: Holzhausen, 2001), 55–64, esp. pl. 30, fig. 2.

[20] J. Dresken-Weiland discusses the Magis's audience with Herod in *Italien mit einem Nachtrag Rom und Ostia, Dalmatien, Museen der Welt* (ed. T. Ulbert; Repertorium der christlich-antiken Sarkophage 2; Mainz: von Zabern, 1998), 57, no. 15 and pl. 60.2. If one compares this with the refusal to worship Nebuchadnezzar depicted in the Catacomb of Saints Marcus and Marcellinus (in J. Fink and B. Asamer, *Die römischen Katakomben* [Sonderhefte der Antiken Welt; Mainz: von Zabern, 1997], 36, fig. 56) this interpretation is highly unlikely.

[21] Reproduced in M. Borda, *La pittura Romana* (Milan: Società Editrice Libraria, 1958), 375.

[22] For more detailed information, see Dresken-Weiland, *Italien*, 49–50, no. 143 and pl. 51.1.

[23] Cf. also F.W. Deichmann, "Zur Erscheinung des Sternes von Bethlehem," in *Vivarium: Festschrift für Theodor Klauser zum 90. Geburtstag* (ed. E. Dassmann and K. Thraede; JAC Ergänzungsband 11; Münster: Aschendorff, 1984), 98–106, and D. Calganini Carletti, "Nota iconografica: La stella e il vaticinio del V. T. nell'iconografia funeraria del III e IV sec.," *Rivista di archeologia cristiana* 64 (1988): 65–87.

[24] Cf. e.g. J.J. Collins, *The Scepter and the Star: The Messiahs of the Dead Sea Scrolls and Other Ancient Literature* (ABRL; New York: Doubleday, 1995), 269 s.v. "star."

[25] For more detailed information, see I. Knohl, "'By Three Days, Live': Messiahs, Resurrection, and Ascent to heaven in *Hazon Gabriel*," *JR* 88 (2008): 147–158.

Having illustrated some of the features shared between the community of the Dead Sea Scrolls and the early Christians, we can now turn
to some of the deviations. Controversial even to this day is the role
of *John the Baptist*. That he belonged to the members of the Qumran or Dead Sea Scroll community is not yet a supportable conclusion.[26]

Admittedly, like the Qumran community, Luke 1:80 tells that John the
Baptist spends his childhood in the desert, which is where we find him
also later in life: teaching and baptizing—from which the appellation "the
Baptist" derives. According to Matt 3:1–17 and the synoptic parallels
in Mark 1:2–11 as well as Luke 3:1–22, for the early Christians, John
the Baptist is the preacher of repentance who prepares the way for the
Messiah, additionally called the "Lamb of God" in John 1:29 and 36.
Matthew 3:4 and Mark 1:6 describe him wearing camel hair clothes
and eating locusts as well as wild honey. In fact, in early Christian
iconography the Baptist is usually recognizable by his pelt garment, as
we can see in the two Ravenna baptisteries.[27] In the Neonian baptistery,
John holds a cross with inset gems in his left hand. The upper portion
of the cross has been augmented like the upper torsos of John and Jesus.
In the Basilica of Euphrasius in Poreč[28] the Baptist carries a cross-staff
in his left hand, probably as a reference to the coming Messiah. On the
ivory *kathedra* of Maximian,[29] he is depicted similarly with a fur collar
and the *Agnus Dei* in his left hand. The Baptist is always shown bearded,
as the encaustic Sinai icon[30] shows.

With respect to the numerous *miqwaot* found at Qumran, the only
shared characteristic with the baptism of John lies in the type, namely
an immersion. The Qumran *miqwaot* are not even exceptional because
similar finds were made on the Masada, in Jericho, and in Jerusalem.
As prescribed in the Mosaic Law (Lev 12–15), their purpose was for

---

[26] Here see R.L. Webb, "John the Baptist," *Encyclopedia of the Dead Sea Scrolls* (ed. L.H
Schiffman and J.C. VanderKam; 2 vols.; Oxford: Oxford University Press, 2000), 1:418–
421, with the most important literature.

[27] Color images can be found, among others, in A. Paolucci, *Ravenna: Una guida d'arte*
(Florence: SCALA, 1973), 53 and 55.

[28] In M. Prelog, *Die Euphrasius-Basilika von Poreč* (*sic!*) (trans. G. Popović; Monumenta artis Croatiae 1.4; Zagreb: Udruženi izdavači, 1986), fig. 22.

[29] Fig. 227 in W.F. Volbach, *Frühchristliche Kunst: Die Kunst der Spätantike in West-
und Ostrom* (München: Hirmer, 1958).

[30] Cf. A. Bank, *Byzantine Art in the Collections of Soviet Museums* (Leningrad: Aurora
Art Publishers, 1977), pl. 110.

ritual cleansing and preparation (*miqwah*).[31] In contrast, the baptism of John, to which Jesus also deferred, is distinctively oriented to the coming judgment, as described in Matt 3:13–17, Mark 1:9–11 and Luke 3:21–22.

Unique is a miniature illumination on Folio 4b of the Rabbula Gospels (fig. 17)[32] dating to 586, where the baptism of Christ is pictured with a manifestation of fire or light in the waters of the Jordan, corresponding to Matt 3:11 ("I will baptize you with water … he will baptize you with the Holy Spirit and with fire").[33]

Distinct from Qumran is also the Christian sacrament of baptism, which Jesus establishes (according to Matt 28:19 and John 3:5) and which prefigures the resurrection. In the post-apostolic period this is with increasing frequency administered through the pouring of water (fig. 18). Because of its occurrence also in the Qumran writings, the enduring emphasis on the "living water" as in *Did.* 7 remains very noteworthy.

The *communal meal*, which is described in 1QS VI:2–6 and 1QSa (1Q28a) II:17–22, played an equally important role. In 1QS VI:2 we read, "and they shall eat in community." As is still often practiced among some Jews today, the meal is held with at least ten men ranked according to a strict hierarchy. According to 1QS VI:5–6, a priest should give the benediction over the bread and (new) wine.

In seeking a comparison with other religious communities, one might consider the Mithras cult with its exclusive male membership. For these mystics a meal represents a central event, as has been verified by the discovery of reliefs and various bones in Mithraea. The reverse side of such a cultic relief from Konjica (fig. 19)[34] illustrates a hierarchy: those low in the hierarchy, such as the *corax* (left) and the *leo* (right) are servants of those higher in the hierarchy (probably the *pater* and the *heliodromus*), who are reclining on the couch. In front is a wild boar and a bull's head on either side of a three-legged table with four small bread loaves incised with crosses. It was believed that as a result of Mithras' slaying of the

---

[31] Cf. J.D. Lawrence, *Washing in Water: Trajectories of Ritual Bathing in the Hebrew Bible and Second Temple Literature* (Academia Biblica 23; Leiden: Brill, 2007).

[32] In C. Cecchelli, G. Furlani, and M. Salmi, *The Rabbula Gospels: Facsimile Edition of the Miniatures of the Syriac Manuscript Plut. I, 56 in the Medicaean-Laurentian Library* (Monumenta occidentis 1; Olten: Graf, 1959).

[33] See also G. Winkler, "Die Lichterscheinung bei der Taufe Jesu und der Ursprung des Epiphaniefestes: Eine Untersuchung griechischer, syrischer, armenischer und lateinischer Quellen," *OrChr* 78 (1994): 177–229.

[34] Images in E. Schwertheim, *Mithras: Seine Denkmäler und sein Kult* (Antike Welt Sondernummer 10; Feldmeilen: Raggi, 1979), 71–72.

bull, which is depicted on the front side of the relief, the consumption of animal meat and blood would achieve new life.

If one examines descriptions of meals in early Christian literature one must conclude that, especially in the initial period, it is impossible to determine whether these meals were Eucharistic or *agape* meals, that is, a community meal. The same holds true for the images depicting meals.

Such is the case for a fresco in the Cappella Greca of Rome's Priscilla Catacombs (fig. 20), which depicts seven figures, some even women. The figure to the far left (*in dextro cornu*) appears to be sitting differently than the rest and has both arms extended, perhaps in a blessing gesture. In front of the participants are a two-handled cup, one plate with two fishes and one with five loaves, as well as seven baskets to the left and right of the sigma. An interpretation of this scene is very difficult. Despite the depiction of the processional offering (*Anbringung*) on the front wall of the apse's arch, Joseph Wilpert's[35] liturgical interpretation of this fresco as a Eucharist is highly questionable. More probable is that the five loaves and two fish, as well as the seven baskets, allude to the miracle of the Multiplication of the Loaves. Furthermore what remains noteworthy is that only one female, the third from the right, wears a veil, which customarily in the catacomb frescoes is an indicator of the deceased individual. In fact, we must not forget that here we are in a burial site, in which only a liturgy for the dead—if even any liturgy at all—would be celebrated.

The same holds true for the so-called sacramental chapels in the Catacombs of Calixtus (fig. 21). Their designation as such is also credited to Joseph Wilpert, and must currently also be reconsidered. In the paintings are again seven reclining figures at the sigma, in front of which are two plates with fish and eight baskets of bread.

The numerous paintings in the Catacombs of Marcellinus and Petrus[36] are configured entirely differently, with servants and the frequent and highly symbolic names AGAPE and IRENE; these paintings perhaps reflect the deceased.

We will close this brief examination with the *resurrection*,[37] which emerges as a theme in the Qumran scrolls in 4QMessianic Apocalypse

[35] J. Wilpert, *"Fractio Panis": Die älteste Darstellung des eucharistischen Opfers in der "Cappella greca," entdeckt und erläutert* (Freiburg: Herder, 1895).

[36] See J.G. Deckers, H.R. Seeliger, and G. Mietke, *Die Katakombe "Santi Marcellino e Pietro": Repertorium der Malereien* (Roma Sotterranea Cristiana 6; Münster: Aschendorff, 1987), pls. 24b, 30b, 33c, 59a, 64a and b.

[37] For more detailed information, see G.W.E. Nickelsburg, *Resurrection, Immortality,*

Fig. 1. Vienna, Österreichische Nationalbibliothek, Cod.
theol. graec. 31 (Vienna Genesis): pictura 3 (Weitzmann,
Spätantike und frühchristliche Buchmalerei, fig. 23)

Fig. 2. Paris, Bibliothèque Nationale, Nouv. acq. lat.
2334 (Ashburnham Pentateuch): folio 9ʳ (Weitzmann,
Spätantike und frühchristliche Buchmalerei, fig. 45)

Fig. 3. Rome, S. Maria Maggiore (H. Karpp, ed., *Die frühchristlichen und mittelalterlichen Mosaiken in Santa Maria Maggiore zu Rom* [Baden-Baden: Grimm, 1966], fig. 29)

Fig. 4. Ravenna, S. Vitale (R. Vantaggi, *Ravenna und seine Kunstschätze* [Narni: Plurigraf, 1987], 24)

Fig. 5. Ravenna, S. Apollinare in Classe (Vantaggi, *Ravenna*, 121)

Fig. 6. Ravenna, So-called Mausoleum of
Galla Placidia (Paolucci, *Ravenna*, 38)

Fig. 7. New York, Metropolitan Museum of
Art: inv. no. 90.5.11 (Stauffer, *Textiles*, 38)

Fig. 8. Ravenna, Museo Nazionale:
Maximian's *kathedra* (Detail) (postcard)

Fig. 9. London, British Museum (P. Metz, *Elfenbein
der Spätantike* [München: Hirmer, 1962], fig. 44)

Fig. 10. Rome, S. Maria Maggiore (Karpp, *Die*
frühchristlichen und mittelalterlichen Mosaiken, fig. 6)

Fig. 11. Ravenna, S. Apollinare Nuovo (G. Bustacchini,
Ravenna: Seine Mosaiken, seine Denkmäler, seine Umgebung
[Ravenna: Fotometalgrafica Emiliana, 1984], fig. 185)

Fig. 12. Vatican City, MPC: inv. no. 31 450 (Photo © Musei Vaticani)

Fig. 13. London, Victoria & Albert Museum: inv. no. 814–1903
(M. Vassilaki, ed., *Mother of God: Representations of the Virgin
in Byzantine Art: Exhibition Benaki Museum, 20 October–20
January 2001* [Milan: Benaki Museum, 2000], 221, fig. 187)

Fig. 14. Riggisberg/Bern, Abegg-Stiftung: inv. no. 3100b
(so-called *Marienseide*/Detail) (S. Schrenk, *Die Textilsammlung der
Abegg-Stiftung*, vol. 4: *Textilien des Mittelmeerraumes aus spätantiker
bis frühislamischer Zeit* [Riggisberg/Bern: Abegg-Stiftung, 2004], 185)

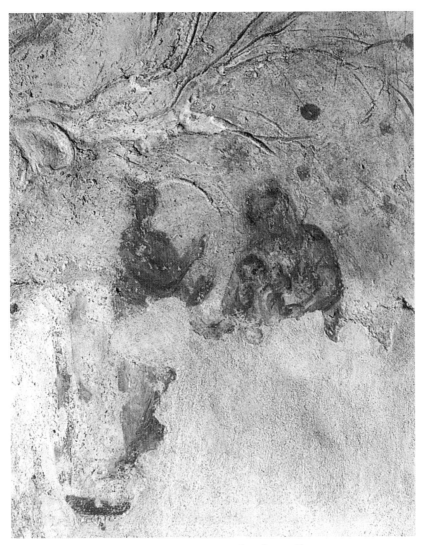

Fig. 15. Rome, Catacombs of Priscilla
(V. Fiocchi Nicolai, F. Bisconti, and D. Mazzoleni, *Roms
christliche Katakomben: Geschichte-Bilderwelt—Inschriften*
[Regensburg: Schnell & Steiner, 2000], fig. 140)

Fig. 16. Rome, New Catacombs in the Via Latina:
Cubiculum O (Detail) (Ferrua, *Katakomben*, fig. 141)

Fig. 17. Florenz, Medicaean-Laurentian
Library, Plut. I, 56 (Rabbula Gospels): folio 4b
(Cecchelli, Furlani, and Salmi, *Rabbula Gospels*)

Fig. 18. Rome, Catacombs of Calixtus, So-called sacramental chapel
A 3 (A. Baruffa, *Le catacombe di San Callisto: Storia-Archeologia—Fede*
[Vatican City: Libreria Editrice Vaticana, 1992], 80)

Fig. 19. Sarajevo, Zemaljski muzej Bosne i Hercegovine:
inv. no. 29 920 (Schwertheim, *Mithras*, fig. 87)

Fig. 20. Rome, Priscilla Catacombs (Detail) (postcard)

Fig. 21. Rome, Catacombs of Calixtus (S. Carletti,
Kurzer Führer durch die Katakombe des Hl. Kallistus
[Rome: Pontificia Commissione di Archeologia Sacra], fig. 11)

Fig. 22. Dura Europos, Synagoge (Detail) (C.H. Kraeling,
The Synagogue [The Excavations at Dura-Europos: Final
Report 8.1; New Haven: Yale University Press, 1956], pl. 69)

Fig. 23. Dura Europos, Synagogue
(Detail) (Kraeling, *Synagogue*, pl. 70)

Fig. 24. Rome, Catacombs of Marcellinus and
Petrus (Deckers, Seeliger, and Mietke, *Katakombe
"Santi Marcellino e Pietro,"* color pl. 30 b)

Fig. 25. Rome, MPC: inv. no. 31 439 (Photo © Musei Vaticani)

(4Q521). Through the victorious Messiah, the new creation begins with the new and eternal Jerusalem, since he is "freeing prisoners, giving sight to the blind, straightening out the twisted" (2 + 4 ii 8), and "he will heal the badly wounded and will make the dead live, he will proclaim good news to the meek, give lavishly [to the need]y, lead the exiled and enrich the hungry" (2 + 4 ii 12).[38] This is, however, the only place in the Qumran scrolls where resurrection is mentioned, and it remains questionable whether a resurrection of all the Israelites in the framework of the *parousia* is truly meant.[39]

Ancient Jewish art provides an analogous image which can be found on the north wall of the synagogue in Dura Europos. Three panels depict the resurrection of the dead as a symbol of the restoration of the Jewish people at the end of days, as described in Ezek 37:1–14. The prophet is shown three times in the first two sections. In the first (fig. 22) he wears Persian clothing (a brown tunic with sleeves and green trousers), and is being apprehended by God; next he listens to the word of God; and lastly he is shown at the revival of bodies. The second section (fig. 23) illustrates the animation of the dead by Psychai. In early Christian art, this motif is especially found on sarcophagi, such as inv. no. 4 = 31 450 (fig. 12) and 31 440 in the MPC. Usually this motif is reflected in the way in which a wonderworker touches with his staff the nude recumbent body or limbs.

The New Testament reports in Luke 4:16–30 that Jesus, when handed the book of the Prophet Isaiah, reads from Isa 61:1, "The Spirit of the Lord is upon me, because he has anointed me to bring good news to the poor. He has sent me to proclaim release to the captives and recovery of the sight to the blind, etc." Matthew 11:4–5 and Luke 7:22 report similar deeds of Christ the Messiah.

In early Christian iconography the resurrection of the individual is initially expressed through images of rescue or liberation, such as the spewing out of Jonah or Daniel in the lion's den. For this reason the biblical figures are frequently pictured together with the portrait of the

---

and Eternal Life in Intertestamental Judaism and Early Christianity (HTS 56; Cambridge: Harvard Divinity School, 2006).

[38] Translation according to F. García Martínez and E.J.C. Tigchelaar, *The Dead Sea Scrolls Study Edition* (2 vols.; Leiden: Brill, 1997–1998), 2:1045.

[39] For the discussion about resurrection in the Qumran Dead Sea Scrolls cf. e.g. É. Puech, *La croyance des Esséniens en la vie future: Immortalité, résurrection, vie éternelle? Histoire d'une croyance dans le judaïsme ancien* (2 vols.; EBib NS 21–22; Paris: Gabalda, 1993) and Knohl, "Three Days"; idem, *Messiahs and Resurrection in The Gabriel Revelation* (Kogod Library of Judaic Studies 6; London: Continuum, 2009).

deceased, as in the example of Susanna as an older woman between two youths in the Catacombs of Marcellinus and Petrus (fig. 24), and Noah as a woman on the sarcophagus of Julia Julianete in the MPC 174B.[40] Further convincing evidence for the belief in the bodily resurrection is offered by a sarcophagus panel (no. 115; fig. 25), in which the raising of Lazarus not only depicts Lazarus with the features of an old woman, but a small, young, nude person stands—as in the Creation scenes[41]—next to his sister at the feet of Jesus.

---

[40] In G. Koch, *Frühchristliche Sarkophage* (München: Beck, 2000), fig. 21.

[41] Cf. H. Kaiser-Minn, *Die Erschaffung des Menschen auf den spätantiken Monumenten des 3. und 4. Jahrhunderts* (JAC Ergängzungsband 6; Münster: Aschendorff, 1981), esp. pls. 10a and 24a.

HERMENEUTICS AND METHODS OF INTERPRETATION IN THE ISAIAH PESHARIM AND IN THE *COMMENTARY ON ISAIAH* BY THEODORET OF CYRUS

AGNETHE SIQUANS
University of Vienna

Interpretation of the Bible, especially of prophetic texts, is important for Jewish and Christian communities who are eschatologically orientated. The same was true for the Qumran community as well as for the early Christians. Interpretations of the book of Isaiah were particularly prominent among early Christians. Generally it was understood in a messianic way as a prophecy of Jesus Christ. This type of interpretation can be found in the *Commentary on Isaiah* by Theodoret of Cyrus. Unfortunately, christological interpretations by the Church fathers often led to anti-Jewish statements. Such interpretations can also be found in Theodoret's commentaries. The impact of Theodoret's anti-Semitism is a serious issue that I have addressed already in a previous article.[1] Here my primary concern is with his hermeneutics in comparison with the pesharim. Theodoret was a monk and bishop of the town of Cyrus in Syria. At the height of the patristic era, in the first half of the fifth century C.E., he interpreted many biblical books. So, his *Commentary on Isaiah* was written several centuries after the Qumran pesharim.[2] Nevertheless, both kinds of texts share common features.

In what follows I first describe the two texts. Secondly, I consider the content of each and ask: How are Isaiah's words interpreted? Thirdly, I analyze the methods and hermeneutics of interpretation and draw some conclusions.

---

[1] For Theodoret's attitude towards Jews, see A. Siquans, "Antijüdisch? Theodorets 'Quaestiones in Deuteronomium' und seine perspektivische Bibellektüre," *BZ* 52 (2008): 19–39.

[2] J.H. Charlesworth, *The Pesharim and Qumran History: Chaos or Consensus*? (Grand Rapids: Eerdmans, 2002), 118 dates the composition of the pesharim to the years between 100 and 40 B.C.E.

1. The Isaiah Pesharim of Qumran
and Theodoret's *Commentary on Isaiah*

Concerning the pesharim, I concentrate on the so-called continuous pesharim on Isaiah. Brooke lists five pesharim on Isaiah from Cave 4 and one pesher from Cave 3.[3] The state of preservation of these texts is different. 3QpIsa (3Q4) is very poorly preserved. It contains a quotation of Isa 1:1. The scantily preserved text shows an eschatological orientation. 4QpIsa³ (4Q161) is a pesher on Isa 10:22–11:5. Portions of the biblical text are preserved with commentary. The citations of Isaiah are extensive and without omissions whereas the commentary is scarce. 1QpIsa^b (1Q162) contains citations from Isa 5 and their pesher. 4Qpap pIsa^c (4Q163) is a document consisting of 57 fragments in a poorly preserved state. Quotations from Isa 8:7–31:1 can be identified. Obviously, this papyrus manuscript was not a commentary on the whole of Isaiah but interpreted selected passages. Besides, there are citations from Jeremiah, Zechariah, and Hosea. 4QpIsa^d (4Q164), consisting of three fragments, contains short citations from Isa 54:11–12 with interpretations. In 4QpIsa^e (4Q165) parts of Isa 11:11–12; 14:19; 15:4–5; 21:10–15; 32:5–7; and 40:11–12 and very little commentary can be found. This pesher is interesting because of its terminology. The extant fragments of the pesharim show that the biblical text of Isaiah is quoted first. Then, either with or without an introduction formula, the pesher is given. Usually the interpretation is considerably shorter than the quotation of the biblical text. This fact emphasizes the importance of the latter. To understand the pesharim and their interpretations of Isaiah, it is necessary to take other Qumran writings into consideration, especially other pesharim, which can help to identify the historical background or the religious ideas of the commentators and their communities.

Interestingly, like the Qumran pesharim, the *Isaiah Commentary* of Theodoret of Cyrus, written between 435 and 447 C.E., was for centuries believed to be lost. Though its existence was known of through Theodoret himself, August Möhle only identified this *Commentary* in an old manuscript in Constantinople in 1929, and edited it. Theodoret's *Commentary*,

---

[3] G.J. Brooke, "Isaiah in the Pesharim and Other Qumran Texts," in *Writing and Reading the Scroll of Isaiah: Studies of an Interpretive Tradition* (ed. C.C. Broyles and C.A. Evans; VTSup 70.2; Leiden: Brill, 1997), 609–632. See also M.J. Bernstein, "Pesher Isaiah," *Encyclopedia of the Dead Sea Scrolls* (ed. L.H. Schiffman and J.C. VanderKam; 2 vols.; Oxford: Oxford University Press, 2000), 2:651–653.

which comprises the whole book of Isaiah, is almost entirely preserved. Theodoret writes in Greek and uses the Septuagint as his Bible. Like the Qumran pesharim, he first cites the biblical text. The following interpretation remains close to the quoted text and is generally longer than the lemma. Thus, the proportion of lemma and interpretation is different from the pesharim. Theodoret is well known to us through his various writings.[4] Therefore, the understanding of his *Isaiah Commentary* is supported by a lot of additional information. Furthermore, we can place Theodoret and his Isaiah interpretation within the Christian exegetical tradition. So, the conditions for understanding the Isaiah pesharim and Theodoret's *Isaiah Commentary* differ considerably. There is much more information about the *Commentary* of Theodoret and its context of production than there is about the Qumran pesharim.

2. The Isaiah Interpretation
of the Pesharim and of Theodoret

We now take a closer look at the contents of the commentaries. How are the Isaiah texts interpreted? Because the pesharim are only partially preserved, these fragments have to be taken as the starting point for the examination. Then the corresponding interpretations from Theodoret's complete *Commentary* can be put alongside. The better preserved passages of the pesharim are chosen for the following comparison, which can be solely exemplary.

4QpIsa[a] (4Q161) quotes and comments on Isa 10:22–11:5, though only parts of the text are preserved.[5] Isaiah 10 announces the destruction of Israel's enemy Assyria. The text originated around the events in 701 B.C.E. when Sennacherib besieged Jerusalem and its king Hezekiah. The pesharim display a double reading of the Isaiah text.[6] The historical meaning is not the only one. As *Pesher Habakkuk* points out, the author assumes that God did not reveal to the prophet the meaning of his word about the last days. Only the Teacher of Righteousness knows the

---

[4] For Theodoret's exegesis, see J.-N. Guinot, *L'Exégèse de Théodoret de Cyr* (ThH 100; Paris: Beauchesne, 1995).

[5] For 4QpIsa[a] (4Q161), see J.M. Allegro in *DJD* V (1968): 11–15; for notes, see M.P. Horgan, *Pesharim: Qumran Interpretations of Biblical Books* (CBQMS 8; Washington: Catholic Biblical Association of America, 1979), 70–86.

[6] Thanks to Hanan Eshel ז״ל for this helpful hint.

definitive meaning of the prophet's words.[7] So, they interpret the
prophet's words in terms of the community's current situation and the
imminent "end of days." The conflicts Isaiah speaks about are seen as conflicts of the interpreter's own time. The Assyrians are called "the Kittim,"
who are usually identified as the Romans.[8] In 4QpIsaᵃ (4Q161) 5–6 10–
13 the Isaiah text is applied to the campaign of Ptomely Lathyrus against
Jerusalem in 103–102 B.C.E.[9] Thus, the interpreter refers to an event in
the recent past. Subsequently, the interpretation focuses on the last days
and on the Messiah. The topics of battle and destruction of the enemies
(i.e. the enemies of the Messiah and of the community itself) are at the
centre of attention.

Theodoret also displays a multiple interpretation. He often reads the
text historically and interprets the events of Isaiah's lifetime as such.
Nevertheless, he points to a metaphorical level of understanding, though
in different way than the pesharim do. His primary concerns are not
the military and political aspects of the text. He does not figuratively
transfer the Assyrians to any group of his own time. He rather prefers
a spiritual and individual interpretation and concentrates on piety. This
for Theodoret implies criticism of the Israelites as well as of the Jews of
later times, because meeting his standard of piety means the acceptance
of Jesus Christ as the Messiah.[10]

Isaiah 11:1–5 predicts a "shoot out of the stump of Jesse" whom
Theodoret, as well as the Qumran pesher, interpret in a messianic way.
For the pesher this shoot is the soon to come Messiah. For Theodoret it
is Jesus Christ. Whereas the pesher speaks of an event in the near future,
Theodoret speaks of a fulfilled prophecy. Both mention the eschatological
judgment. While the pesher anticipates the coming Messiah as the judge,
Theodoret speaks of a second manifestation of Jesus Christ at the end of
days, when he will judge all humans.

4QpIsaᵇ (4Q162) consists of one quite large fragment containing some
verses of Isa 5.[11] The middle column, which is best preserved, contains a
commentary on Isa 5:10, a quotation of Isa 5:11–14 and its short inter-

---

[7] See 1QpHab VII:1–8 in Horgan, *Pesharim*, 16. For a short description, see S.L. Berrin, "Pesharim," *Encyclopedia of the Dead Sea Scrolls* 2:644–647.

[8] See e.g. T.H. Lim, "Kittim," *Encyclopedia of the Dead Sea Scrolls* 1:469–471.

[9] See H. Eshel and E. Eshel, "4Q448, Psalm 154 (Syriac), Sirach 48:20, and 4QpIsaᵃ,"
JBL 119 (2000): 645–659.

[10] See above, n. 1.

[11] For 4QpIsaᵇ (4Q162), see J.M. Allegro in *DJD* V (1968): 15–17; for notes, see
Horgan, *Pesharim*, 86–93.

pretation, as well as a quotation of Isa 5:24c–25, and again a rather short piece of interpretation. Isaiah 5:10 says: "For ten acres of vineyard shall yield but one bath, and a homer of seed shall yield but an ephah." (NRSV) Theodoret quotes vv. 9–10 and comments: "To the menace of desolation he added that of infertility: For different are the lessons (by God), because different are the human faults."[12] One of Theodoret's favourite topics interpreting the Scriptures is God's παιδεία, his solicitous education of the humans. As a result, Theodoret interprets the different menaces in Isa 5 as God's lessons to his people. The pesher in 4QpIsa[b](4Q162) reads the menaces in another way: "[1] Interpretation of the phrase concerns the end of days, at the doom of the earth before the sword and famine; and it shall be [2] in the time of the earth's visitation" (II:1–2). The pesher refers to the end of days, that means to the future. Theodoret speaks about the past, about Israel in Isaiah's times, and implicitly about the present time of his readers. In the eyes of the pesher's author, Isaiah prophesied the desolation of the earth at the end of days.

After these short comments in both texts, the lemma continues. Theodoret cites vv. 11–12 and then adds a commentary. The pesher quotes vv. 11–14 and briefly comments on the text: "These are the Men of Scoffing who are in Jerusalem. Those are they who [quotation of Isa 5:24c–25]. That is the congregation of the Men of Scoffing who are in Jerusalem" (II:6–10). Verses 15–24b are omitted. The Qumram pesher just identifies the ones Isaiah speaks of in 5:11–14 with the "men of scoffing who are in Jerusalem." Horgan, representing the majority opinion, identifies the scoffers referring to the "scoffer" in CD 1:14, who is the enemy of the Teacher of Righteousness. The scoffers are therefore the "allies and followers of the Wicked Priest."[13] The pesher continues quoting vv. 24c–25 as an explanation of the attitude of "the Men of Scoffing." The interpretation is short and only inserts the most necessary identifications. Isaiah himself has already indicated what is to be said about these people. The passage ends with another annotation about the "congregation of the Men of Scoffing who are in Jerusalem." Theodoret's verse by verse commentary on vv. 11–14 refers to the Jews in Isaiah's times. They are accused by the prophet and threatened by desolation. Theodoret quotes the New Testament concerning the accusation of drunkenness and voracity in vv. 11–12: "No one can serve two masters" (Matt 6:24). Then he

---

[12] J.-N. Guinot, ed., *Théodoret de Cyr: Commentaire sur Isaïe* (3 vols.; SC 276/295/315; Paris: Cerf, 1980–1984), 1:236–238, English translation A.S.

[13] Horgan, *Pesharim*, 92.

interprets the meaning of some metaphorical expressions allegorically. For example, he identifies the "hills" (v. 25) with the demons who are worshipped on the hills. God's people will be "like refuse in the streets" (NRSV). To support this prophecy Theodoret quotes Ps 83:11. In the historical details concerning the famine and the captivity he also refers to the writings of Josephus.[14] Theodoret's interpretation is an exhortation of his readers as well as a criticism of the biblical Israel.

What do the two commentaries have in common? They both identify a certain group of people as the ones accused by Isaiah and distance themselves from these groups. Whereas for Theodoret the prophecies have already been fulfilled, for the Qumran pesher the events are just taking place in the present time, and the end is awaited in the near future. Theodoret speaks of the Jews of Isaiah's time, perhaps also about the Jews of Jesus' and of his own time. The Qumran pesher speaks of the "scoffers" as contemporaneous to the author. Whereas Theodoret often speaks to his addressees in an exhorting manner, the pesher seeks to comfort its readers by describing the imminent end of their enemies. Theodoret's *Commentary* often changes between an historical and a spiritual or moral level. 4QpIsa^b (4Q162) is clearly eschatologically oriented. Its interpretations are short and concentrate on a few distinct arguments. Theodoret is more elaborate. He does not speak out of a threatening situation. This is due to the Christian belief that Jesus Christ is the Messiah and salvation has already been accomplished. Furthermore, the Christians are no longer persecuted and thus live in a settled situation within the Roman Empire.

Due to the poor state of preservation of 4Qpap pIsa^c (4Q163), a comparison with Theodoret's *Commentary* is rather difficult.[15] Nevertheless, there is one passage in 4Qpap pIsa^c (4Q163) where a few lines of commentary can be found. It comments on Isa 30:15–18. After the quotation of the biblical text the pesher says: "[10] The interpretation of the passage: at the Last Days, concerning the congregation of the S[eekers-after-]Smooth-Things [11] who are in Jerusalem [...] [12] by the Law and not [...] [13] a heart for to seek [...]" (23 ii 10–13). The following line contains a citation of Hos 6:9.[16] The "Seekers-after-Smooth-Things" are usually

---

   14 Guinot, *Commentaire*, 1:238–248.
   15 For 4Qpap pIsa^c (4Q163), see J.M. Allegro in *DJD* V (1968): 17–27; for the English translation quoted in the following, see J.M. Allegro et al. in *Exegetical Texts* (ed. D.W. Parry and E. Tov; The Dead Sea Scrolls Reader 2; Leiden: Brill, 2004), 31–47; for notes, see Horgan, *Pesharim*, 96–106.
   16 Notably, this pesher also cites or alludes to other prophets, namely Jeremiah and

identified as the Pharisees.[17] It can be assumed that they are meant to be the ones who flee from their enemies. Theodoret, on the other hand, exhorts his readers to repent. He addresses them directly with "you." They shall turn around and abandon their way of iniquity to obtain salvation. He explains single words as metaphors for historical realities, for example "Lebanon" or "Carmel" as symbols for the nations and Israel.[18] Theodoret's interpretation of the "mountain" and the "hill" is especially interesting: "A lot of trees on the mountain are not thus remarkable. Though, if somewhere on the top of a mountain one single pine or cypress is left, it is remarked by those who go by. Thus, he [the prophet] says, you will be left, you, too, a little number out of many thousands, and your mischief will be remarked."[19] Theodoret uses a parable to clarify the meaning of Isaiah's metaphorical language. His point in the comment on the respective verses is God's mercy upon those who repent. The pesher's point seems to be the judgment at the end of days. The pesher's expression "a heart for to seek" could likewise indicate repentance and a return to God.[20]

Isaiah speaks of repentance, of pursuers and flight, and of God's mercy. The pesher applies these words to the Pharisees and to the author's own community. Theodoret refers the words to the people of Isaiah's time and to his Christian addressees. He does not explicitly identify particular enemies. He concentrates on the people of God, in the old and in his own time.

4QpIsa[d] (4Q164) comprises three fragments preserving parts of Isa 54:11–12 and its commentary.[21] Isaiah describes the rebuilding of Jerusalem after the Exile. God himself will build the foundations of the city out of precious stones. The pesher understands this prediction as referring to the community: "[... Its interpretation is [2] th]at they have

---

Zechariah. Also 4QpIsa[b] (4Q162) contains a quotation of another prophet, Jer 32:24. See Brooke, *Isaiah*, 625–627.

[17] See Horgan, *Pesharim*, 160 and 173. In the pesharim this expression only occurs in 4Qpap pIsa[c] (4Q163) and 4QpNah (4Q169). For a short overview see A.I. Baumgarten, "Seekers After Smooth Things," *Encyclopedia of the Dead Sea Scrolls* 2:857–859.

[18] Similarly, 1QpHab XII:3–4 interprets "Lebanon" as the "council of the community" (see Horgan, *Pesharim*, 20). Whereas Theodoret speaks of the past, the pesher refers to the present.

[19] Guinot, *Commentaire*, 2:276, English translation A.S.

[20] For the expression "to seek God with the heart" compare e.g. Deut 4:29; 1 Chr 22:19; 2 Chr 15:12; 22:9; Pss 27:8; 119:2.

[21] For 4QpIsa[d] (4Q164), see J.M. Allegro in *DJD* V (1968): 27–28; for notes, see Horgan, *Pesharim*, 125–131.

founded the Council of the Community, [the] priests and the peo[ple ...]³ a congregation of his elect, like a stone of lapis lazuli among the stones [...]" (1 1–3). Verse 12, which is then quoted, is also applied to the Qumran community: "Its interpretation concerns the twelve [...] ⁵ giving light in accordance with the Urim und Thummim [...] ⁶ that are lacking from them, like the sun in all its light. And ['...'] ⁷ Its interpretation concerns the heads of the tribes of Israel at the [end of days ...] ⁸ his lot, the offices of [...]" (1 4–8). The pesher mentions several groups that are important in the community of Qumran: the council, the priests, the people, the twelve, the heads of the tribes. The congregation is called "elect." These chosen ones are compared to the precious stones that are mentioned in Isaiah. The expression "end of days" is reconstructed and it is the only term that signifies an eschatological orientation. Nevertheless, Horgan states that the pesher speaks of the building of the New Jerusalem at the end of days.²² Theodoret applies the whole passage to the Church. The precious stones signify the different virtues of the saints. The believers are the ones who are precious and chosen. The foundations, the pinnacles, and the gates are the leaders of the Church. That they are made of crystal indicates that their teaching is enlightening.²³ These two interpretations clearly show similarities in their hermeneutic approaches: Theodoret speaks of the saints, the pious, the Church leaders. The pesher speaks of the council, the priests, the congregation of the elect, the twelve, the heads of the tribes. Both assume the metaphorical character of the prophet's words and interpret the precious stones in terms of election of their respective communities' members.

4QpIsaᵉ (4Q165), containing passages of Isaiah 11, 14, 15, 21, 32, and 40, is too fragmentary to be compared to Theodoret's elaborate remarks.²⁴

3QpIsa (3Q4) is a document that was identified as a commentary on Isaiah by R. de Vaux and M. Baillet, although this is not a verified identification.²⁵ The text contains parts of Isa 1:1–2 and some non-biblical material. A typical introductory formula is missing. The interpretation

---

²² She follows D. Flusser who discusses the term "the twelve" in connection with Rev 21 and "the twelve" in the Gospels. Horgan, *Pesharim*, 125–126.

²³ Guinot, *Commentaire*, 3:170–172.

²⁴ For 4QpIsaᵉ (4Q165), see J.M. Allegro in *DJD* V (1968): 28–30.

²⁵ For 3QpIsa (3Q4), see M. Baillet in *DJD* III (1962): 95–96. Cf. A. Lange, *Handbuch der Textfunde vom Toten Meer*, vol. 1: *Die Handschriften biblischer Bücher von Qumran und den anderen Fundorten* (Tübingen: Mohr Siebeck, 2009), 276.

seems to contain remarks on the plain sense of the text. The pesher, as well as Theodoret, seems to focus on the same points concerning the setting of Isaiah's prophecies.

3. METHODS AND HERMENEUTICS

For a description of the methods of pesher interpretation, it is helpful to take a look at the other pesharim. Several scholars summarize the exegetical techniques used in the pesharim. M. Fishbane lists the following methods: citation and atomization, multiple interpretations, paranomasia, symbols, notrikon, and gematria.[26] S. Berrin enumerates paraphrase, allegory, polyvalence, atomization, and allusion to other biblical passages.[27] D. Dimant notes the following techniques: modelling the interpretation on the syntactic and lexical patterns of the citation, using lexical synonyms, punning on words (paranomasia), atomizing, vocalizing or grouping the consonants of words in the citation in a different way, adducing other biblical quotations which share one or more terms with the main citation.[28] Theodoret uses all of these methods except of paranomasia, notrikon, and gematria. We have to keep in mind that he used the Greek text. He was aware of the special character of this text as a translation. He often refers to the translations of Symmachos, Aquila, and Theodotion to clarify the meaning of the text. Therefore, the methods relying on letters, consonants, and vowels are out of question for him.

Generally, the particular methods used by Theodoret in his *Isaiah Commentary* and the Isaiah pesharim from Qumran do not differ so much. Both identify certain persons of the biblical text with persons (or groups) of their own time. Both understand metaphorical terms as applicable to their own situations. Both quote other biblical texts to support their arguments. Now and then Theodoret inserts exhortations into the comment. In the Qumran pesharim such passages cannot be found. Altogether, the pesharim are more homogeneous than Theodoret's

---

[26] This last one can be found as a technique of biblical interpretation, though not in Qumran. M. Fishbane, "The Qumran Pesher and Traits of Ancient Hermeneutics," in *Proceedings of the Sixth World Congress of Jewish Studies: Held at the Hebrew University of Jerusalem 13–19 August 1973 under the Auspices of the Israel Academy of Sciences and Humanities* (ed. A. Shinan; 4 vols.; Jerusalem: World Union of Jewish Studies, 1975–1980), 1:97–114.

[27] Berrin, "Pesharim," 2:644–647.

[28] D. Dimant, "Pesharim, Qumran," *ABD* 5:244–251.

Commentary, which is more complex. Whereas the Qumran pesharim focus on the recent past, the present and especially the near future, Theodoret often explains the historical meaning as if concerning Israel at Isaiah's time. Nevertheless, he frequently switches directly to the situation of his contemporary readers. He knows at least three time levels: the time of Isaiah, the time of Jesus and the Apostles, and his own time.[29]

Taking into account the at least partially identical exegetical techniques, what are the factors that determine the differences in the Qumran and Theodoret interpretations? Both interpreters are convinced that they reveal the true meaning of the prophet's text. The truth of prophecy is an explicit topic of their comments.[30] Of course, the particular understanding of what is truth differs. The pesher claims truth for the Qumran community. Theodoret, on the other hand, applies Isaiah's words to Christ and the Christians. The fulfillment of the prophecies in Jesus and the Church is his basic assumption. Within this frame different interpretations of the textual details are possible. Evidently, the respective communities' beliefs provide the framework which shapes the interpretation.[31] The consciousness of election and the expectation of the end of days determine the understanding of the biblical text, in particular, the eschatological focus of interpretation. As a Christian exegete, Theodoret presupposes the coming of the Messiah, which means the fulfillment of Isaiah's prophecy. In his introduction to the *Commentary* he states that Isaiah is the prophet who predicted most clearly the salvation of the nations and the ruin of the Jews.[32] This fundamental idea underlies his interpretation, although it is not always explicit. Nevertheless, Theodoret is awaiting a second manifestation of Jesus at the end of days. This expectation, however, is not as urgent as in Qumran. The decisive event has already happened. Moreover, the first years of Christian expectation of Christ's imminent return have past. The end of days has become an event of the more remote future.

The Qumran pesher applies the prophecies to the present situation and the expected eschatological salvation of the community and the defeat of the enemies in the near future. Therefore, the Qumran pesher

---

[29] Less specifically these time levels could be referred to as the time of the Old Testament, the time of the New Testament, and the time of the Church.

[30] See 4QpIsa^e (4Q165) 1–2: "ri[ghteous] teaching" (Allegro et al. in *Exegetical Texts*, 47); Theodoret on Isa 29:17: "truth of the prophecy" (Guinot, *Commentaire*, 1:260).

[31] Cf. the contribution of A. Lange and Z. Pleše to the present volume who speak of "transpositional hermeneutics."

[32] Ibid., 1:142–144.

focuses more on the eschatological battle. Theodoret presupposes the eschatological victory of Christ. Therefore, his concern is the present life of the Christians who are not in imminent danger. He exhorts his readers to live according to their redeemed status. The interpretative transfer to a spiritual level and also the individualized view of faith are typical of patristic exegesis. In contrast, the Qumran pesher concentrates on the collective aspects of the eschatological events.

To conclude, the pesharim and Theodoret both assume that the decisive meaning of the prophet's words is the meaning they have for their contemporary readers. This is based on the common assumption that the prophets are inspired by God and that their words predict the future.[33] The actual understanding of this future is indeed different. Therefore, it is necessary to interpret the prophet's words according to the changing situations of those who read the Bible again and again. That is what the pesharim, as well as Theodoret, actually did being participants—as Fishbane put it—in an "honorable, ancient, and well-shared tradition of hermeneia."[34]

---

[33] F.F. Bruce and E. Main, "Pesher," *EncJud* (2nd ed.) 16:9–11, 9 list three principles of Qumran interpretation: "1. God revealed His purpose to the prophets, but did not reveal to them the time when His purpose would be fulfilled; this further revelation was first communicated to the Teacher of Righteousness. 2. All the words of the prophets had reference to the time of the end. 3. The time of the end is at hand."

[34] Fishbane, "Qumran Pesher," 114.

THE DEAD SEA SCROLLS AND
THE ANCIENT MEDITERRANEAN AND
ANCIENT NEAR EASTERN WORLDS

OF HEROES AND SAGES: CONSIDERATIONS
ON THE EARLY MESOPOTAMIAN BACKGROUND
OF SOME ENOCHIC TRADITIONS[*]

Gebhard J. Selz
University of Vienna

"[He who saw the deep, the] foundation of the country,
who knew [the secrets], was wise in everything!
...
he saw the secret and uncovered the hidden,
he brought back a message from the antediluvian age."

From the introduction to the Gilgamesh Epic[1]

The general framework of the "Mesopotamian Background of the Enoch Figure" is quite well established. Since the initial comparison of Berossos' account of Mesopotamian antediluvian kings and heroes to the biblical patriarchs a vast literature has evolved that discusses the possible transfer and adaptation of such Mesopotamian topics as ascent to heaven, the flood story, primeval wisdom, dream-vision, divination and astronomy. I argue in this paper that the respective traditions reach back to a third millennium "origin."

0. Enoch, described in Gen 5:22–25 as great-grandson of Adam, father of Methuselah and great-grand-father of Noah, lived 365 years and "he walked with God: and he was not, for God took him."[2] Enoch became a central figure in early Jewish mystical speculations;[3] *1 Enoch*, or the *Ethiopic Enoch*, is one of the earliest non-biblical texts from the Second

---

[*] I wish to thank Armin Lange for his unfailing help and Bennie H. Reynolds III and Matthias Weigold for their valuable comments.

[1] See A.R. George, *The Babylonian Gilgamesh Epic: Introduction, Critical Edition and Cuneiform Texts* (2 vols.; Oxford: Oxford University Press, 2003), 1:539.

[2] All biblical translations follow the KJV.

[3] See H.S. Kvanvig, *Roots of Apocalyptic: The Mesopotamian Background of the Enoch Figure and the Son of Man* (WMANT 61, Neukirchen-Vluyn: Neukirchner, 1988), 35: "Astronomy, cosmology, mythical geography, divination ... are subjects which in a Jewish setting appear for the first time in the Enochic sources, at least in a so extensive form."

Temple period[4] and, at least in part, was originally written in Aramaic as demonstrated by the fragments found among the Dead Sea Scrolls.[5] They prove that the *Astronomical Enoch* and the *Book of the Watchers* are among the earliest texts collected in *1 Enoch*. *2 Enoch* belongs to the Old Slavonic biblical tradition—a tradition[6] that is still very much alive in the popular religion of the Balkans. Indeed, as F. Badalanova Geller was able to demonstrate, there is an oral tradition still alive in contemporary Bulgaria, incorporating various pieces from the Jewish and apocryphal traditions, which has also considerable impact on orthodox iconography.[7] She further calls the underlying (oral) stories "the Epic of Enoch," arguing methodologically along the lines of V. Propp's *Morphology of the Folk Tale*.[8] This epic was certainly also related to the tradition of the kabbalistic-rabbinic *3 Enoch* which, like other hermetic literature, describes Enoch as *Metatron*, featuring him as the "Great Scribe" (*safra rabba*: *Tg. Yer.*).[9] It cannot be the purpose of this paper to take the entire Enochic tradition into consideration; the references to Enoch are mani-

---

[4] J.C. VanderKam, *An Introduction to Early Judaism* (Grand Rapids: Eerdmans, 2001), 88–94; see also J.J. Collins, *The Apocalyptic Imagination: An Introduction to Jewish Apocalyptic Literature* (New York: Crossroad, 1992), esp. the chapter on "The Early Enoch Literature," 43–84.

[5] On *1 Enoch* see J.T. Milik, *The Books of Enoch: Aramaic Fragments of Qumrân Cave 4* (Oxford: Clarendon, 1976) and cf. the review by J.C. Greenfield and M.E. Stone, "The Books of Enoch and the Traditions of Enoch," *Numen* 26 (1979): 89–103. A modern translation of the text is now published by G.W.E. Nickelsburg and J.C. VanderKam, *1 Enoch: A New Translation* (Minneapolis: Fortress, 2004). For the religious-historical framework of the book see J.C. VanderKam and P. Flint, *The Meaning of the Dead Sea Scrolls: Their Significance for Understanding the Bible, Judaism, Jesus, and Christianity* (San Francisco: HarperSanFrancisco, 2002); cf. also VanderKam, *Introduction*. A thorough study of the Enochic literature should, of course, also take into consideration the many references to Enoch in the so-called apocryphal literature. There are presently two recommendable translations: *OTP* and *AOT*.

[6] At the time when I finished this article I was not yet able to check *The Old Testament Apocrypha in the Slavonic Tradition: Continuity and Diversity* (ed. L. DiTommaso and C. Böttrich with the assistance of M. Swoboda; TSAJ 140; Tübingen: Mohr Siebeck, forthcoming 2011).

[7] F. Badalanova Geller, "Cultural Transfer and Text Transmission: The Case of the Enoch Apocryphic Tradition" (lecture delivered at the Conference "Multilingualism in Central Asia, Near and Middle East from Antiquity to Early Modern Times" at the Center for Studies in Asian Cultures and Social Anthropology at the Austrian Academy of Sciences, Vienna, 2 March 2010). I wish to express my gratitude to Dr. Badalanova Geller for fruitful discussions and additional references.

[8] V. Propp, *Morphology of the Folk Tale* (trans. L. Scott; 2nd ed.; Austin: University of Texas Press, 1968).

[9] *Tg. Yer.* to Gen 5:24; see also *b. Ḥag.* 15a; see further A.A. Orlov, *The Enoch-Metatron Tradition* (TSAJ 107; Tübingen: Mohr Siebeck, 2005), 50–59, esp. 51.

fold in the so-called apocryphal tradition.[10] We only mention here that "the instructor" Enoch, Idris in Arabic, is attested in the Qur'an (19:56–57; 21:85–86) as a prophet, and that in Muslim lore, like in Judaism, he is also connected with the invention of astronomy. We may further mention persisting traditions in Classical Antiquity, especially Claudius Aelianus, who mentions the miraculous birth of Gilgamesh.[11]

0.1. Dating back to the late nineteenth century and the so-called Babel-Bible dispute,[12] the relation of the biblical traditions, especially those concerning the paradise narrative, the flood-story, and the (antediluvian) patriarchs, to the Mesopotamian world received much interest (see below 2.1.2). From a modern scholarly point of view, much of what has been written in this period is obsolete and related to anti-biblical or apologetic motivations. Therefore, we encounter often a general warning against a naïve comparative attitude which is certainly in place.[13] If in the following paragraphs we refer to various Mesopotamian materials, we are fully aware of this warning. We do not intend to establish literal

---

[10] Concerning the book of *Jubilees*, Kvanvig, *Roots*, 146, writes e.g.: "Jubilees deals with a tradition about the origin of Babylonian science. This science was revealed to men in primordial time. The revelators were angels who descended from heaven and acted as sages among men. Enoch as the first sage is found in Pseudo-Eupolemus."

[11] Claudius Aelianus, *De Natura Animalium* 12.21: "At any rate an Eagle fostered a baby. And I want to tell the whole story, so that I may have evidence of my proposition. When Seuechoros was king of Babylon the Chaldeans foretold that the son born of his daughter would wrest the kingdom from his grandfather. This made him afraid and (if I may be allowed the small jest) he played Acrisius to his daughter: he put the strictest of watches upon her. For all that, since fate was cleverer than the king of Babylon, the girl became a mother, being pregnant by some obscure man. So the guards from fear the king hurled the infant from the citadel, for that was where the aforesaid girl was imprisoned. Now an Eagle which saw with its piercing eye the child while still falling, before it was dashed on the earth, flew beneath it, flung its back under it, and conveyed it to some garden and set it down with the utmost care. But when the keeper of the place saw the pretty baby he fell in love with it and nursed it; and it was called Gilgamos and became king of Babylon." (Claudius Aelianuns, *On the Characteristics of Animals* [trans. A.F. Schofield; 3 vols.; Cambridge: Harvard University Press, 1958–1959], 3:39–41). We may further note that in the subsequent text Aelianus explicitly refers to Achaemenes, the legendary founder of the first Persian dynasty, who is also said "to be raised by an eagle."

[12] For an overview over this politically remarkable dispute and the involvement of the German emperor Wilhelm II see R.G. Lehmann, *Friedrich Delitzsch und der Babel-Bibel-Streit* (OBO 133; Fribourg: Universitätsverlag, 1989). Delitzsch's hypotheses were sharply criticised by Christian and Jewish theologians of the time and soon became a political issue. Finally the emperor was even requested to make a public profession of his faith.

[13] Cf. R. Liwak, "Bibel und Babel: Wider die theologische und religionsgeschichtliche Naivität," *BTZ* 2 (1989): 206–233. An extensive bibliography of "Articles by Jewish Writers on the Babel-Bibel Controversy" is published in Y. Shavit and M. Eran, eds., *The Hebrew*

dependencies, but would rather draw attention to some parallels with selected Mesopotamian motifs. We will neither address the question of a common Near Eastern origin of such motifs, nor will we attempt to reconstruct the ways of transmission in the necessary detail. The latter were certainly manifold, and that orality played a major role is very likely but, of course, hard to prove.

0.2. The most important contributions concerning the relationship be-tween Berossos,[14] the Sumerian King list, and the biblical patriarchs as well as the connected literary motifs are presently those of R. Borger,[15] J.C. VanderKam,[16] H. Kvanvig[17] and A.A. Orlov.[18] I shall return to them later. The discovery of the Qumran manuscripts put *1 Enoch* in the cen-tre of these discussions and their connections to the related Jewish-Hellenistic texts and to Mesopotamian forerunners have been widely dis-cussed.[19] The Qumran manuscripts of the *Book of Giants* mention the hero Gilgamesh among the Giants who were offspring of the evil (fallen) angels who had intercourse with human females.[20] Starting from this fact,

---

Bible Reborn: From Holy Scripture to the Book of Books: A History of Biblical Culture and the Battles over the Bible in Modern Judaism (trans. C. Naor; SJ 38; Berlin: de Gruyter, 2007), 531–566.

[14] Cf. G.P. Verbrugghe and J.M. Wickersham, *Berossos and Manetho, Introduced and Translated: Native Traditions in Ancient Mesopotamia and Egypt* (Ann Arbor: University of Michigan Press, 1996).

[15] R. Borger, "Die Beschwörungsserie *Bīt Mēseri* und die Himmelfahrt Henochs," *JNES* 33 (1974): 183–196; for an abbreviated English version see idem, "The Incantation Series *Bīt Mēseri* and Enoch's Ascension to Heaven," in *I Studied Inscriptions from Before the Flood: Ancient Near Eastern, Literary, and Linguistic Approaches to Genesis 1–11* (ed. R.S. Hess and D.T. Tsumura; Sources for Biblical and Theological Study 4, Winona Lake: Eisenbrauns, 1994), 224–233.

[16] J.C. VanderKam, *Enoch and the Growth of an Apocalyptic Tradition* (CBQMS 16; Washington: Catholic Biblical Association of America, 1984).

[17] See Kvanvig, *Roots.*

[18] See Orlov, *Enoch-Metatron.*

[19] For *1 Enoch*, cf. the literature listed in n. 5.

[20] The following excerpts of the reconstructed *Book of Giants* are taken from the edition of The Gnostic Society Library (online: http://www.gnosis.org/library/dss/dss_book_of_giants.htm [14 March 2010]) (MSS: 4Q203, 1Q23, 2Q26, 4Q530–532, 6Q8).

The wicked angels, bringing both knowledge and havoc.

2 [...] they knew the secrets of [...] 3 [... si]n was great in the earth [...] 4 [...] and they killed many [...] 5 [... they begat] giants [...] (1Q23 9+14+15)

The outcome of the demonic corruption was violence, perversion, and a brood of mon-strous beings.

I attempt to show that not only did the generally late Mesopotamian traditions about the primeval sages and related matters form a background for the mythical imagery of the Enochic system of thought, but that the much earlier epic traditions about the kings Gilgamesh and Etana should also be considered. We might not be able to avoid some of the traps of this sort of intertextual studies, however, we are by all means entitled to

1 [...] they defiled [...] 2 [... they begot] giants and monsters [...] 3 [...] they begot, and, behold, all [the earth was corrupted ...] 4 [...] with its blood and by the hand of [...] 5 [giant's] which did not suffice for them and [...] 6 [...] and they were seeking to devour many [...] 7 [...] 8 [...] the monsters attacked it. (4Q531 2)

The giants became troubled by a series of dreams and visions. Mahway sees a tablet being immersed in water. When it emerges, all but three names have been washed away. The dream evidently symbolizes the destruction of all but Noah and his sons by the Flood. ... The giants realize the futility of fighting against the forces of heaven. The first speaker may be Gilgamesh.

3 [... I am a] giant, and by the mighty strength of my arm and my own great strength 4 [... any]one mortal, and I have made war against them; but I am not [...] able to stand against them, for my opponents 6 [...] reside in [Heav]en, and they dwell in the holy places. And not 7 [... they] are stronger than I. 8 [...] of the wild beast has come, and the wild man they call [me]. 9 [...] Then Ohya said to him, I have been forced to have a dream [...] the sleep of my eyes [vanished], to let me see a vision. Now I know that on [...] 11–12[...] Gilgamesh [...] (4Q531 1)

[From] Ohya's dream vision ...

1 concerns the death of our souls [...] and all his comrades, [and Oh]ya told them what Gilgamesh said to him 2[...] and it was said [...] "concerning [...] the leader has cursed the potentates" 3and the giants were glad at his words. Then he turned and left [...] (4Q530 II)

More [ill-foreboding] dreams afflict the giants. ... Someone suggests that Enoch be found to interpret the vision. [... to Enoch] the noted scribe, and he will interpret for us 12 the dream. Thereupon his fellow Ohya declared and said to the giants, 13 I too had a dream this night, O giants, and, behold, the Ruler of Heaven came down to earth 14 [...] and such is the end of the dream. [Thereupon] all the giants [and monsters] grew afraid 15 and called Mahway. He came to them and the giants pleaded with him and sent him to Enoch 16 [the noted scribe]. They said to him, Go [...] to you that 17 [...] you have heard his voice. And he said to him, He will [... and] interpret the dreams [...] III:3[...] how long the giants have to live. [...] (4Q530 II–III)

After a cosmic journey Mahway comes to Enoch and makes his request.

3 [... he mounted up in the air] 4 1ike strong winds, and flew with his hands like ea[gles ... he left behind] 5 the inhabited world and passed over Desolation, the great desert [...] 6 and Enoch saw him and hailed him, and Mahway said to him [...] 7 hither and thither a second time to Mahway [... The giants await 8 your

look after the pre- and the post-texts, especially if we remember that any reading implies a recreation of new texts. To put it metaphorically, texts are not stable entities but living beings undergoing all sort of philological and interpretative changes.

1. My contribution is an outsider's view, neither pretending to do justice to the ongoing discussions in biblical studies, in particular in the studies of the Dead Sea Scrolls, nor dwelling on the highly complicated matter of the Babylonian background of the astronomical Enoch tradition.[21] O. Neugebauer, one of the pioneers working on Babylonian astronomical texts wrote in 1981: "The search for time and place of origin of this primitive picture of the cosmic order can hardly be expected to lead to definitive results. The use of 30-day schematic months could have been inspired, e.g., by Babylonian arithmetical schemes (of the type of 'Mul-Apin'), or by the Egyptian calendar." He then continues: "But [sc. in *Astronomical Enoch*] there is no visible trace of the sophisticated Babylonian astronomy of the Persian or Seleucid-Parthian period."[22] The opinion "that the astronomical part of the Book of Enoch is based on

---

words, and all the monsters of the earth. If [...] has been carried [...] 9 from the days of [...] their [...] and they will be added [...] 10 [...] we would know from you their meaning [...] 11 [... two hundred tr]ees that from heaven [came down ...] (4Q530 III)

[Then,] Enoch sends back a tablet with its grim message of judgment, but with hope for repentance.

With this text, compare Gen 6:1–2, 4. See further L.T. Stuckenbruck, *The Book of Giants from Qumran: Texts, Translation, and Commentary* (TSAJ 63; Tübingen: Mohr Siebeck, 1997) and K. Beyer, *Die aramäischen Texte vom Toten Meer: samt den Inschriften aus Palästina, dem Testament Levi aus der Kairoer Genisa, der Fastenrolle und den alten talmudischen Zitaten: Aramaistische Einleitung, Text, Übersetzung, Deutung, Grammatik/ Wörterbuch, deutsch-aramäische Wortliste, Register* (2 vols. and Ergänzungsband; Göttingen: Vandenhoeck & Ruprecht, 1984/1994/2004), 1:225–258 (*1 Enoch*), 258–268 (*Book of Giants*), Ergänzungsband: 117–118 (*1 Enoch*), 119–124 (*Book of Giants*), 2:153–155 (*1 Enoch*), 155–162 (*Book of Giants*). We note that Beyer postulates a Jewish Old-Palestinian language for these earliest Enoch fragments (ibid., 1:229). He understands these fragments as an early translation from a Hebrew original. Especially important is É. Puech, *Qumran Grotte 4.XXII: Textes araméns, première partie: 4Q529–549* (DJD XXXI; Oxford: Clarendon, 2001).

[21] Cf. M. Albani, *Astronomie und Schöpfungsglaube: Untersuchungen zum astronomischen Henochbuch* (WMANT 68; Neukirchen-Vluyn: Neukirchener, 1994), 1–29; cf. furthermore the works of Milik, *Books of Enoch*, and O. Neugebauer, *The "Astronomical" Chapters of the Ethiopic Book of Enoch (72 to 82)* (Det Kongelige Danske Videnskabernes Selskab: Matematisk-fysiske Meddelelser 40.10; Copenhagen: Munksgaard, 1981).

[22] Ibid., 4.

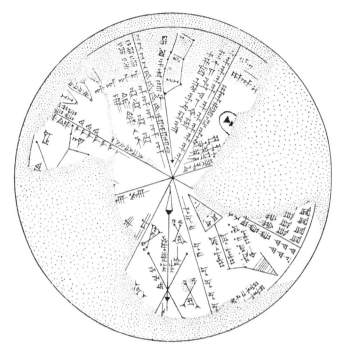

Fig. 1. The Neo-Assyrian star-map K 8538 according to the illustration in H. Hunger, ed., *Astrological Reports to Assyrian Kings* (SAA 8, Helsinki: Helsinki University Press: 1992), 46.

concepts extant in the Old Testament is simply incorrect: the Enoch year is not an old semitic calendaric unit; the schematic alternation between hollow and full months is not a real lunar calendar, and there exists no linear scheme in the Old Testament for the length of daylight, or patterns for 'gates,' for winds, or for 'thousands' of stars, related to the schematic year. The whole Enochian astronomy is clearly an *ad hoc* construction and not the result of a common semitic tradition."[23]

1.1. Neugebauer's opinion sharply contrasts the statement of VanderKam that "Enoch's science is a Judaized refraction of an early stage in the development of Babylonian astronomy—a stage that finds varied expression in texts such as the astrolabes, *Enūma Anu Enlil*, and ᵐᵘˡAPIN. In it astronomical and astrological concepts are intermingled and schematic

---

[23] Ibid.

arrangements at times predominate over facts."[24] Here VanderKam comes back to an early view of H. Zimmern from 1901,[25] who saw the Enochic tradition anchored in stories around the primeval king Enmeduranki, to whom the gods granted mantic and astronomical wisdom.[26]

1.2. The main arguments against Neugebauer's position are provided by the Enochic Aramaic fragments from Cave 4, the careful evaluation of which prompted Milik already in 1976 to suggest that the astronomical parts of the Enoch tradition do belong to the oldest stratum of the Enoch literature in concordance to the 365 (originally) year life span allotted to Enoch in Gen 5:23.[27]

1.3. I cannot discuss here the philological evidence that anchors the biblical tradition in the historical charts. This is a different, albeit very important field which may support my arguments: I just mention one recent example: Jer 39:3 may go back to an eye witness's account of Nebuchadnezzar's conquest of Jerusalem in 589 B.C.E. This is indicated by my colleague Michael Jursa's identification of the chief-eunuch *Nabu-sharrussu-ukin*, the biblical נבו שרסכים רב־סריס or Nebu-Sarsekim, in an economic document from the sun-god temple in Sippar, dated to the "Month XI, day 18, year 10 [of] Nebuchadnezzar, king of Babylon."[28]

1.3.1. The Babylonian exile[29] had a major impact on the development of Judaism, possibly even on the moulding of the apocalyptic traditions.[30]

---

[24] VanderKam, *Enoch and the Growth*, 101.

[25] H. Zimmern, *Beiträge zur Kenntnis der babylonischen Religion: Die Beschwörungstafeln Šurpu, Ritualtafeln für den Wahrsager, Beschwörer und Sänger* (Assyriologische Bibliothek 12; Leipzig: Hinrichs, 1901).

[26] See Albani, *Astronomie*, 27.

[27] Milik, *Books of Enoch*, 8–10.

[28] M. Jursa, "Nabû-šarrūssu-ukīn, rab ša-rēši, und 'Nebusarsekim' (Jer. 39:3)," *NABU* 5 (2008), online: http://www.achemenet.com/document/Nabu2008-05.pdf (1 July 2010). Jursa's translation of the document runs as follows: "[Regarding] 1.5 minas (0.75 kg) of gold, the property of Nabû-šarrūssu-ukīn, the chief eunuch, which he sent via Arad-Bānītu the eunuch to [the temple] Esangila: Arad-Bānītu has delivered [it] to Esangila. In the presence of Bēl-usāti, son of Alpāya, the royal bodyguard, [and of] Nādin, son of Marduk-zēru-ibni. Month XI, day 18, year 10 [of] Nebuchadnezzar, king of Babylon." We may note here that the evaluation of this document provoked a broad discussion in scholarly literature and in the Internet.

[29] Jer 39:3 gives account of Nebuchadnezzar's conquest of Jerusalem and his victory over the Judean King Zedekiah: The passage reports that all of the officers of the king of Babylon made their entry, and occupied the middle gate.

[30] Kvanvig, *Roots*, 612 writes: "The emergence of the apocalyptic traditions and lit-

The background of this "knowledge transfer," however, is the scholarly situation as just described. I say this not to deny the contribution of mere story-telling and fantastic lore to the growth of the corpus of apocalyptic literature, but we cannot neglect the scholarly and even empirical background of the underlying world-view. Indeed, this may provide the best explanation for why so many different topics and stylistic features are fused in the extant Enochic traditions.

1.4. What concerns us here is the heuristic attitude of Mesopotamian scholarship. Even in the late Seleucid period this scholarship remains basically "holistic" or "monistic" in the way that it links alls sorts of empiricism, as may be demonstrated with examples from the famous "Astronomical Diaries."[31] In the fifth year of Darius III (331 B.C.E.) we find a series of astronomical observations:[32]

> Day 13 [20 September]: Sunset to moonrise: 8. There was a lunar eclipse. Its totality was covered at the moment when Jupiter set and Saturn rose. During totality the west wind blew, during clearing the east wind. During the eclipse, deaths and plague occurred. Day 14: All day clouds were in the sky …

The reports then continue with observations from the "Burse of Babylon"; commodity prizes are given together with the positions of the planets in the zodiacal signs.

> That month, the equivalent for 1 shekel of silver was: barley … at that time, Jupiter was in Scorpio; Venus was in Leo, at the end of the month in Virgo; Saturn was in Pisces; Mercury and Mars, which had set, were not visible.

The reports further continue with the famous account of the downfall of the Persian empire in the same year, after the battle at Gaugamela, north of Mossul (331 B.C.E.).

---

erature presupposes both a direct contact with Mesopotamian culture in the Babylonian diaspora, and the syncretistic tendencies in Palestine in the post-exilic centuries." See also S. Robinson, "The Origins of Jewish Apocalyptic Literature: Prophecy, Babylon, and 1 Enoch" (MA diss., University of Florida, 2005; online: http://etd.fcla.edu/SF/SFE0001120/Robinson-Sarah-thesis.pdf [30 October 2010]).

[31] We follow here the unpublished manuscript of G. Graßhoff, "The Diffusion of Knowledge: From Babylonian Regularities to Science in the Antiquity" (paper presented at the 97th Dahlem Workshop on Globalization of Knowledge and its Consequences at the Dahlem Konferenzen, Berlin, 18–23 November 2007).

[32] H. Hunger, ed., *Astronomical Diaries and Related Texts from Babylonia*, vol. 2: *Diaries from 261 B.C. to 165 B.C.* (Denkschriften der philosophisch-historischen Klasse 210; Wien: Verlag der Österreichischen Akademie der Wissenschaften, 1989), 175–176.

On the 11th of that month, panic occurred in the camp before the king. The Macedonians encamped in front of the king. On the 24th [1 October], in the morning, the king of the world [Alexander] erected his standard and attacked. Opposite each other they fought and a heavy defeat of the troops of the king [Darius] he [Alexander] incited. The king [Darius], his troops deserted him and to their cities they went. They fled to the east.

1.4.1. As I have learnt from the Swiss philosopher and historian of science, Gerd Graßhoff, these collections of data were systematically made in order two obtain knowledge about the possible connections of various events, and more specifically in order to get information of how one could interfere and prevent an otherwise probable future event.[33]

1.4.2. The Astronomical Diaries are certainly a latecomer within the cunciform tradition; there is, however no reason to postulate a fundamental change in the methodological attitude of Mesopotamian scholars, at least after the Old Babylonian period. In comparison to our approaches, "there is no methodological difference for Babylonian scholarship compared to causal reasoning to obtain knowledge about causal regularities with causes indicated by signs. This counts for all sorts of domains of knowledge—from medical, over meteorological, economic to astronomical knowledge."[34]

2. Numerous articles and books deal with Enoch and "Enochic literature." From the viewpoint of a cuneiform scholar, Helge Kvanvig's book *Roots of Apocalyptic: The Mesopotamian Background of the Enoch Figure and the Son of Man* must be considered a major contribution.[35] The Babylonian surroundings of the forefathers of apocalyptic literature, Ezekiel and Deutero-Isaiah, led to the hypothesis that other apocalyptic texts may have their roots in the Babylonian exile.[36] Be that as it may, the great impact the Babylonian mantic and astronomical tradition had on the growing Hebrew apocalyptic texts remains beyond dispute.

---

[33] I refer to Graßhoff, "Diffusion"; see also idem, "Babylonian Metrological Observations and the Empirical Basis of Ancient Science," in *The Empirical Dimension of Ancient Near Eastern Studies—Die empirische Dimension altorientalischer Forschungen* (ed. G.J. Selz with the assistance of K. Wagensonner; Wiener Offene Orientalistik 6, Wien: Lit, 2011), 25–40.

[34] Graßhoff, "Diffusion."

[35] Cf. also the literature quoted in n. 5.

[36] VanderKam, *Enoch and the Growth*, 6–15; Robinson, "Origins," 38–51.

2.1. Since the times of Flavius Josephus, the first century Jewish historian who also recorded the Roman destruction of the second temple on 4 August 70 C.E., the relationship of the Jewish prehistory to the similar traditions of the neighbouring cultures became a pivotal point for all sorts of discussions.

2.1.1. While not very widely distributed initially, the *Babyloniaca* of Berossos[37] gained increasing influence on the picture of the earlier Mesopotamian history in antiquity, despite the fact that the primary source for all Hellenistic scholarship remained Ctesias of Cnidos (in Caria) from the fifth century B.C.E. The interest in Berossos' work was mainly provoked by his account of Babylonian astronomy, and, in the Christian era, by his record of the Babylonian flood lore. His report of the ten antediluvian kings was paralleled apologetically to traditions from the Hebrew Bible. In this way Eusebius, bishop of Caesarea (ca. 260–340 C.E.), used the *Babyloniaca* in order to harmonize the biblical and the pagan traditions, whereas Flavius Josephus used it for Jewish apologetics. Therefore, the controversial debate over the reliability of biblical stories about the patriarchs and their relation to the mytho-historical accounts of Mesopotamian prehistory have persisted for two millennia.

2.1.2. After an increasing wealth of Mesopotamian cuneiform tablets was excavated and translated in the middle of the nineteenth century, critical evaluation of the biblical traditions gained great momentum. In 1872 George Smith delivered a paper to the *Society of Biblical Archaeology* in London, announcing the discovery of a Babylonian version of the biblical flood story, hereby renewing the interest in the extra-biblical traditions of Antiquity and eventually supporting the account of Berossos' *Babyloniaca*. A few years later, in 1876, Smith published his book *The Chaldean Account of Genesis*, in which he included translations of excerpts from fragments of *Atraḥasīs*,[38] a text which, together with the so-called "Creation Epic *Enūma Elīsh*," soon became a corner stone for all comparisons between the biblical and Mesopotamian accounts of the "history" of primeval times.[39] To cut a long story short, when S. Langdon published

---

[37] A Hellenistic priest from Babylon, living during Alexander's reign over the capital (330–323 B.C.E.), that is less than 200 years before the alleged earliest Qumran manuscripts!

[38] See W.G. Lambert and A.R. Millard, *Atra-ḥasīs: The Babylonian Story of the Flood* (London: Oxford University Press, 1969), 3.

[39] The comparison of the Mesopotamian flood story with its Noah-related figure of Ziusudra/Utnapishtim and the Babylonian *Epic of Creation* in conjunction with Berossos'

the Weld-Blundell (WB) copy of the *Sumerian King List* in 1923, a thorough revision of earlier opinions became necessary.[40] It became clear, in particular, that the names of (most) of Berossos' early Babylonian rulers were of Sumerian origin. Zimmern himself revised his earlier theories and Pater Anton Deimel even disputed any connection of the cuneiform tradition to the biblical patriarchs.[41]

2.1.3. The biblical patriarchs and the kings before the flood according to Gen 5 and 4, Berossos and the *Sumerian King List*.[42]

[Gen] 5	[Gen] 4	Berossos	WB 62
1 Adam	23 Adam	Ἄλωρος	Alulim
6 Set	25 Set	Ἀάπαρος	Alalgar
9 Enosch	26 Enosch	Ἀμήλων	[...] Kidunnu
12 Qenan	17 Kain	Ἀμμένων	[...] -alimma
15 Mahalalel	18 Mehi(u)jael	Ἀμεγάλαρον	[Dumu]zi, d. Hirt
18 Jered	18 Irad	Δάωνος ποιμήν	[Enm]entuanna
21 Henoch	17 Henoch	Εὐεδωράγχος	[E]sipazianna
25 Methuschelach	18 Methuschael	Ἀμεψινός	Enmeduranna
28 Lamech	18 Lamech	Ὠτιάρτης	Uburtutu
32 Noah	—	Ξισούθρος	Ziusudra

account of Babylonian History fostered many hypotheses and any originality of the biblical stories became disputed. In 1902 H. Zimmern published his influential article "Urkönige und Uroffenbarung," in E. Schrader, *Die Keilinschriften und das Alte Testament* (ed. H. Zimmern and H. Winckler; 3rd ed.; 2 vols.; Berlin: Reuther & Reichard, 1902–1903), 2:530–543, in which he attempted to parallel the names of the biblical primeval patriarchs and similar figures from extra-biblical traditions. Great influence gained F. Delitzsch who with his lectures on "Babel und Bibel" (1902–1905) provoked the so-called "Babel-Bibel Streit"; see F. Delitzsch, *Babel und Bibel* (Leipzig: Hinrichs, 1921). Later he took an even more open hostile stand against the traditional theologians in his work *Die große Täuschung: Kritische Betrachtungen zu den alttestamentlichen Berichten über Israels Eindringen in Kanaan, die Gottesoffenbarung vom Sinai und die Wirksamkeit der Propheten* (2 vols.; Stuttgart: Deutsche Verlagsanstalt, 1920–1921).

[40] A. Deimel, "Die babylonische und biblische Überlieferung bezüglich der vorsintflutlichen Urväter," *Orientalia* (Rome) 17 (1925): 33–47; cf. further H. Zimmern, "Die altbabylonischen vor- (und nach-)sintflutlichen Könige nach neuen Quellen," *ZDMG* 78 (1924): 19–35, 24. W.G. Lambert, "A New Fragment from a List of Antediluvian Kings and Maruk's Chariot," in *Symbolae Biblicae et Mesopotamicae: Francisco Mario Theodoro de Liagre Böhl dedicatae* (ed. M.A. Beek et al.; Studia Francisci Scholten memoriae dicata 4; Leiden: Brill, 1973), 271–280, 271, pointed out that the connection of the patriarchs to the tradition of the *Sumerian King List* was first established by Josephus who again depended on Berossos.

[41] A. Deimel, "Urväter," 43 states: "(Es) dürfte besser ehrlich einzugestehen sein, dass bis jetzt kein Zusammenhang irgendwelcher Art zwischen der babylonischen und der biblischen Überlieferung bezüglich der vorsintflutlichen Urväter erwiesen ist."

[42] C. Westermann, *Genesis*, vol. 1: *Genesis 1–11* (BKAT 1.1; Neukirchen-Vluyn: Neukirchener, 1974), 473.

2.1.4. The most important information we can draw from this table is: 1. Berossos' account of the primeval history of Mesopotamian is clearly based on an emic tradition reaching back almost two millennia. 2. The Mesopotamian tradition dates back to an environment of Sumerian literary tradition; this is corroborated by the newly found Ur III version of the *Sumerian King List*.[43] 3. The position of Noah and Ziusudra/Utnapishtim asserts the interrelation of the biblical and Mesopotamian stories about the Flood.

2.2. As already mentioned, hypotheses on the interrelation of these biblical and Mesopotamian sources have flourished for millennia. In our context the alleged connection of the biblical tradition with the Gilgamesh reception deserves mentioning. Alfred Jeremias, who published the first German translation of the Gilgamesh Epic in 1891, and Peter Jensen supposed that the Gilgamesh material is indeed the blue-print for all related biblical stories, denying them any originality. From the present state of research this seems, at first sight, not even worth mentioning. It is, however, well-known that Gilgamesh's fame, how much mixed and distorted the various Babylonian traditions may have become, exerted influence on many stories of ancient authors all over the Near East. Thus the attestation of Gilgamesh's name in the Dead Sea Scrolls does not come as a surprise. The name is mentioned in the *Book of Giants*, which was later adopted by the followers of Mani. In the *Book of Giants*, Gilgamesh is the name of one of the giants—offspring of the fallen heavenly watchers and human women. Another giant mentioned besides Gilgamesh[44] is Hobabis,[45] who may well be a distortion of the name of Gilgamesh's adversary, Hu(m)baba (Assyrian)/Huwawa (Babylonian), the famous

---

[43] P. Steinkeller, "An Ur III Manuscript of the Sumerian King List," in *Literatur, Politik und Recht in Mesopotamien: FS Claus Wilcke* (ed. W. Sallaberger, K. Volk, and A. Zgoll; Orientalia Biblica et Christiana 14; Wiesbaden: Harrassowitz, 2003), 267–292.

[44] In the fifteenth century c.e. al-Suyūtī collected conjurations against evil demons mentioning amongst them a certain Jiljamiš (see George, *Gilgamesh*, 60–61). George also mentions a certain Theodor bar Konai (ca. tenth century c.e.) who "passed on a list of twelve postdiluvian kings that were held to have reigned in the era between Peleg, a descendant of Noah's son Shem, and the patriarch Abraham. Both the tenth, *gmygws* or *gmngws*, and the twelfth, *gnmgws* or *glmgws*, who was king when Abraham was born, probably represent garbled spellings of Gilgamesh" (ibid., 61).

[45] See also C. Grotanelli, "The Story of Kombabos and the Gilgamesh Tradition," in *Mythology and Mythologies: Methodological Approaches to Intercultural Influences: Proceedings of the Second Annual Symposium of the Assyrian and Babylonian Intellectual Heritage Project Held in Paris, France, October 4–7, 1999* (ed. R.M. Whiting; Melammu Symposia 2; Helsinki: Neo-Assyrian Text Corpus Project, 2001), 19–27.

monster guarding the cedar forest, who was finally killed by Gilgamesh
and his comrade Enkidu. The alleged Elamite origin of the monster's
name would nicely fit the observation that, from a Mesopotamian view,
the localization of the cedar forest in historical times moved from the
Eastern Zagros to the Western Libanon. Proof, however, is lacking.[46] The
name of the Babylonian flood hero Utnapishtim/Ziusudra is, so far, not
attested in the extant manuscripts from Qumran. The name does occur,
however, in the form of At(a)nabīš (*'tnbyš*) in fragments of the *Book of
Giants* found at Turfan.[47]

2.3. A central figure in the discussion about the alleged Mesopotamian
model for the antediluvian patriarchs soon became Enoch, who lived for
365 (364) years and of whom we read in Gen 5:24 "Enoch walked with
God then he was no more, because God took him away." The verb *lāqaḥ*
in this context has received numerous comments.[48] Biblical sources offer
three interpretations: a) the liberation of a dead person from the power
of the underworld, b) a final removal from earth (cf. Elijah) or c) an act
of temporal transference, as in dream visions.[49]

The name Enoch has found several interpretations: It has been argued
that J derived the name from *ḥānaq*, "to dedicate" and "to train" which
comes close to an the interpretation of "the sage" (cf. also Arabic Idris!),
and it may well be that the two values attributed to Enoch in Gen 5 is a
"babilistic" interpretation of "a man dedicated to and trained by God."[50]
In the light of Gen 4:17 the name was also thought to convey the meaning
of "founder," referring to the eponymous city Enoch.[51] This Enoch is
possibly entering the rank of those patriarchs who, according to biblical
tradition, were perceived as a sort of cultural heroes.

---

[46] George, *Gilgamesh*, 147.
[47] Ibid., 155 with n. 93 (and literature).
[48] Kvanvig, *Roots*, 48–53.
[49] Ibid., 48–49.
[50] Ibid., 46.
[51] Westermann, *Genesis*, 443–445 suggests that Enoch may refer to the foundation of
a city or sanctuary. Westermann writes: "In Israel wurde die Erinnerung daran bewahrt,
daß der Städtebau zum dem gehört, was vor und außerhalb der Geschichte Israels
geschah. Die Gründung der ersten Stadt gehört der Urgeschichte an" (444). Discussing
Gen 4:17 most exegetes remark that it seems unlikely that Kain, the tiller, condemned to
a nomadic life, could be renowned as the founder of a city. In an attempt to harmonize
the alleged discrepancies, they even assume that the said founder was originally Enoch
(cf. e.g. Westermann, *Genesis*, 443).

2.4. With the publication of a Seleucid text from Uruk, W 20030,7[52] the comparison between Berossos, the Old Testament, and the *Sumerian King List* reached a new level:

1 [ina ta]r-[ṣ]i?	¹a-a-lu lugal	¹u₄-ᵈan	abgal
[ina ta]r-[ṣ]i	¹a-lá-al-gar lugal	¹u₄-ᵈan-du₁₀-ga	abgal
[ina tar-ṣ]i	¹am-me-lu-an-na lugal	¹en-me-du₁₀-ga	abgal
[ina tar-ṣi]	¹am-me-gal-an-na lugal	¹en-me-galam-ma	abgal
5 [ina tar-ṣi]	¹e[n-m]e-ušumgal-an-na lugal	¹en-me-bulùg-gá	abgal
[ina tar-ṣi]	¹ᵈdumu-zi sipa lugal	¹ᵈan-en-líl-da	abgal
[ina tar-ṣi]	¹en-me-dur-an-ki lugal	¹ù-tu-abzu	abgal

[egir-mar-uru?₅] ina palê^e ¹en-me-kár	¹nun-gal-pirìg-gal	abgal
[šá ᵈištar iš-t]u šamê^e ana é-an-na ú-še-ri-du balag-si_x-par		
10 [šá x x] x x^meš-šú ^na4za-gìn-na ina ši-pir ᵈnin-á-gal		
[i-pu-uš ina] x-kú^ki šu-bat dingir-lu-ulù? balag ina maḫ-ri ᵈan ú-kin-nu		

[	¹ᵈbilga-m]èš	¹ᵈsîn-liq-unninnī ^lu um-man-nu
[ina tar-ṣi	¹i-b]i-ᵈsîn lugal	¹kabtu-il-ᵈmarduk ¹ᵘum-man-nu
[ina tar-ṣi	¹iš-bi]-ᵈèr-ra lugal	¹si-dù ša-niš ¹ᵈ en-líl-ibni um-man-nu
15 [ina tar-ṣi	¹a-bi]-e²-šú-uḫ lugal	¹šu-ᵈME.ME u ¹ta-qiš-ᵈME.ME um-man-nu^meš
[ina tar-ṣi	¹x x]-x lugal	¹é-sag-gil-ki-ni-apla um-man-nu

This document establishes an important link between Berossos' account of the primeval kings and his story of the sage Oannes. In this text the names of Mesopotamian rulers are accompanied by names of advisors, sages, the so-called *apkallū* which play an important role in Mesopotamian iconography and have been known, up until now, chiefly from the so-called *Etiological Myth of the "Seven Sages"* studied by Erica Reiner in 1961.[53]

2.4.1. This list is certainly fictional, it is, however, based on scholarly traditions: the name of the well-known compiler of the standard version of the Gilgamesh Epic, ᵈsîn-liq-unninnī, functions as an *apkallu* to Gilgamesh himself. Further, a certain *Kabtu-il-Marduk*, perhaps referring to the author of the *Erra Epic Kabti-ilāni-Marduk*, is mentioned as a sage

---

[52] Published by J.J.A. van Dijk, "Die Tontafeln aus dem Resch-Heiligtum," in *Uruk-Warka Vorberichte* 18 (1962): 43–52, from which the following transcription is taken.

[53] E. Reiner, "The Etiological Myth of the 'Seven Sages,'" *Orientalia* 30 (1961): 1–11; eadem, *Astral Magic in Babylonia* (Transactions of the American Philosophical Society 85.4; Philadelphia: American Philosophical Society, 1995). See further S. Parpola, "Mesopotamian Astrology and Astronomy as Domains of the Mesopotamian 'Wisdom,'" in *Die Rolle der Astronomie in den Kulturen Mesopotamiens: Beiträge zum 3. Grazer Morgenländischen Symposium* (ed. H. Galter and B. Scholz; Grazer Morgenländische Studien 3; Graz: RM Druck- und Verlagsgesellschaft, 1993), 23–27.

during the reign of Ibbi-Sîn (ca. 2028–2004 B.C.E.), the unlucky last king
of the Ur III empire.

2.4.2. The correspondance between Enmeduranki, for a long time considered to be the Mesopotamian Enoch, with an *apkallu* named Utu-abzu,
proved highly informative.[54] In 1974 Borger observed in an important
article, that in tablet III of the omen series *Bīt Mēseri* ("House of Confine-
ment") a list of these *apkallū* is provided and that the *apkallu* Utu-abzu
who is, as we have just seen, associated with the primeval ruler Enmeduranki is explicitly said to have "ascended to heaven."[55] In Borger's words
we can therefore say: "The mythological conception of Enoch's ascension
to heaven derives ... from Enmeduranki's counselor, the seventh antediluvian sage, named Utuabzu!"[56]

2.4.3. The iconographic evidence for these *apkallū* is manifold and best
known from various Assyrian reliefs. We usually refer to them as *genii. Bīt
Mēseri*, however, describes them as *purādu*-fishes, and this coincides with
iconographic research undertaken by Wiggerman some twenty years ago
in his study on *Mesopotamian Protective Spirits*.[57] Wiggerman could distinguish between basically three types of *genii*, attested in the Mesopotamian art: First, there is a human faced *genius*, second, a bird *apkallu* who
occur only in "Assyrian" contexts, and third, a fish *apkallu*, the original Babylonian *apkallu*, as described by Berossos; according to the texts
the last two groups of *apkallū* are coming in groups of seven. The first
type, the human faced *genius* must be kept apart because these *genii*
are depicted wearing a horned crown which explicitly marks them as
divine.

2.5. I cannot dwell here on the complicated issue of a possible intertextual relation between these *apkallū* and the "fallen angels" of the biblical tradition. Instead I will add some remarks concerning the following

---

[54] See W.G. Lambert, "Enmeduranki and Related Matters," *JCS* 21 (1967): 126–138;
idem, "New Fragment."
[55] "Beschwörung. U-anna, der die Pläne des Himmels und der Erde vollendet, U-
anne-dugga, dem ein umfassender Verstand verliehen ist, Enmedugga, dem ein gutes
Geschick beschieden ist, Enmegalamma, der in einem Hause geboren wurde, Enmebu-
lugga, der auf einem Weidegrund aufwuchs, An-Enlilda, der Beschwörer der Stadt Eridu,
Utuabzu, der zum Himmel emporgestiegen ist, ..." (Borger, "Beschwörungsserie," 192).
[56] Borger, "Incantation Series," 232.
[57] F.A.M. Wiggermann, *Mesopotamian Protective Spirits: The Ritual Texts* (Cuneiform
Monographs 1; Groningen: Styx, 1992).

feature of the Enochic tradition, especially the *Book of Giants*. *1 Enoch* 6:1–3 gives account of the siring of giants; men had multiplied and the watchers, the sons of heaven, saw their beautiful daughters and desired them. Therefore, "they said to one another, 'Come, let us choose for our-selves wives from the daughters of men, and let us beget children for our-selves.' And Shemihazah, their chief, said to them, 'I fear that you will not want to do this deed, and I alone shall be guilty of a great sin.'"[58] *1 Enoch* 7:1–2 describes that the women conceived from them and "bore to them great giants. And the giants begot Nephilim, and to the Nephilim were born ... And they were growing in accordance with their greatness."[59]

2.5.1. This passage reminds one of the old Mesopotamian concept—and I am convinced it *is* a Mesopotamian concept, not a mere invention of modern scholarship—according to which a (mythical) ruler is thought to cohabite with a goddess or with her priestly incarnation.[60] Accordingly, the kings of the Ur III empire depict themselves in their hymns as divine scions, as sons of the mythical ruler Lugalbanda and the Goddess Ninsu(mu)na-k. In the present context it is not without interest that these kings were thus becoming "brothers of Gilgamesh," profiting somehow from the hero's legendary fame.

2.5.2. The divine sonship, however, can be trace back to the middle of the third millennium. An Old Sumerian ruler of the south Mesopotamian city state Lagash depicts himself in his text as follows:

> (The god) [Ni]n[gir]su-k [imp]lanted the [semen] for (the ruler) E'[a]na-tum in the [wom]b ... rejoiced over [E'anatum]. (The goddess) Inana-k accompanied him, named him "In the E'ana (temple) of Inana-k from (the sacred precinct) Ibgal I bring him (= E'ana-Inana-Ibgal-akak-atum)" and

---

[58] Nickelsburg and VanderKam, *1 Enoch*, 23.

[59] Ibid., 24.

[60] This is a much disputed issue, best known under the heading "Sacred Marriage" concept. What is interesting here is the feature of a divine-human interaction in the sexual life and the consequences thereof. We are not concerned here with the hypothesis of a purely metaphorical interpretation or with a possible actualization in an alleged ritual. For a comparative evaluation of this topic see P. Lapinkivi, *The Sumerian Sacred Marriage in the Light of Comparative Evidence* (SAAS 15; Helsinki: Neo-Assyrian Text Corpus Project, 2004); see further E. Cancik-Kirschbaum, "Hierogamie-Eine Skizze zum Sachstand in der Altorientalistik," in *Gelebte Religionen: FS Hartmut Zinser* (ed. H. Piegeler, I. Pohl, and S. Rademacher; Würzburg: Königshausen & Neumann, 2004), 65–72; G.J. Selz, "The Divine Prototypes," in *Religion and Power: Divine Kingship in the Ancient World and Beyond* (ed. N. Brisch; Oriental Institute Seminars 4; Chicago: Oriental Institute of the University of Chicago, 2008), 13–31.

set him on the legitimising knees of (the mother goddess) Ninchursag(a). Ninchursag(a) [offered him] her legitimising breast.[61]

Ningirsu-k rejoiced over E'anatum, semen implanted into the womb by Ningirsu-k. Ningirsu-k laid his span upon him, for (a length of) five forearms he set his forearm upon him: (he measured) five forearms (cubits), one span! (*to the reconstructed measurements of this period ca. 2.72 metres*). Ningirsu-k, out of his great joy, [gave him] the kin[gship of Lagash].[62]

Hence, the ruler is the one "who has strength,"[63] a precondition for his successful rule.

2.5.3. The aforementioned size of 2.72 meters makes just a small giant. However, this size is an outward sign designating someone who transgresses human measurements and norms. Accordingly it became possible to attribute to such an extraordinary ruler a sort of functional divinity, as can be corroborated by several additional arguments. We can therefore say that the ruler is perceived as an Avatar, a manifestation of the state god Ningirsu-k.

2.5.4. A further consequence is that the appearance of the ruler was perceived as perfect in every sense, physically and mentally, he is strong and wise, these being the preconditions for his rule.[64] Such perfection is also mentioned repeatedly as a feature of the kings of Ur III; the best sources for this are provided by their hymns.[65] Therefore it does not come as a surprise that in the texts from the last years of his reign, king

---

[61] Ean. 1, 4:9–12 (H. Steible, ed., *Die altsumerischen Bau- und Weihinschriften* [2 vols.; Freiburger altorientalische Studien 5; Wiesbaden: Steiner, 1982], 1:122) = RIME 1.9.3.1, 4:9–12. See D. Frayne, ed., *Presargonic Period (2700–2350 BC)* (RIME 1; Toronto: University of Toronto Press, 2008), 129–130.

[62] Ean. 1, 5:1–5 (Steible, *Die altsumerischen Bau- und Weihinschriften*, 1:123) = RIME 1.9.3.1 (Frayne, *Presargonic Period*, 129).

[63] Ean. 1, 5:21 *et passim* (Steible, *Die altsumerischen Bau- und Weihinschriften*, 1:124) = RIME 1.9.3.1 *et passim* (Frayne, *Presargonic Period*, 130).

[64] Compare, for example, I.J. Winter, "The Body of the Able Ruler: Towards an Understanding of the Statues of Gudea," in *DUMU-E2-DUB-BA-A: Studies in Honor of Ake W. Sjöberg* (ed. H. Behrens, D. Loding, and M.T. Roth; Publications of the Samuel Noah Kramer Fund 11; Philadelphia: University of Pennsylvania Museum, 1989), 573–584.

[65] See already S.N. Kramer, "Kingship in Sumer and Akkad: The Ideal King," in Le palais et la royauté: Archéologie et civilization: Compte rendu de la XIXᵉ Rencontre Assyriologique Internationale organisée par le Groupe François Thureau-Dangin, Paris, 29 juin–2 juillet 1971 (ed. P. Garelli; Paris: Geuthner, 1974), 163–176; J. Klein, *The Royal Hymns of Šulgi, King of Ur: Man's Quest for Immortal Fame* (Transactions of the American Philosophical Society 71.7; Philadelphia: American Philosophical Society, 1981); and numerous other works.

Shulgi-r was marked with the divine classifier,[66] which was traditionally reserved for all sorts of deities. Roughly two centuries earlier the Old-Akkadian king Narām-Sîn established this practice when he asserts that after rescuing the land from dire straits the people from various cities asked their gods to name him as their god and built him even a temple in the capital city Agade.[67] Such (self-)deification of the ruler was not accepted unanimously in Mesopotamia: In the later cuneiform tradition Narām-Sîn's attempt to obliterate the border between the human and the divine spheres was branded as blasphemous.

2.6. Like the giants, the rulers of Mesopotamia could have dreams. Dreams do, of course, play a major role all over the ancient Near East. For lack of space I just mention some very early examples here. The observable parallels may speak for themselves.

2.6.1. The earliest attestation for a dream is attested in the famous stele of vultures of the pre-Sargonic king of Lagash, E'anatum. In Ean. 1, 6:28[68] we read: "to the one who has lain down, to the one who has lain down (the deity) stood at (his) head."[69] For our purpose, here it is noteworthy, that a deity was the sender or transmitter of the dream. The dream was of divine origin, considered as revelation of the divine will.[70] Whereas the

---

[66] Cf. D. Frayne, ed., *Ur III Period (2112–2004 BC)* (RIME 3.2; Toronto: University of Toronto Press, 1997), 91.

[67] See D. Frayne, ed., *Sargonic and Gutian Periods (2334–2113 BC)* (RIME 2; Toronto: University of Toronto Press, 1997), 113–114.

[68] Steible, *Die altsumerischen Bau- und Weihinschriften*, 1:125 = RIME 1.9.3.1 (Frayne, *Presargonic Period*,130).

[69] We note that this passage follows the miraculous birth of the ruler E'anatum; presumably he was thus especially fitted for the dream message.

[70] The clearest reference to the divine relevation of a text is attested in the late *Erra Epic* with his evident "apocalyptic" theme where the author Kabti-ilāni-Marduk actually asserts in the colophon of the text: (5:40) "For (the god) Erra had burned with wrath and planned to lay waste the countries and slay their peoples, but Ishum, his counsellor, appeased him and (Erra) left a remnant! Kabti-ilāni-Marduk, the son of Dabibi, (was) the composer of this tablet (= of this poem): (The deity) revealed it to him during the night, and in the morning, when he recited (it), he did not skip a single (line) nor a single line (of his own) did he add to it …." (5:55) [Erra speaks] "The scribe who commits it to memory shall escape the enemy country (and) shall be honoured in his own country. In the sanctuary of (those) sages where they constantly mention my name, I will grant them wisdom. To the house in which this tablet is placed—however furious Erra may be, however murderous the Sebettu (pleaiades or seven sisters) may be—the sword of destruction shall not come near." (English translation by L. Cagni, *The Poem of Erra* [Sources of the Ancient Near East 1.3; Malibu: Undena Publications, 1974).

giants sent Mahway to Enoch for an interpretation of their dreams,[71] in earliest parallels from Mesopotamia the deities undertake this task: The Sumerian ruler Gudea had difficulties to understand the precise meaning of his dream and addresses the goddess Nanshe, firstly describing his visions:

> (4:8) Nanshe, mighty queen, lustration priestess, protecting genius, cherished goddess of mine, ... *You are the interpreter of dreams among the gods, you are the queen of all the lands, O mother, my matter today is a dream.*
>
> *There was someone in my dream, enormous as the skies, enormous as the earth was he.*
>
> *That one was a god as regards his head, he was the Thunderbird as regards his wings, and a floodstorm as regards his lower body.* There was a lion lying on both his left and right side ... (but) I did not understand what (exactly) he intended. Daylight rose for me on the horizon.
>
> (4:23) (Then) there was a woman—whoever she might have been—she (the goddess Nissaba[k]) held in her hand *a stylus of shining metal, on her knees there was a tablet (with) stars of heaven,* and she was consulting it.
>
> (5:2) Furthermore, there was a warrior who bent (his) arm holding *a lapis lazuli plate on which he was setting the ground-plan* of a house. He set before me a brand-new basket, a brand-new brick-mould was adjusted and he let the *auspicious brick* be in the mould for me.[72]

2.6.2. Using much the same words the goddess explains the dream:

> (5:12) My shepherd, I will interpret your dream for you from beginning to end: The *person who you said was as enormous as the skies, enormous as the earth,* who was *a god* as regards his head, who, as you said, was the *Thunderbird* as regards his wings, and who, as you said, was *a floodstorm* as regards his lower parts, at whose left and right a lion was lying—he was in fact my brother Ningirsu-k; he talked to you about the building of his shrine Eninnu. The daylight that had risen for you on the horizon—that was your (personal) god Ningishzida-k: like *daylight* he will be able to rise for you from there.
>
> *The young woman* coming forward, who did something with sheaves, who was *holding a stylus of shining metal,* had on her knees a tablet (with) stars, *which she was consulting* was in fact my sister Nissaba-k—she announced to you the bright star (auguring) the building of the House.

---

[71] "Thereupon] all the giants [and monsters! grew afraid 15 and called Mahway. He came to them and the giants pleaded with him and sent him to Enoch 16 [the noted scribe]" (4Q530 II:18). Translation taken from the edition of The Gnostic Society Library (online: http://www.gnosis.org/library/dss/dss_book_of_giants.htm [14 March 2010]).

[72] The translation from Cylinder A follows D.O. Edzard, ed., *Gudea and his Dynasty*

Furthermore, as for the warrior who bent his arm holding a lapis lazuli plate—he was Ninduba: *he was engraving* thereon in all details *the ground-plan of the House.*[73]

2.6.3. Certainly, the setting of this dream is very different from those of the Enoch tradition. We note, however, that the dreams in the *Book of Giants* also show a clear connection with the scribal art, especially the "Tablets of Heavens," to the dreams as a message of God and also to the flood. The latter motif as found in the *Book of Giants* shows a clear connection to the story of the *Erra Epic*, where to Marduk's horror, the deity of pestilence and destruction, Erra, decides to annihilate mankind and its foremost sanctuaries. The reason for the annihilation of the world and the expression of a certain degree of hope looks very similar indeed. It is important to note that this text from the eight century B.C.E. had a considerable audience as can be deduced from the *over* 35 tablets unearthed so far. In many respects, the wording of the text and its attitude ask for elaborate comparison with the Jewish apocalyptical tradition, but this would be another article.[74]

2.7. The story of Etana, one of the oldest tales in a Semitic language,[75] was, as I have argued elsewhere, modeled after the then extant Sumerian tales of the Gilgamesh Epic. Gilgamesh's search for "the plant of life," the ú-nam-ti-la (*šammu ša balāṭi*) was, however, replaced by Etana's search for the plant of birth-giving (*šammu ša alādi*). The entire story runs as follows:

2.7.1. The gods build the first city Kish, but kingship is still in heaven. A ruler is wanted (and found). Due to an illness, Etana's wife is unable to conceive. The plant of birth is wanted. In the ensuing episode eagle and snake swore an oath of friendship. Suddenly the eagle plans to eat up the

---

(RIME 3.1; Toronto: University of Toronto Press, 1997), 71–72 (emphases are mine, G.J.S.).

[73] The translation follows Edzard, *Gudea*, 72 (all emphases are mine, G.J.S.).

[74] For an overview of Mesopotamian "apocalyptic motifs" see C. Wilcke, "Weltuntergang als Anfang: Theologische, anthropologische, politisch-historische und ästhetische Ebenen der Interpretation der Sintflutgeschichte im babylonischen Atram-ḫasīs-Epos," in *Weltende: Beiträge zur Kultur- und Religionswissenschaft* (ed. A. Jones; Wiesbaden: Harrassowitz, 1999), 63–112.

[75] See G.J. Selz, "Die Etana-Erzählung: Ursprung und Tradition eines der ältesten epischen Texte in einer semitischen Sprache," *Acta Sumerologica* (Japan) 20 (1998): 135–179; a different opinion is expressed by P. Steinkeller, "Early Semitic Literature and Third Millennium Seals with Mythological Motifs," in Literature and Literary Language at

snake's children; a baby eagle, with the name of *Atraḫasīs* opposes this plan, but eagle executes it. Now, the weeping snake seeks justice from the sun-god. With the god's help the eagle is trapped in a burrow, and now the eagle turns to the sun-god for help. He receives the answer that, because of the taboo-violation he cannot help, but will send someone else.

Etana prays daily for the plant of birth and in a dream the sun-god tells Etana to approach the eagle. In order to get the eagle's support Etana helps him out of his trap. Now the eagle, carrying Etana on his back, ascends to the heavens. On the uppermost level of the heavens Etana becomes afraid and the eagle takes him back to the earth.

The end of the story is missing, but that Etana finally got hold of the plant of birth is very likely, since other sources mention his son.

3. To summarize: I have tried to show that some features of the Enoch tradition are a re-writing of very ancient concepts. I do not claim that they all can be explained assuming dependencies, as earlier scholarship has done. I do not intend to idolize "origins," but what might eventually come out of such a research—if the topics mentioned here are thoroughly worked out and elaborated in detail—is, that our texts implicate many more meanings than tradition may have supposed. In my opinion there can be little doubt that the official transmission of texts in Mesopotamia was supplemented by a wealth of oral tradition. Indeed, the situation may be comparable to the one attested in the (still) living oral tradition on Enoch in the Balkanian vernaculars.

Ebla (ed. P. Fronzaroli; Quaderni di Semitistica 18; Florence: Dipartimento di linguistica Università di Firenze, 1992), 243–275 and pls. 1–8. Further remarks on the ruler's ascension to heaven are discussed by G.J. Selz, "Der sogenannte 'geflügelte Tempel' und die 'Himmelfahrt' der Herrscher: Spekulationen über ein ungelöstes Problem der altakkadischen Glyptik und dessen möglichen rituellen Hintergrund," in *Studi sul Vicino Oriente Antico dedicati alla memoria di Luigi Cagni* (ed. S. Graziani; Naples: Istituto Universitario Orientale, 2000): 961–983.

LEVI IN THE THIRD SKY:
ON THE "ASCENT TO HEAVEN" LEGENDS WITHIN THEIR NEAR EASTERN CONTEXT AND J.T. MILIK'S UNPUBLISHED VERSION OF THE *ARAMAIC LEVI DOCUMENT*

Ursula Schattner-Rieser

ICP-ELCOA Paris and University of Zurich

1. Introduction

This paper presents the reconstructed text of the Aramaic version of the vision of Levi and his ascent to heaven, as described in the monograph dealing with the *Aramaic Levi Document* (*ALD*), written by Józef T. Milik in the eighties, and rediscovered by Z. Kapera in 2006. In his manuscript, Milik offers some improved readings of 1Q21 and identifies the fragment 1Q37 as a remnant of the vision of the ascent to heaven.

Milik's work on the *ALD*, as initially reported by him in 1976 and 1978 and thought by him to be from the first part of the *Book of the Patriarchs* (*Livre des Patriarches*) includes: 1. the primary text of a monograph on the *Testament of Levi*, 2. an edition of the existing fragments of the text, 3. notes for the preparation of tables providing a reconstruction of the Qumran Aramaic fragments, 4. an appendix consisting of a French translation of his reconstruction of the *Testament of Levi*, and 5. the original handwritten manuscript, partly typed, and his notes from library research, which bear the title "Testament de Lévi: Ma copie: I."[1] Regrettably, the introduction, the conclusion and some footnotes are lacking.

Milik's version differs from those of other editors in many details. For example, the mention of three visions and the opening title, which Milik

---

[1] See Z.J. Kapera, "Preliminary Information about Jozef T. Milik's Unpublished Manuscript of 'The Testament of Levi,'" *Polish Journal of Biblical Research* 6 (2007): 109–112 (110); J.T. Milik, *The Books of Enoch: Aramaic Fragments of Qumrân Cave 4* (Oxford: Clarendon, 1976), 24; idem, "Écrits préesséniens de Qumrân: d'Hénoch à Amram," in *Qumrân: Sa piété, sa théologie et son milieu* (ed. M. Delcor; BETL 46; Paris: Duculot, 1978), 91–106 (95 n. 9).—On the *ALD* see my edition and translation in which some of Milik's readings are already incorporated: U. Schattner-Rieser, "Document araméen de

reconstructs as follows: פרשגן כתב מלי חזות לוי בר יעקב בר ישחק בר אברהם "copie du livre des paroles des visions de Lévi fils de Jacob fils de Isaac fils d' Abraham," as in the introductory formula to the *Visions of Amram* (4Q543 1a–c 1 par. 4Q545 1a i 1). In *T. Levi*, the title was shortened to three words: Ἀντίγραφον λόγων Λευί "copy of the words of Levi" (1:1) and replaced elsewhere in the *T. 12 Patr.* by the word "Testament."[2]

Like other scholars,[3] Milik believes that the Greek *T. Levi* depends upon the original Aramaic document and that there are few Christian interpolations. For him, the "original form" contained 1) the autobiographical introduction, 2) a first short vision concerning the city of Evil (see below, in 5,1 according to Milik's counting), 3) the prayer, followed by 4) the second vision of the three or seven heavens, Levi's ascent to heaven and matters dealing with the priesthood, 5) the commandment of the angels concerning vengeance upon Shechem, the Shechem incident, Jacob's wrath, the justification of the Shechem slaughter, the laws governing the espousal of a violated or raped woman, 6) a third vision in which seven angels depict the consecration of the eternal Levitical priesthood, sacrificial laws and rules governing the wood to be used etc.,[4] 7) Levi's visits to Bethel and Isaac, Isaac's benediction of Levi, Levi's investiture in the priesthood by his father Jacob, Isaac's instructions regarding certain rituals, 8) a life story and 9) the wisdom speech.

For unknown reasons, Milik abandoned the idea of publication some time during the 1990s. It may be that poor health prevented him from completing it. It is also possible that he recognized that his edition differed significantly from the official edition of the Qumran fragments pre-

---

Lévi (Aramaic Levi Document): CL Cambridge a–f; CL Bodléienne a–d; 1Q21; 4Q213–4Q213a–4Q213b–4Q214–4Q214a–4Q214b," in *La Bibliothèque de Qumrân*, vol. 1: *Torah: Genèse: Edition bilingue des manuscrits* (ed. K. Berthelot, T. Legrand, and A. Paul; Paris: Cerf, 2008), 421–467 (448–457).

[2] Due to the use of the Aramaic verb פקד "to attend, deposit, recommend, order, ordain," which is translated by διατίθημι "to place, dispose of by a will" in *T. Levi*. Only *T. Reu.*, *T. Naph.*, *T. Gad*, *T. Ash* and *T. Jos.* use the title "Copy of the Testament of ..."; other "Testaments" begin like the original Semitic *Vorlage* with "Copy of the words of ...," so do the *Assumption of Moses* and *2 En.* 31:1. Only in late Jewish Aramaic (דִּיאָתִיקִי, דְּיָיתִיקִי) and in Syriac, do we have the Greek borrowing (ܕܝܬܩܐ) < διαθήκη.

[3] For example, P. Grelot, "Notes sur le Testament araméen de Lévi," *RB* 15 (1956): 391–306, esp. 405; M. Philonenko, *Les interpolations chrétiennes des Testaments des Douze Patriarches et les Manuscrits de Qoumrân* (Cahiers de la Revue d' histoire et de philosophie religieuses 35; Paris: Presses Universitaires de France, 1960), esp. 3, 7, 59–60.

[4] Confirmed by Milik's v. 165 "C'était une vision—l' une comme l' autre," cf. the Cairo Genizah Levi manuscript in the Bodleian Library in Oxford (CL), col. a line 11: חזוא הוא דן וכדן אנה.

pared by J. Greenfield and M. Stone[5] as well as from É. Puech's critical edition of the Cairo Genizah Levi fragments.[6] Moreover, since his
commentary was based upon his reading of the manuscripts (e.g. col.
b of the Cairo Genizah Levi manuscript in the Cambridge University
library [CL]), many texts had to be changed or rearranged, so as to be
in agreement with those of the official editors. In addition, the numbering system for Qumran fragments had been changed recently, and Milik
had employed his own sigla, incorporated several other fragments and
improved or occasionally corrected his initial readings, which had been
published in *DJD* I.[7] Milik proposes a reconstruction of the supposed
original *ALD* using five scrolls from Qumran[8] (1Q21, 1Q63, 4Q213–
4Q214, 4Q540,[9] 4Q548),[10] the overlapping Aramaic Levi material in the
Cairo Genizah fragments from the Cambridge University Library and the
Bodleian Library in Oxford (CL), the eleventh century Greek manuscript
of the *Testaments of the Twelve Patriarchs* from Mount Athos Koutloumousiou 39 = MS *e* (GL) and a ninth century Syriac fragment, as well
as isolated material from the Greek *Testaments of the Twelve Patriarchs*,
which he supposed to have been omitted in *ALD* (AL) and the Greek
T. Levi (GL). Although Puech first shared Milik's view and proposed
the sigla 4QTestLevi[c] for 4Q540 and 4QTestLevi[e] for 4Q548[11] by adding
an additional fragment from 4Q541, which received the designation

---

   [5] J.C. Greenfield and M.E. Stone in *DJD* XXII (1996): 1–72. For example Milik's
deciphering of 4Q213a 3–4 offers a more important and quite different text from that
of the official edition.

   [6] É. Puech, "Le Testament de Lévi en araméen de la Geniza du Caire," *RevQ* 20 (2002):
511–556.

   [7] J.T. Milik in *DJD* I (1955): 87–91 and pl. XVII.

   [8] Milik had already confirmed verbally to Robert A. Kugler that his identification of
the five scrolls belonging to the *ALD* included 1Q21, 4Q213, 4Q214, 4Q540 and 4Q548,
see R.A. Kugler, *From Patriarch to Priest: The Levi-Priestly Tradition from* Aramaic Levi
to Testament of Levi (SBLEJL 9; Atlanta: Scholars Press, 1996), 27 and 30 n. 22.

   [9] Contrary to Kugler, *From Patriarch to Priest*, 188.

   [10] For Milik, 4Q540, which he entitled 4QLevi[c], is an integral part of the *ALD* (vv. 354–
366). He inserted the fragment between the apocalyptic passage of the "seven jubilees"
(*T. Levi* 17:6–10) and the verses concerning the "new priest" (*T. Levi* 18:1–14), in the
Wisdom speech. Furthermore, using the remains of 4Q548, to which he assigns the
siglum 4QLevi[d] and which describes the final destinies of the sons of light, he suggests
to insert vv. 386–403 in the final part of *ALD*, due to its parallels with *T. Levi* 19, the
Levitical paraeneses. He had reported this previously in an article in which he discussed
the "doctrine des deux voies," see J.T. Milik, "Écrits préesseniens de Qumrân: d' Hénoch
à Amram," in *Qumrân: Sa piété, sa théologie et son milieu* (ed. M. Delcor; BETL 46; Paris:
Duculot, 1978), 91–106 (95). For a differing view, cf. Kugler, *From Patriarch to Priest*, 189.

   [11] É. Puech, "Fragments d' un apocryphe de Lévi et le personnage eschatologique:

4QTestLevi[d], he revised this hypothesis later, and 4Q548 is currently identified as 4QVisions of Amram[f].[12] This was initially Milik's hypothesis.[13] On the other hand, Puech confirms the closeness of 4Q540–541 to *T. Levi* and calls the remnants an "Apocryphon of Levi."[14]

Milik considers *ALD* to be one of the oldest pseudepigraphic pre-Maccabean and pre-Qumranic texts, including material that goes back to the Persian exile. Therefore, he suggests that its composition took place during the third or fourth century B.C.E.[15] The linguistic archaisms retained by the second century B.C.E. copyists are the best proof of an original dating from the Hellenistic or even the Persian period. The orthography is usually defective and the scribe forgot, in one instance, to replace the archaic demonstrative pronoun די by the contemporary form די (4Q213a 3–4 5). An additional archaism is found in 4Q214b 2–6 3, where one reads עעין "wood" and not אעין as in Biblical Aramaic and later Aramaic dialects.[16] Another unusual orthography exists in 1Q21 11 1,[17] where the third person masculine singular imperfect verb יהוה is prefixed with *yôd* and not "corrected" by adding the prefix *lāmed* and changing it to להוה.

4QTestLévi[c–d](?) et 4QAJa," in *The Madrid Qumran Congress: Proceedings of the International Congress on the Dead Sea Scrolls, Madrid 18–21 March, 1991* (ed. J. Trebolle Barrera and L. Vegas Montaner; 2 vols.; STDJ 11.1–2; Leiden: Brill, 1992), 2:449–501 (490–491).

[12] É. Puech in *DJD* XXXI (2001): 391–398 (391).

[13] J.T. Milik, "4QVision de 'Amram et une citation d'Origène," *RB* 79 (1976): 77–97 (esp. 90–92).

[14] Puech, "Fragments d'un apocryphe de Lévi."

[15] Already in Milik, *Books of Enoch*, 24 and 56; See also U. Schattner-Rieser, "Observations sur l'araméen de Qumrân—la question de l'araméen standard reconsidérée," in *Józef Tadeusz Milik et Cinquantenaire de la découverte des manuscrits de la Mer Morte de Qumrân* (ed. D. Dlugosz and H. Ratajczak; Warsaw: Centrum Upowszechniania Nauki Polskiej Akademii Nauk, 2000), 51–62, esp. 54–55. As an excellent epigraphist and philologist Milik differentiated between the date of the *Vorlagen* of different origins, and the current compositions found in caves one and four, which are late copies of older texts.

[16] U. Schattner-Rieser, *Textes araméens de la mer Morte. Édition bilingue, vocalisée et commentée* (Langues et cultures anciennes 5; Brusells: Safran, 2005), 2; eadem, *L'araméen des manuscrits de la mer Morte, I. Grammaire* (Instruments pour l'étude des langues de l'Orient ancient 5; Lausanne: Zèbre, 2004) 64 (α–β) and 65 (VI.b). Incidentally, we notice the strange language in the *ALD* text as given in J.C. Greenfield, M.E. Stone, and E. Eshel, *The Aramaic Levi Document: Edition, Translation, Commentary* (SVTP 19; Leiden: Brill, 2004), 22. See also U. Schattner-Rieser, "L'apport de la philologie araméenne et l'interprétation des archaïsmes linguistiques pour la datation des textes araméens de Qumrân," in *Aramaica Qumranica: Proceedings of the Conference on the Aramaic Texts from Qumran in Aix-en-Provence 30 June–2 July 2008* (ed. K. Berthelot and D. Stoekl Ben Ezra; STDJ 94; Leiden: Brill, 2010), 101–123.

[17] [...]אֹוהי אדין ה ○[...] "... thus he/it will be ..."

Thus, one should always consider the linguistic evidence before assigning a date to a text based upon purely palaeographic considerations. In addition, it should be stressed that what later became *T. Levi* is a composite work, combining typically Jewish beliefs with Mesopotamian and Persian material. The apocalypse of the ascent to heaven, as well as other extraterrestrial journey legends, are based upon ancient and widely disseminated myths that are well attested in Mesopotamian literature. They are very similar to Enoch's ascent to heaven, which is undeniably a very old text, not only conserved in Judeo-Christian literature but also in a Mandaic legend.[18] Another common ancient Near Eastern tale is the narrative of the sage and the praise of wisdom (for example, Aḥiqar, the Seven Sages and Adapa, and the seven angels in *ALD*).[19] Only later, the various literary elements in the *ALD* consolidated and shaped into a "testamentary" narrative, perhaps by Essene or Qumran copyists.

In comparison to others, Milik makes quite extensive usage of *T. Levi* and it is obvious that, for him, *ALD* relied on a text very close to *T. Levi*. Thus his reconstruction of the *ALD*'s text is modelled upon *T. Levi*. Milik also borrows from and/or discusses textual evidence based upon many other Qumran fragments, such as *Jubilees* and the testamentary literature. He even retranslates the passage CD 4:15–19 from Hebrew to Aramaic, with which he fills in vv. 404–407 of his French translation, followed by 1Q21 30.[20] Although Milik shares some views with the other editors of *ALD*, his reconstruction differs from Drawnel's interpretation,[21] as it does, in many ways, from those of Kugler and Greenfield, Stone, and Eshel.[22] Milik also demonstrates the dependence of *Jubilees* upon the *ALD* material.[23]

---

[18] U. Schattner-Rieser, "Reminiszenzen an Henochs Himmelfahrt in der mandäischen Literatur: Ein Beitrag zum Entstehungsmilieu apokrypher Texte aus Qumran," *Sacra Scripta* 9 (2011), forthcoming.

[19] H. Kvanvig, *The Roots of Apocalyptic: The Mesopotamian Background of the Enoch Figure and of the Son of Man* (WMANT 69; Neukirchen-Vluyn: Neukirchener, 1988), containing precious data concerning Akkadian dream visions and primeval sages; see also Henryk Drawnel's chapter about the influence of elementary metro-arithmetical exercises common in the training of Mesopotamian scribal apprentices on *ALD*, in H. Drawnel, *An Aramaic Wisdom Text from Qumran: A New Interpretation of the Levi Document* (JSJSup 86; Leiden: Brill, 2004), 81–96.

[20] See below and J.T. Milik, "Traduction continue du Testament de Lévi [Précédée d'une note de l'éditeur Z.J. Kapera]," *QC* 15 (2007): 5–24 (23).

[21] Drawnel, *Aramaic Wisdom Text*.

[22] Kugler, *From Patriarch to Priest*; Greenfield, Stone, and Eshel, *Aramaic Levi Document*.

[23] This is at variance with Kugler's thesis, see Kugler, *From Patriarch to Priest*, 33.

2. The Account of the Second Vision

The different editors of the *ALD* generally disagree as to whether the original text contains one or two visions. Milik mentions *three* visions. For him, the first two visions, according to *T. Levi* 2:3–4a, took place on Mount Aspis, a mountain near Ebal (ἐγγύς Γεβάλ, *T. Levi* 6:1) the modern et-Ṭûr, in the south of Abel-Mayin (ἐκ δεξιῶν Ἀβιλᾶ, *T. Levi* 6:1), the Abel-Maoul[24] of GL, which he identifies as Mount Gerizim. Milik also expresses his conviction that *ALD* is of Samaritan origin. Whether one agrees with his opinion or not,[25] his arguments are interesting. The first vision, a very short one, occurred due to the influence of the "spirit of prophetic intelligence" (which he calls in French "l'esprit prophétique d'intelligence") and contains a vision of the "city of evil."

The second vision, dealing with the "ascent to heaven," is a dream beginning with a prayer in the Aramaic *Vorlage*, is limited to only two verses in *T. Levi* (2:5–6). However, the prayer is conserved completely in the Greek fragment of Mount Athos (Koutloumousiou E) and partially in the Aramaic Qumran fragment 4Q213a. With the help of the Athos manuscript, Milik retranslates the entire prayer into Aramaic.

After the prayer, the gates of heaven are opened and an angel speaks to Levi.[26] Contrary to the views of other editors of *ALD*, Milik proposed to integrate the following account of the ascent to heaven into the Aramaic reconstruction. And the vision and ascent to heaven from Greek *T. Levi* 2:7–9 fill in vv. 39–48 in Milik's reconstructed text. Milik himself noted that a reconstruction using the minute fragments of 1Q21 is plausible, but nevertheless remains hypothetical. Due to disparities with other manuscripts of *ALD*, he estimated that 1Q21 consists of eleven columns, corresponding to the beginning and the middle of *ALD*. He calculated a total of 30 lines with 64 letters each. He seems to have identified other fragments of 1Q21 not published in *DJD* I, which cannot be identified at present. For Milik, there is no doubt that Levi's vision of the heavens mentions three firmaments (v. 39). This understanding resulted from

---

[24] Due to the confusion between A and Λ < ΑΒΕΛΜΑΟΥΛ < ΑΒΕΛΜΑΟΥΑ, which corresponds to אבל מיא, the Aramaic emphatic form of מין.

[25] For an opposite view, see Greenfield, Stone, and Eshel, *Aramaic Levi Document*, 20 n. 60; R.A. Kugler, *The Testaments of the Twelve Patriarchs* (Guides to Apocrypha and Pseudepigrapha; Sheffield: Sheffield Academic Press, 2001), 51.

[26] Cf. 4Q213a 2 17–18: [. . .] וארו אתפתחו לי תרעי שמיא ומלאך חד which corresponds to vv. 33–34 according to Milik: "[Et voici] que s'ouvrirent devant moi les portes du ciel et *un* ange [m'appela disant: 'Lévi, entre donc!']."

correcting his initial reading[27] of 1Q21 37a 1 from [...]מן תלה[...] to
ש[...], a reading confirmed by Puech.[28] In my opinion,
the reconstruction of vv. 39–42 proposed by Milik is too long. If the
reading can be generally accepted, the reconstruction of v. 41 in 1Q21
32–33 + 37 1–3 should be shortened as follows:

1 [ואעלני מלאכא לש[מ]ין תלי]ת[מ]ין מן עלה וחזית תמן נהו]ר שמיא ל[חדה זהיר מן]
2 [תרין שמי]ן ולא אית[י]כל משחה ל[
3 [ושאלת א[נה אי דן ...]מ'רת מה דן שמיא א]לין [

1 [39 [And the angel led me into] the thir[d hea]ven, [(which was) higher,
   40 and I saw there] the heavenly [ligh]t, [(which was) much brighter than
   (that)]
2 [of the (first) two 41 heav]ens and there was no 42 limit ...
3 [43(44) and I asked] what is the [signi]fication of th[ese] heavens?

There can be no doubt about the reading of "three firmaments," which
has been confirmed by the independent examination of E. Puech.[29] Milik
corrected the reading of 1Q21 32 1 from [ה שמיא ל] to ר שמיא[נהו, which
seems to imply that there are other heavens above these first three, which
are brighter and less gloomy.

For Milik, the priestly scribe of *ALD* proposes an image of the other-
world that is somewhat different from that described in *1 Enoch*. Under
the Mesopotamian influence of Babylonian astronomy, the scribe pro-
mulgates the idea of seven heavens. He retains the traditional teaching of
the threefold division of the universe, namely: a first, gloomy heaven, a
second heaven of waters, and a third heaven of eternal light, identical with
paradise and the place of judgement. To these three heavens, the scribe
added a vertically positioned heavenly four-part realm, which contains
the temple palace.

Milik's thesis is shared by Henk Jan de Jonge, who has demonstrated
that seven is the original number of firmaments described in *T. Levi*.
For him, the three firmament concept is a later transformation based
upon the importance of their contents. Indeed, the third firmament is
identified with paradise in 2 Cor 12:2–4, 2 *En.* 8:1–8 and in *Apoc. Mos.*
37.

---

27 Milik in *DJD* I (1955): 87–91 and pl. XVII.
28 É. Puech, "Notes sur le *Testament de Lévi* de la grotte 1 (1Q21)," *RevQ* 21 (2003–
2004): 297–310 (305).
29 Ibid.

3. Ancient Near Eastern Traditions[30]

The beliefs in the existence of seven heavens originated in Mesopotamia
at a rather late date, but the idea of three heavens was not less common
than that of seven.[31] In Mesopotamian mythology, heaven is, in general,
not a place for humans. This is evident from the words of Gilgamesh to
his friend Enkidu: "Who can go up to heaven, my friend? Only the God
dwells with Shamash forever …"[32] This reservation is also found in the
Hebrew Bible, as one can see in Ps 115:16: "The heavens are the Lord's
heavens, but the earth He has given to the sons of men" (RSV). Similar
statements may be found in Deut 10:14 and 30:12 or in Prov 30:3–4.[33]
There is no need for one to ascend to heaven to learn the "secret things,"
which belong to God only (cf. Deut 29:28 and Sir 3:21–23). A direct
condemnation of this desire to ascend to heaven is found in Isa 14:13–
15.[34] There, the prideful King of Babylon, who wants to ascend to heaven
and become like God, is cast down to the netherworld of worms and
maggots.

(Dream) Visions of the heavens or the netherworld and journeys
thereto are well represented in Mesopotamian mythology. Adela Yarbro
Collins writes: "Support for the conclusion that the motif of seven heavens derives from the Babylonian tradition is its combination with the
notion of the correspondence between the earthly and the heavenly Paradise."[35] Although the seven heaven motif is to be found in Sumerian

---

[30] For a general overview, see J.D. Tabor, "Heaven, Ascent to," *ABD* 3:91–94.

[31] A. Yarbro Collins, "The Seven Heavens in Jewish and Christian Apocalypses," in
Death, Ecstasy, and Other Worldly Journeys (ed. J.J. Collins and M. Fishbane; Albany: State
University of New York, 1995), 57–92 (60).

[32] Quoted from J.E. Wright, *The Early History of Heaven* (Oxford: Oxford University
Press, 1992), 47.

[33] "3 I neither learned wisdom Nor have knowledge of the Holy One. 4 Who has
ascended into heaven, or descended? Who has gathered the wind in His fists? Who has
bound the waters in a garment? Who has established all the ends of the earth? What is
His name, and what is His Son's name, If you know?" (Prov 30:3–4 NKJV).

[34] "13 For you have said in your heart: 'I will ascend into heaven, I will exalt my throne
above the stars of God; I will also sit on the mount of the congregation On the farthest
sides of the north; 14 I will ascend above the heights of the clouds, I will be like the Most
High.' 15 Yet you shall be brought down to Sheol, To the lowest depths of the Pit" (Isa
14:13–15 NKJV).

[35] As in Yarbro Collins, "Seven Heavens," 70. Elsewhere she also states that Culianu
showed that there was never a link between the vaults of heaven and the planets (ibid.,
60).

literature, W.G. Lambert claims that the most common number of heavens in second and early first millennia B.C.E. Babylonia was three.[36]

4. ON THE ASCENT LEGENDS

There are some hundred magical incantation texts, called Maqlu, which relate to the ascent to heaven (and the decent to the netherworld).[37] Another text from the seventh century B.C.E. recounts a terrifying vision, in a dream, in which the legendary Kummaya descends to the netherworld.[38]

The tale most closely related to our ascent legend is to be found in the Akkadian text of Adapa. The son of Ea, attempts to ascend to heaven in order to obtain eternal life, but is cast back down to earth.[39] A somewhat similar story is told in the popular myth of Etana, one of the legendary antediluvian kings of the Sumerian dynasty of Kish.[40] There, heaven is depicted as a three level structure.[41] Etana, riding on the back of an eagle, ascends to heaven, but he has to interrupt his journey and is unable to enter the heavenly realm, because humans have no place in this restricted place.[42] Myths concerning seven firmaments are a well known motif in a number of Sumerian incantations.[43] On Assyrian and Babylonian tablets, the heavenly region consists of three heavens of precious stones and bordered by gates.[44] Anu, the king of heaven, dwells in the highest one, where he sits on a throne.

---

[36] Ibid., 64.

[37] T. Abusch, "Ascent to the Stars in a Mesopotamian Ritual: Social Metaphor and Religious Experience," in *Death, Ecstasy, and Other Worldly Journeys*, 15–39.

[38] Kvanvig, *Roots of Apocalyptic*, 390–391.

[39] *ANET*, 101–103.

[40] Ibid., 114–118. The text is known from six exemplars in Neo-Assyrian and Middle-Assyrian.

[41] W. Horowitz, *Mesopotamian Cosmic Geography* (Mesopotamian Civilizations 8; Winona Lake: Eisenbrauns, 1998), 59–60.

[42] Wright, *Early History of Heaven*, 46.

[43] Horowitz, *Mesopotamian Cosmic Geography*, 208–222 (esp. 208); Wright, *Early History of Heaven*, 41.

[44] Horowitz, *Mesopotamian Cosmic Geography*, xiii, 3, 7, 9, 266–267; Wright, *Early History of Heaven*, 33–35.

5. The Persian Period

According to Wilhelm Bousset, it was the Persian context where the notion of the ascent of the soul developed.[45] Thus also in Israel, interest in a heavenly world originates during the Persian period, as a consequence of the removal of God's presence (*shekhinah*), the destruction of His temple, the exile of His people and the cessation of temple worship. Indeed, apocalyptic views and Jewish mysticism overlap. Apocalyptic tales always contained mystical aspects and mysticism developed to satisfy a different religious need. The main purpose of the ascent is a vision of God, the Great Glory, who sits upon the heavenly throne (*merkavah*), "a likeness with the appearance of a man high above it" (Ezek 1:26 NKJV).

We will not discuss here the possible techniques for "ascending." It seems evident that the rhythmic repetition of words and/or sounds and behaviours, such as mourning, weeping, recitation of hymns, invocations or prayers, ascetic practices and fasting may result in a "state of trance," which enables the righteous one to make the ascent.[46]

When the Persians rose to dominate the Near East, between 538 and 333 B.C.E., a change occurred in popular imagery of the human being, the human soul and celestial phenomena. Although the Persians built upon older Assyrian and Babylonian traditions, they developed a different belief pattern. They combined the Babylonian concept of seven, or at least multiple, firmaments with their belief that the soul indeed does enter those heavens. From 600 to 300 B.C.E., Babylonian astrology developed and the zodiac was invented.[47]

As John J. Collins has written, it is widely assumed that Persian thought heavily influenced Jewish apocalyptic beliefs.[48] Most scriptural texts were compiled late in the Sassanian period (221–642 C.E.) but their roots may be found in Persian literature from the pre-Christian period (at least

---

[45] W. Bousset, "Die Himmelsreise der Seele," *AR* 4 (1901): 136–169, 229–273.

[46] See M. Himmelfarb, "The Practice of Ascent in the Ancient Mediterranean World," in *Death, Ecstasy, and Other Worldly Journeys*, 121–137; P. Alexander, "3 (Hebrew Apocalypse of) Enoch (Fifth–Sixth Century A.D.): A New Translation and Introduction," in *OTP* 1:223–302 (233).

[47] Cf. the development of personal horoscopy, which related astronomy to a "science" that determined calendrical issues. Qumran texts such as 4Q186, 4Q318, 4Q534, etc. or Noah's encounter in 1QapGen ar V or 4Q204 (*1 En.* 106) are good examples of this kind of science.

[48] J.J. Collins, *The Apocalyptic Imagination: An Introduction to Jewish Apocalyptic Literature* (2nd ed.; The Biblical Resource Series; Grand Rapids: Eerdmans, 1998), 29.

as early as the Seleucid dynasty 312–247 B.C.E. or the Parthian dynasty 247 B.C.E.–226 C.E.).

Throughout Persian history, visionary journey narratives, as for example Zarathustra who seeks immortality or the heavenly journey of Arda Viraf (Artai Viraz), seem to be derived from more ancient literature. According to Anders Hultgård, the vision and ascent to heaven of Vishtaspa is obviously based upon Avestic material.[49] In the case of the visionaries Vistaspa and Artai Viraz, the soul leaves the body while the body remains on earth.[50] Arda Viraf was supposedly selected by the assembly to test the truth of Zoroastrianism. After seven days, he awakes joyous, bringing greetings to the assembly from Ahura Mazda, Zarathustra and the gods of the dead. The number seven is often mentioned in the text of Arda Viraf.[51]

Yet another ascension to heaven myth is that dealing with the magi Kartir, mentioned in a fragmentary inscription dating from the beginning of the Sassanian period (third century C.E.). This legend describes Kartir's journey to the East, where, at last, he reaches heaven and is shown the place that has been reserved for him in paradise. Then, he travels through hell and crosses the bridge of Cinvat. On the way, he traverses three levels and then is shown a throne of gold, a throne reserved for the soul of the righteous one.[52] The *Videvat* (19–20) mentions the ascension of the soul. On the third day after death, the soul is taken by a young girl, bright and white, and then travels, finally crossing the bridge into paradise. Vohu Mana rises from his golden throne and speaks with the soul of the Righteous Person, who then continuous his journey to the throne of Ahura Mazda.[53]

A combination of older Persian traditions and later apocalyptic material is found in the Mandaic tale of Dinanukht, who ascended to the

---

[49] A. Hultgård, "Mythe et histoire dans l'Iran ancien: Étude de quelques thèmes dans le *Bahman Yašt*," in *Apocalyptique iranienne et dualisme qoumrânien* (ed. G. Widengren, A. Hultgård, and M. Philonenko; Recherches intertestamentaires 2; Paris: Maisonneuve, 1995), 63–162 (145 n. 164).

[50] Ibid., 148.

[51] M. Haug and E.W. West, eds., *The Book of Arda Viraf: The Pahlavi Text Prepared by Destur Hoshangji Jamaspji Asa, Revised and Collated with further MSS., with an English Translation and Introduction, and an Appendix Containing the Texts and Translations of the Gosht-i Fryano, and Hadokht-nask* (Bombay: Government Central Book, 1872).

[52] A. Hultgård, "Trône de Dieu et trône des justes dans les traditions de l'Iran ancien," in *Le trône de Dieu* (ed. M. Philonenko; WUNT 69; Tübingen: Mohr Siebeck, 1993), 1–18 (12–13).

[53] Ibid., 8–9.

seven heavens. Islamic legends also mention the seven firmaments.[54] Not only are they cited several times in the Koran, but also in a long legend called Miradj-Nameh, preserved in Turkish, which relates the ascension of Mohammed and his journey through seven heavens. The seven heavens are also described in detail in the Babylonian Talmud (*b. Ḥag.* 12b; *b. Menaḥ.* 39a) and in *2 Enoch*.

6. THE HEBREW BIBLE, POST-BIBLICAL LITERATURE, AND QUMRAN

Although the Hebrew Bible itself is silent with regard to the number of heavens, it would seem that, during their Babylonian exile, the Jews adopted Babylonian cosmogony[55] and the sevenfold division of the heavenly realm[56] and incorporated them into their belief systems. Milik posits this idea already in his *Books of Enoch*, where he tries to explain that the ascent of Enoch and his extraterrestrial journey was strongly influenced by Mesopotamian cosmic geography.[57] Milik expresses the same opinion regarding Levi's ascent to heaven. He often refers to the similarities between Enoch and Levi. The apocryphal literature and later Jewish writings show an increasing interest in the heavenly realm.[58] Several Jewish and Christian apocalyptic texts, written between the second century B.C.E. and the second century C.E., use the same motifs and the existence of seven heavens is depicted not only in *T. Levi*, but also in the Babylonian Talmud (*Ḥagigah*), the *Ascension of Isaiah* (preserved in Ethiopian), *2 Enoch*, and the *Apocalypse of Abraham* (preserved in Slavonic), although other ascension legends, such as the *Apocalypse of Baruch*, speak of five firmaments.

Milik mentions the world view of the church father Irenaeus of Lyon who wrote: "Now this world is encompassed by seven heavens, in which dwell powers and angels and archangels, doing service to God, the Al-

---

[54] C.J. Gruber and F.S. Colby, *The Prophet's Ascension: Cross-Cultural Encounters With the Islamic* Miʿrāj *Tales* (Bloomington: Indiana University Press, 2010), 231–232, 299, etc.

[55] See E. Unger, "From the Cosmos Picture to the World Map," *Imago Mundi* 2 (1937): 1–7; Horowitz, *Mesopotamian Cosmic Geography*, 20–42.

[56] See ibid., 208–222.

[57] Milik, *Books of Enoch*, 15–16; P. Grelot, "La géographie mythique d' Hénoch," *RB* 65 (1965): 23–69.

[58] The biblical expression "heaven of heaven" indicates at least two firmaments. If we translate the expression as "heaven of heavens," it implies at least 3 firmaments. But, certainly, in pre-exilic times the heavens are reserved for the Lord (Deut 10:14: "Indeed

mighty and Maker of all things, not as though He was in need, but that they may not be idle and unprofitable and ineffectual."[59] On the other hand, he also states that the three heaven theory is cited in 2 Cor 12:2, a text from the first century C.E.

7. CONCLUSION

These reconstructions give an idea of J.T. Milik's work on the *Testament of Levi* and his views as to the oldest form of the text and its composition. As with any reconstruction, its *Vorlage* cannot be determined absolutely, given the present state of research. Therefore, it must be considered hypothetical and in some ways speculative.[60] I hope that Milik's reconstruction of the Aramaic text based upon tiny fragments will not arouse controversy as was the case with his reconstruction of the text of *1 Enoch*. As long as no other new texts are found, Milik's version, following the order of the Greek *T. Levi* in *T. 12 Patr.*, is justified and merits being presented to the scholarly world.

With Milik's decipherment of 1Q21 37 1 (and Puech's corroboration), the existence of three firmaments in *ALD* is confirmed, which by no means excludes the possible seven heaven concept suggested by Milik. The Greek *T. Levi* (2:1–5:3) includes two versions, one involving three heavens and one containing seven heavens. According to Charles, Bietenhard, and Kee, the Greek text evolved from a three heaven to a seven heaven schema. On the other hand, H.J. de Jonge,[61] in agreement with

---

heaven and the highest heavens belong to the Lord your God, also the earth with all that is in it." [NKJV]). From Qumran we have the fragmentary text of the Book of Mysteries, and the Songs of the Sabbath Sacrifice that prove an increasing interest in the heavenly realm. Also, in John 14:2, Jesus reveals that "in My Father's house are many mansions" (NKJV).

[59] Irenaeus, *Epid.* 9. Translation according to J. Armitage Robinson, *St Irenaeus: The Demonstration of the Apostolic Preaching: Translated from the Armenian with Introduction and Notes* (Translations of Christian Literature, Series IV: Oriental Texts; London: SPCK, 1920), 77.

[60] See Drawnel, *Aramaic Wisdom Text*, 13: "It must be stressed that, notwithstanding all the painstakingly undertaken restoration, the *Document* still remains a fragmentary composition. Its beginning and end are lacking, the results of the text reconstruction are, therefore, not a final word concerning the textual form of the whole work. Further research and, hopefully, further manuscript discovery, may shed a new light and change many of the conclusions delineated in this study."

[61] H.J. de Jonge, "Die Textüberlieferung der Testamente der zwölf Patriarchen," *ZNW* 63 (1972): 45–62 (esp. 60).

Hunkin,[62] whose edition improved upon that of Charles, demonstrates that a seven heaven cosmography was the original concept.[63]

The motifs of three and seven firmaments are of Mesopotamian origin and are also part of Mandaic cosmogony.[64] They reflect a wide spread eastern tradition well represented in the Babylonian Talmud (*b. Ḥag.* 12b–13a; *b. Menaḥ.* 39a), in *3 Enoch* and in the Koran.[65]

The idea that the soul returns to the heavenly realm was common to both Persia[66] and Greece.[67] However, both the Jewish and Christian ascent to heaven legends have so much in common with Persian legends and Babylonian cosmography in the vocabulary, the architectural representation of the heavenly realm, and the belief in a final judgement of the righteous that one should not deny a certain dependence from ancient oriental sources.

APPENDIX 1

MILIK'S TEXT AND TRANSLATION

Where Milik's readings differ from other editions, it is hoped that they will give rise to re-examination of the fragments in question. Émile Puech has already corrected many of these tiny fragments and his reconstructions are generally in agreement with Milik's. Puech confirms that they all belong to a scroll of the *Testament of Levi* and comes to the conclusion that the scroll 1Q21 is more recent than the *ALD* copies coming from Cave 4 (4Q213, 213a, 213b, 4Q214 and 214b) and dates it's fragments to the beginning of the first century B.C.E.[68]

Below, we present Milik's reconstruction of the first 48 verses of the document, from a total of 432.[69] The first three "verses" are borrowed

---

[62] J.W. Hunkin, "The Testaments of the Twelve Patriarchs," *JTS* 16 (1915): 80–97.

[63] See the detailed discussion in Wright, *Early History of Heaven*, 143–148 and 262 nn. 38–39.

[64] E.S. Drower, *The Mandaeans of Iraq and Iran: Their Cults, Customs, Magic Legends, and Folklore* (Oxford: Clarendon, 1937; repr. Leiden: Brill, 1962), 253 n. 33 and 254 fig. 14.

[65] See also the late Islamic legend of Mohammed's ascent to the seven heavens in A. Pavet de Courteille, ed., *Mirâdj-nâmeh: Récit de l'ascension de Mahomet au ciel composé A.H. 840 (1436/1437): Texte turc-oriental, publié pour la première fois d'après le manuscript ouïgour de la Bibliothèque Nationale et traduit en français* (1882; repr. Amsterdam: Philo, 1975).

[66] For the epigraphic evidence of the belief in an afterlife, see P. Lecoq, *Les inscriptions de la Perse achéménide* (L'aube des peuples; Paris: Gallimard, 1997).

[67] Wright, *Early History of Heaven*, 109.

[68] Puech, "Notes sur le *Testament de Lévi* de la grotte 1 (1Q21)," 310.

[69] Milik, "Traduction continue du Testament de Lévi," 5–24.

from *T. Levi* 1:1–2; 2:1–3 (resulting in v. in1–3), which is followed by the Aramaic prayer of Levi of 4Q213a (v. 4) and, lastly, by a retranslation of the Greek fragment Koutloumousiou 39[70] (the vision and ascent to heaven of Levi; it is similar to *T. Levi* 2:7–12). Verses 40–48 are a hypothetical reconstruction based upon 4Q213a and the minute fragments of 1Q21.

The symbols as employed by Milik are:

– in(itial or incipit?)1, in4, in6 = *T. Levi* 1:1–2:4?
– 1, 133, 402: verses conserved in *ALD* or Greek *T. Levi*, and sometimes only in *T. Levi*
– (67), (113), (346): verses of Greek *T. Levi* reworked or summarized;
– ?115, ?413, ?419: fragments of *ALD* or citations of Greek *T. Levi* of uncertain origin;
– [[alternative reading]]

Concerning the Greek it should be mentioned that the accents are missing in Milik's unfinished manuscript, hand typed by his wife Y. Zaluska.

in1 (= *T. Levi* 1:1–2) /¹ Ἀντίγραφον λόγων Λευί, ὅσα διέθετο τοῖς υἱοῖς αὐτοῦ, κατὰ πάντα ἃ ποιήσουσι, καὶ ὅσα συναντήσει αὐτοῖς ἕως ἡμέρας κρίσεως.
in2/² Ὑγιαίνων ἦν ὅτε ἐκάλεσεν αὐτοὺς πρὸς ἑαυτόν· ὤφθη γὰρ αὐτῷ, ὅτι μέλλει ἀποθνήσκειν. Καὶ ὅτε συνήχθησαν, εἶπε πρὸς αὐτούς·
in3 (= *T. Levi* 2:1–4) /¹ Ἐγὼ Λευὶ ἐν Χαρρὰν συνελήφθην, καὶ ἐτέχθην ἐκεῖ, καὶ μετὰ ταῦτα ἦλθον σὺν τῷ πατρὶ εἰς Σίκιμα.
in4/² Ἤμην δὲ νεώτερος, ὡσεὶ ἐτῶν εἴκοσι, ὅτε ἐποίησα μετὰ Συμεὼν τὴν ἐκδίκησιν τῆς ἀδελφῆς ἡμῶν Δίνας ἀπὸ τοῦ Ἐμμώρ.
in5/³ Ὡς δὲ ἐποιμαίνομεν ἐν Ἀβελμαούλ, πνεῦμα συνέσεως Κυρίου ἦλθεν ἐπ' ἐμέ, καὶ πάντας ἑώρων ἀνθρώπους ἀφανίσαντας τὴν ὁδὸν αὐτῶν, καὶ ὅτι τείχη ᾠκοδόμησεν ἑαυτῇ ἡ ἀδικία, καὶ ἐπὶ πύργους ἡ ἀνομία κάθηται,
in6/⁴ καὶ ἐλυπούμην περὶ τοῦ γένους τῶν ἀνθρώπων ...

4Q213a

1   ‏[באדין שחית לבושי ומדכא]אנה ⁷ [להן במין דכין
2   ‏וכל בשרי במיין חיין רח[ע]ת וכל ⁸ [ארחתי עבדת קשיטן
3   ‏אדי]ן נטלת לשמיא ⁹ [עיני ואנפי ופומי פתחת ומללת]
4   ‏ואצבעת כפי וידי ¹⁰ [פרשת בקשט מן קדם קדשיא וצלית ו]אמרת
5   ‏מרי אנתה ¹¹ [מתבנן כל לבבין וכל מחשבת יצר א]נתה בלחודיך ידע
6   ‏[וכען ברכני ובני בתרי והב לי כל ¹² [ארחת קשט
7   ‏ארחק ¹³ [מני מרי רוח רשע ומחשבת יצרא ביש] וזנותא דחא מני

⁷⁰ J.T. Milik, "Le Testament de Lévi en araméen: Fragment de la grotte 4 de Qumrân (Pl. IV)," *RB* 62 (1955): 398–406; Drawnel, *Aramaic Wisdom Text*, 98–99.

8   מרי חזא לי רוח קדשא וח[כמה ומנדע וגבורה ¹⁵ [הב לי ¹⁴[

9   מעבד די רעא לכה ולא]שכחה רחמיך קדמיך ¹⁶ [מרי

10   למדכר ככל רעותך[ד]שפיר ודטב קדמיך ¹⁷ [ולאודיה מליך עמי מרי

11   [אל תשלט בי כל שטן ¹⁸ [לאטעותני מן ארחך

12   רחם ע]לי מרי וקרבני למהוא לכה [למהוא עבדך ולשמשותך בטב]

13   ור שלמך להוא סחור ² [סחור לי ומטלת שלטנך תטללני מן כל באיש]

14–16   [הב לי מרי ...]⁴ [... ³

17   דכר מרי] לע[בדך אברהם ואל תסתר אנפיך מן בר עבדך יעקב ⁵

18   אנתה] ⁶ מרי ב[רכת לאברהם אבי ולשרה אמי

19   ואמרת למהב להן] ⁷ זרע דק[שט מתברך לעלמיא

20   ושמע קל צלות יעקב וצוחת] ⁸ צלות עב[דך לוי

21   למהוא לכה קריב אן משתף עבדך לעבדיך כדי]⁷¹

22   דין קשט ל[כ]ל עלמא לי ולבני לכל דרי עלמיא ⁹

23   ואל תרחק] ¹⁰ לבר עבדך מן ק[דמיך כל יומי עלמא

24   ושתקת ולא צלית עוד [

25   באדין נגדת ב[ה שעתא לשכם ואזלת לדרת ביתנה ¹¹

26   ועלת ¹² על אבי יעקוב וכד[י] אחוית לה חזוי

27   אמר לי אבי למתב] ¹³ מן אבל מין

28   אדין] סלקת אנה על טור גרזין ועל ראשה] ¹⁴ שכבת

29   ויתבת אנה ע]ל כף חד והא חלמין עלי נפלו] ¹⁵ vacat

30   אדין חזוין אחזית] בחלמי וחזית עבדין רברבין] ¹⁶ בחזית⁷² חזויא

31   וחזית שמ[יא מן עלא פתיחין וטור חד מן] ¹⁷ תחותי

32   רם עד דבק לשמי[א והוא אנה עלוהי

33   וארו אתפתחו] ¹⁸ לי תרעי שמיא ומלאך חד [קרא לי

34   ואמר לוי עול

4Q213+1Q21

35   באדין עלנה] בשמין קד[מין וחזית תמן חשוכא רבא

36   ועברונה מן שמיא ועלת לשמין קדמיא תנינן

37   וחזית תמן מין מתלין במציע אלן שגיאין לאלן

38   תלג וכפור מן תחתי ואשה משתלהבה מן מיא עליהון

39   ואעלוני מל[אך] אלה [לש]מין תליתי[ן מן עלה ⁴

40   וחזית תמן נהו[ר שמיא ל[חדה זהיר מן תרין

41   ברקין ש[גיאי]ן וזיקין רהטי[ן ולא אית]י להון ⁵

42   כל משחה ל[מנין דגליהון ולא הוה כל קץ]

43   ברומי [שמיא אלן   איך די] הוין ש[מיא תרין

44   ושאלת א[נה אי די ן [מנהון פריש וא]מרת מה דן⁷³ שמיא א[לן ⁶

45   וענה לי מלאכא אמר אלן ואמ]ר לי עד [תנה

46   ואמ]ר לי עד [תנה תלתת ⁷ שמיא אנה אח[זי]ת ל[ך

47   ועוד תחזה ארבעת שמיא נהירין] שגיא [מן אלן

48   ולא תכול לאדמיה עליהון על פר[שא [די שמיא אנון

      כדי תעול תמן ...] ⁸

---

⁷¹ We corrected Milik's suggestion: ומשתף עבד במליך למעבד.

⁷² Milik reads בחזות which is grammatically more correct.

⁷³ Milik's initial reading of 1Q21 37 3 is:]○ מה○○ שמיא ○ל[. Puech reads 1Q21 37b:

French Translation:

in1 Copie des paroles de Lévi qu'il recommanda à ses fils concernant ce qu'ils auront à faire et ce qui leur arrivera jusqu'au jour du jugement. in2 Il était encore en bonne santé lorsqu'il les convoqua chez lui, et cela en raison de la vision où il lui avait été montré qu'il allait mourir. Et quand ils furent réunis il leur dit: in3 Moi Lévi, je fus conçu à Harran et ce fut là que je naquis. in4 J'étais tout jeune— j'avais dix-huit ans, tandis que Siméon mon frère avait vingt ans, lorsque nous vengeâmes notre sœur Dinah sur Sichem et Hamor. in5 Quand je faisais paître mon troupeau à ʾAbel Mayîn, l'esprit d'intelligence vint sur moi et je vis tous les hommes en train de corrompre leurs voies, et l'injustice se construire des tours. in6 Je me mis donc en deuil pour pleurer le genre humain, et je priai Dieu.

1 Alors je nettoyai mes vêtements et les purifiai dans de l'eau pure 2; et je lavai mon corps entiers dans de l'eau vive et toutes mes voies je les rendis droites. 3 Puis je levai mes yeux et mon visage vers le ciel et j'ouvris ma bouche et je parlai; 4 j'étendis les doigts de mes mains et de mes bras comme il le faut en face du sanctuaire céleste et je priai et je dis:

5 «Mon[74] Seigneur, tu connais tous les cœurs et toutes les intentions cal- culées, toi seul tu (les) sais. 6 Et maintenant bénis-moi et mes enfants après moi[75] et accorde-moi tous les chemins de justice.[76] 7 Eloigne de moi, mon Seigneur, l'esprit d'impiété et écarte de moi des pensées de mauvais penchant et la concu- piscence écarte-(la) de moi. 8 Mon Seigneur, montre moi l'esprit saint et sagesse, connaissance et force accorde-(les) moi 9 pour accomplir[77] ce qui te plaît et trou- ver ainsi ta miséricorde devant toi, mon Seigneur; 10 et pour commémorer selon ton plaisir ce qui est beau et bon devant toi et louer tes actes à mon égard, mon Seigneur. 11 Qu'aucun Satan ne me domine pour m'égarer hors de ta voie. 12 Aie donc pitié de moi, mon Seigneur, et laisse-moi t'approcher pour devenir ton serviteur et fidèle ministre. 13 Que le rempart de ta paix m'entoure et que l'abri de ta domination m'abrite de tout mal. 14 Livre, mon Seigneur, mes ennemis ... 15 Pour ceci, efface l'iniquité de dessous le ciel et élimine l'iniquité de la face de la terre. 16 Purifie mon cœur, mon Seigneur, de toute impureté et je m'élèverai vers toi, moi-même Lévi. 17 Souviens-toi, mon Seigneur, de ton serviteur Abraham et ne détourne pas ta face du fils de ton serviteur Jacob. 18 Toi, mon Seigneur, tu avais béni Abraham mon père et Sarah ma mère 19 et tu as promis de leur donner une descendance[78] juste bénie pour les siècles. 20 Exauce donc la prière de ton serviteur Lévi 21 pour qu'il te devienne proche si tu associes ton serviteur à tes

---

מ]ן דן שמיא ו[א]מרת מה ר], cf. Puech, "Notes sur le *Testament de Lévi* de la grotte 1 (1Q21)," 304.

[74] With the Aramaic, the Greek has κύριε "O Lord! (Seigneur!)"

[75] Or with the Greek "my children (which) are with me."

[76] Or "ways of justice"; Milik, "Le Testament de Lévi en araméen," 402, translates "chemins de vérité."

[77] Lit. "to make, to do."

[78] Lit. "seed of justice."

affaires comme 22 afin qu'une loi juste soit accomplie pour toute l'éternité par moi et par mes fils pour toutes les générations des siècles. 23 Et n'écarte aucun fils de ton serviteur loin de ta présence, tous les jours de l'éternité».

24 Puis je me tus et ne priai plus.

25 Ensuite je me rendis rapidement à Sichem et j'entrai dans la cour de notre maison 26 et pénétrai chez mon père Jacob. Et lorsque lui racontai-je ma vision, 27 mon père m'ordonna de rentrer de ʾAbel Mayîn.

28 Puis je montai sur le mont Garizim et sur son sommet je me couchai; 29 je m'assis donc sur une pierre et voici que les songes m'assaillirent. 30 Puis des visions me furent montrées dans mon songe et je vis des grandes merveilles à travers la vision. 31 Je vis les cieux en haut qui s'ouvraient et une montagne qui apparaissait en bas, 32 si haute qu'elle touchait les cieux, tandis que moi je me trouvais sur elle. 33 Et voici que s'ouvrirent devant moi les portes du ciel et un ange m'appela 34 disant: «Lévi, entre donc!»

35 Ensuite nous entrâmes dans le premier ciel et je vis là-bas une grande obscurité. 36 Alors nous passâmes du premier ciel et j'entrai dans le deuxième, 37 et je vis là-bas des eaux abondantes suspendues entre les deux cieux; 38 neige et glace étaient au-dessus des eaux et un feu brûlant au-dessus d'elles. 39 Et en plus l'ange de Dieu m'introduisit au troisième ciel, plus haut, 40 et je vis là la lumière du ciel, beaucoup plus brillante que celle des deux (premiers) cieux, 41 (ainsi que des tonnerres nombreux et des grands éclairs qui parcouraient le ciel) sans qu'ils mettent 42 mesure au nombre de leurs apparitions. Et il n'y avait aucune limite 43 à la hauteur de ce ciel-ci comme il y'en avait à celle des deux cieux. 44 Et je demandai: «Lequel de ces trois cieux est plus important?» Et je dis: «Quelle est la signification de ces cieux?» 45 Et l'ange me répondit disant: «Ne t'émerveille pas tellement sur ceux-ci!» 46 Et il me dit: «Jusqu'ici je t'ai montré trois cieux, 47 mais tu verras encore quatre autres cieux beaucoup plus lumineux que ceux-ci 48 et tu ne seras pas à même de les décrire, encore moins de saisir l'importance de ces cieux-là. 49 Quand tu y entreras …

APPENDIX 2
THE FRAGMENT ABOUT THE THREE HEAVENS
(1Q21 37) IN COMPARISON WITH 1Q21 1 AND 39

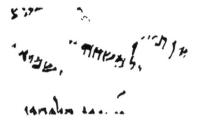

Fig. 1. Drawing of 1Q21 37 according to
PAM 40.540[79]

The mention of the third sky in 1Q21 37 1[80] fills in vv. 39, 44 and 46 of
Milik's reconstructed text by using 1Q21 32–33 + 37 1–3.

1 [ואעלני מלאכא לש[מין תלי]ת[מין עלה וחזית תמן נהו]ר שמיא ל[חדה זהיר מן]

2 [תרין שמי[ן ולא אית[י]כל משחה ל[ ]

3 [ושאלת א[נה אי דן [...] א[מֹרת מה דן שמיא א[לין]

Comparison of 1Q21 37 with 1Q21 1 and 39

Fig. 2. Drawing of 1Q21 1 according to PAM 40.540

Fig. 3. Drawing of 1Q21 39 according to PAM 40.540

---

[79] The images are easily accessible in E. Tov, ed., *The Dead Sea Scrolls Electronic Reference Library* (rev. ed.; Leiden: Brill, 2006).

[80] Puech, "Notes sur le *Testament de Lévi* de la grotte 1 (1Q21)," 305; U. Schattner-Rieser, "J.T. Milik's Monograph on the Testament of Levi and the Reconstructed Aramaic Text of the Prayer of Levi and the Vision of Levi's Ascent to Heaven from Qumran Caves 4 and 1," *QC* 15 (2007): 139–155; Milik, "Traduction continue du Testament de Lévi," 5–24; Kapera, "Preliminary Information," 109–112.

QUMRAN BIBLICAL INTERPRETATION IN THE LIGHT OF ANCIENT NEAR EASTERN HISTORIOGRAPHY

Ida Fröhlich

Pázmány Péter Catholic Univesity, Budapest-Piliscsaba

Modern Historiography— Historical Memory in the Ancient Near East

Ancient Near Eastern cultures, which have produced a bulk of written material, have not left us detailed reports about their own history. Ancient Mesopotamia is a well documented culture, but the noticeable absence of historical literature has been noted repeatedly: "texts are lacking that would attest to the awareness of the scribes to the existence of a historical continuum in the Mesopotamian civilization of which they themselves and their tradition were only a part."[1] Qumran was a particular site of ancient Israelite culture. The library of the community living on the site contained, besides biblical manuscripts, works reflecting their worldview and works expressing their ideas, some of them referring to conflicts within their social spheres. Unfortunately, nothing about the background of these conflicts or the history of the writers has been found. Any regular historiography is absent. According to the expectations of modern history writing—or at least, in view of what ancient historiographers like Herodotus and his Greek colleagues did—no detailed narrative in chronological order was written on the history of the community. Still, one cannot say that they were not interested in history—in biblical history, as well as their own history—since *pesharim* were written as interpretations of prophetic revelations. Nevertheless, the forms for the expression of interest in the past were very different from ancient Greek ones (and from modern ones).

Ancient Israel had a long historical tradition, and a particular tradition of history writing. The history of Israel's past is shaped in various books

---

[1] A.L. Oppenheim, *Ancient Mesopotamia: Portrait of a Dead Civilization* (rev. ed.; Chicago: University of Chicago Press, 1964), 19.

focusing on various eras of history. These are not always reliable to the standard of modern historiography; the narratives are presented with the help of literary and folkloristic patterns and miraculous events.[2] The desire to present a historical description and the reliability of the product are not the same. For that purpose, it is necessary to distinguish the aim of the historiographer and the historical facts which can be reconstructed on the basis of other sources.[3] "We may therefore conclude that to qualify as a historiographic work, it is only necessary for the author to be consciously seeking to describe the past. Whether or not it belongs to this specific genre is determined neither by its historical reliability nor by the degree of its objectivity."[4]

The historical sequence, which opens in the book of Genesis and concludes at the end of 2 Kings, was written to perpetuate historical memory. The genre historiography represents a large portion of biblical literature, and thereby acquires qualitative importance.[5] At the same time, these works are very reticent. Even historical texts (i.e., in texts which, according to Huizinga's definition, were intended to accurately depict events of history) are very laconic.[6] Aside from some highlighted figures like Saul, David and Solomon, the books of Kings and Chronicles do not go into details concerning the history of the monarchy. The authors might have worked from royal annals, more exhaustive materials than what

---

[2] Fundamentalist interpretation tries to prove miraculous events with the help of phenomena and results drawn from natural sciences. This is not necessary, since the works had a special purpose, to express special ideas. The intention of the authors was not to present reliable natural facts, but to convey an idea through the example of the supernatural.

[3] Works with the expression "biblical historiography" in their titles usually deal with the difference between events narrated and the background reality of these events. Ideas and ideology appearing in biblical history writing are treated more infrequently. For a general overview of ancient Near Eastern and biblical historiography in the above sense, see R.C. Dentan and J.J. Oberman, eds., *The Idea of History in the Ancient Near East* (AOS 38; New Haven: Yale University Press, 1955; re-edition New Haven: American Oriental Society, 1983); D.N. Freedman, "The Biblical Idea of History," *Int* 21 (1967): 32–49; H. Tadmor and M. Weinfeld, eds., *History, Historiography and Interpretation: Studies in Biblical and Cuneiform Literatures* (Jerusalem: Magnes, 1983). Y. Amit, *History and Ideology: An Introduction to Historiography in the Hebrew Bible* (Sheffield: Sheffield Academic Press, 1997) is a new overview on history writing in the Bible. See also H. Cancik, *Grundzüge der hethitischen und alttestamentlichen Geschichtsschreibung* (Abhandlungen des Deutschen Palästinavereins 4; Wiesbaden: Harrasowitz, 1976).

[4] Amit, *History and Ideology*, 14.

[5] Ibid., 11.

[6] J. Huizinga, "A Definition of the Concept of History," in *Philosophy and History: Essays presented to Ernst Cassirer* (ed. R. Klibansky and H.J. Paton; Oxford: Clarendon, 1936; repr. New York: Harper & Row, 1963), 1–10, esp. 10.

has been preserved in the biblical text. The history of the kingdom of Israel and then the divided monarchy was redacted for the first time in the Deuteronomistic History.[7] Chronicles, the re-telling of the history of the kingdoms in the frame of a world history, is another historical work—with sometimes different, but not more detailed description of the divided monarchy. Both works contain a series of stereotyped descriptions and not detailed historical narratives à la Herodotus, which had become the basis of European historiography.[8] It is worthy of note here that "history is not how things happened, but an incomplete account, written toward a specific end, of selected developments. This is an important point, ignored in the survey of Near Eastern historiography previously mentioned."[9]

Historiography is an important form of cultural memory. Remembering the past in a community constitutes a form of self-definition.[10] Biblical and ancient Near Eastern writings with historical concern—although they represent a form different from that of Greek history writing—are extremely important since they give an insight into the thinking and identity of the group that produced them. It reflects how they were thinking about the process of history, the causes and consequences of events, and what they considered important (important things were meant to be motives of events). Special narrative forms used as historiography are also informative of the concepts of the culture in which they were written.[11] My aim here is to give a short overview of the specific forms and methods of pieces of historical memory preserved in Qumran writings,

---

[7] On the Deuteronomistic History and its problems, as well as Deuteronomistic history writing, see T. Römer, *The So-Called Deuteronomistic History: A Sociological, Historical and Literary Introduction* (London: T&T Clark, 2005). On history writing in the Chronicles, see S. Japhet, *The Ideology of the Book of Chronicles and its Place in Biblical Thought* (trans. A. Barber; BEATAJ 9; Bern: Peter Lang, 1989).

[8] On questions related to Greek history writing and modern historiography, there is A. Momigliano's very inspiring *The Classical Foundations of Modern Historiography* (Berkeley: University of California Press, 1990).

[9] B. Halpern, *The First Historians: The Hebrew Bible and History* (Philadelphia: Pennsylvania State University Press, 1996), 7. Modern comprehensive works deal only with "Greek" and "European" types of historiography, see E. Breisach, *Historiography: Ancient, Medieval, and Modern* (Chicago: University of Chicago Press, 1983). The introductory part devotes but a few sentences to ancient Near Eastern history writing.

[10] Jan Assmann gives an overall picture on the forms of historical memory. See the chapter "Formen kollektiver Erinnerung: Kommunikatives und kulturelles Gedächtnis" in his *Das kulturelle Gedächtnis: Schrift, Erinnerung und politische Identität in frühen Hochkulturen* (München: Beck, 1997), 48–66.

[11] For an overview on Mesopotamian historiography, see J.J. Finkelstein, "Mesopotamian Historiography," *Proceedings of the American Philosophical Society* 107 (1963):

in the background of ancient Near Eastern historiography—that is, how much specific the Qumran view is and how it correlates with forms and methods of historical memory which are known from other ancient Near Eastern cultures.

Investigated herein are concepts of historical time and ideology manifested in the descriptions of the course of history as they are reflected in the texts bearing the historical memory of the Qumran community. Historical tradition here has an overall meaning, including both traditions of the patriarchal age (which meant a real history for the Qumran reader) and the historical memory of the community of Qumran. The present study aims to examine the attitudes towards history that the authors of these texts held, what the writers thought to be important in history, what they thought to be the engine of history, and what they thought about the causes of events and corollaries of human deeds.

HISTORICAL MEMORY IN QUMRAN

The basic form of Qumran historical memory is interpretation. Biblical history is frequently interpreted in Qumran works. Qumran interpretation has two basic forms: one is the paraphrasing of biblical narratives, the other an explicit interpretation of texts. Biblical historical tradition is paraphrased and interpreted in a number of so-called para-biblical texts and "rewritten Bibles."[12] The explicit interpretation form is represented in the *pesharim*,[13] a special form of historical memory in the life of the Qumran community. The *pesharim* interpret continuous biblical texts verse by verse by means of various literary devices. Interpretations

---

461–472. For principles and methods in Hittite historiography, see H.G. Güterbock, "Hittite Historiography: A Survey" in *History, Historiography and Interpretation*, 21–35.

[12] Para-biblical texts are considered those paraphrasing biblical texts with an interpretative aim. The term "rewritten Bibles" refers, according to G. Vermes, to narratives that follow Scripture, but include "a substantial amount of supplements and interpretative developments." Not everything is retold, while other pericopae are retold with additions and changes. See E. Schürer, *The History of the Jewish People in the Age of Jesus Christ (175 B.C.–A.D. 135): A New English Version* (rev. ed. G. Vermes et al.; 3 vols.; Edinburgh: T&T Clark, 1973–1987), 3.1:326.

[13] The name is the plural form of the noun *pesher* or "interpretation." It designates a group of continuous interpretations written on prophetic books (Isaiah, and five, possibly six of the Minor Prophets) and Psalms. For the *pesher* method and interpretative forms resulting from this method, see S.L. Berrin, "Pesharim," *Encyclopedia of the Dead Sea Scrolls* (ed. L.H. Schiffman and J.C. VanderKam; 2 vols.; Oxford: Oxford University Press, 2000), 2:644–647.

are introduced by the word *pesher* (pl. *pesharim*). These texts were written with the aim of interpreting prophetic and psalm texts as references to events contemporary to the author of the interpretation. The interpreted texts contained meaningful revelations for their intended sectarian audience. Events referred to in the interpretation are episodes memorable in the history of the community. The authors' concept-of and attitude-to history were certainly defined by the community's general attitude toward history. The interpretations themselves speak in veiled terms (for example, using nicknames for real persons) about the history of the community. Thus, the interpretations refer in a coded form to certain events of the history of the community, as well as their conflicts with enemies, supposedly over the second and first centuries B.C.E.

a. *Para-Biblical Texts and Rewritten Bibles*

Let us begin our overview with the so-called para-biblical texts and rewritten Bibles, with works which retell the Bible in some form. 4Q252, 4Q253, 4Q254, and 4Q254a are four fragmentary manuscripts from Qumran Cave 4.[14] They contain implicit commentaries on selected pericopae of the book of Genesis and explicit commentaries on selected passages therein. The most extensive of these texts is 4QCommGen A (4Q252).[15] The text of its first fragment can be divided into two parts of different character: a narrative part, which retells (or, rather only refers to) biblical pericopae, following the biblical order of the narratives; and a second part formed by a series of *pesharim* (i.e., interpretations of biblical citations introduced by the formula *pšrw ʾl*).[16] In spite of its literary diversity, the text as a whole is homogeneous. Arranged in the chronological order of the events found in Genesis, it has a consistent structure throughout.[17] The text of the manuscript seems to be divided into

---

[14] Published by G. Brooke in *DJD* XXII (1996): 185–212, 217–236.

[15] Formerly called "Pesher Genesis" and "Patriarchal Blessings," *4QCommentary on Genesis A* contains six fragments in an early Herodian hand.

[16] H. Stegemann, *Die Essener, Qumran, Johannes der Täufer und Jesus: Ein Sachbuch* (Freiburg: Herder, 1993), 170–172, considered the fragments of 4Q252 as belonging to two different works. G.J. Brooke argued for the unity of the text that begins with col. I of the present text and ends with col. VI, see "The Genre of 4Q252: From Poetry to Pesher," *DSD* 1 (1994): 160–169, esp. 161–165. Sharing this opinion, I will refer to the fragments as parts of the same work.

[17] For a detailed analysis of the sequences in the text, its formal setup and thematic structure, see I. Fröhlich, "Themes, Structure and Genre of Pesher Genesis," *JQR* 85 (1994): 81–90. M.J. Bernstein argues against reading the text in a thematic way and sees it

paragraphs separated by *vacats* (at times in the middle of the line). Each paragraph comprises two pericopae or, respectively, two *pesharim* (except paragraph IV:1–2, which contains a single explicit interpretation referring to Amalek). The pericopae and the *pesharim* illustrate examples of opposite characters. The content of the paragraphs is following:

1. The short introductory sentence—"[In] the four hundred and eightieth year of Noah's life, the end came for Noah" (I:1)—refers to the history of antediluvian mankind. It can be supposed that their history is described according to the Enochic tradition, focusing on the sins of antediluvian humankind, which are sexual misdemeanors (the mixed marriages of heavenly beings with earthly women), practicing sorcery and magic. Events following the deeds of antediluvian humankind are skipped in 4Q252, and the text goes, without mentioning the beginning of the Flood and the events preceding it, to a description of the Flood (with calendar-like addenda about the exact times of the events of the Flood). The second part of the paragraph is formed by a report of Noah's "landing" after the Flood (II:2).[18]

2. The second paragraph cites the biblical mention of the curse of Canaan, his subjection to his relatives (cf. Gen 9:25–26). The background of the cursing of Canaan in the Bible is the violation of a sexual taboo committed by Canaan's father Ham who "saw the nakedness of his father [i.e., Noah] and told his two brethren outside" (Gen 9:22). The next event mentioned in the second paragraph of 4Q252 is a report of Abraham's arrival to Canaan, and the covenant that God made with him (Gen 15) (II:5–13).

3. The sin of the inhabitants of Sodom and Gomorrah forms the content of the beginning of the third paragraph (the background of the story is their sin and homosexuality, which is the violation of a sexual taboo penned in biblical legislation).[19] The second part of the paragraph is formed by a reference to the *Aqedah* (where Abraham merits the covenant) and the blessing of Isaac (cf. Gen 22) (III:1–5, 6–14).

---

as a running biblical commentary in a non-esoteric, simple sense. See his "4Q252: From Rewritten Bible to Biblical Commentary," *JJS* 45 (1994): 1–27.

[18] Unless otherwise indicated, translations from the Hebrew Bible are according to the NRSV and translations of the Dead Sea Scrolls are taken from the *DJD* series.

[19] Cf. Gen 19. Homosexuality is strictly banned in Old Testament legislation, see Lev 20:13; 20:13; cf. 18:22.

4. An oracle on the future seems to form a kind of dividing line in the text. At the same time, it introduces a new form, the *pesher*. The paragraph begins with a citation from Deut 25:19, an oracle about the annihilation of Amalek, enemy of Israel (IV:1–2).[20] From here to the end, the following paragraphs contain a series of explicit quotations followed by interpretations introduced by the term *pesher*.

5. The first fragment of the historical interpretations in *pesher* form is introduced by a citation from the Blessing of Jacob, the disapproval of Ruben, because he had violated a sexual prohibition by having a forbidden relationship with the concubine of his father (cf. Gen 34:22). The second part of the paragraph consists of a citation from the same biblical text, an oracle on the eternal reign of Judah and blessings on the other sons of Jacob (IV:3–7).

Obviously, the series of paragraphs (articulated by *vacats*) of 4Q252 are comprised of contrasting traditions about the sinners and the righteous.[21] In the examples of 4Q252, the sin is connected with the violation of a sexual taboo. The punishment of the sinner is destruction or subjection. The reward of the righteous is rescue from danger and/or taking possession of land. Contemporary readers who were socialized in biblical ethical tradition might have been well aware of the underlying meaning of the references.[22]

4QCommGen B (4Q253) and 4QCommGen C (4Q254) are further fragmentary works which contain Genesis interpretations. The three fragments of 4Q253 are too fragmentary for any thematic structure to be established.[23] There are no overlaps of this text with that of 4Q252. However, some themes are identical, like the story of the Flood. In 4Q253, revelation is given to Noah (1 4), and instructions about clean animals (2 3) are referred to. Besides, the name of Belial is mentioned (3 2). The fragments labeled 4QCommMal (4Q253a) contain a prophetic citation from Mal 3:16–18:

---

[20] The destruction of Amalek has been a theme since the early Jewish interpretative tradition. It can be found in *T. Sim.* 5:4–6:5, and *L.A.B.* on Judg 19. Later Jewish tradition associates Amalek with various sins, foremost with magic and astrology.

[21] The labeling of groups "sinners" and "righteous" goes in the spirit of the Mosaic law. The author of 4Q252 uses Deuteronomic language and shows an apparently strong legal interest. See G.J. Brooke, "The Thematic Content of 4Q252," *JQR* 85 (1995): 33–59.

[22] The punishment of certain sins (sexual sins, bloodshed, magic and cultic impurity) is expulsion from the land and/or extinction of the family (*kārēt*). See P.D. Wright, "Unclean and Clean: Old Testament," *ABD* 6:729–741, esp. 739.

[23] The fragments are written in a late Hasmonean or early Herodian hand.

> [Then those who revered the Lord spoke, each to] his [neighbor. The Lord]
> attended [and listened, and a book of remembrance was written before him
> of those who reveared the Lord and thought on his name.] They shall be
> mine, [says the Lord of hosts, a special possession on the day when I act,
> and I will show pity o]n them as [a man shows pity on his son who serves
> him. Then once more you shall see the difference] between the righteous
> and the wicked, [between one who serves God and the one who does not
> serve him.]   (4Q253a 1 i 2–5)

It is inferential that the prophetic words provide a key to the content
of 4Q253.[24] In all probability, its text contains biblical examples about
the righteous and the wicked, about those who are considered a "special
possession" of the Lord, and those who are not.[25]

The prophetic text provides a key to 4Q252, too, since the concept of
the work matches perfectly with that of Mal 3:16–18 when giving clear
historical examples of the righteous and the wicked—the righteous being
the heir of the land and the wicked the one who losses it. The prophetic
text makes mention of a "book of remembrance." This calls to mind the
fragmentary overviews from Qumran which might have served as *aide
memoires* for historical examples of the sinner and the righteous.

The content of 4QCommGen C (4Q254)[26] partly overlaps with that
of 4Q252. Thus, it might be a variant of the first[27] and a compilation of
historical examples to the prophetical words of Zech 4:14 cited in the text:
"[These are] the two anointed sons who [stand by the Lord of the whole
earth ...]" (4 2). The pericopae examples in the text are the following:
Noah's drunkenness and the cursing of Canaan (1 2–4, based on Gen
9:24–25); a mention of Hagar (2 2); the events leading up to the binding
of Isaac (3 4); promise of the land given to a patriarch (3 6); and the theme

---

[24] The editor of the text thinks that it rather belongs to a commentary on Malachi, see
G. Brooke in *DJD* XXII (1996): 213–215. He further thinks that the quotation refers to
the Teacher of Righteousness, see idem, "Prophecy," *Encyclopedia of the Dead Sea Scrolls*
2:694–700, here 697. Dorothy M. Peters, supposing that 4Q253 and 4Q253a may have
belonged together, argues that the quote from Mal 3:16–18 "may signify a retrospective
view of the flood in Genesis to a time when the first differentiation was made between
the righteous and the wicked" (*Noah Traditions in the Dead Sea Scrolls: Conversations and
Controversies of Antiquity* [SBLEJL 26; Atlanta: SBL, 2008], 165).

[25] The noun *nḥlh* occurs 105 times in the Qumran scrolls, mostly in the works found
in Cave 4.

[26] Written in an early Herodian formal hand, see G. Brooke in *DJD* XXII (1996): 219–
220.

[27] 4Q254 cannot be a second copy of 4Q252, but a parallel text to the work—either a
reworked, complementary version of it, or an interpretation of its narrative material from
a different point of view. In the following, I will deal with the text as a variant of 4Q252.

of the desecration of something (3 8).[28] These are followed by the words of the blessing of Judah and the blessings given to the rest of the sons of Jacob (5–6 1–6 and 7 1–5, based on Gen 49).

4QCommGen D (4Q254a)[29] contains (partly citing Gen 6:15) a description of the measurements of Noah's ark (frgs. 1–2), Noah's debarkation (frg. 3),[30] and something that the raven makes known to the latter generations.

In view of the fragments contained in texts 4Q252–4Q254a, it is 4Q252 alone where the text's formal structure and content, as well as the idea behind this ordering, can be reconstructed. The hypothetical reconstruction of this idea is confirmed by the prophetic citation of 4Q254. The examples of the historical survey in 4Q252 serve as examples for the justification of the idea shaped in the prophetic words, while expressing an unambigous attitude toward history. This attitude is centered around the theme of the land and its appropriation by the righteous. The land provides structure to the survey of the history of humankind, and the history of Israel from the beginning, including the time of the settlement of the Israelite tribes. Three phases are distinct in this process (represented in three paragraphs): sinful humanity lost the land; Canaan lost his right to the land; Ruben lost his birthright and his claim to the land. Moreover, the righteous like Noah, Abraham, and Isaac obtain the land. The oracle about the final doom of Amalek is equal to a symbolic elimination of all those who could endanger the righteous offspring's chances of taking possession of the land. This idea about history is apparently Deuteronomistic. The text might have served those who identified themselves with Judah with historical examples, and it seems to be intended for internal use by the community to reinforce its identity and ideology.[31] Of course, the text does not refer explicitly to this idea. This idea is expressed by the way historical tradition is interpreted and referenced. The series of references and interpretations gives a "skeletonised" overview of history with the recurring manifestation of certain regularities—that of the loss of land by the sinners (especially those committing sins of a sexual nature) and that of the acquisition of land by the righteous, by those who do not violate the Law.

---

[28] *Ḥwll* meaning "pierced" or "profaned" or "trembled." The verb reflects a purity-centered outlook; it is not used in the pertinent part of Genesis.

[29] Three fragments in a developed Herodian formal hand.

[30] Cf. 4Q252 II:1–5.

[31] D.K Falk, *The Parabiblical Texts: Strategies for Extending the Scriptures in the Dead Sea Scrolls* (Library of Second Temple Studies 63; London: T&T Clark, 2007), 139.

b. *Historical Surveys*

The historical survey of the *Damascus Document* (CD 2:2–3:12)[32] is headed by a "theoretical introduction" in the form of the paraphrase of a biblical verse: "and not follow after thoughts of the guilty inclination and after eyes of lust (*'ny znwt*)" (CD 2:16).[33] The expression could contain a primary and a figurative meaning. The primary sense covers the violation of any taboos of sexual character. In a figurative sense (as in many biblical metaphors), the expression is meant as infidelity to God, the practice of cults celebrating alien gods. In the survey of the *Damascus Document*, each example of "*zěnût*" is introduced by the formula "for many went astray through these" (or a variant of this sentence). In the following part of the text, periods characterized either by sin or by righteousness are listed. Unlike 4Q252, each period has here a homogenous character.

1. The first example is the story of the fallen angels (CD 2:17–21), not referred to according to the tradition of Gen 6:1–4, but that of *1 Enoch*, "the heavenly Watchers fell."
2. The second historical symbol is the biblical tradition about the sons of Noah and their families (3:1). Its background could be the story of Noah's drunkenness, the sin of Ham, and the curse of Canaan instead of Ham (Gen 9:18–27). The story refers to the violation of a prohibition of sexual character.[34] Since it is the breaking of a commandment, the tradition referred to in the text of the *Damascus Document* is an example of both: breaking the commandments and committing a sin related to sexuality.
3. The third symbol is the age of Abraham, Isaac, and Jacob—a sinless period due to Abraham, who kept the commandments.
4. The period of the sons of Jacob is interpreted as an age of erring in disobedience, referred to as the age in which "Jacob's sons erred" (3:4–5). The sin behind the reference could be Reuben's lying with

---

[32] The earliest Qumran manuscript of the *Damascus Document* is dated to the beginning of the first century B.C.E. On the basis of the *terminus ante quem* provided by the earliest manuscript and the events referred to in the text, the date of the composition might have been the middle of the second century B.C.E.

[33] The reference is from Num 15:39 with transformations. Num 15:39 says, "And whenever you see this in the tassel, you will remember all the Lord's commands and obey them, and not to go your own wanton ways, led astray by your own hearts and eyes."

[34] Exod 20:23 and 28:42. Prohibition of sexual relations with parents and relatives in Lev 18:7–17.

Bilhah, the concubine of his father (Gen 35:22), which can be interpreted as an example for the sin of *'ny znwt*.

5. The fifth symbol is the example of the Egyptian captivity, when "their children in Egypt walked in the stubbornness of their hearts, in taking counsel against the commandments of God, and doing each one as he thought right" (3:5–10). Thus, the sins committed in Egypt probably consist of infidelity to Yahweh.

In the overview of the *Damascus Document*, periods of sin are listed. All of them are related to sins such as the violation of sexual taboos, the transgression of Noah's laws, and idolatry. An example of the violation of sexual taboos is to be found in four out of five examples. The biblical pericopae referred to are the same as in 4Q252–4Q254a (except the reference to the Egyptian captivity which does not figure in these texts). Nevertheless, using the same examples of sexual sins, supplemented by an example of idolatry, the author of the overview of the *Damascus Document* creates a different system of historical ages from that of 4Q252. In the system of the *Damascus Document*, two sinful periods (and respective falls) are followed by a sinless period. The latter one is followed again by two sinful periods. The sinners are not contrasted with any other contemporary group or person representing a different ethical background. Both Jacob's sons, as well as the generation under Egyptian captivity, are uniformly declared as sinners. The sins serving as a basis for labeling groups and persons as sinners are sexual sins and idolatry.

4Q183 is a fragment of an interpretation on historical events.[35] Two examples for the sinners and one for the righteous are given in the manuscript dated to the late Hasmonean or early Herodian era. The sins are related to bloodshed (1 ii 2) and to cultic offenses, each example of the sin being introduced by this statement: "And they defiled their sanctuary" (1 ii 1). The righteous are told not to commit these sins, to despise wicked property (1 ii 5), and not to walk in "erring spirit" (1 ii 6).

---

[35] Edited under the title *Catenae*, together with 4Q177 and 4Q182, by J.M. Allegro in *DJD* V (1968): 67–74 and 80–81. The bad state of preservation does not allow any relationship to be established between the fragments. A. Steudel, *Der Midrasch zur Eschatologie aus der Qumrangemeinde (4QMidrEschat^{a.b}): Materielle Rekonstruktion, Textbestand, Gattung und traditionsgeschichtliche Einordnung des durch 4Q174 ("Florilegium") und 4Q177 ("Catena A") repräsentierten Werkes aus den Qumranfunden* (STDJ 13; Leiden: Brill, 1994), 155–157, supposes that they form a composition with 4Q182 and 4Q178. This supposition is not confirmed by the text, since there is no overlap between the compositions. See also the comments of M. Kister, "Marginalia Qumranica," *Tarbiz* 17 (1988): 315–325, 321–324 (Hebrew).

The examples cited in the text cannot be identified with any historical
event with any certainty. Mention is made to a cultic sin that is supposedly
followed by a war. A possible biblical candidate for identification could
be 1 Kgs 17, where the Assyrian victory over Israel and the subsequent
exile are interpreted by the Deuteronomistic Historian as a result of
"the sin of Jeroboam"—i.e., the establishment of a state religion in the
northern kingdom with its royal temples, cultic calendar, iconography
and priesthood.[36] From post-biblical period, the rule of the Hasmonean
dynasty and the Roman conquest following it could be candidates for an
historical example.[37]

4Q180 and 4Q181 are fragments of two separate interpretative works
(pesharim) on the historical tradition of Genesis.[38] The title of the work
attested by 4Q180, "pesher on the periods" (pšr 'l hqṣym), is very indicative of the concept of history in the work. In light of the term qēṣ (meaning
"fixed time," "length of time" or "period"), history is a sequence of precisely determined periods.[39] The question is the principle of articulating
historical process, which can be answered on the basis of the content of
the text. The text in the manuscript is divided into paragraphs, separated
by vacats.

The first paragraph might have been a general introduction roughing
in larger chronological units of the history. The text speaks about divine

---

[36] Later prophetic and Deuteronomistic tradition had created from Jeroboam a negative type of ruler, see C.D. Evans, "Naram-Sin and Jeroboam: The Archetypal *Unheils-
herrscher* in Mesopotamian and Biblical Historiography," in *Scripture in Context II: More
Essays on the Comparative Method* (ed. W.W. Hallo, J.C. Moyer, and L.G. Perdue; Winona
Lake: Eisenbrauns, 1983), 97–125. On the northern cult practice and its Deuteronomistic
reception, see J. Debus, *Die Sünde Jerobeams: Studien zur Darstellung Jerobeams und der
Geschichte des Nordreichs in der deuteronomistischen Geschichtsschreibung* (FRLANT 93;
Göttingen: Vandenhoeck & Ruprecht, 1967).

[37] The temple cult under later Hasmonean rulers was considered in Qumran *pesharim*
(middle of the first century B.C.E.) as improper and illegitimate, as shown by recurring
refences to "the evil priest" (*khn hrš'*), an epithet used probably with a collective meaning
for several Hasmonean rulers. See R.A. Kugler, "Priests," *Encyclopedia of the Dead Sea
Scrolls* 2:688–693, esp. 691–692 ("Significance of Priests for the Qumran Community").

[38] The first editor, J.M. Allegro, gave the name "Ages of Creation" to the fragments
belonging to 4Q180–181. The relation of 4Q180 and 4Q181 was discussed by J. Strugnell,
"Notes en marge du volume V des 'Discoveries in the Judaean Desert of Jordan,'" *RevQ* 7
(1970): 163–276 (252–254); J.T. Milik, "Milkî-ṣedeq et Milkî-reša' dans les anciens écrits
juifs et chrétiens," *JJS* 23 (1972): 95–144 (109–124). The fragments belong in fact to two
works, 4Q180 (frgs. 1–12, called also "Pesher on the Periods") and 4Q181, see D. Dimant,
"The 'Pesher on the Periods' (4Q180 and 4Q181)," *IOS* 9 (1979): 77–102.

[39] The concept is known in biblical literature, see Dan 9:24–27, and in several Qumran
writings, see 1QS III:15, 23; IV:3; 1QHᵃ I:24; 1QpHab VII:13. The term is used in the
Animal Apocalypse (1 *En.* 85–90), and the *Apocalypse of Weeks* (1 *En.* 93:1–10).

determination preceding the act of the creation: "... before He created them, He set up their activities" (4Q180 1 2). The exact nature of the "activities" is not known. Functioning and movement of luminaries, as well as human activities in history are both equal candidates for the meaning.[40] The following part of 4Q180 presents history as a sequence of precisely predetermined periods engraved on the heavenly tablets age by age (4Q180 1 2–3) according to the "ages of their dominion" (qṣy mmšlwtm) (4Q180 1 4).[41]

The following words refer, in all probability, to the particular system of history: "this is the order (zh srk) of the so[ns of Noah to Abraham un]til he bore Isaac, the ten ('śrh) [generations]" (4Q180 1 4–5). The number "ten" refers to the number of generations which lived before and after the Flood, and this mention serve as a general introduction for the overview. This is followed by a report on the birth of Isaac (4Q180 1 5). This event marks the beginning of the next series of ten generations. Accordingly, it is to be supposed that the first and second periods were the ten plus ten generations from Adam to Abraham, the Flood being the divider between them. The surviving fragments concern episodes that fall within these two periods.

The second paragraph (4Q180 1 7–10) begins with a "pesher on Azazel and the angels." This is the beginning of the concrete examples for the historical scheme. The events of antediluvian mankind's history are referred to according to the Enochic tradition (1 En. 6–11) with mention of the giants and their fathers, the fallen angels. The author of the pesher in 4Q180 identifies the leader of the angels with Azazel.[42]

Fragments 2–3 and 5–6 concern episodes from the life of Abraham. The author clearly follows the biblical sequence of the episodes as they

---

[40] On the idea that the working of heavenly luminaries is predetermined by God, see 1QHᵃ (1QHᵃ) I:7 and CD 2:7. 1 En. 1–5 gives a description of a perfectly regular functioning of the natural phenomena according to eternal rules which were determined by God in the act of creation.

[41] Dan 9:24–27 writes about a final period determined in seventy year-weeks. The idea that history is a consequent series of determined periods is clearly worded in 1QpHab VII:13. The underlying idea on determined periods (or generations, year-weeks) in human history is quite general in Qumran writings, see e.g. CD 2:9 and passim; 1QS I:14 and passim; 1QHᵃ I:24 and passim; and ancient Jewish apocalypses like 1 En. 85–90 (Animal Apocalypse) and 1 En. 91:1–10 (Apocalypse of Weeks).

[42] The passage reflects a good acknowledgement of the traditions related in 1 Enoch (the Aramaic text of which has remained in Qumran fragments). The author of the pesher combines two traditions, that of 1 En. 6–7 and 1 En. 8:1–2 when giving the name Azazel to the leader of the angels. According to 1 En. 6–7 the leader of the angels who went to earth, begot children with women, and taught humans to sorcery was Shemiḥazah. The

are narrated in Gen 17–18. Biblical events referred to in 4Q180 are possibly to be identified with the sin of the angels (4Q180 1 7–8), the change of Abraham's name (4Q180 2–3 i 3–5), the visit of the three angels to Abraham (4Q180 2–3 ii 3–4), and the destruction of Sodom and Gomorrah (4Q180 2–3 ii 5–7). The mention of Mount Zion (2–3 ii 1–2) preceding the angels' visit to Abraham (cf. Gen 18) may have to do with Gen 13:14–17, where Abraham is promised the land that was not chosen by Lot. That would also account for the mention of Lot in this context (4Q180 2–3 ii 2) and for the fact that the story about the destruction of Sodom and Gomorrah follows it directly. All these events took place before the birth of Isaac, which marks the beginning of the second series of ten generations.[43]

Fragments 5–6 cannot be interpreted in the context of our theme. Certainly, interpretation was going on in reference to later ages. Unfortunately, there is no material to reconstruct the scope and chronology of the overview, which is seemingly built upon the opposition of the sinner and the righteous. The special connection of human groups (the righteous and the sinner) with the land is referred to in the two citations in the text.[44]

4Q181 is a work separate from 4Q180, having a distinct subject matter and literary form. The opening words of the text speak about the opposition of the *yaḥad* and the sinners whose activity began with the sin of the Watchers, who brought uncleanness to the earth. Sin will be active in history until its end. Sins in the world will call up divine punishments: "... severe diseases in their flesh, according to the mighty deeds of God and corresponding to the sinners' wickedness, according to their uncleanness caused by the council of the sons of h[eaven] and earth, as a wicked association until the end" (4Q181 1 1–3). The opposite of the sinners is the gathering of the righteous, "a holy congregation, destined for eternal life and in the lot with His holy ones" (4Q181 1 3–4).

The detailed interpretation of the first period of ten generations, from the beginning until the generation of Isaac, is to be read on frg. 2:

---

list of the leaders of ten mentions Asael. According to 1 *En.* 8:1–2 Azazel (who is not said here to be an angel) is the originator of various sins among men and women. The above data suggest a dual leadership of the rebel angels.

[43] See Dimant, "The 'Pesher on the Periods' (4Q180 and 4Q181)," 77–102; eadem, "Ages of Creation," *Encyclopedia of the Dead Sea Scrolls* 1:11–13.

[44] Two biblical references are made, unfortunately both are fragmentary: "that is wr]itten concerning the ear[th" (4Q180 5–6 2), and "th]at is written concerning Pharaoh[" (4Q180 5–6 5).

"[Abraham until he sir]ed Isaac, [ten generations" (4Q181 2 1). The detailed interpretation begins with the antediluvian age, the activity of the fallen angels whose leader is again identified here with Azazel: "[The prophetic interpretation concerning Azazel and the angels who went in to the daughters] of man, so that [they] bore mighty me[n] to them" (4Q181 2 2; cf. Gen 6:4). The period of Azazel and the angels is determined in seventy year-weeks (4Q181 2 3).[45] This is equal to 490 years. Tallying this data with the biblical chronology (the data that Noah was 600 years old at the beginning of the Flood, cf. Gen 7:6), one can conclude that the fallen angels came to the earth in the 110th year of Noah's lifetime.[46] Azazel's realm is with "those who love deceit ('wlh) and possess guilt" (4Q181 2 4). Unfortunately, the rest of the text was lost, and further periods and historical chronology are not known. The text must have contained a detailed interpretation on at least two periods, that of antediluvian mankind and the period from the Flood until the generation of Isaac. Opposition of the sinner and the righteous is highlighted in the text. Furthermore, deeds of the sinner are mentioned as historical examples, with a chronology in generations and jubilees.

4Q180 and 4Q181 are two separate works, each possessing a distinct system of periodization and chronology. In 4Q180, a chronology based on generations is used, and the history of mankind is divided into periods according to generations. Two of these periods are known: the ten generations before the Flood and the ten generations following the Flood until Abraham. The following part of the work is not known (but it is

---

[45] It is to be noted that both 4Q181 and 2Q252 understand the generation of Isaac (and not his birth) as a marker of the fulfilment and a new era. This phenomenon may have related to the astrological view rather common in the era, that human life is determined with generation. Qumran physiognomic texts (4Q186; 4Q561) reflect the belief that the character of a person's "spirit" is determined, and it can be recognized on the basis of the person's physical characteristics. 4Q186 links physiognomy with astrology. On the questions of Qumran physiognomy and astrology, see M. Popovic, "Reading the Human Body and Writing in Code: Physiognomic Divination and Astrology in the Dead Sea Scrolls," in *Flores Florentino: Dead Sea Scrolls and Other Early Jewish Studies in Honour of Florentino García* Martínez (ed. A. Hilhorst, É. Puech, and E. Tigchelaar; JSJSup 122; Leiden: Brill, 2007), 271–284; idem, "4QZodiacal Physiognomy (4Q186) and Physiognomics and Astrology in Second Temple Period Judaism," *Henoch* 29 (2007): 51–66.

[46] The *Genesis Apocryphon* seemingly follows a different chronology when recounting Lamech's anxiety about the origin of the pregnancy of his wife Batenosh. Lamech is worried that his wife (who is about to give birth to Noah) had conceived by one of the Watchers. Thus the Watchers' coming to earth (described in *1 En.* 6–7) would have preceded Noah's birth.

to be supposed that the series of generic computation continued). The borders of historical periods are determined by the generations. The text speaks of a history preordained, a history written on heavenly tablets. This idea is not comprehensible without the Enochic tradition, where heavenly tablets are mentioned several times. According to one of the ideas in Enochic tradition, history is written on heavenly tablets, and Enoch controls them. In the other tradition, Enoch is visualized as sitting in heaven and writing history on heavenly tablets.[47] 4Q181 uses for periodization the cycle of year-weeks (seven-year periods of sabbatical years). This unit is known from the Bible and is used mainly in post-exile works.[48] 4Q181, besides chronological periods, is acknowledged with a periodization based on ethics, mentioning a period (or rather periods) of sin, equal to an era of seventy year-weeks.

c. *History in* 1 Enoch

The idea of preordained history is shaped in *1 Enoch*, the Aramaic text of which was well known in Qumran.[49] This collection contains, among others, two historical overviews, both of them being part of the Qumran Aramaic tradition. In *1 En.* 85–90, the *Animal Apocalypse*, a short review of human history is given, characterized and periodized with the help of a system of symbols.[50] Fragments of this part of the collection are to

---

[47] F. García-Martínez, "The Heavenly Tablets in the Book of Jubilees," in *Studies in the Book of Jubilees* (ed. M. Albani, J. Frey, and A. Lange; TSAJ 65; Tübingen: Mohr Siebeck, 1997), 243–260.

[48] The system is known in Dan 9:24–27; *1 En.* 93:1–10; 91:11–17 (*Apocalypse of Weeks*). The chronology of the book of *Jubilees* is built on a system of jubilees, cycles of seven sabbatical years. On the system, see M. Weinfeld, "Sabbatical Year and Jubilee in the Pentateuchal Laws and Their Ancient Near Eastern Background," in *The Law in the Bible and in Its Environment* (ed. T. Veijola; Helsinki: Finnish Exegetical Society, 1990), 39–62.

[49] This is true for chs. 1–36 (*Book of the Watchers*), and chs. 72–106 which belonged to the core Enochic tradition formed by the middle of the second century B.C.E. The *Astronomical Book* and the *Book of Giants* were also parts of this tradition (they have not been retained by the translations). Chapters 37–71 are not represented in the Qumran manuscript tradition and probably were not known in Qumran (they might have resulted from later additions to the work).

[50] A commentary to the text is P.A. Tiller, *A Commentary on the Animal Apocalypse of I Enoch* (SBLEJL 4; Atlanta: Scholars Press, 1993). See also I. Fröhlich, "The Symbolical Language of the Animal Apocalypse of Enoch (1 Enoch 85–90)," *RevQ* 14 (1990): 629–636; eadem, *"Time and Times and Half a Time": Historical Consciousness in the Jewish Literature of the Persian and Hellenistic Eras* (JSPSup 19; Sheffield: Sheffield Academic Press, 1996), 82–88.

be found among the Aramaic Enoch fragments from Qumran (4Q201–4Q212). The Enochic *Animal Apocalypse* uses earlier Enoch tradition (*1 En.* 6–11) as well as biblical, historical and prophetic tradition up to the age of the Maccabean uprising. Human figures in the overview are symbolized by animals. The symbols change in the course of the narrative, and the appearance of a new symbol indicates the beginning of a new period in human history.

1. The first period (from Adam to the antediluvian era) is characterized by the symbol of the bull. The colour of the animal indicates the character of the given human figure: white bulls and cows stand for the elect (Adam, Eve), while people considered as sinners (Cain and his descendants) are symbolized by black bulls and cows. The colour red has a neutral significance; figures symbolized by this colour are victims (Abel) or play no important role in the further narrative.

2. With the story of the fallen angels (related according to the tradition in *1 En.* 6), there is a change of symbols. The children born from the union of women (symbolized by black cows) with the Watchers (symbolized by stars) are wild animals (*1 En.* 86:4; 87:3; 88:2; 89:6). The elect (Noah, Shem, Abraham, and Isaac) are symbolized by white bulls (with the exception of Noah, who is transformed into a human being, cf. *1 En.* 89:1). The sinners (children of the Watchers, identified with peoples foreign to Israel and other foreign peoples descended from Ham and Abraham) are symbolized by wild animals.

3. The third historical period is characterized by the symbol of the sheep. This period begins with Jacob, father of twelve sons, ancestors of the tribes of Israel. The elect are characterized by the colour white and additionally by changes in their size and form. Moses appears as a big ram who is transformed later into a human being (*1 En.* 89:3). Samuel and Saul, too, are symbolized by rams (*1 En.* 89:41–44). David appears as a lamb growing into a ram. God is called the Lord of the Sheep. The most important figure of this period is Elijah. According to *1 En.* 89:52, the Lord of the Sheep takes a ewe, Elijah, up to Enoch, who lives in a tower (that is, in a heavenly sanctuary). The end of this period is marked by Elijah.

4. The figures of the fourth period are sheep and shepherds. Sheep stand for the people of Israel, and seventy shepherds stand for their rulers. The shepherds are commissioned by the Lord of the Sheep. When they accomplish their work, they have to give an account of it

to their followers. In heaven, Enoch bears witness to the shepherds'
work, and he will also be their witness "in the end of times," when
they will be judged, together with the Watchers.

The fourth period, the activity of the seventy shepherds, is subdivided
again into four periods:

   a. The rule of shepherds for twelve "hours," the time of the Babylonian
      captivity. The shepherds deliver the sheep to wild animals—that
      is, to hostile peoples. The animals destroy "the house," which is a
      reference to the historical event of the destruction of the Temple of
      Jerusalem (586 B.C.E.), and the mark of the first sub-period (1 En.
      89:65–72a)

   b. The activity of further shepherds working for twenty-three "hours,"
      the Persian period. In this epoch, "three are returning to the flock"
      (a possible reference to Zerubbabel, Ezra, and Nehemiah). Comple-
      tion of "the house" (rebuilding of the Second Temple in 516) marks
      the end of the second sub-period (1 En. 89:72b–90:1).

   c. The rule of further shepherds for twenty-three "hours," domination
      by the Greeks. During this time, wild animals keep on ravaging
      the sheep. No historical events are referenced specifically and it is
      unclear when the period ends (1 En. 90:2–5).

   d. The flock is tended (consecutively) by twelve shepherds during the
      time between the Hellenistic religious reforms of Antiochus IV and
      the final judgment. During this time, white lambs appear in the
      flock and they begin to open the eyes of the other sheep, which were
      blind until that time.[51] Reference is made to the murder of the high
      priest Onias III (170 B.C.E.). The period ends with the events at the
      beginning of the Maccabean revolt expressed in symbolic terms.
      Some white lambs grow horns on their heads, then a white ram
      appears with a large horn—the figure of Judas Maccabeus (1 En.
      90:6–19).

The series of periods of human history are closed by a divine judgement
over the Watchers and the shepherds. A white bull appears and the sheep
change into white bulls and cows (1 En. 90:37–38). According to the
views of the author(s) of the overview, human history is divided into dis-

---

[51] On the symbolism, see J.C. VanderKam, "Open and Closed Eyes in the Animal
Apocalypse (1 Enoch 85–90)," in The Idea of Biblical Interpretation: Essays in Honor of
James L. Kugel (ed. H. Najman and J.H. Newman; JSJSup 83; Leiden: Brill, 2004), 279–
292.

tinct periods and sub-periods. Periods are characterized by human activity that can be evaluated ethically. Symbols (figures and colours) are used in the work to express this ethical evaluation. Sins referred to are violations of divine ethical commands (bloodshed, mixing of races and delivering the elect to destroyers). Unlike other surveys, the overview uses, besides ethical evaluation, a chronological scheme with explicit numerical values. The four-part division (repeated in the fourth period) is characteristic of the literary works of the Danielic collection, the redaction of which might have been roughly contemporaneous with the Enochic survey.[52] This four-part division is combined with the symbolism of seventy, epitomized in the description of the activity of the seventy shepherds, which covered a period of seventy "hours." This seventy-scheme is an interpretation of Jeremiah's prophecy of the seventy years of exile. The image of the seventy shepherds shifts the emphasis to a more synchronic or cosmic idea of the seventy nations and their heavenly counterparts.[53] The overview is a political allegory where animals represent nations or ethnic groups. The final transformation of animals back into white cattle must be understood as the ultimate elimination of the separate identities of the different nations. Foreign nations originate from the sinful relationship of the Watchers with earthly women. Thus, in the Enochic conception of post-exilic imperialism, Israel is at the mercy of demonic powers represented by rapacious animals assisted by bad shepherds.[54]

It seems that history is a recurring system. This system is expressed by the appearance of the white bull following the divine judgement. With

[52] On the *Animal Apocalypse* and Daniel, see Fröhlich, "Symbolical Language," 629–636; J.R. Davila, "The Animal Apocalypse and Daniel," in *Enoch and Qumran Origins: New Light on a Forgotten Connection* (ed. G. Boccaccini; Grand Rapids: Eerdmans, 2005), 35–38.

[53] A. Yarbro Collins, *Cosmology and Eschatology in Jewish and Christian Apocalypticism* (JSJSup 50; Leiden: Brill, 1996), 73. Differently G.W.E. Nickelsburg, *1 Enoch 1: A Commentary on the Book of 1 Enoch, Chapters 1–36; 81–108* (Hermeneia; Minneapolis: Fortress, 2001), 391. To be consulted: K. Klaus, "The Astral Laws as the Basis of Time, Universal History, and the Eschatological Turn in the Astronomical Book and the Animal Apocalypse of 1 Enoch," in *The Early Enoch Literature* (ed. G. Boccaccini and J.J. Collins; JSJSup 121; Leiden: Brill, 2007), 119–137.

[54] L.T. Stuckenbruck, "'Reading the Present' in the Animal Apocalypse (*1 Enoch 85–90*)," in *Reading the Present in the Qumran Library: The Perception of the Contemporary by Means of Scriptural Interpretations* (ed. K. De Troyer and A. Lange; SBLSymS 30; Atlanta: SBL, 2005), 91–102; P.A. Tiller, "Israel at the Mercy of Demonic Powers: An Enochic Interpretation of Postexilic Imperialism," in *Conflicted Boundaries in Wisdom and Apocalypticism* (ed. B.G. Wright III and L.M. Wills; SBLSymS 35; Atlanta: SBL, 2005), 113–121.

the appearance of the white bull, however, it is to be expected that the renewal will bring a substantial change: the disappearance of sin.

Another overview, the *Apocalypse of Weeks* (*1 En.* 93 + 91), might have been known in Qumran, too. No fragment of this part of the Enochic collection is preserved in the Aramaic manuscript tradition except for a fragmentary commentary written about it. 4Q247 is an interpretation of the *Apocalypse of Weeks* from the Enochic collection—a lengthy review of history in the guise of a prophecy based on the Enochic periodization of history. Seven historical periods are presented in the work. The periods themselves are not characterized in detail; the main character of the period is given by the event occurring at the end of the period. The seven historical periods are followed by three eschatological ones and the whole history is concluded by a divine intervention and final judgment.[55] The apocalypse is composed of traditional materials, but in its present form, it is a unified product of a single author, reflecting his views and attitudes toward history. The Apocalypse concerns the righteous community, especially the community of the end time. The idea of "righteousness" (*qšt'*) is perhaps the key concept in the Apocalypse. The naming of the group of the righteous is known only from the Greek text of the work: *hoi dikaioi*, "the righteous."[56] It is Enoch, a prototype of righteousness, who reads the history from a book. Thus, the "weeks" (i.e., the periods of human history) are the following:

1. Primeval period concludes with the time of Enoch. This period is generally characterized as a time of righteousness (93:3).
2. The second period is that of "wickedness and deceit." Sinful times are divided by the Flood conceived as a first end, and the time of iniquity after the flood (93:4).
3. The third period is not well determined. At the end of the period "a man shall be elected as the plant of righteous judgment, and his posterity shall become the plant of righteousness for evermore." The third period is characterized by God choosing Abraham and symbolized as the plant that engenders Israel (93:5).

---

[55] Weeks 7–10 form a narrative on meta-history. On the structure of the work, see M.E. Stone, "Apocalyptic Literature," in *Jewish Writings of the Second Temple Period: Apocrypha, Pseudepigrapha, Qumran Sectarian Writings, Philo, Josephus* (ed. idem; CRINT 2.2; Assen: Van Gorcum, 1984), 383–441, esp. 405. History narrated in the *Animal Apocalypse* (*1 En.* 85–90) is also periodized with the help of the symbols used for human characters in the overview, see Fröhlich, "Symbolic Language," 629–636.

[56] Cf. 1QS III:20, 22 (*bny ṣdq*).

4. The main characteristic of period four is that "visions of the holy and righteous shall be seen" at its end. The period concludes by the giving of the Law following the exodus (93:6).

5. At the end of the fifth period, "the house of glory and dominion shall be built for ever." This period is characterized by the building of the Solomonic temple (93:7).

6. Period six is characterized generally by sins resulting in blindness. Only one positive event breaks with the general character of the period: "and in it a man shall ascend" (a reference to the ascension to heaven of the prophet Elijah, cf. 2 Kgs 2:11). The period is concluded by a divine punishment, the burning of the Temple, followed by the exile (93:8).

7. Period seven is the longest and describes the rising of "an apostate generation." At the end of the period, the righteous elect will be elected as an "eternal plant of righteousness, to receive sevenfold instruction concerning all His creation." This period concludes with the author's own time, when his community becomes the recipient of "sevenfold wisdom and knowledge." No mention is made either of the rebuilding of the temple or of Zerubbabel (93:9–10; 91:11).

8. The eighth week will be characterized by righteousness, and "a righteous judgement may be executed on the oppressors"—that is, "sinners shall be delivered into the hands of the righteous," and "they shall acquire houses through their righteousness" (91:12–13).

9. In the ninth week, the righteous judgement is revealed to the whole world. This means the extermination of sin, and "all the works of the godless shall vanish from all the earth" (91:14b).

10. The tenth week is divided into seven parts, and at the end of the seventh part, "there shall be the great eternal judgement." This will be the time of the final judgement of the Watchers when God "will execute vengeance amongst the angels." Simultaneously, it will be the time of the renewal of heaven and earth. The heavenly bodies will give sevenfold lights, and sin will cease (91:15–17).

The commentary in 4QPesher on the Apocalypse of Weeks (4Q247) concerns the events of weeks five and six (line 2). Periods are prearranged, and "en]graved [in the heavenly tablets]" (line 1). Periods five and six are contrasting periods, the foregoing being the era of the temple building of Solomon (line 3), the subsequent one that of the exile of the last Judean king Zedekiah (line 4). The mention of the sons of Levi and the Kittim (lines 5–6) might refer to a later period that cannot be identified with certainty.

d. Chronologies and Lists

4Q559 is a biblical chronology patterned according the "chronology of the generations of the righteous." The text is fragmentary; the only known mark of its putative era is that of Isaac's generation at Abraham's age of 99, the mark between the first and second period (frgs. 2 and 1).

The periodization is seemingly made on an ethical basis, combined with a periodization by generations, following biblical tradition. A re-markable point in the text is the counting of the new generation begin-ning with Isaac. According to Gen 21:5, "Abraham was a hundred years old when his son Isaac was born to him." The temporal aspect of the promise given to Abraham about the birth of a son is indefinite.[57] The mention of Abraham's 99 years of age as the time of the beginning of the period of Isaac in 4Q559 means that the author antedated Isaac's gener-ation about one year—that is, he counted Isaac's lifetime either from the promise (supposed to be about one year before his birth) or his concep-tion (nine months before birth, which is not a full year).[58]

4Q339 is a list of "false prophets" (line 1), according to the chronology of biblical tradition.[59] Nothing but names are mentioned in the list—names of prophets who mislead their contemporaries when giving false interpretation of the divine word.

---

[57] According to Gen 18:10 "Then one said, 'I will surely return to you in due season, and your wife Sarah shall have a son,'" thus, the time of the angels' visit preceded Isaac's birth at least by nine months.

[58] The same concept is to be found in 4Q180 1 4–5 which mentions a period of ten generations after Noah, from Shem to Abraham, until the time "when he begot Isaac." Similarly, the dividing line between the two periods of the life of Abraham is the begetting of Isaac in 4Q252; the text of II:5–13 refers to events preceding the begetting of Isaac (the last event mentioned here is the promise of the land to Abraham and his descendants), while the subsequent paragraph (II:14–III end) refers to Abraham as to the father of Isaac (the scene of the *Aqedah*, the willingness of Abraham to sacrifice his son).

[59] The four prophets at the end of the list are all known as the enemies of Jeremiah. Ahab and Zedekiah from Judah were accused by Jeremiah of false prophesying and adultery (Jer 29:21–24). Shemaiah from Babylonia prophesied a near end of the exile (Jer 29:24–32). Jeremiah's main enemy, Hananiah, uttered prophecies against those of Jeremiah. His prophecies remained unfulfilled and the prophet himself died the next year (Jer 28).

2 Balaam [son of] Beor;
3 [The] old man from Bethel;
4 [Zede]kiah son of Che[na]anah;
5 [Aha]b son of K[ol]aiah;
6 [Zede]kiah son of Ma[a]seiah;
7 [Shemaiah the Ne]helamite;
8 [Hananiah son of Az]zur;
9 [Yohanan son of Sim]on.[60]

The activity of some of these prophets is documented from biblical tradition.[61] Their prophecies did not come true; consequently, their words were not inspired by God. They were not the transmitters of the divine word though they styled themselves as prophets. The list of the prophets begins with Balaam, the false prophet *par excellence*, and continues with names from consequent periods. It is obvious that the list of sinners (the false prophets) serves to demonstrate the activity of the wicked in a certain period. The chronology of the prophets extends from the age of wandering in the wilderness (according to biblical chronology) to the Maccabean era, ending with Yohanan son of Simon, ancestor of the Maccabean dynasty. Putting his name on the list means a critique by the compiler of the list against the Hasmonean regime.

---

[60] The reconstruction and transcription of line 9 is debated. Immediately after publication, Alexander Rofé and Elisha Qimron independently suggested that the line be supplemented to read "[Yohanan ben Sim]eon" the Hebrew name for John Hyrcanus, the Hasmonean prince who ruled 135–104 B.C.E. See E. Qimron, "On the List of False Prophets from Qumran," *Tarbiz* 63 (1994): 273–275 (Hebrew); A. Rofé, "A List of False Prophets from Qumran: Two Riddles and their Solution," *Haaretz* April 13, 1994 (Hebrew). This suggestion is taken into consideration by M. Broshi and A. Yardeni, "On *netinim* and False Prophets," in *Solving Riddles and Untying Knots: Biblical, Epigraphic, and Semitic Studies in Honor of Jonas C. Greenfield* (ed. Z. Zevit, S. Gitin, and M. Sokoloff; Winona Lake: Eisenbrauns, 1995), 29–37 (33–37). Other contributions to the understanding of this text include A. Shemesh, "A Note on 4Q339 'List of False Prophets,'" *RevQ* 20 (2000): 319–320; K. Beyer, *Die aramäischen Texte vom Toten Meer: samt den Inschriften aus Palästina, dem Testament Levis aus der Kairoer Genisa, der Fastenrolle und den alten talmudischen Zitaten: Aramaistische Einleitung, Text, Übersetzung, Deutung, Grammatik/Wörterbuch, deutsch-aramäische Wortliste, Register* (2 vols. and Ergänzungsband; Göttingen: Vandenhoeck & Ruprecht, 1984/1994/2004), 2:128.

[61] On Balaam, son of Beor, see Num 22–24; "the old man from Bethel" is to be identified with a nameless prophet from Bethel mentioned in 1 Kgs 13:11–30; Zedekiah son of Chenaanah was a prophet who promised Ahab victory against the Arameans at Ramoth-gilead (cf. 1 Kgs 22:1–28; 2 Chr 18:1–27); Ahab ben Kolaiah and Zedekiah the son of Maaseiah, were condemned by Jeremiah for their false prophecies (Jer 29:21–23). Shemaiah the Nehelamite was a false prophet in Babylon and contemporary of Jeremiah (Jer 29:24, 31–32); Yohanan ben Shimon from the clan of Joarib was the grandfather of Judas Maccabeus (1 Macc 2:1; cf. 14:29 and Josephus, *Ant.* 12.265).

A parallel of the list is 4Q340, a list of temple servants (*netinim*). None of the names on the list can be identified with names known from other sources. The last line of the fragment holds the names "Kawik" (?) and "To[biah]" (line 6), the latter being a possible reference to the Tobiad family. Unfortunately, there are no further data to support this identification. Although the negative attitude of rabbinic Judaism towards temple-servants may not have been true for earlier ages,[62] it can be supposed that the list bears a kind of negative genealogy.[63]

Further names on the list are those of temple-servants (*netinim*), so the text in itself is not a historic overview. Nevertheless, being a list of sinners, it might have served as a basis for such a work, and perhaps it was compiled with such a purpose, serving as the preliminary work (an *aide memoire* or a reference) towards the composition of an overview or a detailed narrative.

e. Eschatological Texts

11QMelch (11Q13) is an eschatological work dealing with the end of history, the (pre-ordained) time of "the final days" (*'ḥryt hymym*)[64] and "the Day of Atonement (*ywm hkpwrym*) at the end of the tenth jubilee,"[65] in which atonement shall be made "for all the sons of [light and for] the men [of] the lot (*gwrl*) of Mel[chi]zedek" (II:7–8). Their opposite, the sinners, are mentioned as belonging to Belial's lot (*gwrl*). The nature of their sins is not specified; neither is the role they played during the course of previous human history.

Thus, the text concentrates on the end of history. Events preceding the final judgement are not known. The only system revealed in human history is a chronological one, that of the jubilees, a system for which the book of *Jubilees*—a work very well known in Qumran[66]—provides

---

[62] On temple-servants, see B.A. Levine, "The Netînîm," *JBL* 82 (1963): 207–212; idem, "Later Sources on the Netinim," in *Orient and Occident: Essays Presented to Cyrus H. Gordon on his Sixty-Fifth Birthday* (ed. H.A. Hoffner; AOAT 22; Kevelaer: Butzon & Bercker, 1973), 101–107; J.P. Weinberg, "N^etînîm und 'Söhne der Sklaven Salomos' im 6.–4. Jh. v.u.Z.," *ZAW* 87 (1975): 355–371.

[63] Broshi and Yardeni, "On *netinim* and False Prophets."

[64] The eschatological idea expressed in this term occurs 48 times in the scrolls, most often in basic texts like CD 4:4; 6:11; 1QSa I:1; 1QpHab II:5; IX:6.

[65] *Jubilees* is an overview of fifty jubilees, the last one being that of the exodus from Egypt and the lawgiving on Mount Sinai (*Jub.* 48:1).

[66] Fragments of the original Hebrew of the book were found in fourteen (possibly fifteen) manuscripts, see J.C. VanderKam, "The Jubilees Fragments from Qumran Cave

copious evidence.[67] *Jubilees* gives an overview of a long historical period (from the creation to the giving of the Law at Sinai) in jubilees—that is, in chronological units of forty-nine years (= jubilees), each of which consists of seven "weeks of years."[68] 11QMelch mentions just one period of ten jubilees, which is the last one, followed by the Day of Atonement (II:7–8). Ten jubilees are equal to five hundred years.[69] It is not known if this is a period to be counted from the author's time to the end, or if the author expects a near eschatological end. In the latter case, the data relate to his past,[70] and considering the age of the manuscript (dated to the first half of the first century C.E.),[71] which might not be very far from that of the composition of the work, one can suppose that the beginning of the ten-jubilee period was thought to be the destruction of the Temple. Thus, the end was expected around the beginning of the first century B.C.E.[72]

ETHICAL IMPURITIES AND SEMIOTIZATION OF THE HISTORY

Looking over the texts treated here, one can conclude that they present various attitudes to history and historical time. Periodization in the

---

4," in *The Madrid Qumran Congress: Proceedings of the International Congress on the Dead Sea Scrolls, Madrid 18–21 March, 1991* (ed. J. Trebolle Barrera and L. VegasMontaner; 2 vols.; STDJ 11.1–2; Leiden: Brill, 1992), 2:635–648, esp. 642.

[67] The system of jubilee years is detailed in Lev 25:8–17. It was the end of the cycle of seven sabbatical years (the fiftieth year) when liberty to Israelites who had become enslaved for debt was given back, and land propriety was restored to families who had been compelled to sell it out of economic need. The chronological system of the book of *Jubilees* is based on a system of jubilees and year-weeks. 11QMelch II:2 cites Lev 25:13 on jubilees, and II:4 cites Isa 61:1 on the proclamation of the end of a jubilee.

[68] Besides chronological periodization there is a periodization with the help of literary motifs, see Fröhlich, "*Time and Times and Half a Time*," 97–99.

[69] The year of jubilee came at the end of the cycle of seven sabbatical years. Lev 25:8–10 specifies it as the fiftieth year. There was also in biblical tradition a counting system based on sabbatical years, of 49 and 490 year periods, see Dan 9:24–27.

[70] The manuscript of 11QMelch can be dated paleographically to the middle of the first century B.C.E. or slightly later. The work itself may have been written earlier, the end of the second century B.C.E.

[71] A.S. van der Woude, "Melchisedek als himmlische Erlösergestalt in den neugefundenen eschatologischen Midraschim aus Qumran Höhle XI," *OtSt* 14 (1965): 354–373, esp. 357.

[72] A system identical with that of Dan 9. A remarkable parallel is the system of the *Damascus Document* counting a period of 390 years beginning with 586 the end of which was the beginning of the history of the "covenanters." The number was, in all probability, chosen consciously from one of the manuscript traditions of Ezek 4:4. Based on these countings the beginnings of the school were the beginning of the second century.

works is made sometime on a chronological basis (years, generations, weekdays), but more often on some other basis, especially on an ethical qualification of the characters of historical times. The two systems— the chronological and the ethical one—may be combined among them. Ethical qualification of the eras means an opposition of the sinner and the righteous. The righteous are characterised by the keeping of the Mosaic Law. No specific virtues are mentioned in the texts. Contrary to this, sins are always appraised. Sins referred to in the historical surveys may be placed in three categories. The first is cultic sin (including false prophecy and improper religious practice labeled as walking in "erring spirit"). The second sin is bloodshed. The third category comprises various kinds of sexual sins. These sins have a special place in the religious worldview of the Deuteronomic legislation. They are sins which pollute the land.

Polluting the Sacred—the presence of unclean objects in the sanctuary and inappropriate cult practices make the sanctuary impure. Priests are not to come into contact with anything impure in order not to bring impurity into the sanctuary.[73] Priests, priestly households and Israelites are not to contaminate sacrificial meat and other offerings.[74] If they do, they are liable to the *kārēt* or "cutting-off" penalty.[75] Non-legislative literature gives several examples for the view that illicit forms of the cult were considered as polluting the sacred.[76]

Sexual sins are usually described as "fornication" (*zĕnût*). *Zĕnût* means the violation of any of the prohibitions concerning sexual relations— in particular, those listed in Lev 18. These are incest, i.e., sexual rela- tion between blood relatives and persons in the place of a blood rela- tive such as a stepmother (vv. 6–18), adultery (v. 20), homosexual rela- tions and prostitution (v. 22) and bestiality (v. 23). The basis for this

[73] This is the rationale of the law prohibiting the priests to contact death impurity, see Lev 21:1–4 (prescriptions for priests), and Lev 21:10–11 (prescriptions for the high priest). Legal texts do not mention, but it is obvious, that contact with other impurities like blood was also forbidden. See e.g. Luke 10:25–37, the parable of the Good Samaritan where the priest and the Levite making for a service in the Temple of Jerusalem avoid even the sight of the bleeding man who lies by the roadside.

[74] Lev 7:19–21; 22:3–7; Num 18:11, 13; Lev 7:19–21; 22:3–7; Num 18:11, 13.

[75] The punishment of *kārēt* (noun from the verb *krt* "to cut off") means not only the death of the sinner, but also the discontinuance of his progeny.

[76] During Josiah's cultic reform objects considered as improper to the cult were eliminated from the temple, and defiled, and after that the sanctuary was ritually cleansed, see 2 Kgs 23:8, 10, 13, 16. Prolonged illicit cult practice—Canaanite cults and "Jeroboam's sin," the Northern form of Yahwism—were interpreted as causes of the fall of the kingdom in 722 B.C.E., and cause of the exile of the Northern tribes (cf. 2 Kgs 17:7–18).

biblical view is the sum of biblical laws concerning sexuality. According to Lev 18, sexual sins pollute persons (vv. 20, 23, 24, 30) and the land (vv. 25, 27, 28). Polluting the land results in expulsion from it (vv. 25, 28) and *kārēt* or "cutting-off" for the people (v. 29). Overlapping with permitted impurities is the case of intercourse with a menstruant (v. 19).[77] This sexual relationship is forbidden with a penalty of *kārēt* attached.[78]

Bloodshed and homicide (*ḥamās*) mean shedding innocent blood. Institutional forms of bloodshed, like war or blood feud, do not fall into this category.[79] Yet, any corpse, including any that results from homicide, pollutes persons and objects for seven days.[80] According to the priestly legislation, homicide brings pollution on the land whether the killing was intentional or unintentional.[81] The death of the murderer removes the pollution.[82] The rite described in Deut 21:1–9 serves to remove the pollution of the earth caused by a murder in which the culprit is not known. The polluted earth becomes barren; the land is said not to produce well for Cain because of Abel's murder.[83] The corpse of a hanged person left on the tree for the night also defiles the land.[84]

Idolatry and magic (considered often as *zěnût*) mean further ethical impurities. Offering a child to Molek pollutes the sanctuary.[85] The offender is to be put to death by stoning. A divine punishment to the person for the same sin is the *kārēt* ("cutting-off"). Consulting the dead, an idolatrous act, also defiles a person.[86] Non-P literature generally attests

---

[77] Also Lev 20:18; cf. Lev 15:24.

[78] A special case in Deuteronomy is the prohibition of the re-marriage with a divorced wife after her second marriage. The woman is considered as impure for her first husband; should she marry him, the land would be defiled (Deut 24:1–4; cf. Jer 3:1–10).

[79] This impurity is distinct from that of corpse contamination. Corpse contamination arises from the *state* of the corpse itself; homicide pollution arises from an illicit *act* of killing.

[80] Cf. Num 31:13–24.

[81] Num 35:33–34.

[82] Num 35:12, 16–21, 31; cf. Gen 9:5–6. In the case of manslaughter, the slayer must reside in a city of refuge until the death of the high priest. The priest's death apparently purges the pollution (Num 35:12, 15, 22–25, 28, 32).

[83] Gen 4:10–12; 2 Sam 21:1–14; Hos 4:2–3; Ps 106:38.

[84] This prohibition occurs only in Deut 21:22–23. Notwithstanding this it was considered in everyday practice, and this was the reason for asking for Jesus' body from Pilate and burying it before night, see Mark 15:42–45; Matt 27:57–61; Luke 23:50–56; John 19:38–42 (the last two sources explain the practice with the beginning of the Shabbat).

[85] Lev 20:2–5.

[86] Lev 19:31; 20:6.

that idols were considered as impure and polluting for the devotees,[87] the
sanctuary[88] and the land.[89] Deuteronomy places idolatrous implements
under ḥērem ("extreme dedication") status. This is why the Israelite con-
querors of Canaan are to destroy the implements (Deut 7:5, 25).

Moral impurities have special consequences concerning the relation of
the sinner and the land. The redactor of the Holiness Code considered the
territory of Canaan not only a "promised land"—a land that the chosen
people will inherit as a result of a divine promise—but also as holy, and as
such, bound by certain obligations related to holy things. Other parts of
the legal literature of the Bible also reflect a similar attitude to these sins.
The observance of special laws means a prerequisite of the maintenance
of the purity of people and the land, as well as a precondition for the
survival of human beings on the land.

In summary, ethical impurities are generally considered in the biblical view as polluting the person and the land on which the sin was
committed. The punishment of the ethical impurities in the legislative
parts of the Bible is kārēt, annihilation of the sinner and his offspring.
In non-legislative texts, punishment for sinful impurity is often exile or
other destruction.[90] This punishment serves as a means of rectification
and purification. Another consequence may be agricultural failure.[91] The
people's repentance and their restoration from exile may be discussed in
terms of purification.[92]

Ethical impurities have an important and constant element: their relation to the land.[93] It is a general anthropologic phenomenon that peo-

---

[87] Josh 22:17; Jer 2:23; Ezek 20:7, 18, 26, 31; 22:3–4; 23:7, 13–14, 17, 30; 36:25, 29, 33;
37:23; Ps 106:36–40; cf. Gen 35:2; Hos 5:3–4; 6:10.

[88] Jer 7:30; 32:34; Ezek 5:11; 23:37–39; 2 Chr 36:14.

[89] Jer 2:7–9; Ezek 36:17–18; cf. Jer 13:27 of Jerusalem.

[90] Cf. Isa 64:4–11; Ezek 20:38; 22:2–14, 24, 31; 24:11–13; 39:23–24; Mic 2:10; cf. Ezra
9:11.

[91] Cf. Gen 3:17; Isa 24:5–7; Jer 12:4.

[92] Cf. Jer 33:4–9; Ezek 20:43–44; 36:25–32.

[93] The relation of any people to the land they live on is a basic anthropological concept.
This relation is regulated in human cultures by special rules and prescriptions. Human
groups were thought to be enabled to live on the land only by keeping these rules. On the
biblical concept of the land and rules enabling people to live on it, see W.D. Davies, *The
Territorial Dimension of Judaism* (Berkeley: University of California Press, 1982), 127–
143 ("Reflections on the Doctrine of The Land"); G. Strecker, ed., *Das Land Israel in
biblischer Zeit: Jerusalem-Symposium 1981 der Hebräischen Universität und der Georg-
August-Universität* (GTA 25; Göttingen: Vandenhoeck & Ruprecht, 1983); B. Halpern-
Amaru, *Rewriting the Bible: Land and Covenant in Post-Biblical Jewish Literature* (Valley
Forge: Trinity, 1994); W.D. Davies, *The Gospel and the Land: Early Christianity and Jewish
Territorial Doctrine* (Berkeley: University of California Press, 1974).

ple living in a country have a special relation with the land they live on, and they formulate their right to the land in cosmic and legal terms. The idea of the relation of certain sins with the rule over the land is very well known in the historiographies of several ancient Near Eastern cultures.[94] The Old Babylonian Chronicle (the so-called Weidner Chronicle) relates the history of several Old Babylonian dynasties one after another, giving with it an evaluation of the rule of each king and dynasty.[95] The events that happened under various kings are evaluated from the point of view of the Esagila, the temple of the god Marduk in Babylon. The destiny of the dynasties is determined by the relation of their kings to the cult of Marduk. The kings—with rare exceptions—commit some cultic sin during their rule: they confiscate the fish caught for a sacrifice for Marduk, eat the fish prepared for the offering or fail to perform the ritual sacrifice for the god. Another type of sin mentioned in the account is bloodshed. According to the chronicle, "Naramsin destroyed the creatures of Babili." Ritual sin or bloodshed in each case calls for punishment, which is the attack of foreign hordes and/or the fall of the dynasty. The Weidner Chronicle, actually a *Fürstenspiegel*, a literary letter written by one Babylonian king to another "aiming to warn the reader to take care to provide for the Esagil cult, lest he suffer the fate of former rulers who were not so careful. . . . The emphasis is on maintaining ritual performance in order to insure the throne."[96] The aim of its author was describing the past and showing regularities in it. The text is the clearest example for the idea of the semiotization of history in the name of ethics.[97] The underlying idea is that history consists of a series of similar periods, and each period ends with a fall caused by ritual sin or bloodshed.

This principle seems to be a constant element in Mesopotamian historiography. The Cyrus Cylinder, issued by the Persian ruler Cyrus after the capture of Babylon in 539, also mentions cultic sins and bloodshed as causes of the fall of the last Babylonian king. Nabonid "removed the images of the gods from their thrones and had copies put in their

---

[94] On Mesopotamian Historiography, see Finkelstein, "Mesopotamian Historiography."

[95] For the full text and *Sitz im Leben* of the chronicle, see B.T. Arnold, "The Weidner Chronicle and the Idea of History in Israel and Mesopotamia," in *Faith, Tradition, and History: Old Testament Historiography in Its Near Eastern Context* (ed. A.R. Millard, J.K. Hoffmeier, and D.W. Baker; Winona Lake: Eisenbrauns, 1994), 129–148.

[96] Ibid., 145.

[97] Expression of Jan Assmann, see the chapter with the identical title "Semiotisierung im Zeichen von Strafe und Rettung" in his *Das kulturelle Gedächtnis*, 229–248.

places," "introduced improper cults in the city of Ur and other holy cities," "failed to supply the holy cities with necessary things" and made Babylon's inhabitants suffer. These were the reasons why Marduk left the city and gave Babylon's kingdom to Cyrus, King of Ansan. (Of course, the text was composed by Babylonian priests, adherents of Cyrus.)

Hittite historiography is characterized by the same principles, albeit in a somewhat different form.[98] In a work known as *Murshili's Prayers*, the country is afflicted with pestilence, drought and famine. The ill fate is due to divine punishment. The king asks for an oracle concerning its cause, which turns out to be a sin committed against the gods. This is followed by expiation: a huge sacrifice, the public confession of the sin and praise for the offended deity.

The Egyptian Demotic Chronicle, written in the third century B.C.E., relates the history of the twenty-eighth to thirtieth dynasties. According to the chronicle, the reason why a king loses his throne to another is always the sin he has committed. Chinese historiography institutionalized this principle. In China, the new king had to write down the history of his predecessors and to prove that the predecessor had forfeited the support of the gods.[99]

BIBLICAL HISTORIOGRAPHY AND QUMRAN *PESHARIM*

As to biblical historiography, the most common example of this principle is the justification of the fall of the northern kingdom Israel in 722 B.C.E. in 2 Kgs 17. The chronicle attributes the fall of the northern kingdom to a steady-state cultic impurity resulting from "Jeroboam's sin" (i.e., the northern form of the cult of Yahweh, considered by the chronicler as illicit).[100] This sin was committed by each of the Israelite kings (even by Jehu, the devotee *par excellence* of Yahweh) (2 Kgs 17:22–23). The same principle is present in the historical narratives on the first kings. Saul's story comprises a series of narrative elements relating to his cultic offences and bloodshed. David's three sons commit ethical sins of a sexual character and will be disinherited (the rape of Tamar by Amnon,

---

[98] See the seminal article of H. Güterbock, "Die historische Tradition und ihre literarische Gestaltung bei Babyloniern und Hethitern bis 1200," ZA 42 (1934): 1–91; 44 (1938): 45–149.

[99] Assmann, *Das kulturelle Gedächtnis*, 253.

[100] On Jeroboam's figure as a "bad king" in Deuteronomistic historiography, see Evans, "Naram-Sin and Jeroboam."

Absalom lying with his father's concubines, and Adonijah asking for his father's concubine as a wife).[101]

Historical outlines from Qumran continue this tradition. They interpret historical tradition in the name of ethics, highlighting events and periods characterized by the above types of sins and glorifying people known from biblical tradition as righteous for not committing these sins.

If one considers the *pesharim* in the light of the results presented above, one might have more insight into the intellectual background of these very distinctive writings. The *pesharim* cite prophetic writings (and not historical narratives!) verse by verse, and "translate" the text, identifying its textual elements one by one with persons and events of a later age. It is generally known that the interpretations relate to the events and persons of the age of the author of the interpretation. However, the interpretation represents again a kind of coded language where nicknames are used for real persons and events. These nicknames are in most cases typological names originating from a common tradition (and almost never from the texts commented upon) and attributed with a collective sense. The prophetic text often becomes a pretext for the author of the commentary, which secedes from the text commented upon. Accordingly, the commentary read alone has its own meaning, referring to various events in the history of the community. The author's attitude to history—and, accordingly, the reason for the commentary— is that the prophet's world relates not only to his own time, but also to a remote era which is identical with the present of the author of the commentary. According to this, the figures and persons mentioned in the prophecy are to be identified with those of the author of the commentary. Thus, the events referred to in the coded text are fulfilled prophecies, and this fact assigns to the events a much greater significance.

Although the names cover real historical persons (sometimes, having a collective meaning, they can refer to several persons), we do not make here any attempt to identify any of these names with historical persons. What we intend to examine here are the types of events mentioned in these sources and the opinion of the authors about their significance, their role in the course of the process of human history, the reason why even these events were mentioned, and the reason why others were not. *Pesharim* refer continuously to the history of the community in a coded

---

[101] 2 Sam 13; 16:20–23; 1 Kgs 2:16–18, respectively.

way. They usually present a situation where the wicked and the righteous are opposed. The following are sins of the wicked:

"Cultic offences" were religious practices considered illicit, expressed in terms such as erring, lies, false teachings, lack of knowledge, as well as symbolical names like "the Liar" (*'yš hkzb*), "the Scoffer" (*'yš hlṣwn, 'nšy hlṣwn*), "the Spreader of Lies, who deceived many" (1QpHab X:9).[102] The designations of the Pharisees as "Seekers after Smooth Things" (*dwršy hḥlqwt*) refer to their halakhah, considered erroneous (4QpNah [4Q169] 3–4 i 7).[103] For a similar reason, they are also called "the misleaders of Ephraim" (4QpNah 3–4 ii 8).[104] The Wicked Priest (*khn hršʿ*) "forgot God who had f[ed them,] His ordinances they cast behind them, which He had sent to them [by the hand of] His servants the prophets" (4QpHos [4Q166] II:3–5). "The priests of Jeru]s[al]em which went astray" (1QpMic [1Q14] 11 1). The atrocity of the Evil Priest against the Righteous Teacher, when he tried to force his ideas on the Teacher and his community and wanted to cause them stumbling (*lkšylm*) (1QpHab XI: 4–9), can again be labeled as a "cultic sin."

A more literal cultic offence is the sin of the Wicked Priest who "committed his abhorrent deeds, defiling the Temple of God" (1QpHab XII:8–9).

Violence was committed when "the Young Lion of Wrath" hanged people alive (4QpNah 3–4 i 7–8). Ephraim, the city of the Seekers after Smooth Things, whose sins are lies, deceit and looting, is called "city of bloodshed" (Nah 3:1; 4QpNah 3–4 ii 2–3). The Hasmoneans are mentioned as the Wicked Dynasty (*byt 'šm[tm]*) who called in the Kittim, the enemy ravaging the land (1QpHab IV:10–13). They are guilty of "building a worthless city by bloodshed (*dmym*) and forming a community by lies (*šqr*)" (1QpHab X:10).[105] The oppression of the holy people is often mentioned in other places in the *pesharim*.[106]

---

[102] "The Scoffer" is based on Isa 29:20; "the assembly of the Scoffers (*'dt 'nšy hlṣwn*) who are in Jerusalem" (4QpIsa^b [4Q162] II:10).

[103] The name originates from Isa 30:10 *halāqôt* "smooth things."

[104] They "mislead many (*ytʿw rbym*) by their false teaching, and their lying tongue and their wily lip; kings, princes, priests, and populace together with the resident alien" (4QpNah 3–4 ii 8–9).

[105] The Wicked Priest had a reputation for reliability at the beginning of his term of service but later on, when he became ruler over Israel, "he became proud and forsook God and betrayed the commandments for the sake of riches" (1QpHab VIII:9–11).

[106] The oppressors are the Man of the Lie who turned against the elect (4QpPs^a [4Q171] 1–10 iv 14), and "the wicked princes who oppress his holy people, who will perish like smoke that is lost in the wind" (4QpPs^a 1–10 iii 7–8).

A new element among the sins is looting, the collecting of "ill-gotten riches from the plunder of the people" by the "later priests in Jerusalem" (1QpHab IX:5). The looting of the Wicked Priest (although he collected the goods of the sinners) and his other deeds are characterized as "impurity" (*kwl ndt ṭm'h*) (1QpHab VIII:12–13). The Evil Priest "stole the assets of the poor" in Judah (1QpHab XII:9–10). This sin recalls the second item of the list called the "three traps of Belial" mentioned in CD 4:15–18 otherwise known from a fragment of the *pesharim* as the "traps of Belial" (*pḥy bly'l*) (4QpPs^a [4Q171] 1–10 ii 10–11) which the "Community of the Poor" will escape. The "traps of Belial" mean fornication (*znwt*), wealth (*hwn*) and defiling the sanctuary (*ṭm' hmqdš*) (CD 4:17–18). Looting and gathering of riches by force is a specific form of the sin of violence (*ḥms*) considered by Essenes as leading to destruction.

The Righteous

The righteous are mentioned in the *pesharim* as "those who obey the Law among the Jews" (1QpHab VIII:1–3). They are those who observe the Law correctly "in the House of Judah" in every situation. They are the "loyal ones, obedient to the Law, whose hands will not cease from loyal service even when the Last Days seem long to them" (1QpHab VII:10–12). Righteous "have not let their eyes lead them into fornication during the time of wickedness" (1QpHab V:7–8).

The righteous are characterized by the authentic interpretation of the Law, in a special way. Authentic interpretation of the Law by the (Righteous) Priest is interpretation that he received from "the Priest in whose [heart] God has put [the abil]ity to explain all the words of his servants the prophets, through [whom] God has foretold everything that is to come upon his people and [his] com[munity]" (1QpHab II:8–10); "the Teacher of Righteousness to whom God made known all the mysterious revelations of his servants the prophets" (1QpHab VII:4–5). Thus, the prophetic revelations are valid for the history of later generations, according to the Essenes' concept of historical time.

Periodization and Endtime

History in the *pesharim* is a continuous time divided in periods. The periods are determined by God; their coming end is a divine secret. "All the times fixed by God will come about in due course as He ordained that they should by his inscrutable insight" (1QpHab VII:13–14). The sins of the wicked "will be doubled against them in the time which precedes the judgment, 'But the righteous man is rewarded with life for his fidelity' (Hab 2:4b)" (1QpHab VII:17). Their proper religious practice, their fidelity to the Righteous Teacher, and the authority of the right practice are the basis of their rescue in the future, "whom God will rescue from among those doomed to judgement, because of their suffering and their loyalty to the Teacher of Righteousness" (1QpHab VIII:1–3).

Punishment and Reward

The evil deeds of "the misleaders of Ephraim" and their deceit "will be *revealed* at the end of time to all Israel" (4QpNah 3–4 iii 3). The "sack of the later priests of Jerusalem will be handed over to the army of the Kittim"(1QpHab IX:6–7). The wicked, together with the idolatrous gentiles, will be exterminated from the land. "In the day of judgement, God will exterminate all those who worship false gods, as well as the wicked, from the earth" (1QpHab XIII:1–4). "The wi[c]ked princes ... will perish like smoke that is los[t in the win]d" (4QpPs^a 1–10 iii 7–8). The wicked ones of Israel will be cut off and destroyed forever (4QpPs^a 1–10 iii 12–13).[107]

The Righteous will be rescued "from among those doomed to judgement, because of their suffering and their loyalty to the Teacher of Righteousness" (1QpHab VIII:1–3). "The congregation of the Poor Ones" will inherit the land (of Israel) (4QpPs^a 1–10 iii 10–11). The "righteous ones" will possess the land for thousand (generations) (4QpPs^a 1–10 iv 2–3). Similarly, 4QpPs^b (4Q173) speaks of "those who] take possession of the inheritance" when interpreting Ps 37 (4QpPs^b 1 7).

CONCLUSIONS

The views according to which the history of the community is interpreted in the *pesharim* are the same as in the narrative exegesis. Some notions have slightly changed. For example, the idea of "cultic offence," here indicates a false interpretation of the Torah, and the religious observance based on this halakhah. This cultic offence, together with bloodshed and

---

[107] The interpretation is based on a Psalms verse (Ps 37:21–22) in which the ethical principle of the possession of the land is formulated.

looting, leads to disinheritence of the sinner. Narrative exegesis (related immediately to the text) and *pesharim*, a coded history of the community based on interpretations alienated from the text interpreted, explain the fall of the sinners on the same basis as the ancient Near Eastern texts. The basis on which historical facts and events are evaluated is an ethical viewpoint; the overviews they give represent a "semiotization of the history in the name of ethics."[108] This attitude manifests itself in both forms of historical interpretation, the short overviews, and the explicit interpretation of the *pesharim*. It is in line with the ancient Near Eastern tradition of historical memory, trying to show the essential motives that rule history—a schema meant to be effective in giving responses to questions of later ages.

---

[108] Assman, *Das kulturelle Gedächtnis*, 229–248.

PROTECTION OF OWNERSHIP IN THE DEEDS OF SALE: DEEDS OF SALE FROM THE JUDEAN DESERT IN CONTEXT[*]

Jan Dušek
Charles University in Prague

1. Introduction

Ownership is "the legal relation between a person (individual, group, corporation, or government) and an object."[1] The deeds of sale record the process of transmission of ownership from one contracting party to another.

The transfer of ownership from the vendor to the buyer generally has, in Aramaic deeds of sale, these phases: 1. declaration of the sale, 2. payment receipt clause, 3. description of the property, 4. withdrawal clause, 5. investiture clause, 6. guarantees, and 7. witnesses.[2]

Many aspects of the transmission of ownership and its protection in the Aramaic and Hebrew deeds of sale in antiquity have already been studied.[3] The purpose of this study is to analyze the principles

---

[*] I am grateful to Prof. Sophie Démare-Lafont for reading this manuscript and for helping me to improve the concept of my argumentation. I am entirely responsible for possible errors in the article. This study is the result of a research activity which is part of the grant project GAČR 401/07/P454 "Critical Analysis of the New Epigraphic Evidence Related to the History of the Province of Samaria from the 4th Century BCE to the 1st century CE," which has provided financial support for its editing.

[1] *The New Encyclopaedia Britannica: Micropaedia: Ready Reference* (ed. R.P. Gwinn et al.; 15th ed.; Chicago: Encyclopaedia Britannica, 1991), 9:26.

[2] Cf. also E. Cussini, "The Aramaic Law of Sale and the Cuneiform Legal Tradition" (PhD. diss., The John Hopkins University, 1992), 167–199.

[3] I list some of the most important of these studies in chronological order: R. Yaron, *Introduction to the Law of the Aramaic Papyri* (Oxford: Clarendon, 1961), 79–92; Cussini, "Aramaic Law of Sale"; H.M. Cotton and J.C. Greenfield, "Babatha's Property and the Law of Succession in the Babatha Archive," *ZPE* 104 (1994): 211–224; E. Cussini, "Transfer of Property at Palmyra," *Aram* 7 (1995): 233–250; Y. Muffs, *Studies in the Aramaic Legal Papyri from Elephantine* (HO 66; Leiden: Brill, 2003); L.H. Schiffman, "Reflections on the Deeds of Sale from the Judaean Desert in Light of Rabbinic Literature," in *Law in the Documents of the Judaean Desert* (ed. R. Katzoff and D. Schaps; JSJSup 96; Leiden:

of legal protections of ownership behind the terminological unity and diversity in the deeds of sale discovered in the vicinity of the Dead Sea in the light of documents discovered in other places. This effort is enabled by the fact that all important corpora containing Aramaic and Hebrew deeds of sale related to ancient Palestine are published. I analyze Aramaic, Hebrew, Nabataean, Greek and Syriac deeds of sale discovered in Elephantine, Wadi Daliyeh, Naḥal Ḥever, Wadi Murabbaʿat, Dura Europos and belonging to the Seiyâl Collection in chronological order.

I focus on the final stage of the process of the acquisition of ownership by the buyer: the definition of the rights of the new owner (buyer) over the acquired property in the investiture clause,[4] and the description of the duties of the old owner (vendor) concerning the protection of the buyer's rights over the acquired property in the guarantees.

The guarantees in deeds of sale protect the buyer's party against eviction by the vendor's party or by a third person. The vendor is presumed of *bad faith* in protecting the buyer's party against eviction by the vendor's party: this guarantee requires the vendor to refrain. The vendor's party cannot contest the sale. If the vendor's party contests the sale, he acts in *bad faith* and must pay a *penalty* to the buyer. The vendor is presumed of *good faith* in protecting the buyer's party against eviction by a third person. The vendor sold his property in *good faith* and he must be able to prove it. This guarantee requires the vendor to act: he must assist the buyer and clear the sold property from claims of a third person before the court.

The deeds of sale contain different methods of protecting the buyer's ownership. The presumption of *good* or *bad faith* as well as the penalty and compensation as the means of protection are not represented in these deeds in the same way. Their combinations can vary from place to place and from period to period.

Brill, 2005), 185–203. The Aramaic legal tradition was recently studied, with an in-depth analysis of the warranty clause, by A.D. Gross, *Continuity and Innovation in the Aramaic Legal Tradition* (JSJSup 128; Leiden: Brill, 2008), 151–193. I am not able to discuss Gross's study in this article: I received the book when the article was already prepared for the press. Nevertheless, the perspective and results presented by Gross are different from mine.

[4] For the analysis of the *šallīṭ* clause, see D.M. Gropp, "Origin and Development of the Aramaic *šallīṭ* Clause," *JNES* 52 (1993): 31–36; A.F. Botta, "The Legal Function and Egyptian Background of the שליט Clause: A Reevaluation," *Maarav* 13 (2006): 193–209.

2. Elephantine (Egypt, Second Half of Fifth Century b.c.e.)

Two deeds of sale from Elephantine, *TAD* B3.4 and *TAD* B3.12, stipulate the protection of the buyer's ownership against claims raised by the vendor's party, as well as by a third person.[5]

2.1. TAD B3.4: *Sale of Abandoned Property*

The document *TAD* B3.4, dated to 14 September 437 b.c.e., concerns the sale of an abandoned house, situated in the fortress of Elephantine, by Bagazushta, son of Bazu, and lady *Wbyl*, daughter of Shatibara, to Ananyah, son of Azaryah, for the price of one karsh and four shekels of silver by the stone of the king.

The ownership of the abandoned house is transferred in the clauses of withdrawal of the vendors[6] and investiture of the buyer. The investiture clause gives rights to the buyer over the bought property, as well as the right of disposal of the property to the buyer's children or in case of gift to a third person.[7]

The investiture clause is followed by a double guarantee of protection against the vendor's party, containing two waivers of suit or process in the matter of the sold property:[8] each waiver is followed by a stipulation of a penalty in case of violation of the waiver.

The first guarantee forbids to the vendors to intend suit or process against the buyer,[9] his sons and daughters and a third person,[10] determines the penalty of twenty karsh of silver to be paid by the vendors to

---

[5] I quote the texts from Elephantine under abbreviation *TAD* according to B. Porten and A. Yardeni, *Textbook of Aramaic Documents from Ancient Egypt*, vol. 2: *Contracts* (Jerusalem: The Hebrew University, 1989).

[6] אנה בגזשת ואובל כל 2 אנחן זבן ויהבן לך ורחקן מנה מן יומא זנה ועד עלמן "I, Bagazushta, and *wbl*, all 2, we sold and gave to you, and we withdrew from it from this day and forever" (*TAD* B3.4:10–11).

[7] אנת עניה בר עזריה שליט בביתא זך ובניך מן אחריך ולמן די צבית למנתן "you, Ananyah, son of Azaryah, have right to this house, and your sons after you, and to whom you desire to give it" (*TAD* B3.4:11–12).

[8] For the analysis of this "double clause," see Yaron, *Introduction*, 85.

[9] אנחן לא נכל נגרנך דין ודבב בשם ביתא זנה זי אנחן זבן ויהבן לך ורחקן מנה "we shall not be able to institute against you suit or process in the name of this house which we sold and gave you and from which we withdrew" (*TAD* B3.4:12–13).

[10] ולא נכהל נגרה לבר לך וברה ולמן זי צבית למנתן "and we shall not be able to institute against son of yours or daughter or to whom you desire to give" (*TAD* B3.4:13–14).

the buyer in case of violation of the waiver,[11] and ends by the reaffirmation of the investiture of the buyer's party.[12]

The second guarantee forbids the suit or process lead by the children of the vendors against the buyer,[13] stipulates the penalty of twenty karsh of silver in case of violation of this waiver[14] and finishes by the reaffirmation of the investiture of the buyer's party.[15] This second guarantee does not protect the third person in the case of gift.

In these two guarantees protecting the buyer's party against eviction by the vendor's party, the vendor is presumed of *bad faith*: the vendor's party is not supposed to act and to raise claims concerning the sold property. If the vendor's party acts and contests the transaction, it is consequently penalized by the payment of twenty karsh of silver to the buyer. The buyer does not lose the purchased property.

The status of a third person is different: suit or process in the matter of the buyer's ownership is allowed to a third person. The third person is not a contracting party and his claims are not followed by penalizing the claimant. In the case of claims raised by a third person, the vendor must act to protect the buyer's property. The vendor's party is presumed of *good faith*: they sold the property in *good faith* so they are able to protect it against other claims. The vendor's party must cleanse (פצל) the property and give it back to the buyer or his children within thirty days.[16] If they do not cleanse, they are liable to pay compensation—not a penalty—to the buyer. The compensation consists of either another similar house or

---

[11] הן גרינך דין ודבב וגרין לבר וברה לך ולמן זי צבית למנתן אנחן נגתן לך כסף כרשן 20 כסף זוז לעשרתא "if we institute against you suit or process or institute against son or daughter of yours or to whom you desire to give, we shall give you silver, 20 karsh, silver zuz to ten" (*TAD* B3.4:14–16).

[12] וביתא זילך אם וזי בניך מן אחריך ולמן זי צבית למנתן "and the house is moreover yours and your children's after you and to whom you desire to give it" (*TAD* B3.4:16).

[13] ולא יכהל בר וברה לן יגרנך זין חבב בשם ביתא זנה זי תחמוהי כתבן מנעל "and son or daughter of ours shall not be able to institute against you suit or process in the name of this house whose boundaries are written above" (*TAD* B3.4:16–18).

[14] הן גרורו וגרו לבר וברה לך ינתנון לך כסף כרשן 20 כסף זוז 10 "if they institute against you or institute suit against son or daughter of yours, they shall give you silver 20 karsh, silver zuz to the 10" (*TAD* B3.4:18).

[15] וביתא זילך אם וזי בניך מן אחריך "and the house is moreover yours and your children's after you" (*TAD* B3.4:19).

[16] והן גבר אחרן יגרנך ויגרה לבר וברה לך אנחן נקום ונפצל ונגתן לך בין יומן 10 20 "and if another person institute against you or institute against son or daughter of yours, we shall stand up and cleanse and give to you within 30 days." (*TAD* B3.4:19–20).

of the price of the sold property (one karsh and four shekels of silver) and other expenses.[17]

I have summarized the status of the persons who can attack the ownership of the buyer's party. I shall now summarize the status of the persons who are protected by the contract. The protection of the ownership of the buyer, of his children and of any other owner who receives the property from the buyer as a gift, is not equal. The buyer and his children are protected by the vendor and his children against suit or process instituted by the vendor, his children and by a third person. The third person—owner of the sold property in the case of gift—is protected only by the vendor against suit or process instituted by the vendor. The third person is not protected against the vendor's children and against the claims of another third person.

In sum, the means of protection in the case of acting in *bad faith* by the vendor's party is the payment of a penalty fixed by the contract to the buyer. In the case of impossibility to defend the sold property in a process instituted by a third person, the vendor is simply required to recompense the buyer; he is not penalized, because he is presumed of *good faith*. In cases of penalization or compensation, the vendor or his children are liable only to the buyer, not to his children or to the person who receives the ownership as a gift. The persons mentioned in the investiture clause—buyer, his children, third person in case of gift—are separately considered in the stipulation of their protection: their protection is nuanced and very precisely determined.

2.2. TAD B3.12: Sale of Apartment to Son-in-Law

The document *TAD* B3.12 was written on 13 December 402 B.C.E. in Elephantine and concerns a sale of a house by Anani, son of Azaryah, and his wife Tapamet, to Anani, son of Haggai, son of Meshullam, son of Besas.

---

[17] והן לא פצלן אנחן ובנין נתן לך בית לדמות ביתך ומשחתה בר מן בר זכר ונקבה זי אפולי או ברה לה יתה לה ולא כהלן פצלן נתן לך כספך כרש 1 שקל 4 ובנינא זי תבנה בה וכל אשרן זי יהכן על ביתא זך "and if we do not cleanse (it), we or our children shall give you a house in the likeness of your house and its measurements, unless a son, male or female, of ʾpwly or a daughter of his should come and we will not be able to cleanse (it. Then) we shall give you your silver, 1 karsh, 4 shekels and the (value of) the building (improvements) which you will have built in it and all the fittings that will have gone into that house" (*TAD* B3.4:20–23).

The investiture clause gives the authority over the bought property to the buyer as well as to his children after him, or to a third person in the case of gift or sale.[18] All these potential owners are protected against suit or process instituted by the vendors, by their sons or daughters, brother, sister, partner-in-chattel, partner-in-land and guarantor: none of these persons can institute suit or process.[19] The vendor's party as well as other persons are bound by this guarantee: they have to abstain. Consequently, whoever (vendor's party or a third person) institutes a suit, whoever complains in front of the prefect, the lord or the judge, or whoever would like to contest the sale by another deed of sale, acts in *bad faith* and is liable to pay the penalty of twenty karsh of silver to the buyer or his children, not to the other persons in the case of gift or sale.[20]

The contract does not admit claims concerning the sold house presumed of *good faith*, thus the clearance of the property is absent as well as the possibility of compensation of the lost property. The protection of the ownership is absolute, nobody can contest. The vendor is not responsible for a suit or process instituted by other persons: he cannot be penalized in case of suit or process concerning the buyer's ownership by the vendor's relatives or other persons.

---

[18] ביתא זנה (...) אנת עני עני שליט בה מן יומא זנה ועד עלמן ובניך אחריך ולמן זי רחמת תנתן או זי תזבן לה בכסף "this house ... you, Anani, have right to it from this day and forever and your children have right after you and anyone to whom you give it affectionately or to whom you sell it for silver" (*TAD* 3.12:22–24).

[19] לא נכהל נרשנך דין ודבב בשם ביתא זנה זי זבן ויהבן לך ויהבת לן דמוהי כסף וטיב לבבן בגו אף לא נכהל נרשה לבניך ובנתך וזי תנתן לה בכסף או רחמת אף לא יכהל בר לן וברה אח ואחה לן הנגית והנבג ואדרנג זילן "we shall not be able to bring against you suit or process in the name of this house which we sold and gave you and you gave us its price silver and our heart was satisfied; moreover, we shall not be able to bring against your sons or your daughters or to whom you give it for silver or affectionately; moreover, son of ours or daughter, brother or sister of ours, partner-in-chattel or partner-in-land or guarantor of ours shall not be able" (*TAD* B3.12:25–27).

[20] זי ירשנך דין וירשה לבניך ולאיש זי תנתן לה וזי יקבל עליך לסגן ומרא ודין בשם ביתא זנה זי משחת כתב מנעל וזי ינפק עליך ספר חדת ועתיק בשם ביתא זנה זי זבן ויהבן לך יחוב ויתן לך ולבניך אביגרן כסף כרשן 20 באבני מלכא כסף צרף "whoever shall bring against you suit or bring against your sons or against a man to whom you give, or whoever shall complain against you to prefect or lord or judge in the name of this house whose measurements is written above, or whoever shall take out against you a new or old document in the name of this house which we sold and gave you, shall be liable and shall give you or your children a penalty of silver, 20 karsh by the stone of the king, pure silver" (*TAD* B3.12:27–30).

3. Wadi Daliyeh (ca. 375–332 b.c.e.)

The Wadi Daliyeh manuscripts, written in the city of Samaria in the fourth century B.C.E., before 332, are quite fragmentary. Not one of the preserved documents is complete.[21] So the analysis of protection of ownership in deeds of sale is based upon a reconstruction.[22] Most of the deeds of sale concern sales of slaves; two deeds seem to concern a sale of immovable property, other fragmentary deeds seem to concern a lease of the services of slaves, loans etc.[23]

As far as we can reconstruct the texts from the fragments, it seems that the investiture clause does not determine particular rights of the new owner of the property. It simply states that the buyer took possession of the slave,[24] that the slave belongs to him,[25] that he has the right of disposal of the slave,[26] and that the vendor is no longer owner.[27] Other specific rights (to sell, to give, etc.) are not specified.

The clauses concerning protection of ownership are two: the "defension"[28] clause and the contravention clause. These guarantees contain,

---

[21] F.M. Cross, "Samaria Papyrus 1: An Aramaic Slave Conveyance of 335 B.C.E. Found in the Wâdî ed-Dâliyeh," *ErIsr* 18 (1985): 7*–17*; idem, "A Report on the Samaria Papyri," in *Congress Volume: Jerusalem 1986* (ed. J.A. Emerton; VTSup 40; Leiden: Brill, 1988), 17–26; D.M. Gropp in *DJD* XXVIII (2001): 3–116; J. Dušek, *Les manuscrits araméens du Wadi Daliyeh et la Samarie vers 450–332 av. J.-C.* (Culture and History of the Ancient Near East 30 Leiden: Brill, 2007).

[22] I use the reconstruction published in Dušek, *Les manuscrits araméens du Wadi Daliyeh*; for the overview of the legal formulary of the Wadi Daliyeh documents see pp. 105–114. See also J. Dušek, "Formulaires juridiques dans les contrats du wadi Daliyeh," in *Trois millénaires de formulaires juridiques* (ed. S. Démare-Lafont and A. Lemaire; Hautes études orientales 48; Moyen et Proche Orient 4; Geneva: Droz, 2010), 279–316.

[23] Dušek, *Les manuscrits araméens du Wadi Daliyeh*, 65–66.

[24] ‫זך (עבד) (החסן) (קדמהי)‬ B-‫ו‬ S-‫ל‬ "and B(uyer) took possession of the said S (slave) (before him)" (WDSP 3:3–4; 4:4; 8:3–4; 15:8).

[25] ‫עבד יהוה\הוה לה (ולבנהי מן אחרוהי) לעלמא‬ "he will be/has become his slave (and his sons' after him) in perpetuity" (WDSP 1:3[–4], 2:3; 3:4; 5:5; 6:[3–]4).

[26] ‫זך‬ S-‫ל‬ B ‫שליט‬ "the B(uyer) has authority over the said S(lave)" (WDSP 1:4; 4:5; 20:7).

[27] ‫לא שליט‬ V ‫או מן אחרי זנה בנן ואחן זילה‬ "V(endor) has no authority nor his sons and brothers of his hereafter" (WDSP 4:6; 6:[4–]5; 15:10).

[28] The term "defension" clause is a transposition to English of the German "Defensionsklausel" used by H. Petschow for example in *Die neubabylonischen Kaufformulare* (Leipziger rechtswissenschaftliche Studien 118; Leipzig: Weicher, 1939), 55–68. The term "defension clause" is used in the English terminology for the Aramaic legal texts for example in Cross, "Samaria Papyrus 1"; Gropp in *DJD* XXVIII (2001): 3–116; Y. Yadin et al., eds., *The Documents from the Bar Kokhba Period in the Cave of Letters: Hebrew, Aramaic and Nabataean-Aramaic Papyri* (JDS; Jerusalem: Israel Exploration Society, 2002), 226–228, etc.

according to D.M. Gropp, some features of the Neo-Babylonian legal tradition of deeds of sale.[29] The guarantees with penalties are not identical in all deeds of sale, but we present here their summary overview.[30]

The "defension" clause protects property acquired by the buyer against eviction in processes (דין) and stipulates the clearance of the property in such a case by the vendor. The buyer, his sons or a third person who owes the deed of sale,[31] can be protected against a process instituted by the vendor or by the vendor's party (one of his men, one of his colleagues or servants),[32] or by other persons.[33] The vendor is presumed of *good faith*: he sold his property and he must be able to protect it before a tribunal: the vendor must cleanse (מרק) the property from claims and give it back (נתן) to the buyer.[34] The case of non-clearance is perhaps mentioned in WDSP 3:6–7,[35] but it is only a fragment of the formula and does not allow possible conclusions.

The contravention clause concerns the violation (שנה "change") of the contract by the vendor presumed of *bad faith*.[36] The vendor acts in *bad faith* if he contests the sale[37] and the receipt of payment.[38] In this case, the

---

[29] Gropp in *DJD* XXVIII (2001): 24–30; idem, "The Samaria Papyri and the Babylonio-Aramaean Symbiosis," in *Semitic Papyrology in Context: A Climate of Creativity: Papers from a New York University Conference Marking the Retirement of Baruch A. Levine* (ed. L.H. Schiffman; Culture and History of the Ancient Near East 14; Leiden: Brill, 2003), 23–49, esp. 34–40.

[30] For a more in-depth description see Dušek, *Les manuscrits araméens du Wadi Daliyeh*, 78–88.

[31] הן (...) דינן יעבד עם גבר זי שטרא זנה מהחסן (...) "if (...) enter into litigation with a man who owes this deed" (WDSP 6:6; 7:9).

[32] (זי) הן אנה V (או איש זילי כנותי או מן עבדי) דינן אעבד עם B (ובנוהי) (על טעם S זך) "if I, V(endor) (or one of my men, my colleagues or of my servants), enter into litigation with B(uyer) (and his sons) (concerning the said S[lave])" (WDSP 1:5; 2:4[–5]; 4:7; 5:7[–8]; 8:6; 9:[7–]8; 11ʳ:11; 15:11; 19:3).

[33] (ועם בנוהי מן אחרוהי) B והן גבר אחרן דינן יעבד עם "and if someone else enter into litigation with B(uyer) (and his sons after him)" (WDSP 1:[5–]6; 3:5; 8:7–8).

[34] אנה V אמרק אנתן לך "I, V(endor), will cleanse and give (the sold object) to you" (WDSP 1:6; 2:5; 3:6; 4:8; 6:[6–]7; 18:4; 21:10).

[35] והן לא [אמרק] "if I do not [cleanse ...]" (WDSP 3:6[–7]).

[36] (במליא אלה) או אשנה באסרא זנה "or if I change this bond (in these terms)" (WDSP 1:[6–]7; 2:5; 3:7; 6:7; 7:11; 9:9; 15:13; 19:4; 25:1).

[37] (לך) ואמר S-ל כזי זנה עבדא לא זבנת לך "and I say (to you) that I did not sell to you this S[lave]" (WDSP 1:7; 3:7[–8]; 4:9; 5:9[–10]; 8:6–7; 14:15[–16]; 15:14).

[38] (B מניד \\ מנך אנה מקבל לא (זנה) (ש X) וכספא "and I do not receive from you (this) (X shekels of) silver (/from the hand of B[uyer])" (WDSP 1:[7–]8; 2:6; 3:8[–9]; 4:9[–10]; 9:[9–]10?; 15:14; 18:5; 25:2); or וכספא זנה לא יהבת לי "and I have not given to you the silver" (WDSP 6:[7–]8).

buyer is quit,[39] the vendor is in debt[40] and penalized. The vendor must return to the buyer the price of the purchased property.[41] He is liable to pay the penalty fixed by the contract to the buyer[42] and the buyer must accept it.[43] The vendor must pay an additional penalty for each slave in case of sale of more than one slave.[44] The restitution of the price and the payment of the penalties by the vendor to the buyer do not cancel the transaction: the buyer is not deprived of his rights of ownership over the purchased property.[45] It means the restitution of the price to the buyer is not compensation for lost property, as in Elephantine, but constitutes part of the cumulative penalty.

In sum, the contract presupposes that the vendor sold the property in *good faith* and is able to clear it before a tribunal in the event of claims raised by his party or by a third person. This is the sense of the "defension" clause. According to the contravention clause, if the vendor contests the sale, his contesting is presumed of *bad faith* and he is penalized. The sense of the contravention clause and of the cumulative penalties seems to be to prevent the vendor from declining his responsibility for the sale, presupposed in the "defension" clause.

4. Cave of Letters (First–Second Century c.e.)

The Cave of Letters in Naḥal Ḥever produced Nabataean, Greek and Aramaic deeds of sale from first and second centuries c.e.

---

[39] תש×תּ‹בק קדמי "you are quit before me" (WDSP 2:7; 6:[8–]9; 9:[10–]11).

[40] חיב אנה (ואחר) "(and afterwards) I am liable" (WDSP 1:9; 2:7; 6:9; 9:11).

[41] (אנת B) אף כספא ש X זי יהבת לי אהתיב אנתן לך "also the silver, X sh(eqels), which you gave to me, I return to you (you B[uyer])" (WDSP 1:8; 4:10; 5:10[–11]; 6:8; 7:13?; 8:8–9?; 15:[14–]15; 21:13; 35 frg. 5:3).

[42] אשלם אנתן לך B (ובניך מן אחריך) כסף מנן X "I will pay, I will give to you, B(yuer), (and your sons after you), X silver minas silver" (WDSP 1:9; 3:9; 4:11; 5:11[–12]; 15:[15–]16; 18:6).

[43] תהחסן זי לא דינן (ולא חובן) כסף מנן X "you will take possession of X silver minas without litigation (and without liabilities)" (WDSP 1:[9–]10; 2:8; 6:[9–]10; 15:16?).

[44] אשלם ל-B לנפש 1 כסף מנה X "I will pay to B(uyer) 1 silver mina for each person" (WDSP 2:9; 5:12[–13]; 6:10[–11]; 8:9–10?; 9:[11–]12).

[45] ולא שליט אנה V ל-S זך "and I, V(endor), have not authority over the said S(lave)" (WDSP 1:10; 4:12; 6:11; 7:16); (ובנוהי מן אחרוהי) B ושליט "and B(uyer) (and his sons after him) has authority" (WDSP 1:[10–]11; 14:18[–19]).

4.1. *Nabataean-Aramaic Deeds of Sale:*
P. Yadin 2, P. Yadin 3 and XḤev/Se Nab. 2

Two double Nabataean deeds concerning a sale were discovered in the Cave of Letters:[46] P. Yadin 2 (97/98 C.E.)[47] and P. Yadin 3 (97/98 C.E.).[48] P. Yadin 2 concerns the purchase of a date palm plantation by Archelaus, the commander, from Abiʿadan; P. Yadin 3 is a deed of purchase of a date palm plantation by Shimʿon. These two documents were written in the Nabataean kingdom before its Roman annexation (106 C.E.).[49]

The third Nabataean deed of sale, listed as XḤev/Se Nab. 2, records the sale of a parcel of a real estate by a woman Shalom to Šʿdʾlhy; this document was dated by A. Yardeni to ca. 100 C.E.[50]

The investiture, "defension" and contravention clauses are preserved: they are identical in all three documents. According to the investiture clause, the buyer acquires in the purchase the rights forever to buy, to sell, to pledge, to inherit and grant as gift and to do with these purchases whatever he wishes.[51] Like in the Wadi Daliyeh documents, the clauses protecting the buyer's ownership are two: the "defension" clause and the contravention clause.

The "defension" clause presupposes that the vendor sold the property in *good faith* and is able to protect it. This clause forbids lawsuit (דין), process (דבב), or oath (מומא) in the matter of the bought property,[52] stipulates the vendor's obligation to cleanse (צפא)[53] the property from all

---

[46] Yadin et al., *Documents from the Bar Kokhba Period*, 201–246.

[47] 3rd of Kislev, year 28 of Rabʾel II, Nabataean king.

[48] 2nd of Ṭebet, year 28 of Rabʾel II, Nabataean king.

[49] Aspects of language and formulation of the Nabataean documents were compared to the Jewish-Aramaic documents by B.A. Levine, "The Various Workings of the Aramaic Legal Tradition: Jews and Nabataeans in the Naḥal Ḥever Archive," in *The Dead Sea Scrolls Fifty Years After Their Discovery: Proceedings of the Jerusalem Congress, July 20–25, 1997* (ed. L.H. Schiffman et al.; Jerusalem: Israel Exploration Society, 2000), 836–851.

[50] A. Yardeni, *Textbook of Aramaic, Hebrew and Nabataean Documentary Texts from the Judaean Desert and Related Material* (2 vols.; Jerusalem: The Hebrew University, 2000), 1:290–292 and 2:95.

[51] למקנא ולוזבנה ולמרהן ולמנחל ולמנתן ולמעבד בזבניא אלה כל די יצבה B דנה מן יום די כתיב שטרא דנה ועד עלם "to buy and to sell, and to pledge, and to inherit and grant as gift, and to do with these purchases all that he wishes (accrues to) this B(uyer) from the day on which this document is written and forever" (P. Yadin 2:9–10, 30–32; P. Yadin 3:10–11, 33–35; XḤev/Se Nab. 2:13–15).

[52] די לא דין ולא דבב ולא מומא (כלה) "that it not be subject to lawsuit or contest or oath (whatsoever)" (P. Yadin 2:10, 32; P. Yadin 3:11, 35; XḤev/Se Nab. 2:15).

[53] See Y.C. Greenfield, "The 'Defension Clause' in Some Documents from Naḥal Ḥever and Naḥal Ṣeʾelim," *RevQ* 15 (1992): 467–471; repr. in *ʿAl Kanfei Yonah: Collected Studies*

claims[54] and states that the purchased property is clean from the vendor's claims or from claims in vendor's name.[55] Compared to the Wadi Daliyeh deeds of sale the "defension" clause is more developed.[56]

The contravention clause protects the buyer's ownership against the actions of the vendor presumed of *bad faith*. Like in the Wadi Daliyeh documents, the vendor is penalized in the contravention clause in case of violation (שנא "change") of the contract. If the vendor contests the sale, he must give back to the buyer the price of the purchase, must pay all that the vendor may claim or that may be claimed in vendor's name against the buyer and the vendor will pay an undetermined penalty also to the Nabataean king.[57] This means that the penalty consists of the price, of other expenses and of payment to the ruler. This penalty against the vendor has no consequences for the buyer's party: the buyer, his heirs or another person who owns the deed of sale, has the right of disposal over the bought property and remains clean.[58] The return of the price—which corresponds to the compensation in the Elephantine documents—has the role of penalty. The compensation of the lost property itself is not considered in the contract.

---

of Jonas C. Greenfield on Semitic Philology (ed. S.M. Paul, M.E. Stone, and A. Pinnick; Leiden: Brill, 2001), 1:460–464.

[54] ודי אצפא אנה V דנה זבניא אלה מן כל אנוש כלה רחיק וקריב ואשבק לך אנת B דנה לך ולבניך מן אחריך עד עלם "and that I will clear, I, this V(endor), these purchases from anyone at all, distant or near, and I will free them up to you, you, this B(uyer); to you and to your sons after you, forever" (P. Yadin 2:10–11, 32–33; P. Yadin 3:11–12, 35–36; XḤev/Se Nab. 2:15–17).

[55] וכות דכי ומ°°°א אנת B דנה מני אנה V דנה מן כל די אבעא ויתבעא בשמי עליך בזבניא אלה (...) "and as well, clean and ... are you, this same B(uyer), from me, I this V(endor), from all that I may claim or that may be claimed in my name against you regarding these purchases (...)" (P. Yadin 2:11–12, 33–34; P. Yadin 3:[12–]13, 37–38; XḤev/Se Nab. 2:17–18).

[56] וחלק ותעין ועדי\ועּרי ומותו די עד יתבעה בהגן ... ותצדיק כחליפין ומענמין ... זבנין ובראון כחליקת זבניא ובראונא די מתכתב לעלם "clearance and specification and accounting and oath concerning what may still be claimed regarding ... And (there is) agreement regarding exchange rates and profits ... (regarding) purchases and clearances, as is customary for purchases and clearances, as is written, forever." (P. Yadin 2:12–13, 35–37; P. Yadin 3:13–14, 38–40; XḤev/Se Nab. 2:18–20). For the commentary, see Yadin et al., *Documents from the Bar Kokhba Period*, 227.

[57] והן אנה V דנה ... ואשנא מן דנה די לא ברשא אחוב לך אנת B דנה כל דמי זבניא אלה ובכללכל די אבעא ויתבעא בשמי עליך בהם ולמראנא רבאל מלכא כות "And if I, V(endor), this, shall deviate from this (agreement) without authority, then I shall owe to you, you, this B(uyer), the entire price of these purchases, and all and everything that I may claim or that may be claimed in my name against you regarding them. And to our lord Rabʾel the King, as well" (P. Yadin 2:14–15, 38–40; P. Yadin 3:16[–18], 43–44; XḤev/Se Nab. 2:[21–]22).

[58] ושליט ודכי ... "and empowered and clean ..." (P. Yadin 2:16, 40–41; P. Yadin 3:46–47; XḤev/Se Nab. 2:[23–]24).

4.2. *P. Yadin 8: An Aramaic Deed of Sale*

Aramaic contract P. Yadin 8 was written in 122 C.E. in the Roman
Provincia Arabia. According to the *editio princeps*, this contract is a deed
of purchase for an ass or donkey and a female animal, by Yehoseph, son
of Shimʿon, from his brother, whose name is lost.[59] The interpretation of
the text was reconsidered and rightly corrected by Hillel I. Newman: the
contract is a deed of sale where Yehoseph, son of Shimʿon, acts as vendor
and pronounces the guarantees for the sold property on lines 6–9.[60]

The "defension" clause seems to be in the lines 6–7,[61] and the contravention clause concerning the violation (שנה "change") of the contract
by the vendor, punished by the penalties, is attested in lines 8–9.[62] The
penalty should be paid also to Caesar.[63]

This form of legal protection of the buyer's ownership seems to belong
to the same legal tradition as the Nabataean deeds of sale.

4.3. *Greek Deeds of Sale from the Cave of Letters*

Two deeds of sale recording the same transaction were discovered in the
Cave of Letters: a deed of purchase of a date crop (P. Yadin 21) and deed
of sale of a date crop (P. Yadin 22). Both documents were written on
11 September 130 C.E., in Maoza, district of Zoara (Roman *Provincia
Arabia*), and belong to the Babatha's archive.[64] These two deeds do not
contain the investiture clause. A. Radzyner identified in these deeds of
sale some elements of a labor-lease agreement.[65]

P. Yadin 21, belonging to the buyer, contains a clause concerning
payment of a penalty by the vendor to the buyer in case of default of
fulfillment of the contract, and the buyer's right of execution (πρᾶξις).[66]

---

[59] Yadin et al., *Documents from the Bar Kokhba Period*, 109–117.

[60] H.I. Newman, "P. Yadin 8: A Correction," *JJS* 57 (2006): 330–335.

[61] א◦◦◦ לי עמך מנדעם לא אז זעיר ולא סגי[א] אנה ◦ [ ] [בז]בניא אלה מן כל אנוש כלה רחי[ק וקריב]
] "I will [not] have with you anything neither small nor larg[e ...] I, ... [] ... [regarding]
these purchases, from any person whomsever, fa[r or near ...]" (P. Yadin 8:6–7).

[62] [ ]◦ והן א◦◦◦◦ואשנה מן דנה ◦ יהוא לך עמי כול[ ] "And if I ... and deviate from this, you will
have with me (= I will owe you) the entire [... (= *amount*)]" (P. Yadin 8:8).

[63] ולמראנא קיסר כות "and to our lord, Caesar, as well" (P. Yadin 8:9).

[64] N. Lewis, ed., *The Documents from the Bar Kokhba Period in the Cave of Letters:
Greek Papyri* (JDS 2; Jerusalem: Israel Exploration Society, 1989), 94–101.

[65] A. Radzyner, "P. Yadin 21–22: Sale or Lease?" in *Law in the Documents of the Judaean
Desert* (ed. Katzoff and Schaps), 145–163.

[66] "And if I do not provide you with the aforesaid dates in full and drying time, I will

P. Yadin 22, belonging to the vendor, contains a "defension" clause stipulating the vendor's obligation to cleanse (καθαροποιεῖν) the property in case of claims (ἀντιποίησις "claim").[67] This "defension" clause is followed by the contravention clause for the case when the vendor does not cleanse the property from the claims: in this case the vendor must pay a penalty of twenty silver denarii.[68] Apparently, the non-clearance of the property of the claims is considered proof of the vendor's *bad faith*: he is penalized by a fixed sum; the contract mentions no compensation of the lost property because of claims.

It is very interesting to see that the guarantees in two documents concerning the same transaction, pronounced both by the vendor, are different. The copy belonging to the buyer (P. Yadin 21) is focused on the non-fulfillment of the contract by the vendor with the buyer's right of execution upon the vendor's property. The copy belonging to the vendor (P. Yadin 22) reflects a different legal tradition of guarantees with clauses of "defension" and contravention focused upon the vendor's duties. In sum, the buyer's copy informs the buyer about his right of execution (πρᾶξις) on the vendor's property, and the vendor's copy informs the vendor concerning his duties to protect the sold property against other claims.

5. Hebrew and Aramaic Deeds of Sale from Wadi Murabba'at, Wadi Seiyâl/Naḥal Ḥever and 4Q346

The other deeds of sale from Judean Desert, written in Aramaic or in Hebrew, which contain clauses protecting the buyer's ownership, reflect a different legal tradition than the Aramaic/Nabataean deeds of sale mentioned previously. It concerns deeds of sale from Wadi Murabba'at

---

give you for each several talent [of "splits"] two denarii and of Syrian and Naaran (?) one "black." Both upon myself and upon my property or from my guarantor, from whichever the person acting through (you) or for (you), (your) right of execution (πρᾶξις) shall be valid everywhere, the formal question having in good faith been asked and acknowledged in reply" (P. Yadin 21:21–28).

[67] "I shall clear (καθαροποιεῖν) the right to the aforesaid orchards for you of every counterclaimant" (P. Yadin 22:20–23).

[68] "And if anyone enters a counterclaim (ἀντιποίησις) against you because of your purchase and I do not firmly validate [it] for you as aforesaid, I shall be owing to you in return for your labors and expenses twenty silver denarii, interposing no objection" (P. Yadin 22:23–25).

and from the Seiyâl Collection.[69] All these deeds of sale contain the same type of guarantee concerning legal protection of the buyer's ownership, with some variants.[70] The deeds of sale from Wadi Murabbaʿat are dated between 131 and 134 C.E., to the era of "liberation of Israel" (גאולת ישראל).[71] The deeds of sale from the Seiyâl Collection are dated to the third year of "freedom of Israel" (חר[ו]ת ישראל) under Shimʿon bar Kosiba, the prince of Israel (134–135 C.E.).[72]

The investiture clause is wholly or partially preserved in Mur 30 and in XḤev/Se 8, 8a, 9, 21, 23 and 50: these contracts express authority over the purchased property, in Aramaic as well as in Hebrew, by the term רשה "to have power."[73] This term רשה appears together with the term שליט "to have authority" in XḤev/Se 9,6.[74] The investiture clause can give to the buyer and to his inheritors—with small variants—the right to buy, to sell, etc. and to do with the purchased property whatever they desire.[75]

The vendor is responsible for and guarantor of the transaction,[76] by the means of property that he owns or may acquire,[77] for the protection of the buyer's ownership: the vendor will defend the buyer's property against a dispute and challenge,[78] in some cases also against damage[79]

---

[69] Mur 26; Mur 30; XḤev/Se 8, 8a, 9, 21, 23 and 50.

[70] The guarantee clauses are not preserved in some deeds of sale from Wadi Murabbaʿat (Mur 22, 23, 27, 29).

[71] Deeds of sale are dated to 131 C.E. (Mur 22), 132 C.E.? (Mur 23), 133 C.E. (Mur 29) and 134 C.E. (Mur 30).

[72] חר[ו]ת ישראל לשם (\על ימי) שמעון בר כסבה נשיא ישראל. Deeds of sale are dated to the third year of the freedom of Israel: 134 or 135 C.E. (XḤev/Se 7 and 8a) and 135 C.E. (XḤev/Se 8). The date of subscription of the contract is not preserved in the other Aramaic and Hebrew deeds of sale belonging to this corpus.

[73] Mur 30:22; XḤev/Se 8a:6; 9:6; 21:6; 50:12.

[74] See also P. Yadin 47a:9–10.

[75] In Hebrew: לעשות בו כל שתחפץ "to do whatever you wish" (Mur 30:23). In Aramaic: למקנה ולמז[ב]נה ול[מ]עבד בה כל די "to dig and to deepen" (XḤev/Se 8:6); למחפר ולמעמקה תצבה "to buy and to se[l]l, and to [d]o with it whatever you desire" (XḤev/Se 9:7); למחפר ולהעמקה למב[נה] ולהרמא למקנה ולמזבונה "to dig and to deepen, to bu[ild] and to erect, to buy and to sell" (XḤev/Se 21:7–8); למעבד בה כול די תצבה "to do with it whatever you desire" (XḤev/Se 23:3); למקנה ולמזבנה ולמעבד בה כל די יצבן "to buy and to sell and to do whatever they desire" (XḤev/Se 50:12–13).

[76] Hebrew: אחראים וערבים (Mur 30:24). In Aramaic: אחראין וערבין (XḤev/Se 8:6; 9:8; 23:4; 50:14), אחריא וערביא (Mur 26:4), אחרי וערב (XḤev/Se 8a:11).

[77] Aramaic: וכל די איתי לי ודי אקנה "and all that I own and whatever I will acquire" (XḤev/Se 8:6; 23:4; 50:14); [פר]ען תשלמתה מן נכ[סי ודי אק[נה "[The fulfill]ment of my payment from my prop[erty and whatever I will acq]uire" (XḤev/Se 8a:13; 9:10). In Hebrew: וכל שיש לי ושאקנה (Mur 30:23).

[78] חרר ותגר (Mur 26:5; 30:25; XḤev/Se 8:7; 9:9).

[79] נזק (XḤev/Se 9:9).

and annulment.[80] In case of these attacks on the buyer's ownership the vendor will cleanse (שפה or מרק)[81] and establish (קים) the sale before the buyer and his inheritors.[82] The vendor as a guarantor of the transaction is presumed of *good faith*.

We can see that, compared to the other deeds of sale from Elephantine, Wadi Daliyeh and Naḥal Ḥever, the clauses concerning protection of the buyer's ownership in the Aramaic and Hebrew deeds of sale from Wadi Murabbaʿat and from the Seiyâl Collection are considerably simplified and can be compared to P. Yadin 21 (see above, § 4.3). The concept of presumption of the vendor's *bad faith* is absent. The buyer is implicitly protected against all attacks on his acquired ownership: the vendor must cleanse the sold property from all attacks and warrants this protection by all his property that he owns or may acquire.

The guarantee, by the means of property that the vendor owns or may acquire, is interesting. In Palestine we find this principle especially in the context of the right of execution in the Greek deeds from the Cave of Letters published by N. Lewis[83] and in other contracts from Wadi Murabbaʿat and from the Seiyâl Collection:[84] in the Greek marriage contracts,[85] in a Greek contract of deposit,[86] in Aramaic and Greek deeds of acknowledgement of debt,[87] in a Greek deed of loan of hypothec,[88] and in a Greek deed of sale.[89] All these deeds were written under Roman administration. This clause gives to one contracting party, or to a person

---

[80] בטלן (Mur 26:5); בטלה (XḤev/Se 9:9).

[81] Greenfield, "'Defension Clause.'"

[82] למשפיה ולמקימה אתרא קדמך ול[קד]ם ירתה[י]ך "to cleanse and to establish the place before you and be[fo]re your inherit[o]rs" (XḤev/Se 9:8–9); למרקא ולקימא זבנה דך קדמ[כן] "to cleanse and to establish the sale before you and before your inheritors"]וקדם ירתכן (XḤev/Se 50:15 and Mur 26:4–5).

[83] Lewis, *Documents from the Bar Kokhba Period*.

[84] The promissory note XḤev/Se 49:11 is an exception: it contains the guarantee by all property, but the reference to the execution is absent.

[85] In the Cave of Letters: P. Yadin 18:16–20, 51–56 (Babatha Archive, 5 April 128 C.E., in Maoza, Zoara disctrict, *Provincia Arabia*). In the Seiyâl Collection: XḤev/Se 65 (P. Yadin 37) (Salome Komaïs Archive, 7 August 131 C.E., in Maoza, Zoara district, administrative region of Petra, *Provincia Arabia*); XḤev/Se 69:11 (130 C.E., in Aristoboulias, *Provincia Judaea*). In Wadi Murabbaʿat: Mur 115:16–18 (124 C.E., in Bethbassi, toparchy of Herodion, *Provincia Judaea*).

[86] P. Yadin 17:12–[15], 34–38 (21 February 128 C.E., in Maoza, district of Zoara, *Provincia Arabia*).

[87] Mur 18:7–8 ar (55/56 C.E., year two of Caesar Nero, in Ṣiwata); Mur 114:17–21 gr (171? C.E.).

[88] P. Yadin 11:8–11, 23–29 (6 May 124, in Ein Gedi village of lord Caesar).

[89] For the Greek deeds of sale, see above, § 4.3.

who is not a party to the agreement, the right of execution (πρᾶξις) upon
present and future property of the other contracting party,[90] in case of
default of fulfillment of the obligations stipulated in the contract.

The practice of execution, in case of default of fulfillment of obligations, stipulated in the contract is known in the Greek papyri from
Ptolemaic and Roman Egypt. These contracts—and especially the marriage contracts—contain the *praxis* clause concerning the right of execution. This *praxis* clause concerning execution seems to be—according to
H.J. Wolff—a result of the actions of Greek tribunals in Ptolemaic Egypt
in cases concerning personal claims.[91]

H. Cotton mentions that the clause of guarantee by present and future
property exists in some Demotic marriage contracts from Egypt,[92] and
states that this clause is not known in the Greek marriage contracts from
Egypt.[93] According to H. Cotton, the formula concerning the guarantee
by present and future property is among the Greek contracts attested
only in deeds contracted by Jews and discovered in the Judean Desert.[94]
Nevertheless the combination of the *praxis* clause with the guarantee by
present and future property is also attested in Syria, in four deeds from
Dura Europos written in the second and third centuries C.E.[95] Thus the
deeds from the Judean Desert probably reflect a legal practice common
to Syria and Palestine which is not exclusively Jewish.

The principle of absolute guarantee by the vendor's property, which
evokes the right of execution of the Greek contracts, was probably adopted to the Aramaic and Hebrew deeds of sale from the legal formulary
from Ptolemaic Egypt. It is not proven if the Greek influence comes
from the time of Ptolemaic rule over Palestine or if it was later. One
Greek deed of sale, written in the Ptolemaic period in Transjordan (*birta*
of Ammanitis), is preserved in the archive of Zenon from Caunos: it

---

[90] ὧν τε ἔχει καὶ ὧν ἂν ἐπικτήσηται κυρίως "both those which he possesses and those which he may validly acquire in addition" (P. Yadin 17:36–37).

[91] H.J. Wolff, "The *Praxis*-Provision in Papyrus Contracts," *TAPA* 72 (1941): 418–438.

[92] P.W. Pestman, *Marriage and Matrimonial Property in Ancient Egypt* (Leiden: Brill, 1961), 115–128, esp. 115–117. H.M. Cotton refers to this text in *DJD* XXVII (1997): 270.

[93] H. Cotton, "A Cancelled Marriage Contract from the Judaean Desert (*XHev/Se Gr.* 2)," *JRS* 84 (1994): 64–86, esp. 79–80.

[94] Ibid., 80.

[95] P.Dura 20:17–19 (Antichretic Loan, 121 C.E.); P.Dura 21:6–8 (Antichretic Loan, first half of second century C.E.); P.Dura 22:9–12 (Loan on Security, 133/4 C.E.); P.Dura 29:12–14 (Deposit, 251 C.E.). According to C.B. Welles et al., *The Excavations at Dura-Europos: Final Report*, vol. 5.1: *The Parchments and Papyri* (New Haven: Yale University Press, 1959).

is a deed concerning the sale of a Babylonian slave girl Sphragis by Nicanor to Zenon, written in April–May 259 B.C.E.,[96] but unfortunately this contract does not contain any guarantee. The situation is similar in P.Dura 15 from the second century B.C.E. written under the Seleucid administration.[97] The oldest Aramaic evidence of guarantee by present and future property seems to be attested in a small fragment of an Aramaic deed of sale: 4Q346. The text may be dated paleographically to the late first century B.C.E.[98] In Palestine, the oldest Aramaic evidence of the right of execution upon present and future property in case of default of payment is in an acknowledgement of debt from Wadi Murabbaʿat Mur 18:7–8 written 55/56 C.E., in the time of Caesar Nero, under Roman administration.

6. Dura Europos (Second–Third Century c.e.)

One Syriac and four Greek deeds of sale were discovered in Dura Europos, in Syria.[99]

6.1. Syriac Deed of Sale of Female Slave

One Syriac deed of female slave written in 243 C.E. in Edessa under Roman rule[100] was discovered in Dura Europos (P.Dura 28).[101] In this deed of sale we find the structure that is already known from the deeds of sale from Wadi Daliyeh and from the Nabataean deeds of sale (P. Yadin 2

---

[96] P.Cairo Zen. 59003. X. Durand, *Des Grecs en Palestine au IIIe siècle avant Jésus-Christ: Le dossier syrien des archives de Zénon de Caunos (261–252)* (CahRB 38; Paris: Gabalda, 2003), 45–48.

[97] See below, § 6.2.

[98] A. Yardeni in *DJD* XXVII (1997): 296–298.

[99] Welles et al., *Parchments and Papyri*.

[100] "In the year 6 of Autokrator Caesar Marcus Antonius Gordianus Eusebes Eutuches Sebastos …" (P.Dura 28:1–2).

[101] C.C. Torrey, "A Syriac Parchment from Edessa of the Year 243 A.D.," *ZS* 10 (1935): 33–45; C. Brockelmann, "Zu dem Syrischen Kaufvertrag aus Edessa," *ZS* 10 (1935): 163; Welles et al., *Parchments and Papyri*, 142–149 and pls. LXIX–LXXI; J.A. Goldstein, "The Syriac Bill of Sale from Dura-Europos," *JNES* 25 (1966): 1–16; H.J.W. Drijvers, ed., *Old Syriac (Edessean) Inscriptions: With an Introduction, Indices and a Glossary* (SSS 3; Leiden: Brill, 1972), 54–57; idem and J.F. Healey, *The Old Syriac Inscriptions of Edessa and Osrhoene: Texts, Translations and Commentary* (HO 42; Leiden: Brill, 1999), 232–235.

and 3, XḤev/Se Nab. 2), from the Aramaic P. Yadin 8 and Greek P. Yadin 22: the investiture clause is followed by the "defension" and contravention clauses.

In the investiture clause, the buyer receives the right of disposal of the bought property and the right to purchase, to sell or to do whatever he wishes.[102]

The "defension" clause protects the buyer against any person who enters into litigation (ܢܕܘܢ) or raises complaint against (ܩܒܠ in eth-pa'al) the buyer or his inheritors: in this case, the vendor or his inheritors will cleanse (ܡܪܩ) and clear (ܢܕܟܐ) the property and will give it back to the buyer.[103] The vendor is presumed of *good faith*.

The contravention clause forbids the revocation (ܠܡܗܦܟܘ) of the contract by the vendor:[104] denial of sale by the vendor is not admitted and the determination of penalty is absent. The absence of penalty and the simple prohibition of contestation of the sale by the vendor seem to indicate that the contract knows the presumption of *bad faith*, but does not admit it.

6.2. *Greek Deeds of Sale*

Four Greek deeds of sale were discovered in Dura Europos: P.Dura 15 (second century B.C.E.) written under the Seleucid administration, P.Dura 25 (180 C.E.), P.Dura 26 (227 C.E.) and P.Dura 27 (ca. 225–240 C.E.), written under Roman administration.

P.Dura 15, written more than three centuries before the other deeds of sale from Dura Europos, contains only a statement concerning the penalty for default equal to the price of the sold property.[105]

---

[102] ܕܢ ܥܒܘ ܐܢܬ ܐܢܬܬܐ ܐܢܬ ... "that from this day and forever you, Tiro, the buyer, and your heirs will have authority over this female slave whom I have sold to you, to keep or to sell or to do with her whatever you wish" (P.Dura 28:11–12).

[103] ... "and if anyone shall enter into litigation or raise complaint with Tiro, the buyer, or with his heirs on account of this slave whom I have sold to him, I, Matarʿata, the seller, and my heirs will arise and make legal declaration and cleanse and clear (her) and I will confirm her in the possession of Tiro, the buyer" (P.Dura 28:12–15).

[104] ... "And I will not be empowered to revoke the words of this document" (P.Dura 28:15).

[105] "(Date. Place. Philip, son of Amynander, citizen of Europos?, has sold lands belonging to him) together with fruit trees and farm buildings and gardens and all appurtenances which lie in the *ekas* of Arybbas in the *kleros* of Conon according to the existing

The rights over purchased property acquired by the buyer are defined in the investiture clause only in P.Dura 26: the buyer has the right to acquire, to employ, to sell and to administer as he pleases.[106]

The guarantees are well preserved only in P.Dura 26 and 27: they contain the guarantees with "defension" and contravention clauses, similar to the Syriac P.Dura 28. The "defension" clause compels the vendor to cleanse (καθαροποιεῖν) the property if somebody lays claim (ἐμποιεῖν).[107] The contravention clause determines specific cumulative penalties in case of non-clearance by the vendor, and the property belongs to the buyer.[108] The cumulative penalty consists in P.Dura 25 of the double amount of whatever loss and an additional penalty of 500 drachmae (= price of the sale),[109] and of double the price of the sale and other loss in P.Dura 26.[110]

The guarantees in P.Dura 27 are fragmentary, but seem to reflect the same schema as in P.Dura 25 and 27.[111] This schema, where the price of the property is not a compensation of loss, but a part of the penalty, fits the schema known in the manuscripts from Wadi Daliyeh and in the Nabataean deeds of sale.

---

records of survey against the sum of 120 drachmae as principal and the like amount as penalty for default ..." (P.Dura 25:1–2).

[106] "... which the price the seller has received from the buyer, and he has transferred to him the land to have it as owner securely for all time, to acquire (κτᾶσθαι) and to employ (χρᾶσθαι), to sell (πωλεῖν) and to administer, in such fashion as he pleases (δι[οι]κεῖν τρόπῳ ᾧς ἂν αἱρῆθαι)" (P.Dura 26:13–15).

[107] "Lysias, the seller, acts as guarantor and broker according to the law and has undertaken, if anyone lays claim to the objects of sale, the slave and the half-share of the vineyard, that he will oppose it and establish a clear title for Heliodorus" (P.Dura 25:9–10, 30–32); "the seller furnishes to the buyer the above purchase unencumbered, unmortgaged, free from any title dispute, and clear of claims; if he does not so furnish it, and if anyone raising a claim gets possession of the above mentioned purchase or any part of it, then the seller will contest the claim in the courts and clear the title for the purchaser" (P.Dura 26:20–24).

[108] "While this deed of sale shall be valid nevertheless" (P.Dura 25:33–34).

[109] "If he does not establish a clear title, and Heliodorus suffers any loss in consequence, he will pay to him double the amount of whatever loss has occurred and an additional penalty of 500 drachmae" (P.Dura 25:10–11).

[110] "If not, he will pay him double the amount of the price and the loss similarly" (P.Dura 26:24–25).

[111] "... he undertakes thus, that if anyone [laying claim, shall gain possession of the above purchase or a part] thereof, he himself will take a stand [... and clear the title] and free it for [((the purchaser), or if not, he will pay him] the price which he received doubly [and the damage in addition; and this] sale shall remain [valid even so ...]" (P.Dura 27, frgs. a–b).

7. Conclusions

I have analyzed legal texts written during approximately 700 years, from the fifth century B.C.E. (Elephantine) until the third century C.E. (Dura Europos), in Aramaic, Hebrew, Nabataean, Greek and Syriac, especially in Palestine, but also in Egypt and in Syria. Over such a long period and large area, we admit that the available evidence is very scanty. It is nevertheless possible to distinguish—within the analyzed texts—three main groups, according to the form and content of the guarantees.

7.1. *Elephantine*

The deeds of sale from Elephantine compose the first and oldest group written in the Persian period, like the Wadi Daliyeh documents. The form of their guarantees is different from the group of the Wadi Daliyeh documents and other later documents; the principles are similar but not the same.[112] This means that, within the Persian Empire, the law protecting purchased property was not identical in all satrapies: it was at least different in Egypt and in Palestine (satrapy of Transeuphrates).

The guarantees in the two deeds of sale from Elephantine are perhaps the most logical. The principle of protection of the buyer is very simple: the vendor is *penalized* by a high sum of silver, fixed by the contract, in case of an act in *bad faith*, but he must *recompense* the buyer when acting in *good faith* and the buyer is evicted, without other penalizations. This simple principle is in both deeds of sale, *TAD* B3.4 and B3.12, with the difference that the actions of all persons (vendor's party and third person) are presumed of *bad faith* in B3.12.

7.2. *Aramaic Tradition in Palestine and Syria*

The second group, which is the most impressive, consists of the following deeds of sale:

– deeds of sale from Wadi Daliyeh from the fourth century B.C.E. (province of Samaria under Persian rule);

---

[112] The form of final clauses (clauses concerning the protection of the buyer's ownership) of the deeds of sale from Elephantine and from Wadi Daliyeh were compared by D.M. Gropp: these two corpora represent two different legal traditions. D.M. Gropp, "The Wadi Daliyeh Documents Compared to the Elephantine Documents," in *The Dead Sea Scrolls Fifty Years After Their Discovery* (ed. Schiffman et al.), 826–835.

- Nabataean deeds of sale from the Cave of Letters (P. Yadin 2 and 3) and from the Seiyâl Collection (XḤev/Se Nab. 2) written at the end of the first century C.E. in the Nabataean kingdom;
- Aramaic P. Yadin 8 written in 122 C.E. (Roman *Provincia Arabia*);
- Greek P. Yadin 22, written in 130 C.E. in Maoza (Roman *Provincia Arabia*);
- Greek deeds of sale from Dura Europos (P.Dura 25, 26, and 27), written in 180 C.E., 227 C.E. and ca. 225–240 C.E., under Roman administration;
- Syriac deed of sale from Dura Europos (P.Dura 28) written in 243 C.E. in Edessa, under Roman rule.

These deeds of sale from Syria-Palestine, written during approximately 600 years (fourth century B.C.E.–third century C.E.), seem to reflect the same—or similar—legal tradition of the protection of the buyer's rights. This legal tradition is attested in Palestine and Syria, especially in Aramaic or its later dialects, but also in Greek texts, under Persian, Nabataean and Roman administration. This overview shows that the Roman administration in Palestine and Syria probably did not interfere excessively with local legal traditions of sale. The oldest corpus belonging to this tradition consists of the deeds of sale from Wadi Daliyeh with Neo-Babylonian legal features.[113]

The rights of the buyer over the bought property are defined in the investiture clause: the Nabataean documents and P.Dura 28 define specific rights of ownership acquired by the buyer's party (authority over the property, right to buy, to sell, to give, etc.), Wadi Daliyeh documents are more brief and Greek P. Yadin 22 does not contain an investiture clause. Unlike the Elephantine documents the "defension" and contravention clauses seem to be independent of the content of the investiture clause.

Protection of buyer's ownership consists of the "defension" and contravention clauses. The "defension" clause stipulates the vendor's duty to cleanse the buyer's property if somebody raises a claim concerning it. This clause presumes that the vendor sold the property in *good faith*. The contravention clause prevents the vendor from contesting the sale (verb שנה is often used), against an action in *bad faith*. This contravention clause is the condition *sine qua non* of the application of the "defension" clause. The threat of penalties in the contravention clause forces the vendor to execute the clearance stipulated in the "defension" clause.

---

[113] Gropp in *DJD* XXVIII (2001): 19–32; idem, "Samaria Papyri," 23–49.

The principle of the vendor presumed of *good/bad faith* known in the Elephantine documents also exists in these deeds, but the consequences of the action in *good* and *bad faith* are different. The vendor's action in the "defension" clause is presumed of *good faith*, and his action concerned in the contravention clause is presumed of *bad faith*.

The main difference from the Elephantine texts is in the use of the return of the price of the sold property by the vendor to the buyer. In deeds of sale from Elephantine, it has the role of *compensation* of the lost property paid by the vendor to the buyer in the event of his eviction. But in the texts from Syria-Palestine, and especially in the Aramaic documents from Wadi Daliyeh, in the Nabataean deeds of sale and in the Greek deeds of sale from Dura Europos, the return of the price of the sold property is part of the penalty that is to be paid by the vendor to the seller in case of violation of the contract by the vendor's party. An attempt at eviction of the buyer, when the vendor cannot clear the property, seems to be considered as proof of the bad faith of the vendor and he is penalized; without consequences for the buyer's ownership.

7.3. Greek Influence in Aramaic and Hebrew Texts

The third group consists of Aramaic and Hebrew deeds of sale from Wadi Murabbaʿat and the Seiyâl Collection written during the second Jewish revolt against Rome, in the "free Israel" of Shimʿon bar Kokhba between 131–135 C.E.[114]

The investiture clause in the deeds from Wadi Murabbaʿat and the Seiyâl Collection reflect the same legal tradition as the documents from the second group (see above, § 7.2).

The guarantees protecting the ownership in these deeds seem to be influenced by the clauses concerning the right of execution (*praxis*) well attested in the Greek documents from the Judean Desert written under Roman rule and from Syria (Dura Europos).[115] This influence in the Aramaic and Hebrew deeds of sale perhaps came from Ptolemaic Egypt and might be older than the Roman occupation of Palestine, but we are unable to prove it.[116]

---

[114] Mur 26; Mur 30; XḤev/Se 8, 8a, 9, 21, 23 and 50.

[115] See above, § 5.

[116] H. Cotton came to a similar conclusion in the matter of the Greek marriage contract P. Yadin 18 concluded between two Jews but reflecting a Greek legal practice from Egypt: H. Cotton, "XḤev/Se ar 13 of 134 or 135 C.E.: A Wife's Renunciation of Claims," *JJS* 49 (1998): 108–118, esp. 117.

This legal tradition seems to have coexisted in the deeds of sale, at least in first and second centuries C.E. in Palestine, together with the older Aramaic legal tradition (see above, §7.2). The Greek deeds P. Yadin 21 with the buyer's right of execution and P. Yadin 22 with "defension" and contravention clauses prove that both types of guarantees (see above, §§7.2 and 7.3) were used in the contract concerning the same transaction, according to the owner of the contract (vendor and buyer).

PUBLIC MEMORY AND PUBLIC DISPUTE: COUNCIL MINUTES BETWEEN ROMAN EGYPT AND THE DEAD SEA[*]

BERNHARD PALME

University of Vienna

Approximately one million papyri and similar handwritten documents, one would guess, are preserved in museums and collections all over the world. After 120 years of papyrological research some 80,000 papyri (in various ancient languages) have been published, and the number grows by ca. 700 new texts each year.[1] The bulk of those documents originates and was discovered in Egypt, of course. The diversity of texts and types of documents could too easily create the impression that the papyrological evidence in its entirety offers a fairly representative view of almost all aspects of life in antiquity. But even in Egypt the geographical and chronological distribution of preserved papyri is very uneven and concentrates on a few sites, mostly situated on the fringe area of ancient settlements.[2] Most of the material which survived from the Ptolemaic and Roman periods was produced and found in villages, while nearly all papyri from the Byzantine period come from cities, mainly the *metropoleis*—that is, the chief towns in each district, *nomós*. Equally uneven is the spreading of preserved papyri over the centuries.[3]

---

[*] The papyrological abbreviations used in this article follow J.F. Oates et al., *Checklist of Editions of Greek, Latin, Demotic and Coptic Papyri, Ostraca and Tablets* (5th ed.; BASP-Sup 9; Oakville: American Society of Papyrologists, 2001). An updated electronic version of this list is available online: http://scriptorium.lib.duke.edu/papyrus/texts/clist.html

[1] These calculations are based on P. van Minnen, "The Millennium of Papyrology (2001–)?" in *Akten des 23. Internationalen Papyrologenkongresses, Wien 22.–28. Juli 2001* (ed. B. Palme; Wien: Österreichische Akademie der Wissenschaften, 2007), 703–714, and idem, "The Future of Papyrology," in *The Oxford Handbook of Papyrology* (ed. R.S. Bagnall; Oxford: Oxford University Press, 2009), 644–660, esp. 645.

[2] The most comprehensive treatments are still K. Preisendanz, *Papyrusfunde und Papyrusforschung* (Leipzig: Hiersemann, 1933), 40–185, and E.G. Turner, *Greek Papyri: An Introduction* (2nd ed.; Oxford: Oxford University Press, 1980), 25–53. An excellent recent overview is provided by H. Cuvigny, "The Finds of Papyri: The Archaeology of Papyrology," in *The Oxford Handbook of Papyrology*, 30–59.

[3] W. Habermann, "Zur chronologischen Verteilung der papyrologischen Zeugnisse," *ZPE* 122 (1998): 144–160, based on the *Heidelberger Gesamtverzeichnis* (HGV): http://

From the point of view of a documentary papyrologist, one could ask: What is the value of the comparatively small number of papyri, wooden panels and ostraca preserved from other parts of the Graeco-Roman world? Even an optimistic estimation would count hardly more than thousand documents from outside Egypt—slightly more than one percent of the published evidence available at the moment.[4] Probably all papyrologists would agree though, that the scientific value of those documents cannot be estimated high enough.[5] First, they provide very welcome information about some parts of the ancient world that are much less well documented—and less well known—than Egypt. Second, and even more important, they give us the possibility to compare and sometimes to correct our historical conclusions based on the evidence from Egypt.[6] Granted that Egypt stands somewhat apart from the other provinces of the Roman Empire and that analogy is a tool to be used with caution, papyri from outside Egypt are of essential methodological importance, even if their limited number and restriction to a handful of finding places offer hardly more than some selective spotlights.

Literary and documentary papyrology—or let's say: classical philology and ancient history—equally profited from the new texts from outside Egypt. To quote just the most prominent discoveries: Who could now-a-days imagine the papyrological world without the orphic papyrus found in Derveni near Thessaloniki in northern Greece,[7] or without the literary and philosophical texts from the Villa dei papiri in Herculaneum? No

---

aquila.papy.uni-heidelberg.de. On peculiarities of the papyrological evidence cf. B. Palme, "The Range of Documentary Texts: Types and Categories," in *The Oxford Handbook of Papyrology*, 358–394.

  [4] H.M. Cotton, W.E.H. Cockle, and F.G.B. Millar, "The Papyrology of the Roman Near East: A Survey," *JRS* 85 (1995): 214–235 provide a catalogue of more than 600 papyri written outside of Egypt. Since then, the corpora P. Euphr., P. Petra I and III, as well as some single documents from outside Egypt have been published (see e.g., F. Mitthof and A. Papathomas, "Ein Papyruszeugnis aus dem spätantiken Karien," *Chiron* 34 [2004]: 401–424).

  [5] Cf. the considerations of J. Gascou, "The Papyrology of the Near East," in *The Oxford Handbook of Papyrology*, 473–494.

  [6] For the spread of papyrus in the ancient world, see N. Lewis, *Papyrus in Classical Antiquity* (Oxford: Clarendon, 1974), 84–94, focusing on the Greek papyri. On the importance of Hebrew and Aramaic papyri, see the brilliant surveys in L.H. Schiffman, ed., *Semitic Papyrology in Context: A Climate of Creativity: Papers from a New York University Conference Marking the Retirement of Baruch A. Levine* (Culture and History of the Ancient Near East 14; Leiden: Brill, 2003).

  [7] T. Kouremenos, G.M. Parássoglou, and K. Tsantsanoglou, eds., *The Derveni Papyrus: Edited with Introduction and Commentary* (Studi e testi per il Corpus dei papiri filosofici greci e latini 13; Florence: Olschki, 2006).

legal historian would ignore the *tabellae* found in Pompeji, and certainly no historian of the Roman and post-Roman period would miss the Latin letters on the wooden tabletts from Vindolanda at Hadrians Wall and Vindonissa in Switzerland, or the Latin ostraca from BuNjem in Libya, the papyri from Byzantine Ravenna or the *Tablettes Albertini* from the Vandalic kingdom in Africa.[8] The Near East has, of course, the lion's share of handwritten documents from outside Egypt. Besides the treasures from the Judean Desert and Dead Sea area—the core subject of the present volume—one should mention the famous papyri from Dura Europos in the Roman province Mesopotamia. And we still may hope for sensational new discoveries like the carbonised papyri from Byzantine Petra or the small dossier from the Euphrates (but this time in the Roman province Syria) that turned up some years ago.[9]

Sometimes even a single line may open a totally new chapter in the endless story of what we call cultural history. To give just one example: A small scrap, found in a Roman camp at Masada turned out to contain the beginning of Dido's first speech in Virgil, *Aen.* 4.9; at the other end of the Empire, at Vindolanda, a military camp at Hadrians Wall, a verse of *Aen.* 9.473 was identified on a small wooden tablet; and in the Desert between the Nile Valley and the Red Sea someone copied *Aen.* 1.1–3. Probably all three attempts to write down some lines of Virgil were done by Roman soldiers.[10] Occasionally *Agathe Tyche*, the patroness of papyrology, provides us with a group of connected text— that's what papyrologists call an "archive."[11] Dozens of such papyrus

---

[8] Corpora of papyri, ostraca, and wooden tablets from outside Egypt: Europe: P. Ital. I–III, T. Sulpicii, T. Vindol. I–III, T. Vindon., O. Cret. Chers.—North-Africa: T. Alb., O. BuNjem.—Near East: P. Petra, P. Murabbaʿat, P. Ḥever, P. Jud. Des. Misc., P. Babatha = P. Yadin I, P. Yadin II, P. Ness. III.—Mesopotamia: P. Dura, P. Euphrates.

[9] In addition to P. Euphrates, cf. the preliminary report of D. Feissel and J. Gascou, "Documents d'archives Romains inédits du Moyen Euphrate (IIIᵉ siècle après J.-C.)," *CRAI* 133 (1989): 535–556, and the Syriac texts in J. Teixidor, "Deux documents syriaques du IIIᵉ siècle après J.-C., provenant du Moyen Euphrate," *CRAI* 134 (1990): 144–163, and idem, "Un document syriaque de fermage de 242 après J.-C.," *Semitica* 41–42 (1993): 195–208.

[10] P. Masad. 721 (MaspapVirgil lat [Mas721]); T. Vindol. II 118; O. Claud. I 190. On the back of PSI XIII 1307 = ChLA XXV 786—another military document—the words *Aeneas Dardaniae* resemble Virgil as well.

[11] For the terminological problems, see A. Martin, "Archives privées et cachettes documentaires," in *Proceedings of the 20th International Congress of Papyrologists, Copenhagen 23–29 August 1992* (ed. A. Bülow-Jacobsen; Copenhagen: Museum Tusculanum Press, 1994), 569–577, and A. Jördens, "Papyri und private Archive: Ein Diskussionsbeitrag

archives survive from Egypt, but we are lucky enough to have archives also among the documentary texts from the Judean Desert as well as from Mespotamia.[12]

Both the documents from the Bar Kokhba sites in the Judean Desert and the documents from the Euphrates are rich in evidence for the routine functioning of the Roman provincial administration. Ancient historians and legal historians have extensively studied and discussed all texts of major interest, like the petitions, summons, declarations of property and various types of legal contracts.[13] Comparative studies of similar types of documents from Egypt and the Judean Desert— e.g. census declarations, marriage contracts or deposits—have brought particularly rich results.[14]

In what follows I would like to focus on one document: P. Yadin 12— otherwise also known as P. Babatha 12 or 5/6Ḥev papExtract from Council Minutes gr (5/6Ḥev12)—and one specific aspect of this document: the city council. P. Yadin 12 contains an extract from council minutes of Petra, written in spring 124 C.E., when Petra was the capital of the Roman province Arabia.[15] P. Yadin 12, like many other documents from the so-called "Babatha archive," has received considerable attention.[16] Thus,

---

zur papyrologischen Terminologie," in *Symposion 1997: Vorträge zur griechischen und hellenistischen Rechtsgeschichte* (ed. E. Cantarella and G. Thür; Köln: Böhlau, 2001), 253–268.

[12] The main papyrus archives from outside Egypt are described by Gascou, "Papyrology of the Near East," 477–481. On papyrus archives in general cf. K. Vandorpe, "Archives and Dossiers," in *The Oxford Handbook of Papyrology*, 216–255. An important electronic tool on archives is provided by W. Clarysse and K. Vandorpe at "Papyrus Archives in Graeco-Roman Egypt": http://www.trismegistos.org/arch/index.php.

[13] The scholarly literature on these manuscripts is extensive; in addition to a long series of articles by H.M. Cotton, numerous important contributions are collected in R. Katzoff and D. Schaps, eds., *Law in the Documents of the Judaean Desert* (JSJSup 96; Leiden: Brill, 2005).

[14] For a brilliant overview, see H.M. Cotton, "The Impact of the Documentary Papyri from the Judaean Desert on the Study of Jewish History from 70 to 135 CE," in *Jüdische Geschichte in hellenistisch-römischer Zeit: Wege der Forschung: Vom alten zum neuen Schürer* (ed. A. Oppenheimer unter Mitarbeit von E. Müller-Luckner; Schriften des Historischen Kollegs: Kolloquien 44; München: Oldenbourg, 1999), 221–236.

[15] The document dates between February 27th and July 28th 124 C.E. Additional information is provided in BL X 285 and XI 292. Photographs of the papyrus are available in N. Lewis, *The Documents from the Bar Kokhba Period in the Cave of Letters: Greek Papyri* (JDS 2; Jerusalem: Israel Exploration Society, 1989), pls. 5–6 and in E. Crisci, *Scrivere greco fuori d'Egitto: Ricerche sui manoscritti greco-orientali di origine non egiziana dal IV secolo a.C. all'VIII d.C.* (Pap.Flor. XXVII; Florence: Gonnelli, 1996), pl. XXIII.

[16] Especially the legal aspects of the text have been studied: H.M. Cotton, "The Guardianship of Jesus son of Babatha: Roman and Local Law in the Province of Arabia,"

my contribution will concentrate on just a minor point. The "Babatha archive" consists of papyri in the possession of a Jewish woman called Babatha, who lived in both Arabia and Judaea. When she went hiding in the Cave of Letters during the revolt of Bar Kokhba, she had with her a group of 37 personal documents in Greek, Nabatean, and Aramaic spanning the period from 94 to 132 C.E. Babatha's documents constitute the single most precious repository of evidence that we have for private life and landholding in Roman Arabia and Palestine.[17]

Before analyzing P. Yadin 12 in detail and comparing it with Egyptian documents, I should say some preliminary things on the *boulai*. The βουλή (*curia*) or city council was a characteristic feature of many of the Greek cities of the Hellenistic period. Modeled more or less on the pattern of the Athenian *boule*, the *boulai* of the Hellenistic cities were in a large degree responsible for the internal administration of their community. Many of these cities eventually succumbed to Roman rule, but in most of them the *boule* was retained. It remained hence an important institution in the Greek cities throughout the eastern Roman provinces.[18]

In Egypt, however, the situation was different.[19] During the Ptolemaic period, only two cities, apart from Alexandria, possessed a *boule*: Naucratis in the Delta and Ptolemais in Upper Egypt. When Egypt was added to the Roman Empire in 30 B.C.E., Augustus and his successors kept an especially close watch upon its administration.[20] Despite requests from

---

JRS 83 (1993): 94–113, esp. 95–97 and eadem, "Language Gaps in Roman Palestine and the Roman Near East," in *Medien im Antiken Palästina: Materiale Kommunikation und Medialität als Thema der Palästinaarchäologie* (ed. C. Frevel; FAT 2/10; Tübingen: 2005), 151–169; T.J. Chiusi, "Babatha vs. the Guardians of her Son: A Struggle for Guardianship: Legal and Practical Aspects of P. Yadin 12–15, 27," in *Law in the Documents of the Judaean Desert*, 105–132.

[17] Cf. the introduction to the archive by Lewis, *Documents from the Bar Kokhba Period*, 3–29 and the critical review of G.W. Bowersock, "The Babatha Papyri, Masada, and Rome," *Journal of Roman Archeology* 4 (1991): 336–344; repr. in *Studies on the Eastern Roman Empire: Social, Economic and Administrative History, Religion, Historiography* (Goldbach: Keip, 1994), 213–228.

[18] There is ample discussion on the subject; the basic studies are still F.F. Abbot and A.C. Johnson, *Municipal Administration in the Roman Empire* (Princeton: Princeton University Press, 1926), and A.H.M. Jones, "The Cities of the Roman Empire: Political, Administrative and Judicial Institutions," *Recueils de la Société Jean Bodin* 6 (1954): 135–173; repr. in *The Roman Economy: Studies in Ancient Economic and Administrative History* (Oxford: Blackwell, 1974), 1–34.

[19] The *locus classicus* is P. Jouguet, *La vie municipale dans l'Égypte Romaine* (Paris: de Boccard, 1968).

[20] Cf. A.K. Bowman and D. Rathbone, "Cities and Administration in Roman Egypt," *JRS* 82 (1992): 107–127, see also the critical remarks by A. Jördens, "Das Verhältnis der

the Alexandrinians to the Emperors Augustus and Claudius, Alexandria did not receive the permission to set up or reinstate its *boule*. Neither did the *metropoleis* of the nomes possess councils during the first and second centuries C.E.[21] Only Antinoopolis, a city founded in Middle Egypt in 130 C.E. by Hadrian, was organized as a Greek city, complete with a *boule*.[22] And only in 200 C.E., when Septimius Severus visited Alexandria in person, a *boule* was granted to this famous town. Shortly afterwards evidence begins to appear for the existence of *boulai* in several *metropoleis* of Egypt as well.[23] The position and character of the new *boulai* of the *metropoleis* appear to owe little to predecessors in Egypt and elsewhere. Rather they took over many of the functions of the κοινὸν τῶν ἀρχόντων in the *metropoleis*, a number of elected or appointed magistrates who functioned in concert with the officials of the local administration, namly the *strategos* and the *basilikos grammateus*, and with representatives of the central government, the *procuratores* and the *praefectus Aegypti*.[24] These *boulai* were invested, however, with a much wider competence. The most important tasks of the *boulai* of the third (and fourth) century C.E. were the supervision of finance and the election of the officials and liturgists who played an essential role in the administration of the *metropolis*. The *boule* was responsible to the central government for

<hr />

römischen Amtsträger zu den 'Städten' in der Provinz," in *Lokale Autonomie und römische Ordnungsmacht in den kaiserzeitlichen Provinzen vom 1. bis 3. Jahrhundert* (ed. W. Eck unter Mitarbeit von E. Müller-Luckner; Schriften des Historischen Kollegs: Kolloquien 42; München: Oldenbourg, 1999), 141–180.

[21] A.H.M. Jones, *The Cities of the Eastern Roman Provinces* (ed. M. Avi-Yonah et al.; 2nd ed.; Oxford: Clarendon, 1971), see esp. 295–348 for Egypt. On the development of the cities in Egypt see more generally R. Alston, *The City in Roman and Byzantine Egypt* (London: Routledge, 2002).

[22] M. Zahrnt, "Antinoopolis in Ägypten: Die hadrianische Gründung und ihre Privilegien in der neueren Forschung," in *Provinzen und Randvölker: Afrika mit Ägypten* (ed. H. Temporini; ANRW II.10.1, Berlin: de Gruyter, 1988), 669–706; on the political context cf. also M.T. Boatwright, *Hadrian and the Cities of the Roman Empire* (Princeton: Princeton University Press, 2000), esp. 190–196.

[23] For the following, see Jouguet, *La vie municipale*, 344–350 and A.K. Bowman, *The Town Councils of Roman Egypt* (American Studies in Papyrology 11; Toronto: Hakkert, 1971), esp. 15–19 for the installation of the *boulai*, and D. Hagedorn, "The Emergence of Municipal Offices in the Nome-Capitals of Egypt," in *Oxyrhynchus: A City and Its Texts* (eds. A.K. Bowman et al.; London: Egypt Exploration Society, 2007), 194–204.

[24] This interaction is analysed by A. Jördens, "Der *praefectus Aegypti* und die Städte," in *Herrschaftsstrukturen und Herrschaftspraxis: Konzeption, Prinzipien und Strategien der Administration im römischen Kaiserreich: Akten der Tagung an der Universität Zürich 18.–20. 10. 2004* (ed. A. Kolb; Berlin: Akademie Verlag, 2006), 191–200.

the payment of taxes and the demands for the supply of the army (*annona militaris*).[25]

The procedure of the meetings may be described briefly.[26] They apparently opened with εὐφημίαι, *acclamationes*. The meetings were chaired by the *prytanis*, and he took a prominent role in opening discussions, introducing business and forcing decisions. P. Oxy. I 41 is probably the best example of the opening rituals of a council meeting in the presence of the governor (lines 1–7):[27]

> [- - -] when the assembly had met, (the people cried) [- - -] the Roman power for ever! lords Augusti! good fortune O governor, good fortune to the *catholicus*! Bravo *prytanis*, bravo the city's boast, bravo Dioskoros chief of the citizens! under you our blessings still increase, source of our blessings, [- - - Isis] loves you and rises, good luck to the patriot! good luck to the lover of equity! source of our blessings, founder of the city … bravo
> …

And after some other acclamations, the *prytanis* replyed (lines 16–21):

> "I welcome, and with much gratification, the honour which you do me, but I beg that such demonstrations be reserved for a legitimate occasion when you can make them with authoritative force and I can accept them with assurance." The people (ὁ δῆμος) cried: "Many votes does he deserve, lords Augusti, all-victorious for the Romans, the Roman power for ever! …"[28]

We understand from the phrase "The people cried" (ὁ δῆμος ἐβόησεν) here, and other evidence from elsewhere, that meetings of the *boulai* were not (or not necessarily) closed sessions, but in fact open to the public. The system in debate is rather obscure. There does not seem to be any fixed order of speaking. Any problem was simply discussed until a decision was reached or postponed until the next meeting.[29] The evidence shows that the city councils were also the stage for petitions and complaints. The

---

[25] For the variety of businesses of the *boulai*, cf. A.H.M. Jones, *The Greek City from Alexander to Justinian* (Oxford: Clarendon, 1940), 211–250; Jouguet, *La vie municipale*, 399–454; and Bowman, *Town Councils*, 69–119.

[26] For these meetings, see ibid., 32–39 and Jones, *Greek City*, 185–188, quoting instructive passages from various sources.

[27] P. Oxy. I 41 = W. Chr. 45 = Sel. Pap. II 239 (Oxyrhynchus, early fourth cent. C.E.), cf. BL IX 176–177, on the dating: K.A. Worp, "Further Chronological Notes," *ZPE* 151 (2005): 153 n. 3.

[28] Translation according to A.S. Hunt and C.C. Edgar, *Select Papyri*, vol. 2: *Official Documents* (LCL 282; London: Heinemann, 1934), # 239.

[29] The record and the situation in P. Oxy. I 41 is extensively analyzed by T. Kruse, "The Magistrate and the Ocean: Acclamations and Ritualized Communication in Town Gatherings in Roman Egypt," in *Ritual and Communication in the Graeco-Roman World*

boule was called upon to confirm exemption from liturgy by persons of privileged status, like Roman citizens, soldiers or athletes. The subject of most petitions adressed to the *boulai* were complains against nomination to liturgies or similar duties. All this was discussed in public. Moreover, every business of the *boule* was not only a thing of the moment, but something for the public memory. Naturally the business meetings of the councils were recorded and each *boule* kept the minutes of her meetings for decades, maybe even longer. P. Oxy. XVII 2110 is probably the most instructive example of council minutes we have; though dating from 370 C.E., it illustrates the procedure which we may assume was not substantially different from that of the second and third centuries C.E. A complaint is made:[30]

> In the 3rd consulship of our masters Valentinian and Valens, eternal Augusti, Phaophi 9, at a meeting of the *boule*, in the *prytany* of Claudius Hermeias, son of Gelasius, ex-*gymnasiarch* and councilor; after the *plaudits* Theon, son of Ammonius, councilor, represented by his son Macrobius, came forward and made the following statement:—"Fellow councilors, you know as well as I that my name is on the tablet about to come into force and that I am one of the twenty-four ordained by our lord the most illustrious Tatianus (= praefect of Egypt) for the *pagarchies* and contractorships. Perhaps in ignorance, the president has appointed me to the administration of the soldiers' woolen clothing for the 14th indiction, at the very time when I have horses to keep; wherefore I put it to you that the ordinances ought not to be infringed."—The councilors cried: "What is on the tablet is valid; what has been rightly ordained must not be infringed."— Ptoleminus, ex-*logistes*, said: "What has been ordained by our lord the most illustrious Tatianus with the approval of the whole council must stand fast and unshaken, whence it follows that the twenty-four are not to serve in any other service whatever but keep to the heavier liturgies, not only in this but in future *prytanies*. If, however, anyone wishes to serve in another service, he does not do so on the responsibility of the council, and Macrobius ought not to be burdened."—Gerontius, ex-*exactor*, said. "What has been rightly ordained and legally done by my lord Tatianus and referred to our sovereigns and to my lords the most illustrious *praefects of the praetorium* has its validity from them, and hence it is not proper for Macribius to be burdened by either the *prytanis* or the future *prytanis* with other administrations" ...[31]

(ed. E. Stavrianopoulou; Kernos Supplément 16; Liège: Centre International d'Etude de la Religion Grecque Antique, 2006), 297–315.

[30] P. Oxy. XVII 2110 = Sel. Pap. II 240 (Oxyrhynchus, 6 October 370 C.E.), cf. BL IX 193; X 146; XI 159.

[31] Translation according to Hunt and Edgar, *Select Papyri*, # 240.

The complainant is supported by statements from nine other councilors until the *prytanis* finally yields and upholds the complaint. The situation is typical: Acclamations and disputes—every business of the *boule* was done in public. We understand that—like today—publicity was desired because it would make all actions more "transparent." But we also can imagine that publicity could well give an even more harsh tone to every dispute: being successful (or not) in escaping public duties was one thing for a councilor, being victorious or defeated in a public discussion was still another thing.

The written minutes of the meetings, kept by each *boule*, grew in importance, as the financial responsibilities of the town council increased.[32] Much more than simple "public memory," the records could in cases of dispute get some legal bearing, as the entries clearly displayed each action and every decision made by the *boule*. In Egypt, the terms ὑπομνήματα and ὑπομνηματισμοί are used to describe those reports and could probably best be translated into English as "proceedings." U. Wilcken[33] demonstrated an equivalent between the terms ὑπομνηματισμοί and Latin *commentarii*, the day to day *journal* in which Roman magistrates recorded each and every official activity. E. Bickerman[34] attempted to bring the term ὑπομνήματα close to Latin *acta*, a second step in recording the official business. The *acta* were compiled at the end of the day from the *commentarii* and contained in short form the results and decisions of the magistrates or the *boule*. But this distincion is not always clear in our documents—and maybe was not always observed. Structure and style of the records are known from quite a number of original minutes of *boulai* that survived in more or less fragmentary conditions. Two substantial bodies of evidence come from Oxyrhynchos and Hermoupolis.[35] The majority of the reports is written in *oratio recta* and contains vivid accounts of the meetings, interspersed with acclamations

---

[32] On the proceedings see Bowman, *Town Councils*, 32–39 with a list of recorded meetings or references to meetings on pp. 32–33.

[33] U. Wilcken, "Ὑπομνηματισμοί," *Philologus* 53 (1894): 80–126.

[34] E. Bickerman, "Testificatio Actorum," *Aegyptus* 13 (1933): 333–355.

[35] Oxyrhynchos: P. Oxy. XII 1413–1419 (end of third cent. C.E.); XXVII 2475–2477 (298); Hermoupolis: SPP V preserves an extensive convolute of proceedings from the middle of the third century C.E.; this important evidence is analysed by Bowman, *Town Councils*, esp. 32–39; M. Drew-Bear, "Les archives du conseil municipal d'Hermoupolis Magna," in *Atti del XVII Congresso Internazionale di Papirologia: Napoli, 19–26 maggio 1983* (3 vols.; Naples: Centro Internazionale per lo Studio dei Papiri Ercolanesi, 1984), 3:807–813, and eadem, "Contenu et intérêt historique des archives du conseil municipal d'Hermoupolis sous Gallien," in *Egyptian Archives: Proceedings of the First Session of the*

and interjections. Discussions, motions, and comments were recorded verbatim and therefore present an insight into the routine business of the city councils—like the two examples just cited.

Proceedings of this kind were of course no Egyptian peculiarity. P. Yadin 12 proves that the *boulai* of other cities kept their minutes too, and they did so even before the Egyptian *metropoleis* had a *boule*. Moreover, containing an extract from council minutes of Petra, P. Yadin 12 proves that such extracts were put on public display and by this—similar to legal judgments of Roman governors—served as formal publications of council decisions. Those published extracts are abbreviated versions of the verbatim council proceedings (the Egyptian ὑπομνηματισμοί) and resemble the *acta* of Roman magistrates. P. Yadin 12 reads as follows (lines 1–11):

> (*Inner text*): Verified exact copy of one item from the minutes of the council of Petra the *metropolis*, minutes displayed in the temple of Aphrodite in Petra, and it is as appended below in the outer text.

> (*Outer text*): Verified exact copy of one item of guardianship from the minutes of the council of Petra the *metropolis*, minutes displayed in the temple of Aphrodite in Petra, and it is as appended below:

> (*line 6*) "And of Jesus, a Jew, son of Jesus, of the village Maoza, 'Abdobdas son of Illouthas and John son of Eglas [i.e. are appointed guardians]."

> Done in Petra, *metropolis* of Arabia, four days before the kalends of …, in the consulship of Manius Acilius Glabrio and Gaius Bellicius Torquatus …[36]

> (On the back signatures of the witnesses)

This small sheet of light-colored papyrus contains a double document.[37] At this type of contract the text—styled as objective minutes—was written two times on the same sheet of papyrus. One copy remained visible (*scriptura exterior*), the second one was rolled up and sealed (*scriptura interior*). The stitched-up upper (now inner) text exists to verify that the exposed or lower text, accessible to all, has not been manipulated. In cases of litigation the seals could be broken at court and the original

---

International Congress on Egyptian Archives / Egyptological Archives (ed. P. Piacentini and C. Orsenigo; Quaderni di Acme 111; Milan: Cisalpino, 2009), 187–195.

[36] Translation by Lewis, *Documents from the Bar-Kokhba Period*, 49.

[37] On this form of the document see ibid., 6–10; H.M. Cotton, "'Diplomatics' or External Aspects of the Legal Documents from the Judaean Desert: Prolegomena," in *Rabbinic Law in Its Roman and Near Eastern Context* (ed. C. Hezser; TSAJ 97; Tübingen: Mohr Siebeck, 2003), 49–61.

text could be read. The double document was a common style for legal documents in Hellenistic Egypt,[38] but became relatively rare in Roman Egypt—fewer than a hundred among the thousands of contracts published so far.[39] But the papyri from Wadi Murabbaʿat and Dura Europos include numerous double documents from the Roman period. Moreover, all but one of the private documents from the Euphrates area are of the double form—confirming the prevalence of this type in Palestine, Arabia, and Syria at least into the middle of the third century c.e.[40] Nevertheless, we detect a first sign of decline in P. Yadin 12: The inner text does not repeat the relevant text any more (as it should), but simply refers to it "and it is as appended below in the outer text."[41]

P. Yadin 12 belongs to the legal documents of Babatha—a wealthy woman from Maoza at the south end of the Dead Sea.[42] When she fled to the cave at the time of the uprising of Bar Kokhba, she kept with her documents concerning her property[43] and the raising of her son Jesus from her first marriage.[44] By the time P. Yadin 12 was set

---

[38] H.J. Wolff, "Zur Geschichte der Sechszeugen-Doppelurkunde," in *Akten des XIII. Internationalen Papyrologenkongresses: Marburg/Lahn, 2.-6. August 1971* (ed. E. Kießling and H.-A. Rupprecht; MBPF 66; München: Beck, 1974), 469–479; idem, *Das Recht der griechischen Papyri Ägyptens in der Zeit der Ptolemaeer und des Prinzipats*, vol. 2: *Organisation und Kontrolle des privaten Rechtsverkehrs* (Handbuch der Altertumswissenschaft X.5.2; München: Beck, 1978), 57–71; M. Amelotti and L. Migliardi-Zingale, "Osservazioni sulla duplice scritturazione nei documenti," in *Symposion 1985: Vorträge zur griechischen und hellenistischen Rechtsgeschichte* (ed. G. Thür; Köln: Böhlau, 1989), 299–309.

[39] For double documents from the Roman period, see D. Rathbone, "PSI XI 1183: Record of a Roman Census Declaration of A.D. 47/8," in *Essays and Texts in Honor of J. David Thomas* (ed. T. Gagos and R.S. Bagnall; American Studies in Papyrology 42; Exeter: American Society of Papyrologists: 2001), 99–106.

[40] Cf. Gascou, "Papyrology of the Near East," 482; for the use of double documents in the papyri from outside Egypt, see ibid. 485.

[41] This "presentation" of the content of the document does not, to be sure, provide much possibility for controlling the outer text.

[42] For the Babatha Archive and its context, see the literature quoted in nn. 13 and 17; for additional remarks, see M. Goodman, "Babatha's Story," *JRS* 81 (1991): 169–175; B. Isaac, "The Babatha Archive: A Review Article," *IEJ* 42 (1992): 62–75; repr. in *The Near East under Roman Rule: Selected Papers* (Mnemosyne Supplementum 177; Leiden: Brill, 1998), 159–181.

[43] H.M. Cotton and J.C. Greenfield, "Babatha's Property and the Law of Succession in the Babatha Archive," *ZPE* 104 (1994): 211–224.

[44] In addition to the literature cited above in n. 16, cf. A.E. Hanson, "The Widow Babatha and the Poor Orphan Boy," in *Law in the Documents of the Judaean Desert*, 85–103, and generally J.G. Oudshoorn, *The Relationship between Roman and Local Law in the Babatha and Salome Komaise Archives: General Analysis and Three Case Studies on Law of Succession, Guardianship and Marriage* (STDJ 59; Leiden: Brill, 2007).

up (124 C.E.), Babatha was widowed and the boy orphaned. In the first half of the year 124 C.E. the *boule* of Petra had appointed two men to be guardians of the orphan.[45] The purpose of the present document was to copy from the minutes (ἀπὸ ἄκτων) of the *boule* of Petra the names of the two guardians appointed by the *boule*. Unlike similar proceedings from Egypt, P. Yadin 12 "from the beginning to end ... reads like a Greek translation of a Latin original."[46] Even the date is given in Latin and the formula ἐγγεγϱαμμένον καὶ ἀντιβεβλημένον (probably *scilicet* ἀντίγϱαφον) in lines 1 and 4 renders the Latin *descriptum et recognitum* at copies of edicts issued by Roman authorities and indeed the excerpt from minutes of the city council of Caere in Italy which survived in a Latin inscription.[47]

As the Greek and Roman practice normally required only a single guardian, the naming of two guardians presumably followed local custom.[48] Appointed by the *boule* in one of its meetings, the whole affair of naming guardians for Babatha's orphan son became public. The fact was memorized publicly in the *acta* of the *boule*, and it was displayed in the center of the city. According to lines 5–6, the *acta* of the *boule* were posted at the Aphrodeision, the temple of the Arabian Aphrodite (al-Uzza) in Petra.[49] In the Roman Empire, edicts and decrees of the emperors and governors as well as the *acta* of the city councils were routinely posted at centrally located public buildings for the information of those concerned. The interested parties could have copies made during the period of posting. This practice is very well known from Egyptian papyri as well, but the posting is expressed by πϱοτίθημι, not πϱόκειμαι, as here. Babatha took care that the veracity of her copy of the *acta* of the *boule* concerning

---

[45] Thus lines 6–8 of the document quoted above (see p. 890).

[46] Lewis, *Documents from the Bar-Kokhba Period*, 48; cf. also J. Adams, *Bilingualism and the Latin Language* (Cambridge: Cambridge University Press, 2003), 267–268, and H.M. Cotton, "The Languages of the Legal and Administrative Documents from the Judaean Desert," *ZPE* 125 (1999): 219–231.

[47] CIL XI 3614, lines 4–6 (113/4 C.E.): "Descriptum et recognitum factum in pronao aedis Martis | ex commentario, quem iussit proferri Cuperius Hostilianus per T. Rustium Lysiponum | scribam, in quo scriptum erat id quod infra scriptum est ..."; and lines 8–9: "Commentarium cottidianum municipii Caeritum, inde pagina XXVII kapite VI ..."

[48] Babatha was dissatisfied with the performance of both guardians. Only a couple of months after their nomination, she petitioned the governor and later summoned the guardians: P. Yadin 13 (5/6Ḥev papPetition to Governor gr [5/6Ḥev13]; second half of 125 C.E.), P. Yadin 14 (5/6Ḥev papSummons gr [5/6Ḥev14]; October 125 C.E.); P. Yadin 27 (5/6Ḥev papReceipt gr [5/6Ḥev27]; 132 C.E.).

[49] The Aphrodeision is best identified with the Temple of the Winged Lions; cf. G.W. Bowersock, *Roman Arabia* (Cambridge: Harvard University Press, 1983), 87.

the guardians of her son were attested by witnesses. Five witnesses signed on the back of P. Yadin 12, the first four in Nabatean, the fifth in Greek.

In Roman Egypt, in fact all legal proceedings that survive on papyrus are such "copies from the *commentarii*" (ἀντίγραφον ὑπομνηματισμοῦ τοῦ δεῖνος or simply ἐξ ὑπομνηματισμῶν). Court proceedings and legal judgments were never stand alone documents, but just entries in the *commentarii* of the judging official.[50] If one party wanted to have a written document on the results of a *causa*, the posted *acta* had to be copied— just the way Babatha did it. Those extracts frequently were cited in court or included in petitions. For the same reason P. Yadin 12 was also styled as a legal contract with witnesses.

Despite those similarties, there are, however, some differences between the Egyptian extracts ἐξ ὑπομνηματισμῶν and P. Yadin 12. First: the extracts ἐξ ὑπομνηματισμῶν from Egypt are *verbatim* records of the proceedings and thus may, as Wilcken already thought, indeed be copies from the lenghty *commentarii*.[51] P. Yadin 12, on the other hand, is taken ἀπὸ ἄκτων βουλῆς Πετραίων, and the way it briefly states just the facts (and not the discussions) may indicate, that it really was taken *ab actis*, presumably the summaries of the ὑπομνήματα of the *boule*, as Bickerman suspected.[52] Second: The administration of the Egyptian *metropoleis* before 200 C.E. had been vested in the κοινὰ τῶν ἀρχόντων, but the operations of these bodies had been largely dependent upon co-operation with officials of the central government, like the *strategos*. It is striking that the *boule* of Petra—also styled as *metropolis* (lines 2 and 5) and maybe organized as a Greek polis only shortly before[53]— had the capacity to name the guardians; in Egypt we would expect the *strategos*, chief administrator of the *nomós*, to be responsible for appointing guardians.[54] This is an important point: The *boule* of Petra perfoms legal actions on her own authority already in 124 C.E., while the *boulai* of the Egyptian *metropoleis* even in the third century C.E.—when

---

[50] R.A. Coles, *Reports of Proceedings in Papyri* (Papyrologica Bruxellensia 4; Brussels: Fondation Égyptologique Reine Élisabeth, 1966).

[51] See above, n. 33.

[52] See above, n. 34.

[53] It remains unsure whether Petra had the constitution of a *polis* before 114 C.E. Cf. G.W. Bowersock, review of A. Spijkerman, *The Coins of the Decapolis and Provincia Arabia*, JRS 72 (1982): 197–198, 198; on the meaning of *metropolis* in this contexts cf. idem, "Babatha Papyri," 340 n. 7.

[54] R. Taubenschlag, *The Law of Greco-Roman Egypt in the Light of the Papyri (332 B.C.– 640 A.D.)* (2nd ed.; Warsaw: Państwowe Wydawnictwo Naukowe, 1955), 153–162, esp. 161–162; Cotton, "Guardianship," 96.

Petra had already advanced to the status of a *colonia*[55]—still act only together with and probably depending on the *strategos*.

P. Yadin 12 attests to activities by the *boule* of Petra in the province Arabia in 124 C.E., which the *boulai* of the Egyptian *metropoleis* and Alexandria were able to perform only three generations later, after 200 C.E. Twenty years after the incorporation of Arabia in the Roman Empire in 106 C.E., the *boule* of Petra functions as if it would be a free Greek city. Thus, this small papyrus document proofs that the city council of Petra had retained the important role the councils of Greek cities played in the Hellenistic period before the coming of Rome. Not only city administration and taxation, but also a variety of private legal actions, like the appointment of guardians, were on the agenda of the public meetings of Petra's city council.

---

[55] Petra became *colonia* under Elagabal; cf. S. Ben-Dor, "Petra Colonia," *Ber* 9 (1948–1949): 41–43; F. Millar, "The Roman *coloniae* of the Near East: A Study of Cultural Relations," in *Roman Eastern Policy and Other Studies in Roman History: Proceedings of a Colloquium at Tvärminne, 2–3 October, 1987* (ed. H. Solin and M. Kajava; Commentationes humanarum litterarum 91; Helsinki: Finnish Society of Sciences and Letters, 1990), 7–58, 51.

THE QUMRAN PESHARIM AND THE DERVENI PAPYRUS: TRANSPOSITIONAL HERMENEUTICS IN ANCIENT JEWISH AND ANCIENT GREEK COMMENTARIES[*]

ARMIN LANGE[a)] AND ZLATKO PLEŠE[b)]
a) University of Vienna
b) University of North Carolina at Chapel Hill

Already in 1953, Karl Elliger stated in his commentary to *Pesher Habakuk* that the text often resorts to allegorical interpretation.[1]

> Es wird allegorisiert, wiederum nicht durchgängig, aber da, wo der Wortsinn sich der Konzeption des Auslegers nicht fügt, und gelegentlich auch sonst.

Ten years later, after more pesharim were published, Asher Finkel compared the pesharim with rabbinic sources and characterized their exegetical approach as allegorical in nature.[2]

> The method of applying pesher to the Scriptures indicates traditional lines of interpretation in Qumran and Rabbinic sources. The central feature is the understanding of the inspired words of the past in the context of a present or future situation, or in relating them to a given case. To achieve these purposes the exegete allegorically interprets the significant words.[3]

Finkel's understanding of the pesharim has been reasserted by a number of scholars, including Bilha Nitzan,[4] Devorah Dimant,[5] Menahem

---

[*] We are indebted to Dr. Nóra Dávid for editing this article according to the stylesheet. If not indicated otherwise, translations of ancient sources are our own.

[1] K. Elliger, *Studien zum Habakuk-Kommentar vom Toten Meer* (Studien zur historischen Theologie 15; Tübingen: Mohr Siebeck, 1953), 142, cf. 142–143.

[2] See A. Finkel, "The Pesher of Dreams and Scriptures," *RevQ* 4 (1963–1964): 357–370 (364–370).

[3] Ibid., 370.

[4] B. Nitzan, *Pesher Habakkuk: A Scroll from the Wilderness of Judaea (1QpHab): Text, Introduction and Commentary* (Jerusalem: Bialik Institute, 1986), 51–54 (Hebrew).

[5] D. Dimant, "Pesharim, Qumran," *ABD* 5:244–251 (249). Dimant speaks of "symbolic or allegorical equations" (ibid.).

Kister,[6] and Shani Berrin.[7] The recent publication of the *editio princeps* of the Derveni papyrus[8]—a lemmatic allegorical commentary on an Orphic poem which, due to its archeological context and its paleography, can be dated to the late fourth century B.C.E.—allows now for a comparison between the Qumran pesharim and a relatively early firsthand witness of Greek allegoresis. In this article, we would like to revisit Finkel's characterization of the pesharim as allegorical in light of such a comparison. In choosing the Derveni papyrus and the Qumran pesharim for our comparison, we have been guided by the affinities between the cultural status of their respective producers and by their similar hermeneutical objectives and procedures. As our study intends to show, these two "metatexts"[9] represent the dissenting attitudes of religious groups or individuals, each feeling increasingly estranged from their cultural matrix and its approaches to founding texts and authoritative traditions. As a result of this estrangement, they each resorted to a transpositional kind of hermeneutics by presupposing a new signification of the authoritative texts and traditions beyond their culturally endorsed meaning. Since our objectives reach far beyond a simple answer to the question of whether the pesharim practice allegoresis or not, we begin with some general observations about the nature and scope of transpositional hermeneutics.

TRANSPOSITIONAL HERMENEUTICS

Transpositional hermeneutics designates an interpretative procedure that seeks to redescribe and thereby recontextualize the authoritative texts of a specific culture. The procedure itself comprises three distinctive

---

[6] M. Kister, "A Common Heritage: Biblical Interpretation at Qumran and its Implications," in *Biblical Perspectives: Early Use and Interpretation of the Bible in Light of the Dead Sea Scrolls: Proceedings of the First International Symposium of the Orion Center for the Study of the Dead Sea Scrolls and Associated Literature, 12–14 May, 1996* (ed. M.E. Stone and E.G Chazon; STDJ 28; Leiden: Brill, 1998), 101–111. Kister characterizes pesher-exegesis as a "historical-eschatological allegory" (111).

[7] S. Berrin, *The Pesher Nahum Scroll from Qumran: An Exegetical Study of 4Q169* (STDJ 53; Leiden: Brill, 2004), 17: "It is our contention that the author of pesher perceived his biblical base-text as polysemous, allegorical, and generally cohesive."

[8] For the Derveni papyrus, see below, 899–908.

[9] According to G. Genette, *Palimpsests: Literature in the Second Degree* (trans. C. Newman and C. Doubinsky; Lincoln: University of Nebraska Press, 1997), 4, metatextuality is "the relationship most often labeled as 'commentary.' It unites a given text to another, of which it speaks without necessarily citing it (without summoning it), in fact sometimes even without naming it."

moments: (i) the anticipatory movement of fore-understanding (*Vorverständnis*)[10] as a basic notion of reality that every reader brings as a presupposition to a text and finds it either confirmed or contradicted; if the text contradicts this presupposed basic notion of reality, the reader next resorts to (ii) atomization, or isolation of individual elements from the text, which serves the purpose of (iii) recontextualization, or the systematic one-by-one matching of the elements isolated from the authoritative text with those belonging to a chosen referential paradigm. In this way, transpositional hermeneutics confirms the reader's fore-understanding and realigns a seemingly contradictory authoritative text with it.

Formally, transpositional hermeneutics corresponds to the practice of allegoresis, or allegorical interpretation, inasmuch as both operate within the same hermeneutical dichotomies of surface vs. hidden meaning, whole vs. part, conventional semantics vs. conceptual transformation, and normative vs. deviant reading of the text.[11] At the same time,

---

[10] The term *Vorverständnis* was introduced into hermeneutics by Rudolf Bultmann ("Ist voraussetzungslose Exegese möglich? [1957]," in *Glauben und Verstehen: Gesammelte Aufsätze* [4 vols.; Tübingen: Mohr Siebeck, 1933–1965], 3:142–150; "Das Problem der Hermeneutik [1950]," in *Glauben und Verstehen*, 2:211–235) in conversation with Martin Heidegger (*Sein und Zeit* [15th ed.; Tübingen: Niemeyer, 1979]). While Bultmann restricted his own hermeneutical discourse of *Vorverständnis* to the interpretation of biblical texts—although he envisioned a wider hermeneutic framework—Hans-Georg Gadamer made it an integral part of his hermeneutical theory (*Hermeneutik*, vol. 1: *Wahrheit und Methode: Grundzüge einer philosophischen Hermeneutik* [6th ed.; Tübingen: Mohr Siebeck, 1990], 272–312).

[11] For many modern scholars, atomization is a recurrent but not necessary moment in allegorical exegesis. For example, R. Pfeiffer in his *History of Classical Scholarship* (Oxford: Oxford University Press, 1968), 35–56, argued that the fifth-century "Sophists" used a detailed word-by-word analysis but showed no interest in allegoresis. In his monograph *Spätantike Dichtungstheorien: Untersuchungen zu Proklos, Herakleitos und Plutarch* (Stuttgart: Teubner, 1990), W. Bernard distinguished between "substitutive" and "diairetic" allegory, the former roughly corresponding to the Stoic practice of atomization, or a one-to-one matching of the individual elements of the base text with those belonging to a chosen referential paradigm, and the latter to the method of later Platonists who sought to reveal the concealed meaning of "whole" narratives or their episodes. But see N.J. Richardson, "Homeric Professors in the Age of the Sophists," *Proceedings of the Cambridge Philological Society* 21 (1975): 65–81 (67), who suggests that "it may be wrong to attempt to draw too hard and fast a line between detailed word-by-word analysis of a text with a view to eliciting its true meaning, and the more extended form of interpretation which seeks to reveal the underlying purpose or hidden significance of whole scenes, or even of whole poems." Such a neat division between two procedures also runs counter the idea of the hermeneutical circle already formulated in the Neo-Platonist theories of textual "scopus" and more recently elaborated in the hermeneutical theories of Schleiermacher, Heidegger, and Gadamer. As pointed out by H.-G. Gadamer, *Truth and Method* (trans. J. Weinsheimer and D.G. Marshall; 2nd ed.; New York: Continuum, 1989),

allegoresis in its traditional sense of a physical, ethical, or psychological exegesis is only a segment, or subspecies, of transpositional hermeneutics. The range of referential paradigms available to transpositional hermeneutics is practically indefinite, and it includes not only physical or psychological phenomena but also any concrete historical situation, political ideology, or religious belief and projection.

Before proceeding to a detailed analysis of transpositional hermeneutics in our exemplary metatexts, we want briefly to examine the ways in which each of these metatexts envisages the purpose and meaning of the base text as a whole—that is, their idea of how a given base text relates to the set of their anticipatory presuppositions (*Vorverständnis*). To start with the Derveni papyrus, its author formulates this preliminary insight at the very beginning of his detailed line-by-line exegesis of the Orphic "sacred discourse":

> This poem is strange and riddling for people, even though [Orpheus] himself did not intend to say contentious riddles, but rather great things in riddles. In fact, he is telling a holy discourse from the very first word to the last, as he also makes clear in the well-chosen verse: for having ordered them to "put doors to their ears," he says that he is not legislating for the majority [but teaching those] who are pure in hearing …
>
> (P. Derveni VII:4–11)

The initial recognition of an overarching tension between the literal and non-literal meaning of the Orphic poem leads the Derveni author to postulate a set of important exegetical assumptions about the poem's intent. As indicated in the above passage, "Orpheus" understood the value of concealment and deliberately cultivated the "riddling" style. In this way, the legendary singer restricted his wisdom to a particular audience, "those pure in hearing," at the expense of the ignorant majority confined to the explicit content of his poem. And finally, "Orpheus" was telling a riddling story "from the very first word to the last," as though he wished to warn "those pure in hearing" to attune their ears not only

---

291, "the movement of understanding is constantly from the whole to the part and back to the whole … The harmony of all the details with the whole is the criterion of correct understanding." Even the Stoics did not draw too hard a line between atomization and a more extended analysis of whole stories; cf. Cicero, *Nat. d.* 3.63 (= *SVF* 2.1069): "A great deal of quite unnecessary trouble was taken [by the Stoics] to rationalize these purely fanciful myths *and* explain the reasons why each of (divine) names was thus called." In the allegorical treatises of Philo of Alexandria, atomization is also a necessary step toward a correct understanding of the whole biblical lemma, as he constantly moves from the whole to the part and back to the whole; cf. D.T. Runia, "Further Observations on the Structure of Philo's Allegorical Treatises," *VC* 41 (1987): 105–137.

to an overall intent of the poem but also to its narrative line and to its individual elements—to each verse and every word therein. Taken together, these assumptions lay the ground for the specific exegetical method of the Derveni author, which amounts to a systematic matching of the verses, phrases, and individual words of the Orphic poem with specific extratextual referents.

A similar set of assumptions indicative of transpositional hermeneutics characterizes the Qumran pesharim, the earliest line-by-line Jewish commentaries. The *Pesher Habakkuk* from the Qumran community is a good case in point. As 1QpHab VII:1–5 explains,

> 1 And God told Habakkuk to write down what will come over 2 {over} the last generation; but the end of that period, He did not let him know. 3 *vacat* When it says, "so that he can run who reads it" (Hab 2:2), 4 its interpretation is about the Teacher of Righteousness to whom God made known 5 all mysteries of the words of his servants the prophets.

In this case, the true meaning of God's prophecy is hidden even to the prophet himself. Although "God told Habakkuk to write down" what would happen to "the last generation," דור האחרון, Habakkuk does not know when the *eschaton* is coming. This deeper level of meaning is enclosed in his prophecy, yet only the Teacher of Righteousness has access to it.

How can we explain the parallels between the Derveni papyrus and the pesher? What circumstances led to the development of such strikingly similar hermeneutical agendas? To answer these questions, we first study the Derveni papyrus and its detailed word-by-word interpretation of an Orphic poem. Next, we will look at the hermeneutics of the pesharim from the Qumran library. At the end of our article we will draw some conclusions.

Transpositional Hermeneutics in the Derveni Papyrus

For many reasons, the Derveni papyrus represents one of most significant recent manuscript finds from the ancient world.[12] It is arguably the oldest surviving Greek literary manuscript, one of the earliest surviving

---

[12] The ensuing summary of the archaeological and paleographical aspects of the find draws on an excellent monograph by G. Betegh, *The Derveni Papyrus: Cosmology, Theology and Interpretation* (Cambridge: Cambridge University Press, 2004), 56–73, and on the introductory section in the first critical edition of the papyrus by T. Kouremenos,

Greek papyri, and the only papyrus found in mainland Greece. As far as
its content is concerned, the papyrus casts a new light on the relationship
between philosophical speculation and religious thought in the fourth
century B.C.E., and provides new evidence for the history of Orphism and
the ritual function of exegetical texts in this revisionist religious movement. For our study, the text of the papyrus is particularly significant
as the earliest preserved running commentary with verbatim quotations
(*lemmata*)—a predecessor of the continuous commentaries (*hypomnê-
mata*) produced by the Alexandrian philologists.

The Find and Its Content

The papyrus was discovered in 1962, in the course of the excavation of
a group of graves near Derveni, a narrow mountain pass twelve kilome-
ters north of Thessaloniki. The burial site was located on the territory
of the ancient town of Lete and its nearby sanctuary of Demeter and
Kore. The papyrus scroll was found in the debris of the pyre belonging
to tomb A of this burial site. The archaeologists involved in the excavation of the burial site and the study of the individual graves and their
contents favor a date for the burials in the late fourth to early third century B.C.E. Thus the actual papyrus scroll might also date from the same
period. Paleographical dating has proven inconclusive, but the affinities
of the papyrus script with late fourth-century pottery inscriptions and
the copyist's systematic use of *paragraphoi* does not exclude an earlier
date between 340 and 320 B.C.E. The text transmitted on the papyrus may
belong to roughly the same period, but most scholars think that it dates

---

G. Parássoglou, and K. Tsatsanoglou (henceforward KPT), *The Derveni Papyrus* (Studi
e testi per il corpus dei papiri filosofici greci e latini 13; Florence: Olschki, 2006), 1–
10. Our translation of individual sections follows K. Tsantsanoglou's diplomatic and
critical edition in KPT, 62–125 and the edition with an extensive apparatus (absent in
KPT) by A. Bernabé, *Poetae epici Graeci: Testimonia et fragmenta*, vol. 2.3: *Musaeus,
Linus, Epimenides, Papyrus Derveni, Indices* (Teubner; Berlin: de Gruyter, 2007), 171–269.
Among an ever-increasing number of studies on the Derveni papyrus, we have especially
benefited, besides the aforementioned monograph by Betegh, from the following: A. Laks
and G.W. Most, eds., *Studies on the Derveni Papyrus* (Oxford: Clarendon, 1997); A. Laks,
"Between Religion and Philosophy: The Function of Allegory in the Derveni Papyrus,"
Phronesis 42 (1997): 121–142; F. Jourdan, *Le papyrus de Derveni* (Vérité des mythes 23;
Paris: Les Belles Lettres, 2003); C. Calame, "Pratiche orfiche della scrittura: itinerari
iniziatichi?" in *Orfeo e le sue metamorfosi* (ed. G. Guidorizzi and M. Melotti; Rome:
Carocci, 2005), 28–45; A. Bernabé, "Autour de l'interprétation des colonnes XIII–XVI
du Papyrus de Derveni," *Rhizai* 4 (2007): 77–103; M. Frede, "On the Unity and the Aim
of the Derveni Text," *Rhizai* 4 (2007): 9–33.

from the end of the fifth to the beginning of the fourth century, mostly on the basis of its numerous allusions to cosmological theories of various fifth-century Greek natural philosophers, from Diogenes of Apollonia to Anaxagoras and Heraclitus.

The preserved top portion of the papyrus varies in hight, with the beginning of the scroll suffering more damage than the inner layers. As a result, the opening three columns (*selides*) of the papyrus survive only in small fragments of 9–10 lines. The ensuing twenty-three columns have 14 to 17 lines of writing, of which the upper 10–11 lines yield an almost continuous text with occasional small lacunae. It is impossible to determine the original height of the scroll, but comparison with the height of early literary papyri suggests that approximately half of the text is missing. A large block of space following the last column and the conjectured number of 20 *kollemata* typical for a standard croll indicate that we possess the fragments of all columns of the papyrus.

There is a noticeable change of tone, style, and content from the top of col. VII, where the author launches his systematic exegesis of a poem he attributes to Orpheus. In contrast with this impersonal exposition which, with the exception of col. XX, continues to the end of the text, the style of the first six columns is forceful, occasionally polemical, and ridden with rhetorical questions.[13] The columns are concerned with propitiatory rituals, with the magi performing sacrifices and the initiates, with the Erinyes and the Eumenides, the impending daemons and the avenging souls of the deceased, with oracles and dream interpretation, and with the interconnectedness of impiety, injustice, and the lack of understanding among people, including even the initiates.

The atmosphere evoked in the first six columns is reminiscent of Plato's unfavorable description of the itinerant Orphic priests "who present a noisy throng of books by Musaeus and Orpheus, … in accordance with which they perform their rituals, and persuade not only individuals but

---

[13] A similar shift in tone, from an engaging polemic to a dry explanation of words, phrases, and grammatical construction of a literary text, can be observed in the second-century *hypomnêma* on Thucydides from Oxyrhynchus (P.Oxy. 853). For the comparison of the Derveni papyrus with ancient hypomnematic commentaries and later scholia, cf. A. Lamedica, "La terminologia critico-letteraria del Papiro di Derveni ai *corpora* scolio-grafici," in *Lessici technici greci e latini* (ed. P. Radici Colace and M. Caccamo Caltabiano; Messina: Accademia Peloritana dei Pericolanti, 1991), 83–91; idem, "Il Papiro Derveni come commentario: problemi formali," in *Proceedings of the XIXth International Congress of Papyrology, Cairo 2–9 Sept. 1989* (ed. A.H.S. El-Mosallamy; Cairo: Ain Shams University Center of Papyrological Studies, 1992), 1:325–333; Betegh, *The Derveni Papyrus*, 94–108.

also entire cities that the unjust deeds of the living or the dead can be absolved or purified through ritual sacrifices and pleasant games" (*Resp.* 2.364e–365a). The Derveni author does not appear to share Plato's general resentment toward the religious professionals who conduct private religious ceremonies, for in col. V:4–5 he seems to speak of himself as a member of one such group ("we"), that of diviners (μάντεις), who "go into the oracular shrine to inquire for oracular answers" on behalf of their clients. What he profoundly resents, however, is people's disbelief in the post-mortem punishments and their inability to understand premonitory dreams sent by gods. And he shows even less sympathy for the conduct of "those who make a craft of the holy rites" but cannot, or do not wish to, explain the rituals they are performing, leaving the initiates ignorant of "what they have seen or heard or learned" (P. Derveni XX:4–8). The ensuing commentary of an Orphic poem—the latter presumably an instance of what the initiates "have heard or learned" in the ritual—is thus intended as a corrective move on the part of a rival practitioner, dissatisfied with the low professional and intellectual standards of his colleagues.

The poem with which the author is occupied from col. VII onwards provides yet another among many versions of the Orphic theogony. The lacunous state of the papyrus does not allow full reconstruction, but the remaining lines, some fully preserved and others recoverable from the author's partial quotations, reveal significant divergences from the other known Orphic accounts. In this curious reworking of the succession myth recorded in Hesiod's *Theogony*, the oldest deity appears to be Night (col. XI:1–3), and not Konos as in some other Orphic versions. Her son is Ouranos, who is to be the first king (XIV:6). Kronos supplants his father Ouranos after chopping off his sexual organ (XIV:5), only to be himself deposed by Zeus (VIII:4–5; XV:6). Following the advice of Night (XI:10) and Kronos (XIII:1), Zeus swallows Ouranos' sexual organ (XIII:4) and, remaining the sole ruler (XVI:9) with absolute power (XVII:12), contrives a new generation of gods. The last episode in the story, as given in the papyrus, deals with Zeus' incestuous desire for his mother Rhea.

Compared with the plot of Hesiod's *Theogony*, the Orphic poem of the Derveni papyrus brings two important innovations: one is Zeus' swallowing of Ouranos' sex and the other his mating with Rhea. By the former act, Zeus absorbs within himself all previous cosmic stages, and by the latter he breaks the pattern of previous succession and thereby secures his everlasting supremacy. As one line in the poem describes him, "Zeus is the head, Zeus is the middle, and from Zeus all things have their being" (XVII:12). As a result, the cosmos is no longer ruled by a number of gods, each assigned a different function in generating and maintaining the existing order, but has a single source, a single ordering principle, and a single point of convergence. In this model, the traditional gods of Homer and Hesiod are assimilated to a transcendent divine designer, Zeus, and play the role of his various creating powers immanent to the world. Based on this preliminary insight into the general scope and purpose of the Orphic poem, the Derveni author begins his detailed interpretation of the Orphic poem by transposing its individual episodes and characters into the framework of Greek natural philosophy.

Transpositional Hermeneutics in the Derveni Papyrus

The cosmology that underlies and guides the Derveni author's exegesis is not systematically expounded, but given in a series of snapshots, each linked to a particular verse, or a group of verses, of the poem. It is also eclectic, made up of the bits and pieces taken from various fifth-century B.C.E. physical theories, but it does not lack internal coherence, drawing as it were on those physical theories which argue for a single intelligent principle governing the cosmogonic process. The only natural philosopher mentioned by name is Heraclitus (IV:5), whose statement about the size assigned to the sun, the Erinyes, and Dike (Justice) is subsequently quoted (IV:7–9) and later paraphrased (XXV:9–12). But the influence of two other naturalists, viz. Anaxagoras of Clazomenae and Diogenes of Apollonia, is more tangible, and especially of their respective theories of a single corporeal and intelligent substance, air and mind respectively, informing and governing phenomenal reality.[14] The indebtedness to these two thinkers is particularly noticeable in the middle section of the Derveni commentary:[15]

> And the following verse: *Ouranos, son of Night, who reigned first.* By naming Mind that strikes (κρούοντα) existing things against each other Kronos (Κρόνον), he (sc. Orpheus) says that it did a great deed to *Ouranos*, for the latter was thereby deprived of *the kingship.* And he named it Kronos after its action and the other (names), too, according to the same principle. For when all the existing things [were not yet being struck, Mind,] dividing as it were the nature of things, [received the designation *Ouranos*].
>
> (XIV:6–13)

---

[14] For the eclectic cosmology underlying the Derveni author's individual comments, see esp. Betegh, *The Derveni Papyrus,* 224–348, and Frede, "On the Unity," passim.

[15] All words typeset in italics mark the original Orphic poem.

And in the next verse, *Since then in turn Kronos, and next contriving Zeus*, he (sc. Orpheus) says something like this: the rule has been *since the time* he has been the king. And this rule is explained as [his] striking (κρόυων) the existing things against each other and setting them apart into their current reconfiguration—not different from different ones but rather [different]iated.   (XV:6–10)

[*Zeus was first to be born, Zeus the last, with the flashing bolt.*][16] [...] It existed *before* it was named, and then it was named. For air existed even *before* the present things were set together, and will always exist. For it did not come to be, but existed. And why it was called air has been made clear in the previous sections. But it was thought to be born after it got the name Zeus, as if it did not exist before. And he (sc. Orpheus) said that it will be *the last* after it was named Zeus, and this will continue to be its name until the present things have got set together into the same state in which the former things were floating.   (XVI bottom–XVII:9)

The passages exhibit rather clearly the hermeneutic procedure adopted by the Derveni author—a mixture of a detailed elucidation of individual names or common words (typed in italics) and the more extended physical reinterpretation of whole episodes from the Orphic poem. The author first sets apart a verse or verses, and then either breaks open the lemma by means of an initial comment, often in the form of a paraphrase, or immediately picks up those words or phrases in the lemma whose semantics or grammar he finds obscure. Having isolated them out of the verse (atomization), he matches each of these words or phrases with the corresponding elements of his cosmological doctrine. This "atomization" of a lemma is a crucial moment in the whole exegetical procedure, for it not only allows the Derveni author to proceed with a more extended interpretation of the larger narrative units but also works as a protective shield against possible accusations of his arbitrary choice of the philosophical framework.

The above quoted sections from the Derveni commentary show that etymology plays an important role in matching the gods involved in the Orphic story of succession with the particular modalities of the intelligent air, or air/Mind. Ouranos thus signifies the initial attempt at separating (ὁρίζειν) elementary particles within the original lump of elemental mixture, and Kronos the subsequent stage of "striking" (κρούειν) these "existing things" against each other—a vortex-like action which

---

[16] This is a possible restoration of the Orphic verse from the destroyed lower part of col. XVI, based on a fragment from an Orphic poem preserved in multiple sources; cf. Bernabé, *Poetae epici Graeci*, 2.3:228.

entails further division and diversification of matter and causes like particles to tend toward like particles. The conjunction of these particles leads to the present world order—a process that the Orphic poem (XXI:5–12) assigns to Zeus and his divine progeny, viz., Aphrodite, Peitho, and Harmonia, who make particles "mate" (ἀφροδισιάζειν), "persuade" (πείθειν) each other, and stay "closely attached" (ἁρμόζειν). But etymology is not the only interpretive tool at the author's disposal—he often detects cosmological references in ambiguous grammatical constructions (*hyperbaton* in VIII:6), in phonetic assonances of words (ἐπικλῶσαι and ἐπικυρῶσαι in XIX:4–5; cf. XXIII:11–13), or in unexpected combinations of nouns and adjectives ("long Olympus" in col. XII passim). The range of interpretive procedures employed by the Derveni author is impressive, showing not only his philosophical competence but also advanced knowledge of semantics, grammar, and all sorts of rhetorical devices.

Hermeneutics of the Derveni Author and Early Greek Allegoresis

As mentioned eaerlier, it has become customary to situate the hermeneutics of the Derveni author in the context of the Presocratic allegoresis of Homeric poetry. Early Greek allegorists also employed the atomizing strategy already observed in the Derveni papyrus, matching individual Homeric gods and heroes with specific natural phenomena, bodily parts, or psychological processes. The first known practitioner of this method was the early sixth-century grammarian and Homeric scholar Theagenes of Rhegium, whose exegetical program is recorded in a scholion that probably goes back to Porphyry (schol. B *Il.* 20.67 = DK 8.2):

> Homer's discourse of the gods is generally incongruent and also inappropriate, for the myths he relates about the gods are unbefitting. Against this sort of accusation, some people offer a solution from the diction (ἐκ τῆς λέξεως), thinking that all was said in an allegorical mode (ἀλληγορίᾳ) and has to do with the nature of the elements, as in the confrontation of the gods. For they say that the dry clashes with the wet, the hot with the cold, and the light with the heavy, and that, moreover, water extinguishes fire while fire evaporates water. In a similar fashion, there exists a mutual opposition between all the elements that constitute the universe: they may occasionally suffer partial destruction, but they all remain eternally. And he (Homer) arranges these battles by calling fire Apollo, Helios, and Hephaistos, water Poseidon and Scamander, the moon Artemis, air Hera and so on. In the same way, he sometimes gives names of gods to dispositions: that of Athena to wisdom, Ares to folly, Aphrodite to desire, Hermes to

discourse, and so on as it is appropriate to each. This type of defense is quite ancient and goes all the way back to Theagenes of Rhegium, who was the first to write on Homer. Such is the solution from the diction.

Theagenes' method of a one-by-one matching could also account for his attested interest in the Homeric usage, as he is cited for a variant reading of *Il.* 1.381 (DK 8.3), and for his pioneering study of the correct usage of the Greek language (DK 8.1a). As in the case of the Derveni author, Theagenes' transpositional hermeneutics represents a medley of extended allegorical interpretation in a physical or psychological key and the semantic study of individual words. A similar dual tendency can be observed in the Homeric scholarship of the fifth-century critic Metrodorus of Lampsachus, simultaneously engaged in the explanation of Homeric glosses (DK 61.5) and in a rather extravagant procedure of explaining the heroes of the *Iliad* as parts of the universe and the gods as parts of the human body (DK 61.3–4). Thus, a sharp distinction that is often drawn between the narrative dimension of allegoresis and a systematic word-study does not always hold true. In fact, both the earliest allegorists and the Derveni papyrus seem to suggest exactly the opposite. Allegorical interpretation is the combination of a word-by-word matching and the search for broader correspondences between the text as a whole and the complex structure of its referent.[17]

But despite their close agreement in matters of exegetical methods and procedures, the Derveni author and the early allegorists of Homer appear to differ rather significantly both in their intentions and in their achieved results. If Porphyry's account of Theagenes is accurate, then he must have resorted to allegoresis in order to "defend" Homer's anthropomorphic representations of the gods against the charges of irreverence and moral impropriety brought by his philosophically minded contemporaries.[18] For Theagenes, Homeric allegories are essentially a stylistic choice—the

---

[17] Cf. *supra*, n. 11, and esp. W. Bernard, *Spätantike Dichtungstheorien*, who distinguishes between "substitutive" and "diairetic" allegory, the former roughly corresponding to Theagenes or the Derveni papyrus, and the latter to the method of the later Platonists who take the narratives or their episodes as a "whole." For a "dual tendency" in Theagenes and Metrodorus, see Richardson, "Homeric Professors," 65–81, where he counters the argument made by R. Pfeiffer in his *History of Classical Scholarship* (Oxford: Oxford University Press, 1968), 35–56, namely that the fifth-century "Sophists" used detailed word-by-word analysis but showed no interest in extended allegoresis.

[18] The first preserved attack on traditional anthropomorphic representations of gods comes from Xenophanes, who asserts that "Homer and Hesiod attributed to the gods everything blameworthy and disgraceful among men: stealing, adultery, and deceiving one another" (DK 21 B11).

poet's concession to the way the people of his time thought and talked. Theagenes' allegoresis consequently serves a double function. On the one hand, it endorses the culturally dominant way of reading Homer by neutralizing the shocking aspects of the surface meaning as a simple matter of Homeric usage (ἐκ τῆς λέξεως). On the other hand, by offering an alternative reading of Homeric poetry in a physical or psychological key, it accommodates this important repository of cultural memory to a new conceptual framework of natural philosophy and thereby bridges the gap between traditional and more recent modes of cultural communication. Following our definition of transpositional hermeneutics in the introductory section, we could say that Theagenes reached a new understanding of the Homeric text that simultaneously endorsed and went beyond the common (and his own) *Vorverständnis* of Homer. In formulating this compromise solution, Theagenes resorted to two complementary exegetical methods, allegoresis and word semantics (etymology, explanation of glosses), and applied both of them to individual elements isolated from the Homeric text—the former in order to transpose these elements into new physical or psychological frameworks, and the latter to ground his interpretation into the linguistic conventions of Homer's own time.

Contrary to Theagenes, the Derveni author employs transpositional hermeneutics to promote all sorts of radical separations—first, the separation between the Homeric-Hesiodic polytheistic model and the Orphic lore of one divinity, Zeus, who is "first and last" and both transcendent and immanent; then, the separation within his own fringe movement between the initiates who "understand" and those who remain "ignorant"; and finally, the separation within his own religious craft between the strict ritualists and those who, like him, believe that initiatory rituals are ineffective without the proper understanding of their hidden intent. For the Derveni author, Orpheus' "riddling poetry" is not a stylistic choice, but rather the way of concealing the truth from the unworthy. While Theagenes was a literary-minded intellectual engaged in the contemporary discussions about the value of traditional sources of authority, the Derveni author, in turn, is an itinerant religious specialist involved in a revisionist reappraisal of his divinatory craft and its underlying written lore. Thus, even though he clearly draws on the tradition of physical and moral allegory, the background of his exegetical procedure is primarily religious and, as is the case with the sources of the pesharim, appears to lie in the ancient practices of oracular divination and omen interpretation. We have discussed the divinatory background of the Qumran pesharim and the Derveni commentary elsewhere.[19] In this contribution, we are more interested in the concrete historical and ideological motives that prompted the Derveni author and the Qumran pesharists to adopt a similar hermeneutical model of atomization and transposition.

TRANSPOSITIONAL HERMENEUTICS IN THE QUMRAN PESHARIM

As mentioned in our introduction, the Qumran pesharim, which are dated to the first half of the first century B.C.E., represent the earliest preserved line-by-line Jewish commentaries. As has been shown by Michael Fishbane and others, the Qumran pesharim were inspired by ancient Near Eastern omen interpretation in their hermeneutics of isolation and recontexualization.[20] The difference between Ancient Near Eastern omen lists and the Pesharim lies in the choice of material used as primary and secondary narratives. In the pesharim, the quoted biblical lemma is the equivalent of the *protasis* in an omen list (e.g. a brief description of a dream in an ancient dream book) and the lemma's interpretation is the equivalent of the omen list's *apodosis* (e.g. the interpretation of a dream in an ancient dream book). But the pesharim are interested in interpreting not the life of an individual in light of scripture but rather the history of the Essene movement as the only true remnant of Israel. In pesher

---

[19] A. Lange and Z. Pleše, "Derveni-Alexandria—Qumran: Transpositional Hermeneutics in Jewish and Greek Culture," in *Palimpsestes Deux: Symposium international sur la littérature de commentaire dans les cultures du Proche-Orient ancien et de la Méditerranée anciennt, Aix-en-Provence* (ed. P.S. Alexander and S. Aufrère; OLA; Leuven: Peeters, forthcoming). For valid suggestions pointing to the same direction, see Betegh, *The Derveni Papyrus*, 364–370.

[20] For the pesharim and ancient Near Eastern omen-interpretation, see L.H. Silbermann, "Unriddling the Riddle: A Study in the Scripture and Language of the Habakkuk Pesher (1QpHab)," *RevQ* 3 (1961–1962): 323–364 (330–335); A. Finkel, "The Pesher of Dreams and Scripture," *RevQ* 4 (1963–1964): 357–370; I. Rabinowitz, "Pesher/Pittaron: Its Biblical Meaning and Its Significance in the Qumran Literature," *RevQ* 8 (1972–1975): 219–232 (230–232); M. Fishbane, "The Qumran Pesher and Traits of Ancient Hermeneutics," in *Proceedings of the Sixth World Congress of Jewish Studies: Held at the Hebrew University of Jerusalem 13–19 August 1973 under the Auspices of the Israel Academy of Sciences and Humanities* (ed. A. Shinan; 4 vols.; Jerusalem: World Union of Jewish Studies, 1975–1980), 1:97–114; M. Nissinen, "Pesharim as Divination: Qumran Exegesis, Omen Interpretation and Literary Prophecy," in *Prophecy after the Prophets? The Contribution of the Dead Sea Scrolls to the Understanding of Biblical and Extra-Biblical Prophecy* (ed. K. De Troyer, A. Lange, and L.L. Schulte; CBET 52; Leuven: Peeters, 2009), 43–60.

hermeneutics,[21] this history of the Essene movement as the true remnant of Israel living in the last days functions as a secondary narrative. To achieve their exegetical objective, the pesharim employ the same mechanism of isolation and recontextualization as the Derveni papyrus. A good example is 1QpHab III:2–6, which quotes the rather cryptic verse Hab 1:7:

> Terrible and dreadful are they; their justice and dignity proceeds from themselves.

In the book of Habakkuk, this verse is part of a description of the Neo-Babylonian empire, which God has raised as an instrument of punishment for his people.[22] But for *Pesher Habakkuk*, written in the middle of the first century B.C.E., the long gone Neo-Babylonian Empire was of little interest. Following its revisionist agenda, the pesher isolates the phrase "dreadful and terrible" from the primary narrative of Hab 1:7 and recontextualizes it into the secondary narrative of the Essene-Jewish history:

> Its interpretation is about the Kittim: the fear and dread of whom are over all the peoples; intentionally all their plans are to do evil, and with deceit and treachery they walk among all the nations.

By way of this transposition, the phrase "terrible and dreadful" refers now to the fear and dread experienced by an encounter with the Roman army—the Kittim being the pesher's name for the Romans.[23] This transposition allows the pesher to find a deeper signification of the primary text. Pesher hermeneutics is governed by the presupposition (*Vorverständnis*) that Jewish prophetic scriptures carry two meanings, a surface meaning and a hidden deeper meaning. This deeper meaning was not understood by the prophet Habakkuk, but only by the initiated interpreter.[24] Shani Berrin has aptly summarized this approach to the interpretation of Jewish scriptures as follows:

---

[21] For the interpretative and hermeneutic strategies of the Qumran pesharim, see E. Osswald, "Zur Hermeneutik des Habakuk-Kommentar," *ZAW* 68 (1956): 243–256; Fishbane, "Qumran Pesher," 98–100; S.L. Berrin, "Qumran Pesharim," in *Biblical Interpretation at Qumran* (ed. M. Henze; Studies in the Dead Sea Scrolls and Related Literature; Grand Rapids: Eerdmans, 2005), 110–133; eadem, *The Pesher Nahum Scroll from Qumran: An Exegetical Study of 4Q169* (STDJ 53; Leiden: Brill, 2004), 9–19.

[22] For the interpretation of Hab 1:7 as concerned with the Neo-Babylonian Empire, see e.g. R.L. Smith, *Micah-Malachi* (WBC 32; Waco: Word Books, 1984), 101–102.

[23] For "Kittim" as a cipher for the Romans in Qumran literature, see e.g. T.H. Lim, "Kittim," *Encyclopedia of the Dead Sea Scrolls* (ed. L.H. Schiffman and J.C. VanderKam; 2 vols.; Oxford: Oxford University Press, 2000), 1:469–471 (470).

[24] See our discussion of 1QpHab VII:1–5 in the introduction of this article.

A form of biblical interpretation peculiar to Qumran, in which biblical poetic/prophetic texts are applied to postbiblical historical/eschatological settings through various literary techniques in order to substantiate a theological conviction pertaining to divine reward and punishment.[25]

When Berrin claims that pesher is "a form of biblical interpretation peculiar to Qumran," she is well aware of hermeneutical parallels in ancient Near Eastern omen exegesis and in rabbinic *petirah* midrashim. It should also be pointed out that the hermeneutics of atomization and recontextualization can be found in various interpretative passages inside the Hebrew canon as well. Examples include Jer 23:33–40[26] and Dan 9:23.[27] What was not yet available to Berrin though was the Derveni papyrus. But before comparing pesharim with the allegorical exegesis of the Derveni papyrus, we will analyze other pesher interpretations of Jewish scriptures.

Transpositional Hermeneutics in 4QpPsᵃ (4Q171) 1–10 i 25–ii 20

To develop a better idea of how pesher exegesis applied transpositional hermeneutics to prophetic Jewish scriptures, we turn to a passage of 4QpPsᵃ (4Q171). 4QpPsᵃ is one of the three extant manuscripts of a pesher on selected Psalms.[28] This *Psalms Pesher* can be dated to the early first century B.C.E.[29] The passage in question, 4QpPsᵃ (4Q171) 1–10 i 25–ii 12, interprets Ps 37:7–11.

---

[25] Berrin, "Qumran Pesharim," 110; eadem, *Pesher Nahum*, 9.

[26] Cf. A. Lange, "Reading the Decline of Prophecy," in *Reading the Present in the Qumran Library: The Perception of the Contemporary by Means of Scriptural Interpretations* (ed. K. de Troyer and A. Lange; SBLSymS 30; Atlanta: SBL, 2005), 181–191.

[27] Cf. e.g. A. Lange, "Interpretation als Offenbarung: Zum Verhältnis von Schriftauslegung und Offenbarung," in *Wisdom and Apocalypticism in the Dead Sea Scrolls and in the Biblical Tradition* (ed. F. García Martínez; BETL 168; Leuven: Peeters, 2003), 17–33 (17–22).

[28] Whether 1QPs (1Q16), 4QpPsᵃ (4Q171), and 4QpPsᵇ (4Q173) are three copies of one *Psalms Pesher* (thus e.g. H. Stegemann, *Die Essener, Qumran, Johannes der Täufer und Jesus* [4th ed.; Freiburg: Herder, 1994], 179) or attest to three different pesharim to selected Psalms (thus T.H. Lim, *Pesharim* [Companion to the Qumran Scrolls 3; London: Sheffield Academic Press, 2002], 38–39) is still debated. Due to missing overlaps between the three manuscripts and the bad stage of preservation of 1QPs and 4QpPsᵇ, no certainty can be reached on this issue. It seems more probable though that the Qumran library contained one *Psalms Pesher* in several copies rather than three different Psalms pesharim.

[29] Cf. Stegemann, *Essener*, 179–180. For a recent survey of 4QpPsᵃ and its history of research, see N. Crisanto Tiquillahuanca, *Die Armen werden das Land besitzen: Eine exegetische Studie zu Psalm 37* (Beiträge zum Verstehen der Bibel 16; Münster: Lit, 2008), 22–44.

Psalm 37 belongs to the group of wisdom psalms in the Psalter. It emphasizes the validity of the sapiential concept of act-consequence correlation in the context of short-term gains by the wicked. Gerhard von Rad summarizes the theme of the psalm as follows:

> Do not grow heated at the prosperity of the wicked (vv. 1, 7b), trust and hope in Yahweh; the righteous will not be ruined, but will possess the land (vv. 3, 7, 19, 22, 34). The wicked, however, come to a bad end; in a short time the wicked man is no longer there (vv. 2, 10, 20). The thoughts in the psalm are simple and are not developed in any complex way. Its conclusion is that it is the end that is important. The end ... of the wicked is destruction, the end of those who trust in Yahweh is salvation (vv. 37 ff.). By 'end' the psalm obviously means the conclusion of a way of life in which God's salvation and judgment are then finally visible to men.[30]

For the Essene interpreter of Ps 37 this simple message contradicted his experiences. The illegitimate Hasmonean high priests of the Jerusalem temple had been in power for several generations. The—in the eyes of the pesharist—schismatic Pharisees became increasingly influential in Jewish religious and political life. The Essenes, who perceived themselves as the only true remnant of God's chosen people and as the only part of Israel that truly observed his Torah, were isolated and marginalized. Transpositional hermeneutics allowed the Essene pesharist to find a deeper meaning in the Psalm, one that was related to the history of his movement and concerned his own experiences and expectations. For this purpose, the pesharist structured his pesher into larger interpretative units, separated from one another by large blank spaces (*vacat*) extending up to a whole manuscript line.[31] A section commenting on Ps 37:7 runs as follows:[32]

> "[Be resigne]d to [the LORD and] wait for him, do not be angry because of the one who is successful on his way, because of the man 26 [who carri]es out (his) wicked schemes" (Ps 37:7). Its [interpretation] is about the Man of the Lie who led astray many with words 27 of deception because they

---

[30] G. von Rad, *Wisdom in Israel* (trans. J.D. Martin; Harrisburg: Trinity, 1972), 203–204.

[31] Preserved *vacats* can be found in 4QpPs[a] (4Q171) 1–10 i 24; ii 6, 12, 21; iii 6, 13; iv 6, 12, 22 and 4QpPs[b] (4Q173) 1 6. For the *vacats* in 4QpPs[a], see G.L. Doudna, *4Q Pesher Nahum: A Critical Edition* (JSPSup 35; London: Sheffield Academic Press, 2001), 240–243.

[32] All translations of 4QpPs[a] (4Q171) 1–10 i 25–ii 20 are based on the edition of M.P. Horgan, "Psalm Pesher 1," in *The Dead Sea Scrolls: Hebrew Aramaic, and Greek Texts with English Translations*, vol. 6b: *Pesharim, Other Commentaries, and Related Documents* (ed. J.H. Charlesworth et al.; The Princeton Theological Seminary Dead Sea Scrolls Project; Tübingen: Mohr Siebeck, 2002), 6–23.

> choose swift things and did not list[en] to a translator of knowledge, so
> that ii 1 they will perish through sword, and through famine, and through
> plague.   (4QpPsᵃ [4Q171] 1–10 i 25–ii 1)

Out of Ps 37:7, the pesher isolates two elements, viz. the man who carries
out his wicked plans and the success on his way. Both elements are identified with the "Man of Lie" and his followers. The *Damascus Document*
(CD B 20:15; cf. 1QpHab II:2; V:11; 4QPsᵃ 1–10 iv 14) shows that the
phrase "Man of Lie" is a slanderous way of designating the adversary of
the Teacher of Righteouness in the Essene-Pharisaic schism. The "Man
of Lie" is the one "who carries out his wicked schemes" in Ps 37:7. His
success in Ps 37:7 is understood by the pesharist as his "leading astray of
many with words of deception." The phrase "swift things" hints at a liberal
Pharisaic halakhah as the means of promoting this deception. Instead
of following a Pharisaic dignitary, the "many" should have listened to
the "translator of knowledge." A passage in one of the so-called Teacher
Songs in the *Hodayot* (1QHᵃ X:15) shows that "translator of knowledge"
was a self-designation of the Teacher of Righteousness.[33] Thus, by way of a
transposition of two elements from Ps 37:7 into the history of the Essene
movement, the *Pesher on Psalms* turns the general statement about the
brief success of the wicked from Ps 37:7 into a concrete prophecy about
the shortlived Pharisaic success in the Essene-Pharisaic schism. This
interpretation of Ps 37:7 could well be influenced by the persecution
of the Pharisees by Alexander Jannaeus. Such an understanding of the
Pesher would be in line with *Pesher Nahum*'s reading of this persecution
(see 4QpNah 3–4 i 6–8).[34]

The interpretation of Ps 37:8–9a expresses the hopes of the pesharist
that the Pharisees might eventually return to the Essene movement.

> "Desist from anger and abandon fury, do not 2 be angry, it can only cause
> evil. Indeed, evil men will be cut off" (Ps 37:8–9a). Its interpretation is
> about all those who turn back 3 to the Torah, who do not reject to turn
> back from their evil, because all who resist 4 to turn back from their sin
> will be cut down.   (4QpPsᵃ [4Q171] 1–10 ii 1–4)

---

[33] Cf. e.g. J.H. Charlesworth, *The Pesharim and Qumran History: Chaos or Consensus?*
(Grand Rapids: Eerdmans, 2002), 83, 97.

[34] H. Eshel, *The Dead Sea Scrolls and the Hasmonean State* (Studies in the Dead Sea
Scrolls and Related Literature; Grand Rapids: Eerdmans, 2008), 147–148, thinks that
"they will perish through sword, and through famine, and through plague" refers in 4QPsᵃ
1–10 ii 1 to a famine attested in Coile-Syria for the year 65 B.C.E. But the language of 4QPsᵃ
1–10 ii 1 is rather idiomatic at this place and employs biblical rhetoric (cf. e.g. Jer 14:12;
21:9; 24:10; 27:8, 13; 29:17, 18; 32:24, 36; 38:2; 42:17, 22; 44:13; Ezek 6:11; 12:16). Contra
Eshel, the pesharist has therefore no concrete famine in mind at this place.

Again, the pesharist isolates two elements out of Ps 37:8–9a: (i) "desisting from anger" and "abandoning fury," and (ii) "cutting down." Transposed into the history of the Essene-Pharisaic schism, "desisting" and "abandoning" signify a Pharisaic return to the true interpretation and fulfillment of the Torah as practiced in the Essene community. While Ps 37:9a proclaims that the sapiential act-consequence correlation will lead in the long run to the "cutting off of evil men" (כיא מרעים יכרתו), the pesher sees this as a prophecy that the Pharisees will be cut off: "because all who resist to turn back from their sin will be cut down (יכרתו)." As in the previous passage, transposition of individual elements from Ps 37 into the history of the Essene-Pharisaic schism turns the Psalm's description of the ethical structure of the universe into a prophecy concerning the history of this schism. Some Pharisees will return to the Essene understanding of how to fulfill the Torah because of the threat of (eschatological) punishment.

This eschatological dimension of Ps 37 is emphasized in the following paragraphs of the pesher:

> "And those who wait for the LORD, they will take possession of the land" (Ps 37:9b). Its interpretation is: 5 they are the congregation of his chosen ones, those who do his will. "And only a little time and there will be no wicked one" (Ps 37:10a). 6 vacat   (4QpPsᵃ [4Q171] 1–10 ii 4–6)

After discussing the issue of the Pharisees who will return to the Essene movement and its halakhah, the interpretation of Ps 37:9b focuses on the future of the Essenes themselves. For this purpose, the pesharist isolates the Hebrew word המה ("they") out of Ps 37:9b: "They (המה) are the congregation of his chosen ones," and applies it to the Essene community. Transposed into the history of the Essene movement, their "waiting for the Lord" is explained as doing God's will, viz. observing the Lord's Torah according to its Essene interpretation. "Waiting for the Lord" becomes in this way the observance of the correct halakhah. Possession of the land mentioned in Ps 37:9b as the reward for the patient sage remains uninterpreted at this place, and it will be explained later in the pesher's detailed interpretation of Ps 37:11. Instead, the *Psalms Pesher* ends the section dedicated to Ps 37:9b with an uninterpreted quote of Ps 37:10a: "And only a little time and there will be no wicked one." In the context of the preceding and following paragraphs, this quotation addresses the demise of the Pharisees and all other wicked people in the imminent eschaton.

In the second preserved paragraph of its interpretation of Ps 37, the *Psalms Pesher* addresses the eschatological future of both the Essenes and the Pharisees. The interpretation of Ps 37:10b is concerned with the eschatological fate of the latter group:

> 7 "And when I will regard his place, he will be no more" (Ps 37:10b). Its interpretation is about all of wickedness at the end of 8 forty years: they will end and in the land not one wicked man will be found.
>
> (4QpPs[a] [4Q171] 1–10 ii 7–8)

To understand what will become of the Pharisees, the pesharist isolates the Hebrew word איננו ("and he will be no more") out of Ps 37:10b. The Psalm itself emphasizes the short-lived prosperity of the wicked at this place. Transposed into the eschatological thought of the Essene movement, this one-word statement gains a new signification. All the wicked, including the Pharisaic violators of the Torah, will perish. In the opinion of the pesharist, after forty years there will be no more wickedness. This period of forty years evokes the forty years of Israel's wandering in the desert until it was delivered into the Promised Land. Like Israel after the Exodus, the Essene movement will also experience the destruction of its enemies after forty years. But the meaning of the forty years is not exhausted by the pesher's typological reading of Israel's time in the desert. The *Damascus Document* shows that the span of forty years was of key importance in the eschatological hopes of the Essene movement.

> And from the day the unique Teacher was gathered in until the end of all the men of war who turned away 15 with the Man of the Lie, there will be about forty years. And during that time God's 16 anger will be kindled against Israel, as he said, "There is no king and no prince" (Hos 3:4) and no judge and no reprove in righteousness.   (CD B 20:14–17)[35]

Like the *Psalms Pesher*, the *Damascus Document* connects the period of forty years with the end of the "Man of the Lie" and the Pharisaic movement. After the death of the Teacher of Righteousness there will come a time when the Essenes will have no leader and when God's anger will be lit against Israel. The *Psalms Pesher* shows in its preceding paragraph (4QpPs[a] [4Q171] 1–10 i 24–ii 5) that persevering in Torah observance is the appropriate conduct during this forty-year period.[36]

---

[35] Translation according to J.M. Baumgarten and D.R. Schwartz, "Damascus Document (CD)," in *The Dead Sea Scrolls: Hebrew, Aramaic, and Greek Texts with English Translations*, vol. 2: *Damascus Document, War Scroll, and Related Documents* [ed. J.H. Charlesworth; The Princeton Theological Seminary Dead Sea Scrolls Project; Tübingen: Mohr Siebeck, 1995], 4–57 (35).

[36] Thus Stegemann, *Essener*, 174, 180. For the motif of a forty-year period in Essene

After forty years, in the soon-to-come eschatological end, the Pharisees and all other wicked ones will be destroyed. Only the Essenes as the true observers of God's law will be rewarded.

This second aspect of the eschatological future is addressed in the interpretation of the following lemma:

> 9 "And the poor will possess land and they will enjoy abundant peace" (Ps 37:11). Its interpretation is about 10 the congregation of the Poor Ones: they will accept the appointed time of humiliation and they will be delivered from all the snares 11 of Belial. And afterwards they will enjoy all [...] of the land and they will become fat [...] 12 flesh. v[acat]
>
> (4QpPsᵃ [4Q171] 1–10 ii 9–12)

The pesharist isolates three elements out of Ps 37:11. The "poor" (ענוים), the "possession of land," and the "enjoyment of abundant peace." Transposed into the Essene history and eschatology, the ענוים are identified with "the poor ones" (האביונים). In Essene literature, האביונים is a self-designation of the Essenes in general and the followers of the Teacher of Righteousness in particular.[37] For the pesharist, it is thus the Essenes to whom possession of the land and enjoyment of abundant peace are promised according to Ps 37, because they endured forty years[38] of affliction prior to the eschaton in true observance of the Torah.[39] Transposed into the Essene eschatological worldview, this promise of Ps 37 signifies the deliverance from the Essene archdemon Belial as the dominant negative force before the eschaton.

Once saved, the Essenes will enjoy the possession of the land. In Ps 37, the "possession of the land" is not to be understood as a concrete conflict with (violent) potentates over the land of Israel.[40] The parallel usage of the verbs ירש and שכן in Ps 37:29 demonstrates that a more general

---

literature cf. also H. Eshel, "The Meaning and Significance of CD 20:13–15," in *The Provo International Conference on the Dead Sea Scrolls: Technological Innovations, New Texts, and Reformulated Issues* (ed. D.W. Parry and E. Ulrich; STDJ 30; Leiden: Brill, 1999), 330–336.

[37] See 4QpPsᵃ (4Q171) 1–10 iii 10; 1QpHab XII:3, 6, 10; cf. 4QMᵃ (4Q491) 11 i 11; 1QM (1Q33) XI:13; XIII:14. For the Essenes' self-description as "the poor" in the *Psalms Pesher*, see J. Jokiranta, "The Social Identity Approach: Identity-Constructing Elements in the Psalms Pesher," in *Defining Identities: We, You, and the Other in the Dead Sea Scrolls: Proceedings of the Fifth Meeting of the IOQS in Groningen* (ed. F. García Martínez and M. Popović; STDJ 70; Leiden: Brill, 2008), 85–109 (98–102).

[38] See above the commentary to lines 7–8.

[39] Jokiranta, "Social Identity," 105.

[40] Contra K. Seybold, *Die Psalmen* (HAT 1/15; Tübingen: Mohr Siebeck, 1996), 155–156.

experience of well-being and safety is meant: "The phrase ... seems to be a kind of shorthand for salvation and prosperity in general."[41] But in the light of Essene eschatology, the pesharist understands the general statement of Ps 37 as a concrete promise that the Essenes, being as it were the only true remnant of Israel, will possess the land in the eschaton because all wicked parts of the Israel will be destroyed. The "enjoyment of abundant peace" from Ps 37:11 also has a concrete eschatological signification for the pesharist. In the eschaton, the Essenes will "grow fat" like fat cows on good land. By combining the "possession of the land" with the prospect of "growing fat" out of it, the *Psalms Pesher* reflects eschatological expectations of the *Damascus Document*:

> And at the end of (his) wrath, three hundred 6 and ninety years after giving them into the hand of Nebuchadnezzar, king of Babylon, 7 he turned his attention to them and caused to grow out of Israel and Aaron a root of planting, to inherit 8 his land (לירוש את ארצו) and grow fat in the goodness of his soil (ולדשן בטוב אדמתו).[42]   (CD A 1:5–8)

Transpositional Hermeneutics in the Pesharim

The two sample paragraphs from the Qumran *Psalms Pesher* on Ps 37 provide a good illustration for the issues addressed by pesher hermeneutics. Psalm 37 speaks of the wicked as of ethically defunct persons and addresses the problem of theodicy by claiming that their successes are short lived. The righteous, who are currently poor and oppressed by the wicked, will be rewarded by God in the future and their wicked opponents destroyed. Psalm 37 has thus no specific group of wicked people in mind and shows no interest in eschatology.

As is the case with other psalms, the Essenes regarded Ps 37 as scripture. It was thus for them a key constituent of Jewish cultural memory. And yet, the views expressed in Ps 37 agreed neither with the Essene worldview nor with Essene thought. In contrast with the general statements of Ps 37, the Essenes knew exactly who the wicked in Israel were— those who broke God's laws, including all non-Essene Jews, and especially the Pharisees. Furthermore, Ps 37 does not address eschatological concerns but promises the demise of the wicked during the lifetime of the righteous. But the Essenes were convinced that they lived in a

---

[41] Cf. N. Lohfink, "יָרַשׁ *yāraš*; יְרֵשָׁה *yᵉrēšâ*; יְרֻשָּׁה *yᵉruššâ*; מוֹרָשׁ *môrāš*; מוֹרָשָׁה *môrāšâ*," *TDOT* 6:368–396 (394); and H.-J. Kraus, *Psalmen*, vol. 1: *Psalmen 1–59* (6th ed.; BKAT 15.1; Neukirchen-Vluyn: Neukirchener Verlag, 1989), 441.

[42] Translation according to Baumgarten and Schwartz, "Damascus Document," 13.

time of eschatological trial shortly before the final judgment. The lack of eschatology in a key part of their cultural memory was all the more a problem for the Essenes because the Teacher of Righteousness died some time after the Essene-Pharisaic schism and because the importance of the Pharisees within Judaism continued to grow. According to the surface meaning of Ps 37, the righteous Teacher should have experienced the downfall of Pharisaic opponents during his lifetime. As a memory space of Jewish cultural memory, Ps 37 thus contradicted the key assumptions of Essene thought and worldview.

As a result, the Essenes found themselves increasingly estranged from their scriptures as the memory spaces of the Jewish cultural memory. There were two possible ways for them to address this growing sense of estrangement: either descripturalize Ps 37 or adjust it to Essene thought and worldview by way of either rewriting the original text or interpreting its manifest meaning. The evidence of the pesher on this psalm indicates that the Essenes chose to adjust the meaning of Ps 37 to the central tenets of their worldview and thought by way of transpositional hermeneutics. This adjustment was possible inasmuch as the Essenes approached Ps 37 with the presupposition (*Vorverständnis*) that the Jewish scriptures are indispensable to a right understanding of Jewish history. Another Essene presupposition was that this historical dimension of the Jewish scriptures is not easily accessible but hidden behind their surface meaning. Transpositional hermeneutics provided the Essenes with a necessary tool to disclose a deeper historical meaning of the Jewish scriptures. In order to overcome truisms of the psalmic text they regarded as highly authoritative, the Essenes transposed its individual elements into the secondary narrative of their own history and thought. Transposition of these individual elements into Essene history and thought allowed the pesharist to assign them new meanings and hence to elicit a whole new meaning to Ps 37. In the three sample paragraphs of 4QpPs[a], which were analyzed above, the psalm prophecied the respective pre-eschatological and eschatological fates of the Essenes and the Pharisees.

But transpositional hermeneutics did not only allow for a rereading of Ps 37; it also asigned a new meaning to the Essene history and to the present situation of the Essenes as well.[43] In other words, the

---

[43] For this phenomenon, see the contributions to de Troyer and Lange, *Reading the Present in the Qumran Library.*

Essenes interpreted their own history in light of Ps 37. The employment of transpositional hermeneutics in the pesharim enabled the Essenes to overcome not only their estrangement from authoritative scriptures but also the hiatus between their thought and the historical and political realities of their times. The Essenes' radical observance of the Torah and the events leading to their separation from the Pharisees raised the (eschatological) expectations for a reward that would correspond to their suffering. But the successes of the Pharisees contradicted the Essene hopes for such a reward. Transpositional hermeneutics, such as applied in pesher-commentaries, was nevertheless able to explain the hiatus between Essene expectations and historical realities and thereby reintegrate the Essenes and their thought into their contemporary historical context.

To summarize: As evidenced by the extant pesharim, transpositional hermeneutics enabled the Essenes to overcome their dual sense of alienation, from the Jewish scriptures on the one hand and from their contemporary context on the other.

1. Books such as Habakkuk or texts such as Ps 37 addressed past historical or theological contexts, not the situation of the first century B.C.E. Prior to that time, Essene eschatological readings of prophetic texts had sometimes been disproved by history. Very much like ancient Greek allegorists, the Essenes faced the challenging task of simultaneously communicating a primary and a secondary narrative with each other. In the particular case of the pesharim, we can distinguish two such narratives: the primary narrative, or the literal meaning of the prophetic texts, and the secondary narrative about a reality that disagreed both with the literal meaning of the prophetic texts and with the Essene hopes created by their historical experiences.

2. Historical developments contradicted the Essene worldview and estranged the Essenes from their own present. Although they perceived themselves as the true remnant of Israel, which alone observed the Torah and fulfilled Israel's covenantal obligations, the Essenes had no political power and suffered persecution from their enemies. Transpositional hermeneutics allowed the Essenes to reassess their reality in the light of their scriptures. Thanks to this exegetical procedure, events like the Essene-Pharisaic schism were understood as a necessary eschatological cleansing in the period of assessment prior to the final eschatological judgment.

Conclusion

The principal objective of our study was to point to a common hermeneutical pattern underlying the exegetical techniques of two culturally heterogeneous metatexts—the Orphic Derveni papyrus and the Qumran pesharim. We are now ready to ask whether in their respective use of transpositional hermeneutics and its methods of atomization and recontextualization, these metatexts could have influenced each other or whether they are historically independent phenomena. If we accept the last proposition, then their commonalities go back to a basic structure of human understanding and to such universal hermeneutical preconditions as the historical situatedness of the interpreter or, even more abstractly, a general human tendency to re-describe reality and invent new ways of relating an object to other objects. While acknowledging the presence of these transcendental elements of hermeneutic experience in the two metatexts under our investigation, we would still like to propose a more concrete, historical explanation of their common interpretative strategies.

In our examples, a common problem of the relevance of authoritative religious traditions was addressed by resorting to the same technique of atomization and recontextualization. The Derveni papyrus isolates individual elements from an Orphic theogony and recontextualizes them into the discourse of philosophical cosmology. The Qumran pesharim isolate individual elements from the prophetic scriptures of Judaism and recontextualize them into the (eschatological) history of the Essene movement. These hermeneutical undertakings are transpositional in that they transpose individual elements of primary narratives into secondary narratives. What the Derveni papyrus and the pesharim share in common is the need to transpose one narrative into the context of another one. Their shared hermeneutical approach can therefore be best described as *transpositional hermeneutics*.

Transpositional hermeneutics is a dialectical process in which both the primary and secondary narratives undergo structural adjustments and acquire new meanings. In the Derveni papyrus, a cosmology that underlies and guides the author's exegesis of Orphic theogony is a creative reworking of various fifth-century B.C.E. physical theories necessitated by the narrative logic of the base text. The example of the *Psalms Pesher* shows how the pesharist was able to find the righteous Essenes and their wicked opponents lurking beneath the surface meaning of the archetypal conflict of the just and the wicked in Ps 37. At the same time, it was precisely this universality of Ps 37 that enabled the pesharist to provide an eschatological dimension to the history of his movement and its present sense of failure and disappointed hopes. While the basic method of transposing isolated items out of one narrative into another guides both the allegorical project of the Derveni papyrus and the Qumran pesher exegesis, the two metatexts are quite distinct in their aims. The Derveni papyrus transposes elements out of an Orphic poem into the narrative of various fifth-century B.C.E. physical theories. The pesharim transpose elements out of prophetic texts into the history of the Essene community.

Transpositional hermeneutics is a cross-cultural phenomenon, which developed independently in Greek and Jewish cultures. There is no common historical archetype to the methods of exegesis employed in the Derveni papyrus and the pesharim. What we have here are two metatexts without direct historical contiguity, yet sustained by the same hermeneutical presupposition (*Vorverständnis*) and driven in their exegetical endeavor by a similar sense of estrangement from the normative understanding of authoritative texts within their respective cultures.

It is precisely this sense of cultural estrangement that serves as a necessary precondition for the employment of transpositional hermeneutics. Cultural estrangement may be triggered by various reasons, and these reasons, in their turn, determine the selection of a particular referent, or a secondary narrative, into which the elements isolated from a base text will be transposed. The range of referents, or secondary narratives, is practically indefinite, from historical (pesher) to philosophical referents (Theagenes, the Derveni papyrus). In this process, the only stable element is a threefold structure of the transpositional procedure (*Vorverständnis*—atomization—recontextualization), while both the initial impetus for resorting to transpositional hermeneutics and its concrete realizations are historically specific and thus infinitely diverse.

For the Derveni author, a systematic application of philosophical allegoresis to the riddling language of the Orphic theogonical poem reflects his profound sense of estrangement from all sorts of prevailing norms, both in the society at large and in his own religious group—first, the estrangement from the Homeric and Hesiodic polytheistic model, at the time still dominant in Greek culture; second, the estrangement within his own Orphic movement from the majority of initiates, deprived of the correct hermeneutic attitude towards the cathartic and telestic rites in which they participate and towards the sacred lore they pretend to observe; and finally, the estrangement within his own religious craft from the strict ritualists, those who believe in the effectiveness of their rituals without understanding their hidden intent. By transposing the Orphic lore into the categories of contemporary philosophy, the Derveni author opens up the way to modernize his own religious tradition, accommodate it to new conceptual frameworks, and distance it even further from the mythological discourse of traditional polytheism.

In the case of pesher-exegesis, the Essene pesharists experienced a dual estrangement from the prophetic texts and from their own history. The author of the *Psalms Pesher*, for example, is confronted in his reading of Ps 37 with its universal claim that the sapiential act-consequence correlation is only temporarily valid, and that the short-lived gains of the wicked will soon be recompensed by their eternal punishment and by the lasting rewards for the just. The Essenes' own history, and especially their disappointment over Pharisaic successes which led to their increasing marginalization, not only countered the optimistic theodicy of Ps 37 but also made the present reality of the movement devoid of any positive signification. Transpositional hermeneutics offered the pesharist a way out of this hermeneutical deadlock. By transposing the elements of Ps 37 into the turbulent history of his movement, he identified the archetypical figures of just and wicked in Ps 37 as the Essenes and their Pharisaic and Sadducean opponents, respectively. The rewards and punishments that Ps 37 projected into an immediate future became rewards and punishments in the imminent eschaton. By way of this simple transposition, the pesharist assigned an eschatological dimension to the retributive theodicy of Ps 37 and simultaneously gave his own movement a much needed hope in the imminent resolution of its tribulations.

What, in the end, is the purpose of transpositional hermeneutics, and what wider cultural goals does its technique of atomization and recontextualization of authoritative texts attempt to achieve? In the two ancient Mediterranean societies covered in this study, texts and especially authoritative texts, both oral and written, represent the reservoirs and transmitters of cultural memory.[44] They are the memory spaces[45] which make up

---

[44] For the concept of cultural memory, see A. Assmann, *Erinnerungsräume: Formen und Wandlungen des kulturellen Gedächtnisses* (München: Beck, 1999), J. Assmann, *Das kulturelle Gedächtnis: Schrift, Erinnerung und politische Identität in frühen Hochkulturen* (2nd ed.; Müchen: Beck, 1997), and A. Erll and A. Nünning, eds., *Cultural Memory Studies: An International and Interdisciplinary Handbook* (Media and Cultural Memory 8; Berlin: de Gruyter, 2008).

[45] For texts as memory spaces, see e.g. R. Lachmann, "Mnemonic and Intertextual Aspects of Literature," in *Cultural Memory Studies*, 301–310.

the totality of cultural memory in these societies. But authoritative texts remain static as their respective societies undergo political, social, and cultural transformations. The consequence of these changes is a gradual alienation from the founding texts as repositories of cultural memory. A natural response to this historical process of cultural alienation is to rephrase outdated master-narratives. Such attempts at rephrasing frequently took place already in the oral stages of both Greek and Jewish culture. Numerous redactions of Homeric and biblical narratives indicate that the same readjustment of cultural memory was also applied to its written versions.

But the increasing authority and importance assigned to written texts made the practice of rephrasing and rewriting utterly problematic. It can hardly be a coincidence that philosophical allegoresis evolved along with the first attempts to standardize the Homeric text in Pisistratean Athens.[46] Likewise, it can hardly be a coincidence that *pesher* exegesis began after Judaism developed the concept of sacred scripture during the Hellenistic religious reforms of the years 175–164 B.C.E.[47] The increasing authority of written traditions asked for a method that would simultaneously maintain their fixity and adapt them to changing cultural models and new discursive modes. The transpositional hermeneutics of isolation and recontextualization, such as attested in pesher exegesis and in the philosophical allegoresis of the Derveni papyrus, was ideally suited for this double task of simultaneously preserving and readjusting the written repositories of cultural memory.

---

[46] For the textual history of the Homeric epics, see G. Nagy, *Homer's Text and Language* (Traditions; Urbana: University of Illinois Press, 2004).

[47] See A. Lange, "From Literature to Scripture: The Unity and Plurality of the Hebrew Scriptures in Light of the Qumran Library," in *One Scripture or Many? Canon from Biblical, Theological, and Philosophical Perspectives* (ed. C. Helmer and C. Landmesser; Oxford: Oxford University Press, 2004), 51–107.

WHY DOES 4Q394 BEGIN WITH A CALENDAR?

GEORGE BRANCH-TREVATHAN
Emory University

4QMMT[a] (4Q394) 3a includes a solar calendar and the beginning of a sectarian halakhic discussion. Regardless of whether that calendar "originally" belonged to *MMT* or was later added by a scribe, someone in antiquity associated the solar calendar with the halakhic and hortatory sections of *MMT* and so placed it before them. In this paper, I address why someone would make that association.

I argue that sections B and C of *MMT* portray the *yaḥad* as the utopian or eschatological community and that by connecting the solar calendar to this idealistic depiction of the community, the original author or subsequent scribe participates in the fairly widespread use of solar symbolism in utopian and eschatological discourse of the late Hellenistic and early imperial periods. In other words, the text features the sort of use of solar symbolism we find in Iambulus' travel narrative *Commonwealth of the Sun*, Aristonicus' *Heliopolitae* (at least according to Strabo), and the propaganda of the Roman emperor Augustus.

To put this paper in a broader context, by focusing here on *MMT*, I hope to highlight the importance of one discursive context of the *yaḥad*'s deployment of a solar calendar. And by studying *MMT*'s sectarian calendar in light of the discursive contexts that encouraged its rhetorical use—rather than, say, claiming that *MMT* includes a calendar *only* because *MMT* indexes the major disagreements between the *yaḥad* and its rivals—I adopt an approach to Qumran sectarianism that Albert Baumgarten has suggested. In *The Flourishing of Jewish Sects in the Maccabean Era*, Baumgarten contends that explanations of why the Dead Sea Scrolls' sect split from other Jews too easily equate boundary markers with boundary creators, what the group used to distinguish itself from what actually gave rise to the sect.[1] The community ("we") of 4QMMT, for instance, distinguished itself from other Jews on the

---

[1] A. Baumgarten, *The Flourishing of Jewish Sects in the Maccabean Era: An Interpretation* (JSJSup 55; Leiden: Brill, 1997), 75–78.

basis of its halakhah. But in the late Second Temple period, more Jewish sects existed than did positions on most disputed laws. The legal opinions of distinct groups overlapped and 1QS even witnesses conflicting judgments within one sectarian vision.[2] Therefore, legal stances, while important secondary expressions of difference, cannot account primarily for the *yaḥad*'s or any other sect's origins or foundations, Baumgarten argues.[3] Opinions on the source(s) of legal authority probably cannot either, since 1QS suggests that these too may differ within a single community expression.[4] Concerning the calendar, Baumgarten writes, "Calendar differences are neither a necessary reason for nor an inevitable expression of separatist trends. They can play either role under the appropriate circumstances, but it is precisely those circumstances which it is the task of the investigator to discover and comprehend."[5] Hence Baumgarten proceeds to describe how several sociological circumstances promoted sectarian divides along certain lines. Similarly, I highlight how a specific discursive condition of the Greco-Roman world, the frequent employment of solar symbols and solar calendars in utopian visions, encouraged the *yaḥad*'s deployment of one particular boundary marker: the solar calendar. Put another way, I attempt here to shed light on why the *yaḥad* stressed the solar calendar (and not some other symbol)[6] as a

---

[2] It includes, for example, three penal codes and two admissions protocols, some of which contradict each other. In addition to Baumgarten, *Flourishing of Jewish Sects*, 77, see S. Metso, "In Search of the *Sitz Im Leben* of the *Community Rule*," in *The Provo International Conference on the Dead Sea Scrolls: Technological Innovations, New Texts, and Reformulated Issues* (ed. D.W. Parry and E. Ulrich; STDJ 30: Leiden: Brill, 1999), 306–315.

[3] Baumgarten, *Flourishing of Jewish Sects*, 77. Cf. E. Qimron and J. Strugnell in *DJD* X (1994): 131: "MMT deals primarily with the three topics that stood at the center of the controversy between the Jewish religious parties of the Second Temple period. All are issues with regard to which a lack of consensus would make it impossible to coexist within a single religious community. Disagreement on these issues is what created the sects."

[4] Baumgarten, *Flourishing of Jewish Sects*, 78–79. On 1QS, see Metso, "In Search of the *Sitz Im Leben*." For the view that opinions on the source of legal authority may have defined and distinguished Jewish communities, see M. Smith, "What is Implied by the Variety of Messianic Figures?" *JBL* 78 (1959): 66–72 (72).

[5] Baumgarten, *Flourishing of Jewish Sects*, 78.

[6] Morton Smith points out that within several ancient Jewish groups, members maintained widely diverging notions of the Messiah and the eschaton. "What faces us, therefore, is an unreconciled diversity, within single groups, of opinions which are nevertheless considered important, at least by many members of the groups concerned. Recognition of this diversity raises far-reaching problems as to the organization of these groups and the significance of their ceremonies. If a group had no single eschatological

critical distinction between themselves and outsiders by highlighting the ancient cultural trends that encouraged the use of this particular symbol as a boundary marker. I do not pretend that these trends alone explain the appearance of the solar calendar in 4Q394 3a (or elsewhere at Qumran). I merely describe here one of the historical circumstances that illuminate why in one manuscript a solar calendar precedes parts B and C of *MMT*.

1. 4Q394

Of the six reconstructed manuscripts[7] that constitute 4QMMT (4Q394–399), only one, 4Q394, contains a calendrical section before the more discursive legal section. What fragments belong to 4Q394—and so the extent of its calendar—and whether that calendar originally or ever formed part of *MMT* remain disputed.[8] My argument depends only on

---

myth, it cannot have been organized as a community of believers in the myth it did not have" ("Messianic Figures," 71). For my purposes, Smith's observation shows that messianism did not become a boundary delineating Jewish groups. As with explaining why the solar calendar did, answering why messianism did not requires understanding the discursive spaces, the total range of signifying possibilities and the power relations buttressing each, within which each group's members expressed themselves.

[7] Themselves consisting of one hundred or so fragments. See E. Qimron, "The Nature of the Reconstructed Composite Text of 4QMMT," in *Reading 4QMMT: New Perspectives on Qumran Law and History* (ed. J. Kampen and M.J. Bernstein; SBLSymS 2; Atlanta: Scholars Press, 1994), 9–13 (9).

[8] Qimron and Strugnell in their *editio princeps* attribute ten fragments to 4Q394, the first two of which contain only calendrical material, and print a twenty-three line calendar at the beginning of *MMT* (*DJD* X [1994]). But most editors have not assigned what Qimron and Strugnell consider frgs. 1–2 of 4Q394 to that manuscript because, compared with frgs. 3–7, 1–2 are written in smaller letters (2.5–3 mm, on average, vs. 3–3.5 mm, on average), with less distance between the lines (4.8 mm vs. 5.5 mm), in much shorter columns (7–9 cm vs. 16–18 cm), and by a different hand using different orthography. See F. García Martínez, "Dos notas sobre 4QMMT," *RevQ* 16 (1993): 293–297; Qimron in *DJD* X (1994): 201; L.H. Schiffman, "The Place of 4QMMT in the Corpus of the Qumran MSS," in *Reading 4QMMT*, 80–98 (82); J.C. VanderKam, "The Calendar, 4Q327, and 4Q394," in *Legal Texts and Legal Issues: Proceedings of the Second Meeting of the International Organization for Qumran Studies, Cambridge 1995* (ed. M. Bernstein, F. García Martínez, and J. Kampen; STDJ 23; Leiden, Brill, 1997), 179–194.

On rhetorical and material grounds, Strugnell maintains that the calendrical section of 4Q394 belongs to a different text than the legal and exhortative sections of MMT. On rhetorical grounds, he argues that "[t]he legal and hortatory parts of MMT are addressed by one group to another and have a notably polemic tendency to them. The calendar, however, is clearly only a list, not addressed to anyone, and with no internal indicators

what scholars generally agree upon regarding the manuscript: 1) that it includes calendrical material that represents the solar calendar assumed in other Qumran texts and 2) that it includes calendrical material *and* the beginning of the legal section, section B, of *MMT*.

First, 4Q394 3–7 begins with slightly over two lines of calendrical material in the form of a Sabbath list of the sort found also in 4Q320–327:

שבת ע[ל] ו אחר [ה]ש[בת ויומ השני השלישי] [נו]סף ושלמה השנה שלוש מאת וש[שים וארבעה] יום ("Sabbath. To it, after [the] Sa[bbath, the second day and the third day are ad]ded. And the year is complete, three hundred and six[ty four] days").[9] These lines show that this list refers to the 364-day solar[10] calendar: if the Sabbath plus three days marks the end of the year, then

---

of polemical intent" (*DJD* X [1994]: 203; see also idem, "MMT: Second Thoughts on a Forthcoming Edition," in *The Community of the Renewed Covenant: The Notre Dame Symposium on the Dead Sea Scrolls* [ed. E. Ulrich and J. VanderKam; Christianity and Judaism in Antiquity 10; Notre Dame: University of Notre Dame Press, 1994], 57–73). Others, however, see a 364-day calendrical list as inherently polemical and thus in keeping with the rest of *MMT* (see, for example, S. Talmon, "Calendar Controversy in Ancient Judaism: The Case of the 'Community of the Renewed Covenant,'" in *The Provo International Conference*, 394–395). Strugnell buttresses his argument about rhetoric with an appeal to the physical nature of *MMT*'s fragments, insisting that there was simply no space on 4Q394 for a polemical preface to the Sabbath list: "if one reconstructs the entire calendar in 4Q394, it would be difficult to postulate anything before it except an incipit of a calendar." He maintains, furthermore, that 4Q395, which also contains the beginning of the legal section, lacked a preceding calendar: "enough uninscribed leather is preserved before Section B to make it highly probable that no text ever stood before it" (*DJD* X [1994]: 203). But, according to Schiffman ("The Place of 4QMMT," 84 n. 14), the photograph of 4Q395 published in *DJD* X as pl. III contradicts Strugnell's assertion and VanderKam argues that since we do not know the width of the space between columns on 4Q395—only one column is extant—and since the uninscribed space to the right of the text on 4Q395 is comparable to the space between columns in 4Q394 and 4Q327, "it is possible that another column (or more) appeared before the only preserved one" ("The Calendar, 4Q327, and 4Q394," 184).

[9] Throughout I follow the Hebrew text in *DJD* X (1994). All translations of ancient sources are my own.

[10] Uwe Glessmer argues that because several calendrical documents coordinate a 364-day scheme with the moon and not the sun, "if a comprehensive heading for the concept of calendar at Qumran is to be chosen, the oft-used term 'solar calendar' is certainly inappropriate and should be avoided." The essence of the calendar, in his view, was the 364-day year, which enabled "schematic assignment of weeks or Sabbaths," and not any solar basis ("Calendars in the Dead Sea Scrolls," in *The Dead Sea Scrolls after Fifty Years: A Comprehensive Assessment* [ed. P.W. Flint and J.C. Vanderkam; 2 vols.; Leiden: Brill, 1998–1999], 2:213–278 [231]). Glessmer is certainly right that the 364-day year's suitability for schematization (days of the year always fall on the same days of the week) made it attractive. But, solar associations were also a crucial part of the 364-day year's symbolic potential and hence its appeal; in addition to the arguments about *MMT* below, see also *Jub.* 2:9.

Tuesday concludes the year and the new year begins on Wednesday—just as other Qumran texts lead us to expect.[11] Thus, the solar nature of 4Q394's calendar is evident whether one includes or omits the disputed calendrical material of frgs. 1–2.[12]

Second, 4Q394 3a includes both the calendar and the legal section of *MMT* and so this conjunction does not depend on textual reconstruction. At some point in antiquity, the calendrical and halakhic discussions of *MMT* were joined.

Such a conjunction invites explanation. Qimron and Strugnell consider it meaningless, imagining that a scribe happened to copy a distinct and banal calendrical document before an epistle or treatise. The Sabbath list "appears as uncontroversial in its intention as our 'thirty days hath September,'" they claim.[13] Schiffman, however, believes a later scribe very intentionally prefixed the calendar to a halakhic-hortatory text, just as, in his view, the redactor of the *Temple Scroll* incorporated a calendar into that text—the very same calendar, in fact.[14] Schiffman's scribe senses the calendar's inherent polemic (one has a reason after all for saying even hackneyed phrases like "thirty days hath September"): "it may very well be that the scribe copied the calendar before MMT precisely because calendrical issues were to him determinative and he could not imagine that they were not a factor in the initial schism" that *MMT* reflects.[15] I agree with Schiffman that whoever placed the calendar next to sections B and C of *MMT* associated it with those passages and in what follows I offer an additional reason that 4Q394 begins with a calendar.

---

[11] In the *Songs of the Sabbath Sacrifice*, for example, the first Sabbath falls on the fourth day of first month (4Q400 1 i 1) and so the year must begin on Wednesday. On calendars at Qumran, see J.C. VanderKam, *Calendars in the Dead Sea Scrolls: Measuring Time* (New York: Routledge, 1998).

[12] VanderKam, "The Calendar, 4Q327, and 4Q394," 183: "[I]t is worth emphasizing that even if the fragments of 4Q327 [= 4Q394 1–2] do not belong to 4Q394, that does not eliminate the presence and important place of a calendrical statement in the first preserved passage in 4Q394." See also S.D. Fraade, "To Whom It May Concern: *4QMMT* and its Addressee(s)," *RevQ* 76 (2000): 507–526 (521–522).

[13] *DJD* X (1994): 110–113. The quote is from p. 113.

[14] Schiffman, "The Place of 4QMMT," 83–86. He points out that, by themselves, the legal and hortatory sections constitute a complete rhetorical unit that never mentions the calendar; אלה מקצת דברינו ("these are some of our precepts," B 1) forms an *inclusio* with אנחנו כתבנו אליך מקצת מעשי התורה ("We have written down for your benefit some deeds of the Torah," C 26–27).

[15] Ibid., 85. See also Fraade, "To Whom It May Concern," 522–523.

2. The Utopian *Yaḥad* of 4QMMT

Like some of the first scrolls published, 4QMMT describes an eschatolog-ical community ("we"), a community, that is, that sees itself as to some degree already constituting humans', or at least their own, ultimate *telos*.[16] The legal section (B) lists specific *halakhot* concerning which the *yaḥad* differs from its addressee ("you"),[17] the Pharisees ("they"),[17] and "the mul-titude of the [people]" (מרוב ה[עם], C 7). At the beginning of the hor-tatory section (C), the author of 4QMMT explains that to avoid involv-ing themselves in the majority's incorrect keeping of the law, פרשנו מרוב ה[עם ... ומהתערב בדברים האלה ומלבוא ע[מהם]לגב אלה ("We have sepa-rated from the multitude of the [people] … and from sharing in these practices and from associating wi[th them] on these principles," C 7–8). Given that most of the matters (בדברים) discussed in section B concern the Temple,[18] "we have separated" probably means the *yaḥad* has forged for itself some alternative to participating in the Jerusalem Temple.

Interpreting this separation in light of the closing chapters of Deuter-onomy,[19] *MMT* casts the *yaḥad* as a religious paragon (ואתם י[ודעים שלוא]מצא בידנו מעל ושקר ורעה, "Now you k[now that no] unfaithfulness, false-hood, or evil may be found in us," C 8–9) and others as the apostasizers whom Moses predicts: כתוב ש[תסור]מהד[ר]ך וקרת[ך]הרעה ("It is written that you [will turn aside] from the p[at]h and evil will summon yo[u]," C 12).[20] It then turns Deut 30:1–3 on his addressee: וכת[וב]והיא כי]יבו[א

---

[16] For other definitions of eschatology, see Baumgarten, *Flourishing of Jewish Sects*, 173; Smith, "Messianic Figures"; Y. Hoffman, "Eschatology in the Book of Jeremiah," in *Eschatology in the Bible and in Jewish and Christian Tradition* (ed. H. Graf Reventlow; JSOTSup 243; Sheffield: Sheffield Academic Press, 1997), 75–97 (75–78). The *yaḥad(im)* of 4QMMT, the *Damascus Document*, and *Serekh ha-Yaḥad* might also be described aptly as "millenarian," a subgroup of "eschatological" that emphasizes the "*imminent* com-mencing of the eschatological era" (Baumgarten, *Flourishing of Jewish Sects*, 154, empha-sis mine). But I wish to stress here the idealized and realized-eschatological dimensions of the *yaḥad*'s self-understanding and so employ "utopian" and "eschatological."

[17] The *halakhot* that *MMT* attributes to "them," rabbinic literature attributes to the Pharisees. Therefore, "they" in 4QMMT likely refers to Pharisees or their predecessors. See Qimron and Strugnell in *DJD* X (1994): 175 and especially Y. Sussmann in *DJD* X (1994): 180–200.

[18] See the summary by Qimron and Strugnell in *DJD* X (1994): 131.

[19] *MMT* broadcasts its reworking of Deuteronomy in section B's opening words; אלה מקצת דברינו (B 1) echoes Deut 1:1: אלה הדברים אשר דבר משה אל־כל־ישראל. It thus portrays itself as another normative address to its audience, a *Triteronomy* if you will, an exhortation to keep the law properly by adopting *MMT*'s halakhah.

[20] Cf. Deut 31:29: כי ידעתי אחרי מותי כי־השחת תשחתון וסרתם מן־הדרך אשר צויתי אתכם וקראת אתכם הרעה באחרית הימים כי־תעשו את־הרע בעיני יהוה ("For I know that after my

עליך [כו]ל הדברי[ם] האלה באחרי[ת] הימים הברכה [וה]קללא [והשיבות]ה אל
לבבך [ובכו]ל נפשך ("And it is writt[en], 'When [al]l
of these things [com]e upon you at the en[d] of days, the blessing [and
the] curse, [you will move] it into your heart and return to him with all
your heart [and with al]l your soul," C 12–16). The authors of *MMT* write
in order to facilitate this eschatological repentance, which they equate
with understanding scripture as the *yaḥad* does: כתב[נו אליכה שחבין בספר]
מושה [ו]בספר[י הנ]ביאים ובדוי[ד] ("we have [written] to you so that you
may study carefully the book of Moses [and] the book[s of the Pr]ophets
and of Davi[d]," C 10–11). The addressees should "scrutinize all these
things" (הבן בכל אלה, C 28), "so that you may rejoice at the end of time
in finding some of our precepts correct" (בשל שתשמה באחרית העת במצאך
מקצת דברינו כן, C 30). Doing so, "will be counted to you as righteousness in that you will be doing what is right and good in his eyes" (ונחשבה
לך לצדקה בעשותך הישר והטוב לפנו, C 31). Thus, the *MMT yaḥad* already
possesses the conduct and knowledge that the eschaton will vindicate,
already enjoys the moral purity for which others must pray (ובקש מלפנו
שיתקן את עצתך והרחיק ממך מחשבת רעה ועצת בליעל ["Ask him to set you
in order and he will remove from you evil's purposes and Belial's will"],
C 28–29). It embodies the end-time repentance or "return" that it believes
others Jews will make. It is a community that prefigures the eschatological state. 4Q394 joins this depiction of the *yaḥad* to a solar symbol, the
solar calendar.

3. Solar Symbolism in Three Contemporaneous Eschatological Projects: Iambulus' and Aristonicus' *Heliopolitai* and Augustan Propoganda

Iambulus, Aristonicus, and Augustus attest a discourse that employed
solar symbols to characterize the ideal (Iambulus, Aristonicus) or eschatological (Augustus) society. Roughly contemporaneous with the composition and use of the Dead Sea Scrolls, they represent a part of the discursive contexts within which the *MMT yaḥad* depicted itself as a separate,
ideal, and morally superior community with a solar calendar.

---

death you will certainly go to ruin, turning aside from the path that I have commanded
you. Evil will summon you at the end of days because you will do evil in the sight of the
Lord").

Iambulus' travel narrative, *Commonwealth of the Sun,*[21] describes a
social and natural utopia, a set of islands on which geography, flora,
and fauna, and human physiognomy, knowledge, conduct, and community are perfected.[22] The extant portions of the work do not mention
the islanders' calendar but Iambulus seems to have termed the island
Heliopolis, its residents *Heliopolitae,* or "citizens of the Commonwealth
of the Sun," not merely because the islanders worship the Sun (Diodorus
Siculus, *Bibliotheca historica* 2.59.2) but because in antiquity solar symbols carry particular utopian associations. As David Winston states,
"Iambulus' Sun symbolism is especially understandable when we realize its specific connection with justice and righteousness. The prophet
Malachi (3.20) spoke of 'the Sun of Justice,' a figure of speech then current
in the Near East, from the ancient Babylonian literature to the Orphic
hymns."[23] Solar symbols, for Iambulus, convey that a community is ideal.

In 133 B.C.E., Attalus III died and bequeathed the Pergamene kingdom
to Rome. In the wake of or just before Attalus' death,[24] Aristonicus, claiming to be an illegitimate son of Eumenes II, attempted to seize control
of the area. According to Strabo's account of the campaign, Aristonicus,
"went up into the interior and quickly assembled a multitude of resource-
less people and slaves, invited with a promise of freedom, whom he called

---

[21] The work is known to us only through Diodorus Siculus' *Bibliotheca historica* (2.55–
60) and brief remarks in Lucian's *True Histories* and John Tzetzes' *Chiliades* but was likely
composed in the second or first century B.C.E. On the narrative and its date, see D. Winston, "Iambulus' *Islands of the Sun* and Hellenistic Literary Utopias," *Science Fiction
Studies* 10 (1976). Cited 29 July 2006. Online: http://www.depauw.edu/sfs/backissues/
10/winston10art.htm.; idem, "Iambulus: A Literary Study in Greek Utopianism" (Ph.D.
diss., Columbia University, 1956); and N. Holzberg, "Novel-like Words of Extended Prose
Fiction II," in *The Novel in the Ancient World* (ed. G. Schmeling; Leiden: Brill, 1996),
619–653 (621–627). See also Doron Mendels' enumeration of the systematic similarities
between the Qumran *yahad,* the Essenes, and Iambulus' *Heliopolitae* ("Hellenistic Utopia
and the Essenes" *HTR* 72 [1979]: 207–222).

[22] In antiquity, accounts of the ideal society often belonged to travel narratives (e.g.,
the account of the island of Scheria in the *Odyssey,* Herodotus' fantastic tales, Hecateaus
of Abdera's Hyperboreans, Euhemerus of Messene's *Sacred Inscription*); Josephus refers
to this convention in *Ag. Ap.* 2.220–224. For discussion see E. Gabba, "True and False
History in Classical Antiquity," *JRS* 71 (1981): 50–62 (58–60); T. Engberg-Pedersen,
"Philo's *De Vita Contemplativa* as a Philosopher's Dream," *JSJ* 30 (1999): 40–64 (45–46,
64).

[23] D. Winston, "Iambulus' *Islands of the Sun.*" W.W. Tarn identifies many ancient texts
that associate the Sun and the ideal human community ("Alexander Helios and the
Golden Age," *JRS* 22 [1932]: 135–160 [140, 147–148]).

[24] On the timing of Attalus' campaign, see E. Gruen, *The Hellenistic World and the
Coming of Rome* (2 vols.; Berkeley: University of California Press, 1984), 2:594–596.

Heliopolitae," or, "citizens of the Sun-city" (εἰς δὲ τὴν μεσογαίαν ἀνι-
ῶν ἤθροισε διὰ ταχέων πλῆθος ἀπορῶν τε ἀνθρώπων καὶ δούλων
ἐπ' ἐλευθερίαι κατακεκλημένων, οὓς ἡλιοπολίτας ἐκάλεσε).[25] Perhaps
inspired by Iambulus' account of the *Heliopolitae*,[26] Aristonicus, at least
on Strabo's account, attempts to forge a utopian community, in this case
a more socially just community, and to communicate his utopian intent,
he employed solar symbolism.[27]

In 10 B.C.E., the Emperor Augustus erected the obelisk that today
stands in front of the Italian Parliament building. Its height and original
location demanded attention. At 30 m tall, it was a vertical land-marker.
Located in the Campus Martius off the Via Flaminia, it dominated the
initial visual impression that the capital made upon those entering the
city from the North. Surrounding it were inlaid bronze markers and
astrological signs that rendered the obelisk the gnomon of the largest
sundial ever constructed. It is likely also the most ideological sundial
ever. Imported from Egypt, adorned with hieroglyphics, and bearing
an inscription on its base referring to "victory over Egypt," the obelisk
memorialized Augustus' defeat of Antony and Cleopatra, a victory that
ended a century of civil wars and inaugurated a "new era" of peace, or at
least this is how some contemporaneous Roman literature portrays the
victory (i.e., Horace's *Carmen Seculare* and Virgil's *Aeneid, inter alia*).

The obelisk/sundial claimed that with Augustus the eschatological[28]
age had begun not only by memorializing the inauguration of that new
age but also by associating Augustus with the Sun sign (Capricorn) and

---

[25] Strabo, *Geogr.* 14.1.38 is the only evidence for this title, though other evidence suggests Aristonicus did recruit slaves. The historical sources for Aristonicus are collected
and translated in Z. Yavetz, *Slaves and Slavery in Ancient Rome* (New Brunswick: Transaction, 1988), 47–66 and R.K. Sherk, ed., *Rome and the Greek East to the Death of Augustus*
(Cambridge: Cambridge University Press, 1984), 39–45. I quote the Greek text of Strabo
from the Loeb Classical Library edition.

[26] Tarn argues that Aristonicus strives to implement Iambulus' vision ("Alexander
Helios," 140) or some version of it (*Alexander the Great* [2 vols.; Cambridge: Cambridge
University Press, 1948], 2:413–414).

[27] O. Patterson, *Freedom in the Making of Western Culture* (New York: Basic, 1991),
270. The meaning and value of Strabo's report is heavily debated and many scholars do
not believe that Aristonicus sought social transformation; for discussion and bibliography, see Gruen, *The Hellenistic World*, 2:597; V. Vavrinek, "Aristonicus of Pergamum: Pre-
tender to the Throne or Leader of a Slave Revolt?" *Eirene* 13 (1975): 109–129.

[28] On eschatology as a dimension of Greek and Roman cultures, see D. Georgi, *The
City in the Valley: Biblical Interpretation and Urban Theology* (Studies in Biblical Literature
7; Atlanta: SBL, 2005), 25–52, 301 (cf. 218); H. Koester, "Jesus the Victim," *JBL* 111 (1992):
3–15 (10–13).

the Sun God (Apollo). According to Pliny the Elder (*Nat.* 36.72), the sundial's bronze markers established the beginning of the year at the winter solstice and so under the sign of Capricorn. Augustus claimed to have been conceived under Capricorn (Suetonius, *Aug.* 94) and from at least 41/40 B.C.E. and especially after 28 B.C.E., he minted coins that featured Capricorn alongside images and text depicting him as "born to save the Roman state" and as herald of a new, pacific (and hence superior) age.[29] Furthermore, obelisks were sacred to the Sun God, Apollo, and this obelisk was taken from the Sun Temple in the Sun City (*Heliopolis*) of Egypt and dedicated to Apollo.[30] Augustus likely promoted the stories that later appear in Suetonius claiming that Augustus' mother spent the night in the Temple of Apollo and was impregnated with Augustus by the God (*Aug.* 94), that Augustus' earthly father dreamed that the sun rose from his wife's womb (ibid.), and that Augustus was born just before sunrise (*Aug.* 7). Apollo also appeared at the top of the cuirass of the widely disseminated *Prima Porta* portrait type of Augustus, which, by assimilating Augustus' physiognomy to that of Polyclitus' Doryphorus, represented the *princeps* as the ideal (male) human form and so captured visually Augustan propoganda's eschatological claims. And Augustus further stressed the eschatological nature of his reign by having the Temple of Actium Apollo built next to his house on the Palatine Hill, which itself recalled the myth of Romulus' founding of Rome there in the eighth century B.C.E. The architectural configuration cast Augustus as the new founder of the city.

Thus, the Sun, the Sun sign, and the Sun God (Apollo) formed a symbolic repertoire on which the sundial in the Campus Martius drew to make eschatological claims. Every winter solstice, when the Sun was reborn (i.e., the days began to lengthen) under Capricorn, the sundial commemorating Augustus' victory announced the beginning of a new year and a new, ideal age.[31]

---

[29] T.S. Barton, *Power and Knowledge: Astrology, Physiognomics, and Medicine under the Roman Empire* (Ann Arbor: University of Michigan Press, 1994), 42. See also P. Zanker, *The Power of Images in the Age of Augustus* (trans. Alan Shapiro; Ann Arbor: University of Michigan Press, 1988), 101–166; W. Eck, *The Age of Augustus* (trans. Deborah Lucas Schneider; Malden: Blackwell, 2003), 122–123.

[30] Zanker, *Power of Images*, 144.

[31] Ibid., 46.

4. Conclusion

I am, of course, not the first to describe the Dead Sea Scrolls *yaḥad* as utopian and/or eschatological. Helmut Koester epitomizes this interpretation well:

> The eschatological orientation of the community appears in all aspects of its life. The Essenes not only anticipate the promised future of the true people of God, they already are these elect people and God's temple. Every new member had to assign his possessions to the community. Personal poverty and communal living represent the messianic age, which knows no difference between rich and poor. The liturgy of the common meals, regularly celebrated every day, mirrors the messianic banquet. While holy war ideology is clearly evident, there are also strong correspondences with Hellenistic utopian concepts. Retreat to a secluded place, common meals of simple food, community of goods, sharing all labor, strict moral obligations and penance for offenders, rejection of temple worship, and finally the preference for a solar over a lunar calendar are also ingredients of Iambolous' utopian Hellenistic romance *Commonwealth of the Sun*.[32]

And Philip Davies argues that 1QS is not a rule of an actual community but Jewish utopian literature.[33]

Koester and Davies have in mind texts other than 4QMMT. I have tried to show here that *MMT* belongs in the same utopian, eschatological vein and that vein itself takes part in a larger discourse that associated solar symbolism with ideal community.[34] One reason then that the sectarian text 4Q394 begins, originally or secondarily, with a solar calendar is that, in the discursive context of the Hellenistic and early Roman periods, a solar calendar powerfully symbolized the utopian and eschatological claims made in the rest of *MMT*.

---

[32] H. Koester, *Introduction to the New Testament*, vol. 1: *History, Culture, and Religion of the Hellenistic Age* (2nd ed.; Berlin: de Gruyter, 1995), 225.

[33] P.R. Davies, "Redaction and Sectarianism in the Qumran Scrolls," in *The Scriptures and the Scrolls: Studies in Honor of A.S. van der Woude on the Occasion of his 65th Birthday* (ed. F. García Martínez, A. Hilhorst, and C.J. Labuschagne; VTSup 49; Leiden: Brill, 1992), 152–163 (157–160).

[34] For other ways in which the solar calendar is eschatological, see M. Albani, *Astronomie und Schöpfungsglaube: Untersuchungen zum astronomischen Henochbuch* (WMANT 68; Neukirchen-Vluyn: Neukirchener Verlag, 1994).

SELECT INDEX OF ANCIENT SOURCES

DEAD SEA SCROLLS

See also Greek and Latin Literature as well as Papyri, Ostraca, and Inscriptions.

Rabbinic and Medieval Jewish Literature

New Testament

PAPYRI, OSTRACA, AND INSCRIPTIONS

CONTRIBUTORS

JEFF S. ANDERSON is Professor of Religion at Wayland Baptist University's Anchorage, Alaska campus. He is author of *The Internal Diversification of Second Temple Judaism* (2002) and *The Old Testament: Its Story and History* (2009). He is a participating member of the Enoch Seminar.

RUSSELL C.D. ARNOLD, Ph.D. (2005), UCLA, is Assistant Professor of Religious Studies at DePauw University in Greencastle, Indiana, and serves as co-chair of the Ritual in the Biblical World Section of the Society of Biblical Literature.

MOSHE BAR-ASHER, Ph.D. (1976) in Hebrew and Aramaic Studies, Hebrew University, is Hayyim Mahman Bialik Emeritus Professor of Hebrew and Aramaic and Jewish Languages at the Hebrew University and President of the Academy of Hebrew Language in Israel.

MEIR BAR-ILAN, Ph.D. (1983), Bar-Ilan University, is Professor of Jewish History in Antiquity and Professor of Talmud at Bar-Ilan University.

MOSHE J. BERNSTEIN, Ph.D. (1978) in Classical Languages, Fordham University, is Professor of Bible, Yeshiva University, and was a member of the international editorial team for the Dead Sea Scrolls.

PIERPAOLO BERTALOTTO, Ph.D. (2007), University of Bari (Italy), is an independent researcher and secretary of the Journal *Henoch*.

GEORGE BRANCH-TREVATHAN is a doctoral candidate in New Testament at Emory University.

ESTHER G. CHAZON, Ph.D. (1992), Hebrew University of Jerusalem, is Senior Lecturer in Hebrew Literature and Academic Head of the Orion Center for the Study of Dead Sea Scrolls & Associated Literature at the Hebrew University.

EDWARD DĄBROWA, Ph.D. (1977), is Professor of Ancient History and the head of the Department of Jewish Studies at the Jagiellonian University in Kraków. He is Editor-in-Chief of *Scripta Judaica Cracoviensia*.

NÓRA DÁVID, Ph.D. (2009) in Ancient History, Pázmány Péter Catholic University Piliscsaba, is an assistant at the University of Vienna, Institute of Jewish Studies.

KARL PAUL DONFRIED, Dr. theol. (1968), University of Heidelberg, is Elizabeth A. Woodson Professor Emeritus of New Testament at Smith College and former Fulbright Professor at the Hebrew University.

JAN DUŠEK, Ph.D. (2005) in History and Archaeology of Ancient Worlds, École Pratique des Hautes Études, Paris, works as researcher at the Centre for Biblical Studies of the Academy of Sciences of the Czech Republic and the Charles University in Prague.

J. HAROLD ELLENS is a scholar of Second Temple Judaism and Christian Origins, as well as a Clinical Psychologist, holding a Ph.D. in each of those two disciplines. His entire professional life has been devoted to studying and publishing on the interface between Psychological and Biblical Studies.

JOHN ELWOLDE, formerly executive editor of the Dictionary of Classical Hebrew, University of Sheffield, is a Translation Consultant of the United Bible Societies.

ESTHER ESHEL, Ph.D. (2000) in Bible, Hebrew University of Jerusalem, is a Senior Lecturer in the Bible department and in the Martin (Szusz) Department of Land of Israel Studies and Archaeology at Bar-Ilan University. She is an acting head of the Jeselsohn Epigraphic Center of Jewish History at Bar-Ilan University.

HANAN ESHEL (1958–2010), Ph.D. (1993), Hebrew University of Jerusalem, was Professor in the Martin (Szusz) Department of Land of Israel Studies and Archaeology at Bar-Ilan University and the head of the Jeselsohn Epigraphic Center of Jewish History at Bar-Ilan University.

STEVEN E. FASSBERG, Ph.D. (1984), Harvard University, is Caspar Levias Professor of Ancient Semitic Languages at the Hebrew University of Jerusalem and a member of the Academy of the Hebrew Language.

IDA FRÖHLICH, Ph.D. (1984) in History, Oriental Institute of the Academy of the USSR, St. Petersburg (Leningrad), is Professor of Ancient Judaism and Ancient Near Eastern History at the Pázmány Péter Catholic University Budapest.

RUSSELL FULLER, Ph.D. (1988) in Hebrew Bible, Harvard University, is Professor in the Department of Theology and Religious Studies at the University of San Diego and a member of the international team editing the Dead Sea Scrolls.

MILA GINSBURSKAYA, Ph.D. (2009), University of Cambridge, is currently working on transforming her dissertation on purity in biblical and early Judaism into a monograph. Her postdoctoral project at the University of Birmingham focused on temple and identity in the Dead Sea Scrolls.

NOAH HACHAM, Ph.D. (2003) in Jewish History, is lecturer of Second Temple Jewish History at the Hebrew University of Jerusalem.

PAUL HEGER, Ph.D. (1996) in Judaic Studies, University of Toronto, is a research reader affiliated with the University of Toronto, working on the exegesis of the Dead Sea Scrolls.

JAMAL-DOMINIQUE HOPKINS, Ph.D. in Dead Sea Scrolls and Qumran Studies, University of Manchester, is Chair of Biblical Studies and Languages and Assistant Professor of Biblical Studies at the Interdenominational Theological Center in Atlanta.

TAL ILAN, Ph.D. (1992) in Jewish History at the Hebrew University, Jerusalem, is Professor of Jewish Studies (Judaistik) at the Freie Universität Berlin, Germany.

SANDRA JACOBS, Ph.D. (2010) in Biblical Law, University of Manchester, is an Honorary Research Associate in the Department of Hebrew and Jewish Studies, University College, London.

ALEX P. JASSEN, Ph.D. (2006) in Hebrew and Judaic Studies, New York University, is Assistant Professor of Early Judaism at the University of Minnesota. He is the author of *Mediating the Divine: Prophecy and Revelation in the Dead Sea Scrolls and Second Temple Judaism* (Brill, 2007), which won the 2009 John Templeton Award for Theological Promise.

AARON KOLLER, Ph.D. (2009), is Assistant Professor of Bible, Semitics, and Jewish Studies at Yeshiva University.

ARMIN LANGE, Dr. theol. (1995), University of Münster, is Professor of Second Temple Judaism at the University of Vienna and a member of the international team editing the Dead Sea Scrolls.

JAMES ALFRED LOADER, D.Litt., Th.Dr., D.Th. in Semitics, Old Testament Exegesis and History (Pretoria and Groningen, 1973–1984), is Professor of Old Testament at the University of Vienna and Professor Extraordinarius of Theology at the University of South Africa and of Biblical Literature at the University of Pretoria.

EKATERINA MATUSOVA, Ph.D. (2000), is Associate Professor of Classics at the Institute for Oriental and Classical Studies at the Russian State University for the Humanities, Moscow.

ULRIKE MITTMANN, Dr. theol (1996), University of Tübingen, is Professor of New Testament and History of Ancient Religion at the University of Osnabrück.

CHRISTA MÜLLER-KESSLER, Dr. (1988), Freie Universität Berlin, Dr. phil. habil. (2002), Friedrich-Schiller-Universität Jena, is Privatdozentin at the Friedrich-Schiller-Universität Jena.

BERNHARD PALME, Dr. phil. (1989), University of Vienna, is Professor of Ancient History and Papyrology at the University of Vienna and the Director of the Papyrus Collection of the Austrian National Library.

ZLATKO PLEŠE, Ph.D. (1996) in Classics, Yale University, is Associate Professor of Ancient Mediterranean Religions (Greco-Roman world and early Christianity) at the University of North Carolina at Chapel Hill.

Renate Pillinger, Ph.D. (1976) *sub auspiciis praesidentis rei publicae*, University of Vienna, is Professor of Early Christian Archaeology and real member of the Austrian Academy of Sciences.

Stefan C. Reif, Ph.D. Litt.D., is Emeritus Professor of Medieval Hebrew Studies and Fellow of St John's College in the University of Cambridge. He founded the Genizah Research Unit at Cambridge University Library and directed it from 1974 until 2006.

Bennie H. Reynolds III, Ph.D. (2009) in Ancient Mediterranean Religions, University of North Carolina at Chapel Hill, is Visiting Assistant Professor of Religious Studies at Millsaps College.

Alexander Rofé, Ph.D. (1970), is Professor Emeritus of Bible at the Hebrew University, editor of *Textus: Studies of the Hebrew University Bible Project*, vols. XVIII–XXIV, and author of *Introduction to the Literature of the Hebrew Bible* (Hebrew: 2006, 2007; English: 2009; Italian: 2011).

Ursula Schattner-Rieser, Dr. phil. habil. (1998), University of Sorbonne, Paris, is lecturer of Semitic languages at the Theologicum of the Catholic University of Paris (ICP) and of Ancient Judaism at the University of Zurich.

Lawrence H. Schiffman, Ph.D. (1974) in Near Eastern and Judaic Studies, Brandeis University, is Ethel and Irvin A. Edelman Professor of Hebrew and Judaic Studies and chairman of the Skirball Department of Hebrew and Judaic Studies at New York University.

Michael Segal, Ph.D. (2004) in Biblical Studies, Hebrew University, is Senior Lecturer in the Department of Bible at the Hebrew University, and Editor of the Hebrew University Bible Project.

Gebhard J. Selz, Dr. phil (1985), Freiburg University, is Professor of Ancient Near Eastern Languages and Oriental Archaeology at the University of Vienna.

Agnethe Siquans, Dr. theol. (2001), University of Vienna, is Associate Professor of Old Testament studies at the University of Vienna and works in the field of the reception of biblical texts.

GÜNTER STEMBERGER, Dr. theol. (1967), is Emeritus Professor of Jewish Studies at the University of Vienna.

DANIEL STÖKL BEN EZRA, Ph.D. (2002) in Comparative Religion, Hebrew University, is Research Director for Hebrew and Aramaic Language, Literature, Epigraphy and Palaeography (Fourth Century B.C.E. to Fourth Century C.E.) at the École Pratique des Hautes Études in Paris.

LOREN T. STUCKENBRUCK is Richard Dearborn Professor of New Testament Studies at Princeton Theological Seminary. His published work has focused on Aramaic Dead Sea materials and on their implications for the understanding of evil and theological anthropology.

HANNA TERVANOTKO is a doctoral student in the Department of Biblical Studies, University of Helsinki, and the Department of Jewish Studies, University of Vienna.

EMANUEL TOV, Ph.D. (1974) in Biblical Studies, Hebrew University, is J.L. Magnes Professor of Bible at the Hebrew University and the former Editor-in-Chief of the Dead Sea Scrolls Publication Project.

CECILIA WASSEN, Ph.D. (2004), McMaster University, is Associate Professor of New Testament at Uppsala University.

FRANCESCO ZANELLA, Ph.D. (2006) in Semantics of Ancient Hebrew, University of Florence, is research assistant at the Universities of Siegen and Bonn in the framework of the ThWQ Project (Theologisches Wörterbuch zu den Qumrantexten).

CONTENTS VOLUME ONE AND TWO

ANCIENT SEMITIC LANGUAGES
AND THE DEAD SEA SCROLLS

THE HEBREW BIBLE AND OTHER SECOND TEMPLE JEWISH
LITERATURE IN LIGHT OF THE DEAD SEA SCROLLS

ANCIENT JEWISH LITERATURE IN
GREEK AND THE DEAD SEA SCROLLS

THE DEAD SEA SCROLLS AND
JEWISH LITERATURE AND CULTURE OF THE
RABBINIC AND MEDIEVAL PERIODS

THE DEAD SEA SCROLLS AND EARLY CHRISTIANITY

THE DEAD SEA SCROLLS AND
THE ANCIENT MEDITERRANEAN AND
ANCIENT NEAR EASTERN WORLDS